The Care Guide

The Care Guide

A handbook for the caring professions and other agencies

Edited by
Michael Jacobs

CASSELL

Cassell
Wellington House, 125 Strand, London WC2R 0BB
215 Park Avenue South, New York, NY 10003

First published 1995

British Library Cataloguing-in-Publication Data
A catalogue record for this book is available from the British Library.

ISBN 0-304-33569-X (hardback)
     0-304-33380-8 (paperback)

Typeset by York House Typographic Ltd, London
Printed and bound in Great Britain by Mackays of Chatham plc

Introduction

Despite cuts both in the statutory provision of care and in the funding of other (often voluntary) agencies, there has perhaps never been a time when so many people have sought help, and when there has been such a wide variety of resources for them. No-one in either the caring professions or the voluntary sector is of course unaware of the long waiting lists and swelling demands; but it is a remarkable feature of our times that there has developed so much expertise and knowledge about the many and complex issues which people bring to those who offer the promise of care, counsel and concern. Those who seek help tend to present specific problems – indeed they may feel they have to knock on a particular door in order to be heard in the first instance. The initial presenting issue sometimes reveals other anxieties and difficulties. The person who offers care – whether professional or unpaid, whether generic or specialized – needs to be able to distinguish those issues for which he or she may be able to offer help, and those which need another's expertise. The supreme value of this book is that it brings together, in summary form, knowledge about and recommendations for responding to most of the most obvious situations which are likely to be presented.

The Care Guide draws upon the expertise and knowledge of those who specialize in these many fields. Only closer reading of the contributions will reveal what is unique to each situation, and what might be in common with others; where specialist help is necessary and where the non-specialist (in that field) can help. Because there are different presenting problems each requires recognition of the knowledge that is currently available to us. It is important to be able to identify particular issues, and it is useful to have some understanding of the principal factors to be borne in mind. If there is any risk that a little knowledge may be dangerous, the authors in the articles in this book make it clear where specialist help is necessary, and often where it can be found. At the same time there are other presenting issues discussed in these articles, where the benefit of a little more expert knowledge helps the person offering care or counsel both to sharpen their focus and to develop a more sensitive approach to the situation. Modestly applied, this knowledge may enable a more comprehensive service to be offered.

Each of the contributors to *The Care Guide* has divided their article into a number of headings, which provides a common format throughout. Some headings do not apply to every subject, in which case the lettered sections may jump in sequence. Each article is therefore set out with most, if not all, of these parts:

(a) The article starts with a straightforward definition or description of the issue or the presenting problem.

(b) This section describes the topic in more detail – such as the different ways in which the issue is likely to be presented; or signs and other indications that may alert the reader to the possible presentation of a particular issue; or different aspects related to the topic.

(c) Although this does not apply to all entries, the precipitating factors and other underlying causes for many of the issues are described in this section.

(d) The core of each article is normally to be found in this section. It may include practical considerations for the person offering care, whether directly related to presenting problems or more generally applicable to the practice of care and counselling. Particular features of caring in the situation addressed are described in such a way as to assist the responsible but non-specialist professional or unpaid worker. Practical suggestions may be made. In the case of particular problems, where specialist help is recommended, this section also looks at how these might be handled in the interim, and the extent to which the helper can work with such clients.

(e) Organizations and services offering specialist help, care or counselling for the particular situation are listed in this section, sometimes with addresses and telephone numbers. These resources may be appropriate for the client, and in some instances also for the care-giver who is wanting supervision, consultancy or advice in their own work with particular issues.

(f) This section raises particular issues in the relationships between the professional and caring agencies, the client and the specialist resources to whom the client may be referred – such as liaison and involvement with or letting go of the client by the person making the referral. This part may also highlight particular issues for the care-giver in working with the issues raised in the article.

(g) Each article concludes with up to three currently available books recommended for further study. Other books and articles may be cited in the main text. Where these are *not* listed as one of the recommended texts, the full reference can be found in the bibliography at the end of the guide.

In reading all these articles in the course of my editorial function I have learned a great deal. The authors have introduced me to new aspects of each subject, including deeper understanding of the issues involved; they have encouraged me to respond more confidently to a variety of presenting problems; they have helped me confront my ignorance and prejudice; and they have pointed me in the direction of specialist resources that in some cases have much more to offer than I can. Because the authors represent so many professions, and so many different ways of working – a variety of therapies, philosophies and outlook – I have also had a deepening sense of the richness of which is available to those who seek help.

For most readers this is a book to be consulted as need arises; or to dip into when a particular subject becomes relevant. Few will read it from cover to cover as an editor inevitably does. But from my reading of every article I know that the reader will find in *The Care Guide*, as I have found, a wealth of careful and caring expertise. For this the reader will be as grateful as I am to all those who have contributed their knowledge and their experience.

MICHAEL JACOBS
Leicester
September 1994

Readers who find addresses and telephone numbers changed from those listed in this book will render a future reprint or new edition more accurate if they can so inform the editor via the publishers.

The contributors

ANNE ABEL SMITH is a research psychologist (*mid-life crisis*)

PETER AGULNIK is a consultant psychiatrist at Littlemore Hospital and to the Isis Centre, an NHS counselling service in Oxford (*psychosis and severe mental disorders*)

TIM BOND is Staff Tutor in Counselling at the University of Durham and current Chair of the British Association for Counselling (*confidentiality*)

PAUL BROWN is a consulting clinical and occupational psychologist (*mid-life crisis*)

TONY CHESTERMAN is the Clergy in-Service Training Adviser in the Diocese of Derby, and a Canon Residentiary of Derby Cathedral (*spiritual direction*)

DAVID CLARK is Team Rector in the parish of Oadby, Leicestershire; founder-chairman of the Leicester branch of Cruse – Bereavement Care; and a trained counsellor (*funerals*)

PENNY CLOUTTE is a mother, freelance counsellor, trainer and writer (*self-help groups*)

KAY CLYMO is a tutor, trainer and counsellor on loss, death and bereavement (*loss; suicide and attempted suicide; terminal illness*)

IAN COOPER is Chair of the British Association for Counselling Trauma Care Sub-Committee, a psychotherapist and a trainer of support teams (*major incidents and disasters*)

KENNETH CRACKNELL is the President of the Cambridge Theological Federation and Senior Tutor at Wesley House, Cambridge where he teaches systematic and pastoral theology (*faith differences; fanaticism*)

DOMINIC DAVIES is BAC accredited, has a Diploma in Person Centred Counselling and Psychotherapy, is a Senior Lecturer in Counselling at Nottingham Trent University and specializes in sexuality and AIDS work (*AIDS/HIV; gay men and lesbians*)

GUY DEANS is a counsellor and psycho-sexual therapist (*sexual deviation; sexual difficulties; transvestism and trans-sexualism*)

ALAN DUCE is prison chaplain at HM Prison, Lincoln (*prisoners and ex-offenders*)

ROGER ELLIS is an independent counsellor, consultant and trainer (*fees and gifts*)

DOREEN FINNERON is a Community Work Officer with Manchester Diocesan Board for Social Responsibility (*community politics*)

MAGGIE GARSIDE is Victim Support Co-ordinator for Dunstable, Bedfordshire (*victims of crime*)

DAVID GOODACRE is Vicar of Ovingham, Northumberland, and Pastoral Adviser in the Anglican Diocese of Newcastle (*forgiveness of sin; prayer and ritual*)

TONY GOUGH is a pastoral consultant working in private practice in Leicester; and the author of several books dealing with positive aspects of human relationships (*couples, working with; divorce*)

PETER HAWKINS is Managing Director of Bath Consultancy Group helping organizations manage change and development; and a founder of the Bath Centre for Psychotherapy and Counselling (*supervision*)

PETA HEMMINGS is Senior Practitioner in the Barnardo's Orchard Project, and specializes in working with young children in families affected by serious illness or bereavement (*children's experience of loss and death*)

SUE HOPTON is an accredited member of the Association of Christian Counsellors, counsellor, supervisor and trainer of home visitors, pastoral carers, counsellors and supervisors (*home visiting*)

PAM HORROCKS works part-time as Staff Counsellor for Staffordshire Social Services Department and is also part-time Tutor in Counselling at the University of Keele (*counselling, suitability for*)

HILARY INESON is Adviser in Adult Education and Training for the Church of England Board of Education (*adult learning*)

PAUL JACKSON is a nurse therapist at Mount Zeehan Unit, Canterbury, Kent (*alcoholism*)

MICHAEL JACOBS is Director of the Counselling and Psychotherapy Programme at the University of Leicester (*editor; advocacy; cross-cultural awareness; legal advice; money advice; racism and prejudice; religious belief*)

DOROTHY JERROME is Senior Lecturer in Social Gerontology, University of Southampton (*old age*)

RON JOHNSON is a chartered educational psychologist (*children with learning difficulties*)

BRETT KAHR is Lecturer in Psychotherapy at Regent's College London, a registered psychotherapist and a clinical associate with the Mental Handicap Team at the Tavistock Clinic London (*learning disabilities*)

PENNY LEWIS is a systemic psychotherapist and training consultant (*pain and illness*)

PATRICK LOGAN has been Housing and Homelessness Adviser for the Anglican Diocese of Southwark since 1976, where his role is primarily education, development and support (*homelessness*)

DAVID LYALL is a Senior Lecturer in the Department of Christian Ethics and Practical Theology at the University of Edinburgh; and former chaplain to the Northern Group of Hospitals in Edinburgh (*hospital visiting*)

JAN MCLAREN is the Director/Senior Counsellor of the Laura Centre, Leicester (*death of a child*)

JOHN MCLEOD is Director of the Centre for Counselling Studies at Keele University (*counselling and psychotherapy, forms of*)

FELICITY MADDEN trained as a nurse and health visitor; and is now a counsellor and trainer (*cancer*)

JIM MONACH is a lecturer in Mental Health Studies, Department of Psychiatry, University of Sheffield: and Committee Chair of the British Infertility Counselling Association (*infertility*)

EMANUEL MORAN is a consultant psychiatrist at Grovelands Priory Hospital, London and Chairman of The National Council of Gambling (*gambling*)

ANNA MOTZ is Principal Clinical Psychologist for Forensic Services, West London Healthcare (*violent clients*)

WANDA NASH is the UK Chair of the International Stress Management Association (*stress*)

JOHN ORMROD is a clinical psychologist based at the Leicester General Hospital (*depression; obsessive compulsive behaviour; phobias and anxiety*)

FRANK PARKINSON is a counsellor and trainer with wide experience of working with victims and helpers following traumatic and violent incidents of all kinds (*post-traumatic stress; redundancy and unemployment*)

JANET PERRY is a counsellor, trainer and writer (*gender issues*)

DAVID PETERS, a former GP, is a Senior Lecturer at the University of Westminster, course director of an MA in Therapeutic Bodywork and an MSc in Complementary Therapy Studies, and Chair of the British Holistic Medical Association (*holistic medicine*)

BARBARA RAYMENT is Co-ordinator of Wandsworth Youth Advisory Service (*adolescents*)

JUDY RYDE is a psychotherapist in private practice and a staff member of the Bath Centre for Psychotherapy and Counselling (*abortion and miscarriage; mothers and infants*)

MICHAEL SADGROVE is Provost of Sheffield Cathedral (*marriage customs, preparation, etc.*)

PETE SANDERS is a freelance counsellor, trainer, supervisor and author of counselling books (*telephone, use of*)

FRANCES SCOTT teaches at Nottingham Trent University on the diploma and certificate courses in Careers Guidance (*careers guidance*)

JANET SEDEN is a lecturer and practice co-ordinator in the School of Social Work, University of Leicester (*child abuse*)

JULIA SEGAL is a counsellor for people with multiple sclerosis and their families at the MS Unit, Central Middlesex Hospital; and a consultant for professionals and volunteers involved with disabilities and illnesses (*physical disabilities*)

MARTIN SHAW was formerly Senior Lecturer in Social Work at the University of Leicester (*adoption*)

IVAN SOKOLOV is creator of Parent-Link, and a personal and organizational development consultant (*children with behavioural difficulties*)

DAVID STOTER is Senior Chaplain and Manager of the Chaplaincy and Bereavement Centre at the University Hospital, Nottingham (*recovery from major surgery*)

GABRIELLE SYME is an independent counsellor and psychotherapist in Leeds, and is a supervisor, trainer and writer (*bereavement*)

IRA UNELL is a lecturer in Substance Misuse at the University of Leicester and with the Leicestershire Health Authority (*substance misuse*)

MOIRA WALKER is Head of the University of Leicester Counselling Service, a registered psychotherapist with the UK Council for Psychotherapy and a writer and trainer (*adult survivors of abuse; eating disorders; single parents; violence towards women*)

SUE WALROND-SKINNER is a family therapist and Adviser for Pastoral Care and Counselling in the Anglican Diocese of Southwark (*families, working with*)

JOHN WHEWAY is a psychotherapist in private practice and a staff member of the Bath Centre for Psychotherapy and Counselling (*guilt and shame*)

CLAIRE WINTRAM is a freelance tutor and groupworker, with a particular interest in issues as they affect women's lives (*pre-menstrual syndrome*)

RICHARD WOOD is a counsellor and trainer based in Leicester (*gender issues*)

HARRY WRIGHT is clinical nurse specialist in psychotherapy based at The Hazel Centre, Llandrindod Wells (*groups, use of*)

VAL YOUNG is a women's psychotherapist, equal opportunities trainer and author (*menopause*)

Index of articles and subjects

Titles in **bold type** indicate that a full article on this subject is included within the text.

Abortion and miscarriage

(a) With abortion or miscarriage a baby has been lost before it has been born, and before it has been seen or held by the parents. Superficially it seems that an abortion is a desired event and miscarriage is an undesired event. It is not necessarily as simple as this.

This is an area full of multi-layered and strong emotions and complicated by contentious issues. Having a political 'opinion' on whether abortion is 'murder' or 'a woman's right to choose' can mask deeply and closely felt feelings. Similarly, miscarriage can be seen as a 'medical event' rather than a terrible bereavement. These issues are explored below.

(b) Practically every woman who has an abortion or a miscarriage is seen by a doctor. With legalized abortion now available it is rare for a woman to seek a 'back street' abortion. It is important for doctors to understand that in the case of either an abortion or a miscarriage this is a crisis in the woman's life even if she approaches the event with enormous *sang-froid*. She may be unaware of any more complicated feelings. A clumsy attempt by those around her to suggest they exist may push the woman into a more entrenched position. Denying her feelings may be the best way she knows of handling them at the time. It may be only possible for a professional who attends her to stress that distressing feelings are often inevitable, and help is available if the need arises.

It may be that those who show the least emotion are the most at risk. Some judgement may be needed in distinguishing these people from others who, being very well defended, still carry on normal life, maybe for years, before the anguish surfaces that was not felt at the time. Most counsellors and psychotherapists have seen these patterns from their practices.

Other women may be extremely distressed and open to receiving help if it is offered. This distress may manifest itself in the open expression of emotion – a circumstance which has the best prognosis for recovery in the long term. Or it may be displaced in some way, which results in the woman finding life hard to cope with. In this case more specialized help may be needed, which is discussed below.

A miscarriage or an abortion does involve a potential father as well as a mother. Although the father will not have experienced the reality of the child growing in the womb or the physical event of the abortion or miscarriage, he has experienced a loss which may be very significant to him. This may well be overlooked by both carers and friends and even by himself, particularly if he sees his role as taking care of the woman. Many of the difficult and ambivalent feelings experienced by women may well be experienced by men too. It may be difficult for men to allow these feelings, particularly as carers and friends may not expect or recognize their distress.

It is important for a carer to remember that a father is often involved in the loss of a child and that there can be stress on the relationship between the parents of the lost child. Issues lying dormant in their relationship may come to the fore at this time. They may also blame each other for the event; and the bitterness that ensues may be hard to survive with the relationship intact. Couple counselling (see *couples, working with*) could be very helpful in assisting the couple in expressing their feelings safely and in re-owning what each has projected on to the other.

(c) The precipitating factors and circumstances under which a woman has an abortion vary enormously. Miscarriage is different from abortion though there are factors in common. In the case of abortions it is impossible to list them all. I can only indicate some of the possibilities:

1. It may be essential for the mother's health.
2. She may be seriously injured or made unwell by experiencing pregnancy and childbirth or it may even threaten her life.
3. The child may be known to have physical defects which would make life difficult for both mother and child.
4. The mother may feel that her life circumstances are such that it would not be right to bring a child into her world, or having the child may require sacrifices on her part that she feels unwilling to make.

Whatever the circumstances surrounding an abortion, they are rarely made without agonizing thought. Even when the decision seems to be thoughtless, it may well be a desperate step, where thought and feeling have been repressed for fear of the depth of the distress that might otherwise be experienced. Feelings or potential feelings include a sense of **loss** and **guilt**. Both of these are hard to face for any woman who has an abortion.

Many women feel they cannot allow themselves to mourn the loss of a child they have chosen to lose. But the loss is often very keenly felt and may take a woman by surprise. She may have considered herself to be decisive and clear in her choice of an abortion, only to find that she feels a sense of loss and ambivalence which is hard to bear or even to admit. Guilt may be even more difficult to come to terms with, preventing her from allowing herself to mourn. Her inner conscience may question her right to have these feelings, as if she has killed her own child.

In the case of miscarriage, the obvious difference is the precipitating factor: a woman does not consciously choose to have a miscarriage. In spite of this, she may well have a similar feeling of guilt to the woman who has had an abortion. She may wonder if she took sufficient care to carry the child successfully to term. Indeed, the miscarriage may confirm, or appear to confirm, that a lack of care (such as smoking, drinking or taking vigorous exercise) was an expression of her ambivalence about carrying the child. Some women may even be aware of feeling some relief, which might reinforce their feelings of guilt.

A woman who has a miscarriage may therefore feel she has killed her child in a surprisingly similar way to those who have had an abortion. Many of her emotions can be closely linked to feelings about abortion. Those who have had an abortion in the past are often told they will subsequently find it harder to carry a child to term. Whatever the physical realities, this appears to set up anxieties which may make it a self-fulfilling prophecy. These complicated and distressing feelings have to be taken into account when working with women who have experienced such a loss. For whatever reason, when women in this position ask for help, it is necessary to be aware that they are bereaved and that they will experience this in much the same way as any other **bereavement**.

(d) The quality of a woman's contact with professionals is all-important at this time. Although it may be inappropriate for medical, nursing or social workers to explore her feelings in great depth, the quality of empathy shown at this heightened and vulnerable time can make a significant difference to how her experience is integrated into her life.

As I have noted, there is a danger here that the woman can cut off her feelings or be overwhelmed by them. If she cuts them off they may re-emerge in an indirect way. This might impoverish her life by the development of symptoms such as **phobic** or **obsessional** states. If her feelings overwhelm her it may mean that creative or lively responses to everyday experience become difficult or impossible.

At a time of crisis we are in fact at our most open to experience (Hawkins, 1991). It is a time of the most likelihood of damage and the greatest possibility of learning. By 'learning' I mean responding to life's experiences in such a way that our understanding of, and contact with, ourselves is deepened and strengthened. Meeting with a helper at this time can assist or hinder this process. Although family and friends are similarly supportive, the carers are often invested with a quality similar to parenting. They are associated with greater knowledge and expertise. There is often a sense of surrendering to their care. They are turned to when the woman feels, as a child might, that she is unable to care for herself. Although she may present an adult front, she is likely to feel panicky and desperate for help. Her body may feel beyond her control and may put her in touch with a great sense of vulnerability. She will need people to take care of her in a way which is sensitive to the complexity of her emotional state.

Women with less extreme responses may nevertheless find counselling or psychotherapy useful in helping them to understand their responses and to make sense of their experience. To do this they may need the time and space counselling or psychotherapy provide, with the encouragement to experience fully whatever they are feeling however illogical or unacceptable it may seem to them. The therapist or counsellor can provide an opportunity to explore the experience and real meaning of an abortion or miscarriage which has occurred. Counselling is more likely to focus directly on this particular experience, and encourage the mourning that needs to be completed in order that the woman can continue with life.

I have developed a three-stage model that can be used in the counselling of women who have had abortions and miscarriages. This model is particularly applicable for women who are not deeply disturbed or psychotic, but need counselling to help with the mourning process. Often women feel they will not be able to go on to have a live child after this event and feel very distressed by this.

A client whom I call Ruth explained why she felt the need of counselling: 'I felt haunted. I had an idea in my mind that I wouldn't be able to carry a child successfully until I dealt with it.' The three stages may be only three one-hour sessions, but each stage may be given longer as seems appropriate. I usually describe the process we go through to the woman in an initial interview, so that we can start on the material at the beginning of the first meeting. This model also shows that the work does not always have to be long-term to be effective.

Stage one
It is necessary to establish a good, trusting relationship with the woman before or alongside embarking on the main focus of this stage. This may take longer with some women than others. In practice the relationship can be built up while attending to the main focus, but has to be taken more slowly with some women.

The purpose of this stage is to bring the child or children that have been aborted or miscarried symbolically into the room. If it helps, cushions can be used to represent each child. Often the woman has had more than one miscarriage or abortion. There may be one, or some of each. Ruth had one abortion and four miscarriages with no live births. Although they were not recent events she was amazed at how well she remembered each child. They all had definite personalities and characteristics. In this session the customary denial of the child is fully reversed. The child is not only acknowledged but is remembered as completely as possible. Each mother finds that she knows the child in surprising detail. They are each given a name. Ruth had no difficulty at all in naming and describing each of her five children. Being able to fully own, explore and share this knowledge is of course enormously painful, but also a relief. Ruth later recalled that it was helpful to 'give them life; and by that I mean give them some reality, a personality. . . . It was bringing them alive and articulating my relationship with them – conversing with them and getting to know them a bit or bringing out the relationship I already had with them.'

Having brought the child fully into the room the mother can then say what needs to be said to each child. An enormous mixture of feelings can be owned – love, anger, guilt, pain, resentment. In the case of an abortion it is important for the mother to explain her actions to the child. The mother can sit in the place of the child and reply as the child. I encourage the mother to feel her way into the role before replying so that she really feels herself to be replying from the child's position. From this perspective the mother often taps depths of wisdom that are surprising to her. The ensuing conversation is always deeply healing to her. At the end of the session I encourage her to put the child somewhere in the room, as it were, and let the child know that she will return the following week. If she is ready to go on to the next stage I ask her to bring to the following session anything she thinks could contribute to a ritual for saying good-bye to the child.

Stage two

In this stage the child or children are given a place in the psyche of the mother, without denying their existence but in such a way that the mother can freely move on and continue life.

First the child or children are brought back into the room and re-contacted. I then encourage the mother to find an internal space where the child could live in peace for both of them. Although we must say good-bye to the child it is important that the child is not again denied. This time the child is laid to rest and, as it were, given an internal resting place within the mother that feels right for both of them.

I find that ritual helps to give a good sense that this is really done. The ritual must match the dignity and solemnity of the situation. Each mother designs her own ritual. She is providing a **funeral** that was never had. The lost child is fully recognized and mourned. I encourage the mother to make definite statements which describe the truth of their relationship and how the child will now be carried internally in a different manner or in a different place. The child is acknowledged but is now at peace and will no longer affect the mother's development as an individual, except in so far as she has deepened and has grown in wisdom through her experiences.

This is Ruth's account of the ritual she made: 'I can remember taking all week, desperately trying to think of something for the ritual. I walked all round the house looking at everything, trying to find an object that I could use in it. Not until the last minute did I find something. It was a brass candlestick. I also brought a little box of children's birthday cake candles. I wasn't sure how I was going to put them together. I had some idea it was lacking, and you went into the garden and got a sprig of blossom and we put it into the candlestick and that completed it. I lit two or three candles. I kept these items together for a long time and put them in what is now the baby's room.' (Ruth now had a child who sleeps in that room.) 'For a period I used to go in there, light the candles and sit and look and think. I felt very pleased with the items I brought for the ritual because the ritual felt good. I remember reaching the moment when it was time to say good-bye and I said I didn't want to say good-bye. I didn't want them to go away – for that to be it. I did want them to *be* somewhere still. You said, "Yes, fine". I addressed myself to each one in turn You asked me what message I wanted to give each one. I can remember from that time onward an immediate and profound sense of relief and resolution that has remained ever since.'

Stage three

The general purpose of this stage is to reflect on the process that the woman has been through, in order that she may give voice to the internal changes that have occurred. This helps the woman to own the experience fully and to feel the reality of it in her everyday world. We may also at this stage pay attention to the woman's relationship to her womb and fallopian tubes if she is hoping to conceive or stop mis-carrying. The woman can picture her womb as a nurturing and welcoming environment and not one 'haunted' by a dead child. Psychological factors seem to be significant in **infertility** in women. Unresolved feelings about abortion can be an important factor in the list of prob-lems leading to infertility.

One year after the session I had with Ruth she carried a child to term and had a little girl. About that pregnancy she said she felt 'positive and optimistic from the start and all the way through. Although there was some anxiety it was almost token. Somewhere inside me I felt a certainty that this one would go through successfully and I had the child I now do have.'

(e) For some, an abortion or miscarriage may have an even more devastating effect. It may rock the very foundations of their sense of self – particularly if that foundation is already not well based.

Those whose own early experiences in infancy have not fostered a clearly defined and stable sense of self may be predisposed to feelings of disintegration as the death of the child reminds them of destructive and persecutory feelings and experiences in their early relationships with carers (Klein, 1987). A psychotic episode (see *psychosis*) may be precipitated in which persecutory or grandiose ideas are believed in a literal way. There may alternatively be a deep and immovable **depression** which is characterized more by withdrawal than by sadness. The woman may become unreachable in her own private hell. In this case **suicide** or suicide attempts may be a real danger as she is overwhelmed by a sense of **guilt**.

In these cases more expert help will be needed. In an emergency situation the psychiatric services will need to be contacted and may be able to help restore the woman to a more even keel.

If the woman is to really heal the trauma of this experience then a psychotherapist will be able to help the woman understand her own distress and provide the reparative situation necessary to rebuild a strengthened sense of self. This may be provided within the statutory services, or be available privately.

(f) Although counselling can be relatively short term, it is important to understand when referring to a counsellor or psychotherapist that the work is often slow and careful as it touches areas that are painful and can only come to light in a trusting relationship. This also means the counsellor or psychotherapist cannot talk about the work with the client in detail to the referee or referral agency. It is important that this is understood and respected for the work to continue satisfactorily.

(g) Hey, V., Itzin, C., Saunders, L. and Speakman, M. A. (eds) (1989) *Hidden Loss*. London: The Women's Press; Klein, D. and Kaufmann, C. (1992) *Unplanned Pregnancy*. London: Penguin Books; Phillips, A. and Townsend, R. (1992) *Bitter Fruit*. London: Hunter.

JUDY RYDE

(See also *bereavement; death of a child; guilt and shame; loss*)

Adolescents

(a)   Adolescence is a formative part of life's experience. It is the process which transforms the child into an adult – a period in which young people make the transition from dependence to independence.

(b)   While it is important not to be prescriptive about what constitutes 'normal' adolescent development, there are some tasks which are common to the majority of young people. Adolescence is centrally concerned with change: physical, social, emotional and psychological. There are, however, no rules about when adolescence begins or ends, the feelings which accompany it or how each individual copes with the process. The common tasks which face young people in adolescence are additionally complicated by the crises and pressures in society – unemployment, family breakdown, lack of housing. And, for those young people who may have experienced a damaging childhood, adolescence may also precipitate major psychological crises. For each young person adolescence is a unique experience. At some point, most young people experience some degree of stress or anxiety as major physical changes coincide with the move towards establishing themselves in the adult world. Many will seek help and reassurance of one kind or another, either through books, magazines, 'agony aunt' columns, helplines or from trusted adults in their communities.

Adolescence is a period of challenge – both for the young people involved and for all those who come into contact with them. It is a time to test out how their emotional, physical, psychological and social self can develop and enable the process of change from a girl or boy to a woman or a man. While human development includes a number of transitions throughout the life-cycle, no other period is likely to be as potentially turbulent as this process. It is the experience of adolescence which propels young people into forming (or not forming) their ideal of the adult they want to become. The options available during adolescence, and the decisions and choices made about both practical and personal lives, have a profound effect on young adulthood. During adolescence young people begin defining their own level of need and the process of getting those needs met for themselves. This is a difficult process for most of them, and for some it may be a painful and fearful task. But it can also be an exciting task as young people confront and challenge the adult world.

(c)   The outward and most obvious signs of the onset of adolescence are the physical changes occurring to young people's bodies. Changes at puberty often bring a mix of emotions: embarrassment and feelings of awkwardness, together with some sense of relief and pride. Young people in early adolescence are normally intensely preoccupied with their bodies and the way they are changing. They are indeed acutely concerned that their development is 'normal'. In coming to terms with their physical development, young people have to learn to accept a new body image and gain a sense of control over their body, which often feels bigger than they are. In addition to dealing with their own feelings, young people also have to face the reactions of others around them. In families, there may well be shifts and changes in parent–child relationships and an increase of teasing by siblings. Their changing shape may also provoke sexual comments and invitations. Handling other people's reactions to their own body changes adds to the stress and lack of confidence that many young people feel.

Until they reach the age of 16, whether young people choose to attend school or not, there is a statutory expectation that they will be in full-time education. For most young people school represents a major part of life's certainties. It may be a place to belong, to feel safe in, a place where there is predictability and some consistency. (Young people who experience bullying will of course have other feelings.) While some young people may not feel very positive about school and may behave disruptively, it is somewhere to go, a situation where they at least know what is expected of them. The prospect of leaving school, even for those desperate to do so, can provoke fears and anxieties, coupled with excitement and a sense of freedom. Unfortunately, for significant numbers their leaving school or college leads only to unemployment. Since large numbers of young people expect to be unemployed for considerable periods of time, even that most tangible evidence of a young person's entry into the adult world is now denied them. Employment is not only a passport to meeting many of life's practical needs; it still defines to a large extent who we are in society, and thus affects a range of emotional, psychological and social needs. Young people are increasingly caught in a world in which the social structures extend the time they will spend in an impoverished adolescent state. Little wonder then that some young people seek other escape routes and ways to meet their needs, e.g. drugs (see *substance misuse*), parenthood, petty crime.

A further part of the process of becoming an independent person requires a re-definition of the relationship between parent (or carer) and child. Both sides have to be willing to negotiate the process of adjusting to and accommodating the emerging independence of the young person. Intense feelings are likely to be experienced on both sides. Parents may feel a sense of loss as their children move away from them. Young people may be so preoccupied with their own physical and emotional changes that they have little sense of their parents' feelings. For many more children and young people **divorce** or separation and the introduction of a new partner by a parent into the family home is becoming common. This can leave a young person, who already feels confused and experiencing volatile emotions and mood-swings, also feeling increasingly isolated and unwanted. He or she may no longer feel safe and loved (although in some cases that may rarely if ever have been felt). Frequent and painful arguments may erupt. There may also be physical violence. For a significant number the way out is to leave home. The issue most frequently presented by young people to youth counselling and advisory services is housing and **homelessness**, and this is often due to family difficulties.

Another factor contributing to young homelessness, as well as to significant mental health and relationship difficulties, are the numbers of young people who have experienced abusive relationships with adults – sexual, physical and emotional (see *child abuse*). They may have negotiated childhood without any real sense of safety. Adult care may have been provided in ways which only compounded their sense of confusion. Clearly in these kinds of family settings young people's needs are unlikely to be satisfactorily met.

In trying to establish their adult identities, young people may reject the models offered by family members and seek out alternatives. Often these role models represent more seemingly successful or glamorous life-styles – teachers as well as the rich and famous may equally well feature in their fantasies. In addition to looking for other adult role models, young people's relationships with their peers also begin to change. Peer relationships often assume greater significance in adolescence – the views and opinions of peers tend to hold greater value than those of family members. A sense of belonging to, and of being liked and accepted by, a group of peers is often felt to be more important at this time than relationships with any other groups. One of the little-acknowledged effects of unemployment is that young people tend to spend considerably more of their time with peers. They miss out on the experience of learning to be with and working alongside different adult groups. As a consequence, there is likely to be an increased distance and greater misunderstanding between different age groups.

In looking beyond family groups for love and acceptance, young people may also begin to experiment emotionally and physically with their emerging adult sexuality. Sexual experimentation, whether it is heterosexual or homosexual (and it may be both), frequently creates concerns and anxieties about sexual practices and performance, as well as more practical considerations of contraception and 'safe sex'.

In general, the hope is that young people will pass through the transition from child to adult and emerge relatively unscathed, with family relationships more or less intact. Some, and perhaps arguably a rising number, find the transition considerably more difficult, as (for example) family breakdown and youth unemployment become an increasingly prevalent experience. The social, political and economic changes during the post-war period have placed children encountering adolescence in a situation where personal change is a daily hazard. In addition, young people's adult carers are themselves experiencing difficult changes in their own lives – unemployment, financial problems, family and partnership breakdowns, and isolation from local communities. Many of these issues are not of themselves new and were of course experienced in previous generations. Perhaps what is different is the sheer number of people experiencing a combination of all or many of these issues, together with a level of expectation about their personal and working lives that we have not seen before. It is against this broad background that many young people are facing this significant transition from child to adult. As young people undergo their struggle for independence they need to push against solid and firm boundaries, yet many of them are finding that all too frequently the adults in their lives are feeling as vulnerable, confused and fearful as themselves. There is no-one they really dare push against with any conviction of finding the reassurance of resistance.

Furthermore, the reality of many young people's lives is often at odds with the kinds of life-style and image portrayed in certain sections of the media. The pressure to do it all and to get it all right in a competitive world, which then denies them access to the opportunities it seems to hold out, leaves many young people feeling insignificant and undervalued. For young people in minority groups, these feelings are compounded by discrimination levelled at personal factors that are not just to do with their age. While there are clearly solutions that need to be found over and above the provision of helping interventions by the caring professions, there is still much that workers can achieve in enabling young people to feel supported and helped.

(d) It is important to recognize the diverse range of practical and emotional needs and concerns that adolescents have. We also have to accept that their needs do not stand in isolation from one another, but are interdependent. Young people's practical and emotional concerns are inextricable: decisions about education and employment, leaving home, etc. have a significant impact on the way they feel about themselves and about their relationship with others. For a young person to feel and be healthy requires a self-determined, optimum level of their needs being met.

Since adolescence creates the opportunity for young people to begin to meet *their own* needs as independent people, positive experiences and influences at this critical period enable them to make up for some of the deficits of the past. This is especially true, and is more likely to take place, when young people can determine for themselves that they want help. Understanding their needs, and satisfying them in ways which are neither self-harming nor harming to others, can be an especially difficult task for young people who have had little positive experience during their childhood. Young people need access to help which enables them to articulate what they want, which helps them to feel skilled and which enables them to take control. The help and support which is made available to them therefore has to be sensitive to, and to acknowledge, the transition from the comparatively powerless child to the, hopefully, empowered adult. Young people frequently shift between the two roles of being a child and an adult. Sometimes this comes from their own internal struggle. However, they also have to carry out a juggling act in the context of some confusing social policy signals regarding their rights as autonomous and independent beings: e.g. welfare benefit entitlements, access to housing, legislation on homosexuality, etc. The helping responses offered to young people must respect them as individuals and value their experience.

Young people are most likely to turn to outside help when they find themselves in a crisis, such as being homeless, or because of an increasing unease or dissatisfaction with the way they feel about themselves and their relationships with others There are a number of core skills which any helper needs to possess in order to offer the most effective level of help: the ability to listen and convey understanding are the primary skills. Experience suggests that there are a number of important elements which should also be present in offering help to young people. These are that the help is confidential, impartial, informal and accessible. These areas have most recently been highlighted in research around young people's access to youth counselling and advisory services (Feaviour, 1994).

While there is certainly a need for specialist youth counsellors and advice workers, in practice this may not always be possible. Thus people who are able to offer more general support within the context of a relationship which respects a young person's desire for confidential and impartial help can go a long way to providing good quality help.

One of the key skills in working with young people is the ability to really listen to what they are saying. It is of course a skill which is essential in any helping intervention, and which workers need to remain aware of regardless of their status or experience. Listening is an important way in which adults can communicate respect. Sadly, many young people do not feel listened to and they are therefore reluctant to speak, for fear that they will be dismissed or that their problems will be ignored. Young people want to be heard in a way which demonstrates that they have been understood and accepted, and their experiences validated. This requires helpers who are able to be straight in their dealings with them, and who can be open and honest about what they can and cannot offer. It also requires adults who are able to be consistent and reliable. If a young person's experience of adults has been one in which they have felt let down or where there have been confusing messages about boundaries and expectations, it is vital when they choose to seek help that the person they ask can maintain consistency in their actions, and can deliver what they promise. Adolescence provides an opportunity to gain some of the experience that has been lacking in childhood. Helpers chosen by young people to support them in this process need to remain conscious of just how much they can provide.

For young people seeking help in a crisis or for those who are feeling scared, vulnerable and uncertain it is critical that their helpers have a very clear sense of their own professional and personal boundaries. Professional boundaries are very clearly linked to the issue of **confidentiality**. It is vital that helpers are absolutely clear about the parameters of the helping relationship and the degree of confidentiality they are able to provide. This in turn needs to be communicated clearly and explicitly to young people, so that they are in a position to make a choice about the kinds of information they want to bring. While there are issues about protection when working with young people, these need to be balanced against the growing autonomy of adolescents and their right to receive help which respects their privacy. Unless specifically requested, young people do not want family members or others informed about their need for help. Young people, like adults, wish to retain control of their personal information. Schools, social services and some other statutory services may not be able to offer this, and therefore other services need to be available to support young people.

Since young people want access to help which is informal, accessible and impartial, an authoritarian approach, which appears to make judgements of a young person and about their difficulties, is totally inappropriate. Young people respond well to people who are warm and accepting of them, who treat them and their problems seriously, and who do not belittle or deny their problems and concerns. This does not preclude the helper from challenging any behaviours which are harmful or damaging. For individual helpers, being informal and accessible demands flexibility and adaptability in the way they work. While helpers are responsible for maintaining a good sense of their professional helping role and the limits that this places on their relationships with young people, they must also be able to allow themselves to be seen for who they are. Often young people will want to have a sense of who their helpers are. They are uncomfortable and uneasy with workers who appear to hide themselves behind a professional role. A friendly and open approach with an appropriate level of humour and self-disclosure can be important in allowing young people to express how they are feeling and in enabling a relationship of trust to develop.

(e) While teachers, youth workers and other adults in the community may be the first people to whom a young person turns for help, it may be that ongoing help and support is better delivered by a specialist service. On a national basis young people's access to confidential counselling and advisory services is variable. Many of these services are affiliated to Youth Access (Magazine Business Centre, 11 Newarke Street, Leicester LE1 5SS, Tel: 0116 255 8763). Although Youth Access does not promote a prescriptive model in the delivery of services to young people, it seeks to encourage some common features both in practice and procedures. Many of these youth counselling and advisory services are part of the voluntary sector. Unlike the Citizens Advice Bureaux they are not easily identifiable, and the easiest method of contact and referral is via Youth Access. Essential ingredients in these agencies are the notions that young people self-refer and that the agency holds to an explicit statement on confidentiality. Agencies often offer a range of helping interventions: information, advice, counselling, sexual health services, group work and telephone counselling. But it is important to check with an individual agency regarding the particular type of help they can offer.

Regardless of whether help is offered by the individual care-worker or the specialist agency, a person-centred rather than a problem-centred approach is best able to meet young people's needs. Young people do not want to feel that they are either 'mad' or 'bad' just because they choose to seek help. Feelings during adolescence are often strong and confusing. Helpers who are able to listen to young people can offer some relief and release from the intensity of their feelings, and perhaps help towards some understanding and insight into ways of resolving their difficulties.

(f) Feaviour, K. (1994) *Who's Really Listening?* Leicester: Youth Access; Rayment, B. (1994) *Confidential Policy and Practice in Youth Counselling and Advisory Services*. Leicester: Youth Access; The Children's Legal Centre (1992) *Working with Young People: Legal Responsibility and Liability*. The Children's Legal Centre (20 Compton Terrace, London N1 2UN).

BARBARA RAYMENT

Adoption

(a) Adoption is the permanent legal transfer of all the parental rights and responsibilities relating to a specific child from one person to another. Adoption is quite distinct from fostering in which parents share their responsibilities with foster carers, either directly or by arrangement with local authority social services or a voluntary child care agency. A fostering arrangement may last for years but it may be ended at any time at the instigation of parents, foster carer or agency, and parents at no time lose their parental responsibility. An adoption order, which transfers all the original parents' responsibilities to the adoptive parent(s), can be made only by a court, and ended only by the making of a subsequent adoption order to other adoptive parents.

To be an adoptive child or parent does not inevitably lead to problems requiring professional help, despite the impression given by some of the early and often crude research derived from psychiatric or court records. Most recent research shows positive outcomes for the great majority of adoptions, a good deal more positive than the other available options of fostering, residential care or even growing up in the average one-parent family. It is unsafe and unhelpful to assume that adoptive families will have problems or that any problems they do have necessarily relate to their adoptive status.

That being said, people who give up a child for adoption, adoptive parents, children and adults who have grown up in adoptive families are faced with a number of specific tasks over and above those to be addressed in 'normal' families. The natural parents often are left to deal with a chronic sense of **loss** and **guilt** over their decision, reduced but perhaps never totally eradicated by sensitive counselling at the time of the adoption. For adoptive parents, the main tasks revolve around developing a sense of 'ownership' towards the adopted child (as they would to a child of their 'own') and encouraging a sense of belonging in the child, while acknowledging the differences between 'natural' and adoptive parent–child relations.

For the child, the major task is to recognize and deal with the fact of having been given up by (or removed from) the birth parents for adoption. For the adoptive family as a whole, there are issues around perceiving themselves and being seen as deviating from the image of the 'normal' family – even though the normal family is now less the norm in our society than is often supposed. (The frequent use of quotation marks in this section is an indication of the difficulties we experience in thinking and talking about different family patterns and relationships.)

(b)   A parent who has given up a child for adoption will at the time experience a range of emotions, depending on the circumstances – grief, guilt, anger, helplessness, etc. Unresolved feelings of **guilt** and **loss** may linger for many years, to be triggered by major or minor crises involving loss or the threat of loss in later life. Although the emphasis has been on mothers, there is evidence that many fathers who have lost a child through adoption (a process in which they are generally left on the sidelines) experience similar reactions.

Adopted children may experience a range of problems expressed in a variety of ways: from emotional and behavioural problems arising from life events prior to placement or difficulties in their relationship with the adoptive parents; to insecurities in their adoptive status which may reverberate well into adult life. Where adopters have attempted to conceal or minimize the facts about their child's origins, the child may experience a sense of betrayal and loss of trust when the truth emerges. Where their adoptive status has been over-emphasized, they may have a sense of rootlessness, belonging to neither their original nor their adoptive family.

People who have grown up adopted may wish to investigate their origins, sometimes to the extent of seeking out their original parents. The quest may be due simply to natural curiosity from a secure base in their adoptive family; or, where adoptive relations are less satisfactory, it may reflect an idealized fantasy around recreating a lost childhood.

Particular problems may arise for black or Asian children placed with white families, a practice now frowned upon professionally but almost encouraged in the 'liberal' climate of the late 1960s and 1970s. The risk for such children is of growing up belonging to neither community and ill-equipped to deal with life in a racist society.

Adoptive parents may also experience the normal challenges of child-rearing, compounded by difficulties around telling the child about their adoptive status. Parents who adopted because they were unable to produce their 'own' children may have unresolved feelings about their own **infertility**, which in turn may lead to problems in dealing positively with issues of sexuality in their adopted children.

Some of the difficulties for all parties arise from the tradition of 'closed' adoption, with its aim of maximum secrecy and minimal contact between natural and adoptive parents before and after the adoption. Such secrecy has come to be seen as undesirable as well as difficult to maintain in older child adoptions. The recent trend towards open adoption, with sharing of information and continuing contact, should reduce some of these problems. Only time will tell whether other problems will take their place, in particular some of the sense of confusion, insecurity and divided responsibility generally associated with long-term foster care.

(c)   To have a child placed for adoption is clearly a crisis in a parent's life, however rational the decision may appear to be. It is an experience akin to **bereavement**, though often without benefit of the normal social supports offered following a death.

For the child or adoptive parents, problems may have their roots in any phase of their lives. Adoption involves a radical disruption in a child's life and relationships, which can result in what has been called 'genealogical bewilderment' (confusion over origins) for the child. Nowadays most children available for adoption are older, perhaps even of school age, with a pre-adoption history of abuse or neglect, and with memories of earlier family relationships which will be significant even when unsatisfactory. Many such children also suffer from chronic illness or multiple disabilities (see *physical disabilities; learning disabilities*) requiring – though not necessarily receiving – continuing professional help for themselves and for their adopters.

The nature-versus-nurture debate has swung widely over the years and many people now adult would have been adopted at a time when it was believed that a loving home would overcome most obstacles. Matching children and adopters is a far from exact science, much depending on a post-adoption chemistry which cannot readily be predicted. Genetic research has indicated the importance of heredity in relation to mental health (especially schizophrenia) and alcoholism, and more general personality characteristics such as extraversion/ introversion and intelligence.

Adoptive parents tend to have high expectations of themselves and may unconsciously transmit these expectations to the child in the form of unrealistic demands in terms of behaviour, school achievement, career ambition, etc. Although adopted children are sometimes unhelpfully referred to as 'chosen', it is in fact the adoptive parents who are chosen (by the agency) and they may harbour residual doubts as to their entitlement to be parents. There is probably less of a tendency nowadays to talk of the risk of 'bad blood' in adopted children but some adopters may still be inclined to lay on natural parents the blame for behaviour which others would tolerate as part of the rough and tumble of family life.

(d)   When a problem is presented as specifically related to adoption, the obvious first port of call for the person concerned is an adoption agency, preferably (although not necessarily) the one involved in the original placement, where the relevant information and expertise should be available. But often issues of adoption arise in the course of counselling on other personal or family matters, and it may be neither necessary nor desirable to refer the person on – they may indeed be unwilling to be referred further. It is important for a helper to recognize that, while there is specialist knowledge in this field, the human problems in adoption are those common to other situations – **loss** and change, identity and self-esteem, blocked or faulty communication with families (see *families, working with*).

Adoption is not a once-for-all event, but a process which becomes part of the continuing fabric of adoptive family life. The obvious challenges are those in the early stages when child, parents and other family members have to adjust and adapt to their new relationships with one another. Some of these adjustments occur during the period between placement and the court hearing, when adoption agency involvement is greatest. Other crucial points may arise around talking with the child about his or her origins – again not once-for-all, but an updating process in line with the child's or young person's emotional and intellectual development; or arise when starting school, during adolescence, when the adopted adult marries or is preparing to become a parent themselves.

Talking to adopted children about their origins is generally recognized as one of the major worries for adopters. An apparently simple exercise (akin to telling the 'facts of life'), it re-activates memories of a possibly difficult time in the adopters' lives, draws attention to the child's loss of first parents and 'differentness' within the adoptive family, and may be felt to threaten the stability of the family itself. Little wonder that some earlier authorities advised adopters to keep the fact of adoption secret from the child! It is now generally recognized that openness and honesty are essential to the parent–child adoptive relationship and that children have a right to an understanding of their situation. As with other painful communications, parents may at times have difficulty in communicating, and children may have difficulty in 'hearing' this information.

Facts are only part of the matter: perhaps more important are the feelings which the parent or the child attaches to these facts. Exploring what adoption means to the person concerned may reveal misunderstandings and misconceptions, which with help can be overcome. Given the relative tolerance with which unmarried parenthood is now regarded it is not difficult for any adopted person to regard their position as evidence of rejection or lack of care by the original parent: 'Why me? What was so wrong with me that I was given up for adoption?' It is hard now to understand the degree of social stigma attached to unmarried parenthood and illegitimacy as recently as the 1960s, and the heavy social and financial pressures on unmarried mothers to give up their babies. Even now, bringing up a child single-handed (see *single parents*) is no easy matter; and for some young parents who recognize their limitations, placing their baby for adoption remains a loving rather than selfish action.

Much harder to come to terms with is the discovery that one's adoption was a sequel to incest, abuse or neglect. At one level, what may be needed is support while seeking further information, following the maxim that, however painful knowledge may be, it is generally better to know than not to know, and so be left with fears and fantasies. Beyond this again is the importance of the meaning of it all in terms of the sense of self – you are not the victim of your autobiography, but you may become the victim of the way in which you interpret your autobiography.

(e) Local authorities are required by law to provide a service to anyone involved in adoption – birth parent, adoptive parent or adopted child – not just around the time when the placement and adoption order are being made but at any time afterwards as well. This service is normally provided through the social services department, often through a specialist adoption team. Adoption work is also carried out by voluntary child care agencies such as Barnardo's, the National Children's Home, the Church of England Children's Society and the Catholic Children's Society.

The key organization in the adoption field in the United Kingdom is British Agencies for Adoption and Fostering (BAAF) with its headquarters at 200 Union Street, London SE1 0LY, and a number of regional offices. BAAF seeks to promote good standards of practice in adoption and fostering by means of its publications, seminars and courses, and through its information and advisory services. Its list of publications includes clear, concise leaflets addressed to birth parents, children and adopters as well as research material intended for professionals. BAAF also publishes a quarterly journal *Adoption and Fostering* containing articles, news, medical and legal notes and book reviews on a broad range of relevant topics.

The Post-Adoption Centre (5 Torriano Mews, Torriano Avenue, London NW5 2RZ) also publishes pamphlets and offers occasional workshops for adopters and others involved in adoption. Parent to Parent Information on Adoption Services (PPIAS) (Lower Boddington, Daventry, Northants NN11 6YB) offers, among other services, support and information to families adopting – or considering adopting – children deemed 'hard-to-place', i.e. children who are older or suffering from disabilities. Some areas have adoption **self-help groups** of various kinds, and information about these is best obtained from local social services departments.

(f) Adoption records are highly confidential and agencies are not permitted to disclose their contents to third parties without the consent of the Lord Chancellor's Office. People seeking information about an adoption in which they were involved (either as natural or adoptive parent or as an adopted person) should be referred to their social services department where they should receive guidance and information as well as appropriate counselling support.

(g) Brodzinsky, D. M. and Schechter, M. D. (eds) (1990) *Psychology of Adoption*. Oxford: Oxford University Press; Shaw, M. (ed.) (1994) *A Bibliography of Family Placement Literature*. London: British Agencies for Adoption and Fostering; Winkler, R. C., Brown, D. W., Keppell, M. V. and Blanchard, A. (1988) *Clinical Practice in Adoption*. Oxford: Pergamon Press.

MARTIN SHAW
(See also *infertility; mothers and infants*)

Adult learning

(a) Learning describes gaining knowledge and new skills, self-development and changing or challenging values. It happens throughout life in informal ways and at particular times through more formal structures. It takes place in an individual working alone, through one-to-one contact, in small groups or in large gatherings.

(b) Adults do not all learn easily. There are both internal and external blocks to learning. Change brings with it fear, anxiety and resistance, which in their turn inhibit learning. *Internal* blocks are embarrassment, feelings of insecurity, bad memories of previous learning experience, lack of motivation and fear of failure. Lack of access to learning institutions and educators who do not provide appropriate methods of learning constitute *external* blocks.

(c) Adults are not empty receptacles waiting to be filled with knowledge or trained in skills. They bring their experience which includes negative feelings from previous learning. Memories of school evoke feelings of powerlessness, boredom or anxiety; as adults, their fear of appearing ignorant or stupid may be emphasized by the lack of more recent formal learning. They can overcome their initial reluctance when there is a strong motivation to learn, but may continue to feel anxious that they will not be able to keep up with the others, that their ignorance will be unacceptable and that they may fail.

Open access is one of the values of adult education, but some learning institutions present learners with obstacles when the provision focuses on the content of what is to be learned at the expense of an appropriate process of learning.

Individuals learn in different ways and need a variety of methods for effective learning.

(d) When designing learning for adults, the teacher or facilitator needs to ask the following questions:

- what is to be learned?
- what are the learners' needs and how will they be supported?
- what experience and knowledge do the learners bring with them?
- what styles or preferences for learning do the learners have?
- how will learning be achieved most effectively?

What is to be learned   refers to the content of the specific learning event. This can be chosen by the educator, by the learner or by negotiation between the two. The aim of the learning should be clear and the content should be presented in manageable units with space for reflection and assimilation. The learner should be encouraged to generalize from the learning experience and to make connections, which lead to application. Any effective learning will take account of the different learning styles or preferences of the learners and of their capacity to learn (Mackie, 1981).

The learners' needs: Adults learn best when learning is geared to their own particular needs and interests. As they recognize their own steps forward, their confidence grows and this in turn leads to more learning. Clearly formulated learning outcomes or goals aid this progress. Learners need to feel that their experience is being valued and used. They need to have their new learning reinforced by practice, by positive affirmation, by challenge and by accurate feedback which focuses on the learning rather than on the learner.

There must be a supportive climate in the learning group or between the learner and the teacher. Adults need a climate where failure is not only possible but is seen as a necessary step on the way to further learning. Unlearning of old habits or facing challenges to deeply held convictions is both difficult and meaningful. It only becomes possible when the learner recognizes the need to learn (change) and where the climate and environment are sufficiently supportive to enable risks to be taken. The task of the educator is to provide such a climate. The educator must also be aware of the balance of power in this relationship and provide learners with the opportunity to express their own learning needs.

Experience   in this context includes events from the past and in the here and now. Experience includes both having and knowing. 'Having' points to the immediacy of contact with the events of life happening at this moment. 'Knowing' relates to the interpretation of events. Not all experience leads to immediate learning. It is accepted and stored away, because its relevance is not apparent. When it becomes relevant as an aid to learning, it returns to consciousness and is reflected on.

One of the skills of the educator is to offer a structure which enables learners to reflect critically on their experiences and learn from them. She helps learners to think about previous experience as a base for current learning. Learners are then more focused on how the new learning fits with existing frameworks. They can then cope more easily with the discomfort which results when those frameworks come under threat from new information or changing values.

Learning style   refers to the learner's characteristic ways of processing information, feeling and behaving in learning situations.

Honey and Mumford (1992) have developed a learning style questionnaire which describes four basic learning preferences in adult learning:

> *Activists* learn by doing and enjoy being asked to experience new things. They are impatient with theory and too much stepping back.
>
> *Reflectors* stand back from any experience in order to consider its implications. They need space and time in which to assimilate what has happened and do not learn well when there is too much activity. They need space alone to begin to make links for themselves.
>
> *Theorists* need to be clear about the theory underlying the subject. They like to be able to look in depth at the abstract concepts involved.
>
> *Pragmatists* need to relate learning to their everyday lives. They like to practise and to see clearly how what they learn is able to be applied.

Learners use all four ways of learning, but show a preference for one or two styles. When designing for others it is important to be aware of your own natural preferences, to consider the preferences of the learners and to provide appropriate learning methods. It is difficult to provide what every learner needs when learning happens in a group. The educator should use a variety of methods and material, and try to ensure that each style finds something which suits. Learners should be encouraged to develop their less natural learning styles, and each learning experience should include all four elements.

Effective learning: A number of theories have been formulated around the idea of learning as a cycle.

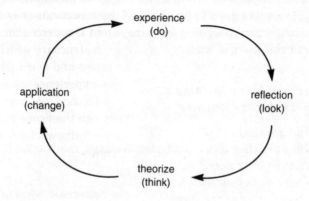

Based on Kolb and Fry, 1975.

In this model, learning is described as a cycle which has four kinds of activity. Experience, reflection, theorizing and application are all necessary to effective learning, but learners will find it easier to enter the cycle at the place which fits most easily with their preferred learning style. The activist likes to 'do', the reflector to observe and reflect, the theorist enjoys thinking about abstract concepts and generalizations, and the pragmatist likes to put into action what he or she has learned.

For learning to be effective, adults must exercise some control over what and how they learn. As learning progresses and confidence grows people move from dependence on the educator towards more self-direction. Those offering learning need to hold the balance between their own needs to share information or skill and the learners' actual needs. Education is not value-free, and recognizing the power relationship between learner and teacher is important.

The educator can develop a *learning contract* between the learner and the educator in which needs are diagnosed, objectives (learning outcomes) formulated, learning strategies and resources identified and progress evaluated. In the relationship between learner and teacher power remains with the learner (Knowles, 1975). The task of the educator is to provide the resources for learning, and to respond to educational need in ways which improve the quality of the self-directedness of learners.

Challenging the external blocks to learning requires a recognition that changing individuals may only enable them to live more happily with oppressive institutions within an oppressive society. Freire's work (1972, 1974) suggests that individuals can also learn to challenge and change the structures. Freire's methods are especially useful when working with people who are disadvantaged by society or educational provision. Educators need to be aware of their own values and political understanding when designing learning, and to be clear about the aim of any particular piece of work.

A checklist for effective learning
Information about the learners:

- Who are they?
- What are they like – attitudes, feelings, motivation?
- What do they need?
- What do they already know?
- What skills do they have?
- What experience will they bring?

Information can be gathered by written questions or interview, through a pre-course meeting or from previous experience of the educator, which must be checked with the learners.

- from the information gathered define a clear *aim*:
    short and sharply focused, relevant, clear and concise
    specific, measurable and manageable in the time available
- check that you have the skills, knowledge and resources to achieve the aim
- develop a learning contract with the learners:
    agree learning outcomes (objectives)
    methods
- from the aim and learning outcomes design a method of evaluation
- design a learning experience:
    using a variety of methods

      beginning with the learner's own experience
      containing adequate reflection time
      with appropriate theory to be given verbally or on handouts
      ensuring the opportunity for practice and application of
         learning

- check the venue. Is it:
      warm and well lit?
      comfortable?
      near public transport?
      safe for people arriving alone?
- does it have flip chart and pens, overhead projector?
      spaces for sub-groups to meet?
      the right sort of seating for the methods to be used?

Any of these elements can make the difference between effective and ineffective learning.

(e) There is a body of knowledge and expertise which relates to enabling and supporting learning. Many colleges of further and higher education run courses or offer diplomas and certificates in adult education. The Open University has a number of modules relating to the education and training of adults. National Vocational Qualifications are available in training and development from levels 3 to 5. The Open College Networks recognize learning programmes and award credits to individual learners. Credits gained in one area are increasingly transferable through the Credit Accumulation Transfer System. The National Institute for Adult and Continuing Education (NIACE) (19b De Montfort Street, Leicester LE1 7GE) offers useful publications and information. The Open University and the Church of England Board of Education both offer schemes for professional development. The churches have recently developed Adult Network, an ecumenical network for those involved in adult learning. Its aim is to support those working in both full-time paid work and volunteers to develop their skills and to disseminate good practice.

(g) Boud, D., Cohen, R. and Walker, D. (eds) (1993) *Using Experience for Learning*. Buckingham: Open University Press; Craig, Y. (1994) *Learning for Life*. London: Mowbray; Smith, R. (1982) *Learning How to Learn*. Buckingham: Open University Press.

HILARY INESON

Adult survivors of abuse

(a) 'Abuse' nowadays is most likely to be understood as referring to sexual abuse, and adult survivors as having therefore experienced as children this type of exploitative behaviour. However, the term covers a wider range of ill treatment (see *child abuse*), and it is important to recognize that adults presenting as survivors of abuse may have been tragically exposed to a horrific range of damaging events. These can encompass physical, sexual and psychological abuse, as well as neglect. The term 'survivor' is generally preferred to 'victim' when referring to an adult. It is felt to be more positive and a less negative label. However, no word is ideal in that it cannot adequately encompass the horrors of the experience, or the agony of those who have been made to suffer.

(b) The recognition of the existence of large numbers of adults who need help in adulthood as a result of abuse in childhood is a fairly recent one, although abuse itself is neither a new nor a modern phenomenon. There is now much wider acceptance of child abuse as a major social ill, although services for the adult have been slower to develop, and remain inadequate.

Both women and men present as adult survivors. The gender difference in abuse rates is not possible to ascertain accurately. However, it is now generally recognized that far more men have been sexually abused in childhood than was previously thought. Similarly, it is recognized that women abuse as well as men. It still seems that more girls are at risk of sexual abuse than boys and that their abusers are very much more likely to be men. As a result a large number of those presenting for help as adults are women who have been abused by men. The picture of neglect and physical abuse is more complex. Many clients who present primarily as survivors of physical abuse were abused by mothers as young children. This may reflect the current style of child care in society: small children are predominantly cared for by women. However, men also physically abuse children. Another pattern is survivors who have been sexually abused by the father or other close male relative, and physically abused or neglected by the mother.

Some have even been abused in many ways by many people, continuing over years sometimes even into adulthood. For others the abuse has occurred on one or two occasions only. Commonly, abusers are family members or someone known and trusted by the child and the family: for instance, abuse occurs in children's homes, schools, churches, nurseries, hospitals and with child-minders. Abusers and their victims come from all walks and classes of life. It is clear that many abusers insinuate themselves carefully into trusted positions where they can have easy access to children. Abuse can be meticulously planned, especially where this is part of an organized ring.

It is essential to recognize that adults who have been abused carry with them the legacy of a spoilt childhood in which their belief in the trustworthiness of others has been demolished. Often the survivor believes or fears that *she or he* is the bad, wicked or dangerous person, rather than their persecutor. This reflects what she or he has often been told by the abuser: statements such as 'You're bad; you deserve this'; 'It's your fault I'm doing this'; 'You like it really – it's what you want'; and 'You made me do this' are expressions frequently used. The abuser conveniently denies his own responsibility, placing it on the innocent victim, who internalizes the badness that is unacknowledged by the perpetrator. To understand the extent, impact and ongoing consequences of abuse it is essential to understand the depth of denial by abusers, and the powerful consequences of this on the child, and subsequently on the adult.

Abuse is often accompanied by threats: for example, children are told that if they say anything, their siblings, friends or pets will be harmed; or the family will be destroyed; or their mother will be heartbroken; or they will not be believed and they will be taken away. Abusers are inventive in their threats. Fear is effectively instilled into the child, and does not go away in adulthood. In many ways, in working with the adult survivor, the helper also works with the terrified, mistrustful and hurt child who hides inside the adult.

Some survivors present in adulthood with very sad experiences of how either as adults or as children they tried to tell and to find help, but to no avail. Some will have had earlier and very negative experiences of the caring professions. Those who have been in care as children or received psychiatric care as adults are often suspicious of professionals. Too many have either been re-abused within the system or simply not been heard. Some speak more positively, but the numbers who do not is extremely worrying, and needs noting by all those working in the care system, in whatever capacity. Too many who have been betrayed as children are betrayed again as adults. It is crucial that very careful attention is paid to clinical practice and methods of care. It should never be abusive, repressive or invasive. Yet the experience of many is just that.

Others present to agencies as adults who have told no-one before. The pain of revealing abuse for the first time should never be underestimated. Some cover the pain by appearing very distant from their experience. Horrific details can be recounted in a calm, controlled and objective manner. It may feel confusing to the helper that such horrors are so coolly recounted. It is as if the experiences were nothing to do with the survivor, as if they are talking about someone else. However, this may reflect a psychological mechanism called 'dissociation' that has been essential for their very survival. The person has learnt to move away from what is happening to them in order to avoid a degree of pain that would otherwise be intolerable.

Others who have never told before express their pain more obviously. Their distress can be extreme: beginning to talk can unleash feelings and memories that feel unbearable. Some feel relief and release as hidden and secret experiences are revealed and shared; others find that for a while the pain is intensified. Acknowledging secrets is highly problematic for the survivor: once spoken they cannot be easily hidden away again; they now have to be faced. Abuse survivors often experience ambivalence about potential helpers. Once they have disclosed details about their abuse, anxieties and doubts abound: Will the helper be trustworthy? Will they believe? What will they do with the information? Will they be able to cope? Will they maintain confidentiality? Are they competent to help? Do they really understand? Are they really interested?

Not all abuse survivors, however, come for help clearly presenting that as the issue. The abuse may be hidden behind other physical or psychological problems; memories may be hazy or repressed; or the survivor may not initially feel safe enough to reveal what has happened. Presentations vary: many people with a history of abuse misuse drugs or alcohol (see *alcoholism, substance misuse*); others self-harm in other ways, e.g. self-mutilation and overdosing. **Eating disorders** have been linked to childhood abuse, although research varies in estimating the degree of significance. Sexual and relationship difficulties (see *sexual difficulties*); extreme feelings of low self-esteem; lack of self-confidence, and a sense of shame (see *guilt and shame*) and badness; self-loathing, and a deep sense of lack of trust – all *may* be symptomatic of abuse in childhood. For some, their childhood is a blank, as if it had not existed. They have little recall – only a sense of depression, anxiety and loss that cannot be attached to specific events. It is crucial to note that while all these *may* be symptomatic of earlier abuse, it should *never* be assumed or suggested that this is the case. It is also important to note that many abuse survivors have been, and still are, admitted to psychiatric hospital with such presentations. For far too many, this is still either not being recognized, or not given an adequate and helpful response.

(c)   It is popularly believed that abuse breeds abuse, and that victims are likely to become perpetrators. It is clear that for some this is true: child victims sometimes become adolescent and adult abusers. Many young adult survivors express enormous anxiety in case they as future parents abuse their own children.

It is perhaps easier to document and trace families where the cycle of abuse is apparent: these situations are more likely to come to both agency and media attention. However, there is a hidden story elsewhere. Those who work with survivors, who are survivors or who have friends who have come through abuse, know that for many their triumph is that they have broken this pattern: they have not abused either their own children or anyone else's. They are proud of their own parenting or care-taking of other children. They have done it differently. They do not appear in the statistics, nor find themselves in the newspapers. Their victory is silent and invisible except to those helpers who are privileged to share their pride.

The question remains why some people do abuse children. It has to be accepted that what was comfortably considered as a societal taboo – incest – is for many not a taboo. Clearly it is broken frequently. Abuse can be understood as the inability to perceive a child as having any separate rights and value. The child is an extension of the adult abuser, existing primarily to meet the adult's needs. Certainly where sexual abuse occurs within a family the boundaries between appropriate adult and child contact behaviour are demolished by the adult. Experiences that should be reserved for adults are imposed on children; and their significance is denied by the adult.

Power is also relevant. In the same way as violence to women disempowers and humiliates them, while bolstering the abuser's sense of power and vengefulness, the same can occur in violence perpetrated against children. Perpetrators, through superiority of physical size and bodily and psychological maturity, get their way: for that moment they are powerful.

Abuse of children can be wrapped up in false ideological nonsense: e.g. the Frank Beck scandal in Leicester where the abuse in children's homes was rationalized by him as 'regression therapy'; or the claims of paedophiles that sex with children is a legitimate activity. These claims, and others like them, are often persuasively expressed but do not convince. They represent the smooth talking of those who refuse to see the damage and pain they cause. Their own needs are paramount, and the reality of children's damaged lives is twisted conveniently to suit their own desires.

It is obvious that abusers frequently lead double lives. Many survivors have lived with horrific abuse within the home, while having to cope with a public image of their abuser that is the absolute converse of their own experience. Abusers can be pillars of the local community: respected, trusted and highly regarded. The violent part of their self is successfully split off; erupting in the home, and leaving their public persona convincingly respectable.

(d)   There are a large number of abuse survivors wanting and needing help, and insufficient resources available to meet their needs. As a consequence many receive no help; others go on to long waiting lists for counselling or psychotherapy; others see a variety of helpers in voluntary agencies or **self-help groups**. It is not unusual for voluntary workers to find themselves working with situations they feel unqualified to handle because no other service is available. It is easy to say, given the complex range of issues thrown up by abuse, that all those who work in the field should be adequately trained and supervised. However, the reality of scarce resources and service cuts means that this is often not the case. Many helpers are left to struggle as best they can.

In whatever capacity care takes place, there are some key areas that are essential to acknowledge and recognize. Helpers will hear terrible things in the course of this work and have to take care of their own well-being if they are to be effective. A helper who is overwhelmed or over-tired has little left to offer. If help is made available it is crucial to be clear regarding what is offered, and not to offer more than can be definitely given. Abuse survivors have experienced a terrible assault on the boundaries of their self and their world, and those offering help must be clear of their own boundaries, and able to hold to these. Offering what cannot be fulfilled betrays the survivor yet again. The implication is that helpers sometimes have to say 'No': however much they would like to help, they recognize that they cannot. In this instance referral to another agency, even if it means a wait, is most appropriate.

Enormous care has to be taken not to repeat the abusive pattern under the guise of offering help. There are twin dangers here. One is of the helper being invasive in his or her approach. The client is given no choice: a particular approach or helper is thrust upon them. They may be subjected to questions they do not want to answer, or cannot answer. They may be expected to agree to a way of working that is not explained, and that is prescribed by the practitioner, from an agenda arising from agency policy or theoretical orientation rather one that responds to client needs. Some agencies offer very limited time contracts, carrying the danger of stirring up issues for the survivor, without sufficient time allowed for resolution. Helpers can be invasive in other ways, too: for instance, sexual abuse of clients is more common than most like to believe.

The other danger is of repeating the pattern of being another person in authority who does not hear, does not believe or does not take the abuse seriously. I have heard comments such as: 'It only happened to her once or twice; it wasn't that serious'; 'It wasn't very bad sexual abuse; he didn't penetrate her'; and 'This abuse thing is simply being

exaggerated. It's a band-wagon. A lot of them make it up.' It appears to
be more comfortable for many people (including abusers and those who
failed to intervene) to believe such statements; but they are a denial of
the truth and further damage survivors. Helpers can also appear not to
take abuse seriously because of their anxiety not to be abusive. As a
result, they can be paralysed into inaction or silence, fearing that their
response is bound to be insufficient. Their motivation is positive, but
their lack of response can be experienced as disinterest or disbelief.

It is important that survivors work with a person they are comfortable with; and that they, not the helper, control the process in terms of
how much they say, about what and at what time. This has implications
for how helping services are organized. Care has to be taken over issues
relating to the gender and culture of available helpers (see *gender
issues; cross-cultural awareness*). Many women abused by men do not
want to see a man. Others feel it is important to see a helper from the
same culture as their own, while some may wish to see someone from
outside of it. The key word is *choice* and the client may exercise this in a
number of directions. It is not sufficient to allocate a helper, and then
ask the client if this is acceptable. This presupposes a degree of
assertion from the survivor that at that stage is unlikely to exist. Abuse
does not encourage self-assertion and saying 'No' to a perceived authority figure can be impossible. It is the responsibility of the agency to be
sensitive to these areas.

Working with anyone who has been very hurt by abuse can feel a
demanding task. Time and patience are needed. Those who have been
abused find trust of others extremely problematic – and for very good
reason. Helpers should not expect their good intentions to be easily
accepted by their client. Trust has to be earned; and it will even then be
tried and tested: trusting a stranger is not easy when those near to you
have let you down so badly. The assurance of **confidentiality** is crucial.
The survivor needs to be sure that the helper will not be shocked,
frightened or damaged by what they say and recall. There must be no
pressure to explore or examine areas before the client is ready. Clients
may fear they will not be able to cope as some aspects of the abuse are
revealed. For some this reflects their feelings at the time of the abuse
that they would not survive. They discover that the re-telling is less
fearful than imagined. However, some may not be able to cope even
with the most supportive and gentle care. Helpers should be aware of
this possibility and have knowledge of other locally available resources.
One survivors' support organization was fortunate in having access to a
local psychiatrist with a particular interest and expertise in this area.
They worked co-operatively with her and she was able to make psychiatric beds available in the event of a survivor needing temporary respite:

an asylum in the true sense of the word. This may be unusual but is an example of excellent and creative use of resources.

(e)   Specialist resources vary enormously in different localities. Some are well served by a combination of voluntary bodies and National Health Service provision; others have little. The Child Abuse Survivors' Network offers contacts and information for survivors of all types of abuse: PO Box 7, London N3 6XJ (Tel: 0181 992 5522). Local Citizens Advice Bureaux often have local information. Women's Therapy Centres offer counselling and therapy and some offer specialized training and supervision in this field. They can be contacted at 6 Manor Gardens, London SW9 6DZ.

(g)   Ainscough, C. and Toon, K. (1993) *Breaking Free: Help for Survivors of Child Sexual Abuse*. London: Sheldon Press; Herman, J. L. (1992) *Trauma and Recovery*. New York: Basic Books; Walker, M. (1992) *Surviving Secrets: The Experience of Abuse for the Child, the Adult and the Helper*. Buckingham: Open University Press.

MOIRA WALKER
    (See also *child abuse; groups, use of; guilt and shame; learning disabilities; violence towards women*)

Advocacy

(a)   Advocacy in the sense in which it is used in this article is a more recent form of offering help, although there is of course a long tradition of advocacy, which for the most part is associated with the legal profession – indeed in Scotland barristers are called advocates. An advocate in a court speaks for another person, representing their interests. Advocacy as it has come to be used since the early 1990s also means speaking for someone, although it has essentially broadened its meaning now to include many other kinds of advocate other than lawyers. The use of advocacy has been particularly pioneered by disadvantaged or disempowered groups such as those diagnosed as mentally ill, those who have **physical disabilities** or **learning disabilities**, and the elderly (see *old age*). Advocacy in this sense means either representing another, or supporting and/or accompanying another. This can take place in many kinds of situation where the 'client' – through lack of knowledge, confidence or status – is in a relatively powerless position *vis-à-vis* those who are in positions of authority, and whose decisions affect the lives of those who need help and other resources. As one booklet describes it, advocacy is 'about redressing the balance of power' (Anfilogoff, 1993).

(b) Although the citizen and the consumer are represented officially through district and county councillors, MPs and representatives on local bodies and boards, as well as through consumer organizations and other such groups, it can be very difficult to access those who make decisions and exercise control, etc. including even such representatives. Such representatives become part of the system – indeed, in order to function effectively this is inevitable. But in doing so they either themselves assume an authority which makes them less approachable, or they find themselves in a position where the 'ordinary' person views them as remote or inaccessible, should such a person wish to put forward a request or a complaint. I know of examples of parents making a complaint in a school to find the head teacher accompanied by three other members of staff – clearly very intimidating to the individual parent involved. Advocacy reverses this power imbalance. The need for support in such positions is recognized in many complaints or grievance procedures, where the opportunity is provided to be accompanied by a colleague, friend or union representative; and this is a form of advocacy. The presence of another is itself supportive, and the colleague may choose to add his or her own voice to the discussions, to ensure that the person's interests are best and fully represented.

The recognition of the value of advocacy has led to a more precise typology. The different forms which advocacy can take are listed (by Anfilogoff (1993) from which much of this information is taken) as:

1. *self-advocacy*, where the person speaks up for him or herself;
2. since this is often hard to do, the person may be supported by an adviser. This is called *supported self-advocacy*;
3. sometimes it is better to get together with others in the same position, which is called *group advocacy*; *collective advocacy* is similar; this is where a group campaign for themselves or for others, although in this instance this is more likely to be an established project;
4. *peer advocacy* is where those who help people to put their case are drawn from others who have experienced similar problems;
5. *citizen advocacy* involves the use of someone who is more able to get heard, working with the person who does not feel heard. This does not always mean speaking on the person's behalf; it can also involve imparting the necessary skills to enable them to be heard more clearly;

6. *crisis advocacy* occurs when help is given for a one-off occasion, probably in this case with the advocate speaking for the person, so that short-term concerns can be dealt with immediately. Thereafter, once the crisis has been negotiated, the person can handle things for herself or himself;

7. *professional advocacy* is where an expert in a particular field, or someone who is professionally employed, but who is independent, speaks up for the person. Care needs to be taken not to confuse independent professional advocacy with situations where those employed by an organization take up a case within the institution. Anyone who is in this position always risks conflicts of interest, since the threat to their conditions of employment and career prospects may make it impossible to push as hard as the person they represent would wish.

(d) There are certain principles involved in advocacy in the sense in which it is used in this article, which provide helpful pointers to the way in which advocacy might be entered into with and on behalf of a person or a group.

1. The starting point of any advocacy work is what the person or group wants to say – not what others are saying (even if sometimes they are apparently more knowledgeable). The advocate does not therefore deter the person from making a complaint on the grounds that the advocate knows what the reply will be. People have the right to raise any issue they wish, and the advocate helps them do this in the most effective way. This point needs to be understood in conjunction with the next, that an advocate helps the person to secure all the necessary information that might make a claim or an argument more effective.

2. It is vital to help people make informed choices. This may include checking out that they recognize the options, as well as ensuring that they understand what any professionals or experts with whom they are dealing are telling them. This may include calling in the services of an interpreter to ensure that the most accurate information is imparted.

3. An advocate does not have to agree with the person, but needs to respect their view; and then put it across faithfully, or help the person to put it across accurately. 'The important thing is that the voice that gets heard is theirs, not mine' (Anfilogoff, 1993).

4. An advocate does not raise issues unless it is quite clear that the person wants them raised – it is important to check this out, especially where confidential information is involved. Advocates need to respect privacy as well as confidentiality.

5. As indicated above, it is vital that an advocate has no conflict of interest. They therefore need to be independent of the organization or

institution with which the person is dealing. This does not simply apply to professionals. One of the difficulties for some local caring groups who may assist clients of local authority departments is that they are themselves funded or partly funded by local government. This itself could give rise to some conflict of interest, which needs to be thought through in case it jeopardizes the advocacy even of a volunteer working for the project. Similarly organizations should be careful about using their own members as advocates in support of appeals or complaints against the organization or another member. Such people are again not fully independent. If an advocate is not sure whether or not there may be a conflict of interest, he or she should seek advice from an established advocacy group.

6. The best type of advocacy puts the person or group in a better position to take on issues for themselves. It is obviously therefore preferable that a person or group representative should be helped to state their own case, and supported in carrying through their own arguments, rather than speaking for them. This can mean taking time preparing the person. While it could be quicker sometimes to take up an issue as a helper, this is not always good advocacy. Alternatively it means acting in the short term on another's behalf to enable that person or group thereafter to take the current or similar issues on for himself or themselves. As one pamphlet puts it, 'Advocates should do themselves out of a job'.

7. Although the above point may represent the most desirable practice, it is even more important that people are able to choose the advocacy that is best for them. One person wants another to act on their behalf; some may want to do it themselves, with enough support and information to give them confidence; others prefer to be part of a group.

8. Although an advocate's first loyalty is to the person being represented, advocacy does not involve attacking others involved in any issue in a personal or emotive way. An advocate tries to carry through the task in a thoughtful and energetic way, but also as dispassionately as possible.

(e)   Although these guidelines may be sufficient to enable the reader, at least in some instances, to engage in advocacy of one of the types listed above, clearly there is value in being trained; there is strength in working with others; and there is wisdom in drawing upon the experience of those more professionally engaged in advocacy. There are already a considerable number of advocacy groups in many different parts of Britain, and they are growing fast. Some of them are specifically for disabled people. These groups are able to offer individual advice, and training for advocacy. Their task is also to ensure that the opportunities for advocacy are made known to those who could benefit from such services.

Some national networks exist, focused on specific types of advocacy for particular groups of people. At the time of writing, however, there is as yet no comprehensive national organization in Great Britain dealing with all types of advocacy, although there is now an annual conference of advocacy groups; and arising from it a development working party is looking at the possibilities of a national network. Tim Anfilogoff is convening this, and can for the time being send details of local advocacy groups on receipt of a stamped addressed envelope (Advocacy Development Project, Cell Barnes Hospital, Highfield Lane, St Albans, Herts AL4 0RG). The Scottish Advocacy Forum is likely to join this larger network. For people in Scotland with learning disabilities and connections with Barnardo's, the Barnardo's Advocacy Service has offices in Edinburgh, Glasgow and Dundee (write enclosing s.a.e. to The Barnardo's Advocacy Service, Corstophine Road, Edinburgh EH12 7AR). Contacting area social services may be a further way of identifying such advocacy resources as may exist within a particular locality.

(g)   Anfilogoff, T. (ed.) (1993) *An Advocacy Handbook*. Advocacy Development Project in association with Hertfordshire Social Services (Cell Barnes Hospital, Highfield Lane, St Albans, Herts AL4 0RG); *The Mind Guide to Advocacy in Mental Health* (1992) available from Mind, Granta House, 15–19 Broadway, Stratford, London E15 4BQ.

MICHAEL JACOBS

AIDS/HIV

(a)   AIDS stands for Acquired Immune Deficiency Syndrome – a generic name for a collection or *syndrome* of bacterial, protozoan, fungal and viral infections many of which are ordinarily quite common and responsive to treatment but, in a person who is immune compromised, may be more troublesome, sometimes fatal. HIV stands for the Human Immunodeficiency Virus. It causes a gradual collapse of the body's ability to fight illness, which for some people can lead to death from infections which the body is unable to defend itself against. There has been some debate about whether HIV is the cause of AIDS and whether AIDS inevitably leads to death. It does seem fairly widely accepted that HIV is the cause of AIDS, and that AIDS *eventually* leads to death. However, it should be remembered that there are an increasing number of long-term survivors of HIV infection.

The current practice is to refer to those infected with the virus as *people*, rather than patients, sufferers or victims; as this is non-pathologizing and more empowering.

(b)
1. People infected with HIV or symptomatic with AIDS
The most obvious group of people who might present for help are those with HIV infection. This group can be divided into those who are well (asymptomatic) and those who are unwell (symptomatic). There are references elsewhere to AIDS Related Complex (ARC). This term has now been replaced by the above categories. People who are symptomatic may have had severe opportunistic infections which may be grouped together under the diagnosis of AIDS. AIDS is a syndrome, a collection of illnesses, each with its own treatment. 'Opportunistic infections' simply means infections which take the opportunity of revealing themselves when a person's immune system is weakened. These may be existing illnesses that have previously been held in check by the immune system, or they may be new infections.

2. Family, friends or partners of people with HIV/AIDS
The second group who might present for help are friends, partners and family members of people with HIV infection. They may also have HIV, but in this instance, I include them as presenting with concerns about their friend, or family member. This group's worries may centre on the practical and emotional difficulties of supporting someone with a life-threatening condition; but they are likely to be overlaid by homophobic prejudice and discrimination against gay men and drug users.

3. 'Worried well' with or without good cause
There are also those who have come to be known as the 'Worried well'. They can be divided into two groups: the first is what someone described as the 'I-once-kissed-the-office-manager-at-a-party-in-1956' brigade! They are people who are at practically no risk of infection, who may feel guilty about past misdemeanours. Their guilt gets focused on HIV as a 'punishment' for their wrongdoing. When HIV first started coming to the general public's attention around 1986, clinical psychologists around the country were inundated with clients who had previously presented with obsessive-compulsive disorders, but now presenting with 'AIDS phobia'.

A second group may indeed have been involved in risk activities, but are currently well. They may wish to explore the implications of taking an HIV test, or they may need further information about HIV routes of transmission, etc.

4. 'Unworried well' – those at risk, but unconcerned

The last group may not immediately be associated with HIV worries, because they themselves are not presenting as concerned about that. This group consists basically of anyone who is sexually active and who does not have safer sex (i.e. anyone having unprotected penetrative intercourse). Potentially this group is very large, and may include yourself, your colleagues, most of your friends and family members! Shernoff (1989), a psychotherapist and HIV education consultant in New York, suggests that counsellors and by extension other helpers can play a vital role in HIV education and prevention. He argues that because of our training in helping people explore difficult feelings, as long as we become comfortable in discussing sexual matters explicitly, and are informed about HIV transmission, we are perfectly placed to help our clients explore how they feel about having to protect themselves and their partners from HIV infection.

(c)   Why do people get infected?

1. Denial

HIV strikes at the core of our major societal taboos – sex, death, disability and illness. Many of us are particularly uncomfortable about discussing these issues openly, and so it becomes easier to try and ignore the threat of getting infected with HIV. By placing the epidemic in a few 'other' groups: gay men, intravenous drug users, prostitutes, Africans, etc. we can deny the threat to ourselves. This is a dangerous, yet common way of protecting the self. By attributing blame to others one can try to 'magically' protect oneself. AIDS clearly has no in-built bias for such groupings; and while it is true that in the UK gay men and intravenous drug users are the most common groups affected, there is plenty of evidence to show that members of these groups do not have sex only with other gay men or drug users.

2. Perception of risk

One of the reasons people are infected with HIV is that Parliament has failed to amend the age of consent for gay male sexual activity from 21 to 16. This means that many gay teenagers are not getting culturally sensitive and effective health education. It is unclear whether politicians ignore the fact that gay young men will fail to abide by the law, or they do not care about these young men's lives because they are homosexual. What is clear however, is that HIV infection *is* rising among young gay men.

There are of course other reasons why young gay men are not heeding the health education messages targeted at older gay men – they may not consider the message applies to them. Many young people see HIV and AIDS as applying to older people, and falsely believe that by having sex with their own age range, they are not at risk. There may also be adolescent risk-taking mentioned below.

There are of course other people who do not perceive themselves to be at risk, for example married couples (who may later discover their partner's bisexuality or extra-marital affair); and young heterosexuals who may feel immune to the risk, because they see HIV as a gay or drug users' problem.

3. Risk-taking behaviours

If one were to try and design a life-threatening virus which seeks to undermine attempts at realistic health education, then a sexually transmitted virus would be an excellent place to start. Young people at the beginning of their sexual lives want to experiment, to discover, to rebel and to take risks. HIV provides a challenge to risk-taking young people – a risk that may even be unacknowledged or is consciously denied, both in sexual behaviours and in terms of injecting drug use.

4. Poverty, race, class, etc.

In many countries HIV is fast becoming a disease of the poor, of people of colour, of the working classes. In New York for example, there are currently more black people with HIV than gay men. In Glasgow, there are more intravenous drug users infected with HIV than gay men. Lack of access to housing and health care has led disenfranchised people to turn to drugs as an escape from the pressures of alienation and discrimination. The epidemic may well follow a similar pattern over here, hitting the homeless who, because of inadequate housing and health care, have much poorer chances of recovery or long-term survival.

5. Sexual behaviours

One thing is for sure, the *quantity* of sexual partners one has has no bearing on one's risk of infection. It is perfectly possible to have a high number of sexual partners and, by having non-penetrative sex or protected sexual intercourse with them, to remain free of infection. One encounter of unprotected vaginal or anal intercourse with an infected person can, however, lead to infection. It is not *who* you have sex with, it is what you *do* that counts. HIV is a virus, it is not a punishment for sinful living.

(d) In caring for and helping any of the groups listed above it is important to remember the following:

1. You are not yourself going to get infected through professional contact. Since HIV is only passed on through the blood or semen of someone infected getting into the bloodstream of another person, there is no chance of a helper getting contaminated. This may be an obvious statement to make, but there has been much fear and misinformation around, and it is important to state this clearly at the outset.

2. Many people are frightened and may feel helpless, so the client may present with a history of people avoiding them. The client may mistrust you too, not least perhaps because of the societal prejudice towards gay men and intravenous drug users.

3. Your family and colleagues may be over-concerned for you. You may end up sharing with your client a view of AIDS as a 'magical terror' – threatening to strike all in its path.

4. Practical concerns are relevant. Housing, transport and money are important. There may be a need for welfare rights advice. Benefit arrangements may need to be hurried up. **Legal advice** regarding wills, issues about child custody and wishes regarding ongoing medical support may also be relevant.

5. Maintenance of hope is a primary concern for anyone living with HIV, and clients may want to live in a state of denial – which is understandable. Challenge denial sensitively and empathically, and only when life is put at risk. The defence is the psyche's way of protecting the self, until the self can face the full impact of what lies ahead. Try to find ways to help clients feel in control of their lives, as this will help maintain their hope, and reduce some of the stresses associated with living with an ever-changing condition.

6. The whole process of living with HIV infection is a grief reaction. Most people will come to terms with it in their own time with supportive help. And if there was maladaptive behaviour beforehand, it is unlikely to have disappeared in such people (see *bereavement; loss*).

(e) People get sick because the immune system eventually breaks down. The virus, which has fed off the white blood cells by infecting them and multiplying like mad, leaves the body unable to fight disease. People may then see the emergence of illnesses which they have been carrying and which the immune system has kept under control (for example, cold sores from the *herpes simplex* virus) as well as new infections. These may become virulent quite quickly and difficult to treat.

There is a range of treatments available, both allopathic (medical) and complementary, which may alleviate symptoms and improve the quality of life. Complementary therapists include practitioners of traditional Chinese medicine, homoeopathy, aromatherapy. Any of these may have an important role in helping strengthen the immune system and manage opportunistic infections (see *holistic medicine*).

The Terrence Higgins Trust is Britain's first and foremost HIV charity, named after one of the first people to die with AIDS in this country. The Trust was originally set up by his gay friends to provide education and services to other gay men affected by AIDS. It now employs 60 paid staff and 1,500 volunteers offering a wide range of services for both prevention and care to *anyone* affected by HIV. The address is 52–54 Grays Inn Road, London WC1X 8JU. Tel: 0171 831 0330 (Administration), or 0171 242 1010 (Helpline: 1200–2200 daily).

The National Aids Line, funded by the Department of Health in 1987 as a response to the need for widespread public education, is a free 24-hour helpline that provides telephone counselling to anyone wanting to talk over any issue around HIV. They also have a service in minority ethnic languages and a Minicom line for hearing-impaired callers with text phones: Tel. 0800 567123 (24 hours daily); 0800 521361 (Minicom line).

Many towns and cities now have their own local HIV voluntary services. These may be around an AIDS helpline, offering telephone information and support to people worried about HIV; or they may also provide home care support and befriending in the form of trained 'buddies'. Many HIV voluntary services are also involved in education and prevention initiatives. Every health authority in the country has a designated officer, usually a health promotion officer responsible for HIV education. These services may also offer loans of education materials and training resources to community groups and schools wanting to study the issues further.

(f)   Caring for people who have HIV infection is extremely stressful, yet can be very rewarding. It is important to consider seriously support needs, and if they are not currently good enough, to seek out sources of support for yourself which are. This may be possible from specialist HIV social workers or counsellors; or from your local HIV voluntary agency. Consider these needs seriously and discuss them with your managers or supervisors if you are embarking on this work. Survivor guilt is sometimes experienced by close friends, partners and family members and those carers working closely with people with HIV. You may find yourself feeling guilty that you are going to survive your client. This guilt is akin to the 'bargaining' one can sometimes see in grief reactions (see *bereavement*).

Working with a primarily young population and seeing people becoming progressively ill can tear at the heart-strings of most people. It is healthy to be angry at a virus that pulls down fit young people in their prime of life; and also at the apparent lack of resources allocated either to prevent HIV from being passed on to the young (primarily young gay men), or to treat those who have been infected with the care and sensitivity that all people deserve.

The whittling away of the health service and the social security provision means that many people do not get the help they need. This is of course not just relevant for people with HIV/AIDS – in fact some people with HIV/AIDS have had better treatment than others who may have less sex-related illness – but it is a sad indictment of one of the most developed countries in the world that so many people suffer purely through lack of money and provision.

Many families experience a great reluctance to be open about their loss due to negative public reaction to homosexuality, drug use and HIV/AIDS. It is important to be sensitive to this and to help preserve their right to **confidentiality**, while still trying to help them through any feelings of **guilt or shame** they may be experiencing.

(g)   Anderson, C. and Wilkie, P. (eds) (1992) *Reflective Helping in HIV and AIDS*. Buckingham: Open University Press; Dilley, J. W., Pies, C. and Helquist, M. (eds) (1989) *Face to Face: A Guide to AIDS Counseling*. San Francisco: AIDS Health Project, University of California.

DOMINIC DAVIES
(See also *gay men and lesbians; terminal illness*)

Alcoholism

(a)   Response to the term 'alcoholism' is often negative, and those perceived to be alcoholics can be dismissed as victims of nothing more than their own excesses: that is, their suffering is a consequence of their drinking, which as self-inflicted behaviour they could readily choose to stop. Even the more compassionate view, that alcoholism is a disease, means that those drinkers thus labelled are viewed as being intrinsically different from everyone else.

Within the helping professions, the use of such definitions as 'alcoholism', 'addiction' and 'alcohol dependence' also implies a great deal, but in reality explains little. It is more useful to think in terms of 'problem drinking' rather than 'alcoholism' and a continuum of alcohol use rather than those who drink safely and those that are alcoholics.

> For there is no dividing line where alcohol use ends and alcohol abuse begins; where drinking stops giving benefit and starts creating problems instead. Alcohol can have good and bad effects at the same

time; it can, in some senses, be both used and abused simultaneously. (Shaw et al., 1978: 41)

A helpful working definition is, therefore, 'problem drinking is repetitive use of beverage alcohol causing physical, psychological or social harm to the drinker or to others' (Heather and Robertson, 1989: 7). Despite the scope of this definition, it remains client-centred in that it seeks to relate alcohol use to the problems it is causing, rather than attempting to match symptoms to diagnosis. On a continuum, therefore, the person who drinks once weekly, but always gets into trouble at the end of the evening, and the habitual drinker who consumes a bottle of spirits daily, can both legitimately seek help with their alcohol use.

(b) Those with drinking problems present their difficulties in many ways to a variety of helping agencies. Many clients can accommodate very heavy drinking in their lives and maintain the semblance of normality. For those that present directly to specialist alcohol units, this façade of functioning has usually gone and the client often appears in a distressed, chaotic state. While in crisis, clients can be very demanding, which may leave helpers feeling the onus is on them to produce immediate solutions. Sometimes, clients have made changes to their drinking between initiating contact and being seen. In these instances there is less pressure on the helping agency to find solutions and more emphasis is put on helping the client to further changes already made.

However, often the route to specialist agencies is more circuitous and the client's drinking may be seen as secondary to other difficulties. A major example is that of ill health. A client may visit their GP for many years suffering various ailments without the connection with their alcohol use being made. Causation is obscured by the progressive rather than the acute, physical complications of excessive alcohol use, and as virtually any aspect of the body's functioning can be affected, it is difficult to establish a drink-to-harm relationship. A variation, but by no means rare example, of the drink and health connection can come to light in a crisis situation. There have been many incidents of heavy, but secret, drinkers being admitted to hospital due to some physical problem. After one or two days of enforced sobriety, the client has started to withdraw from alcohol, which may become a medical emergency if the client suffers alcohol withdrawal fits or delirium tremens.

Commonly, clients present to a variety of agencies such as GPs, mental health services, social services and other statutory or voluntary organizations, with psychological problems. Invariably the symptoms are those of **depression** or anxiety. Heavy drinking exacerbates feelings of depression, although often the drinking started in an attempt to alleviate primary feelings of depression. Likewise, initially alcohol may help moderate anxiety, but as tolerance to alcohol increases, so often does the experience of anxiety. If the client drinks to the extent of suffering withdrawal symptoms, then this will both exacerbate and mimic anxiety. As drinking progresses, cause and effect become indistinguishable.

Sometimes, as a consequence of drinking, a client withdrawing badly from alcohol and suffering delirium tremens may be so disturbed as to be deemed psychotic and require immediate intervention. Things are further complicated with those clients that have existing mental health problems and use alcohol excessively. They may be reasonably stable when sober, but a period of drinking may push them into an acute psychotic episode.

Similarly, of those that have attempted **suicide** a large percentage have had alcohol in their system at the time of the attempt. While this in itself may not indicate a problem with alcohol, the incidence of drinking in these situations warrants proper assessment of its use. On other occasions, a client's drinking may come to light through someone else's difficulties. Children may be functioning badly at school or having other problems, and when explored the cause may be found in parental drinking. Similarly, spouses may seek help for their own emotional problems that are related to their partner's alcohol use. Alternatively, couples may present with marital problems out of which one's drinking difficulty may emerge.

Finally, the prison and probation services are increasingly being confronted with those whose crimes are related to alcohol misuse, for example, petty crime to fund drinking, repeated violence when drunk or the constant presence of alcohol when offences are perpetrated.

In summary, the client having problems with alcohol can present in a variety of guises to a variety of agencies. This suggests that the exploration of a client's alcohol use should be on the agenda of all helping agencies.

(c) Despite many years of study and research, no single factor has emerged as 'cause' of problem drinking. Increasingly, theories are being modified and synthesized into a more eclectic whole. Evidence does not suggest a total genetic or disease causation, but rather a predisposition to which cultural and social learning factors contribute. Some theories, such as the psychoanalytic idea of a dependent or oral personality, suggest that problem drinking is a symptom of some pre-existing personality structure. Again, this adds texture to the whole, rather than being an explanation in itself.

At present, those who develop problems with alcohol are not thought to be premorbidly different from those who do not. However, they are often premorbidly different in terms of the prevalence of problem drinking in their family history and in their cultural and familial patterns regarding alcohol use. A developmental model of problem drinking highlights three facets (Ellis et al., 1988: 19): first, a specific learning history in which they have developed a reliance upon alcohol as a way of reducing unpleasant emotional experiences or enhancing pleasant ones; secondly, a long history of heavy alcohol use, despite mounting problems associated with it; and thirdly, a series of conflicting beliefs regarding alcohol, themselves and other people, which reinforces their habitual and maladaptive use. This type of model is useful for the helper in that it avoids the frustrating search for cause, and instead concentrates on more tangible areas which can then be responded to appropriately.

(d) In the caring professions, those with drinking problems are often deemed to be one of the most difficult client groups with which to work. Accordingly, they seem to elicit a fairly unique emotional response from workers, which can inhibit the usefulness of interventions made. It is vital, therefore, that all helpers exposed to those with drinking problems have, at the very least, the chance to explore constructively their own feelings around this client group which could otherwise block the change of responding usefully.

> 80 agents in our studies reported feeling that clients with drinking problems were distasteful, embarrassing and threatening. . . . Some believed they were compulsive liars. Such beliefs were easily aroused in agents who lacked information about alcohol and alcohol related problems and had received no training in the skills required to work with clients with drinking problems. (Shaw et al., 1978: 151)

One of the fundamental problems facing helpers is deciding whether to see the client if they have alcohol in their system. Many agencies take the view that it is unreasonable to expect the client with drinking problems to attend alcohol free and the most important thing is to engage them in treatment. Some agencies, such as hospital casualty departments, have no real option but to accept whoever arrives. However, most agencies can define conditions of attendance and avoidance of this can be dangerously collusive. Not to expect the client to attend totally alcohol free may deny their capacity for making healthy choices and changes. Ideally, anyone attending an agency should be alcohol free, irrespective of whether they have a problem with drinking. There are two main reasons for this.

First, if alcohol free, the chances of the client behaving in any way that creates a threat to their own or other's safety are minimized. Secondly, being free from alcohol and with a clear consciousness is the best state for true therapeutic communication to develop. The stumbling block in introducing an 'alcohol free' policy is often the agency's perceived difficulty in enforcing it. It is useful to seek the guidance of specialist agencies in exploring both the practicalities and helpers' feelings around implementing such a policy. Helpers often experience difficulty when faced with the client's reluctance to acknowledge the problematic nature of their alcohol use. This ambivalence can be confusing for the helper who may feel they must convince the client they have a problem. For the problem drinker, alcohol, which causes such difficulties, is often the thing they love most. Therefore, to be rid of these difficulties, they also have to break their attachment to alcohol. However, there are techniques and constructs that aid the helper, at least temporarily, to circumvent the likelihood of becoming enmeshed in such issues.

Such a construct is the 'model of change' (Prochaska and Diclemente, 1986) which is useful in its application to those with drinking problems. It is suggested that when changing behaviour, people move through the stages of pre-contemplation, contemplation, action and maintenance. An awareness of where the client may fit in this model allows for interventions to be tailored more appropriately. At the pre-contemplation stage, the client would feel they do not have any difficulties related to their alcohol use. The evidence and others may differ, but the client takes no heed of this. Rather than trying to convince the client they do have a problem, interventions at this stage are more gentle and aimed at keeping the client interested, harm reduction strategies and offering help to the family or others involved. The next stage is that of contemplation, where the client is considering both the possibility that they may have difficulties and the idea of change. Interventions are aimed at exploring the client's conflicts around change and looking at the costs and benefits of drinking. Generally, clients are amenable to factual information, and the use of self-monitoring aids, such as drink diaries, will establish the reality of their drinking. At the action stage the decision to make changes to drinking has been made and the client is looking at how to implement this at a behavioural level. Interventions are around working with the client in establishing appropriate practical strategies for the initiation of change. Finally, at the maintenance stage, the client is preserving the changes made. Interventions are focused on consolidating these changes and finding ways of coping with further difficulties that arise.

It is important not to think of these stages as fixed or diagnostic. Rather, an awareness of these stages in relation to how the client presents will allow for a more appropriate response.

It is often difficult for the helper when the client presents their drinking as secondary to another problem. The example of a client drinking in an attempt to cope with their anxiety poses a double dilemma for the helper: first, in deciding which aspect of the person's presenting difficulty to address; and secondly, if appropriate, to which specialist agency the client should then be referred. In such instances it is usually wise to address the drinking first as psychological difficulties are invariably exacerbated by alcohol use. To use the example of anxiety again, a period of sobriety often leads to a diminishment in the symptoms experienced, not least, as with a clear consciousness, the client is more able to address the issues that originally contributed to their anxiety. In short, initially the helper need not be concerned with the conundrum of 'do clients have problems because they drink or do they drink because they have problems?', as it is safest to work first towards reducing consumption.

If the helper can establish the presence or not of the following three factors, then a fairly accurate assessment of the severity of alcohol use can be made. First, ask about tolerance: that is, how much has drinking increased in order to maintain the same effect? Secondly, ask about withdrawal symptoms following a period without alcohol. These symptoms are varied, but often include shaking, sweating, anxiety, stomach cramps, etc. Thirdly, ask whether the client takes more alcohol to ease the symptoms of withdrawal. The presence of these factors indicates a severe problem with alcohol that probably requires the help of a specialist agency. Drinkers in the cycle of tolerance, withdrawal and relief drinking are usually scared of stopping their drinking for fear of the trauma of withdrawal. Sometimes a client may present in an acute state of withdrawal, so it is useful for all agencies to have policies such as direct access to specialist agencies, local GPs or casualty departments to support helpers in dealing with such situations. However, most problem drinkers, while being uncomfortable, withdraw safely from alcohol without further intervention. Presenting in a state of withdrawal may be an attempt to coerce the helping agency into effecting some sort of rescue, and again it is useful to seek the help of specialist agencies in such instances.

A further quandary for the helper is agreeing drinking goals, particularly around the conflict between total abstinence or a reduction in drinking as acceptable targets. Those clients who have a long drinking history, who are older, have less family support and present with established tolerance, withdrawal symptoms and relief drinking, are rarely able to drink in a more controlled manner without first achieving a considerable period of abstinence. This is usually the sort of client that would benefit from referral to a specialist agency. However, younger drinkers with more stable backgrounds, without the presence of withdrawal symptoms and relief drinking, often respond to less intensive input and may reduce their consumption to safer levels without the need for total abstinence. Such clients are usually amenable to non-specialist help and would perhaps be scared off by a referral to specialist agencies for fear of being labelled or stigmatized. It is suggested that non-specialist interventions are particularly useful when they are related to the client's drinking in a brief, focused and practical way (Davidson et al., 1991: 63).

In summary, ideally the non-specialist helper should feel confident enough to assist those with less severe drinking problems and be able to refer on appropriately those with more severe difficulties.

(e)   There are many routes through which the client can get help. Most helping agencies can either work directly with the client, or carry out an assessment and refer on to a specialist agency, or assist the client at a practical level in finding an agency that can help. Increasingly, clients can gain direct access through well advertised routes such as help and advice lines or voluntary counselling services. Additionally, the prominent organization Alcoholics Anonymous is present and accessible in all areas of the country. Meetings are always well advertised and the formalities of referral and appointments are unnecessary.

One of the characteristics of the alcohol services is the differing philosophies from agency to agency. In some instances, the differences are quite radical, as between disease theory and social learning based models. Often it is a matter of chance in fitting client to service and it is therefore important that helping agencies have a basic understanding of what local specialist services offer.

Specialist services can be utilized by non-specialist agencies in many ways, such as for basic training, supervision, consultancy and devising policies. Increasingly, alcohol services are seeking to take on training roles, thus helping more generic agencies to respond usefully to those with drinking problems, ensuring treatment does not remain the sole responsibility of the specialists.

(f)   Issues that arise between agencies are often around differing roles and differing professional accountability within multidisciplinary teams. These conflicts need to be sensitively handled by specialist agencies involved in any sort of supervision or consultancy. To a certain extent this can be achieved by dividing the tasks and focusing on specific areas of practice. For example, counselling **supervision** can be offered to the helper and consultancy on policy matters to the agency management. It also has to be accepted that some situations remain unchangeable. A casualty department is unable to turn someone needing help away purely because they have alcohol in their system, even if this is a policy many agencies can implement. Here the specialist agency could offer help to the medical staff in constructively dealing with their feelings around their situation, and in looking towards policies that are as safe as they possibly can be in the circumstances.

These 'loopholes' can often be exploited by clients. They lead to disharmony between services, as one agency may feel the other is off-loading difficult clients on to them, and the other may be frustrated because the client has been able to manipulate the system. This often happens in crisis situations such as severe withdrawal from alcohol, overdoses or other attempts at self-harm while drinking. These incidents are always going to occur, but one of the ways of minimizing the consequences is by multi-agency contact and agreement: that is, by liaison and mutual support between hospitals, voluntary agencies, generic and specialist services.

(g) Davidson, R., Rollnick, S. and Macewan, I. (1991) *Counselling Problem Drinkers*. London: Tavistock/Routledge; Heather, N. and Robertson, A. (1989) *Problem Drinking*. Oxford: Oxford University Press; Shaw, S., Cartwright, A., Spratley, T. and Harwin, J. (1978) *Responding to Drinking Problems*. London: Croom Helm.

PAUL JACKSON
    (See also *substance misuse*)

Bereavement

(a) Bereavement is the reaction to the loss of a person or object. Most commonly it is the result of the death of a person who is loved, and involves the loss of a close relationship. For others it may have been loss of a partner as the result of divorce, or life events such as moving house or schools. Bereavement is also caused by major losses such as miscarriage, infertility, an operation (e.g. mastectomy, orchidectomy), loss of a limb, blindness, deafness, redundancy, unemployment, retirement and by disasters such as fire and burglary or loss of pets. Grief is the complex emotional response to bereavement. To recover, the person has to let go of the bonds that held them to the lost person or animal, place or object. This involves the psychological processes of mourning.

(b) The bereaved most frequently need and may ask for emotional help two months or more after the loss. This is probably because close to bereavement family and friends rally around; but lack of knowledge about bereavement, and a less close relationship with the dead person, means most people assume that 'everything should be back to normal' after about two months. For the bereaved this is the time of most acute despair and fear of madness, and support and comfort is needed. It may not be asked for, because a feature of grief is loss of self-esteem and a belief that people are only being kind for the sake of the dead person and do not really mean it. The bereaved may take some convincing that the offer of help is genuine.

Some never ask for help but worry their family or other people, who then seek out help for the mourner. Some of these worries are well founded, particularly when two years and more after the loss the bereaved are still obviously grieving intensely; or there are other signs of unresolved grief, such as excessive idealization of the dead person, complete denial of the loss or bitterness directed towards anyone involved in the care of the deceased.

In these instances the bereaved person nearly always needs skilled help; the 'worried' person is also likely to need help, if only by being understood and supported. Other worries, such as the bereaved seeing, hearing and talking to the lost person in the first six to nine months after the death, indicate the lack of knowledge in the 'worried' relations. By offering information about the grieving process and how to respond, anxiety can be relieved.

It is quite common for mourning to be prolonged when only part of the grief work has been completed. As a result a seemingly minor further loss can result in an acute bereavement reaction. Unresolved grief is also frequently picked up when counselling someone about an apparently unrelated topic. A clue to this can be great difficulty in terminating the counselling.

(c) A death or loss causes bereavement, but the actual capacity to grieve and complete the process of mourning is related to the external circumstances surrounding the death, as well as the personal history of the bereaved person.

There are five external circumstances that should be taken into account:

1. The actual place of the death is highly significant. If the death occurred in a distant place it is harder to grieve; the more so if the dead person's body was never seen and the grave site never visited. This happened with many wartime deaths from both the First and Second World Wars.

2. If there are simultaneous losses as in a car crash or a community disaster where more than one member of a family or a community is killed, the survivor's grief tends to be prolonged, partly because more than one loss has to be grieved; but also because the people who might form the network of support are dead, or unavailable because they are grieving themselves (see *major incidents*).

3. In a similar way successive deaths or losses result in protracted grief. An example might be when a partner dies close to a young person

leaving home. Both events need to be mourned, but if one happens before the grieving for the other is complete, the significance of the second loss is often denied and the whole grieving process blocked. The mourning of the second loss cannot even start until the first loss has been grieved. The resultant vicious circle is hard to break.

4. The nature of the death or loss is also significant. A sudden, unexpected or untimely one is much more difficult to believe. The **death of a child** before a parent is an example. Such a loss is 'unthinkable'. This denial makes it hard to feel the loss and results in a prolongation of grieving. This is even more pronounced when a death is due to homicide or **suicide**. When someone has been murdered the intense feelings of anger, vengeful thoughts and fantasies of revenge can be overpowering and almost impossible to express (see *victims of crime*). In the case of suicide the survivors frequently feel such a mixed range of feelings that it is again very frightening to acknowledge or express them. One minute they will feel intense anger with someone killing himself or herself, then overwhelming sorrow and then **guilt** that they did not hear the cry for help nor save them (see *suicide and attempted suicide*).

5. A person's social networks and the attitude of the culture to death also affect the grieving process. This is facilitated where there are good support networks and where the mourning rites of the particular culture can be observed. Having evolved over generations they frequently aid grieving. To some extent Britain is a death-denying culture, which often results in the lack of, or withdrawal of, support and the disappearance of many of the helpful mourning rites. Of course in some instances the mourner is unable to use either the cultural mourning rites or the available supportive networks (see *funerals*).

Grieving is also affected by the person's life history and their emotional development – also known as internal factors:

1. An individual's attachment history is important. This was first recognized by John Bowlby (1979) who studied the attachment behaviour between a young animal and a key care-giving adult. It is likely that this behaviour is essential for self-preservation, particularly in human beings who take many years to reach self-sufficiency. Evidence has accumulated that children form either secure attachments with their care-givers or insecure, anxious attachments. Secure attachments occur when the care-giver is sufficiently sensitive and positively responsive to the infant; insecure attachments when the care-giver is either rejecting and unresponsive or singularly insensitive. Children with secure attachments manage separation and the subsequent return of the care-giver more easily than children with insecure attachments, who are more distressed by separations and are slower to re-attach when the care-giver returns. A secure attachment gives individuals a

secure base from which to manage life's vicissitudes. This in turn means they are better equipped emotionally to grieve losses.

Attachment history also affects the way in which multiple separations are managed. If a child with an insecure base is subjected to too many separations, as is often the case with children who are put into care, it is much more likely that she or he will become permanently detached into adulthood, and deny all distressing feelings or the need for a close relationship. Such people are often unable to grieve adequately should a loss occur later in life.

2. Loss history also affects the capacity to mourn. Any unresolved losses accumulate and are 're-awakened' by a further loss; thus the reaction to the most immediate loss may seem disproportionate to the event. There is considerable evidence that children and teenagers whose parents or siblings die are rarely helped to grieve the loss adequately. The result is the greater likelihood of **depression** in adulthood, a prolonged grief reaction or even an inability to grieve.

3. The age, the emotional maturity and the stage in development of the bereaved person affects the grieving process. Children at different ages have very different understandings of death and separation (see *children's experience of loss and death*). Grief is particularly challenging when people are passing through major transitions in their life-cycle. **Adolescence** is one example where the transition from childhood to adulthood involves considerable losses, which need to be grieved. If a death of a close relative happens at this point it is doubly hard to deal with the bereavement, let alone manage the separation from the family of origin, which is the normal developmental task for adolescents in Western cultures. This time is a major transition period for the parents of adolescents as well. They are grieving for the loss of the children and adjustment to the change in the family group. In the case of women, there is probably some loss of their identity as major caretaker of the children, and possibly loss of their capacity to bear children with the onset of **menopause**. If a bereavement occurs at this point the individuals are much more vulnerable.

4. The intimacy of the relationship with the dead person, which is partly related to the quality of the attachment relationship mentioned earlier, markedly affects the grieving process. Obviously the loss of a spouse, partner, child, lover, parent, sibling or close friend results in a more intense grief reaction. But it is important to remember that the loss of a close friend at work might have more impact than the death of a sibling. For a child the death of a grandparent might be a very great loss. Where a close relationship is hidden, such as an extra-marital affair, or not accepted by society in general, such as a gay relationship (see *gay men and lesbians*), the griever may be abandoned, with few people prepared to listen or support.

5. The emotional complexity of the relationship also affects the grieving process. Where the relationship has been loving, affectionate and honest, with expression of both the negative and positive feelings, grieving is relatively straightforward. If the relationship was not direct and open, with denial of the range of feelings, the grieving is likely to be complicated and prolonged. Commonly it is the negative feelings (anger, hate and resentment) that are denied, both during the relationship and after it has ended.

An assessment of the external circumstances surrounding the loss and the personal internal factors of the individual is essential because it indicates whether the grief process is likely to be complicated and prolonged. This type of response is sometimes labelled pathological, morbid or abnormal. Lendrum and Syme (1992) suggest that it is more helpful to consider the range of responses to loss as being along a spectrum. At one end are those whose secure attachments in childhood and capacity to trust others help them tolerate and understand their own strong feelings. This enables them to manage separation and loss, so the grieving process is more straightforward. At the other end are those who were insecurely attached and experienced too many unresolved separations. The lack of capacity to trust others to validate their feelings results in a variety of responses, either prolonging grieving or actually blocking grief work. Examples are excessive idealization of the dead and often an associated feeling of unbearable **guilt**; denial of the death and/or the impact of the death; bitterness; and extreme anger with others associated with the death, particularly hospital staff, employers, family and priests, which can lead to litigation.

The recognition of the likelihood of a complicated response is essential to ensure the person is referred to someone capable of offering a longer-term counselling relationship, in which early separations and losses can be focused upon.

(d)   In the 1960s Colin Murray Parkes asked a group of London widows to tell him in their own words about their bereavement. From this he was able to establish a pattern of normal grief (Parkes, 1975), outlined overleaf. It is important to recognize that while knowledge of the pattern helps a worker assess what parts of the grief work have been experienced and perhaps worked through, it should not be assumed that the phases happen in a strict sequence or over a standard time scale.

This pattern is essentially the same for women and men. Differences are probably related to sex roles. In general men seem to need to regain control of their world more quickly. They frequently experience the loss of a sexual partner as a castration, and their sexual needs re-emerge sooner than women's.

Phases of adult mourning and related feelings

Phases	Predominant feeling	Time from death
1. numbness	shock	2 weeks to 1 month
	disbelief	
2. yearning	reminiscence	
	searching	6 months
	hallucination	
	anger	
	guilt	
3. disorganization	anxiety	
and despair	loneliness	
	ambivalence	1 year
	fear	
	hopelessness	
	helplessness	
4. reorganization	acceptance	2 years or more
	relief	

As with all supportive counselling, active listening is greatly enhanced with knowledge of the psychological process and in particular the features which most distress or confuse the client. For simplicity I discuss each phase.

Numbness: Not many actually seek counselling in the first few weeks after a bereavement, but priests and ministers, for instance, are asked to give very practical support in the organization of the **funeral**. It is important to remember that the bereaved are shocked and numb, particularly if it is a sudden and unexpected death. They frequently feel nothing. One measure of a helpful funeral is its ability to enable people to cry, perhaps for the first time.

Numbness is unique to severe loss and is one of several occasions when the bereaved wonder if they are going mad. Confirmation that the 'cotton-wool' feeling is normal can be comforting. Numbness is probably protective. People can only acknowledge and accept gradually the enormity of what has happened. At this time disbelief in the loss is profound, which is another reason why funerals are so important, as is seeing the body of the dead person.

Yearning: In the early part of this phase disbelief is still manifest, both in the searching and in hallucination. Searching is most frequently shown in the need of the bereaved to reminisce on the loss or death, although some people physically search. It is important for a carer to hear this story repeated as many times as necessary, and to allow tears to be shed, not least because most friends and family will rapidly tire of both; but also because even when not speaking, the story goes on in the bereaved person's head like a stuck record. This is another time when the bereaved fear they are going mad and need the reassurance of the normality of their experience. Hallucination also reflects the disbelief: the bereaved frequently see, feel or hear the dead person. This is often disturbing to the family, but comforting to the bereaved. It is helpful to acknowledge to the bereaved both the vividness of what occurred, and also how it reflects their disbelief in the death. Almost always they also know that the death has occurred and this needs to be recognized.

Sometimes the bereaved seem to be unable to stop reminiscing. Should this persist well past the first six months the bereaved may be frightened that if they were to stop actively remembering they will forget the deceased. They may need permission to stop recalling, and recognize their fears of disloyalty. They may then discover that the person is now inside them – what is called 'internalization'.

The anger associated with bereavement is often hard to express, perhaps because of childhood fears of being punished for being angry, and because of a common view in society that 'one should not speak ill of the dead'. Anger is frequently directed towards helpers, health professionals, family or employers. The task of a counsellor is to enable the bereaved to recognize gradually that they are angry with the dead person for abandoning them. As one widow said, 'He's got the best deal'.

Guilt is usually expressed in terms of 'if only . . . '. This is likely to be a mixture of appropriate and inappropriate guilt. Both need to be expressed and the bereaved encouraged to review the whole relationship with attention to what irritated them, what made them angry or what they hated, just as much as the ways in which the relationship worked well.

The inability to deal with negative feelings about the dead person is most likely to result in complicated grief. The main signs of this are idealization of the dead, and even a shrine, often in the form of their bedroom untouched, or none of the possessions disposed of years after the death. In these instances expert help should be sought to enable the person to move on to the next phase.

Disorganization and despair: At this stage the reality of loss is beginning to be felt, with little sense that they will ever recover. Promises that all will be well are rarely helpful. It is better to let the bereaved talk about their feelings of acute anxiety (often childhood fears, such as fear of the dark or being alone, return), of loneliness, of ambivalence towards the dead person (perhaps swinging between idealization and vilification), of hopelessness and helplessness. This phase may last for many months and is particularly difficult because for each good hour or even day there may be weeks of utter despair. It is hard for the bereaved to believe that they will recover.

Reorganization: Recovery only gradually happens. It normally takes at least two years but can take a lot longer, and may never occur if the grief work of the previous stages has not been done. One landmark is the end of the first year but others are birthdays, anniversaries and Christmas. Surviving these can feel like a major step. Reorganization means acceptance of what has happened and gaining a new identity. Life will never be the same again. Recovery may mean something different for the elderly who may have spent half a lifetime with someone. They frequently say they reach a contentment, whereas younger people say that life returns with its full range of joys and sorrows.

(e)   In cases of complicated grief the person may need the intervention of a psychotherapist or psychiatrist. Cruse (126 Sheen Road, Richmond TW9 1UR. Tel: 0181 940 4818) is a nationwide organization, with branches in most major cities and towns, offering bereavement counselling, advice and information and social contact for the bereaved. The National Association of Widows (54–57 Allison Street, Digbeth, Birmingham B5 5TH. Tel: 0121 643 8348) offers self-help for the bereaved. There are also specialist bereavement groups such as: Gay Bereavement Project (Unitarian Rooms, Hoop Lane, London NW11 8BS. Tel: 0181 455 8894/6844); Jewish Bereavement Counselling Service (1 Cyprus Gardens, London N31 1SP. Tel: 0181 349 0839); Compassionate Friends (for those whose child of any age has died) (53 North Street, Bristol BS3 1EN. Tel: 0117 953 9639); SANDS (Still Death and Perinatal Death Association) (28 Portland Place, London W1N 4DE. Tel: 0171 436 5881); SIDS (Foundation for the Study of Infant Death) (35 Belgrave Square, London SW1X 8QB. Tel: 0171 235 0965 and Cot Death Helpline: 0171 235 1721); Miscarriage Association (c/o Clayton Hospital, Northgate, Wakefield, West Yorkshire WF1 3JS. Tel: 01924 200799).

(g)   Lendrum, S. and Syme, G. (1992) *Gift of Tears*. London: Routledge; Raphael, B. (1984) *The Anatomy of Bereavement*. London: Unwin Hyman; Worden, J. W. (1991) *Grief Counselling and Grief Therapy* (2nd edn). London: Routledge.

GABRIELLE SYME
(See also *children's experience of loss and death; death of a child; funerals; loss*)

Cancer

(a)   The word 'cancer', although slowly losing some of its dreadful connotations, nonetheless continues to provoke fear in many people, and for the sufferer, to hold the idea of a brush with mortality.

Cancer has been defined as:

> a disease in which a family of cells will grow progressively, with permanent impairment of normal growth control, resulting in spread of the primary group of tumour cells – the primary tumour – which penetrates the capsule of the parent organ. Secondly, the cancer cells will penetrate the walls of either lymphatic or blood vessels, and will be capable of implantation and growth in secondary or metastatic sites, especially in lymph nodes from lymphatic spread, and in any organ from blood-borne spread, especially lungs, bones, liver and brain. (Halnan, 1982)

(b)   While some cancers are diagnosed unforeseen, by screening, many are discovered through observation of a bodily change or symptom; some people respond with worry and seek medical reassurance early, and some underplay the significance and await developments. For most, the period of anxiety heightens with a GP's referral for further investigation of the symptom in a hospital setting, which will probably involve waiting. When a definite diagnosis is made and the extent of the disease ascertained, the news is broken either by GP or hospital doctor, and the appropriate course of treatment is explained and commenced.

Initial treatment completed, the paths awaiting patients diverge: for many with primary disease only, there may be a period of recovery and convalescence before full life is resumed. Disease is left behind with complete cure effected. For some there may be remission of widely differing lengths of time before further relapse. For some full health is never entirely regained and the future holds regular hospital visits including further courses of in-patient treatment, culminating in advanced disease and death. All patients face physical examinations, investigations and medical interviews at regular intervals while the course or absence of disease is monitored. Even those who have no further trouble and are able ultimately to pronounce themselves cured, therefore, have months and maybe years of follow-up which may be anxiety-provoking and disruptive.

This brief outline will alert the potential helper to the wide differences in experience lying in store for the cancer sufferer. For all patients, however, suffering from the most minor to the most advanced state of disease, a process of psychological readjustment is set in motion from the time of earliest suspicions or diagnosis.

Even among those patients who have suspected and feared that their symptoms may stem from a malignancy, the initial reaction to the undisputed diagnosis may be one of intense shock: this may last from minutes to several days and interfere with the patient's ability to absorb the explanation of her or his illness and treatment. There may be numbness and a sense of unreality. Generally this gives way to a growing awareness of the implications and significance of the diagnosis, which may be influenced by previous experience of others with cancer. Feelings may be intensely painful such as anxiety, sadness, **depression**, anger, **guilt** and **loss**.

The process of adjustment at this stage can be helped by several factors: the understanding support of close relatives or friends may alleviate distress and give comfort by encouraging sharing of feelings and offering realistic reassurance. Relatives may also have a role in liaising with medical and nursing staff and relaying information to the patient, who may have difficulty in remembering much detail. The single person with no-one to go home to after bad news may be especially vulnerable at this time, and support from nurses and GP may be sought. Where medical and nursing staff are able to give generous time for explanations and discussion, this does much to build confidence and trust and dispel unwarranted fears. There has been a trend towards increasing frankness over the last two decades and the nature of a patient's illness is rarely now hidden from him or her. Sometimes, where there are such resources, an elective counselling interview is made available to patients to offer support at an early stage. This identifies those who may be particularly vulnerable psychologically, such as those who have needed psychiatric treatment in the past.

(c) There has been some research to look at the most common ways people respond cognitively and behaviourally to the diagnosis of cancer. Greer et al. (1979), in a long-term prospective study of patients with breast cancer, observed four categories of mental adjustment:

1. Fighting spirit: here the patient fully accepts the diagnosis, adopts an optimistic attitude, seeks information and determines to fight the disease.
2. Denial: here the patient either rejects the diagnosis or minimizes its seriousness.
3. Stoic acceptance: here the patient adopts a fatalistic attitude.
4. Helplessness/hopelessness: here the patient is overwhelmed by the diagnosis and daily life is disrupted by a preoccupation with cancer and dying.

While patients sometimes fluctuate between these attitudes, inevitably the counsellor commonly sees those whose distress or problems preoccupy and disrupt daily life. This can occur at all stages of diagnosis, treatment and aftercare: some adjust to primary disease with minimal reaction, others are overwhelmed with shock; some experience problems when treatment is over and normal life is not resumed as expected, because of continued anxiety or depression. For many the diagnosis of secondary disease or recurrence is the most traumatic, because the possibility of complete cure is eliminated.

Those who refer patients for help are likely to be those relatives or hospital or practice staff who first recognize the symptoms of distress, or patients may seek help for themselves through their GP or specialist voluntary agencies. When a patient's feelings become intensely painful or prolonged their behaviour may change in some noticeable ways:

> Mrs A found herself low, tearful and unable to manage when she resumed work after her treatment for cervical cancer, and her depression contributed to a deterioration in her marriage; she became distressed during a check-up and the junior doctor began to explore her difficulties.

> Mr B was admitted to hospital for radiotherapy following recurrence of disease. He was aggressive and un-co-operative with the nursing staff and disturbed the other patients, complaining they received better help than him. At the root of his 'difficult' behaviour was intense fear that he would have to return to living alone when his treatment finished. The sister-in-charge discussed her concern with the departmental counsellor.

> Miss C, although successfully treated for early breast cancer, could not 'get over it'. Six months later her anxiety was still intense. She was constantly preoccupied with aches and pains and yet feared to burden her family with her worries in case they got fed up. She hid her distress, but slept badly, and her appetite deteriorated. Her GP was alerted when she frequently attended his surgery seeking reassurance.

All these patients ultimately came into counselling.

(d) Those offering care to the cancer sufferer in a professional or voluntary non-specialist capacity, and who have themselves little experience of the illness at close quarters, may find themselves facing the first contact with apprehension: 'Will I know what to say? Will I put my foot in it?'

Such anxieties usually disappear when the person is first encountered. It is no longer a 'cancer sufferer' with whom we are beginning to engage, but a real person, who from the first contact plays his or her part in a developing relationship. He or she is undergoing a unique experience which we may, if invited, be permitted to share.

It is important to distinguish between the various ways help may be offered. There are degrees of psychological care, which range from befriending to specialist intervention, all of which have the patient's mental well-being as their aim, and comprise many of the same basic characteristics: offering of time, the helper's own warmth and genuine willingness to listen to whatever the patient or client wishes to express. A befriender may enter into a relationship which principally involves listening, sitting alongside and imaginatively understanding what the patient is feeling. Here communication is as it might be between friends, and may involve mutual disclosure of past and present experience. Meetings may be *ad hoc* and take place in the patient's home, in a hospital or in a hospice.

Where a voluntary or professional counsellor engages with the patient, care needs to be taken to provide a therapeutic setting: i.e. to negotiate to meet for a specified time in **confidentiality** without interruption, with due notice of breaks. Here counsellors may feel that disclosure of their own experience of cancer is not particularly helpful. Instead they focus on identifying and working on the particular problems, while offering emotional support and trying to stay in tune with the patient's feelings.

Before the initial session, a referrer may have alerted the counsellor to a patient's particular problem, or nothing much may be known. In either case, it often helps to ascertain early on the patient's understanding of their condition. This can be done by gentle questioning: 'I'm not quite sure . . . I only know a little about what has been happening to you . . . I wonder if you could put me in the picture?'

This gives patients the freedom to say as much or as little as they choose, and for helpers to gauge something of their understanding by the terminology used. Care should be taken to use the patient's own words: if the word 'cancer' is used, the helper should use it also; likewise terms like 'lump', 'tumour', 'growth' or the more vague 'trouble'. The need is first to establish trust that the counsellor will introduce nothing unexpected or threatening.

Hopefully during a first session the counsellor learns something of the patient's history of the illness and reaction to it, what he or she expects of its outcome, something of the family and support network. The setting provides an opportunity for confiding current feelings in all these spheres. It is helpful to know how a patient has reacted to previous crises, and to assess degrees of anxiety and depression. The extent to which these areas are explored depends on the patient's emotional and physical state and their ease at talking. By the end of the first session it is important to have begun to identify particular problem areas. Often anxiety and **depression** is found to be related to some of the following:

1. difficulties in accepting illness and uncertain future;
2. intense and painful feelings proving difficult to manage;
3. fears in relation to treatment;
4. fears of death and manner of dying;
5. dilemmas about confiding feelings to close family and friends because of fears about 'causing distress';
6. relationships disturbed by the patient's illness, e.g. the 'dependent' person suddenly needing to be the 'supporter';
7. trauma and losses from the past which arouse previously unworked-through feelings;
8. loss of a sense of self, and self-esteem.

Particular areas of concern may be summarized by the counsellor, reflected back to the patient for confirmation or revision and time taken to discuss how both see the way forward.

Although initial sessions are largely for assessment, where previously pent-up feelings have been more freely expressed, great relief is often afforded. Mrs D slumped into the chair at the beginning of her session and said 'It's such a relief not to have to go on pretending I'm "fine" – can I just sit here and cry?' At the end of the session, having cried and talked much of her feelings since diagnosis, Mrs D went off cheerfully and did not need another appointment.

While some patients derive benefit from a single session, others are helped by coming over a longer period and working through thoughts and feelings in depth. Counselling is likely to be supportive rather than exploratory, with defences needing rebuilding. There is not much place for direct reference to the transference, but links with the past are useful, especially when they help to clarify emotional reactions and difficulties in accepting help. Mrs E was the eldest of a large family and from an early age had helped her mother with care of the younger children. Her mother seems to have lavished attention on her sons, but her daughter felt unloved and alone when troubled. Mrs E likewise felt alone with her worries about her cancer and felt she should be supporting others rather than 'burdening' them; the link made with her past made sense and allowed her to feel easier with accepting help.

Importantly, counsellors need to allow themselves to be 'used' for the work the patient needs to do: where patients have early disease, the focus of work may be on the fears and feelings arising from diagnosis and treatment. Permanent job loss may affect self-esteem: Miss F had resumed work on finishing treatment for breast cancer, but felt her colleagues expected her to pick up as though nothing had happened; she could not manage, gave up and then sat at home feeling isolated and useless.

Changes in body image may also affect self-esteem: Mrs G felt ugly, overweight and lopsided following her mastectomy, triggering feelings of unlovableness experienced when her husband walked out years before. At one session she produced photographs of herself as a pretty child, slim young girl and attractive, smiling wife. Looking at them together with the counsellor helped her to get back in touch with her sense of self as a worthwhile, whole and pleasant-looking person.

Many patients fear their distressed feelings mean that they are not fighting the disease positively and well-meaning relatives may regularly remind them that a 'positive' attitude will help. While Pettingale, following Greer's research (Greer et al., 1979), suggests that some attitudes are associated with a better prognosis than others in early-stage non-metastatic cancers, it is not conclusive. Such patients may need active reassurance of this and to be told that on the contrary, the more they allow themselves to express all their natural feelings without suppression, the greater the chance of psychological healing.

Sometimes the counsellor may point out how the ways in which patients think about their illness and future may influence them. Mrs H ruminated so long on how her recurrence had robbed her of the chance of cure that she failed to recognize that, at the age of 70 and currently recovered from treatment, her remission allowed her a full life.

Patients whose remissions have given way to advanced disease may defend against their physical decline and protect themselves by a slow withdrawal from close emotional contact. However, those with advanced disease whom the counsellor sees may need to share an inner world that demands much of the counsellor's own capacity for holding and containing. The process of letting go, with its ebb and flow of hope and despair, may be extremely painful for the patient to express and the counsellor to hear. However, rage and grief at what is to be lost may fluctuate with hope that life still holds some joys. Mrs J told the counsellor about her sudden weakness, her terror of being left alone at home and her conviction that she smelt of death. She cried, and then raged against God for allowing her suffering, and the doctors for failing to diagnose her cancer earlier. Then followed a period of calm during which she said how much she was looking forward to sitting in her garden and seeing relatives who would visit. She understood that the two states were connected: that if she could rage and cry, she could also experience some hopeful feelings. 'I won't need to see you again', she said, 'it will be enough to know I can.'

There may be discussion of how quality of life can be improved, with short term goals and activities to afford pleasure and a sense of control and achievement; however, the challenge for the counsellor as terminal illness draws near is expressed by Dreifuss-Kattan as 'not what to say but how to listen' (1990). She movingly describes the patient's need to rediscover the 'good internal object', or good inner experiences and fantasies which sustain and comfort as the outer world is relinquished. Miss K had nearly overwhelmed the counsellor with her rage and distress at the sudden lethal brain tumour diagnosed. However, when the counsellor visited the ward the following week, Miss K was lying in bed calmly and although evidently near death, looked peaceful. She managed a few words about her childhood in the country and her longing to go home and then drifted off to sleep. She died shortly afterwards.

(e) Where difficulties emerge that would be more appropriately dealt with by specialist intervention, such as severe anxiety, **depression**, resurgence of previous mental illness or **phobias**, etc., referral may be made to psychology or psychiatric services. Those too ill to attend in a formal setting may be much helped by home visits from Macmillan nurses or district nurses, or by referral to hospice counselling services.

(f) Often those offering psychological support need to liaise with medical and nursing teams. It may emerge that the patient is struggling to manage poorly controlled pain; that the treatment offered is not fully understood or that ambiguous remarks are causing distress. The counsellor will need the patient's permission to air such concerns with others.

It is clear that counselling people with cancer demands much of the helper's own inner resources and may touch many personal fears and feelings, attitudes to death, **religious belief** and spirituality. It is crucial that adequate support and **supervision** from experienced colleagues is regularly available if counsellors and other helpers are to healthily maintain their function in this ultimately deeply satisfying sphere of work.

(g) Dreifuss-Kattan, E. (1990) *Cancer Stories*. Hillsdale, NJ: Analytic Press; Greer, S., Morris, T. and Pettingale, K. W. (1979) 'Psychological response to breast cancer: effect on outcome', *The Lancet* ii: 785–7.

FELICITY MADDEN
(See also *recovery from major surgery; terminal illness*)

Careers guidance

(a)   Careers guidance seeks to meet the needs of those who are in the process of making and implementing decisions concerning careers and career routes, including training and education. Its aim is to ensure that such decisions are as realistic and well informed as possible. The term 'career' may be understood, in this context, in its broadest sense to refer, not only to 'professional' types of work, but to all issues related to occupational choice, paid and unpaid work and other aspects of life planning that may be relevant to the acquisition of skills and experience that are relevant to work.

Career planning is something which all of us engage in, with varying levels of awareness and clarity, in many cases without the assistance of careers guidance. While the outcome of career planning can never be totally predictable, if it is based upon a realistic understanding of the social and economic context, and follows a rational process, it is more likely to result in decisions that can be put into action and consequent career changes which can be managed with the minimum of difficulty. Careers guidance is therefore concerned with damage limitation and can be supportive of anyone engaged in career planning activities. Typically, this includes those passing through critical transitions, such as school, college and university leavers. In such cases the educational institutions frequently make provision for careers guidance. However, the need for support in choosing new career directions can occur at any time and can be prompted by many personal factors.

(b)   Career planning is essentially a very personal process, throwing up a multitude of presenting problems. Career problems present themselves in a variety of guises, both psychological and practical. Psychological difficulties may include inability to choose a direction, lack of knowledge about opportunities, lack of confidence in oneself or the choices that have been made or dissatisfaction with current employment. Practical career problems include unsuccessful attempts to gain employment or training, difficulties arising from life transitions or unanticipated events such as exam failure or changes in health or financial status.

While any typology of presenting issues is necessarily tentative, for there are probably as many career issues as there are clients, it may be helpful to classify these issues into three main groupings: those concerned with choice and constraint, those concerned with implementation and those concerned with progression.

Problems associated with choice and constraint are generally presented in terms of information needs. However, provision of additional information, by itself, rarely solves the problem and more often elicits a 'yes, but' response, suggesting that further work needs to be done to ensure that the desired outcome or career plan is realistic in every respect. Career choice issues range from 'I have no idea what I want to do', or '. . . what I can do', through to 'there are so many possibilities, how can I choose?' It is often assumed that careers advisers are mainly concerned with matching people to jobs and that their expertise consists of generating viable career ideas. Since the viability of career ideas is dependent upon a whole series of dynamics governing the relationship between the individual and the range of opportunities open to them, the examination and selection of options for serious consideration requires the full and active participation of the client. In addition, people and jobs are necessarily in a constant state of change, so expectations of careers guidance that characterize it as an infallible, once and for all matching exercise are unhelpful and unrealistic. The responsibility for choices clearly rests with the chooser, but an adviser may be able to ensure that the process of choice takes account of the full range of relevant factors and information. This may involve utilizing a variety of techniques including aptitude and interest questionnaires (many are now available in interactive computer packages) which can assist in generating options for consideration.

Realistic career choices cannot be identified in the absence of an analysis of perceived and actual constraints. The presenting problem may be: 'I know what I want to do but it is difficult or impossible because . . . ', the underlying assumption being that the adviser should take responsibility for removing the difficulty. Occasionally this may be possible. The adviser's knowledge of available routes and opportunities may supply a previously unknown means of achieving the desired outcome. However, the likelihood is that the assumed career goal is unrealistic, which may be due to a lack of relevant information about oneself or opportunities, or an unwillingness or inability to apply and integrate this information. In such situations it may be necessary to establish a series of sub-goals which are more closely related to the client's present circumstances, needs and abilities; and thereby enable the person to move forward, possibly at a slower pace but with greater realism.

Repeated failure to put plans into action may indicate, therefore, that the problem has more to do with the mechanics of planning than a simple lack of appropriate skills and strategies. The career goal for which the person is aiming may be unrealistic at the present time, for a whole host of reasons. Presenting issues related to implementation, or the stage of putting plans into action, may also be concerned with developing and applying the skills needed to gain entry to careers or training routes. Selection and testing procedures are often complex, and particular skills and coping strategies may be needed to manage these situations in such a way that the candidate's level of suitability for the position is accurately demonstrated.

In essence all career planning problems are problems of progression: 'What are my options after completing this qualification?', 'How can I return to work?', 'How can I improve my chances of promotion?' Such presenting issues are all legitimate within the parameters of careers guidance but they also beg further questions. In each case issues of progression are concerned with the interface between a unique individual and the actual, as opposed to the perceived, opportunities open to them. It is all too easy to fall into the assumption that objective information alone can answer these needs when in fact issues of career progression can only be genuinely resolved when subjective personal awareness goes hand in hand with accurate information about options.

(c) The essential starting point in the process of career planning is the client's ownership of the process. Career problems can easily be attributed to a range of social and economic factors such as instances of inequity in the education system, discriminatory selection procedures, high unemployment rates, insufficient provision for child care and unhealthy working conditions and practices; to name but a few. These factors and many others serve to disempower people from attempting to solve career problems and it is this very de-motivation that is a major obstacle to career planning. Unless an individual actually wants to resolve issues related to their career for themselves and to their own satisfaction and believes that this is possible, no real progress can be made.

Once an individual is able to take responsibility for their own career planning and is actively engaged in the process, they face the question of how to go about planning rationally. The careers adviser's role is therefore one of providing a rational approach to decision-making and enabling clients to maintain confidence in this approach. It is obvious that all decision-making requires an examination of the relationship between the self and the options available, and yet all too often decisions are made without a conscious realization of the implications of this fact. If decisions are made on the basis of only partial awareness of oneself and opportunities, difficulties are more likely to occur as a consequence. Criteria that result from personal preferences may be linked, illogically, to external options. Thus the young man who vigorously defends his decision to be an accountant despite the fact that his abilities lie in quite different areas may be unaware that his chief motivation lies in the fact that the accountant who lives next door owns a shiny Jaguar! Conversely, discrete aspects of self-knowledge may be linked to a narrow range of known opportunities resulting, for example, in the large numbers of schoolgirls who enjoy exercising responsibility as babysitters wanting to become nursery nurses. One might suspect that in many instances, this has more to do with fostering a healthy sense of self-esteem, selecting a life-style and developing personal responsibility, than making a realistic career choice.

The need to develop self-awareness and awareness of opportunities, and to explore the relationship between the two, is so self-evident that it is frequently neglected. Yet unless people acquire this understanding at a conscious level they are unable to proceed with rational decision-making. Blocks to decision-making can result from confusing the data concerning self and opportunities, from neglecting one side of this equation or from failing to develop sufficient realistic awareness of self and sufficient information about opportunities. The demands inherent in pursuing this simple formula to its logical conclusions are such that one of the key functions fulfilled by an adviser is often related to enabling clients to maintain confidence in the mechanics of the process.

Problems with career decision-making would seem to result from inadequate attention being given to the three stages of development of self-awareness and awareness of opportunities. Initially, sufficient accurate data must be collected. In relation to oneself this probably involves assessing one's abilities, experience, interests, physical capabilities and strength, values, life-style, etc. In relation to opportunities it may mean ensuring that one is aware of a range of linked career options, knows the entry requirements, training routes, key functions and responsibilities involved, is aware of conditions of service, opportunities for progression and psychological and financial rewards. For decisions to be reached on the basis of such data it is necessary for a clear sense of personal priorities to be established regarding objectives, needs and preferences in relation to work and life, and for relevant opportunities to be evaluated in the light of these priorities. This often highlights new factors to be related to the personal priority analysis, which in turn may lead to further research into opportunities. Individuals vary in the extent to which they need and are able to refine this process; in some cases the need to reach decisions quickly in order not to miss opportunities may itself be a high priority and outweigh the need for more detailed planning. For some, personal and financial sacrifices are necessary to achieve the desired outcome, and lengthy and meticulous planning may be essential. Since decision-making essentially involves selecting one route or option to the exclusion of others, compromises are usually necessary and this in itself requires a certain level of realism about personal priorities. If the process is pursued rigorously it inevitably suggests a number of contingency plans which can be called upon should the need arise.

The fact is that few people take responsibility for their career planning difficulties, few are consciously aware of the need to relate self-knowledge to knowledge about opportunities in a rational way and even fewer pursue this process rigorously. Yet the underlying causes and solutions to career problems can generally be traced to some deficiency in the past or present career planning process. This may be related to the self-concept: an under- or over-estimation of personal skills or abilities, an inaccuracy in the individual's understanding of how he or she is perceived by others or a problem of dissonance between the self-concept and self-presentation. Such problems are often difficult for an individual to acknowledge and in some instances may require professional intervention and support. Alternatively, poor career planning may result from inadequate investigation of opportunities: assumptions that particular skills can only be utilized in a narrow range of career options, inaccurate or out of date information about entry and training requirements or lack of appreciation of the psychosocial implications of particular types of work.

(d) The underlying principles and skills required to support clients through the process of career planning are in no way unique to professional careers advisers. Those working in the helping professions will be experienced in the process of establishing purposeful working relationships with clients, in negotiating with clients to achieve clarity about their own role and in setting clear and achievable objectives for working with clients. In the context of careers guidance the focus of these negotiations is essentially concerned with enabling clients to remain in control of their own decision-making process and to work towards career decisions that are well informed, realistic and therefore capable of being put into action. This requires the adviser to be impartial about the outcomes of the guidance process and clear about their right to organize the interaction in order to achieve the most useful outcome for the client.

The adviser faced with a client in the process of making career plans is most likely to be presented with questions that seem to demand information about jobs, entry requirements or availability of training routes. Usually such generalized questions are the tip of the iceberg and further exploration will reveal more detailed personal questions linking the client's assumptions about their current situation and the possible direction in which they can move. The temptation for inexperienced careers advisers is either to move into feeling inadequate because they do not possess the relevant information or to offer premature solutions based on what little knowledge they have. However, further probing and exploration of the client's ideas and concerns will provide a wider perspective about the needs to be resolved in relation to career planning. For instance, a presenting problem about the availability of a college course may throw up a whole range of concerns about personal confidence and competence to study, priorities about interests in different subjects and the usefulness of particular qualifications for entry to particular types of employment. The relative significance of the issues arising out of this preliminary discussion will determine the objectives towards which the adviser and client jointly agree to work. By methodically exploring the way in which the client perceives their problem it is possible for the adviser to help seek solutions that are meaningful to the client. The essential outcome is not that the adviser offers the best solution he or she can, for these will always be limited by the adviser's personal perspective; but rather that clients are supported in gaining insight into the reasons for their difficulties and seeking and utilizing solutions that are satisfactory to them.

Thus the three stages of careers guidance can be characterized as:

1. agreeing and clarifying the issue to be resolved in relation to career planning;
2. identifying the cause of career planning difficulties;
3. developing appropriate strategies to overcome these difficulties.

(e) Clarity about the client's needs in relation to career planning forms a basis for seeking appropriate solutions, one of which may be referral to other agencies. Careers guidance is now provided, free of charge, by a large number of organizations under contract to local Training and Enterprise Councils. The TECs hold a remit to support the provision of high-quality careers guidance by ensuring that careers advisers are adequately trained and regularly monitored. Contracts to provide careers guidance services may be held by a wide range of organizations, some of which have special expertise in working with particular client groups: people with disabilities, particular age groups, ethnic groups, ex-offenders. However, many organizations cater for a wide range of clients and the choice of an agency may be determined more by location and convenience of access than any other factor. Details of local providers are obtainable from local Training and Enterprise Councils, who can advise on suitable agencies to offer guidance to both adults and young people. Traditionally, careers guidance services, especially for young people, have been provided by the local education authority's careers service. Though these services are now moving away from exclusive LEA control, their long-standing experience of providing impartial guidance to their local communities suggests that they will be likely to continue to fulfil this role in the future, particularly in relation to young people.

(f) All accredited careers guidance providers are effectively linked to one another by the requirement to work to the standards set by their local TEC, which is also a condition of their funding. The extent to which co-operative networks of careers guidance providers have been established varies from one area to another, and in some instances competitive tendering for contracts to provide guidance services has emphasized competition rather than co-operation. Systems for referring clients from one agency to another tend to be informal. Consequently reasons for transferring clients and issues of **confidentiality** of information are usually discussed with the client prior to referral, at which time the issue of transfer of any records of guidance can be discussed. Most guidance providing agencies supply a Career Action Plan, a copy of which is given to the client and a copy supplied to the TEC.

(g) Benjamin, A. (1969) *The Helping Interview*. Boston: Houghton Mifflin Company; Egan, G. (1982) *The Skilled Helper: Model, Skills and Methods for Effective Helping*. Monterey, CA: Brooks/Cole Publishing Co.; Hayes, J. and Hopson, B. (1972) *Careers Guidance: The Role of the School in Vocational Development*. London: Heinemann Educational Books.

FRANCES SCOTT
(See also *redundancy and unemployment*)

Child abuse

(a) Child abuse is defined by opinions and values prevalent in society and by culturally conditioned practices of child rearing. While there may be agreement about serious acts of physical and other abuse, there are differing views about some forms of 'discipline' and abuse. A useful starting point is:

> a child is considered to be abused if he or she is treated by an adult in a way that is unacceptable to a given culture at a given time. (Meadow, 1989: 1)

It is helpful to add a further definition:

> The intentional, non-accidental use of physical force or intentional non-accidental acts of omission on the part of a parent or other caretaker, interacting with a child in his care aimed at hurting, injuring or destroying that child. (Gil, 1978: 48)

This definition specifies acts of intention and also omission towards children by carers; and sites abuse not only in the context of society, but clearly in the context of a relationship where the nurture or protection which might be expected is either dangerously absent or has become negative or destructive.

The earlier concept of child abuse as the *battered baby syndrome* (Kempe and Helfer, 1980) has since been developed to 'embrace virtually any problem which may have an adverse impact on a child which could possibly be attributed to an act of commission or omission by an adult' (Parton, 1989: 55).

Child abuse is a well defined concept in some aspects, but complex at the interfaces where culture, values and opinions meet identification, intervention and treatment. It is this complexity which leaves the rights and needs of children set in the context of the rights and responsibilities of their carers, the state and the system. The caring professional's role can therefore become a delicate balancing of all these factors.

(b)   Abused children present to helpers both directly by verbal disclosure and indirectly by behaviour or telling a third party. Often the impact of abuse is not realized until adult life (see *adult survivors of abuse; children with behavioural difficulties*). Establishing that a minor (under 16 years) is being abused and protecting them satisfactorily is a very skilled task. A reading of enquiries such as the one into Jasmine Beckford's death or the Cleveland Report makes this clear (Beckford Enquiry, 1985; Cleveland Report, 1988).

A perusal of the reporting by newspapers or other media of such issues also demonstrates the difficulty of the work and the strong feelings aroused. However, certain presentations of abuse can be identified. In these cases the abuse would be investigated by the social services department of the local authority, the police and in some areas the NSPCC. These cases are as follows:

1. *Physical abuse:*   This usually means an assault on a child which causes injury, e.g. bruising, fractures. It may also include failure to prevent injuries such as burning and scalding, as well as deliberately inflicting burns or scalds. This category includes deliberate poisoning, suffocation, asphyxiation, drowning and Munchausen's syndrome by proxy.

2. *Neglect:*   This can be defined as persistent failure to provide proper care, e.g. failure to feed or clothe a child, or attend to his or her hygiene or seek medical attention. The neglect will have caused impaired or seriously delayed development including non-organic failure to thrive.

3. *Emotional abuse:*   This is emotional ill-treatment which is persistent and severe. It causes behavioural and social outcomes. It is frequently present in other forms of abuse but can be present alone, e.g. verbal bullying or belittling.

4. *Sexual abuse:*   This is the sexual exploitation of a minor for the gratification of the perpetrator. The child may be unable to understand or meaningfully consent.

However, the presentation of abuse is often unclear and there are indicators which may alert caring adults to the possibility of abuse and arouse concern. For instance, children who are suffering abuse can be sad and unable to enjoy life in the same way as their peers. They may be unable to concentrate to learn, or join in games or activities. They might lack trust in adults, and be withdrawn or aggressive, or show other behavioural indicators that all is not well. They might be excitable, low in self-esteem, anxious, enuretic or they might bully other children. They may be pseudo-mature, having developed coping strategies, which are maladaptive but enable survival in a hostile world.

Repeated small injuries, unusual marks or injuries for a child of a particular age, improbable accounts of how injuries happened, vagueness or lack of knowledge or concern about a child's whereabouts on the part of carers may all be significant. Other areas of concern would be verbal hostility and ill-feeling towards a particular child which are consistently negative.

These kinds of indicators, which are complex and contradictory, cannot alone be conclusive. The other difficulty is that most children have sad or angry or excited behaviours from time to time. All kinds of upsets can cause similar behavioural outcomes in children who are developing well and happily, e.g. illness or death or the arrival of a new baby in the family. Equally, most carers experience times of feeling angry with their children, or are tired and stressed and cannot care as well as usual. Accidents happen to most people at some time. However, most of this is either temporary or part of life events which all children need to negotiate as part of growing up.

Where children are being abused, the condition is more likely to be severe and persistent, with many indicators together. For this reason multi-agency collaboration is vital in building up a picture of what may be a cluster of indicators that show serious cause for concern.

These kinds of factors can alert caring professionals to the possibility of significant harm being possible at the hands of carers. Children can be abused by caretakers irrespective of class, culture, religion, race or disability. It is also helpful to keep in mind that very young children, or children who rely heavily on carers for their needs, are more vulnerable to exploitation and abuse. This may include children with disabilities and children in hospitals and other institutions. It is important to be alert to the failure to seek medical attention for a child, or the avoidance of a child being seen by professionals. In particular, if a child about whom there is concern is not present at school or any other activity, it is vital that their well-being be sensitively checked out and not left, on the assumption that someone else will know or will have checked.

(c) It would be comforting to professional carers if there were a nice clear list of factors which predispose parents or other adults to abuse children. It seems clear from social work practice and research that certain contributory factors are significant and re-occur. However, the definition of risk remains a matter of interdisciplinary and detailed assessment, which can never be fully certain in this complex area of inter-generational and human interaction in a multi-cultural society.

For example, socio-economic factors may play a part in the sense that social isolation, poor housing and money problems all create and sustain stress. However, many children are loved and valued and nurtured at home in spite of great material deprivation; and children have been abused in more affluent situations.

The psychopathology of individual caretakers is significant. The feminist analysis of male power and its relevance to abuse is very important in this area in highlighting the vulnerability of women and children in a patriarchal society, where they may be viewed as property or belongings. The work done with offenders in prisons is also illuminating in demonstrating how an offender may select and groom the victim of sexual abuse. Parents who were themselves bullied can have learned an abusive way of child-rearing which is passed on. Parents who were starved of love and nurture themselves may expect a baby to satisfy their own needs. Likewise the unrealistic expectations of small children by immature parents can lead to ordinary developmental stages, such as tantrums or crying, being interpreted as attack or defiance towards a caretaker, and inappropriate 'punishment' being given. Children are also at risk from parents whose coping mechanisms are impaired by **psychosis**, drug or **alcohol** misuse or illness, especially if there is insufficient help and support.

Some children appear to be more vulnerable to abuse than others in the same family; for instance: babies who cry for long periods and/or do not feed well; children whose behaviour is challenging; a child whose birth was difficult or whose presence for some reason is not really wanted. It is important to remember that children with disabilities can be abused and may be more vulnerable to disbelief or the incapacity to tell than others (see *learning disabilities*).

It is unwise to have a simple cause and effect view of the underlying factors around child abuse. All children are potentially vulnerable, especially the very young. However, it is possible to consider risk factors and to work towards holding a body of knowledge as to what these are, and to consider the social, personal and political factors as all having relevance.

(d) Professional carers who encounter disclosures of child abuse work in differing kinds of setting. The main difference of approach is between those with legal powers and duties, and those who operate from a community or private base with no mandatory brief. Helpers in statutory agencies have their roles and responsibilities clearly defined and may have legal responsibility for protecting children. Other professional carers may encounter the issue from time to time, but may not have legal duties, policies or guidelines. Some helpers are in situations where they are totally reliant on their own skills and judgements as to what care and counsel to offer. Both situations have their own dilemmas and it is important to be aware of the likely actions of other professionals, especially those with legal powers and duties, so as not to make referrals without a clear idea of possible outcomes or in a way that leads to unrealistic expectations. Inappropriate and unskilled work can be very damaging to the child or young person and helpers should seek help and support. **Supervision** and consultation are essential.

Disclosure: Children and young people choose whom to tell about abuse. This can be a difficult step to take, as an abused person may feel loyal and protective towards the perpetrator. There is also the possibility of being told of events that the carer defines as abuse, but which have not been recognized as such by the young person. Additionally, a child may be afraid that the consequences of telling will mean the break-up of their home. They may also have been threatened by an abuser that terrible things will happen if they tell. With very young children cues such as sexualized or violent drawing and play are inconclusive alone and difficult to interpret, but can be attempts to bring attention to a child's worries or bad experiences. Such cues need following with great care and by someone with expertise. Children who begin to hint or tell need a great deal of sensitive understanding and to be reassured that they are believed.

They also need to know as far as is possible what will happen, without false assurances about the outcome. Different settings present different issues regarding disclosure. For instance, a voluntary group leader may be unsure how much to listen to before contacting a statutory agency. A statutory agency worker may have the difficulty of establishing rapport with a young person, who does not know them and has already told their story to someone else, and yet have legal responsibilities to investigate the situation.

Interviewing: Further reading and training in this area is essential, but some very basic guidelines can be given here.

It is essential to stay calm and alert, to have a quiet place to talk and to be unhurried and unpressurizing. Listen carefully, taking full account of the child's age and stage of development. Be careful not to ask leading questions or to be shocked; maintaining a neutral, accepting attitude is crucial, as is allowing the story to emerge uninterrupted and interpreted. Where possible give good clear information about what you might do and when. If interviewing an adult bringing information about a child, it is important to be clear what the consequences of telling you are, especially if you think you may be working with someone who is abusing someone else.

Confidentiality: In this area this cannot be easily promised, if at all, although there is often debate between different helpers about this (see *confidentiality*). For helpers with statutory duties and powers there are clear guidelines in place: the child's physical well-being is an absolute priority. For most other agencies, guidelines are like to name child protection as an area where strict confidentiality may be breached in the interests of a child. Children have a right to protection and unless a worker is entirely satisfied that the abuse was in the past or the child is now safely protected by other carers, referral to social workers should be made. Where several professional carers are involved there may be conflicting opinions about what should be kept confidential. Considered decisions need to be made about what information is passed to whom, and what consents are needed or set aside. It is also important that care be taken about sources of information and accuracy.

The helper's feelings: Everyone has been a child and carries within them that experience as well as possible experiences of caring for their own or other people's children. Consequently the helper's feelings can be very strong and it is important to monitor and reflect on these. Doubt, denial, anger, shock, abhorrence, naïvety can all make hearing and helping about abuse difficult. Similarly, feelings about state intervention in family life can affect a helper's views and judgements about how to act (Fox-Harding, 1991). Anyone working with child abuse issues needs support, consultancy, time and resources given to discussing, doubts, anxieties, perspectives and value judgements.

Co-operative working: Child abuse work requires consultation rather than individual action. To achieve the best outcome for an individual requires the combined efforts of all the agencies with resources and expertise. To be effective it is helpful to have a working knowledge of local resources and agencies, their philosophies and services. Such a knowledge avoids inappropriate and unrealistic referral.

Cultural issues: These require sensitive consideration. Cultural variations in child-rearing patterns do exist. Awareness of cultural, racial (see *cross-cultural awareness*), religious (see *faith differences*), class, **gender**, disability issues (see *physical disability; learning difficulties*) and other perspectives are essential. At the same time the knowledge that children are abused in all kinds of families and that their welfare is paramount should be maintained alongside this sensitivity to differing value systems and cultural practices.

The legal framework: Social work and other helping services for children are set in the context of The Children Act 1989. This Act was implemented in October 1991. When it was introduced to Parliament it was described by the Lord Chancellor as 'the most comprehensive and far reaching reform of child care law which has come before parliament in living memory'. It brings together all previous child-care law. A brief summary cannot do it justice, but five key principles are significant. These are: the welfare of the child as paramount; partnership between parents and professionals; the importance of keeping children in their families wherever possible; the importance of the wishes of children and their parents; and the corporate responsibility of the whole local authority for child welfare and protection (Shaw et al., 1990).

Only ongoing research will illuminate how these principles are being implemented to protect and support children. One study of a local authority's work with children considered to be at risk of suffering significant harm at the hands of their carers concludes:

> The Children Act appears to have facilitated both the new approach of minimal court intervention and working in partnership; it has achieved this through its sound underlying philosophies and

principles in partnership with professional social work practice.
(Hardiker and Barker, 1994: 75)

(e)   There is considerable specialist expertise in the area of child abuse
both in statutory agencies and voluntary bodies and private practice.
The main large agencies are: area child protection and review bodies
(see (f) below); local social services departments (intake or child protection); NSPCC; schools psychological services; child psychiatric services;
Family Service Units; Home Start (under-5s); Barnardo's; the Children's Society; Childline; the police – Special Units: trained WPCs.

(f)   Following cases where children have died or been badly injured, or
mistakenly been removed from home, the Department of Health has
acted to improve multi-agency intervention on behalf of children and to
improve child protection services (*Working Together*, Department of
Health, 1988).

   The outcome of this should be that every local authority together
with other agencies has an area child protection committee to co-
ordinate and review services. The agencies represented will usually be
health, education, social services, the police, the NSPCC and other
leading children's voluntary agencies. All these agencies should be
committed to working together to protect children and provide services
which are anti-racist, anti-sexist, anti-oppressive and sensitive to
disability.

   Each has a specific role and a remit to share concerns. Detailed
instructions should be available to staff in their workplaces. Social
services and the police have a legal duty to investigate all allegations of
child abuse and should liaise closely. All information received from the
public must be acted on. It is important that referrers understand this
when contacting these agencies. Workers can help by being clear about
their own role, knowledge, involvement and what assistance they
might offer. They need also to be clear that wherever possible children
should be supported to remain in their own homes and communities
with support services to help. Children should only become subject to
court proceedings if their welfare cannot be promoted in any other way
and it is impossible to protect them from further abuse in any other
way. Local information on services will be available from your local
authority.

(g)   Corby, B. (1993) *Child Abuse: Towards a Knowledge Base*. Buck-
ingham: Open University Press; Fox-Harding, L. (1991) *Perspectives in
Child Care Policy*. London: Longman; Shaw, M., Masson, J. and
Brocklesby, E. (1990) *Children in Need and Their Families: A New*

Approach. University of Leicester School of Social Work and Faculty of Law and the Department of Health.

JANET SEDEN
(See also *adult survivors of abuse; learning disabilities*)

Children with behavioural difficulties

(a)   This article addresses the issues of a child's behaviour that others find difficult. I take my approach to the issues largely from the Parent-Link way of working with parents and children. This can be loosely described as humanistic with a bias towards the person-centred. Parent-Link is a preventive education and support programme offered to parents of children of all ages by facilitators trained and supervised by the national charity Parent Network. I will very briefly consider other approaches, such as behaviour modification, within the narrow set of circumstances where resort to them may be appropriate.

(b)   The assumption here is that the reader may come across relevant issues in two possible ways: first in direct contact with children and young people, and secondly in contact with parents and other adults living and working with children and young people. That is, you yourself may be dealing with children's behaviour that you have difficulty with, or you may be dealing with other people who find children's behaviour difficult.

The starting place is to question what I mean by behavioural difficulties. A lot is spoken and written about *difficult children*, and many might choose to define the issues with this as a starting point. The title of this article takes a more middle of the road approach in referring to *behavioural difficulties in children*, still locating the problem wholly with the child even as it switches from branding the child to branding their behaviour. However, you will have noticed that my bias is to go one step further and write about *behaviour in children that adults find difficult*. I would therefore lump difficult behaviour into the same category as bad behaviour and assert that there is no such thing as bad behaviour in children, only behaviour that adults and other children experience as unacceptable.

(d)   This definition is an essential step for me in working towards the development of effective strategies for bringing about changes in behaviour in others and myself. It leads me directly to two different next steps: one that goes deeper into my understanding of behaviour and human nature and one that helps me ascertain what practical action I can most usefully move towards.

Needs behind behaviour
In common with much of the humanistic field, particularly Carl Rogers and Fritz Perls, I have a working assumption that all behaviour is consciously or unconsciously designed to satisfy fundamental human needs. From this perspective it is easy to see the crying of a baby as an effective strategy for getting fed. At other times such crying may be designed to meet needs for protection from fear or anxiety, or to attract loving attention to meet the child's needs for affection. In an ideal world our children grow up to progress through the learning of a whole host of useful and acceptable strategies for getting their needs met. So a toddler can learn to come and say 'I need a cuddle', rather than lie on the floor crying when they are not getting their affection needs met. If they have effective models for the socially acceptable behaviour that gets their needs met, they can grow up into 'well adjusted' adults who do not lack for any fundamental human need. They are mature, responsible and skilled enough to ask for what they need.

In practice, few of us are this fortunate. We did not have the loving support of aware understanding parents when we were tiny. We were surrounded as children by models of unstraight ways of getting our needs met and encouraged by an over-developed consumer society to totally confuse our needs with the satisfiers of those needs – the *wants* we have been led to expect to receive. As such we have each learnt a whole host of socially acceptable and unacceptable ways to try and satisfy our needs, many of which are ineffective.

The four-year-old who still only knows the screaming tantrum of a baby as a way to get to do what she wants; the ten-year-old who disrupts the class with his constant attempts to attract attention from the teacher; the teenager who believes that the only way to attract affection is to sulk: they have all learnt their ineffective ways of behaving from either the models or the negative reinforcements they received from the significant adults in their lives. Yet the needs they are struggling so hard to meet are valid in and of themselves. The difficulty lies in their use of ways to get their needs met that are not acceptable to others.

Understanding this concept of needs behind behaviour frees me up to relate to issues of difficult behaviour in non-judgemental ways. It also opens up possibilities of responding to behaviour I have difficulty with in genuine problem-solving ways rather than the more normal punitive ways many people living and working with children are used to. Finally, it identifies a potential responsibility for me to find ways to

deal with the issues that are also educative, helping the people concerned to learn more effective and acceptable ways to get their needs
met in future.

Before I can move forward into action around behaviour I find
difficult, it is essential that I also understand a little more about whom
it is difficult for and why.

Problem ownership

Understanding the reasons why children (and adults) behave in ways I
normally find difficult can go a long way towards changing my attitude.
Separating out the child and his or her valid basic needs from the
behaviour often allows me to be accepting of both child and behaviour. I
may no longer find the behaviour difficult. In this case I can see the
child as owning a problem of unmet needs for themselves and effectively doing something about it. I may choose to involve myself in some
way in helping them to get their needs met, or if they are doing fine on
their own, stand back and let them continue.

Even with this changed attitude, I may find the child's chosen way to
meet their need as unacceptable and difficult as ever. At this point it is
useful for me to ask myself 'What need of mine is being interfered with
by the behaviour I find difficult?' If the answer is truthfully none, I need
to challenge myself by questioning what right I have to label the child's
behaviour as difficult or unacceptable. If the answer is truthfully some
need, then I step into the frame as also owning a problem of unmet
needs.

For example: My child is playing loudly with a friend on a cold and
wet day. They are rushing round the house playing at racing drivers.
They are adequately meeting their needs for stimulation, participation,
creativity and who knows what else. If I was brought up to be quiet and
slow around the house, I may find this behaviour difficult if not
downright unacceptable. As such I will react to it as if their behaviour is
causing me a problem. It certainly isn't causing them any kind of
problem. If I am honest and self-aware I can check out my reasons for
labelling their fun as difficult and maybe shift myself into a place where
I can relax and let them continue.

If I happen to be feeling ill and have a terrible headache that is made
worse by the boisterous play of the children, then I have a legitimate
problem in this situation. As such it would be wholly appropriate for me
to confront their behaviour in order to solve my problem and get my
needs met.

This concept of problem ownership challenges me to be clear about
what is going on in any situation both in terms of here and now reality
as well as in terms of the projections and transferences I bring into the
situation:

- Am I finding the child's behaviour difficult because it is inter-fering with a need of mine?
- Am I finding the child's behaviour difficult because of some current state of mind or emotions I brought with me to the situation?
- Am I finding the child's behaviour difficult because of some old triggered response left over from my childhood and what I was or was not allowed to do or feel?
- Am I finding the child's behaviour difficult because of the feelings that it triggers in me here and now?

Moving into action

With the clarity that answering such questions can give, it is possible for me to take a rational adult decision as to what to do:

1. Is it appropriate to stay out of the situation and leave the child to get on with whatever they are doing?
2. Is it appropriate to grant that the child owns the problem and offer to help them find a more useful way to get their needs met?
3. Is it appropriate to own my problem in the situation and confront the child about their behaviour in the hope that they will choose some other behaviour that doesn't interfere with my needs?
4. If as often happens, both I and the child have a problem, it may be appropriate to challenge the child's behaviour, disclose my problem and sit down with them to negotiate a way that we can both get our needs met in the situation.

Some examples

1. I witness an adolescent couple arguing in the community centre and the boy strolls off leaving the girl in tears. My fear and dislike of tears wells up inside and I long to rush over and make it all better for her. Yet I hold back, knowing that the pain she is suffering is normal and her tears are very healing.
2. I have watched Derek being excluded from today's gang and now hear him shouting occasional rude comments at the others. I am aware of his pain at being rejected. His behaviour does not directly impinge on me, yet I know that it will only alienate him further from the group. I do not want to take sides in the matter and yet would like to help this boy learn more effective ways of behaving. I approach Derek and engage him in conversation, listening to his feelings and, as he calms down, helping him think of how he could behave in ways that would endear him to the group rather than alienate him from them.

3. I am trying to clear up at the end of the day. Half a dozen youngsters are having a ball rushing round and round the hall. I am getting more frustrated and angry as I see them undoing the order I am struggling to achieve. Before I totally lose my patience and my self-control, I take hold of my power and send them a strong straight message something like 'I'm trying to clear up while you are all having enormous fun; you are getting in my way, I can't stand it any longer! What are you going to do about it before I lose my temper?' Stunned into a moment's silence, they sheepishly leave to continue their games outside.

4. I recognize the signs of an impending tantrum in Jane. She has been crashing around in the kitchen and passing back and forth along the corridor outside my office. She is obviously in dire need of some attention, and I really have to finish this report. Not wanting to have to deal with the extreme behaviour that comes in her attacks, I put my needs on hold long enough to go and see her in the kitchen. I acknowledge her agitated state and tell her it looks like she needs some time to talk things through. I also tell her that I have 20 minutes' more work to do to finish my report. We discuss what we can do about the situation and agree to meet in my office in 20 minutes and meanwhile she can borrow one of my tapes she particularly likes to listen to.

Through problem ownership I am able to identify when to use my essential listening skills to empower the child to figure out how to get their needs met, satisfying a universal need for acceptance and affection at the same time. I am also able to identify when it is appropriate to be assertive and state my needs. In the last instance I can identify when I need to use a combination of these fundamental communication skills to negotiate a solution to a shared problem.

Supporting others who find children's behaviour difficult
With the understanding and awareness that the two concepts of *needs behind behaviour* and *problem ownership* give us, assisting others who find children's behaviour difficult should be easier than dealing with our own issues. One step removed from the inevitable emotional triggers, clashes of values and burdens of responsibilities that so often bug our relations with young people, I hope it will be possible to put into practice much of what I have written above.

If you come to me with a problem to do with the behaviour of children in your care – be they your own children or children you have a professional responsibility for – I will start by listening to the feelings you will surely have. People invariably feel one or more of a host of emotions when faced with behaviour in children that they find difficult.

These may include frustration, anger, resentment, guilt, helplessness, fear and jealousy, to name but a few. Taking a moment to listen to and even help name the feeling is an essential starting place.

The feelings in the situation will give us both lots of clues as to what is going on underneath. Some of them may be appropriate in the circumstances. A teacher may well have cause to be afraid of behaviour she perceives as aggressive or even violent in 16-year-old youths in her class. Other feelings, like guilt, resentment or jealousy are more likely to be old material that we bring to the present from our own childhood. Sorting out the 'here and now' from the 'there and then' is an important step in examining the issues of problem ownership.

With my help you may be able to see that the problem is actually your perception of the behaviour as difficult. Alternatively, you may see that the child concerned is expressing genuine yet unsuccessful attempts to meet major needs. Yet again, it might be that the behaviour is not difficult in and of itself but for the fact that it is interfering with your own needs in the situation. My role now is to counsel and facilitate you through working out who owns what problem, understanding the whole concept of needs behind behaviour and helping you to decide what if anything to do about the situation.

Dealing with extreme situations
My writing will have identified a firm humanistic bias in my approach to this whole issue that I experience as being more than adequate to grapple with most everyday situations. I recognize that extreme situations do arise where a more controlling and less child-centred approach would bring quicker results, even though it is less empowering in the long run.

As mentioned above, all social behaviour is learned. The ineffective ways a child develops to meet their needs are either modelled from the significant adults around them or developed in response to the behaviour of those adults. If the only way a child can attract the contact and attention all children desperately need is to behave in extremely difficult ways, then they will do so rather than get no contact at all. Negative attention is always better than no attention at all. A child so damaged by lack of genuinely caring human contact may need quite structured practical help to change their patterns of behaviour.

Conventional approaches to behaviour modification focus on how to influence the child directly to change their behaviour through programmes of reward and punishment. Yet more recent developments, particularly in the Maudsley Hospital 'Family Game', work to provide explicit practical instructions to the parents to change their response to the so-called 'problem' child, thereby breaking the patterns of interaction that reinforce the ineffective behaviour.

(e) It is for me critical that I hold on to my understanding that all behaviour is about meeting basic needs. In cases that require more extreme levels of intervention, this concept merges well into either systems theory or field theory that can form the basis for more specific family therapy style interventions in the given situation. In this way we can hold on to the concept that it is the child's behaviour we find difficult, not the child, and work with all concerned to help the child develop more socially acceptable and practically useful ways of coping in the world.

For particular assistance in dealing with behaviour you find difficult in children, you can explore and develop the skills and understanding of the approach I have outlined through attendance at a Parent-Link course. Though usually aimed at parents, many carers and professionals attend and gain enormously from this education and skills training programme. These groups are available in many places in England and Scotland, with the availability expanding all the time. Details of your nearest group can be had from the Parent Network at 44–46 Caversham Road, London NW5 2DS. At the time of writing, the Parent Network is launching a new programme for training professional carers in the Parent-Link approach. Additionally, you can find support from local counsellors and family therapists.

(g) Axline, V. (1975) *Dibs: In Search of Self.* Harmondsworth: Penguin; Bolton, R. (1986) *People Skills.* Melbourne: Prentice-Hall of Australia; Sokolov, I. and Hutton, D. (1988) *The Parent Book: Getting On Well with Your Children.* London: Parent Network.

IVAN SOKOLOV
(See also *children with learning difficulties; families, working with; learning disabilities*)

Children with learning difficulties

(a) There are tasks which most of us find easy and tasks which most find difficult. Thus a child's difficulties must be seen in the context of how most children manage. The 1981 Education Act said that a child has a learning difficulty if he or she has significantly greater difficulty in learning than the majority of children of that age, or has a disability which prevents effective use of facilities generally provided. This definition recognizes context and the difficulties some children have in obtaining access to the curriculum (e.g. the visually impaired).

For a child, the context also needs to include not only age but physical condition, early experiences, present circumstances, motivation, emotional and behavioural functioning and personality factors.

About 20 per cent of children have some form of learning difficulty (Warnock Report, 1978), though many of these will be short term and most will be provided for by 'normally available provision'. About 2 per cent require extra provision, and about 0.1 per cent have severe learning difficulties (Mental Health Foundation, 1993).

(b) A broad range of learning difficulties is found among children. Difficulties may arise from peripheral weakness: vision, hearing, speech or physical handicap (see *physical disabilities*). Other children have general learning difficulties, usually regarded as having three levels: mild, moderate and severe (see *learning disabilities*). Some children have specific learning difficulties, most commonly with reading. Others have learning difficulties associated with emotional or behavioural difficulties (see *children with behavioural difficulties*), and a few have difficulties associated with personality disorders such as autism (see *psychosis and severe mental disorders*). A child may show more than one form of difficulty, and diagnosis is often difficult.

(c) For children with peripheral weaknesses, the cause of the learning difficulty is self-evident. The extent of the effect on learning may require much careful observation.

Mild and moderate levels of general learning difficulties are generally regarded as part of the normal range of human abilities, and these children may show no obvious reason for their difficulty. Severe learning difficulties are more often found in association with a developmental or acquired weakness of central functioning (e.g. a brain injury).

Much controversy surrounds the causation of specific reading difficulties or 'dyslexia'. Reading difficulties arise from a variety of causes, but the controversy relates to a small minority of children whose difficulties are severe (in contrast to their general level of functioning), and very resistant to help. The issue is whether such children are inherently different to others, or simply at the severe end of the continuum of such difficulties. The debate continues.

In some children whose capacity for learning is unimpaired, emotional and behavioural difficulties may interfere with their attention, motivation, relationship with teachers and peers and school attendance. Children with primary learning difficulties may also develop associated emotional and behavioural difficulties. Children with personality disorders or mental disorders may show effective but uneven learning in unrelated areas. Here the difficulty is not just one of poor motivation but often appears to involve distortions in processing information as well.

(d) Helping a child with learning difficulties involves identification and diagnosis of the difficulty and making appropriate arrangements to help the child. Identification needs to establish that the difficulty exists and what areas it covers. Diagnosis needs to establish the severity of the difficulty and its causation. Arrangements to help should be related to the areas of difficulty, the severity and what appears to be the cause. Views formed from initial identification and diagnosis should not be rigid, as ongoing work with the child may lead to revision and hence to changes in the help offered.

The treatment of learning difficulties usually requires arrangements to modify or re-programme the child's learning experiences in accordance with the initial diagnosis. Observation of the child's reaction and progress may suggest changes to the diagnosis and hence to the re-programming, or the need for refinement of the programme itself. Thus there should be an ongoing interaction between diagnosis, planned intervention and the results obtained. This process is likely to require discussion among those involved with the child and sometimes advice from specialists.

The re-programming of learning experiences may be achieved in various ways, but it needs to be selective and systematic for maximum effectiveness. Taking pressure off the child by giving him or her more time, or by temporarily reducing target levels, may be an important first step. Further measures include increasing repetition of new work and giving more practice to consolidate acquisition. This may require the structure of the programme to be tightened, and more frequent, possibly shorter, rest periods introduced. Then more intermediate steps to target may be needed, and essentials identified and highlighted. Increased continuity and closeness of teacher contact may be required to sharpen observation of the child's performance, improve feedback, provide rapid attention to sticking points and, importantly, to improve teacher/pupil rapport and attend to the individuality of the child. All children in state schools now have to follow the National Curriculum, but the speed and level at which children with learning difficulties work will vary a great deal. These children have a great need to experience success.

Children with peripheral difficulties need early identification. It is important to encourage and support them in using whatever facility they have in the area of weakness, including providing appropriate aids to enhance this, and also to encourage the use of other channels for learning and self-expression. Specialist advice is usually needed.

Children with general learning difficulties show weakness in learning capacity. This includes weakness in speed, retention or recall or in understanding what is required as tasks become more abstract. As the amount of material increases a child may have especial difficulty in viewing the material as a whole, being only able to focus on particular parts in isolation. He or she may become quickly overloaded and confused as the number of components increases. Rigidity, distractibility and distortions in learning may also be shown. General learning difficulties are likely to affect performance across the curriculum, though some children show specific talents.

Mild general learning difficulties may sometimes not be identified until some other difficulty (e.g. behavioural) is shown. These children need sympathetic personal attention from parent and teacher to assure them that their efforts are appreciated and expectations of achievement are realistic. Attention to particular difficulties, perhaps plugging gaps in learning, may also be required, plus re-programming to increase repetition of input and enhance consolidation. Strengthening self-confidence is important and experience of success is needed.

The difficulties of children with moderate general learning difficulties tend to become increasingly evident as they move up the age range at school. Their failure to master earlier work may obstruct them in new work, or the speed of the class may leave them with little or nothing accomplished. As the work becomes less immediate and concrete they may become bewildered by concepts which lack meaning for them. Some are good readers, but more often they have difficulty with reading and writing. Sometimes they become overwhelmed by the demands of the ordinary class, and become distressed. Attempts by class and subject teachers to help them may be sufficient, but often they are ineffective as it is not possible for these teachers to give help which is sufficiently personalized, selective, systematic, targeted and sustained. These children need substantial help through re-programming and regular extra personal attention by sympathetic and appropriate staff. This may be provided from within the ordinary school's own resources, but often will need extra resources, including extra teaching help, as well as extra work on parental contact. Where such intervention proves inadequate a transfer to a special school will need to be considered.

Severe general learning difficulties are often quite evident. Impoverished interaction, immaturity of understanding, a striking inability with tasks, rigidity or distractibility in application, inability to understand beyond the narrow immediate and concrete, and lack of foresight are some of the characteristics. There are often associated physical difficulties. These children need a tight programme carefully selected in content, graded in small steps and often highly individualized. Some of these children may be quite successful in the early stages of an ordinary school, but most will eventually need a very specialized learning environment, usually in a special school. Recently there have been attempts to retain more of these children in ordinary schools, but it remains to be seen whether the children obtain greater benefit from this.

Specific reading difficulties (or 'dyslexia') are not always severe, but early identification and initially low-key help are desirable. Mild cases may be assisted by gentle help from a parent in co-operation with the class teacher. More severe cases will need re-programming, including extra attention to reading and writing within class, reinforced by parental support, perhaps use of materials produced with the help of a specialist teacher and perhaps some regular extra help in a small group or individually. Severe cases, fortunately few in number, will need a regular programme of individual help from a specialist teacher in addition to re-programming and parental support. Some will make only weak progress over a long period, and help with reading may need to be supplemented and eventually superseded by help with complementary communication skills such as note taking, use of a computer and oral skills.

The learning difficulties of children with emotional and behavioural difficulties are likely to interact with their primary difficulties. Learning progress may be hard won, yet such progress may help the child's emotional development. School achievement may be poor but learning capacity is usually unimpaired, and re-programming needs to be made within the structure of an overall plan focused on the child's primary difficulties. Content, speed, spacing and the degree of flexibility of the programme are likely to be important. Those working with these children need to be able to discuss their work with others involved, and possibly with specialists.

Children with mental disorders may show very idiosyncratic learning, e.g. the child may read or write fluently but be disassociated from the act (as if somebody else is doing it) or from the meaning of the words. Specialist advice should be sought.

(e) Educational psychologists, usually employed by the LEA, give advice and support on a wide range of learning difficulties and on whether a child may need a statement of special educational need. In addition, LEAs also usually employ specialist teachers of the visually and hearing impaired, who can provide valuable advice and support. For speech difficulties the speech therapy service (usually the Health Authority) should be contacted. Advice on physical handicap may be obtained from physiotherapists and perhaps from an LEA school for physically handicapped pupils. Appropriate LEA special schools may give advice on general learning difficulties, and there may be specialist teachers of reading to advise on specific reading difficulties. Advice on children with emotional and behavioural difficulties may be obtained from specialist teachers or LEA units or special schools. For children with mental disorders, psychiatric advice should be obtained.

There is a variety of voluntary agencies which can provide very valuable help. A list may be obtained from the social services department.

(f) Confidentiality can be an issue, and an understanding may need to be reached about it, e.g. parents may sometimes request that information be withheld, and professionals will need to respect that.

Mutual respect between those involved is needed. Difficulties are often complex and there is a need for sharing and discussion of information and for shared involvement, most importantly with parents, in decision-making. Agreement must be reached on recording discussions and decisions and on arrangements to monitor and review programmes.

(g) Beveridge, S. (1993) *Special Educational Needs in Schools*. London: Routledge; Dockrell, J. and McShane, J. (1993) *Children's Learning Difficulties: A Cognitive Approach*. Oxford: Blackwell; Kerr, S. (1993) *Your Child with Special Needs: A Parents' Handbook*. London: Hodder and Stoughton.

RON JOHNSON
    (See also *children with behavioural difficulties; learning disabilities*)

Children's experience of loss and death

(a) Children who are bereaved in their early years are at risk of developmental disturbance. The risk lies not in the bereavement but in the quality of care afforded them during and after the event. Adults frequently underestimate children's abilities and exclude them on grounds of immaturity when there is clear evidence to the contrary. Given appropriate information and sensitive care all children can be helped to make choices about their involvement in and understanding of the meaning of the death of a family member. It is against this sympathetic background that the child sets their mourning and comes to a personal appreciation of this experience.

All change involves a degree of **loss** and childhood is full of change. Children naturally develop through a sequence of gradual changes towards maturity. These changes are manageable because they build on acquired skills. Bereavement presents a problem for a young child because the degree of loss within the experience, combined with the child's developmental immaturity, demand a developmental shift in the child's abilities: one which, without extra support, asks more of her than she is able to make. Unfortunately, the crisis of **bereavement** stretches a family's resources and often reduces adults' sensitivity to a child's needs. It is this cluster of factors which places the bereaved child at risk of developmental disturbance. If her worries and fears are left unaddressed she will communicate her distress in a number of ways, many of which lead to further problems.

(b)   We would expect a bereaved child to be sad, tearful and less sure of themselves and the world in general; these are recognized responses to loss. The difference between expected responses and those which should alert us to a child's distress lies in their intensity.

Young children do not express themselves primarily through language, which is an adult medium. Children communicate worries and unhappiness in a variety of ways: through increased anxiety, fears and phobias (see *phobias and anxiety*), sleep disturbance, changes in appetite, mood swings, a marked lack of concentration, reluctance to try new activities, restlessness, bedwetting, soiling, increased accidents, inconsolable sadness, lethargy and an increase in general aches and pains. A bereaved child who develops one or more of these is expressing their distress and is in need of help (see *children with behavioural difficulties*).

(c)   There are three elements within the childhood bereavement which have a bearing upon the outcome: the experience of death; the nature of the relationship with the deceased; and the child's developmental age.

1. The experience of the death varies greatly. In the case of death through protracted illness bereavement starts at the point of diagnosis. From the time when the family no longer has an expectation of a shared future they are a bereaved family. Degenerative illness entails a series of losses which culminate in death. The family bereaved through this route enters into mourning with understandably diminished emotional and physical resources and yet they have some of the hardest work ahead of them. It is not surprising that even the most loving parents may be unable to respond to their children as sensitively as they would normally. This is not a criticism or a judgement, merely an observation of what is often the case.

The foundation for a child's mourning lies in the quality of her experience of illness and preparation for the death. It is a paradox that loving parents cause problems for young children facing bereavement because they love them. A parent's role is twofold: one is to nurture and care for their child's physical and emotional needs and the other is to protect them from hurt and harm. The process of watching a loved person deteriorate and die causes immense emotional pain and mental anguish. The loving parent strives to minimize or spare their child that pain and one can readily understand their reasons for doing this. However, in these circumstances, to do so causes the child more rather than fewer problems.

Parents also commonly believe that a young child is protected by their immaturity and cannot appreciate what was happening even if they are told. Both assumptions are understandable but misplaced. The 'protected' child often feels excluded by their parents and has no chance to care for and say good-bye to the dying person. They are given no choices. The most common response seen in such children is one of anger at having been denied this once in a lifetime opportunity, and anger is not an emotion adults tolerate in children of any age (see *children with behavioural difficulties*).

Sudden or traumatic death removes this preparatory time and presents the family with a host of other practical problems and feelings of regret and remorse. These emotions stem from the fact that all human relationships are imperfect and, when a life ends abruptly and without warning, no time is given to make recompense or say sorry. We long for one last meeting in which we could have said and done so much. Those regrets combine with a feeling that there are incomplete plans, half-finished sentences, as though that dead person has gone before they said they would. We are left, bewildered by their absence. The effects of sudden death most closely mirror the experience of the excluded, 'protected' child and is the clearest example of how she feels in the aftermath.

2. The second factor is the quality and nature of the relationship with the dead person. The imperfections within relationships are the most difficult aspects to resolve within mourning. They have to be acknowledged and incorporated within our view of the dead person and ourselves and this is a painful and saddening process. The loss of a relationship that was predominantly happy and mutually rewarding leaves a big gap, but at least the child knows they were loved and appreciated by that person. The relationship which was fraught with bitterness, cruelty and inconsistency will be equally missed for very different reasons. Both are the same in that they are recognized for what they are, although mourning the former is easier.

The relationship which causes most difficulties for the bereaved is the ambivalent relationship. This is one in which neither person is sure whether they love or hate each other and oscillate equally between the two. Bereavement leaves the mourner wondering exactly who has died, was it someone they loved or hated? The question becomes unanswerable because the person who could have answered it is no longer there. The chance has gone, confusion remains and mourning is a profoundly worrying experience.

3. The third factor is that of the child's developmental age. Chronological age alone is not a satisfactory guide because experience affects the child's ability to understand death and its implications. Most children develop a mature understanding of death between the ages of eight and nine. They understand that death is permanent and irreversible, that it is caused by accident, murder, suicide or incurable illness and that every life ends in death. Although this is part of normal development, those who have been bereaved of a parent as a result of illness will be able to understand all these elements at a much earlier age: given the opportunity, children as young as three and four years old can and do understand death. The belief therefore that children are 'protected' by their immaturity is not relevant. The child who can understand needs explanations, not exclusion.

(d) Bereavement undermines our sense of security and forces us to reconsider what can be taken for granted. Bereaved people feel anxious about their safety in a world where loved people can disappear permanently and often without warning. This anxiety is the most common reaction seen in children and is a very reasonable one. There are three ways in which children can be helped to manage their anxiety.

First, they need to be given information. Children develop different ways of thinking as they mature. Four-year-olds think in a linear fashion, connecting one event with another and drawing conclusions from the sequence. If they are left to draw their own conclusions about the meaning of events surrounding illness and death, they will develop a bizarre view of what actually happened and often come to believe they are somehow involved. This happens because a child of this age believes they are very powerful and can cause things to happen by their behaviour, or even by wishing it. For example, if they have been naughty and then, a day or so later, their mother dies they may make a connection between the two events and blame themselves for this catastrophe. To prevent this happening, children need to have their questions welcomed, answered honestly, clearly and concisely and in language they can understand. I have found that very young children who are included in the progress of a family member's illness will observe the changes brought about by the illness. If they are given honest answers to their questions, they will be able to make the connections between what they see and what they come to know. Only in this way can we prepare children for the inevitable outcome and reduce the impact of the shock of bereavement. It is an unkindness to treat them in any other way. Explanations can be related to previous experiences: for example, if a child has observed an animal become ill and die, this experience can be used to help them understand what they are seeing now. Young children learn through experience and can extend their knowledge by making these connections.

Children are fascinated by the facts of death and spontaneously blurt out questions about what happens to the body in cremation or burial when adults would rather draw a veil over the whole affair. Children's curiosity is the spur to exploring and learning about the world and they see no difference between asking about death or why the sky is blue. Adults' unease should not silence or confuse them but unfortunately it often does.

This unease is reflected in adult clichés and ready-made phrases for explaining death to children, the quality of which only serve to create further problems. For example, a six-year-old who is told 'Daddy has gone to heaven to be with Jesus' will think either that if Daddy has gone somewhere he can just as easily come back, or that there must be something wrong with them if Daddy would rather be with Jesus than his family. This example shows how easily a child can be confused by well-meaning but inappropriate images which adults use to avoid the painful reality of death. This quality of explanation spares the adult, not the child.

Secondly, bereaved children need to be given extra affection. Bereaved children live in sad families (see *families, working with*). If their parent has died then the surviving parent is either tearful or depressed most of the time. If it is a sibling who has died then both parents are bereft (see *death of a child*). It is understandable that the child starts to worry about how lovable she is. She can easily start to think either that she is part of the cause of this sadness, or that if she were 'better' in some way she would be able to make her parents happier. Bereaved children need to know that their parents' sadness does not mean that they love them less. This needs to be expressed in two ways, verbally and physically.

The child needs to be told that she is loved as much as she always was and that her parent's sadness is not a reflection of her worth. Children also need to have love demonstrated, but the ways in which this is done vary according to the child and parent. Some children love to be cuddled, whereas others may feel overwhelmed and very uncomfortable with such closeness. It is important to find the right way for each child and to respond sensitively.

Thirdly, children need a greater sense of security in their environment which can be achieved in a number of ways. Families who live with **terminal illness** live with uncertainty, and children often feel that the whole world has become chaotic and threatening. This can be tolerated for a while providing they are able to rely on some things. The guarantee of landmarks in the day, such as mealtimes and bedtimes, creates a sense of routine and reliability. Bedtimes also give the child an opportunity to have a quiet five minutes with their parent, a time when worries can be shared and cuddles given and received. Household routines help to promote the feeling that the parent is able to look after them. When one's world has been profoundly shaken, this is very important. It is a particularly big issue for children because there is commonly a very real fear about their own survival and the survival of other special people. The parent who creates order within the home helps the child to feel that some things can be relied upon. This is perhaps the most important aspect of security, that the child feels not only safe in the present, but that she can also rely on her parent in the future.

(e) Barnardo's Orchard Project, in Newcastle upon Tyne, specializes in working with families where a member is seriously ill (see *terminal illness*) or has died and has a wealth of expertise in these areas. There are other Barnardo's projects which work with families affected by AIDS (see *AIDS/HIV*) which are a resource within that and the wider field of working with illness and **bereavement**. Some agencies offer this service as part of a wider remit. Hospices, child and family psychiatry units, Malcolm Sargent social workers and some Cruse centres are useful sources for referral.

(f) The professional ethics of **confidentiality** and respect for the client which apply within all counselling relationships apply equally to children. The only extra consideration which needs to be stated clearly to the child is that of child protection. If a child were to disclose that someone was physically or sexually abusing her then the counsellor has a legal and moral duty to contact a child protection agency on the child's behalf (see *child abuse*).

(g) Bowlby, J. *Attachment and Loss*, Volumes 1–3. Harmondsworth: Penguin; Furman, E. (1974) *When a Child's Parent Dies*. New Haven:

Yale University Press; Raphael, B. (1984) *The Anatomy of Bereavement*. London: Unwin Hyman.

PETA HEMMINGS
(See also *bereavement; death of a child; funerals; loss*)

Community politics

(a) Community politics describes the ways in which people organize how they live together in their neighbourhood or local community. It is not based on party political slogans, but on how people can work together for change. Britain is a representative democracy. Every citizen has the right to a say in who governs the country and who controls the local authority – and yet about 20 per cent of the electorate at national elections and 60 per cent at local elections do not bother to vote. One of the chief reasons for this is that they do not believe it will make any difference to their lives. (Some individuals may have given up their right to vote for economic reasons. There is evidence to suggest that a considerable number of people did not register to vote for fear of being traced and penalized for non-payment of the Poll Tax.) Community politics is about how people *can* make a difference to their lives. It is about participatory democracy.

It is usually individuals who are presented (or who present themselves) to helping agencies as having problems. However, individuals are not islands; human beings live out their lives, and experience their difficulties, within a complex web of relationships, ranging from family and everyday contacts, through neighbourhood, city and country, right to international level. If there are a number of people presenting with similar problems within a community, this may be an indication that the causes lie, at least in part, outside of the individual; and the most effective form of response may be action in the community.

(b) People have been organizing themselves in communities for as long as history. However, in modern society with its complex bureaucracy and all the weight of government, it often seems that local people have very little power to make significant changes. 'They' take all the important decisions. 'We' don't have any say at all. This is often the feeling, particularly in poor communities where people are even more used to having to do as they are told and accept life as it is. The apparent apathy, and the feeling of being trapped that can result from this, may lead to a range of presenting individual problems – the most common probably being **depression**.

There are many ways in which people can organize themselves to change life in their communities. An important influence has been the work of Saul Alinsky in the United States. His community organizing techniques have had remarkable success and have generated a dedicated following: they are similar to what is termed 'community action' in the United Kingdom (Alinsky, 1969 and 1972; Pitt and Keane, 1984). Methods of organizing in the community usually fall into one of three broad categories:

1. *Community service:*   This covers services provided by one group for another group perceived as needing help. Examples range from the provision of 'meals on wheels', luncheon clubs for the elderly and day care groups for people with Alzheimer's, to facilities for the homeless. The essence of this category is that it is provision by one group for another.

2. *Community development:*   This is used to describe a process in which people come together to discuss, plan and organize collectively ways of having more say over the factors which control their lives. Examples of this are: a group of people setting up and running a community centre or a community newspaper; a group of parents running an after-school club; the setting up of a credit union in which local people finance and run their own saving and loan facility.

3. *Community action:*   This occurs when people come together to work on a specific issue aimed at achieving a limited and easily identifiable change. It is usually over quite a short period of time. Examples include campaigns to change the route of a new road, to get a pedestrian crossing, to oppose the closing of a local facility or to save the old town hall.

These are not hard and fast categories. Some developments span more than one; often during the lifetime of a particular project it moves from one category to another. It is quite common for something which begins with community service (for example, the provision of a luncheon club for the elderly) to develop into more 'political' action (maybe a campaign for a higher level of provision, or increased pensions). However, the broad categories are useful in considering how community politics operates and how work in the community can be encouraged.

(c)   The precipitating factors for activity in community politics are: an awareness of needs or problems in the community; a decision to try to change things for the better; and a growing realization that 'together we can achieve what would be impossible on our own'. This is often accompanied by an anger with the injustice of the situation as it is and a feeling of having been pushed too far. Sometimes the precipitating factor takes the form of an external threat.

(d) Community politics begins to happen when the factors referred to above are followed by a period of bringing people together and planning, organization and, finally, action. This sequence might be rounded off by reflecting on the success or otherwise of the action and further planning (Thomas, 1983; Twelvetrees, 1987; Finneron, 1993: 5–14).

The perception that things are wrong and that change is needed quite often originates from an individual or a small group. Help with this stage of development is often the first contact a worker in the community might have with a group. Small groups, sure that they are right in their perception, may need to be slowed down; first, so that they can check the accuracy of their perceptions; secondly, to give them time to do a thorough analysis and to get to the heart of the problem; lastly, in order to gain support as widely as possible, since this will be a vital factor in any attempt to change things.

Other people will be more likely to support efforts if they have been involved from an early stage. Let me give an example: a group of residents on an estate see young people hanging around on street corners. The residents feel threatened by their presence and also suspect that boredom leads to petty crime. They could go right ahead and set up a youth club in the church hall or other available premises. However, they would stand more chance of success if they check out the answers to a few questions first:

- what facilities are already available?
- if there are facilities, why don't the young people use them?
- what do the young people want?
- has the youth service any plans for developments in the area?
- are there other people or groups in the area who are also concerned about this apparent problem?
- is there anyone or any group they can work with?
- other people in other areas must have had these difficulties: how have they responded? How successful have they been? Can anything be learnt from this?

Time spent looking at the answers to these questions is well worthwhile. This preliminary or research stage can take a period of many months in the case of community development or community service. In the case of community action it is likely to be fairly brief as time is often more pressing. However, it is necessary to all types of political activity in the community and should not be missed out.

The next stage is the coming together of people in organizing and planning. It is usually fairly easy to keep people together when they have a short-term goal in mind, as in community action; but for things which take a longer period of time it can be more difficult. Even for short-term goals it is worth giving some thought to what keeps people together. People do not keep coming to long-winded, boring meetings, where they are never allowed to say what they think, or where everything seems to be all talk and no action. Meetings should be well planned and have a clear purpose. Everyone should know what decisions have been taken and who is going to do what. It is a good idea to break long and difficult tasks into smaller, more manageable segments, so that there can be a sense of achievement. Celebrations along the way help to keep people together and keep up spirits (Adirondack).

Once the group has decided what it is aiming for, the next step is to consider tactics. It is important to know what the forces are opposing the change you want, and at which points you can exert influence. This is particularly vital in the case of community action where time is short. The group must know the timing of important decisions – it is ineffective to mount a demonstration against a new road after the contracts have been awarded. In the case of something less contentious, for example the setting up of a luncheon club, they need to know who controls decisions about the use of suitable buildings.

The choice of tactics depends on the nature of the issue, the goal, the resources of the various parties involved and the relationship between them (Brager and Specht, in Henderson and Thomas, 1981). Where there is a high probability of agreement between the parties, some shared values and a good relationship, the tactics of consensus is most appropriate. For example: a group of local people want a community centre, and approach the local authority to let them have the use of a redundant school building (Finneron, 1993: 48–56). The local authority agrees that the area is lacking in facilities, but has not got the resources to provide them. The authority agrees that the group can use the building, thus making them eligible to apply for various grants to bring extra resources into the area. There may be haggling over the terms of the lease and questions about who is responsible for a leaking roof, but essentially the interests of the authority and the group are similar.

Where there are significant differences, but the possibility of agreement, there may be campaigns of a competitive bargaining nature. The housing department of a local authority may have decided that the houses in a particular area are 'unfit for human habitation'. They begin to move people out and to demolish the houses. Residents agree that the houses are poor, but believe they can be improved to an acceptable standard. This would cost less than the authority's solution and, more important for the people, help keep the community together and prevent the blight which spreads in areas earmarked for demolition. The people campaign, protest to the council and, most importantly, renovate a few properties using a small charitable fund. They create a strong voice which the council must listen to; they propose an alternative strategy and they demonstrate its viability (Finneron, 1993: ch. 4).

If there is no possibility for agreement, the tactics are probably associated with a high degree of conflict and disruption. This is probably most common with community action, for example when decisions are being made about the route of a new road or the demolition of an amenity. Vital council meetings have to be lobbied; and if that fails it is usually necessary to engage in more direct action, perhaps a human cordon to prevent demolition workers from reaching a site. A demonstration of the willingness of local, ordinary people to place themselves in the 'firing line' often causes those in power to think again.

Community politics does not always result in success for the community group; but the better informed, planned and more widely supported any action is, the more likely it is to achieve at least some of the desired goals. Even if they fail in terms of the tasks they set out to do, people often feel some satisfaction that 'at least we had a go'. Participation in community politics frequently changes the people involved. By coming together to act, people learn skills and develop confidence. This in turn leads them to more effective and committed future action. For example, a parent may begin by helping in a local play-group. He or she may then go on to be a member of the local committee which runs the play-group. Experience of organizations in this area, and a perception of the needs of families and children, reinforced by the play-group, may lead that person to press the local council to provide better play facilities. If that is not effective, they may form a local group to raise funds, to design and construct their own play areas.

A word of warning is appropriate here. For the individuals involved, this process of enrichment and self-development may be accompanied by some pain. This seems to be particularly so for women. It is sometimes the case that women who achieve a greater self-awareness and confidence find themselves unable to continue to accept the former pattern of relationships and responsibilities in their family lives. This can lead to tension if they have a partner who is unable to respond to their changing needs (Twelvetrees, 1987).

In order to achieve their aim, a group needs access to resources. This could be access to photocopying and printing for posters and a building in which to hold a meeting; or it could be something more substantial like the services of a specialist worker and the permanent use of a building. This again is often the point at which someone from outside the community, with access to or knowledge of other sources of support, can make a vital contribution.

Within the community itself there will always be groupings with different interests and aims. Sometimes these may be brought together to act with some sort of unity. Here again there is often an opportunity for someone from outside to smooth this process: someone whom all groups recognize as having no factional loyalties, but who may have skills in negotiation and diplomacy at these levels. However, occasionally differences may give rise to fighting between factions. Unfortunately this seems to occur in some instances when a small amount of gain has been achieved, and the group which fought for it ends up in an unseemly squabble about its use. If the issues seem clear to the worker, for example if a community group has managed to gain a resource from which it wants to exclude others on the basis of their racial origin, then the worker will need to be seen to take sides. If the issues are not clear, it may be better to step back from the conflict in order to be able to help progress once it is over. This is always a fine judgement to make. Talking to others who have had similar experience often helps to clarify the possible choices.

Once a particular action or stage is finished it is advisable to hold a 'post-mortem'. This may be painful in the case of failure or may seem unnecessary in the case of success; but much of value will have been learned about strategy, tactics and timing, and skills will have been developed. All this will be needed again because one thing that is certain about community politics is that, once people have experienced the feeling of taking control over some aspect of their lives, they will come back for more.

(e)   There are a number of agencies which offer training for those engaging in community politics. Universities and other higher education establishments may offer courses within an extra-mural department. These typically have titles such as 'Organizing for Local Action', 'Citizen Organizing', 'How to Get Things Done', etc.

National organizations specializing in this type of activity are: the Federation of Community Work Training Groups, 356 Glossop Road, Sheffield S10 2HW; the Standing Conference on Community Development (at the same address as the Federation); the Community Development Foundation, 60 Highbury Grove, London N5 2AG.

These organizations run conferences and training events. They have newsletters and publications and may be able to offer consultancy. The Federation and the Standing Conference also have local branches in many areas.

Most areas are also covered by a council of voluntary service. These vary enormously in character and level of activity and may have workers with local knowledge who can give advice. It is always useful to find out what is going on in the locality. For the name and address of your local CVS, contact the National Council of Voluntary Organisations, Regent's Wharf, 8 All Saints Street, London N1 9RL.

An organization called Community Matters (8–9 Upper Street, London N1 0PQ) has an excellent range of publications relevant to those working in the community.

(f) The chief danger of a professional or an outside person getting involved in community politics is that they tend to dominate in the situation. Their skills, motivation and access to resources can easily push them into a leadership position. Workers from outside agencies inevitably feel some tension between the agenda of the people they are supposed to be working with and that of their employing agency; for example, workers employed by the local authority need to be on their guard against becoming the agents of the local state, and manipulating local people for its benefit.

Generally speaking there is agreement that the worker should help and assist (or in the jargon – 'enable') people in the community. How this works out in practice varies according to the situation. It might be appropriate sometimes to help people to ask the right questions, at others to chair meetings and write applications for funding. The important factor to bear in mind is that control and power over what is happening must remain with the community. If the group decides to do something which seriously conflicts with the values of the worker or agency then it may be time to withdraw.

The important principles are to work with people rather than for them and to start where they are in their thinking rather than where the worker is. This is not being condescending or patronizing – it is good sense. Anything else produces results which depend on the worker and which, even if successful in the short term, do not last. A useful question to keep asking is 'Who is benefiting from this?'

Everyone needs to feel they are needed and people who work for caring agencies are no exception. Sometimes we can feel a little rejected when something we helped to start up continues quite well without us; or when some person who used to rely on us for advice now acts independently. We must learn to view these things as a reflection of our success and professional competence.

While taking all this into account we need to recognize that the roots of many problems experienced by communities lie outside these communities themselves. Community politics as described here can be seen as a first stage in a more widespread movement for change in the way decisions are made in our society. Whether or not this is the case, it is certainly true that community politics can be effectively used to make distinct local differences to the quality of life.

(g) Henderson, P. and Thomas, D. H. (eds) (1981) *Readings in Community Work*. London: Allen and Unwin; Twelvetrees, A. (1987) *Community Work*. Basingstoke and London: Macmillan; Wilson, D. (1986) *Taking Action in Your Community*. London: Longman Self Help Guides.

DOREEN FINNERON
    (See also *self-help groups*)

Confidentiality

(a) Confidentiality protects the privacy of the client and is fundamental to developing sufficient trust between the person being helped and the helper. Confidentiality is one of the major methods for showing respect for a client's autonomy and an ethical principle which operates within all the caring professions.

(b) The management of confidentiality poses a considerable challenge to the caring professions. Some members of the caring professions believe that confidentiality ought to be absolute and therefore totally and permanently secret between the person being helped and the helper. This view has the advantage of simplicity and certainty. However, this view is naïve because it sets confidentiality above all other ethical principles. For example, someone tells you in confidence that he is about to poison the water supply. Is it better to preserve confidentiality or lives? Therefore the principle of confidentiality needs to recognize that there are limitations. This means that an entitlement to secrecy may cease where the autonomy of others is endangered.
    Confidentiality is usually thought of as a personal arrangement between the person being helped and the helper. This is most likely to be true of someone seeking independent help and able to pay for the services of a single professional. However, if that professional is working within an organization or the service can only be provided by a team, does confidentiality rest with the individual service provider, with the team or with a whole organization? Practice varies between professions and individual practitioners. Most counsellors and psychotherapists regard confidentiality as defined by the personal relationship, whereas most providers of social services and health care operate

on confidentiality to a team or agency. These differences in practice are confusing for clients and professionals alike. They can lead to tensions on interdisciplinary teams because of differences in what service providers are willing to communicate to each other. Practice about communication between the same kind of professionals also varies. Doctors will usually assume that a patient consents to the disclosure of confidential material to another doctor provided it is considered to be in the patient's best interests and the recipient of the information needs to know it. In contrast, counsellors are much more restrictive and will not routinely pass personally identifiable information to another counsellor without the client's permission.

However, there are certain issues about confidentiality which apply to all the caring professions, even if they find different solutions. These are:

- how does an obligation of confidentiality arise?
- are there any people who lack the capacity to enter into a confidential relationship?
- when is it defensible, legally and ethically, to disclose a confidence?

I answer these questions below.

(d) The ethics and law of confidentiality are so closely mutually interdependent that it is not possible to separate them into distinct categories. An obligation of confidentiality can arise in any of four situations:

1. there is a legal contractual agreement about confidentiality;
2. the person disclosing information says 'I am telling you this in confidence' or other words to the same effect;
3. the person receiving the information says 'I will keep what you say in confidence';
4. the nature of the relationship implies confidentiality, e.g. doctor/nurse–patient, counsellor/psychotherapist–client, independent financial advice worker–debtor, etc.

Confidentiality created in any of these ways not only carries considerable moral weight, but is also enforceable legally by the common law and in certain specific circumstances by statute. A successful court action could result in a court order to prevent breach of confidence, and the award of damages which can be considerable if someone has had their social reputation damaged, lost employment or career prospects.

As a general principle, an obligation of confidentiality arises in the situations above if the person imparting confidential information is

capable of informed consent. The right of young people to confidentiality even with regard to their parents has been strengthened in recent
years. In a landmark case the House of Lords ruled that some young
people under the age of 16 are capable of a confidential relationship.

One of the reasons why members of the caring professions find
confidentiality so challenging is that it throws up situations which can
be resolved differently according to the ethical analysis used. For
example, a student welfare worker is approached by a tutor who wants
to act in the best interests of a student. He asks the welfare worker
whether she knows what has caused the student to fail an exam in order
to present a case at the exam board with a view to giving the student
another chance. The welfare worker knows about a bereavement which
is not known by the teaching staff. Should the welfare worker say 'I am
sorry but I cannot pass on confidential information with the student's
consent', or 'I can tell you in confidence, the student has been bereaved
but does not want this to be widely known'? The first response would be
appropriate if *respect for autonomy* is the paramount ethical consideration. On the other hand, if *doing the greatest good* (beneficence) is the
guiding principle then the second response may be more appropriate,
particularly if disclosure is considered to be in the *best interests* of the
student and, as in this case, is to someone who *needs to know* in order to
achieve the desired outcome.

Another reason why the management of confidentiality can be so
challenging is the potential for conflicts of interest to arise. For example, a psychologist working for an employment assistance programme is asked to hand over his confidential records to the employer
who is both paying the psychologist's work as well as being the
employer of clients who see the psychologist. When the psychologist
refuses on grounds of confidentiality, the employer insists on access.
What should the psychologist do? Both ethically and legally the psychologist has conflicting duties to her clients and her employer. The
recommendation about working within the agreement about confidentiality provides the best protection for clients. It supports what is
considered to be sound ethical practice, namely that clients ought to be
informed, before receiving a service, of any reasonably foreseeable
circumstances in which confidentiality will not be observed. It also
prevents the employer retrospectively changing his requirements
about confidentiality. However, it does not appear to prevent an
employer prospectively requiring the professional to restrict confidentiality. The arguments that such restrictions should be kept to a
minimum are based on professional ethics rather than the law. Once
such an agreement has been reached, a professional would be obliged to
inform all clients of the restrictions or she could become in breach of her
contract of employment.

A client's consent to waive confidentiality means that disclosures authorized by that consent are defensible in law. The consent may be total or restricted about what can be said and to whom. Kenneth Cohen (1992), a solicitor with an interest in therapy, has observed that

> . . . it is the experience of many counsellors that where the client's express consent to appropriate disclosure is necessary, it is often possible to persuade her to give that consent. Although it may not be ideal to have to try to persuade a reluctant client to agree to disclosure, to do so will often show greater respect for her autonomy than not making the attempt.

However, there must come a point where a forced consent is not consent. For example, it is inappropriate for a counsellor or helper to say to a client who is suicidal 'Either you tell your GP and seek his help or I will have to talk to him'. This places the client in a double bind with no means of protecting confidentiality. In these circumstances, it seems ethically better to acknowledge that the client refuses consent and preferably to find some other way of proceeding which is acceptable to the client. If the counsellor feels she must still contact the GP, then she should take professional responsibility for her actions. There must come a point when coercing or persuading someone to consent becomes less respectful of her autonomy than honestly countermanding her expressed wishes.

Legally it is considered defensible to communicate confidential information which is already in the public domain. Few caring professionals would wish to rely on this defence, because it would be hard to do so without raising doubts in the minds of other clients about the professional's integrity and capacity to maintain confidences. Pragmatically, it is often difficult to discern the difference between information which is held in confidence by many people and that which is truly in the public domain.

The third situation in which it is legally defensible to breach confidence is the most problematic for members of the caring professions. It is determined by balancing the public interest in the keeping of confidence against the public interest in disclosure. 'Public interest' is defined as 'the best interests of society as a whole'. The weighing of the two principles is the responsibility of the individual professional and inevitably involves a degree of uncertainty about what decision would be made by a court. This public interest defence is the most flexible but it is therefore the least predictable. Issues which threaten individual safety fall within this category. The responsibility for deciding where the balance lies rests with the individual practitioner, although she may seek guidance. In deciding whether a breach of confidence is defensible, the court will bear in mind whether the information disclosed was restricted to that needed to meet the public interest and that the disclosure was restricted to someone able to respond in the public interest, i.e. reporting suspected child abuse to the social services, NSPCC or police would be defensible. In most circumstances, passing confidential information to the press would be unlikely to pass this test.

The public interest in the prevention and detection of crime also makes it defensible to break a confidence in order to report a crime to the police. Legally, it is not possible to bind someone to confidentiality in order to conceal a crime.

Anonymous discussions of cases for the purposes of supervision and training are technical breaches of confidence. However, the public interest in the monitoring of standards of service and adequate training probably outweigh this technical breach (Cohen, 1992).

Working with the appropriate code for professional conduct is relevant to a public interest defence. One court case suggests that courts will wish to consider the published codes and guidelines of a profession in their consideration of what constitutes the public interest. It also follows that the public interest may vary according to the needs and constraints associated with a particular profession. For example, doctors are permitted by their code to imply permission to pass confidential information where it is inappropriate to seek prior consent, provided that it is in the patient's *best interests* and the recipient needs to know. In contrast, counsellors have no such provision in their code of professional conduct. It is assumed that the relationship between counsellor and client is more personal. Counsellors are not interchangeable in the same way. Therefore, it is more appropriate to rely on the patient's explicit consent, unless exceptional circumstances such as the counsellor having 'good grounds for believing that the client will cause serious physical harm to others or themselves' (BAC, 1993). In the case of suicide, it has been suggested that the counsellor ought to conduct a careful assessment of the situation rather than automatically consider breaking confidentiality (Bond, 1993).

There are instances where the law requires a member of the caring professions, like any citizen, to break confidentiality. When this arises, the disclosure of confidential information has a defence against being sued for breach of confidence.

Some statutory law overrides the legal right to confidentiality. Three statutes have been of particular concern to members of the caring professions. Generally there is no duty to answer a police officer's questions. A polite refusal is sufficient, although lying or giving misleading information constitutes an offence. However, some statutes create an obligation to answer questions. For example, a doctor was convicted under the Road Traffic Act 1972 of refusing to identify a patient wanted for dangerous driving. He was fined £5 in 1973 but never gave the information. The confidential nature of the relationship with the patient was an insufficient reason for refusing to answer questions. The Prevention of Terrorism (Temporary Provisions) Act 1989 (s.8) makes it an offence to fail to disclose information, without reasonable excuse and as soon as reasonably practicable, which would assist the prevention or investigation of an act of terrorism connected with the affairs of Northern Ireland. The Children Act 1989 (s.47) converts a widely held moral concern to prevent and detect child abuse into an obligation for some members of the caring professions. The provision is complex and considered in more depth elsewhere (Bond, 1993). Briefly it creates an obligation on social workers to investigate allegations, regardless of whether these were given to them in confidence. Professionals in local education authorities, health authorities, housing authorities and any other person authorized by the Secretary of State are required to assist these enquiries by providing relevant information and advice. Courts have ordered the production of confidential health and therapeutic records as part of their investigative role in order to decide what is in the best interests of a child.

A court may require a professional carer, appearing as a witness, to answer questions put to her, even if this means breaking confidence. Refusal to answer may amount to contempt of court. Nonetheless, it is possible to ask a court to use its discretion and not compel an answer or to restrict the information that is requested. A few have appeared as conscientious witnesses and used lawyers to request that they be excused breaking confidences. Sometimes their request has been successful (Hayman, 1965). Courts can order the production of records in court. Under powers given to them by the Police and Criminal Evidence Act 1984, the police can obtain search warrants for confidential records, but in many cases they will need the signature of a circuit judge rather than the more usual magistrate's signature. Appeals against the issue of some of these warrants have been successful, although the reasons have not always been published.

A recent development in allegations of rape and sexual assault has been the involvement of the police, acting on behalf of the Crown Prosecution Service, in seeking access to therapeutic records held by the health service, counsellors and rape crisis centres with the victim's consent. Strictly speaking, the victim's consent should place this activity in the first category of defensible breaches of confidence (above). However, there are serious doubts expressed by the caring professions involved that the victim always gives an informed and autonomous consent. The victim will be aware that a refusal of access to these records would result in the case being dropped. The caring professions also point out that therapeutic records may be rather low quality information from a factual point of view because the therapist's role is to deal with the subjective experience, which may be contained in a mixture of factual recall and fantasy; whereas the courts are exclusively involved in the former. This recent development is causing some therapists to worry that their role is being confused with factual investigators and that any inconsistency in the different versions of a story (a normal occurrence in therapy, especially following rape trauma) is interpreted in court as evidence of the unreliability of the victim and the case is dropped.

A professional's notes and records cannot usually be protected from disclosure and use in court proceedings if a client requires their production.

A legal obligation to disclose confidences may arise from the contract of employment. For example, some employers are extending their employees' obligations to report child abuse by making this a contractual term in circumstances where the Children Act does not impose this.

Clear communication with clients about their entitlement to confidentiality and especially any reasonably foreseeable limitations on confidentiality is the best way of working within the law. It is also sound ethically, because it demonstrates respect for client autonomy. There are situations where breach of confidence would be legally defensible, but is vulnerable to misunderstanding by other clients and could undermine confidence in the service being provided. Keeping confidences (secrets) is an important way of maintaining confidence (trust) with the clients. The management of confidentiality is complex and both ethical and legal practice is still evolving. Anyone who has a major concern about confidentiality with legal overtones is encouraged to seek legal advice.

(e)   The law on confidentiality is a specialized subject and one of the most rapidly evolving legal subjects. This makes it difficult to obtain reliable guidance. Professional associations and legal services provided as part of a professional indemnity insurance scheme may be the best sources of information.

Most of the caring professions have published codes and guidance which provide a useful starting point for resolving ethical dilemmas. However, decisions about confidentiality often turn on the professional judgement of an individual practitioner. Some professions, like counselling, have a system of ongoing and regular **supervision** which provides an obvious forum for support in making that decision. An experienced practitioner may be able to fulfil a similar role for professions which do not have such arrangements.

(f) In agencies where members of different professions are working together, there is the potential for interprofessional conflict over confidentiality, unless the individual practitioners are willing to respect that professional practice may need to vary according to the demands and practicalities of each profession. However, all professions can unite against disclosures of confidences by carelessness or gossip. The protection of confidential material requires periodic review, especially as the technology for record keeping is evolving rapidly and may no longer involve paper records.

(g) Bond, T. (1993) *Standards and Ethics for Counselling in Action.* London: Sage Publications; Cohen, K. (1992) 'Some legal issues in counselling and psychotherapy', *British Journal of Guidance and Counselling* 20 (1): 10–26; Kennedy, I. and Grubb, A. (1994) *Medical Law and Ethics.* London: Butterworths.

TIM BOND

Counselling and psychotherapy, forms of

(a) Counselling and psychotherapy have only emerged in the 1970s and 1980s as significant contributions to caring and helping provision in Britain. Counselling and psychotherapy are forms of helping that basically overlap in terms of their aims, processes and clients. Their main differences tend to exist at the margins of either discipline. For example, although both counselling and psychotherapy are used with clients with a broad range of emotional, self-concept and relationship problems, those clients with more limited and focused problems (such as study skills, **stress** or **careers guidance**) are more likely to be seen by helpers who label themselves as counsellors. Clients who are more deeply troubled or damaged (such as people with personality deficits or long-standing inability to cope) are more likely to find appropriate assistance from psychotherapists. While the training received by counsellors and psychotherapists is on the whole similar, consisting of a combination of theoretical knowledge, practical skills and work on self, it is typical for psychotherapists to have received longer and more demanding training than counsellors. What is unique about counselling is that it includes both professionally trained practitioners and trained but unpaid volunteers. Psychotherapy has had greater status in the medical profession, although in the 1990s counselling has increasingly become a feature of primary health care provision. From the point of view of the client, the fact that the person who is offering help is known as a counsellor or psychotherapist makes little practical difference. In either case, the client receives a 'therapy' using the relationship between therapist and client to promote insight, learning and behavioural change.

(b) It is important to be clear about the distinction between counselling/psychotherapy (or 'therapy') and other kinds of helping relationship. The main aim of therapy is to promote the client's autonomy, empowerment and psychological change. This kind of therapeutic process can only occur if the client voluntarily chooses to engage in it, and if the therapist's primary commitment is to the client. By contrast, in professions such as social work, probation or nursing, the tasks of the helper often include practical assistance, information giving and social control. In these situations it is more usual to talk about the application of *counselling skills* rather than counselling itself. There are variants of this way of working (see *couples, working with; groups, use of; families, working with; telephone, use of*).

(d) The main textbooks on counselling and psychotherapy, such as Corey (1991), Dryden (1990) or McLeod (1993), reveal dozens of approaches to therapy currently in use. This situation has arisen partly because the creativity of people working in this field has resulted in an explosion of ideas and techniques, and also because of the influence of the private practice market-place. It is possible to categorize these alternative approaches as belonging within three broad styles of therapy: psychodynamic, cognitive-behavioural or humanistic.

Psychodynamic   counselling or psychotherapy represents the form of therapy that has been established for the longest time. The origins of psychodynamic therapy lie in the work of Sigmund Freud (1856–1939), the founder of psychoanalysis. While modern psychodynamic counsellors and psychotherapists acknowledge a debt to Freud, it also needs to be recognized that his ideas have been developed and adapted by later generations of therapists working in this tradition. Specifically, some of the ways in which Freud understood the centrality of sexuality and fathers can be seen as products of his time and place, and have been significantly extended by other psychodynamic writers. Daily psychoanalytic sessions in which patients lie on a couch and have their dreams and fantasies interpreted by an analyst out of their line of vision have generally been supplanted by a more practical and active approach.

At the core of the psychodynamic approach to therapy are a set of basic principles:

- people are generally not aware of the true reasons for their behaviour. The goal of therapy is to bring to light the *unconscious* impulses, fears and wishes that guide the ways that a person responds to situations;
- beneath the surface, people struggle with primitive emotions such as love, hate, rage, the need for attachment and coping with loss;
- behaviour in adult life has its origins in childhood events, experiences and fantasies, usually associated with relationships with significant others (such as parents);
- people move through a set of developmental stages. Problems that occur at any stage result in the person being in some way stuck or troubled by that phase of their emotional development, continuing to act out these unresolved fears and needs throughout their life;
- while it is possible to gain insight or understanding of these unconscious processes, and to gain a measure of control over the destructive effects of childhood experiences, specifically psychodynamic therapy helps people to develop greater emotional maturity through the reworking of old relationship patterns in the therapeutic relationship (i.e. transference). At the root of this approach is a sense that awareness and understanding of inner conflict can only be achieved through the relationship with the therapist or counsellor.

From a psychodynamic perspective, the client possesses only a limited *conscious* awareness of why he or she is anxious, lonely, angry or depressed. The painfulness and sensitivity of the true origins of his or her distress leads to *defence mechanisms* such as denial, projection or reaction formation. It is essential, therefore, for the therapist to pick up clues from non-conscious communications made by the client. The classic method used by Freud was to analyse the content of dreams and 'free associations' reported by the client. Similarly, psychodynamic therapists work with the fantasies, images and metaphors in what the client says. However, the most powerful method of identifying unconscious patterns is to observe the way the client feels or acts in relation to the therapist. Psychodynamic therapists present themselves to their clients as relatively neutral and detached. Any reaction the client has towards the therapist can be viewed as indicative of how that client typically relates or related to significant others. For example, one client may get angry with a therapist for being a cold, remote father. Another client of the same therapist may behave in a sexual or seductive manner during sessions. It is as though the therapist functions as a blank screen on to which the client can project his or her ways of being with others. This process is known as *transference*, and the emergence in therapy of this kind of reaction gives the therapist an opportunity to help the client to first of all recognize, then understand, then reframe their deepest feelings in relation to others.

This therapeutic process takes time (although psychodynamic therapists also use specialized short-term techniques) as the client must be allowed to build up enough trust in the therapist to express long-repressed feelings, and the therapist needs time to accumulate information. There will inevitably be phases when the client resists both his or her own feelings and possibly the interpretations made by the therapist. They may test out the integrity of the therapist, and need to express love or rage in the therapeutic relationship, learning that this does not destroy the relationship. It is for these reasons that it is essential to conduct psychodynamic counselling or psychotherapy within strict role and time boundaries. Even apparently trivial attempts by the client to circumvent the strict boundaries of the work, for example by arriving late, going over time, or offering the therapist a gift, can be taken as signifying deeper feelings in relation to the therapist. These events may become material for interpretation. Another critical feature of the psychodynamic approach is that it is necessary for the therapist to have undergone a considerable amount of personal therapy to be able to achieve the level of insight and self-awareness required to avoid becoming entangled in the transference and defensive manoeuvres displayed by the client.

The cognitive-behavioural   approach to counselling and psychotherapy offers a quite different perspective. This approach has its origins in behavioural and cognitive psychology. It therefore takes a more rational and 'scientific' stance. The basis for the approach is the idea that people can learn maladaptive ways of behaving and thinking, and that the role of the therapist is to provide opportunities for re-learning. The relationship between therapist and client resembles that between teacher and student, with the latter being set exercises and homework assignments. The aim of cognitive-behavioural therapy is to bring about changes that are identified as desirable by the client. It is an active, problem-management approach to therapy, with relatively little emphasis being placed on insight or understanding the causes of problems, and a great deal of emphasis being devoted to techniques for bringing about change.

At the beginning of the work with a client, a cognitive-behavioural counsellor usually makes an assessment of the nature, intensity and frequency of the problems reported by the client. They agree a contract for change. Typically, the client is asked to rate the severity of problems, and in later sessions is asked to re-rate these same complaints, providing a way of monitoring change and progress. If possible, the problems identified by the client are framed in terms of concrete, specific behaviours and cognitions. For example, a client with anxiety in social situations may be encouraged to develop specific progressive targets such as attending a social event, engaging in a conversation with someone familiar and then with someone new.

Once the contract for change is established, the therapist initiates exercises or tasks designed to achieve the objectives. Activities undertaken by cognitive-behavioural therapists include systematic desensitization, social skills training and cognitive re-structuring. The therapist expects the client to practise relevant skills between sessions, and may in some instances accompany the client into real-life situations to reinforce and monitor the use of these skills.

Systematic desensitization   is a means of dealing with stimuli that produce anxiety. The aim in much therapy is to replace an anxiety/ fear response to a stimulus or situation with a more comfortable and productive relaxation response. For example, with an agoraphobic client, the fear of going outdoors may result in a greatly restricted lifestyle and multiple relationship difficulties. If the client can learn to feel relaxed when outside, many of these secondary problems are reduced. The first step in systematic desensitization is to teach the client how to relax. Often, the client will be given an audio tape containing instructions on breathing and relaxing different muscle groups, and told to practise relaxation skills for a set time each day. The next phase is to establish a hierarchy of fear-inducing stimuli. Most fearful might be walking down the road and entering a shop. Least fearful might be looking out of the front door, or imagining going to the garden gate. After deciding on a hierarchy, the therapist then asks the client to practise relaxation skills while engaging in the least fearful activity. Once the person has learned to relax in the presence of this stimulus, the next most fearful scenario is tackled, and so on through to the most feared situation. One of the by-products of systematic desensitization is that, in addition to learning how to deal with one particular problem situation, the client also acquires a general set of coping skills, and a belief in his or her ability to deal with difficulties (see *phobias and anxiety*).

Another procedure employed in cognitive-behavioural therapy is *social skills training* or *assertiveness training*, developed to help people who have difficulties in dealing with relationships and social situations. It is assumed that being successful in relationships depends on possessing appropriate social skills, and that many people who are anxious, depressed or lonely have failed to learn these skills. The concept of 'skill' used in this context implies that complex activities such as, for example, refusing an unwanted request can be reduced to a set of micro-skills involving such non-verbal processes as eye contact, tone of voice, movement and posture, and timing. The cognitive-behavioural therapist assesses the particular skill deficits that are causing problems, and uses strategies such as modelling, live practice and video feedback to help the client to acquire and assimilate these skills. For instance, a client who has problems with alcohol may have great difficulty in refusing a drink when it is offered by a friend. Social skills training can enable this person to be confident that he or she can say 'no' effectively without being in danger of losing that friend.

A final example of a technique widely used in cognitive-behavioural counselling is *cognitive restructuring*. Albert Ellis, in particular, is associated with the identification of 'irrational beliefs' as a factor in many behavioural problems. Ellis observed that the response a person makes to a stimulus or situation is typically not automatic or unthinking, but is shaped by the beliefs the person has about the event. He argued that beliefs have important emotional and behavioural consequences, and that irrational beliefs result in self-defeating behaviour. An example of an irrational belief would be 'I *must* have love or approval from all the significant people in my life'. For someone with this belief, an argument with a husband or wife may be experienced as 'catastrophic', and trigger off withdrawal, depression or other forms of emotional disturbance. The aim of the therapist is to assist the client to learn that it is more rational or realistic to believe that 'I enjoy it when significant people give me love or approval, but I accept that there are times when they may not feel this way towards me'. The therapist does this by challenging the client, perhaps drawing on humour and absurdity, and also by teaching more rational ways of thinking about problems.

There also exist a wide range of other techniques and strategies. This approach to therapy is characterized by a high degree of inventiveness and innovation as practitioners strive to find techniques that achieve the best results in the shortest possible time. For example, cognitive-behavioural therapists have been instrumental in developing many self-help books and manuals that can be used by clients with specific difficulties.

The humanistic perspective is the third major approach to therapy. The key figure in the development of this form of therapy has been Carl Rogers, the founder of the approach known as 'client-centred' or 'person-centred' therapy. The emergence of humanistic psychology, and with it humanistic therapy, in the 1950s was in large part due to a rejection of the psychodynamic and behavioural methods that predominated at that time. The main distinctive features of the humanistic approach are the importance given to concepts such as growth, creativity, the self, authenticity and the capacity for choice. These essential human attributes are considered by humanistic therapists to be given insufficient emphasis in other theoretical approaches.

Constructive or creative personality change or growth occurs in an environment in which the person feels understood and accepted by another person who is perceived as honest and trustworthy. By developing these conditions, the therapist enables the client naturally to find ways of exploring their experiencing of problems, and then gradually to arrive at their own solutions to these problems. The task of the therapist is to be as empathic, congruent and accepting as possible towards the client, and to communicate these qualities effectively. For example, a client who enters counselling because of difficulties and stress at work may initially spend time justifying himself or blaming others for his problems. As the therapist reacts to these statements with a genuine interest in the person who is experiencing these pressures, the client may become more open to talking about his own feelings.

It is this personal felt sense or here-and-now experiencing of a problem or issue that is central to the process of humanistic therapy. It places special value on the acceptance of feelings, and on the client's 'internal locus of evaluation' as a guide to action. The implicit message of the humanistic therapist is that feelings can be trusted. The more that a client is able to gain access to and express the whole of how he or she feels about a topic or issue, the more creatively he or she may be able to act in relation to that issue. The role of the therapist is not to interpret feelings, but to assist the client in his or her own struggle to become aware, and to find meaning in that awareness.

Another important feature of humanistic therapy is the notion that the therapist is striving to be as honest or genuine as possible in the relationship. In seeking empathically to enter the world of the client, the therapist is inevitably affected by the client. There is a sense of an encounter between two people, a healing relationship.

Gestalt Therapy is a widely used humanistic approach to therapy that employs a wide variety of exercises and techniques to facilitate the client's awareness of here-and-now experiencing. For example, if a client reports being caught between two opposing feelings, Gestalt therapists might introduce 'two-chair' work, in which one side of the 'split' is placed on one chair, and the other side on the opposing chair, so that a dialogue can take place between them. Another broadly humanistic approach to therapy is Transactional Analysis, which uses the analysis of ego states, games and life scripts to promote personal growth and choice in clients.

Some counsellors and psychotherapists do in fact regard themselves as *eclectic* (choosing ideas or techniques from different approaches) or *integrative* (attempting to develop a creative synthesis of different approaches). Eclecticism should not be an excuse for a piecemeal or haphazard approach to therapy. The client may become confused if the therapist changes tack in mid-treatment, for example abandoning the empathic respectfulness of the client-centred approach and taking control of proceedings by suddenly introducing highly structured behavioural tasks. Integrative approaches drawing on the theoretical models and techniques of psychodynamic, cognitive-behavioural, Gestalt, Transactional Analysis and the person-centred 'core conditions' are becoming increasingly popular.

Hypnotherapy   is an approach to therapy that has gained in influence during the 1980s. This approach relies on the induction of deep relaxation states in clients, and is more directive in orientation than other approaches. While hypnotic techniques are powerful and can be effective, their appropriate use requires substantial specialist training and should always be used under supervision.

(e)   The three mainstream forms of therapy – psychodynamic, cognitive-behavioural and humanistic – represent very different ways of helping people with emotional and behavioural difficulties. The choice between them would be made easier if it could be shown that one was more effective than the others, or if they were each best suited for specific types of client or problem. Unfortunately it is not possible to make any simple statements about which approach is most effective. There has been a great deal of research into the effectiveness of therapy, and it tends to show that on average about two-thirds of clients improve, with the remaining one-third either staying the same or deteriorating as a result of therapy. Studies that have compared groups of people receiving therapy with matched control groups not receiving help generally show that therapy 'works' for a wide variety of client groups. There is little evidence that particular clients or presenting problems respond better to particular forms of therapy. This is probably because any type of therapy can be adapted to deal with most kinds of problems. In everyday practice, however, it is obvious that some clients have very definite preferences regarding the sort of intervention they would see as appropriate or beneficial. It is also apparent that therapists themselves gravitate towards approaches that suit their own personalities and values.

There are a number of practical issues in gaining access to effective counselling. Whether the person seeking access is a client or a professional making a referral, it can be difficult to know where to go for appropriate therapeutic help. In Britain, counselling and psychotherapy is mainly available through a number of voluntary agencies such as

Relate, the Westminster Pastoral Foundation and many smaller alcohol, drug, bereavement, mental health and rape crisis agencies. There is a growing presence of counselling in primary health care teams, in GP surgeries. Some NHS trusts support psychotherapy services. Most colleges and universities employ student counsellors. An increasing number of large organizations provide employee counselling. Finally, there is a vast network of therapists in private practice. At present, there is no single directory that lists all of these services. The most comprehensive directories are those published by the British Association for Counselling (1 Regent Place, Rugby CV21 2PJ) and the UK Council for Psychotherapy (Regent's College, Regent's Park, London NW1 4NS).

Counselling and psychotherapy are not regulated by law in Britain, and anyone can set up in practice. It is therefore very important to check the credentials and qualifications of any therapist to whom one might be referred. Ideally, the person should have received more than 400 hours of training, and be accredited by either the British Association for Counselling, the British Psychological Society or the UK Council for Psychotherapy. However, given the piecemeal nature of therapy training in Britain, there are many excellent therapists who have not gained this type of official accreditation. All competent therapists receive regular **supervision**, and most will have undergone personal therapy. The personal qualities of the therapist, and the therapist–client match are as important as paper qualifications, so it is usual to have an initial interview to allow each participant to decide whether they can engage in therapy together. Individual therapists and particularly agencies often have waiting lists, so this initial meeting may be followed by a waiting period.

(f) Those referring clients to counselling may find that the therapist or agency insists that the client makes the appointment himself or herself. This is done to ensure that participation is voluntary and that the therapist can enter into a contract directly with the client. The **confidentiality** required in therapy usually means that the therapist only reports back to the referring agency any information that the client has agreed can be passed on. Similarly, some therapists may be reluctant to attend case conferences for fear of compromising their relationship with the client. It is normally desirable for the person making the referral to disengage from any counselling relationship with the client while the therapy is in progress.

(g) Corey, G. (1991) *Theory and Practice of Counseling and Psychotherapy* (4th edn). Pacific Grove, CA: Brooks/Cole; Dryden, W. (ed.)

(1990) *Individual Therapy: A Handbook*. Buckingham: Open University Press; McLeod, J. (1993) *An Introduction to Counselling*. Buckingham: Open University Press.

JOHN MCLEOD
(See also *counselling, suitability for; groups, use of*)

Counselling, suitability for

(a) There is no simple formula for defining clearly who is and who is not suitable for counselling. Human beings are complex and diverse as is the variety of problems in living that are presented to counsellors. Within the field of counselling itself there are so many modes and models, it is impossible to give an accurate description of suitability for all situations (see *counselling and psychotherapy, forms of*). Some models such as short-term focused psychotherapy (Malan, 1976) give clearer indications of who is suitable: others may give some idea of the limitations of a particular approach (Dryden, 1990).

(b) The difficulty in deciding who is suitable is compounded by the confusion between what is counselling and what is psychotherapy. One of the most obvious reasons for people coming into counselling is to receive help and support with a stressful or traumatic current life situation such as a bereavement, assault, diagnosis of a serious illness, birth of a disabled child – there are a multitude of stressful life events which can disrupt emotional equilibrium. There is often an obvious counselling agency to refer to and this sort of work is designated as 'counselling'.

People also arrive in therapy for the purpose of changing something about themselves, their manner of thinking, feeling or relating to the world, other people or themselves. The referral may be prompted by a particular current life situation, but the focus of the work is change in the individual rather than the event itself. This sort of work is seen to be at more 'depth', more fundamentally personality-changing, and is called 'psychotherapy'. At either end of the continuum the differences are clear but within the two extremes there is a huge area of overlap. For instance, 'supporting' and helping a client to cope through the experience of a bereavement often leads on to an examination of other significant attachments, which can then lead to significant changes in the way the client handles current and future relationships.

The length and depth of the work can be decided by the model the counselling agency operates – counsellors in some settings (particularly medical) work to a short-term model of six to eight sessions. This sort of work implies a clear focus and contract. Many voluntary agencies and counsellors in private practice adopt an 'as long as it takes' approach and contract accordingly. Even this is no indication of the sort of work that may be happening. Supportive, reflective counselling sometimes goes on for long periods; short-term therapy can be dynamic and life-changing.

Despite the difficulties involved when surveying a whole range of services and approaches I believe there are guidelines which help us make effective decisions about suitability for counselling.

(d) Whatever problem the potential client may be presenting, there are certain key aspects of the therapeutic process to be considered.

Motivation: Counselling is about a client and counsellor working together. It is not a treatment to be administered one to the other. It requires a willing and participative involvement from the client. No matter how much in need of help potential clients may seem, if they have no motivation and/or desire for changing themselves, counselling is unlikely to ever get started. Counselling is rarely helpful when the client is 'sent' or attends either to please or to appease a third party.

Motivation is also about clients' desiring and working towards understanding their own response to their problem or circumstances. Thus the person who rigidly sees the source of all his or her problems in the external world in general or blames another person in particular, and is therefore unwilling to look within, is unlikely to be helped by counselling.

Counselling requires communication between client and counsellor. Some degree of silence and withholding may be part of the client's problem and can be worked with, but a totally withdrawn or monosyllabic client will not engage in the process. Account needs to be taken of clients' fears and expectations about counselling, which may be inhibiting a response or preventing them initiating any communication. People who consistently communicate feelings by acting on them impulsively and perhaps destructively, rather than talking about them and reflecting upon them, are not likely to benefit from counselling.

Counselling as a process: Counselling does not provide any miracle overnight cures. Changes, improvement and gratification are likely to be gradual, possibly slow; thus for anyone looking for immediate alleviation of a particular symptom, counselling is unlikely to be satisfactory.

The process itself can be stressful as feelings are explored, painful past events revisited and the enormous impact of some situations realized. To look honestly at oneself, to share feelings, discuss past and present difficulties and examine one's own part in those difficulties requires some degree of inner resources and strength in itself. Clients also need to be sufficiently self-supporting to cope with their problems between sessions.

If there is an extreme fear and unwillingness to look at the loss or the problem in question, or to discuss any background factors, this may suggest an extremely vulnerable ego. Any attempt at counselling may disturb a fragile inner world causing a breakdown. An alternative mode of helping is more appropriate.

The counselling relationship   is an essential part of the therapeutic process. People who have no previous history of being able to form relationships are unlikely to be able to do so with a counsellor. Past relationships do not necessarily have to have been happy or satisfactory (far from it – this itself may be the presenting problem); but there needs to be some evidence of an ability to have formed at least one relationship to some basic degree. Without this experience the client is unlikely to be able to trust or utilize the space for emotional intimacy that counselling offers.

If the client is an extremely needy, dependent personality who is unlikely, once counselling has started, to ever be able to manage without the counsellor, it would be more appropriate to suggest an alternative form of help such as a 'befriending' service.

There are also some practical issues to consider. Regular weekly counselling sessions will have a financial cost. This may be in terms of the fee if the counselling is private. Certainly there is a cost in terms of a regular time commitment, and perhaps other expenses in terms of child-care costs, transport, time off work, etc. Before starting in therapy it is important to check that the client will be able to work consistently at and complete whatever contract is worked out, rather than have to leave therapy with issues opened up but not worked through. It is irresponsible to start a course of action that cannot be completed.

Each client is an individual and not everyone who suffers a major life crisis or trauma needs counselling. Any assessment needs to take account of the client's overall situation. A network of community and family support can make all the difference between a crisis being manageable or overwhelming. Conversely there are those individuals who already seem to have a system of help around them but for some reason cannot use it effectively. This may be because of a role they have adopted in their family or community which prevents them sharing their own vulnerability and pain. To talk to someone outside and uninvolved may be their only real source of help. It is essential that we look at the needs of the individual carrying the problem rather than just the problem itself.

Who is not suitable for counselling?   The literature gives us few categories definitely to exclude and even these can be challenged by pioneering therapists in specialist centres. However, there seems to be general agreement that those suffering from psychosis, chronic drug or alcohol addiction, severe depression, personality disorder and severe brain damage would not be helped by counselling (see *alcoholism; psychosis, etc.*). Uncomfortable as it is to the counselling profession to label human beings, what we are looking at in all the above categories is some condition or predisposition which prevents the potential client from engaging in a realistic and meaningful dialogue about his problems which also includes some recognition of the part he plays in it. Muddled and disturbed thoughts in themselves do not mean counselling will be unsuccessful. On the contrary, many clients work on 'strange' or 'irrational' thoughts and feelings; if, however, they are not recognized as such, or there is no insight as to how others might perceive them as such, there is no basis for an objective dialogue about them.

People on a high dosage of anti-psychotic or anti-depressive drugs are also unlikely to be sufficiently emotionally free enough to engage in counselling. Counselling can and does work alongside other methods of treatment so long as the client is in touch with their emotions and in realistic contact with the world.

Where there is a long-standing problem or symptom which has been referred to numerous professional helpers in the past it is unlikely that counselling will make the breakthrough that has previously failed to occur, unless there is a serious question that previous help was inappropriate in some way. It is important not to confuse a chronic problem with an unresolved but recently restimulated issue from the past. Often conflicts and feelings around past situations lie dormant for many years, to be resurrected by a present trigger in one's own life or another's. This sort of material can and is worked on very effectively in counselling.

(e)   Counselling services vary from one geographical area to another. Two useful directories to refer to are those published by BAC and UKCP (see *counselling and psychotherapy, forms of*, section (e)).

(f)   *How to refer:* In general it is preferable that clients refer themselves rather than be referred by a third party. The first contact made by the client is important and facilitates engagement in the counselling process. There are occasions when clients are so hurt, fearful or lacking in confidence that it is necessary to support them in making initial contact, provided we are sure this is the client's wish and not our decision. The sooner the client can support himself in maintaining the therapy the better the prognosis. Counsellors very rarely adopt a proactive approach to bring clients into counselling, but there are some rare occasions when it may be appropriate to do so: such as the person who has been involved in a major trauma or disaster. No-one can be forced into a counselling relationship. If in doubt it is probably kinder to the potential client to make an offer which can be refused rather than not.

After referral: Once counselling has started there will be established a confidential relationship and the counsellor will not be free except in extreme circumstances to divulge information about sessions without the client's permission (see *confidentiality*). In situations where counselling is happening alongside other forms of treatment, there need to be clear definitions of each professional's role. Given that counselling includes empowering clients to understand and take responsibility for themselves, any planning meetings should include the client. Counselling does not fit into the old paternalistic model of helping.

Many people's experience of emotional distress is linked in some way to their physical health and psychosomatic presentations. In these situations it is important that medical practitioners, counsellors and the client work in harmony to ensure that the correct form of treatment is being followed and that nothing is being overlooked.

Dual relationships: Counselling works best if the counselling relationship has clear boundaries and there is no role confusion on either side. Unless she is working jointly with a couple or family, it is usually not helpful for one counsellor to be involved with more than one member of a family. Each client needs to feel trust and safety with the counsellor, and if there is any suspicion of divided loyalties this will certainly impair the counselling.

It may also be appropriate to consider whether the counsellor has potentially a dual relationship with the client. In an educational setting she may be both student counsellor and tutor; in a health centre she may be nurse and counsellor. Cross-over of roles cannot always be avoided but will be less detrimental to the counselling if openly acknowledged and the implication discussed on both sides.

(g) BAC (undated) *Counselling and Psychotherapy: Is It For Me?* British Association for Counselling, 1 Regent Place, Rugby CV21 2PJ;

Clarkson, P. and Pokorny, M. (eds) (1994) *The Handbook of Psychotherapy*. London: Routledge; Tyndall, N. (1993) *Counselling in the Voluntary Sector*. Buckingham: Open University Press.

PAM HORROCKS
(See also *counselling and psychotherapy, forms of; groups, use of*)

Couples, working with

(a)   There is enough stress connected with counselling only one person; it increases almost logarithmically as we add others because it puts greater demands on our skills and attention. (Kennedy and Charles 1990: 307)

This article focuses on some important issues that arise for helpers working with couples. The term 'couple' is intended to be a gender-inclusive term, applying to married and non-married heterosexual couples, as well as to those within a homosexual relationship. The context of 'working' with couples may be within a formal counselling or therapeutic contract, or it may be within other professional or non-professional contexts where couples' issues can arise (e.g. social work, schools and hospitals).

(b)   Many problems presented by couples may not, on the surface, appear to concern their own relationship at all. The problems presented may be thought of as 'out there' rather than 'in here'. For example, parents concerned for their anorexic daughter naturally focus upon their child as the 'problem'. Those couples looking after, or responsible for, elderly parents (especially when they are living with their children) can often focus on the 'problem' of their parents, and entertain the view that all the family problems are due to the pressures brought about by this new responsibility. Undoubtedly, there are real issues in such scenarios, but it is all too easy to simplify the family dynamics and attribute all problems to their elderly relatives. Equally, teenage children can be targeted as the 'presenting problem' without which all might be considered well in the family nest. The perceptive helper needs to be aware that other difficulties may lurk beneath. The tendency to 'scapegoat' members of the immediate family can provide a very convenient cover for deep-seated, unhealthy dynamics between the couple concerned.

Where one partner is suffering from unbearable pressure from these internal or external factors, this can often find expression in breakdown and other forms of physical illness. On these occasions the general practitioner may be the first point of contact.

On the other hand, an immediate clash between the couple themselves, or an event involving the security of the marriage or relationship, provokes a readily recognized crisis. On these occasions the 'in here' issues are usually acknowledged more readily by both partners. They then, either together or separately, may seek outside help and advice. Working with couples, of course, means that *both* partners are willing to work together on the relationship. When one partner is reluctant – or even hostile – such defensiveness needs addressing first of all; and if it proves impossible to find common ground for the couple to work together on their own agreed agenda, it is probably more profitable to work with the willing partner on their own. People who sabotage attempts to salvage a threatened relationship usually attribute all the blame to their partners anyway, and refuse to accept any responsibility for the present state of affairs.

(c)   It is all too easy in working with couples for the helper to have an immediate impression that this marriage or relationship was a non-starter from the very beginning! However true this may be, we have only the present to start from. I set out in this section a few of the factors that the helper needs to bear in mind when assessing the *status quo* of the existing relationship.

First, it is important for the helper to have in mind the useful distinction between the conscious and the unconscious factors in any human relationship. It is a common fallacy that 'falling in love' with one's partner is a totally conscious activity, based on 'here-and-now' factors and an existential emotional response to such factors. In spite of much modern research that shows otherwise this fallacy continues. (Skynner and Cleese, 1983: ch. 1; Hendrix, 1990: part 1; Clulow, 1985: ch. 4; Scott Peck, 1978: sect. 2).

Of all the factors in the relationship between any two people, it is the unconscious ones that are most likely to prove the 'fly in the ointment' and the most intractable to deal with. The habits of denial and repression are formidable defences with which the helper is confronted. When such factors are discerned, the future capacity to work with this couple is immediately an important issue for the helper to discuss with their supervisory resources.

Secondly, can the helper discern what kind of partnership these two people are engaged in? In *Couples in Counselling* (Gough, 1989) I suggest that there are 'models of partnership' which often accurately reflect this unconscious relationship. For example, a couple may be acting out a 'Siamese-twin' role, wherein each partner has subjugated their own individual personality and behaviour to the other. They never risk the expression of any differences, or preferences of their own; they are welded together as a unit – inseparable and indistinguishable from one another. Or the couple may be acting out a 'Babes-in-the-Wood' model, that is distinguished by a mutual sense (conscious or unconscious) of their dependency and helplessness; they are both 'lost', but somehow they feel safer together. The 'Peter-Pan-and-Wendy' pattern is marked by a strong emphasis on the childishness of the male and a strong rescuing pattern of the female in these relationships. (See further in the books referred to in section (g).)

Thirdly, there is the factor of 'change' within the relationship. As in all counselling, it is especially necessary for the helper to ask the question 'Why now?' Referring to the factors already mentioned above, the helper may find it useful to ask herself (and eventually the couple) when a part of the unconscious element in this relationship has surfaced and some new level of awareness been reached. Or is the previously satisfactory model of their relationship now proving to be unsatisfactory? Or has some new crisis arisen within their relationship caused either by external or internal factors?

Such internal factors might include personal growth and development on the part of one of the partners, or an illness, or some new responsibility such as the care of sick children or ageing parents. On the other hand, it may concern a crisis precipitated by an extra-marital relationship such as an affair. Crises within a marriage do not have to be considered as inevitably negative, or detrimental to the ongoing relationship. True, they may be extremely uncomfortable for the people concerned, but as Socrates might have said, 'The unexamined *marriage* is not worth living'.

(d)   For the helper, it is important at the outset to remember that working with *couples* differs from working with individuals in at least one important aspect: with couples it is *the relationship between them, not their individual psychopathology* that forms the main focus. If it appears to the helper that individual work needs to be addressed by either of the partners, then professional referral needs to be undertaken to an appropriate resource such as a counsellor or psychotherapist or, in special cases, their GP for referral for a psychiatric report (see section (e)).

Should the presenting problem concern *internal factors* (see above) the helper needs to give patient attention to the ideas, views and feelings of each of the partners. The important counselling skills of listening with attention, empathic responding, genuineness and respect are used by the helper in order to ascertain where each partner stands. It may be, for instance, that the precipitating factor concerns whether or not an ageing parent should come to live with the couple and their family. To some extent of course such crises as these are predictable, but since we have infinite capacities to 'put off the evil day', it is all too easy to feel trapped by a sudden emergency of the kind that elderly parents can provoke. Or the emergency could concern the behaviour of a teenager – thoughts of giving up further education, drugs, bad company, unplanned pregnancies, for example – when parents turn for help and advice to an outside agency. The helper's response will depend upon the kind of agency within which they are working. For example, some agencies are of the 'advice-giving' kind, such as the Citizens Advice Bureaux, social services or other specialist agencies. Counselling skills may be used in order to assist the couple to express their concerns and feelings about their situation and some appropriate course of action decided upon.

Important as these internal factors are, it is often those originating from outside the relationship that can appear to be the most intractable and threatening. Internal factors usually focus upon and utilize the combined strengths of the couple towards the presenting problem. They are often at one regarding both the needs and the means of meeting those needs, especially where their children are concerned. *External* factors, however, usually concern the needs and preferences of only one partner and such unity as may exist facing internal factors is, of course, noticeably absent when, for instance, one of the partners is involved in an extra-marital affair. As mentioned above, it is important for the helper not to take too gloomy a view of such a crisis, since what may be happening below the surface of the awareness of the couple is that some important need – for years, perhaps ignored, avoided or denied – is now surfacing and demands urgent attention. In the case of a sexual affair, it is often found that deep dissatisfaction with the sexual content of the marriage or relationship has been going on for years but at a subliminal level, outside conscious awareness. It is now clearly on the agenda, and the issues that may have been denied or avoided can no longer be ignored.

There are some issues in the helping relationship that can be of value to the helper at this point. The helper needs to bear in mind the following points:

1. *Time-management:*   Ensure that each of the partners has enough time to express their thoughts and feelings. It is easily discernible which of the partners is the most dominant by the 'air-time' they take up in the interview or counselling session. The helper needs to elicit from the silent partner their views and opinions in order to equalize – as far as possible – the space given to each partner.

2. Intervention by the helper: For those trained in the psychodynamic or person-centred schools of counselling, important adjustments will need to be made when faced with working with couples. There is a need for more intervention that would normally be thought appropriate when working within those models of counselling, but – as with time-management – the helper needs to act more forcefully in ensuring the fairness of the use of time, and to point out when the communication needs to be addressed to each other rather than to the helper.

3. Listening to each other: Nowhere is the active intervention needed by the helper more that in assisting the couple to listen to one another. Couples often degenerate into a pattern of filtering out messages from their partner, and avoidance techniques are usually firmly in place by the time the couple seek outside help. Nothing is going to be accomplished or changed unless this vital aspect of their relationship is given urgent and regular attention. A useful suggestion to the couple is to set aside a reasonable amount of time each day, when one partner speaks and the other listens – in silence. This may, at first, be for only five minutes or so, but the effect on their relationship can often be staggering. The time can be adjusted to the needs and importance of the issue(s) that confront the couple, but unless there is a definite willingness to set aside a regular time to address one another, and to hear their pain, there is little chance of any successful outcome to the couple's problem.

4. Gender issues: It is usually found that the gender of the helper forms a focus within the helping relationship when the minority gender feels that there is collusion going on between the two people of the same sex. Male helpers will be regarded as 'on the side of' the husband; female helpers as 'on the side of' the wife. However much this may be true (and the feelings of the helper cannot be totally disregarded in a helping relationship), special attention needs to be given by the helper in order to avoid their own agenda intruding into the issues brought by the couple concerned (see *gender issues*).

5. Multiple emotions: One of the hardest elements of working with couples is the weight of carrying the combined emotional output of two people. One-on-one helping is often stressful enough; but with two people the weight is often found to be surprisingly stressful, even to those who have been working in this field for many years. Those who are new to working with couples always express their surprise and shock at the difference in the dynamic of a couple's relationship. This is quite natural, particularly if they have been working hitherto solely in one-on-one relationships, since everything is doubled: two sets of emotions, two differing views, two differing attitudes towards the helper, two possible aspects of transference (and counter-transference) – plus the special chemistry produced by the often violent expression of emotions and the effect they have on the other partner. The helper tries to contain his or her own feelings, while responding both to the strong emotions of the speaker and the sense of desolation or fear of the listening partner. This is what makes working with couples (and, of course, families) quite unique and faces the helper with surprising reactions to their own experience of this kind of care.

(e) What is true of counselling is manifestly true of all helping relationships: *no one can help everyone*. This is not necessarily a sign of incompetence, still less of failure; it is a question of our own personal and professional boundaries, and in my opinion it is a sign of maturity and strength to recognize when a helping need is beyond our personal resources. While it is often useful and growthful to take up a challenge and extend our boundaries of expertise and competence, this must never be at the risk of further harm to the people who seek our help. If we never took on work that we felt fearful of we would never grow; but this needs to be tempered by common sense, and a quiet word with our supervisor!

When the presenting problems of a couple appear to be outside our experience, or the safe level of our competence, consideration of referral needs to be high on the agenda. This possibility should be made clear at the outset in working with couples. If the helper feels that other agencies could be of more use to them, then there should be no hesitation in making use of referral resources. To whom could we refer?

Perhaps the best-known resource for working with couples in Great Britain is Relate (formerly the Marriage Guidance Council). Relate facilities are fairly widespread (see local telephone directory for details) and they work with both heterosexual and homosexual couples, as well as individuals.

There are some specific religious resources that offer help, such as the Catholic Marriage Advisory Council (Head Office: Clitheroe House, 1 Blythe Mews, Blythe Road, London W14 0NW. Tel: 0171 371 1341) from whom details of local resources can be obtained.

The British Association for Counselling produces an annual Counselling and Psychotherapy Resources Directory which contains both individual and organizational resources for counselling couples, and further details can be obtained from 1 Regent Place, Rugby CV21 2PJ (Tel: 01788 578328).

(f)   It is sometimes found that the material produced in the process of working with couples concerns issues wider than those of the two people who have sought your help. One area of particular importance is that of

child abuse, physical or sexual. Other areas concern harm intended either to one of the partners or to themselves and immediately raises the important question of **confidentiality**. What is the contract within which the helper is working with this couple? Most helping facilities work within agencies governed by strict ethical codes of conduct and these are either implied or clearly stated at the outset of working with couples. Where there is a contract involving strict codes of confidentiality then the helper is clearly in a dilemma. The Code for Ethics and Practice of the British Association for Counselling is worth quoting as a guide to all helpers:

> B.4.4. Exceptional circumstances may arise which give the counsellor good grounds for believing that the client will cause serious physical harm to others or themselves, or have harm caused to him/her. In such circumstances the client's consent to a change in the agreement about confidentiality should be sought whenever possible unless there are also good grounds for believing the client is no longer able to take responsibility for his/her own actions. Whenever possible, the decision to break confidentiality agreed between a counsellor and client should be made only after consultation with a counselling supervisor or an experienced counsellor.

There are also good grounds for seeking the permission of the couple to consult their medical practitioner, especially when the original referral came from that source.

(g)   Freeman, D. R. (1990) *Couples in Conflict*, Buckingham: Open University Press; Gough, Tony (1987) *Couples Arguing*. London: Darton, Longman & Todd; Gough, Tony (1989) *Couples in Counselling*. London: Darton, Longman & Todd.

TONY GOUGH
(See also *divorce*)

Cross-cultural awareness

(a)   Cross-cultural awareness is not simply about working with members of another race. It applies equally to the cultural aspects involved in different religious allegiances; in class background; in having been brought up in or living in different geographical locations; and even between age groups – we speak, for example, of a 'youth culture'. Although it is tempting to use the term 'sub-culture' of further divisions within the principal ethnic or religious groups, this would be to underestimate the powerful distinctions that can exist both within as well as between groups. It is preferable to stay with the single term *culture*, which has been defined as 'that complex whole which includes knowledge, belief, art, morals, law, custom, and any other capabilities and habits acquired by man as a member of society' (Tyler, 1958).

Cross-cultural can be used interchangeably with other terms in the literature, such as *trans-cultural* or *inter-cultural*. Whichever term is employed, it is important to recognize that in most cases it refers not just to the helper as needing to be aware of the implications of working clients of different cultural backgrounds. The term also implies the need to acknowledge that the client too has her or his own cultural perception of the helper's culture and of the setting in which care is offered. In other words cross-cultural awareness is a *reciprocal* process, although it is often the helper who has the greatest opportunity of bringing these issues into focus. Helpers are normally in a stronger position than the client to acknowledge the importance of these issues and assist their further exploration. This is more difficult for the client to do, particularly if she or he already perceives herself or himself as being in an inferior position to the helper. Such a self-perception may itself be culturally reinforced making it more difficult to question openly the helper's assumptions.

In some cases cultural issues are the actual focus of the caring work. The helping relationship can itself reflect these issues, when helper and client are themselves representative of cultural difference.

(b)   In addition to the problems which some clients will bring to the care-giver arising from cultural differences within the community (see *faith differences; fanaticism; gender issues; racism and prejudice; religious belief*) there are also occasions for misunderstanding, and even hurt, in the relationship between the client and helper, caused by their different cultural backgrounds:

1. There are problems of language. Although this is obviously true in the case of different languages, and sometimes of dialects, there are also difficulties about two people conversing in the same language, particularly if for one of them the common tongue is their second language. Each has his or her own understanding of what their common language means. Apart from mispronunciation and mistranslation, helper and client may find themselves using similar words, but attaching to them very different concepts or values. Even slight differences of nuance, such as whether or not 'please' and 'thank you' is used in different cultures, can give rise to feelings in the other party either of impoliteness or excessive politeness. Some cultures are much more expressive than others. The reserved white person may then look upon a group of

black people as noisy, volatile or even aggressive, when they themselves are simply speaking to each other in their own way.

2. There are similar difficulties with respect to non-verbal language.
Physical space between people, for example, is typical of British culture, whereas some other cultures sit or stand much closer. Intimate
contact in public may be shocking to some. Eye contact also varies: some
cultures avoid direct eye contact, and in this case it is a sign not of
insincerity but of respect. Nodding, which to the British tends to mean
'Yes', in some cultures means 'No'.

3. Differing behavioural patterns across cultures can create hostility,
and accusations of bad manners or lack of respect. Eating habits vary
between cultures. Matters of personal hygiene can be quite different (so
that different cultures think others are 'unclean'). Rules of hospitality
vary greatly between but also within cultures. For instance, there are
differences about entertaining strangers between cultures, but also
within the British class system: at the risk of generalizing, working-
class families are more obviously welcoming to and natural with
spontaneous callers, middle-class families more reserved and more
dependent upon prior invitation.

4. Religious festivals and in some cases the principal holy day of the
week are different in various faiths. Therefore what is sacrosanct for
some (such as time off for the British worker at Christmas and Easter,
whether or not religious sentiments attached to the festival are held
important) is very ordinary to another. Yet those of other faiths equally
have times of the year and festivals which are sacrosanct, but infre-
quently acknowledged in the programming and planning of white
organizations. Religious differences also often carry important variations governing food, alcohol, sexual intimacy, gender relationships
and expectations, etc. Forms of worship differ: for example, what some
black Pentecostal churches clearly value as being signs of 'gifts of the
Spirit' are seen by outsiders as suspiciously like indications of group
hysteria.

5. Cultural histories mean different perspectives on the same events or
on the same situations. Thus black history is seldom taught in the
British education system, any more than European history is taught
from a foreign perspective. Not only does this mean that the white
British child grows up with a white British view of historical events and
peoples, but also the black British child grows up with a one-sided view
of their history of their own family, that takes no account of anything
other than their origins as slaves or subjects of European powers,
whether in Africa, the Caribbean, India or elsewhere. The richness of
their own culture, before and during and since domination by European
settlers, is neglected.

6. Lack of a true cross-cultural perspective in our society must also account for the discrepancy in rates of imprisonment of black and white men, the diagnosis of severe mental illness in black and white people, the economic status of black families, their lack of representation in the media and in politics, attitudes towards sexuality, etc. Some of the attitudes which lead to these discrepancies also apply to other equally important groups such as the disabled, or even to large sections of the population, such as women (see *gender issues*).

7. Indeed, it should be stressed that these cultural differences involve many different groups – it is not just colour that needs to be recognized as carrying cultural implications. Differences exist within Europeans, Africans, Indians, etc. and not just between them. 'What is done', 'what we believe' and 'what is important to me' are as likely to differ between areas of a country or continent, and between generations, as they are between races. It should also be emphasized that these potential 'problems' are on both sides. In caring work it is often the helper who regards the client as being the one who has difficulties, who needs to be understood. In the cross-cultural context the client is just as likely to find the helper different and therefore difficult to understand.

(c) The problems of cross-cultural awareness lie rather obviously in helper and client (or in a team or group of helpers, or in a client group) representing in their own persons different cultural backgrounds. Such backgrounds provide a perspective which it is impossible ever to be free from. Attitudes, beliefs and behaviour cannot be separated; each one is reflected in the other. Beyond the individual helping relationship, cultural differences are rooted deep in history and in geographical location, which themselves need to be acknowledged and valued as existing in their own right. Ignorance of each other's culture is the primary cause of misunderstanding and hurt feelings, and perhaps of the wrong type of help being offered.

Learning about cross-cultural differences is not necessarily sufficient to remove deeper-seated prejudices and personal bias. For example, it is difficult to use the word 'black' without associating the term with the dark, the evil, the shadowy, and the dirty. Such is the way we have come to use this term. Such language nevertheless means that at a subconscious level not only a white person, but also a black person associates blackness with these negative connotations. It may appear extreme (especially to white people) to want to remove the word 'black' from common usage, and it may indeed be impracticable to do so; but if you understand the issue, it cannot but help raise awareness of just how pervasive attitudes are, and what they mean to relationships between cultures.

More deep-seated prejudice can make it difficult if not impossible to examine, tolerate and understand difference; and such belief systems can render ways of coping with difference more pathological, giving rise for example to **racism, fanaticism**, chauvinism (see *gender issues*) and other examples of wilful hostility and persecution. This is explored more fully in the article on **racism and prejudice**. It is very different from the unwitting and sometimes unconscious (although pervasive) lack of awareness which is the subject of this article. Unconscious prejudice is likely to be present in any helper. The effects of such prejudice inevitably function at some level in anyone who is not a member of a majority group.

(**d**) Gender, disability, sexual orientation and racial awareness education and ongoing self-analysis is now an essential part of all training for the caring professions and caring work, although 'bolt-on' training, given in a small number of hours, is an insult to other cultures. It assumes that any culture, or even the awareness of cultural difference, can be learned overnight. Some cultural awareness can be a subtle way of claiming to understand the other. It is only proper immersion in a different culture that enables the helper to begin to understand from within how it feels to be a member of it. Commitment to awareness of what is significant within different cultures, both to groups and individuals within them, should be part of the skills base of every helper. Awareness itself is never ending. Learning about differences (and commonalities) is therefore an inevitable part of every caring act and helping interview.

Caring work invariably requires the application of general skills and knowledge to specific situations. Ascertaining and then working with the particular circumstances of each individual is what gives caring work its variety. There is a danger in learning any set of skills or acquiring any body of knowledge that those in the helping professions tend to 'psychologize' others, without always pausing to thing that the norms for a particular culture may be different. Thus what may be a sign of mental disturbance in a white person may not at all be a sign of disturbance in an Afro-Caribbean person. Whether or not the helper is a counsellor, and whether or not they are trained in a particular style, what is technically known as a 'person-centred' approach is relevant to a more general attitude to patients or clients. In all client work the helper must listen for the nuances of the individual client's own background, in terms of family and community, in relation to cultural history as well as in terms of individual history. This truism about listening (and respecting) can be spelled out more precisely in a series of recommendations, to ensure that a helper's working base-line is one that is properly cognizant of the dimensions of the multi-cultural society in which all caring work takes place.

1. All literature which is used either to advertise caring resources, agencies, departments and institutions, or as part of their procedures, must be comprehensible to those who do not speak English. Just as in Wales all official literature and notices are in two languages, so in the areas of Britain where for many people English is not their first language, leaflets, posters and follow-up information must be made available in appropriate languages. This is necessary even when an agency does not have staff who speak these languages. An agency may not itself yet be able to offer adequate help other than in English, but it still needs to attempt to be as accessible as possible, even if contact is made through the client's own interpreter. In some cases agencies may be able to refer on to others which can provide help in the client's first language. Such resources should always be listed.

2. Wherever possible some of those who are employed as caring professionals or volunteers should be able to offer languages other than English. If not, it should be possible to arrange for an interpreter, either with the client's help, or through specialist agencies. Clearly in some situations, such as personal counselling, the use of an interpreter is difficult, and counsellors who speak other languages are very important human resources. Facilities for signing for those with impaired hearing is another useful adjunct for a caring agency.

3. Since cultural issues extend far further than language (or even ethnicity) it is important for a helping agency to be as fully representative as it can be of the 'cultural mix' of the community in which it is located. This applies as much to gender balance and to 'class' as to colour. It is not necessarily (see point 4) that client and counsellor have to be matched: diversity can be as important as similarity. It may sometimes be possible to provide clients with a choice, although they sometimes have to wait longer to be seen by the person they would prefer. But the real value for an agency in having differing cultural backgrounds on its salaried or volunteer staff is that this diversity will be represented in the agency's professional discussions (supervision, training, etc.) and in its management (policy, administration, etc.)

4. Although it is clearly desirable that such facilities for choice of helper be offered, agencies also need to be aware that precise cultural matching of client and helper is not always what a client wants. In particular, experience suggests that young Asian women sometimes do not want to see an Asian counsellor or other helper, because they fear that their story will reach the Asian community and perhaps be heard by their family. Sometimes this anxiety overrides their trust in the counsellor's assurance of **confidentiality**. They may therefore prefer to see someone

of a different cultural background. What is important (if in some places
an ideal that is not easily met) is for the client to be given a choice.
5. On the other hand, there can also be problems when a client from one
culture has no choice, and is allocated to a helper of a different culture.
The caring professional or volunteer needs to be particularly sensitive
to what a client feels about being in the care of someone who is of a
different race, religion or gender, particularly if the last two aspects are
important distinctions to a particular culture. Any of these factors may
complicate a working partnership between client and care-giver. Even
if the helper is personally acceptable to the client, the agency itself may
represent cultural values that are uncomfortably distinct from the
client's own background. These are all factors that may ultimately need
to be accepted, but they will be less damaging when they are acknowledged and talked about. This is especially important if they interfere
with co-operative work – and this can happen from both sides.
6. It should never be assumed that it is only the helper's own cultural
base that offers ways of helping the situations which clients bring to
care professionals or agencies; nor that clients have therefore to be
assisted to take advantage of the helper's own culture's expertise. The
client's culture may equally well be able to provide solutions.

> Life has produced many teachers, many philosophers, many trainers,
> but very few educators. An educator is one whose duty is not only to
> impart knowledge to others, but also he has the task of developing
> the knowledge, skills and the mind of the student, and bring out the
> latent qualities which the student already possesses. (Quoted in
> Akbar, 1982)

One of the tasks of the helper in any cross-cultural situation is therefore
to explore with the client the positive values, beliefs and expertise of the
client's culture, to see what resources are already present in the client's
experience. To this end d'Ardenne and Mahtani (1989: 20–1) list potential desirable resources that can be checked with clients:

a. family: does the client have a same-culture partner, and/or
    family in the area?
b. social network: does the client live in the same area as others
    from her or his culture – or have access to such networks?
c. religious resources: this could be a much more important area
    for the client than, for example, the non-religiously committed
    culture of a helper is personally willing to admit (see *faith
    differences; religious belief*);
d. health care: are there health professionals of the client's cul-
    ture? or are there other traditional healers in their community?
e. political situation: is the person a refugee? and/or in a political
    group which is tolerant of them?

f. education: are there educational establishments which can help in terms of multi-cultural education? or does the client have educational achievements that can cushion prejudice?

g. employment: the cultural attitudes of the employer, and of other people at work; or if the client is unemployed are there other members of the same culture in the same position?

7. Particular issues arise in helping clients in transitions – indeed much helping work can be said to be focused on transitions of one sort or another. These may be more complex for those who are also moving from living in one cultural background into another. The cultural dimensions of such transitions should not be ignored, particularly the **loss** of that which has provided a relatively secure base – together with the anxieties about what is new.

8. Helpers need to be sensitive to the cultural bias which they themselves have. It is not just the client who is different; the helper is too. Clients and helpers need to be encouraged to recognize that differences are not about what is right or wrong (even if some experiences have led them to think that). On some occasions both clients and caregivers (the latter through **supervision**) may also need to be helped to recognize why misunderstandings and conflicts can arise.

9. It needs to be borne in mind throughout training and practice that most of the books about the work of the caring professions, most psychology and much that informs the work of the helper, has been written by white people, even by white men. That includes this book, and indeed this article. Writing about a different perspective (even if it is well researched) can never be the same as writing from within that perspective. This is not a criticism of such writing – one person can only write from within a single perspective, and no single perspective is ever the whole picture. In caring work there is much that is about values, and values are relative to the society and culture in which they occur. No values are universal.

10. Similarly, helpers should never assume that because they know something about a given culture, they can take a particular client's background for granted. Although there may be features which form a backcloth to any presenting issue, individual nuances are unique; what d'Ardenne and Mahtani write of counsellors is equally true of all care professionals and volunteers, that they 'need also to be careful of overemphasising cultural or racial factors to the exclusion of other variables' (1989: 52).

11. None of what is written here implies that it is only helpers who need to adapt themselves to accepting and understanding different cultural behaviours, attitudes and expectations in their clients. Clients may also have at times, and in some matters, to adapt to the dominant

culture, whether or not that culture is right in its basic assumptions. 'When in Rome' in some cases still applies, although, of course, what constitutes the 'home' culture is itself in a steady state of change, in turn influenced by the other cultures with which it interacts.

12. Finally, it should be said that although a wider and deeper cross-cultural perspective makes any helping situation more complex, it also increases the richness of the experience of caring work. The care-giver will not only gain insight into another's culture, but often also find a new perspective on her or his own.

(e) Adult education courses (in university extra-mural departments and community colleges) often run courses in cross-cultural awareness, although, as this article suggests, such courses are only the beginning of the life-long process. Some cities have community centres that cater especially for black and Asian people. There are also courses offered in some centres on subjects such as black history, Indian dance, etc. – all opportunities not just to learn about cultural awareness in general, but to learn about other cultures through experiencing them. There are specialist bookshops in some cities where different cultures are more fully represented in publications, music, gifts, etc. Cultural activities within the community (arts, religious festivals) provide some experience or participation in other cultures. Even visiting other countries, especially when able to get away from tourist-package places, is another way in which some modest insights can be achieved.

Nafsiyat, the Inter-Cultural Therapy Centre (278 Seven Sisters Road, Finsbury Park, London N4 2HY. Tel: 0171 263 4130) runs courses in the principles for inter-cultural therapy. One of the Divisions of the British Association for Counselling is RACE (Race and Cultural Education), which is for members of any ethnic group – write to the Secretary, RACE Division, BAC, 1 Regent Place, Rugby, Warwickshire CV21 2PJ). The Association of Black Counsellors can be contacted at 4 Alexandra Avenue, Sutton, London SN1 2NZ (Tel: 0181 644 5479). The headquarters of the Asian Family Counselling Service are at: 2nd Floor, Rooms 4/5, 40 Equity Chambers, Piccadilly, Bradford, West Yorkshire BD1 3NN (Tel: 01274 720486). They are able to provide training in regional centres for non-Asian workers. The Institute of Transcultural Health Care (15–17 Upper Albert Road, Sheffield 8) co-ordinates and conducts interdisciplinary studies into the health of black and ethnic minority populations resident in Britain.

There are a large number of agencies offering counselling, support and welfare help of different kinds to clients who come from specific cultural backgrounds. Local directories, sometimes available from councils of voluntary service (or their equivalent) or from social services, normally provide details of organizations and groups that can meet particular needs, including those of specific cultural groups.

The development of **self-help groups**, and the use of advisory groups drawn from specific cultural settings, is of immense importance when working cross-culturally. It is often the caring professionals (and sometimes the caring volunteers) who hold both the financial resources and the power to bring about change, but the client group that holds the key to how best to employ those resources. This applies to groups who represent any type of difference, but is obviously even more relevant when a group is able to represent a different culture to that of the dominant cultural group from which the majority of care providers are drawn.

(g) Cheetham, J., James, W., Loney, M., Mayor, B. and Prescott, W. (eds) (1981) *Social and Community Work in a Multi-Racial Society.* London: Harper and Row; d'Ardenne, P. and Mahtani, A. (1989) *Transcultural Counselling in Action.* London: Sage Publications; Rack, P. (1982) *Race,   Culture   and   Mental   Disorder.* London: Tavistock/Routledge.

MICHAEL JACOBS
(See also *gender issues; racism and prejudice*)

Death of a child

(a) Parental loss of a child is considered to be the most traumatic, profound, protracted and complex of all losses. In 1992 9,394 children aged 14 or younger died in England and Wales (OPCS, 1994). Of these, 63 per cent were stillbirths or neonatal deaths (under 28 days) with a further 17 per cent occurring in the first year of life. The incidence rose between 15 and 19 years, with 1,401 deaths, and between 20 and 24 years, with 2,236 deaths. Throughout childhood and early adulthood males are 50 per cent more at risk than females.

Most children and young people survive parents, who may or may not be in relationship together. For as long as parents live, their progeny, *of whatever age*, remain psychologically and biologically their children, and are mourned as the next generation who should succeed them. What follows, therefore, applies to parental bereavement following the death of a child at any age from miscarriage to adulthood.

(b) Every bereavement is unique: even when parents grieve for the same child, their expression of grief and their process of mourning are individual and unsynchronized. At a time when they most need each other for support and understanding they are least accessible. Most grieving parents become preoccupied with their loss and are restricted in their ability to attend to the emotional needs of their partner. Sexual intimacy, which once gave life to the child, may now be unbearable for one or both partners. Help may be sought initially for difficulties in the relationship: helpers may not realize that the precipitating factor is the death of a child. Most partnerships suffer after such a loss: far from bringing parents together, it threatens the stability of even the best relationships.

Bereaved parents may seek help at any time after the death of a child but their expectations of the helper will depend upon their present understanding of the loss. They may hope unconsciously that the helper will resurrect the child. At a conscious level such parents may feel overwhelmed, disempowered, disoriented, terrified and exhausted. Commonly they experience visual, auditory or olfactory hallucinations which bring comfort but also affirm their incipient madness. They may wish for their own death, as life is no longer worth living, and so that they may be reunited with their child. While wary of causing hurt through suicide they often long for a terminal illness or fatal accident.

Family and friends may urge bereaved parents to pull themselves together. Or they may avoid contact because they feel impotent, anxious they will cause further hurt and, at a deeper level, they fear contamination: if this child can die, so too can their child and so too can they. At this point many bereaved parents, feeling abandoned, ostracized and isolated, seek outside help. This may be as early as the first month after the death. Everyone else has returned to normal; their lives have irrevocably changed. But to seek help is to acknowledge the reality of the loss, which some parents resist for months. Many function on automatic pilot, going through the motions of a safe and familiar routine, distancing themselves from the trauma until they are emotionally prepared to experience the anguish of their grief. Sometimes it is not until the first year has passed that they begin their bereavement work. Even then some avoid focusing on their loss and instead embark upon a relentless programme of diversionary activity. The truth is too dreadful to contemplate. But it is rare for this to extend into a third year. After the second anniversary of the death (or the second missed birthday, Christmas, Mother's or Father's Day) the expression of grief may erupt violently and the protective defensive patterns break down: avoidance and denial are no longer possible. By this time, however, others may expect the bereaved parents to have 'recovered' from their loss, so manifestations of their grief may be treated inappropriately as pathological.

The effects of the loss of a child are so pervasive and multifaceted, with a wide range of somatic symptoms, psychological, behavioural and social disturbance, that it is always worth eliciting a bereavement history from someone seeking psychological or medical help (Rando, 1986; Worden, 1991). There remain many older bereaved parents who need to grieve for their stillborn babies or sons killed in combat, whom they have never forgotten. The loss of a child is *lifelong* (Rando, 1986: 86; Rubin, 1993; Knapp, 1986; Klaus, 1993). Whenever the child dies, the parents will not only be reminded of him or her when they see a child of similar age or appearance but, as their peers pass normal developmental milestones, they will be reminded poignantly of what their child should have been and of what they miss. The child is irreplaceable: 'shadow' grief persists (Knapp, 1986).

It is increasingly recognized that traditional criteria used for identifying pathological grief are themselves normal components of parental bereavement (Rando, 1986: xiii). It is, therefore, important for those helping bereaved parents to be informed about the depth and range of parental reactions rather than derive their understanding and therapeutic interventions from conceptual models based predominantly upon the death of a spouse.

(c) Some factors influence all bereaved people (see *bereavement*). Others apply uniquely to bereaved parents and relate either to the parents' response or to characteristics of the child's death.

Parents' response: All parents struggle to find a meaning for this loss. Their sense of what is right and fair is deeply threatened: they seek a purpose for the death which restores meaning to their lives and a belief in the inherent safety of their world. If a child can die anything can happen. A child's death defies the natural order of the world that children succeed their parents.

Parents protect their young until they are capable of independent life. When a child dies, parents feel they have failed as protectors, whether or not they were culpable. This sense of failure results in intense feelings of guilt and low self-esteem. It also leads to their being over-protective of surviving children.

As recipients of their parents' genes, children ensure immortality for the preceding generation. Not only is this denied them but, if children can die, so too can parents, who therefore have to face their own mortality. They have already lost those parts of themselves, biologically, psychologically and socially, which were manifest in the dead child and which were experienced as physical extensions of themselves.

Children are the embodiment of parents' hopes for the future, a narcissistic vehicle for a second chance at life. Practically, children may care for parents in their old age when the protective, nurturing roles are reversed: all this is lost when a child dies.

During the initial period of loss most parents become preoccupied with the dead child to the exclusion of surviving siblings. It is the dead child whom they want and who invariably embodies all that is ideal. The effect on the bereaved siblings, who cannot replace the dead child or compete with this perfect angel, is profound (see *children's experience of loss and death*).

When the dead child is the only child, parents lose their identity, role and status as parents. With those whose first child is miscarried, stillborn or dies neonatally, there is deep frustration at their inability to experience complete parenthood, and both may feel a sense of physiological and social inadequacy at their failure to fulfil the natural expectation of reproduction. This may be remedied if they succeed in giving birth to another child but for those who are unable to do so these feelings may be intractable.

Some theorists attribute significant differences in the experience of parental grieving to gender. I believe it is only one of many contributory variables.

Factors related to the child: The age of the child at death is significant. When a baby or younger child dies emphasis is upon unfulfilled promise. When older children die they have been part of the parents' lives for so long that to survive necessitates a radical reorganization of role, routine and values: memories abound as painful reminders of the wasted potential of an emergent young adult. There is some evidence to suggest that an anticipated death is less complicated to mourn than a sudden death. Although parents resist acceptance of a **terminal illness** they have time to contemplate the unthinkable, to prepare themselves and their child. A sudden death provides no opportunity to resolve unfinished business between child and parents; no time to say good-bye.

The mode of death may ease or exacerbate the grieving process. A violent death, or one resulting in mutilation or in there being no body, presents additional trauma to parents who may be haunted by actual or imagined images. Some deaths, such as suicide, or drug overdose, or accidents for which the parent may feel responsible, lead to intense guilt and shame (see *guilt and shame; major incidents; suicide; victims of crime*).

The nature and quality of the relationship between parent and child, the role the child played in the family and the personal, individual meaning the child had for each parent, are all factors which will affect their bereavement process.

(d)   In the immediate aftermath of a child's death, parents may need practical assistance not only with death-related tasks (registration, **funeral**, etc.) but to maintain the basic routines of life. Everyday activity will be painful, especially when it has previously involved the dead child, or when parents are exposed to other apparently complete families enjoying life together. Active practical support offered spontaneously by calm, competent and caring helpers is incalculable in helping families survive the first traumatic weeks.

It is necessary for helpers to understand the process bereaved parents undergo towards 'recovery'. Most useful is Worden's conceptualization of the four tasks of mourning (Worden, 1991).

1. *To accept the reality of the loss:*   This is the most difficult task and may be the last to be fully accomplished. It may take many years to believe fully that the child has gone forever and will never be experienced again in this life. Parents of older children may fantasize that the child has gone away, on holiday, on a world tour. They miss the child but they do not acknowledge that the child's life has ended. Most parents desperately seek an answer to 'Where is he (or she) now?' If they are certain of an afterlife most parents will accept this and focus upon the missed presence, feeling comforted that one day they will be reunited.

Some parents doubt the child ever lived: they wonder if they have imagined him or her. This is especially so for parents whose baby was miscarried or stillborn because they only have memories of the child *in utero*. It can be helpful if parents see their aborted embryo or spend time with their stillborn baby: cuddling the baby; taking photographs from every angle, clad and naked; taking a lock of hair; making foot and hand prints; keeping the blanket in which he or she was wrapped. Until the reality of the child's life is acknowledged the death cannot be mourned.

Parents may be helped to accept the reality of their child's death by remembering his or her life, reminiscing with photographs, school books and treasured toys, writing or tape recording their memories and keeping a journal of their bereavement journey. They need repeatedly to tell the story of the death: what happened; how they felt; whether or not they saw the body; their experience of the funeral. This process cannot be forced or rushed.

2. *To work through the pain of grief:*   Most parents are frightened by the intensity and unpredictability of their feelings. They need to be reassured that their feelings are normal and that they are not going mad. They need to know that they will not always feel like this, that the wrenching pain will subside and their preoccupation with themselves

and the dead child will ease; that they will be able to eat, sleep, concentrate, smile, laugh and love again. But this will take time and no one can predict how long. It is very important to offer realistic hope for the future. They will never be the same as they were before. They will never forget their child, but they will not always suffer as they do in the early years.

Parents may express feelings through whatever medium is natural for them: writing to the dead child or about the child; art work; any expressive therapy may be facilitative. Contact with other bereaved parents, in a self-help or therapeutic group (see *self-help groups; groups, use of*), may help parents to feel less isolated and more normal; it may provide essential social and emotional support and hope for the future through the example of parents more advanced in their bereavement.

3. *To adjust to an environment in which the deceased is missing:*   This task often involves conflict between parents who may have different needs with regard to how it is maintained. One may banish all reminders of the dead child; the other may wish to fill the house with mementoes. A couple must communicate their individual needs and not take action which provokes a secondary loss for their partner. It is normal for parents to preserve the child's room for two or three years before relocating the possessions, keeping some, giving others away and using the room for another purpose. Precipitate destruction of the child's belongings is invariably regretted later, as apart from memories and photographs, they are all that remain. It is usually unwise for parents to move house immediately after the child dies: although being there may be excessively painful, moving away encourages denial and deprives parents of important memories. The parents' world is full of places and activities beyond the home associated with the child, most of which must be faced. It may be helpful to accompany a bereaved parent to any place which is particularly painful to confront.

4. *To relocate emotionally the deceased and move on with life:*   The realistic aims of parental bereavement are that the dead child should no longer be the primary focus of the parents' life; he or she should be remembered with joy as well as sadness; parents will have found some purpose and meaning in life again, often with very different priorities; they will be able to feel joy in living and re-engage in loving relationships. Parents achieve these aims gradually, sometimes imperceptibly, over several years, but only when they feel free from survivor guilt and are willing to take the risk of loving and losing again. There will always

be a gap in their lives but they often emerge immeasurably streng-thened by the knowledge that through their own resources they have survived the worst fate imaginable.

The accomplishment of these four tasks is not sequentially linear but more circular. For parents to be aware that they can actively engage in grief work provides a sense of control in an otherwise unpredictable world. However, they may be resistant, because to do so is to acknow-ledge the child is dead.

When bereaved parents present as a couple it is important to acknow-ledge that they grieve differently and at a different pace. Both may assume the role of protector and 'try to be strong' for the other, concealing their individual pain for fear of adding to their partner's distress. This is impossible to sustain, does not achieve the desired effect, leads to misunderstanding ('he doesn't seem to feel anything') and a breakdown in communication. A helper may work individually with each parent on his or her personal grief and with both together focusing upon their relationship.

The quality of the helping relationship is fundamental: conveying empathy, acceptance and congruence facilitates healing. It is essential to work within the parents' own frame of reference, entering their individual, subjective world. Most important is an empathic understanding of the depth and breadth of their loss (Leon, 1990). As they strive to construct a new reality in their chaotic world they require contact with others who share these meanings, which 'provides valida-tion of the new system of beliefs, values, assumptions and norms' (Braun and Berg, 1994). If at least one other can understand their experience they are not alone.

To be fully present alongside bereaved parents as they plummet into despair; to neither minimize nor accelerate their journey; to tolerate their violent fluctuations in detachment from the dead child; to be patient with their labile mood swings and inconsistent level of function-ing; to accept unconditionally their intense pain, anger and guilt and to facilitate expression of these agonizing feelings; to be experienced as a genuine, nurturing, reliable, compassionate and safe presence will promote recovery. The helper's essential humanity should prevail.

This takes its toll: working with bereaved parents is stressful. Helpers often feel impotent, overwhelmed, hopeless and ineffective: progress is erratic, pedestrian; newly bereaved parents can no more fully engage with the helper than they can with each other, so the helper may feel unable to make psychological contact and withdraw. Those who persevere should prepare for the work by actively pondering their own mortality; by reading widely in the bereavement literature, especially personal accounts by bereaved parents (e.g. Loizeaux, 1993;

Monckton, 1994; Renouf, 1993; Sarnoff Schiff, 1992); by taking care of their own physical, emotional and spiritual needs; and by acknowledging their personal limitations.

(e) Parents may be referred appropriately to a bereavement counsellor or psychotherapist or, if necessary, a clinical psychologist or a psychiatrist. The National Association of Bereavement Services (20 Norton Folgate, London E1 6DB. Tel: 0171 247 0617) publishes a directory. Three agencies focus exclusively upon bereavement for anyone affected by the death of a child, providing support, counselling, information, consultancy and training: The Laura Centre (4 Tower Street, Leicester LE1 6WS. Tel: 0116 254 4341); The Alder Centre (Royal Liverpool Children's NHS Trust, Alder Hey, Eaton Road, Liverpool L12 2AP. Tel: 0151 252 5392); Sunrise Child Bereavement Centre (83 Stirling Road, Edgbaston, Birmingham B16 9BN. Tel: 0121 454 1705). Most hospices and some hospitals provide bereavement support as do several national self-help organizations (see *bereavement*).

(g)   Rando, T. A. (1986) *Parental Loss of a Child.* Illinois: Research Press Company; Sarnoff Schiff, H. (1992) *The Bereaved Parent* (2nd edn). London: Souvenir Press; Worden, J. W. (1991) *Grief Counselling and Grief Therapy* (2nd edn). London: Routledge.

JAN MCLAREN
(See also *bereavement; children's experience of loss and death; funerals; loss*)

Depression

(a) 'Depression is the common cold of psychopathology' (Seligman, 1973). Seligman's oft quoted analogy certainly has some validity. Depression is a common and recurring complaint which is often time-limited. In any one year approximately one in ten of the population will have an episode of depression. One quarter of episodes of depression last less than a month, a further 50 per cent recover in less than three months and, as with colds, most people cope without seeking treatment.

However, the comparison is unfortunate in that it fails to convey the potential seriousness of depression. It accounts for about three-quarters of psychiatric hospitalizations and one in every seven people who has been hospitalized for major depression will eventually die by **suicide**. In many developed countries suicide is in the top ten most frequent causes of death and, in younger males, it is in the top three. Depression may also reduce life expectancy in disorders like **cancer**. Lastly, its impact clearly extends beyond the sufferer to include family, friends and colleagues.

The term depression is used very often in our day-to-day conversation to describe a normal down-swing of mood. Such down-swings in mood may be adaptive. In rather the same way that normal anxiety and fear can warn of danger and prevent more serious harm, so depression may remind of losses and spur a person to find ways of re-engaging with activities or friends. However, just as anxiety can become abnormally generalized and severe, so depression can pose more problems than it solves.

(b) There is general agreement on the most common signs and symptoms of depression. Davison and Neale (1990) suggest the following list:

1. sad, depressed mood;
2. poor appetite and weight loss or increased appetite and weight gain;
3. difficulties in sleeping (insomnia); not falling asleep initially, not returning to sleep after awakening in the middle of the night, and early morning awakenings; or in some depressed people a desire to sleep a great deal of the time;
4. shift in activity level, becoming either lethargic (psychomotor retardation) or agitated;
5. loss of pleasure and interest in usual activities;
6. loss of energy, great fatigue;
7. negative self-contempt; self-reproach and self-blame, feelings of worthlessness and **guilt**;
8. complaints or evidence of difficulty in concentrating, such as slowed thinking and indecisiveness;
9. recurrent thoughts of death or **suicide**.

Within the diagnosis of depression there exists, however, great heterogeneity. Some individuals have periods of mania interspersed with their depressive episodes and are labelled manic-depressive or as suffering from bipolar disorder. In unipolar depression a distinction has sometimes been made between endogenous depression (arising 'from the inside' – from biochemical disturbance in the brain) and reactive depression (a reaction to external stresses, sometimes called 'exogenous' to parallel the term 'endogenous'). This distinction is, however, often difficult to make and is not very useful clinically.

Psychotically depressed individuals will experience delusions and hallucinations which commonly revolve around either disease, nihilism (the belief that parts of the body have 'gone' where they once

existed), poverty and ruin or guilt and self-denigration. Other categor-
izations include post-natal depression and seasonal affective disorder.

It has long been considered that the period after giving birth is a time
of increased psychiatric risk although there is now some doubt as to
whether post-natal women are at any more risk of depression than
control groups. Three categories of mood disturbance that have been
identified following childbirth are: maternity blues, affecting about
half of all mothers; post-natal depression, occurring in about 10–15 per
cent of women; and puerperal **psychosis**, a comparatively rare condition usually requiring hospitalization.

Hippocrates noted 'whoever wishes to pursue the science of medicine
in a direct manner must first investigate the seasons of the year and
what occurs in them'. It has long been recognized that some individuals
regularly experience depressive episodes on an annual basis. There
appear to be two patterns of seasonal affective disorder with the
depression recurring either in the summer or winter. Interestingly,
phototherapy, sometimes used in the treatment of winter depression,
was first used over 2,000 years ago: 'lethargics are to be laid in the light,
and exposed to the rays of the sun' (Aretaeus).

Physical **pain** almost anywhere in the body, sometimes occurring in
multiple sites, is a frequent symptom in depression. There is also
evidence that people of non-Western cultures present with more somatic symptoms when depressed. However, it is also worth remembering
that certain diseases (for example, thyrotoxicosis and Addison's disease) may produce depressive type symptoms; and also that there is
often an association between depression and physical disease and other
problems such as anxiety disorders. The term 'secondary depression' is
sometimes used to describe depression that is preceded by another
psychiatric or physical disorder.

Just as with anxiety there is also a link between depression and
alcohol consumption. Heavy drinking can lead to mood deterioration,
although conversely alcohol consumption might sometimes represent
an attempt to self-medicate (see *alcoholism*).

(c)   The causes of depression have attracted theoretical attention for
over two millennia. The Greeks believed melancholia was the result of
excess black bile and that this was influenced by diverse processes such
as the seasons, diet, life-styles and life events. Reviewing contemporary
models of depression we see many similarities with the theorizing of the
Greeks. Thus it is widely accepted that the onset of depression and its
course are related to a variety of biological, historical, environmental
and psycho-social variables, and that no one theory can adequately
address its complexity.

This section focuses briefly on some of the psychological and biological factors in depression, since these inform many of our treatment strategies. This in no part reflects the view that socio-political factors are not important. Indeed, it is quite possible that non-professionals can have a greater impact in these areas than people wedded to models of individual pathology. The interested reader is referred to Gilbert (1992) who gives a comprehensive account of theories of depression.

Freudian theory argues that when an individual is confronted by the loss of an ambivalently loved object anger is introjected. For individuals fixated at the oral stage of development, who have a tendency to be excessively dependent on other people for the maintenance of self-esteem, this anger continues to be turned towards the self. This theorizing is the basis for the widespread psychodynamic view of depression as anger turned inward.

The learned helplessness theory of depression suggests that although anxiety is the initial response to a stressful situation, it is replaced by depression if the person comes to believe that control is unobtainable. Later formulations include the concept of attribution. It is not, for example, failure *per se* that is important, but the sense we make of it. The depression prone individual is thought to show a 'depressive attributional style', a tendency to attribute bad outcomes to personal, global, stable faults of character. When persons with this style have unhappy, adverse experiences they become depressed.

The biochemical basis of depression has focused on norepinephrine and serotonin, two chemical messengers within the brain. Two particular groups of drugs, the tricyclics and the monoamine oxidase inhibitors (MOAIs), both commonly used in the treatment of depression, have the initial effect of increasing the levels of these messengers in the brain. However, after several days their levels return to normal. Since for both tricyclics and MAOIs there is a time-lag of one to three weeks before they become effective as anti-depressants, recent theories about their effects suggest that they may work by altering the receptor sites of the messengers.

'People are disturbed not by things, but by the view which they take of them' (Epictetus). The underlying assumption of Beck's cognitive theory of depression (Beck et al., 1979) is that emotional disturbance follows from distortions in thinking. There are three main components.

Negative automatic thoughts 'come out of the blue', often seemingly unprovoked by events and appear 'valid' in the sense that they are often accepted unchallenged by the recipient; examples might include thoughts like 'I'm a failure' or 'everything I do goes wrong'. According to the model these thoughts are not simply symptomatic of being depressed but they themselves are responsible for disrupting mood. There may often exist a whole chain of negative thinking. For example, a specific situation such as an acquaintance passing a depressed person without acknowledging them might precipitate the following series of thoughts:

He's deliberately ignored me
↓
People find me boring
↓
All my relationships seem to go wrong
↓
I'm always going to be lonely
↓
I'm not lovable and not worthy of love

The second component is the presence of systematic logical errors in the thinking of depressed individuals. Several categories have been described of which two examples are: dichotomous thinking (all or nothing: black/white thinking, e.g. 'only a miracle can make me well again'); and arbitrary inference (where a conclusion is inferred from irrelevant or insufficient evidence; exemplified by the above – concluding that one has been *deliberately* ignored if there has been no acknowledgement).

Depressogenic schemas are long-lasting attitudes or assumptions about the world that represent the way in which the individual organizes their past and current experience, and is suggested to be the system by which incoming information about the world is classified. In the chain of thinking outlined above, the last statement, 'I'm not lovable and not worthy of love', might stem from an individual's early relationship with their parents and be an example of a depressogenic schema.

According to Beck such schemas are often latent, only being activated by a specific event. Thus the belief 'I'm not lovable' might only become active after someone had experienced the break-up of a relationship. Once activated they, in turn, produce an upsurge of negative automatic thoughts.

(d) Providing the depressed person already has the necessary skills to cope with their difficulty it may be that offering personal qualities such as warmth, encouragement and understanding are sufficient help. Indeed this may be why some placebo therapies work quite well, by encouraging those who normally use active coping strategies to mobilize their energies. However, for some people, dealing with their difficulties will have exceeded their capacity. In these cases personal qualities will still be important but not sufficient.

Depression can often be a vicious circle. It can slow the person down mentally and physically and everyday tasks can become an enormous effort. The individual may get tired easily, do less than they used to and then be self-critical for not doing enough. Rewards from their environment will decline, and in time they may even begin to think that they cannot do anything at all and that they will never get over this feeling. This in turn deepens the depression, making it even more difficult to do anything. It is no accident that one of the metaphors we use to describe severity of depression speaks of it 'spiralling downwards'. Engaging in activity is one way of breaking this pattern.

Initially keeping a daily record of activity might help identify parts of the day that are particularly problematic. In addition for some people the process of diary keeping in itself stimulates more activity. The next stage might be to begin planning activities in advance. This should serve to boost activity levels and may also help someone develop a sense of control and purpose over their lives. For some individuals even the most simple task feels too difficult, in which case it will need to be broken down into manageable chunks. It may help to build in rewards for the successful completion of certain tasks.

There is a danger that initially such activity may make a person more depressed, triggered by a thought along the lines of 'I'm not doing it as well as I used to'. It may be important to re-emphasize that the goal initially is just to complete the agreed task; although it may be necessary in some instances to plan other activities.

According to the cognitive model it is the thoughts that a person has that either cause or exacerbate their depression. Given this, it can sometimes be helpful for an individual to begin recording their thoughts and feelings. Once automatic thoughts have been identified the challenge is to help the person come up with valid alternatives. It should be emphasized that the task is not simply one of positive thinking. It may be possible to test out a thought by collecting data or carrying out experiments. If, for example, a person believed that 'all my friends are sick of me', it should be possible to plan an assignment to see if this is indeed the case.

Questioning may help someone to generate alternative thoughts (How might someone else view this situation? How would you have viewed it before you got depressed? Are you condemning yourself as a total person on the basis of one event? Are you blaming yourself for something which is not your fault? Would you say that to a friend in a similar circumstance?). There follows a series of automatic thoughts together with an alternative:

When Claire passed by me today she did not say anything. I must have done something to upset her.
It is true that she didn't smile at me but I have no reason to think that I offended her. It was probably nothing at all to do with me. Perhaps she just has a lot on her mind.
Everything goes badly for me.

Everything? Actually I'm not that consistent! Some things do go badly
for me, just as they do for everyone else, but some things go well.
I didn't get the job. I'm just a failure.
Failing in one specific area does not mean that as a person I am a total
failure.

Clearly, this is only a very brief introduction to some of the ideas of
cognitive therapy. For the interested reader Beck et al. (1979) give a
clear, but detailed, account of cognitive-behavioural interventions in
the treatment of depression.

Many people have reservations about taking anti-depressant medication. However, there is evidence that for some people it can have
beneficial effects. The most commonly prescribed drugs for depression
belong to a group called the tricyclics. No therapeutic benefit is discernible for about a couple of weeks when taking these drugs, while certain
side-effects, such as dryness of mouth, may appear immediately. It is
not uncommon for doctors to gradually increase the prescribed dosage
as the person begins to tolerate the side-effects. Given the therapeutic
lag the depressed person may often feel the drugs are not working, and
if the dosage is being increased they may come to believe that they must
be a particular serious or intractable 'case'. Studies have shown that up
to three-quarters of people taking anti-depressants receive sub-thera-
peutic doses. If drugs are to be taken it may be useful to inform, or
remind, the individual about these characteristics of the drugs.

Another item of concern for people is whether they will become
addicted to medication. They can perhaps be reassured that they will
not become physically addicted to them in the same way that some
people are to minor tranquillizers; however, there is always the possibility of psychological dependency. Tricyclics are dangerous in overdose and given the risk of suicide that accompanies depression they are
sometimes only dispensed in small amounts, or relatives or carers are
asked to give them to the patient.

For many carers and counsellors the decision as to whether to
recommend or arrange further help can be fraught. On the one hand
there is often a keenness to encourage the individual's own efforts,
thereby perhaps maintaining the sufferer's self-esteem, and a desire to
avoid the stigma of contact with professional services; in contrast there
are the dangers of re-affirming a person's belief that they cannot cope if
there are continued experiences of failure. It needs to be recognized that
there are risks that depression can present, and that more intensive
psychological and physical interventions can sometimes be effective.

One issue that should always be to the fore when wrestling with this
decision is the risk of **suicide**. Ideally this is a topic that should be
discussed. It is highly unlikely that talking about suicide will put the

idea into the person's head. Instead, most depressed people are relieved to have the subject raised, and from such discussion one can perhaps begin to make an assessment of risk. The old adage that people who really intend to commit suicide do not talk about it is *not* true. It is also the case that many people who commit suicide have made previously unsuccessful attempts. There is sometimes a particular risk when a person seems to be improving since apathy may resolve before hopelessness. Given the real risk of suicide in this group it is perhaps best to err on the side of caution.

(e)   Within the NHS, general practitioners are the point of access to more specialist services such as clinical psychologists and psychiatrists. Clearly, localities vary in terms of the extent and nature of their resources. Where community mental health teams exist these might represent a reasonable first point of contact for further information about the availability of support, supervision or other services.

(g)   Blackburn, I. (1987) *Coping with Depression*. London: Chambers; Rowe, D. (1983) *Depression: The Way Out of Your Prison*. London: Routledge.

JOHN ORMROD
(See also *loss; menopause; phobias and anxiety; psychosis and severe mental disorders; violence towards women*)

Divorce

(a)   While there are religious and social factors involved in divorce, this article focuses on the provision of appropriate care for the two people concerned in this process, with a glance in the direction of the wider effects upon family life. My main concern is to raise important issues that the carer needs to bear in mind; so that, in spite of divorce often being a harrowing experience, receiving help might enable it to become a positive event for both parties involved. My emphasis is on facilitating couples facing divorce to find such an outcome.

(b)   Divorce can be presented to the carer in a number of ways. First, it may be presented either on its own as a clearly defined goal or *fait accompli*, or as one of a number of problems facing the client. Secondly, responses to the subject of divorce depend on what stage clients are at: i.e. are they getting over it? going through it? or intending divorce in the future? The carer's response clearly depends on the stage at which those seeking help find themselves. Thirdly, divorce is often presented as an imagined 'cure-all' for a whole range of problems facing a couple. It is tempting to attribute all one's problems to the marriage and imagine that ending it will solve everything. The carer needs patience and understanding in helping those for whom divorce is in prospect to sort out facts from fantasies, and perhaps to break down the wider problems into manageable 'mini-problems' that might need separate and specialist help. For example, if there are health problems, e.g. **depression**, medical intervention may become necessary. The poor quality of a personal relationship can, of course, be a contributory factor to ill-health, but it needs to be addressed specifically by the most appropriate caring resource (see section (e)).

(c)   The precipitating factors of divorce are as complex and personal as human relationships are in general. Official divorce statistics can only relate to the *legal grounds* upon which the divorce proves to be success-ful: e.g. adultery, unreasonable behaviour, desertion and living apart for either two or five years. While legal grounds offer a starting-place for understanding – for instance, adultery can precipitate a divorce – they are better seen as the *means* of ending a marriage rather than the *reasons* for ending it.

The legal umbrella term, 'irretrievable breakdown of the marriage', is a helpful generalization because it points to the *quality* of a relation-ship that is no longer viable, at least in the view of one of the parties. When one partner is unhappy in a marriage, that *marriage* is neces-sarily unhappy.

If we regard acts of adultery and unreasonable behaviour as the mountain peaks precipitating divorce, there is usually a great deal more happening down in the lowlands of the relationship. Some of the events that can bring a marriage into crisis are predictable: having (or refusing to have) children; changes in the financial structure of the marriage (whether this means moving up *or* down market); children leaving home; care for ageing parents, especially those who come to live in the marital home; loss of sexual libido; and any transitional period that can unleash hidden potential for growth either personally, psycho-logically or vocationally. Any of these have within them the power to change the formerly agreed basis of the marriage. Often, of course, the marriage simply dies, and divorce is the way of certifying death. As John Berryman writes:

> Why people divorce each other is their own business, inscrutable.
> They seldom, in my experience, know why themselves – know what
> was more important, I mean, along the camps of the Everest of
> dissatisfactions nearly any human being feels with any other human
> being he knows inside out. Maybe nothing is most important. It's the

mountain, and you must get too weary to climb on. (Rubinstein, 1990: 290)

(d) For those either considering the possibility of divorce, or in the process of getting divorced, issues of **loss** and leave-taking will become relevant. (On the Holmes–Rahe Social Readjustment Rating Scale, divorce rates 73 stress units. Only a death rates more.) The life *context* in which the divorce is taking place is therefore all-important for the carer. Where does the present crisis fit in with what else is happening in this person's life right now? Taking a careful history probably repays the effort, since divorce needs to be considered by the carer within the wider context of the person's life-history as will as their present situation (not least other divorces that may have occurred within the two families concerned). It is always possible that any crisis can represent a 'bridge too far' for the person to cope with, coming on top of other unresolved crises in their lives, especially those involving loss. These can include miscarriages, **redundancies**, retirement as well as death. Indeed, the wise carer may ask about the care and support given and received by each partner during these crises, and discover hidden resources within the relationship which could mean that divorce is not necessarily the solution it was first thought to be.

The *content* of care needs to relate directly to a wide set of variables, which include the following questions:

Have the couple hit a sticky patch in their relationship and has divorce arisen as one of their options – more in anger and desperation than with serious intent?
In this case, some short-term counselling might be the most appropriate response, providing a breathing-space within which the couple can sort out the immediate problems, as well as the long-term prospects for the durability of the marriage.

Have the couple reached breaking-point, and has one of the partners left the matrimonial home?
Even here all is not lost – and the break could well sharpen their view of the options as to what is important to them and what they actually want to fight for. Sometimes people neither hear nor pay any attention to the distress signals that their partner sends out, and the acting-out of their despair by a temporary withdrawal can focus upon the seriousness of the situation.

Is there an 'eternal triangle' situation?
The existence of a 'third party' always complicates the original relationship, but again this could be as much a sign of frustration at an emotional vacuum as a wish for a permanent change of partners. The

partner who has been left is usually the one who will seek a carer's help, in order to know how to deal with their situation, including practical matters (not least financial) that concern them. Sometimes there is a coming and going of a partner that adds further complications to the relationship. I call this phenomenon the 'Yo-Yo Syndrome' (Gough, 1992: 57f.). Because of indecision or **guilt**, a partner moves backwards and forwards between their spouse and their lover, which adds further pressures to the three people in question, not to mention to the feelings of any children involved.

Did the couple separate some time ago, and now that a new relationship appears to be permanent, does one of the original partners now wish to re-marry?
This is by far the most familiar reason for seeking a divorce. When a marriage is failing, separation is usually the *first* step in order to find some peace or safety. Should the separation become permanent, then the question of re-marriage can present itself. People may then seek the advice and assistance of a carer when a second union is contemplated, chiefly as a 'post-mortem' exercise to discover the 'cause of death' of their previous relationship. They want to become aware of what happened so that their second marriage or partnership does not become contaminated by the same harmful elements in the first. Whereas *every* marriage involves carrying baggage from the past into it, in the case of second or subsequent marriages this is even more important to analyse. Second marriages fail more frequently than first, and the reason for this is not hard to find. The carer needs to give particular attention to the 'unfinished business' of previous relationships. This may include: 1. access to, and care for, any children of former marriages; 2. financial provision for a former spouse and children, or by a former spouse; 3. unexpressed or delayed emotions (e.g. guilt, shame, anger) relating to the past which may be delaying the enjoyment of the new relationship; 4. testing-out of the withdrawal of emotional investment in previous partners, so that fresh energy is available for the new relationship.

Where two people are in existing marriages, or have had previous marriages dissolved, it is possible that these four aspects of 'unfinished business' could apply to *both* people seeking a new marriage. The additional complications in such instances are obvious, since two families are involved.

I have suggested four phases of marital break-up in *Couples Parting* (Gough, 1992) that includes a map of leave-taking that the carer can usefully keep in mind when offering assistance to those seeking divorce. In outline this involves:

1. *The preparation phase*

This phase covers the deterioration in the quality of the marriage over several years and the initial separation, of which divorce might be the outcome. Emotional responses such as shock, fear and anger are some of the normal reactions to a sudden leaving by a spouse. However sudden the separation might be, there are usually predisposing factors that have either been hidden or denied that have contributed to the breakdown of the marriage. Fearing the possibility of a rupture in the relationship, it is usually in this initial phase that some helpers are approached as a desperate bid to prevent a split taking place. The carer needs to listen attentively to the person's perception of the marriage as a whole, and to invite mature reflection on its history. Clearly at this point there might well be the possibility of counselling the couple before final decisions are made; at the very least there may be an opportunity of helping them towards finding a clean break in the situation, if not a resolution of current difficulties.

2. *The intermediate phase*

This period is *ex post facto* to the separation, after the partner has gone. The remaining partner seeks help in dealing with the immediate aftermath of the separation. In other cases, the guilt experienced by the departing spouse can precipitate the need for a carer's support. Either way, feelings of anxiety, **depression**, anger and **guilt** may present themselves to the carer as well as understandable concerns for the financial and physical security of the person presenting, and of their children, especially when the departing spouse was the major 'breadwinner'. At some stage, the carer needs to bring up the subject of *personal responsibility*. How far is the client taking their share of appropriate responsibility for the breakdown of the marriage? Do they seem to be taking too little or too much? Are they involved in the 'blaming game', attributing *all* the blame to their spouse *or* to themselves? The degree of guilt they experience is in direct proportion to the degree of blame they attribute to themselves; and this aspect of care is a vital one to be addressed (see Gough, 1990).

3. *The consolidation phase*

Other issues can present themselves in this later stage, such as coping with singleness and letting go of the past relationship. The issues of this phase may include finding new life apart from their spouse. This often takes place at the same time as the divorce, when the irretrievability of the earlier marriage is now finally accepted. This period can also be one of extraordinary growth, as hidden potential is uncovered and released. Former compromises and accommodations made in order to satisfy the needs of the previous partner no longer apply, and there is sometimes a sense of relief – even excitement – at the prospect of these old limitations being withdrawn. The sense of discovering a 'new me' (as in the case of Willy Russell's unforgettable *Shirley Valentine*) can become an important part of this phase.

4. The future phase

The carer is often approached at this stage with concerns about the future, especially when a new partnership is envisaged. At this time, unresolved issues surrounding any 'unfinished business' with their ex-partner may be high on the agenda. Natural fears regarding trust in an intended partner are usually directly related to the degree of pain experienced by the betrayal of a former spouse.

Other issues in this phase can relate to the complications arising out of the care of children. Recently, the old idea that divorce was better for the children than a bad marriage has been challenged. A small study (Cockett and Tripp, 1994) suggest that children from divorced parents suffer more from psychosomatic illness and perform less well at school, and can be affected by the divorce for life. Even so, many people seeking second or subsequent marriages have children by former spouses, either living with them or with their ex-partner. This can give rise to unavoidable contact with former husbands and wives because of access to their children (in itself appropriate and important for the children). But a great deal of conflict can arise out of such arrangements. While some couples find a reasonably amicable way of dealing with these occasional contacts, others see in them opportunities for revenge. They are an outlet for bitterness towards their former partners for the way they feel they have been treated. The children can become the unwitting and unwilling bridgeheads where their parents fight out old battles. Carers are often approached for practical advice in dealing with divorced partners who constantly act out in hostile ways. Where such children are very young, there is the unwelcome prospect of years of hassle ahead of them, until the children can make choices of their own concerning regular contact with their divorced parents.

Issues surrounding step-children can create further difficulties. Not every family can happily mould into a creative working alliance with the children of their parent's new partner. Much energy and understanding has to go into making the new combined family 'gel' and carers need to emphasize the importance of creative listening to the varying needs of all the children involved in the new family. As in most stages of separation, the ability to communicate openly and directly is an essential factor in tackling these and other issues for step-families (see the bibliography in Gough, 1992).

(e)   Many carers need a support system of consultants who are specialized in specific fields within the wider caring professions. This is true of those dealing with divorce. Such specialist provision can be found in:

Relate

For some time now, the former Marriage Guidance Council has been offering facilities either for couples together or for one of the partners to seek help in ending a relationship creatively rather than destructively. In many parts of Britain there are waiting lists to see Relate counsellors, evidence of the increasing workload that arises out of the social pressures surrounding divorce. However, the carer can refer people to Relate, and perhaps provide them with a 'holding operation' until an appointment is available. (Local offices are listed in the local telephone directory.)

Counselling agencies

Never has there been a time of greater provision of counselling agencies, and most carers will be able to find where these are at a local level. The British Association for Counselling (Tel: 01788 578328) provides enquirers with lists both of counselling organizations and of individual counsellors in local geographical areas. People who find themselves stuck in one of the phases of divorce are most likely to be helped by a professional counsellor, especially where depression is present.

Supervision

Most people who are professional carers have regular access to a supervisor with whom they can unpack their own specific concerns. For those in full- or part-time counselling, this is an essential requirement set by most accrediting agencies. However, this provision is by no means as widespread as it should be. Nurses, police, doctors, clergy and other helping professions would benefit from having a supervisory facility built into their contracts as a condition of service. Indeed, all those who care regularly for others, especially in this difficult area of divorce, would find it helpful to find supportive supervisory facilities (see *supervision*).

Finally, within the process of caring for those contemplating or experiencing divorce two specific areas need to be considered.

Immediate referral to the GP needs to be suggested where the carer becomes aware of psychosomatic symptoms present in those seeking their help. Issues such as **stress**, tension, loss of sleep, change in eating patterns and elements of **depression**, especially when suicidal thoughts (see **suicide**) are expressed, require specialist intervention. Divorce naturally gives rise to some of these symptoms. It need not be seen as a failure when medical advice is suggested.

The care and provision for the children of the marriage is often an all-important element in the presenting concerns of the carer's client, and indeed can be directly related to the precipitating symptoms mentioned above. Most frequently, concern for an adequate financial provision for the most vulnerable people in a divorce – the children – is high on the agenda. In the first instance, the local social services department is an immediate point of contact, as well as a resource for further information concerning legal rights and responsibilities.

(g) Gough, T. (1992) *Couples Parting: How to Find the Good in Goodbye*. London: Darton, Longman and Todd; Spanier, G. and Thompson, L. (1981) *The Aftermath of Separation and Divorce*. London: Sage Publications; Vaughan, D. (1990) *Uncoupling: Turning Points in Intimate Relationships*. New York: Vintage Books.

TONY GOUGH
(See also *couples, working with*)

Eating disorders

(a) This generic term encompasses a range of difficulties relating to food intake and body image. Broadly, these difficulties fall into two categories: anorexia nervosa and bulimia nervosa. Anorexia is characterized by the sufferer refusing food, or by allowing herself to eat only certain quantities of particular foods. This is frequently demonstrated in obsessive or ritualistic behaviour – for instance, peeling and slicing an apple in a specific and precise way before she can allow herself to eat it. Severe weight loss results, accompanied by a disturbance of body image; others see her as wasting away while she perceives herself as gross and overweight. There is an inability to recognize either her own nutritional needs or to perceive herself accurately.

The refusal of food can paradoxically be accompanied by a tremendous interest in it: in its purchase, its preparation and in feeding others while denying it to the self. Food becomes fascinating and all-consuming, without it being consumed by the sufferer. Physical symptoms can result, commonly the cessation or disruption of menstrual periods and the growth of a fine downy hair on the body in severe cases. Hyperactivity and a feeling of physical well-being accompanied by a lack of tiredness are sometimes evident. Anorexics may also abuse laxatives.

Bulimia nervosa is characterized by excessive and uncontrolled over-eating, followed by forced vomiting and/or fasting, and/or misuse of laxatives. Vast quantities of food can be consumed during these 'binges'; some bulimics select certain specific foods, others eat anything in sight. The bingeing usually takes place alone and without others knowing, and is often preceded by hoarding and building up a secret and hidden supply of food. Many bulimics appear to the world around them to eat normally and to be of an average weight and shape. As a result this is a problem many women live with for years, successfully maintaining a secret side to their lives.

To some extent the distinction I have drawn here is a false one. Many who suffer from eating disorders experience elements of both conditions: anorexics also binge, and bulimics also starve themselves. Clinical practice shows that some women move from a predominantly anorexic position towards bulimia, sometimes as a response to earlier treatment that the young anorexic may receive. It is as if the more visible symptom goes underground if not treated helpfully, the problem transferring itself to more hidden territory. Others seem to slide between the two poles of anorexia and bulimia.

As with other issues, estimating the extent of eating disorders is problematic, depending on definitions used and populations studied. It has been reckoned that as many as one woman in ten suffers from some form of eating disorder. It is certainly very familiar to counsellors, psychotherapists and psychologists, particularly those working in a young population: anorexia is most likely to first occur during adolescence and young adulthood. Men are much less likely to suffer from eating disorders, although it is currently estimated that up to 10 per cent of anorexics are male, and a few men are now being treated for bulimia.

(b)   Eating disorders can be variously presented to the caring professions. For instance, younger girls who are not eating may be taken by their parents to their general practitioner. The parents may perceive it as a problem, and she may not. She may insist that she is on a diet because she is too fat. They may fear anorexia. The line between dieting and anorexia may take some time to become clear, and this confusion is reflected in anorexia being popularly known as the 'slimmer's disease'. Enormous family tensions are created by one member refusing to eat, although as we shall see the reverse is likely to be true: that anorexia is a *response* to tensions as well as creating others. Similarly, teachers may become concerned if they notice a girl not eating and becoming visibly thinner. This situation of the sufferer not perceiving herself as suffering creates considerable difficulties for helpers as will be discussed later. If at any age weight loss becomes life-threatening (and a number of anorexics do die from the condition) then hospital admission may result.

Others present for help themselves. They may identify the problem as an eating disorder with a clear request for help with it. Such a request may be prompted by their own recognition that help is needed, or can be triggered by the concern of another. For example, a young bulimic woman in her twenties referred herself for counselling after her doctor had expressed considerable concern over the potential long-term damage to her body that could result from continual forced vomiting. An anorexic in her late teens similarly presented herself when she became involved in a significant relationship. She began to face the fact that her anorexia was a response to other difficulties, and was in itself a problem, not a solution.

Eating disorders may not initially be presented as the difficulty, either because the person is as yet unable to acknowledge this to themselves or the helper, or because another issue is genuinely causing more concern. In the first instance other symptoms may be presented: a generalized sense of depression or anxiety, a lack of self-confidence, low self-esteem, a sense of self-loathing or disgust, of feeling worthless, useless and ineffective. All these may be symptomatic of an eating disorder which may be so habitual that the person is unable to recognize its existence without help to do so. There is also an important point to note: depression can cause weight loss and lack of interest in food, but this is not an eating disorder. In this instance the depression needs treating, not the eating (see *depression*).

In the second instance, the eating disorder is acknowledged but is overtaken by concern for another issue, which may in turn have played a causative role in the development of the eating disorder. For example, a young woman presenting as a survivor of child sexual abuse was also anorexic. Working with the effects of the abuse also involved working with the eating difficulties but the primary focus was on the abuse (see *adult survivors of abuse*). Others can present conversely with eating patterns as the identified difficulty and the abuse emerges at a later stage. It should be noted that there is a link between abuse in childhood and the later development of eating disorders. This does not mean that all those with eating disorders have been abused, but studies indicate that this is the case for about 40 per cent of cases. It is a significant factor.

Many practitioners have commented on how anorexics dress, and this can be an indication where no verbal acknowledgement has been made. Large, baggy clothes may be the fashion of the time; or they may represent an attempt to disguise a body that is piteously thin, even if it may be experienced as grotesquely fat. Hiding the body in this way is very characteristic of anorexia, although not of bulimia, where the actions are hidden rather than the results.

(c) Describing eating disorders is relatively straightforward. Unravelling the causes is more controversial and complex, because ideas and theories abound and often conflict with one another. One set of theories explores how eating disorders can be understood as a reflection of disturbed and disturbing family dynamics. Food becomes a means of expressing emotions, of conveying messages and making statements. In this way the anorexic becomes the spokesperson, through their actions, for what cannot be said or acknowledged directly or in any other way. It may be easier for the family to focus on the individual's difficulty with food than to look at what is occurring elsewhere. Secrets are common in these families – as I have noted above, sexual abuse can be one such secret.

Many writers have explored and examined the family dynamics where one member has an eating disorder. Commonly families of an anorexic or bulimic tend to contain a confusing mixture of passivity, control, distance and apparent closeness, that is invasive rather than supportive. There is often a pattern of a passive, powerless mother and a distant but powerful father. Issues of power and control are very intensely present without being thought through, talked over or fought over. There is little ability to acknowledge or resolve conflict and the anorexic is rendered powerless and out of control. She can, however, control eating or not eating, and so gain some of the power that is denied her elsewhere.

However, family dynamics alone cannot explain the preponderance of girls and women with these disorders. It is here that understanding the social and political context is vital. Feminist clinicians and writers understand eating disorders as a way of protesting in a world in which it remains difficult for a woman to have a place in her own right. Women are seen as being caught in a myriad of conflicting expectations and demands, with little room for manoeuvre or legitimate protest. While on the one hand women are seen as carers and responsible for feeding others, on the other they are all too often denied the care they themselves need.

At the same time there is a pressure to be attractive and sexually desirable, which is nowadays equated with being thin. Women are faced not only with a vast array of food but with the social status that accompanies it. Eating well and eating sophisticated food indicates the financial success so prized in this society. Women are encouraged to cook delectable meals, but not to eat too much: the delectable recipes in magazines are often followed closely by the latest diet and latest fashions displayed by the thinnest models. Food is no longer functional. It is highly symbolic and as such is the focus for the conflict, confusion and unhappiness experienced by many women who struggle to find a place in the world, within themselves and in a relationship.

Anorexia can also be understood as a rejection of adult female sexuality. This understanding links with both the family and societal aspects discussed above. If a girl comes from a family where she is not validated and valued, in a society in which she struggles for a place, the adult world may not seem too attractive. Childhood may seem the lesser of the two evils. The very thin body of an anorexic does appear asexual and pre-pubertal, and as has been noted menstruation is likely to cease. This desire to feel and appear non-sexual can be seen as an extreme rejection of, and rebellion against, the stereotypical portrayal of a woman. In other instances it can ensure that the girl or adolescent is not able to leave home. This may reflect an anxiety to watch over and protect a parent. For example, an anorexic girl was the youngest in a family where her father was very violent to her mother. Her anorexia meant she could not leave home as her older siblings had done. If she left, no-one would be left to care for her mother, and she feared for her mother's life. Developing anorexia was an unconscious move on her part to exert some control over her own destiny, to protest – albeit silently – and to ensure she stayed with her mother.

(d) Eating disorders arise from intense and complex dynamics, and produce symptoms (particularly anorexia) that are powerful and anxiety-provoking. Eating disorders are tenacious. They have often been part of the person's life for a long time and have fulfilled an important function. They are not easily given up and the client is likely to experience deeply ambivalent and conflicting feelings in attempting to do so. Helping someone with an eating disorder is not a rapid process. Time and patience are needed.

Those who come for help face a struggle within themselves. It is important that the struggle does not also become a battleground between the helper and the client, in which they both fight for control without even seeing or acknowledging this. It is all too easy to repeat the family and societal pattern that led to the disorder, and become a controlling, repressive helper who denies the experience of the other.

The task is even more difficult if the girl or woman has been persuaded against her own wishes to seek help. This is more likely to happen with the younger age group, who may be brought or sent by parents or schools. Given that control is a central feature of eating disorders the helper may face an impossible task until the client herself decides she wishes to address her difficulties.

The responses of the caring professions to eating disorders vary greatly. Very judgemental language is frequently heard: anorexics are called 'difficult', 'manipulative', 'secretive' and 'devious' without apparently any awareness that this behaviour may reflect the circumstances that created the problem. Others try to understand the meaning of anorexia and bulimia, and recognize that tracking down the feelings and experiences that triggered this particular response is a difficult task, but an essential one if a caring response is to be given.

Anorexics whose weight becomes dangerously low and who are admitted to hospital frequently encounter an approach that responds simply to the eating and not to the underlying problems. The emphasis is on weight gain: this is the measure of successful treatment. Techniques such as not allowing a woman out of bed until her weight is at a certain level, or restricting her visits, not allowing her to get dressed in her normal day clothes and being under continual nurse surveillance are used. Whilst perhaps understandable in terms of life-threatening weight loss, if the causes are not tackled the situation is either likely to recur on discharge; or it can convert into bulimia. Hospital treatment takes away from the woman power and control over her own body and her own self, issues that are essential to the understanding of eating disorders and their effective treatment.

Approaches that see recovery as resting on weight gain alone are unlikely to have any long-term success, and may alienate the woman from seeking further help. This is a limitation that needs acknowledging. They may work in the short term as most women at some point have to capitulate to a system that is more powerful than they are. They have little choice but to eat at the required level. Although some women are clearly grateful in retrospect for interventions that may have been life-saving, others have experienced hospital treatment as invasive, aggressive, unfriendly and imposed without choice and explanation.

Some hospitals have specialized eating disorder units staffed by multidisciplinary teams in which treatment is more sophisticated, incorporating psychotherapy and counselling. However, provision is patchy and treatment can be limited, sometimes failing to understand the complexity of what it is attempting to treat.

Other approaches operate very differently, especially those developed from the feminist counselling and psychotherapy movement. The work undertaken by the London Women's Therapy Centre has been of particular significance in offering an alternative model of care and treatment. These approaches essentially aim to understand and work with the meaning of food to the woman within the context of a therapeutic relationship that is respectful, encourages dialogue and values the woman in her own right. This model appreciates the complexities that lie beneath the symptoms and recognizes issues such as control, power and abuse, actively working with them.

There is no pressure on the client to gain weight. Control both of this and of the overall process stays firmly with her. Food and eating are explored in terms of their significance to the client. It is understood that use of food can be a way of communicating what is otherwise in-communicable, and that the client may at a deep level be very needy. There is considerable emphasis on the importance of allowing time for a trusting relationship to develop, and in recognizing that, like food, this may be both wanted and feared; needed and rejected. There is a sensitivity to, and recognition of, the difficulty in giving up a familiar symptom that may have provided an identity and sense of safety and control. It is understood that as long as food is experienced as the one aspect of the self that can be contained, controlled and managed, then despair, conflictual feelings and unexpressed need can be kept firmly at bay. This all takes place within the context of an approach that takes account of women's position in the larger world and of the conflicts this engenders.

(e)   It is particularly important that women with eating disorders are able to locate the type of help that they feel comfortable with. Any practitioner who may be the first port of call for someone wanting help would be advised to have checked out the resources in their own locality. Similarly women can be encouraged to ask questions of poten-tial helpers themselves.

For those living in parts of the country where there are established Women's Therapy Centres (London, Leeds, Oxford, Birmingham) these are excellent resources for individual and group counselling and ther-apy, and may also offer specialized training and supervision in eating disorders. Some hospitals have eating disorder units, although the type of help on offer will vary enormously. Most college and university counselling services are very familiar with problems of this nature, although they can only be used by students attending those institu-tions. General practitioners may be a source of help and referral. Groups such as Anorexic Aid offer self-help on a group basis at a fairly low cost, and local areas may have their own **self-help groups**. Clinical psychology departments of the National Health Service may offer individual or group therapy.

(g)   Bruch, H. (1984) *Eating Disorders: Obesity, Anorexia Nervosa and the Person Within*. London: Routledge and Kegan Paul; Duker, M. and Slade, R. (1988) *Anorexia Nervosa and Bulimia: How to Help*. Buck-ingham: Open University Press; Orbach, S. (1986) *Hunger Strike*. London: Faber and Faber.

MOIRA WALKER

Faith differences

(a) In discussing faith differences several factors need to be distinguished. 'Faith' has first to be understood in relation to the concept 'religion', and then a distinction must be drawn between 'religion' and 'culture'.

Faith is our way of discerning and committing ourselves to those centres of value and power which exert the ordering forces in our lives. It is more profound and more personal than religion. As Wilfred Cantwell Smith (1979: 12) defines it, faith is

> an orientation of the personality, to oneself, to one's neighbour, to the universe, a total response; a way of seeing whatever one sees and of handling whatever one handles; a capacity to live at a more than mundane level; to see, to feel, to act in terms of a transcendent dimension.

In this sense it is possible to speak of 'the faith of the counsellors' (Halmos, 1965). Self-awareness about their own faith commitment on the part of members of all helping professions is necessary, because 'faith differences' are part of the normal and everyday interactions between helpers and clients.

(b) The concept of 'religion', on the other hand, stands for the personal commitment and serving of God (or in the cases of Jainism, Theravada Buddhism, and other non-theistic systems, of the 'Real', or some other focus of ultimate concern), in accordance with the commands found in accepted (canonical) sacred writings, and expounded by authoritative teachers within an organized body of believers (see *religious belief*). For example, **marriage** between practising and committed members of the Roman Catholic Church and of the Islamic community represents difficulties which have little or nothing to do with the faith of either party (which in essence may be remarkably similar). In this sense 'faith differences' are to be understood properly as religious differences.

Another distinction has to be drawn between 'faith differences' in the sense of 'religious differences', and the differences which arise from cultural manifestations of religion. 'Culture' here means the accumulated mass of traditions, values, attitudes and prejudices that individuals receive through parenting, schooling and general socialization. Culture has been called a 'silent language', which it is the special task of the social anthropologist to unearth and then to articulate clearly and objectively (see *cross-cultural awareness*). These cultural forces are normally hidden from the consciousness (in popular speech 'taken for granted') yet they deeply affect the ways in which people of different backgrounds interact with each other. Matters of grave importance in

the encounter of Westerners and people of African or Asian background, for example, arranged marriages, mourning customs, food
laws, the education of females, attitudes towards homosexuality and
the use of alcohol and other drugs, are often attributed to faith differences. These differences should be seen as differences in culture, rather
than as arising out of religion or faith. For example, Hindus, Muslims
and Sikhs are likely to share common attitudes to arranged marriages
and common expectations about the upbringing and education of their
daughters.

(c) Differences in faith and religion, rather than in cultural attitudes,
present themselves as a problem for the caring professions at the
following points: the upbringing of children and the role of the father
and the mother within the family; the possibility of marriage with a
member of another religious community, sexual morality and attitudes
towards what is deemed to be **sexually deviant**; **old age** and the
treatment of the elderly; attitudes towards the body which give rise to
special needs in nursing and medical care; concepts of sin, **guilt and
shame** and the related understandings of **forgiveness** and beginning
again; views of mental disorder and especially of depressive illness;
attitudes towards death and their consequences for handling grief and
bereavement. Special care needs to be paid to the faith element in each
of these areas.

(d) Consequently, it is important that carers approach people of
different faith backgrounds from their own with both an awareness of
the complexity of the issues involved and a steadfast refusal to make
any assumptions which have not been tested by in-depth interviews
and/or by first-hand knowledge of the life circumstances of their clients.
A Muslim man may have profound convictions about God and the
meaning of life and be a fully committed member of the Mosque, but
equally the expression of his faith may have little to do with the
organized aspects of Islam. Alternatively, although an émigré from a
Muslim country like Pakistan, he may never have attended the Mosque
with any frequency; and in the West remain only culturally and
sociologically a Muslim (avoiding pork perhaps, but probably consum-
ing alcohol). Likewise, a woman of Roman Catholic background may no
longer be observant, rarely attending Mass or saying her private
prayers; but she may, because of her upbringing in Ireland or southern
Europe, have deep-seated attitudes about contraception, abortion and
euthanasia which need to be taken seriously in a counselling or other
helping situation. Yet again, there are people who have adopted
another religion from the one in they were nurtured, but who in
moments of crisis may revert to cultural and religious patterns from

their past. Questions about faith, religion and culture should in any case be assumed to lie somewhere in the background of every individual and will frequently need to be addressed (see *religious belief; cross-cultural awareness*).

In many of these situations members of caring professions will find that their own value systems have to be held in abeyance, or, in the language used by scholars of religion, 'bracketed'. It is of paramount importance that the religious beliefs of clients be respected, and that nothing is done by helping agencies which may be construed as limiting freedom of religion. Article Nine of the European Convention on Human Rights (itself adopted from the Universal Declaration of Human Rights) insists that:

> Everyone has the right to freedom of thought, conscience and religion; this right includes freedom to change his religion, either alone or in community with others and in public or in private to manifest his religion or belief, in worship, teaching practice and observance.

The second part of the same Article makes it clear that:

> Freedom to manifest one's religion or belief shall be subject only to such limitations as are prescribed by law and are necessary in a democratic society in the interests of public safety, for the protection of public order, health or morals, or for the protection of the rights and freedoms of others.

This statement recognizes the possibilities of serious conflicts of interest in which members of the helping professions may get caught up. A religious group may claim that cannabis smoking or the involvement of minors in sexual activity is integral to their religious outlook; but these and similar matters clearly infringe normal standards of public order, health or morals. More difficult is the case of the young woman who does not wish to be party to an arranged marriage, or wishes to marry a member of another faith community against the wishes of her parents. Still more difficult is the case of young people of either sex who wish to convert to another religion against the wishes of their parents.

(e)   Although it is not possible to set out a simple set of procedures in inter-faith matters, or 'how-to' methods of counselling of people of other religions, for the major religious traditions, help may be sought in specific cases from national agencies or by approaching local leaders of religious communities. The indispensable handbook for this purpose is *Religions in the UK: A Multi-Faith Directory* (1993), which lists addresses and telephone numbers of religious groupings under regional headings. An immediate point of reference for more detailed enquiries is the Inter-Faith Network for the United Kingdom, 5–7 Tavistock Place, London WC1H 9SS (Tel: 0171 388 0008). There are also some 62 inter-faith councils in the UK, any of whom will be helpful in providing necessary contacts.

(g) Augsberger, D. (1986) *Pastoral Counselling Across Cultures*. Philadelphia: Westminster Press; Harris, I., Mews, S., Morris, P. and Shepherd, J. (eds) (1992) *Contemporary Religions: A World Guide*. Harlow: Longman; Weller, P. (ed.) (1993) *Religions in the UK: A Multi-Faith Directory*. Derby: The University of Derby in association with the Inter-Faith Network for the United Kingdom.

KENNETH CRACKNELL
(See also *fanaticism; racism and prejudice; religious belief*)

Families, working with

(a) The family as a focus for care, counselling and concern has grown significantly in importance during the past half century, both within the professional and voluntary sectors. Working with families now involves a spectrum of multidisciplinary approaches ranging from those which focus on the care of individual family members or sub-groups within the family, to those which focus on the family unit as a whole. Working with **couples**, working with parents and children, and working with family members undergoing **bereavement**, **divorce** and **post-traumatic stress** can all be considered types of family work, involving a considerable amount of energy and expertise on the part of professional and voluntary carers. Other approaches are concerned with the difficulties of the family group as a whole.

(b) A further means of discriminating between different ways of working with families relates to the type of intervention which is chiefly employed. We might therefore distinguish between family *counselling or therapy*; family life *education*; practical and material *service provision* for families; *information and advice*; the stimulation of **self-help** and **community** activities for families, and finally *political and social action* undertaken on behalf of and alongside families having particular social needs. Important as all of these are, most of these different approaches will not be considered here since many of them are addressed elsewhere in this book. Instead, the focus of this article will be the counselling and treatment of the family unit as a whole, usually known as family counselling or therapy.

(c)   Working with families effectively involves being as clear as possible as to the nature of the family group itself. There are several kinds of family structures that are now common in our society and which exist in varying degrees throughout Europe. Alongside the nuclear family of married parents with dependent children, we find extended family groups of kin living in single or neighbouring households; co-habiting couples, with or without dependent children; lone-parent households (see *single parents*); living-apart-together families (where the adults live separately but maintain a commitment to each other and to their children); step-families and **gay/lesbian** family groups. Single people, too, living alone or in households may expect and demand that their particular pattern of significant relationships are recognized as a pattern of family living. Our definition of family, therefore, needs to be complex and inclusive if it is to be relevant to those carers seeking to counsel the family group as a whole. In order to include all those who may wish to seek help from a family counsellor, our definition of family might therefore simply state that a family is 'an intimate domestic group, in which individuals are committed to one another by ties of blood, law, habitation or emotional bonds or a combination of all four' (Walrond-Skinner, 1993: 97).

(d)   Whatever the particular family type that is experiencing difficulties, we can approach that family as a unit, as an interacting whole and as a system of interpersonal relationships. Viewed in this way, the behaviour and experiences of each family member and the relationships between them affect every other member of the family group and the whole pattern of relationships. It is this total picture of family members and the relationships between them that is the family therapist's focus of concern.

A major advantage of taking this systemic approach to family problems is that we gain, through the theoretical framework which underpins it, a tool which makes some of our more counter-productive tendencies less easy to indulge. Viewing a family systemically invites us to begin to understand its members and the dynamics of their relationships in a holistic way rather than the either/or polarization between the victim/sufferer and the coping/functional members of the group. It invites us to exercise our curiosity rather than our censoriousness, because we are less sure of our ground when faced with the complexities of a system at work. In Bateson's (1972) famous phrase, we are drawn to focus upon 'the pattern that connects' and upon the 'between', which constitutes for Buber the essential heart of relationship. It also helps us take a broad view of the interplay between family dynamics and external social pressures and to understand how a family's own vulnerabilities may be greatly compounded by poverty,

homelessness, overwork, **redundancy** and **unemployment**, debt (see *money advice*), etc.

In particular, we are helped to focus on *process* rather than on *structure*. This enables us to move beyond our inclination to categorize families into types – some of which we then label as 'successful', 'healthy' or 'normal' and some of which we do not. Instead, we begin to understand that some of the *processes* that occur within family systems are more conducive to the change, growth and development required by a family's inexorable movement through the life-cycle; and others are more inclined to encourage stasis, stuckness and ultimately rigidity and death. Viewed in this way, we begin to be able to consider a family system as functional, not because of the way it has been *structured*, but in terms of the way it *operates* in trying to fulfil its emotional and psychological tasks. We can then begin to ask a variety of 'process' questions in relation to each of the family forms which we have just noted:

- can this family help its members to *attach* themselves to one another and achieve intimacy without fusion?
- can this family allow its members to let each other *go*, and achieve differentation without isolation?
- can this family develop a boundary between itself and the outside world that is both sufficiently firm and sufficiently permeable for the family to create an *identity* for itself, affording its members a sense of belonging, but allowing transactions to take place across the boundary with the wider community?
- can this family foster in its members a belief in their own *value* and an ability to acquire the necessary knowledge and skill to move on to the next phase of their life-cycle?
- can this family tolerate *differences* in age and gender, role, temperament and style?
- can this family *handle conflict* without detouring it through a third party, who then becomes the scapegoat or problem carrier for the group as a whole?
- can this family provide *role models* that 'work' for the culture in which the family is embedded?
- can this family *communicate* and *problem solve* effectively, making use of new information, skill and outside help as necessary?
- can this family enable its members *to contribute* to the well-being of society, through the creation of new members and/or new understanding of what the world is about?
- can this family generate *coping strategies* adequate to manage the stress of accidental and transitional crises?

- can this family experience itself as *having its own place and its own purpose* beyond the more immediate tasks of physical and psychological survival?

This move away from the treatment of the individual in isolation to the treatment of the family as a group has significantly altered the ways in which clinicians working in every setting – medical, psychiatric, social welfare and relational – understand both diagnosis and treatment. Even where clinicians continue to focus on the individual, this focus has been subtly changed by our greater understanding of the dynamic relationship of the individual with his or her psycho-social context – primarily his or her family – and also the wider environmental context in which the family group is itself embedded.

This systemic understanding of relationships has also greatly influenced the way in which marriages and other partnerships are offered help. Couples are much more frequently counselled jointly and where they are seen separately, a 'multidirectional partiality' on the part of the counsellor helps to maintain the therapeutic focus on the couple's *relationship system* (see *couples, working with*). The advent of conciliation and other mediation approaches has been made possible because of the systemic understanding of family members' interrelated needs which continue to exist and which need addressing throughout and beyond the process of family break-up.

Family therapy or counselling is an effective and economical way of helping families, both for people who come for help with obvious *relationship difficulties* (difficulties within a *partnership* or between *parents and children*) as well as for those who are complaining of some form of emotional distress that appears, on the face of it, simply to 'belong' to *that individual* and to no-one else. Despite the sincere intentions and the considerable body of expertise that has been accumulated over the years by individual therapists and counsellors, it remains the case that individual counselling often has a detrimental effect upon that person's significant relationships. On the other hand, by offering help to the family as a whole, the pastoral carer or counsellor is able to act 'preventatively' upon people who would not normally enter the counselling situation; and indeed 'retro-actively' upon others who continue to carry within them the scars of unhealed wounds, whether or not they availed themselves at an earlier stage of counselling or other pastoral help.

The logical, practical manifestation of adopting a systemic approach – the gathering together of the family group as a whole to reflect upon, engage with and try to resolve its difficulties – is in itself a powerful tool of change. It releases the potential for healing and change that lies within the family itself. This energy is often released in a quite extraordinary and powerful way by the simple invitation on the part of the helping person, whether clergy or lay, to come together *as a family* with the outsider helper. It is out of this joining together of the family system as a whole and the outside helping agent that new ways forward are opened up for people to talk and to understand and to change their pattern of relationships.

Working with the family group as a whole poses the worker with a variety of challenges, many of which have been described in detail in the wide-ranging literature that has accumulated over the last 40 years. Most fundamental of all is the way in which the worker must try to engage with the family as a whole rather than simply with the individual family members who are motivated to change. Here, the worker will be helped by remembering that a systemic relationship also exists between the expressions of motivation and reluctance exhibited by different family members. Often a direct approach on the part of the worker to a family member who has been said by another to be implacably opposed to the whole idea reveals instead a person who is only too willing to come and tell his or her own side of the story! Practical considerations must obviously be taken into account when trying to engage the family as a whole, and meetings need to be planned at times when those at work and those at school can most easily attend. The family counsellor needs to make a good relationship with each family member in his or her own right, including children and older family members. The counsellor should not be trying to achieve 'neutrality' or impartiality in her approach but the more demanding stance of 'multidirectional partiality' whereby the family recognizes that she is on the side of the family *itself*. This means in practice that she will be fully engaged and committed to each 'side' of the conflict and to every viewpoint held, but within a context of overall fairness.

Most family therapists make use of the concept of the family life-cycle (Carter and McGoldrick, 1989). This provides a compelling framework for understanding the way in which the family group develops over time, the different tasks which it is normally required to perform and the moments of vulnerability to specific kinds of difficulty which it may experience. The family counsellor can usefully become aware of the kinds of developmental crisis which many families will experience, particularly at those moments when new family members join the system and leave, through death, divorce or reaching adulthood. These moments have been described respectively as crises of 'accession' and 'dismemberment' and are often occasions when a family seeks help. The life-cycle framework has been criticized recently because of its normative tendencies and because it may reduce the perceived importance of macro-social influences such as poverty, racism and gender and their effect upon the family's ability to function satisfactorily.

The length of treatment offered varies according to the particular 'school' of family therapy used. Over the last half-decade a range of different schools or approaches to family therapy have developed including a variety of brief therapy approaches. Here, families might be seen for only one or two interviews, the aim of treatment being some highly focused relational change and/or symptomatic relief. These approaches can be highly effective within their own terms and evaluated against their own objectives (Cade, 1993).

Schools of family therapy can be broadly divided between those which are based on a psychoanalytic approach and those which adopt a communication or behavioural approach. In the psychoanalytic approach the family is viewed as a single psycho-social unit and the diagnostic emphasis is on understanding the psycho-social interior of the family group. The individual's symptoms are understood as entry points to understanding the family pathology. The nature of the symptoms and the choice of symptom bearer are significant pointers to the nature of the family's difficulties. For example, a couple who are experiencing severe sexual difficulties may find that their adolescent daughter expresses this anxiety through her promiscuous behaviour. Solvent abuse by a child may be an expression of the hidden, but deadly, hostility between the parents and the younger generation or within the parental partnership. The symptom and symptom bearer often create a focus for the family's anxiety or anger, and in so doing deflect energy and attention away from underlying conflict in the family. The family's history as an interacting group over several generations means that difficulties which are feared as being too dangerous to face (such as violence, incest, abuse or death) are held in the family's shared unconscious as family secrets and avoided themes. They are expressed through the symptoms of individuals and through jointly-owned family myths. These both conceal and reveal the hidden events of the past, which continue to determine the current interactions of the family group in a covert way.

The family is judged to be dysfunctional to the extent to which family members react to one another in terms of the projections, displacement and transference from past relationships on to the present. For example, a couple, especially in the early stages of their relationship, may respond to each other 'as if' they were a parent, former partner or other significant person and not the real and different human being that is actually now present in this new relationship. Likewise a parent may reject a child because he or she is not like the child he or she is actually replacing. Again, parents may seek to gain from their children the affirmation and even the nurture that they failed to receive from their own parents. In so far as these needs are unacknowledged, they remain a continuous source of potential conflict in the next generation. Some writers speak of the interrelated family transference by which everyone transfers on to everyone else the feelings and expectations of other significant relationships, thus severely limiting the possibility of forming authentic, functional relationships with the real members of the family. (See also Boszormenyi-Nagy's (1986) concept of relational ethics.)

Communication patterns have been the subject of a considerable amount of study because when the family is understood and conceptualized primarily as a social system, it is the communication that *occurs between* family members that needs to be the chief focus of interest and concern. For example, work has been done on the ways in which family members place each other in 'double binds' whereby the individual is progressively disqualified by being the recipient of manipulative and contradictory messages. The scapegoating of one or more family members may occur in this way, or through the election of one person by the family group as a whole to carry this role, Conflict is thus detoured and conflict resolution becomes impossible. Various other roles may be taken on by family members, creating a rigid structure, inflexible to changing needs and circumstances. One person may be identified as the 'patient' or problem carrier and, even though cherished rather than scapegoated, may similarly obstruct the resolution of conflict and the developmental tasks of the family. A common defensive strategy is the formation of triangular relationships, whereby two family members draw in a third to act as a buffer or a go-between. For example, either a child or an elderly parent may become the third party between the spouses. This third party often experiences considerable stress while the couple are shielded from open conflict, and also prevented from developing and resolving their relationship.

Difficulties often arise from the way in which boundaries within the family are handled, as well as the boundary between the family and the outside world. Both boundaries may be either too rigid or too permeable. For example, the boundary between the generations needs to be flexible but firm. This enables parents to function as parents but also as a sexual partnership. It allows children to function according to the developmental stage that they have reached and avoid the confusion engendered by incestuous sexual relationships. Likewise if the boundary between the family and the outside world is too rigid, there will be very little communication, support or stimulation for the family. If it is too permeable, the family will find it difficult to retain its sense of identity as a family, overwhelmed as it may become by the demands and distractions of the outside world. The family's ability to remain simultaneously cohesive and adaptive (to be stable and able to change) determines the extent to which it can tackle the tasks of family life.

Increasing knowledge of the complex ways in which families communicate through systems, their behaviour patterns and the metaphors that they use to make known distress has given rise to a variety of sophisticated methods of helping families in difficulties, including the strategic, structural 'Milan' and solution-focused methods (e.g. Minuchin and Fishman, 1981; Boscoli, 1994).

(g) Skynner, A. C. R. (1976) *One Flesh, Separate Persons*. London: Constable; Treacher, A. and Reimers, S. (1994) *User-Friendly Family Therapy*. Oxford: Blackwell; Walrond-Skinner, S. (1988) *Family Matters*. London: SPCK.

SUE WALROND-SKINNER

Fanaticism

(a) The term 'fanaticism' is derived from the Latin *fanum*, a sacred place, a temple, which gave rise to the adjectival form *fanaticus* to describe a person who had been put into a raging enthusiasm by the deity or spirit of that temple or sacred place. English usage always attaches a pejorative meaning to the word fanaticism, stressing either the condition of being possessed by a demon, and therefore engaging in frenzied and irrational activity, or the single-minded propagation of schemes and ideas (ideology) which arise from excessive and mistaken zeal, especially (although not exclusively) in religious matters. A nineteenth-century definition reads: 'Fanaticism is Enthusiasm enflamed by Hatred' (Isaac Taylor, *History of Fanaticism*, 1843). It is, however, worth noticing that the abbreviated form of 'fanatic' – 'fan' – carries only neutral and beneficial overtones, as in 'a motor racing fan' or 'the Elvis Presley fan club'.

(b) In counselling it is essential to distinguish 'fanaticism' from both 'fundamentalism' and 'bigotry'. Fundamentalism is the religious or quasi-religious response to the challenges posed by modern cultures – challenges that are marked characteristically by preferences for secular rationality, the right of individual judgement in matters of faith and the adoption of religious tolerance with its accompanying tendency toward relativism. It is, however, possible to hold fundamentalist or traditionalist views without engaging in irrational or excessively zealous ways of expressing them. The more usual attitude on the part of

traditionalists is best described as bigotry: the obstinate and unreason-
ing attachment to a creed or opinion or party in the face of all contradictory evidence or alternative views. Some forms of fundamentalism,
however, are extremely militant, and do merit the description 'fanatical'. French (1990) has interpreted fanaticism as an 'adversarial dynamic' having four characteristics: participants are normally in late
adolescence or young adulthood, when ideological absolutes may have
the strongest appeal: such ideological absolutes are legitimized by a
religious institution and reinforced with the authority of some form of
ultimate spiritual sanction (excommunication, damnation); orders and
directives from the supposed higher authority are unquestioningly
obeyed; such activity is normally publicly acknowledged; and arrest or
martyrdom may be courted as offering a platform for 'prophetic utter-
ance', in terms of denunciation of the adversary and its world-view.

(c) Fanaticism has been accounted for in several ways. It has been
seen as a 'disease of the religious emotions'. Murisier (1901) believed
that some social element was implicit in an individual's finding a sense
of unity. In the fanatic the social element is wildly exaggerated. The
fanatics' sense of unity is obtained by their identifying with a given
group or community and accepting unreservedly its teaching and
demands. The urgency of this need for stability is reflected in hostility
shown towards dissidents and the energetic quest for converts, who
themselves must show the same marks of the fanatical personality.

More recently, developmental psychology has focused upon **adolescence** in interpreting the origins of fanaticism. Lifton (1961) has
described adolescence as a time of 'strong enthusiasms, a marked
tendency toward emotional polarization, of great ideological receptivity
and of maximum experiential intensity'. Lifton used the terms 'shared
narcissism' and 'totalism' to encapsulate the experiences which lead to
the creation of the fanatical personality. Erikson (1964) also saw the
period of adolescence as decisive in creating fanatical religious personalities: 'religions offer the adolescent . . . rites and rituals of confirmation as a member of a totem, clan or a faith, a nation or class, which
henceforth is to be his superfamily'. Fowler (1981) affirms 'henotheistic
faith' (the single-minded pursuit of one ideal) as a pattern of belief and
identity-seeking in which an individual 'invests deeply in a transcending center of faith and value'. If not correctly handled by teachers and
counsellors this investment, which is most likely to take place in
adolescent and young adult stages of faith, may develop into what
Fowler calls 'fetishism', a focusing on 'an extremely narrow and exclusive center' of value and power. From the point of view of developmental
psychology, fanaticism is fetishism in an active and aggressive form. In
its benign forms fetishism produces the single-minded and unswerving

'fan' with a lifelong devotion to Chelsea Football Club or to model railways.

From the point of view of other social theorists, fanaticism must be interpreted in terms of power and ideology. All societies need symbolic constructions and models of their world, both for self-legitimization and for the maintenance of the identity of the individual within a given society (see Berger, 1969). Forms of social organization in which the older integrative symbolic systems are perceived to be breaking up, and where 'cognitive dissonance' is setting in, pose enormous problems to individuals who sense 'loss of identity'. The growth of fundamentalism in both political and religious forms takes place when radical questioning of an older 'taken-for-grantedness' within the belief system becomes possible. The greater the shock to the prevalent world-view the greater the intensity of the response which needs to hit out at the new and the strange, because 'perfect fear casts out love'. The immediate political consequences are seen in struggles for cultural and religious autonomy, stressing the right of a group to its own specific mode of development and organization. Fundamentalistic demands for autonomy lead to tension and then to open conflict between cultural and religious minorities and the central political authorities. In such situations tradition, prejudice, stereotype and mythologized history together form a prevalent ideology which allows no criticism or self-questioning. It is within these situations of rapid social change, discernible in all parts of the world, that the condition known as fundamentalism has arisen. (See Marty and Appleby, 1991–93.) Personalities with the psychological needs already described fit perfectly into the framework of the adversarial dynamic outlined by H. W. French above.

For these reasons it is normally the case that there is a religious or quasi-religious element in extremist activity, which may find expression in, for instance, Catholic or Protestant terrorism in Northern Ireland, or in Gush Emunim, the 'bloc of the faithful' in Israel, the Jama'at al-Ikhwan al-Muslimin, the 'Muslim Brotherhood', in Egypt or the Hizbullah, the 'party of God', elsewhere in the Middle East. It has always been possible to interpret fascism, nationalism and Marxist Leninism as substitute religions which have demonstrated the same traits as churches and sects. Men and women have been prepared to die for these and similar beliefs because they function as transcending centres of faith and value, the loss of which would mean loss of identity and self-worth.

(d)   In the nature of the case, fanatics do not present themselves to members of the caring professions for help with their condition. Since their central problems turn upon the nature of the belief system or ideology which they have embraced, the main brunt of dealing with fanaticism falls on educators and opinion-formers, and involves the careful analysis of mistaken world-views and the exposing and correcting or errors in falsely mythologized history.

Yet it is essential that people involved in pastoral and other forms of care are prepared to handle the elements of fanaticism which may be incidental to other forms of behaviour (see *obsessive compulsive behaviour; racism and prejudice; religious belief*). Care of the fanatical personality should be directed towards developing a trust that reflects upon new ideas, and the acceptance of a different outlook that need not undermine personal identity. Clients should be helped to see how their previously strongly-held convictions may be taken forward into a fresh outlook. This must be felt as a development of the previous conviction, elements of which are retained in order to recreate and reconstruct a new world-view. The aim should be towards 'open personal change' (Lifton, 1961: 462) when new ethical and behavioural possibilities emerge. One essential element in counselling practice with such people is to enable reflection upon personal narrative, remembering that the systematic ambiguity of a story is a far more appropriate vehicle than the analysis of a set of propositions for the search for coherence and identity.

In the case of religious fanaticism, advance to a new coherence and self-awareness may take place through reconsideration or rediscovery of those scriptures which may have been part of the development of the original fanaticism. Thus a Hindu fanatic might be encouraged to discover this verse from Bhagavad Gita XI, 55: 'have no hatred for any being at all: for all who do this shall come to me'; the Muslim fanatic, from the Qur'an: 'Do not strut about the land with insolence; surely you cannot cleave the earth or attain the height of the mountains in stature' (Surah 17.37); the Buddhist fanatic, from the Itivuttaka, verse 27: 'None of the means employed to acquire religious merit has a sixteenth part of the value of loving kindness'; the Jewish fanatic, the words of the Prophet Micah: 'do justice, love mercy, and walk humbly with your God' (Micah 6:8) and the Christian fanatic: 'though I give my body to be burned, and have not love, it profits me nothing' (1 Corinthians 13:3). Perfect love then casts out fear and enables a new universalizing form of faith response to other people and other ideas.

In the case of the many political forms of fanaticism, no appeal can be made to 'scripture', and usually extremists are impervious to the reinterpretation of tradition towards any 'conjunctive' or 'open' position. Members of groups like those involved in the Irish struggle, or the militant groups in the Middle East, or the Hindu, Sikh or Buddhist extremists in India and Sri Lanka, need to discover the 'expulsive power of a new affection' before they can move into fresh attitudes. Since this must also be a 'transcending centre of faith and value', capable of affirming identity needs of the individual and offering a new realm of meaning and commitment, members of helping and caring professions must recognize that they here move into the area of pastoral care normally offered by ministers of religion (see *faith differences*).

All the above considerations apply to followers of new religious movements (often called cults), whom some regard as 'brainwashed' and in need of 'deprogramming'. People who offer care are sometimes approached by parents anxious about the 'fanatical' behaviour of their otherwise sensible son or daughter. Extreme caution should be exercised about claims made in this area, because in these cases 'fanatical' usually means merely committed and enthusiastic behaviour in regard to an ideology of which the older person profoundly disapproves. Only in rare cases are the younger people involved in an 'adversarial dynamic' (the David Koresh commune at Waco, Texas in 1993 was a rare example of such a group). At no time, therefore, do followers of new religious movements need the 'shock therapy' offered by the 'deprogrammers', which is often suggested by 'anti-cult' agencies. Rather they need the friendly support and guidance of people who are prepared to let them tell their stories and then to build on their faith commitment, thus helping them grow into a wider outlook. This wider outlook may then include reconciliation with the estranged elders.

(g) Fowler, J. W. (1981) *Stages of Faith: the Psychology of Human Development and the Quest for Meaning.* San Francisco: Harper and Row; French, H. W. (1991) *A Study of Religious Fanaticism and Responses to It.* Lewiston, NY: Edwin Mellen Press; Lifton, R. (1961) *Thought Reform and the Psychology of Totalism.* New York: Norton.

KENNETH CRACKNELL
      (See also *racism and prejudice; religious belief*)

Fees and gifts

(a) Charging a fee for a caring service between one individual and another is an emotionally significant and potentially difficult issue. The receipt of payment is often considered to be in conflict with the values involved with care. The giving of gifts can express indebtedness and gratitude, two allied but different feelings.

(b) Payment for care from the NHS or social services in this country, normally in the form of National Insurance and taxation, has been so distanced from the receipt of it that the two are effectively separated. The growth of medical provision based on insurance schemes has modified this picture of late. Nevertheless, when working within a caring organization it is possible, more in the past than at present, to stand aside from money matters and so make them remote and vague. Charging a fee-for-service directly with the client raises many issues that may affect the relationship between carer and client.

(d) Because I am a counsellor using a psychodynamic framework, and because the topic is general and applies to many different situations, readers will need to adapt and apply what is said here to their own various situations. The dynamics of fees are different from those of gifts, so they are considered separately.

There is an obvious conflict of values in caring for someone and charging a fee for such care. 'For love or money?' catches the opposition concisely even though such an opposition may be false. How can wanting to help people be compatible with taking money from them? Is it possible to care in the context of money? Perhaps most of us are susceptible to feeling considerable emotional discomfort, even distaste, in dealing openly with money matters in the caring context; and the philanthropic roots of many agencies of care can add to this. Freud wrote more than 80 years ago 'Money questions will be treated by cultured people in the same manner as sexual matters, with the same inconsistency, prudishness, and hypocrisy' (1913). Even the recent blatant thrusting of business policy and language to the centre of care delivery (e.g. patients are now consumers or customers, doctors are purchasers and other medical services are providers) is not likely to change radically or quickly the attitude and values of those actually doing the caring rather than managing it. The clash in values remains.

Our rational selves can see clearly that money is the necessary means of maintaining a service to others whether by an organization or by an individual, but we would often nevertheless prefer to avoid the conflicts and tensions it arouses. Primitive feelings around narcissism, entitlement and competitive striving are aroused by charging for care or relating with another. What am I worth? Am I selling myself, prostitute-like? Does charging in the context of a human relationship make my offering pseudo or counterfeit? Without fair exchange may the client feel, or be made to feel, subordinate, dependent or inferior to the giver? Out of debt, out of danger. Such primitive feelings usually produce splits in the way situations are defined so that false oppositions are set up such as self-interest versus client interest; or being liked versus being effective; or being professional versus being 'in trade'. Under the sway of such thinking it is difficult to define helping another in terms of a mutual benefit model in which both parties gain. This in reality is the only stable way of sustaining delivery of care. Thus the issue of money in the caring context makes demands on our grasp of reality, on our sense of self-worth and on our capacity to face and deal with primitive and conflicting feelings in adaptive ways.

An explicit policy about money, clear in both the helper's and the clients' minds, is needed to confront such conflicts. According to Barker (1982) the policy should address at least the following questions: How much is the charge? Is the charge for time with the helper or other factors? How is the fee to be paid? Are the fees based on a flat rate or on a sliding scale? Is there a charge for the first or assessment interview before an agreement is reached about continued contact? Can the fees be raised or lowered during the course of treatment? Are payments from third parties acceptable? If the client cannot pay by an agreed time, how long can he or she have before paying? What will the carer do if payment is not made? Are charges made for talking on the telephone? Are charges made when the carer communicates about the client with other professionals on behalf of the client? What is the best way to bill and collect from clients? Should charges be higher for more desirable times such as evenings? Are charges made for missed appointments? What about seeing some clients for free?

As Barker suggests, there is no right answer to these questions. Practitioners need to think through each question and decide for themselves what their policy will be. This will make consistency more likely and help resist the impulse to bend the rules to suit the circumstances of an individual client. Such a clear policy enables the carer to be more secure and detached about money matters, which itself helps to avoid money becoming a continuous background issue that interferes with the work with the client.

When is money first mentioned? A potential client needs to know from the first contact what the charge will be for the first session, how and when it is paid, how long the session will last. Money policy and any further discussion about it should be made explicit in the first session because this can be an important part of the client's decision to make further appointments or not. It is tempting to avoid doing this under the pressure of the immediate discussion of presenting issues. Subsequent misunderstandings are less likely if this is done, however, and it forms a secure basis for future work.

Setting the fee depends on a number of considerations such as the type of clientele one hopes to reach, the prevailing rates for comparable services in the area, overhead costs, the cost of living in the area of the practice and the counsellor's own reputation and scarcity in particular areas of expertise. The counsellor needs to find the optimum fee to charge to help reach financial goals and still appeal to a large enough group of people to maintain a stable practice. Whenever a fee is charged for anything, some people are unable or unwilling to pay, and high fees clearly reduce the number of potential clients. On the other hand, low fees are likely to be interpreted as indicating that the counsellor is less well trained or somehow second-rate. It is often tempting for beginners to express their doubt about their ability or competence by setting a fee considerably lower than the norm.

The arguments for and against a sliding scale for fees are still debated and no clear resolution is in sight. Those advocating a sliding scale hold the view that each client should be treated as an individual; and that an inability to pay for services should not preclude his or her receipt of the needed service, as this is contrary to the basic values of the caring professions. Those who advocate charging a fixed fee argue that a sliding scale is discriminatory, forcing those able to pay to subsidize those with less resources. They also point out that the sliding scale interferes with the counsellor–client relationship in its initial stages more than does a fixed policy, because some sort of means testing is necessary to establish the level of fees. This can, paradoxically, make money more of an issue than when fees are fixed. Many referrals come from former clients and it can be difficult to justify charging a different amount from what is expected.

There is a convention in professional services that a delay is to be expected between the receipt of a service and paying for it. There is something uncomfortable about the client handing over cash at the end of a session in which sensitive personal issues have been considered. A common practice is to bill at the end of each month with an expectation that the full or partial payment will be made within a prescribed length of time. Giving a statement personally to the client, with or without envelope, is probably the most effective way of assuring payment and of making the double-sided nature of the contract between helper and client explicit. Cheques are probably preferable to cash because they are more easily recorded and the temptation to pocket the cash and spend it before it is fully accounted for is more easily resisted. In organizations such as Relate the billing and/or collection of fees is often done through the administrative staff, so making clear that it is the organization that receives the money, not the individual helper.

Charging for missed appointments is another contentious issue. A rule widely applied is that a charge will be made for appointments cancelled less than 24 hours ahead of time, unless the reasons are compelling to make an exception. In counselling, a judgement needs to be made about the underlying reasons for cancellation – is it part of a pattern, is it quite exceptional, is it linked to a difficult session last time or ambivalence about coming at all? Nevertheless, the principle of consistency and clarity in the helper–client agreement still applies as a background commitment. As an example of these issues, a client was offended by not being charged for a missed counselling session because she felt her freedom to opt out at will was curtailed by a sense of obligation to the counsellor. This was removed if she paid for the session, come what may.

These then are some of the issues that arise in charging fees for a service in the helping professions. Gifts are another matter. The receipt of care often arouses the feeling of gratitude and the wish to express this in some way. It has been suggested that the capacity of a mother to receive 'gifts' from her baby is a significant contribution towards the baby's growing sense of power and sense of self-worth. Likewise to be able to receive a gift graciously is empowering for the client and satisfying for the helper. Nevertheless, it is wise to be aware that gifts are notorious in their capacity to attract and express a whole range of complex and contradictory feelings in the giver and the receiver. An uncomfortable feeling of indebtedness in the client can be discharged by a gift and the receiver may well be aware of this. A gift can be a way of insinuating the giver into the life of the receiver, or may be a bid for a more intimate relationship than a professional one. One counsellor working in an agency with a difficult client was made to feel attacked by a personal gift of money at the end of counselling. It was agreed between them that it should go towards the agency in general rather than to the counsellor herself. In summary, it helps to be aware that the meaning of gifts is likely to be complex and it helps the caring process if the meaning is responded to rather than the gift alone.

(g) Barker, R. L. (1982) *The Business of Psychotherapy*. New York: Columbia University Press; Krueger, D. W. (1986) *The Last Taboo*. New York: Brunner/Mazel; Syme, G. (1994) *Counselling in Independent Practice*. Buckingham: Open University Press.

ROGER ELLIS

Forgiveness of sin

(a) 'Forgiveness' is release from sin, the experience of reconciliation after confession. It is thus a value word, dependent on some religious or philosophical framework, in this entry largely a Christian one. Forgiveness relieves someone from feelings of guilt. Biblical metaphors are of 'covering', 'letting go' and 'lifting up' as the gift of God. The last metaphor is used also of release by human beings of each other.

'Sin' is essentially a theological word to describe the cause and result of the separation of humanity from God. It is taken from a military metaphor, from the action of a soldier throwing a stone in ancient battle, and missing the target, and so means 'falling away from the right way'. In the Old Testament myth in Genesis 3, the origin of sin is attributed to the failure of the first man and woman to obey the fairly minimal requirements laid down by God. In the story they had failed to trust him, and by eating from the tree had become conscious, and able to distinguish good from evil, erroneously believing that they had themselves become God. The myth, in granting that they were able to obey or not, allows that they were responsible for their actions, and at least to some extent free, and that they were therefore persons.

'A sense of sin' is either a general awareness of being less than one could be, or an increasing awareness of being a sinner; if the sense is of having done wrong and of deserving punishment, it is called 'attrition'; if of having done damage to the relationship with God or another, 'contrition'.

'Guilt' is of three kinds: legal, moral and relational. The first is defined by the courts, the second by the moral standards of a religion or people, the third by relationships. In the two latter meanings, guilt is the feeling of attrition, of having sinned and of fearing the likely consequences, especially in the third, the breakdown of important relationships.

'A sense of guilt' is the unreliable feeling which lurks unevenly in the conscious mind of having sinned. It is notoriously inaccurate as a gauge, since unethical behaviour is sometimes attended by no guilt at all; while the depressed, especially those brought up in strongly moral and religious households untempered by love, feel guilt out of all proportion to their 'offences' (see *depression; guilt and shame*).

Far more accurate is the truthfulness of the unconscious mind, where genuine sin, the inner knowledge that the person has betrayed both God and others, evokes genuine guilt.

There are two conditions for forgiveness in the gospel, penitence and a readiness to forgive. Penitence is the attitude of mind of wanting to turn away from sin to a new relationship with God and others. A readiness to forgive is very hard, and sometimes after serious injury is such a struggle that only the hope of grace to forgive some day can be grasped. It still remains an essential for the full experience of forgiveness.

(b) In the Church, a worshipping soul lives within an atmosphere of forgiveness. On the spiritual way, Christian souls grow in awareness, without guilt, of falling far short of what they might be, resting on the grace and love of God to help them to journey towards holiness. They grow in penitence, and therefore acquire a new status as a forgiven sinner.

In a post-Christian society which has lost this prior emphasis on forgiveness, many cannot take this for granted, and would rather not talk about sin at all. They perceive it as being about guilt and condemnation, and therefore more to do with imprisoning than releasing. This is a pity, because people do behave badly, they think they should not have done so and they often feel the need to confess and be forgiven.

Such a person may seek out a priest to talk to. It may then emerge that there are other problems of which the sin is only the presenting story, the best way the person can find of opening up a difficult subject. The need for confession and absolution may still be there, but the primary task will be to listen, and to accept and love and understand the person.

It is different when persons are quite consciously approaching God to confess their sin, whether at the beginning of their spiritual journey, or as they progress and grow in contrition. They will then be discovering the inner truth about themselves in the context of a guilt-free and growing awareness of the love of God for them.

(c)   Why 'sin' and not some less emotive word? It is difficult to find a better concept which combines awareness of behaving badly with personal responsibility. To take a common enough example, a husband shouts at his wife, accusing her of infidelity and cruelty to himself only to find that his suspicions are unwarranted. He feels responsible and is in fact convicted of sin. Whatever the more complicated dynamics of the situation, he feels shame at having given vent to his feelings, fears that he may have damaged their relationship (concern for himself) and that he has maligned his wife and caused her unnecessary pain (concern for her). His guilty feelings as he travels home to seek forgiveness are a mixture of anxiety about the likely outcome of their encounter, with a sense of personal distress at his jealousy and stupid behaviour. He needs her word of forgiveness to free him from his guilt and sin.

If the wrongdoing is of wider application, against society, and because of the ramifications and effect of even the mildest wrongdoing also against God, then the only way to find relief is by owning behaviour and seeking forgiveness.

(d)   Conveying the forgiveness of God is at the heart of the Christian religion. Islam does not believe humans capable of the good life, and believes where there is failure that Allah is merciful. Among Hindus, the spiritual person forgives because what another does to him or her is a matter of indifference.

In Christianity, the history of the ministry of reconciliation reveals very different emphases through the ages, but the fourfold pattern of the process is clear: self-examination, confession, penance and absolution.

The struggle to know the truth in self-examination, if at first conducted in private, is almost always assisted by **counselling**. The counselling is itself a process of confession, a sharing of the truth as the client believes it to be. Penitents will not feel forgiven if they confess what really needs to be accepted; so they must first become strong enough, and come to know themselves before they can know what there is to confess. In counselling, clients are trying to understand in an atmosphere of loving acceptance; in reconciliation they are owning possibly the same things and acknowledging their need for forgiveness.

To the unchurched, the confessional probably conjures up a picture of a forbidding box with a grille in a dark church, but this is only one tradition and by no means the only one in the Catholic Church. In Protestant circles, confession in a group is more common. In both Anglican and Catholic Churches a pastoral setting is often preferred where both penitent and confessor can see each other, and a personal welcome can be given to the penitent. More often than not the setting is a counsellor's room, two or more people facing each other informally as they talk through the problem; but there are times when a ritual setting is helpful.

In a formal confession, the process is simple. The confessor invites the penitent to confess, and the latter does so without fuss or too much obsessional detail, and invites the confessor to give him or her penance and absolution.

The third stage is penance. The natural feeling after doing wrong is to want to make amends, to undo what has been done. This is almost always too late and impossible, and in Christian doctrine has already been achieved by Christ; but the urge persists. The penitent is usually invited to do some very simple exercise of prayer, or more rarely some spiritual training, as a counsellor might ask a client to do a simple exercise appropriate to the care of others.

The final part is the word of forgiveness. The central issue in any imparting of forgiveness is the authority to do it, the very question put to Christ in the gospel. Ordination in the more Catholic Churches gives a specific authority to the priest, a word which means mediator between God and humanity, to proclaim as a sacrament of the presence of Christ the word of forgiveness to the penitent soul. In the Anglican Book of Common Prayer, in the Visitation of the Sick, and in Catholic usage, the words are specific: 'by his authority committed to me, I absolve thee from all thy sins, in the name of the Father, and of the Son, and of the Holy Spirit'.

In general counselling, the whole process of care involves both healing and forgiveness, and has its own pattern of self-examination, confession and indeed penance. It is often only by great courage and determination, in itself an illustration of penitence, that distressed clients find their way to their counsellor's room. The forgiveness is also implicit within the process, but sometimes requires a specific word. To absolve like a priest would be to act beyond the counsellor's authority, but some may pray with the client, or assure him or her that in the counsellor's view, quoting whatever authority he or she can properly claim, God forgives the penitent sinner who is prepared to forgive.

(e) As a counsellor is trained by being counselled, so the priest learns by making his or her confession. The priest must also be a man or woman of prayer, confident in the practice of the rituals to help a person through it, and knowledgeable about human development and the practice of counselling. A formal ministry of reconciliation is not the place for counsel, mainly because the positions adopted (priest sitting down and penitent on his or her knees before God) are not appropriate to equal conversation. Communication should be prayerful, addressed to the relationship of the soul with God, rather than to particular problems which should have been addressed before, or can with the permission of the penitent be addressed afterwards. The basic task is the celebration of forgiveness.

(f) Traditionally, the confidentiality of the confessional has been and is absolute, more demanding than anything required by current codes of counselling ethics (see *confidentiality*). This is important in that it allows anyone to come (as it were) off the street and share his or her wrongdoing without fear of it being revealed. If the priest is faced with confession of serious crimes like murder, rape or sexual abuse of children, the penitent must be advised to take the appropriate action, if necessary making contact with the relevant authorities, before there can be complete absolution.

A great fear among some clients is that they might have committed 'the unforgivable sin' (Mark 3:28–30, Matthew 22:31 and Luke 12:10). If it is brought up either in the context of a counselling session or in the confessional it is always a symptom of **depression**, and should be treated as such. The actual passages are in the midst of a sharp conflict between religious people who are full of hate and envy for Jesus whom they accuse of doing good works by evil means. The verses need to be read in the context of Jesus' teaching that there can be no limit to forgiveness. The only conditions are the usual two: penitence and a readiness to forgive others.

(g) Dudley, M. and Rowell, G. (1990) *Confession and Absolution.*
London: SPCK; Linn, D. and Linn, M. (1993) *Healing Life's Hurts.* New
York: Paulist Press; Smith, M. (1985) *Reconciliation: Preparing for
Confession.* Oxford and London: Mowbray.

DAVID GOODACRE
    (See also *guilt and shame; spiritual direction*)

Funerals

(a) Over 640,000 funerals took place in 1993 in the United Kingdom.
After each one, remarks could be heard ranging from 'that was a lovely
funeral' to 'that was impersonal, hypocritical mumbo-jumbo'. The
strength of feeling indicates that for most people the funeral is a very
important human event, a marker at the end of a life, and that it can
and should reflect the wishes of the deceased and of the deceased's wider
family.

Because funerals have to be planned quickly (unless the deceased has
left behind strict instructions), there is no more than a few days to make
all the necessary arrangements. Some ethnic groups insist on the next
day after the death. The responsibility is in the hands of the next-of-kin
together with other relatives, who work closely with the funeral director and the minister or officiant required.

(b) The vast majority of funerals take place within a religious context.
Less than 1 per cent are secular funerals, though the National Secular
Society and the British Humanist Association (1984) are keen to make
their approach more widely available. (Both have offices at Bradlaugh
House, 47 Theobald's Road, London WC1X 8SP – send s.a.e. for leaflet.)
Thus, people in this country are most likely to experience a specifically
Christian framework at funerals, whether it be the Church of England,
Roman Catholic, Orthodox or one of the Protestant denominations.
Increasingly, in the larger cities of Britain, we are becoming accus-
tomed to seeing the large crowds of people who attend a Sikh, Hindu,
Buddhist or Muslim funeral. This article will not be able to cover the
customs of these other faith communities, but some useful information
may be obtained from Julia Neuberger's book *Caring for People of
Different Faiths* (1994).

It is important to emphasize the freedom that people have in choosing
the sort of funeral they want. The quality of provision is patchy across
the country, but most clergy and ministers are willing to sit down with

the next of kin and other bereaved people and put together a service which will honour the dead person and express some of the thoughts and feelings which call for expression publicly on such an occasion. Ministers may offer help, or they may have to be asked.

The cost of funerals is always a topic for complaint, and many ways may be sought to reduce the cost (Walter, 1990: 78–83), but the most common price range in 1994 was between £600 and £1,500. Where people are living on income support, guidance may be sought from the Department of Social Security. Increasingly, people are asking funeral directors for quotations.

(c) There are sometimes unusual and difficult circumstances involved in arranging and conducting a funeral: e.g. mutilation, death by drowning, non-recovery of the body, a death abroad, when a body has been left to medical research, the **death of children**.

If a body has been mutilated or drowned and a long time in the sea, the funeral director will discourage any viewing of the body before the coffin is closed. Next of kin have a right to see the body, and may have to insist on their right. But they should be warned that the experience could be seriously disturbing. Many people prefer to remember the person who has died as they saw them in life, though it is recognized that, for some people, it provides a sense of completion to see the dead body of the person they loved (see *bereavement*).

If a death has taken place abroad, there are certain procedures that must be followed. Each country into which repatriation is requested has legal requirements, which specialist companies handle through and on behalf of the local funeral director in Britain. Generally speaking, a deceased person is embalmed and all documentation prepared within a week of the death taking place. Alternatively, where possible, cremation can be arranged, returning the cremated remains for disposal later. Similar arrangements are usually followed here for foreign nationals who die in Britain.

If the body has been left to medical research, there is very likely to be a long delay, a maximum of two years, before the remains are released for burial. Some relatives ask a church with which they have some contact for a memorial service, shortly after the death. Customarily, at some time during the two years remains are cremated in coffins following a group funeral service conducted by a clergyman at the crematorium without the relatives.

The **death of children** is the subject of another article. Funerals for children need to be handled with particularly great sensitivity: a special rite is offered by most churches.

(d) What are the main elements of a funeral? To the writer, the ritual (see *prayer and ritual*) of the funeral service and the address are both equally important. The ritual is the framework which the mourners can use to plan a service. It reflects perhaps the views and certainly the individuality of the deceased, and the address is a central personal point which can evoke his or her uniqueness. I usually begin funerals by focusing my own mind on what we are trying to do in the following words (with obvious variations as necessary):

> We have three things to do in this service: the first is to give thanks for N. and all that s/he meant to us. The second is to commend N.'s soul into the hands of her/his Creator (sometimes I expand here to recognize the difficulties this concept may hold for the unbeliever, agnostic or atheist). The third task is to pray for one another as we all grapple with the enormity of death.

This is loosely based on the Church of England's Liturgical Commission's answer to the question 'What should we be doing at a funeral service?'

1. To secure the reverent disposal of the corpse.
2. To commend the deceased to the care of our heavenly Father.
3. To proclaim the glory of our risen life in Christ here and hereafter.
4. To remind us of the awful certainty of our own coming death and judgement.
5. To make plain the eternal unity of Christian people, living and departed, in the risen and ascended Christ.

I reckon that it is a matter of sensitivity over the emphasis to be placed on the last three points, which belong more to doctrinal correctness than to pastoral care. Naturally pastoral care should be the prior guide. Here are two examples of funerals that felt completely appropriate. The important role of music, played and sung in hymns and songs, should be noted:

One was the potentially very sad funeral of a stage and television writer. Only 50 years old, he had collapsed and died while out walking. He left a wife and two talented daughters of eleven and thirteen. The funeral service (Anglican) had been carefully composed by his wife and the parish priest, and as it unfolded with hymns, reading, silences, music on tape and an address, so his unique character and personality was evoked. The address, given by a friend, was not a eulogy: it was honest about the dead man. It was a celebration of a life: it was a thanksgiving. And it brought to the fore the man's infectious sense of fun. It was a happy–sad funeral: perhaps the best kind.

A similarly appropriate event was requested by the widow of a Latin American refugee. Again the death was tragic: her husband had been in a coma for two years following an accident. The refugee community and friends where he and his family lived at the time attended the crematorium chapel in force to support the young widow and her children. A guitarist played the haunting melodies of Chilean freedom songs before the service began: a fellow refugee spoke movingly, and in English, for the benefit of the whole congregation, about the deceased's contribution to the struggle for freedom in his oppressed country. The conventional Church of England service from the Alternative Service Book (1980) was adequate, and I felt I had facilitated an event which was as far as possible congruent both to me and to the participants, with their amalgam of political and religious beliefs. I had shared with people, many of whom I knew reasonably well, in acknowledging the transition, in feeling the necessary feelings of grief, sadness and respect. This was in contrast to many funerals where the feelings are either quenched or forbidden, and where the impression is given that the event is a necessary evil and to be dealt with as quickly as possible. All those in a caring relationship with bereaved people can influence matters in a more constructive direction by contacting the officiant, who is usually receptive to suggestions.

Whether children should attend funerals is often debated by parents. My view is that they should be sensitively encouraged to attend. Not to do so deprives a child of an important understanding of life, its limits and, often, the most serious attention to relationships in families (see *children's experience of loss and death*).

A significant part of the funeral rite is the burial or cremation. This part of the 'reverent disposal of the corpse' is one which has most power to distress, if it is not handled sensitively and appropriately to the cultural group to which the deceased belongs.

The burial may take place in either a public or municipal burial ground, a privately designated burial ground or an 'open' churchyard. For example, there are Muslim and Jewish cemeteries. An 'open' churchyard is one which is still being used for burial as opposed to a 'closed' churchyard, which is full and no longer used. (Such 'closed' churchyards may still, however, be used for the interment of ashes following cremation, at the discretion of the minister in charge.) The coffin may either be placed on supports over the grave for the short graveside service, or lowered on canvas straps into the grave. An Afro-Caribbean custom is for a dozen shovels to be available for male members of the family to bury their dead. Sometimes, in other traditions, grieving families have been pleased to do this last service, and the physical activity has given them a sense of completion, and an opportunity to 'let go'.

Commonly, the cremation takes place as part of the funeral service in a crematorium, where the service itself has not taken place beforehand in another place of worship. The minister or officiant may, at the moment of the committal towards the end of the service, close the curtains to conceal the coffin. This symbolic action is taken to signify the separation of the earthly remains of the deceased from his family and friends. It is often a moment of poignancy, which some people choose to avoid by leaving the curtains open.

Some time after the cremation, the ashes are made available for interment or scattering, according to the wishes of the deceased or her family. Seafarers have been known to direct their ashes to be cast upon the waters; golfers upon the links; ramblers near their favourite paths, and so on. This event can also be important in the work of bereavement.

(e)   Contrary to popular opinion, anyone may conduct a funeral service or observance. It is not compulsory for it to take any particular form. It may be mostly in silence, according to Quaker custom. All that is required of the principal person at a funeral is probably warmth of manner, a genuine interest and concern for people at a time of bereavement, some skills in summarizing, in order to speak appropriately of the deceased, and a sense of the appropriate shape of a public event.

(f)   Stress has here been laid on the role of the officiant, but social workers or counsellors with bereaved client(s) may find it helpful to relate to the minister and/or the funeral director, as well as in certain cases doctors, hospice staff, counsellors or hospital chaplains. For example, a widow had an operation just before her husband died, but was able to attend the funeral, thanks to the hospital authorities. She was visited in hospital with her son and daughter to prepare for the service. It was supportive to refer her to the chaplain as well.

(g)   Clark, D. and Clark, S. (1993) *The Dark Uncertainty: Wrestling with Suffering and Death.* London: Darton, Longman and Todd; Kübler-Ross, E. (1970) *On Death and Dying.* London: Tavistock; Walter, T. (1990) *Funerals, and How to Improve Them.* London: Hodder & Stoughton.

DAVID CLARK
      (See also *abortion and miscarriage; bereavement; loss*)

Gambling

(a) Gambling is an activity involving two or more persons in which some property, usually referred to as the stake, is transferred between the people concerned so that some gain at the expense of others. The result depends on the outcome of a risky or uncertain situation, which may be natural or contrived for the purpose. Participation can be avoided and is typically pursued in an active fashion, often for reasons unrelated to the property staked.

While gambling is an acceptable form of entertainment, it may be taken to excess. In these circumstances, financial, social and psychological problems will result. The effect of this may involve not only the person who has been gambling, but also the family and the broader community. This condition has, in the past, been referred to as compulsive gambling. However, since it is not a true compulsive disorder, it is more appropriately referred to as pathological gambling.

(b) Pathological gambling can usually be recognized by the presence of any of the following features:

1. Concern on the part of the person who is gambling or the family about the amount of gambling because it is considered to be excessive, either in terms of the money spent or the time devoted to it.
2. The presence of an overpowering urge to gamble so that the person concerned may be intermittently or continuously preoccupied with thoughts of gambling: this is usually associated with the subjective experience of tension which is found to be relieved only by further gambling.
3. The subjective experience, on the part of the person who is gambling, of an inability to control the amount, once gambling has started, in spite of the realization that damage is resulting from this.
4. Various disturbances for the person who is gambling and the family because of a felt need for the activity. Among possible consequences are the following:
   (i)   financial disturbances such as debt and shortage;
   (ii) social disturbances such as loss of employment and friends, running away from home, eviction, marital problems, **divorce**, behaviour disorders in the children of the family, criminality and imprisonment;
   (iii) psychological disturbances such as **depression** and attempted **suicide**.

In general, pathological gambling is most easily recognized in men. This seems to be due to the fact that, for various social reasons, horse-race and greyhound-race betting and gaming are more frequently patronized by men. These types of gambling have a high turnover of money and therefore the consequences of excess become evident more quickly. On the other hand, women are more likely to gamble on bingo, football pools and lotteries. These do not involve such large sums of money, and when excessive gambling occurs the presentation is much more subtle with disturbances in the social sphere rather than through the accumulation of large debts.

While pathological gambling is seen at all ages, an increasing number of children and young people have recently found themselves in difficulties as a result of fruit machine gambling. Many of these have subsequently gone on to heavy gambling with horse-race and grey-hound-race betting.

(c)   The factors involved in the causation of pathological gambling are varied and complex and many factors may be involved. Among the more important of these are the following:

1. *Social pressures:*   There is increasing evidence indicating that the extent of the availability of gambling facilities and the social pressures encouraging participation are very important factors in determining the extent of pathological gambling and its precipitation in a particular individual. By the very nature of the gambling contract, the activity is a social one. Indeed, the most common organization of gambling involves the gambling industry which is usually the other party to the contract. Obviously, in gambling as in any other commercial enterprise, those who provide the facilities expect to make a profit. However, this can occur only at the expense of the person who is gambling.

Certain types of work make it more easy for the person concerned to turn to gambling, particularly if the work is rather boring and unstruc-tured. Examples of this are the high incidence of pathological gambling among taxi drivers and travelling salesmen.

2. *Psychological factors:*   In the presence of social pressures, predis-posed individuals are propelled towards pathological gambling. Some of the factors involved in this predisposition are as follows:

  (i)   *Morbid risk-taking:* Since gambling is a type of risk-taking, it lends itself to be used by those who, for reasons related to their personality, have a high need for risk. The person who gambles pathologically spends large amounts of money on the intan-gible commodity of risk and therefore has little to show for it after the experience has faded. The main difference between such a person and one who spends large amounts of money on tangible objects, is that the subjective experience of risk is fleeting and may therefore easily pass unnoticed.

This propensity to take risks shows itself in other morbid ways such as attempted **suicide**. The incidence of the latter is very high among those whose gambling is pathological.

(ii) *Other personality factors:* Psychoanalysts have suggested that psycho-sexual factors, as well as an unconscious wish for self-punishment, play important roles in the causation of pathological gambling (see *sexual deviation*).

(iii) *Processes of learning:* Gambling provides an opportunity for learning by means of reward (operant conditioning) in which the wins are unpredictable at any one time, and thus act as an intermittent reinforcement. This schedule of learning has been recognized to be the most effective in habit-formation. This is well illustrated by the fruit machine, which has been referred to as the one-armed bandit.

The gambling situation itself may affect learning. As far as the random processes inherent in gambling are concerned, all participants, even total failures, stand on an equal footing. This may be the only circumstance in which some individuals have this experience and may therefore provide a means of avoiding pathological anxiety in the presence of feelings of inferiority.

(iv) *Mental disorder:* Pathological gambling is most commonly associated with **depression**. More usually, a neurotic type of depression occurs after a bout of heavy gambling with large losses. Alternatively the depression may be primary, with gambling arising as a response to the symptoms of tension or as a self-destructive expiation of feelings of **guilt** symptomatic of depression.

Pathological gambling may be a manifestation of the broader disorder of psychopathy or may be associated with the excessive use of alcohol (see *alcoholism*).

In addition, those whose gambling has become pathological may experience loss of control similar to that found in psychological dependence on alcohol and other drugs. There is thus a state of psychological dependence on gambling.

(d) Pathological gambling involves more than just the activity of gambling. Quite apart from the effects of this pursuit, it involves a whole way of life which has many ramifications. What is required therefore is management of various aspects of the life of the person concerned and rehabilitation.

1. *Assessment of the problem:*   Pathological gambling is a form of behaviour for which there is no one simple explanation. This point must be emphasized quite strongly at the beginning of the assessment. The latter involves a detailed appraisal of the extent and the amount of the present gambling, as well as a detailed history of the development of the gambling from its early beginnings. Since the history is often very chequered, it is usually found to be more accurate if the person being assessed provides the information by means of a written account. This can subsequently be used as the basis of discussion and amplification.

It is important to attempt to obtain some indication of the person's motivation. Many who seek help to assist them with problems that flow from excessive gambling appear not to recognize the need to even restrict their gambling. Indeed, many of these people readily admit that they enjoy the gambling and are only seeking advice because relatives have insisted that they should do so, or because of impending legal proceedings for some misdemeanour due to excessive gambling. Such people are difficult to help.

2. *Financial management:*   It is important to obtain a detailed statement of all the outstanding debts as well as an inventory of the income and out-goings of the person seeking help and his or her family. In terms of this information, the person who has been gambling pathologically needs to be encouraged to draft a realistic plan of repayment. Since the debts are often considerable, the repayments may have to continue over many years. This can obviously only be achieved by encouraging the person concerned to discuss the whole matter with the creditors involved. However, it is important that the repayments should be consistent with the person's regular income and circumstances. There is a considerable danger that in the first flush of enthusiasm, unrealistic repayments will be contemplated, which may lead to temptations to gamble in order to maintain them (see *money advice*).

Excessive gambling is usually associated with a disturbed appreciation of the value of money. Because of this and the continued temptation to gamble, it is wise for all the finances to be controlled, at least for some time, by the spouse/partner or some trusted person. Regular income from wages or salaries should be paid into a bank account over which the spouse/partner or trusted person has sole control. As the period of abstinence from gambling continues, the person who has been gambling pathologically needs to become more gradually involved in working jointly with whoever controls the finances.

3. Counselling: On the basis of information obtained during the course of the assessment, there needs to be some discussion of the nature of the gambling activity. Attention needs to be drawn to some of the snares involved, such as exaggerated ideas of the importance of luck (superstition) and skill (information from tipsters and various dubious numbers systems), and the subtle ways in which excessive participation can occur.

There needs also to be some discussion about the whole procedure of habit-formation and the development of loss of control. This may involve obtaining advice from a clinical psychologist. In any case, it is important to emphasize that there needs to be at least a period of total abstinence from all gambling.

The person who has been gambling pathologically and the spouse/partner need to be encouraged to review the whole organization of their social life. In particular, they need to consider how they spend their spare time, what friends they cultivate and what interests they pursue. It is often within specific settings that incitement to gambling has occurred in the past; the person concerned and the spouse/partner need to make very careful arrangements to avoid such future temptations. This may be easier to achieve by helping them to draw up a joint contract which spells out in detail those types of behaviour to be avoided as well as those to be encouraged. This needs to be reviewed regularly.

(e)   *Gamblers Anonymous* is a form of self-help for pathological gamblers which is organized in the form of local groups which meet regularly. As well as meetings for those who gamble excessively, there are also separate groups for their spouses/partners. Quite apart from the valuable work done in the group setting, Gamblers Anonymous provides a useful means of establishing alternative social contacts to those that went with the excessive gambling. Indeed, in some people who have been gambling pathologically, Gamblers Anonymous may be the vehicle through which all the necessary forms of help can be provided. Even if this is not the case, Gamblers Anonymous still provides a valuable form of help and support for the individual and the family.

The National Council on Gambling can be contacted at Regent's Wharf, 8 All Saints Street, London N1 9RL.

Specialist help: Since the pathological gambling may be a manifestation of mental disorder and may require specialist treatment such a psychotherapy, referral for psychiatric and/or psychological advice may be appropriate.

(g)   Moody, G. (1990) *Quit Compulsive Gambling.* Wellingborough: Thorsons; Moran, E. (1990) 'Pathological gambling' in R. Blugrass and

P. Bowden (eds.) *Principles and Practice of Forensic Psychiatry*. London: Churchill Livingstone.

EMANUEL MORAN

Gay men and lesbians

(a) The definition I use in this article on working with lesbian, gay and bisexual people is: people who experience an erotic attraction to people of their own sex, although not exclusively so. The last clause recognizes the fact that only a minority of people are over a period of time exclusively lesbian, gay or heterosexual, in terms of both their behaviour and of their sexual thoughts and feelings. However, because of societal prejudice and the need to defend one's own identity from external judgements, the majority of people adopt an identity – a label – to describe their sexuality as either lesbian/gay or heterosexual. People are becoming increasingly open about their bisexuality, but the prejudice from within both the heterosexual and homosexual communities means that bisexuals risk rejection by both groups. As a shorthand throughout, I use the contraction 'lesbigays' to refer to lesbians, gay men and bisexuals since it is briefer, although it is not a term in common usage.

(b) There are many different ways in which lesbians, gay men and bisexuals may present to helpers and counsellors.

1. As ordinary people with ordinary problems (depression, loss, anxiety, etc.) which are sometimes connected to their homosexuality
Most lesbigays are ordinary people leading ordinary lives with ordinary problems. They may be depressed, anxious, bereaved, or lonely just as anybody else. Their problems may have some connection to their sexuality; but unless they see it that way, then it is unlikely to be the case that they are depressed *because* they are gay; *anxious* about being a lesbian, etc. It is more likely that the connection is about society's response to them because of their sexuality, a society that considers same-sex love and affection as sick, perverted, immoral and dangerous. Anyone who had the experience of being despised and vilified would probably be depressed, anxious, etc. too! Disliking yourself, or feeling bad about yourself because of internalizing society's negative messages about your homosexuality, is known as *internalized homophobia*.

2. Identity confusion

Some are uncertain about their sexuality – unsure whether they're lesbian, gay or bisexual. We think of this applying most commonly to adolescents: sometime adults refer to this somewhat patronizingly as a 'crush' or 'phase'. This may be true, in that it may be temporary, although one could ask somewhat cynically whether this is not also true of the majority of love affairs? It is important to convey respect for someone else's experience. By attempting to demean young people's experience as temporary the adult may be saying to the young person, that being attracted to one's own sex is insignificant or unimportant. Or is the underplaying of the possibility of a homosexual orientation deliberate? Whatever the motivation, this is an unhelpful response.

Identity confusion is made worse by a society that polarizes sexuality by its binary thinking. People are expected to 'choose' hetero- or homosexuality. Sexual surveys persistently demonstrate that in both behaviour and fantasy, more people are attracted to both sexes than to one sex alone. Yet it is extremely difficult for most people to feel able to be open about being bisexual. As a result people who are open about their bisexuality are sometimes more isolated and vilified than lesbians and gay men. Heterosexuals seem to dislike bisexuals because of their same-sex attraction, and homosexuals because of the bisexual's desire to 'sleep with the enemy'. This dislike of bisexuals has come to be known as *biphobia*.

(c)   A great deal of poorly conducted 'research' has been carried out into the 'causes' of homosexuality (almost exclusively male homosexuality). This stems from the idea that homosexuality has been thought of as an illness. Therefore if we could find out what causes it, perhaps it could be treated and 'sufferers' made heterosexual. Homosexuality was later shown by psychologists and psychiatrists not to be an illness but a natural and normal variation of sexuality. Homosexuality has been socially constructed by Western society as something abnormal, although in many other cultures and at different times in the past, it has been regarded as perfectly normal. Because the declassification of homosexuality as a mental illness has occurred relatively recently (in the 1970s and 1980s), there are still a number of people who believe that it can be treated; and since research continues to try to find a 'cause', by implication there appears to be the possibility of a 'cure'.

The more recent debates around homosexuality as a disorder have occurred as a result of fundamental and evangelical Christianity setting up 'healing missions'. Some Christian psychologists (Cameron and Ross, 1981; Cameron et al., 1989) are still keen to present homosexuality as a disorder, despite being expelled from the American Psychological Association for breaching their 'Ethical Principles for

Psychologists' (Gonsiorek and Weinrich, 1991). Another quarter that has re-awakened the nature versus nurture debate has been the idea of a genetic bias towards homosexuality, promulgated amongst others by a gay geneticist (Le Vay, 1993). His research has attracted much criticism from both within the gay and scientific communities, and it seems to raise more questions than provide answers. It is worth noting that a question which is rarely seriously asked is: what is hetero-sexuality and what causes it?

(d) The following guidelines for working effectively with lesbigay people have been adapted from those suggested by an American psy-chotherapist, Don Clark (1987):

1. It is important for helpers to have a comfortable appreciation of their own homosexual feelings before they can work successfully with lesbi-gay clients. It is not enough just to acknowledge that those feelings exist. Helpers need to be able to value and appreciate those feelings, and if they choose not to act on them, be clear about their reasons why.

> As for the professional who says he or she has no homosexual
> feelings, they are about as well off as the psychotherapist who says
> he or she never dreams. It indicates you are out of touch with your
> inner emotions and would do well to consider another profession.
> (Clark, 1987: 233)

It is not entirely accurate that everyone has homosexual feelings: statistically speaking approximately 5–10 per cent of the population are likely to be exclusively heterosexual (Kinsey et al., 1948, 1953). It is true that most people have erotic feelings of attraction to some members of their own sex, whether they are unconscious and only come out in dreams, or are conscious erotic thoughts and feelings. A sizeable proportion of people (up to 40 per cent of men) act on these feelings at some point in their adult lives (Kinsey et al., 1948).

Heterosexual helpers have a duty to their clients and themselves to explore their own sexuality and to come to terms with their own homosexual component; and be clear with themselves, if they decide not to act on their feelings, why that is. If helpers keep anti-gay feelings hidden they can act as blind spots and sabotage the work they are doing with their lesbigay clients. Having grown up in a heterosexist culture, none of us is entirely free of these feelings.

2. The resolution of internalized homophobic attitudes and beliefs is central to the healthy self-esteem of lesbigay people. We have all been exposed to homophobic prejudice, to anti-gay jokes and anti-lesbian myths. Homosexuality is conveniently and erroneously linked with paedophilia and child sexual abuse in spite of ample research to the contrary.

Some of the most common negative beliefs about lesbigay people include:

(i) lesbigay people are unable to control their sexual attractions and so may force themselves upon heterosexuals, or recruit children and young people into homosexuality by seduction;

(ii) lesbigay parents are damaging role models for their children. The theory is that children need one parent of each gender, in a monogamous relationship – the implications for single, divorced and widowed parents seem to go unchallenged;

(iii) lesbians and gay men act out traditional heterosexual role playing in their relationships – one partner plays the man's role and the other the woman's.

Due to lack of accurate and accessible information these damaging myths may have been internalized by lesbigay people themselves. It may be that the helper needs to have a broader-based knowledge than many lesbigay people have. This is especially true for those who are 'coming out', or who have had restricted opportunities to meet many other lesbigay people.

Most lesbigay people have encountered heterosexist oppression which has probably had a negative effect on them. Even if not directly subjected to anti-homosexual abuse they can be aware of the possibility that they will also be treated in the same way. Many lesbigay people report a lack of spontaneity in their interactions with heterosexual people. This can be likened to being a visitor to another country. One can learn to think in another language, even to speak it fluently, and feel almost at home in the others' culture, but it is still not one's own 'mother' tongue. Ratigan (1991) equates this to living in an enemy-occupied territory – having to guard against betraying oneself, and being hyper-vigilant about how one speaks and acts. Both of these analogies convey something of the experience of living in Britain as lesbian, gay or bisexual.

3. One implication of this lack of spontaneity is that it may be difficult for the lesbigay person to express strong emotions, in particular being openly angry or affectionate.

4. Encourage your client to establish a lesbigay support system: a half-dozen other lesbigay people with mutual personal caring and respect for each other can make a tremendous difference to the self-esteem and emotional well-being of a lesbigay person. For many lesbigay people there is a tendency to pair up soon after coming out, and to avoid the painful and stressful experience of making *friends*. If their relationship gets into trouble (and whose does not?), then a few supportive friends may be able to help them to sort it out, or provide support should their relationship end. It is also helpful to encourage consciousness-raising

efforts, such as attending lesbigay social and discussion groups, pro-gay readings and involvement in lesbigay community activities, e.g. the annual Gay Pride celebrations in London, or participation in lesbigay political groups.

5. Try to minimize any power hierarchy between yourself and your client. While there will always be some power imbalance, try to work towards an equal relationship. This conveys the message that the client is not a second class or inferior person. While helpers do have some authority, use it to affirm homosexual thoughts, behaviour and feelings when reported by the client. This is important, to counteract the experience of disapproval by authority figures.

6. Encourage the client to question basic assumptions about being gay; to explore their stereotypes about lesbigay people; and to develop a personally relevant value system and moral code. Point out the dangers of relying on society's value system for self-validation. This may be especially relevant to the type of sexual and social relationships the lesbigay person chooses to make. While life-long monogamy is supposed to be the norm among heterosexuals, we know that the reality is quite different. Many lesbigay people manage to develop relationship models which meet their needs more effectively, but which are outside the heterosexual norm.

7. Help can be offered but not forced. Lesbigay people have in the past been on the receiving end of a lot of damage from 'helpers' who have tried to force them into heterosexual norms and values. The lesbigay client may well be rightly suspicious of help offered until they trust you. It can be helpful to describe in advance what sort of help you intend to offer (in detail) and why.

8. The helper's primary goal should be to help the person become more fully herself or himself – which may mean the person becoming more truly gay, developing a conscious self-appreciation and an integrity that includes the integration of gay thoughts and feelings. The helper's goal is to encourage this integrity by encouraging behaviour and attitudes that match inner feelings.

9. Consider carefully before revealing to someone else that your client is lesbigay. Reflect on why you are revealing this information, and how the client might feel about a helper making their sexuality known. Is it relevant to the discussion? If so, has the person you are talking to sorted out their own attitudes to lesbigay identity? Or are you likely to be collecting some of their heterosexism too?

Clark (1987) has also developed some 'psychodynamic generalizations' about lesbians and gay men. They may equally apply to bisexual men and women. Since they are generalizations it would be inappropriate for the helper to have a view of all lesbigay people as sick or damaged.

Undoubtedly it is hard to escape entirely free of damage from the insidious affects of heterosexism and homophobia, although research has shown the majority of lesbigay people do have surprisingly good mental health.

Clark presents the following seven generalizations:

(i)   The lesbian/gay person has learned to feel different. In this society, which values conformity, the lesbian/gay person feels devalued or worthless even though she or he may be outwardly successful and accomplished.

(ii) The lesbian/gay person has learned to distrust her or his own feelings. This process began with the dim awareness of attraction to people of the same gender, and the environmental message that such feelings of attraction are wrong or bad. Added to this has been the fear induced by anti-gay myths, and the specific myth that it is almost impossible for someone with such 'perverted' feelings to control the expression of those feelings in their behaviour.

(iii) The lesbian/gay person is likely to have decreased awareness of feelings. The anger generated in a punitive environment and the anger at self for being different seems unjustified, and therefore must be repressed from awareness, where it continues to accumulate. Other feelings are also affected through a process of generalization, and are given less awareness or attention.

(iv) The lesbian/gay person, being invisible to others, is assaulted daily with attacks on her or his character and ability. These attacks may come in the form of anti-gay jokes and statements, or in the form of omission when heterosexuality is being praised. Awareness of the hurt associated with the assaults (often from friends and family) is kept to a minimum so as to keep anger out of awareness.

(v)   The lesbian/gay person feels alone, wrong, and fears further lack of support and affection if he or she reveals true thoughts, feelings and identity.

(vi) The lesbian/gay person is apt to be the victim of **depression**, that includes some degree of immobility. Much of this stems from the repressed anger, the self-imposed limitation on awareness of feelings and limitations on interpersonal interaction, as well as the lack of emotional self-nurturing.

(vii) The lesbian/gay person is likely to be tempted to dull the pain that surfaces now and again through misuse of drugs (see *substance misuse*) and alcohol (see *alcoholism*), or to end the pain by **suicide**. The use of alcohol is reinforced, since gay bars are one of the few community approved meeting places for gay people. Suicide is implicitly encouraged by the community's failure to recognize the existence of 'respectable' gay people.

There is increasing evidence that being openly lesbigay offers opportunities to participate in a cultural identity which can affect one's values, ideas and identities. There is a gay 'sensibility' or culture, a series of gay 'looks' in terms of fashion, music and art. Popular culture has adopted an increasingly homo-eroticized style, partly to attract the 'pink pound', but also to represent more broadly same-sex interest and attractions. Lesbigay people *may* have different views from heterosexuals on matters of politics, relationships and partnerships, sex, etc. The impact of the AIDS epidemic on the lesbigay community is clearly present: even if one is not personally *infected* with HIV (see *AIDS/HIV*), many if not most have certainly been *affected* by it. Lesbigay people live in at least two worlds, the heterosexual and the homosexual. They therefore have two cultural identities. The helper may not have this experience. If helpers are unclear about something their client says, they should say so, and not pretend to understand when they do not.

(e)   There are three organizations which have been involved in supporting lesbigay people since the early 1970s: Gay Switchboard, Lesbian Line and Friend. Many towns and cities have one if not all three groups providing an information, befriending and sometimes a counselling service to the lesbigay communities. Switchboard tends to be more information based and Friend more counselling oriented, although often both will befriend isolated and lonely lesbigay people – perhaps accompanying them to a local gay pub or club, helping to introduce them to others or supporting them while they find their feet. Lesbian Line clearly exists to support women who may feel isolated from the other two, more male-dominated organizations.

There is a wide range of social and interest groups for lesbigay people, from the regular discussion and social groups through to a variety of specialist groups encompassing a range of sporting or hobby-based activities. The most comprehensive listing can be found in the monthly magazine *Gay Times*.

(f)   There are two issues in particular I want to address briefly: one is *guilt by association*; the other *seduction of vulnerable people*. Fear of guilt by association is where a worker is the subject of much nudging and winking because of their interest in and commitment to supporting lesbigay people. The assumption is that by wanting to work with lesbigays they must themselves be lesbigay. Because of the public scorn and condemnation that seems to surround homosexuality, workers who appear to be publicly supportive of lesbigay rights and willing to help lesbigay people, have sometimes been regarded with some suspicion by friends and colleagues: 'Why is she so keen to help them?' It is a very effective way of preventing all but the most committed supporters. The same argument would never be raised around other equality issues. The prevalent culture that seems to undermine support for lesbigay rights is clearly homophobic and can be extremely damaging. If the reader doubts my argument, then monitor your own internal reaction and how others might respond if you were seen wearing a gay positive badge (such as 'gay is good' or 'lesbians are powerful').

The second myth is that vulnerable people are open to being persuaded or seduced into homosexuality by lesbigay helpers and agencies. It is thought therefore that people who are vulnerable and uncertain should go to 'independent' heterosexual therapists. There is no research evidence to support the seduction theory, and clearly the opposite is not true: lesbigays have not been seduced into heterosexuality, despite all the powerful forces of social and peer pressure. What is so attractive and powerful about homosexuality that might persuade someone to try it? Social disapproval alone is enough to put most people off. Beliefs around seduction are also a dangerous slur on lesbigay therapists and helping agencies, most of whom are members of the British Association for Counselling and as such subscribe to a rigorous code of ethics.

(g)   Clark, D. (1987) *The New Loving Someone Gay*. Berkeley, California: Celestial Arts; Davies, D. (ed.) (1996) *Pink Therapy: A Guide for Counsellors and Therapists Working with Lesbian, Gay and Bisexual Clients*. Buckingham: Open University Press; McDonald, H. B. and Steinhorn, A. I. (1993) *Understanding Homosexuality*. New York: Crossroad.

DOMINIC DAVIES

Gender issues

(a)   From the very moment they are born, maybe before, female and male babies are treated differently. So begins their socialization process into socially constructed, culturally created gender roles. The way children are dressed, the way they are talked to, the toys bought for them to play with, the sort of activities to which they are directed and which are reinforced, as well as the media presentation of male and female roles, are all part of this socialization process. Limits are put on female and male behaviour. Socially constructed views of appropriate female and male behaviour are incorporated in our concept of ourselves.

But within our present patriarchal society these roles are not granted equal importance. Womanhood is not viewed or valued in the same way as manhood: women are viewed as second-class citizens. Women's work, inside or outside the home, women's health and ill-health, women's way of organizing their time to take in their responsibilities as carers, indeed women's way of being, all are afforded low status, are seen as less valuable and less important than that of men. In addition, women are likely to be seen as deviant, inadequate, unreliable, stupid or objects of fun for not being able to fit into a world dominated by male attitudes and male values. Men on the other hand, because male attitudes and values are deemed to be the norm, are trapped within a mindset which seems to them natural and is to their advantage. Since it is reinforced everywhere, it is inevitably difficult for men to step outside it. This mindset, culturally and religiously sanctioned, has evolved over very many generations. Both clients and helpers within the caring professions are influenced by such cultural values and mores, which in turn influences the form of service provision.

(b) Social values which inevitably lead to gender stereotypes for women and for men, as well as less importance being granted to the female role, are oppressive to women and limiting to men. Neither gender can operate as 'whole people', integrating their feminine and masculine sides and valuing both. Both are stuck with roles which become increasingly difficult to transcend. Within the context of the caring professions, gender issues are evident in assumptions about the nature of service provision, in differential reactions and responses to male and female users of the service, in the interactions between helpers and helped and in the way agencies and institutions are managed as well as the underlying belief systems and assumptions of those agencies.

The first assumption frequently made in service provision is that, within families, women are the carers and men are the financial providers. The initial contact, maybe the only contact, between agencies and users is then with women users, viewed as the carers of their families. This is particularly so if the service being provided is for children, elderly people or sick and disabled people. In the 1980s social policy and, for example, social work practice, emphasized its function in 'supporting' women in carrying out their caring and nurturing roles, even where it might be recognized as an unreasonable burden (Bowl, 1985: 4), yet there was no questioning or challenging of role definitions which exacerbated the problems. A decade later there is likely to be less notion of support for women in their role, even less a challenging of such assumptions, with a lack of resources underpinning the principle, in the case of children, of parental responsibility which invariably means *maternal* responsibility. In both decades these policies perpetuate and strengthen the gender role stereotypes which contribute to the problems the policies try to address.

This way of responding to users of the service is somewhat puzzling when it is remembered that it is more likely to be women who are the front line workers in any helping provision. The helping professions are still very much characterized by career structures which are male dominated, with many more men than women in senior management positions (Alban-Metcalf and West, 1991: 154). This means too often that men control resources and take decisions, at one step removed from the users of the service. It means that women front line workers do not challenge male assumptions about delivery of resources. This is either because the women workers' role carries little status and therefore little power or because, for whatever reason, they collude with agency notions of service delivery. It inevitably means that male values predominate in the way service delivery is organized and offered. Male values, such as competition, task-setting, goal-orientated rather than process-orientated ways of working, fast results, easily quantifiable results, value for money, face-saving with little emphasis on the concept that the nature of the work has any effect on the helpers, are very much prized and valued in British society in the 1990s, with its free-market economy, contract culture and payment by results. The assumption that such values are relevant when working with humans, rather than machines, is rarely challenged.

(c) Gender issues have become prominent in recent years through a number of factors. Throughout the development of patriarchal societies, spanning a period of several thousand years, gender stereotyped roles have changed and evolved, been more or less rigid, but have always given the male values the greater emphasis and legitimacy. This has led, for example, to women's contribution to society being overlooked or discounted. With the ever increasing importance of the women's movement in the 1970s and 1980s, much has been done to reclaim 'women's history'. Prior to this the history of this country was the history of the actions of some men; and women's contribution, along with that of other powerless groups, remained invisible.

For several hundred years in Western society there has been an increasing emphasis on individual self-determination, alongside a challenge and critique of traditional socially accepted attitudes. And with the very recent economic and legal changes enabling women individually and collectively to assert their rights to self-determination, the inequality inherent in traditional attitudes and practices has been made very clear. Gender issues come into focus as old values are breaking down and old power structures and inequalities no longer can be accepted as legitimate. However, in the 1990s, even though economically and legally progress towards gender equality has been made, much remains to be done and the extent of the necessary attitude changes still needed, both in women and men, is very marked.

(d) Particular attention needs to be paid to:

1. Gender stereotyping
The practice of the caring professions often reflects existing gender stereotyping. Social work in day centres for the elderly and physically disabled, for example, can mean that men are encouraged to participate in production orientated activities, women to knit, sew and chat; self-help in old people's homes means the *women* participating in domestic work (see *old age*). Agencies which provide help for children and their parents invariably offer services for mothers rather than fathers. Similarly, child protection social work may mean that mothers are offered help, even when fathers are the abusers. When working with **child** sexual **abuse**, the mother can be targeted as the responsible parent or the one who fails to protect rather than any effort made to modify the father's actions. When working with child physical abuse, if fathers explain that they cannot talk about problems like a woman or show little interest, these can still be accepted as legitimate reasons for excluding them (see *families, working with*).

Gender stereotyping is very much in evidence in health care provision. Time and again we are reminded of how the health care issues of women are granted less importance and value than those of men. The current debate about breast **cancer** is a good example. Each year around 16,000 women in Britain die from breast cancer, which is apparently more common here than anywhere else in the world. Many of these women are young mothers bringing up families. A pertinent question is whether the general discounting of women is one of the reasons for the patchy resources available for treating this disease.

It is generally the case that women's illnesses are more likely than men's to be perceived as psychosomatic (Telford and Farrington, 1991: 169), and that definitions about mental health are more likely to include mentally healthy adult male characteristics than female (Walker, 1990: 114). An exploration of referrals for **depression** raises interesting questions. Many more women than men present as depressed both to GPs and outpatient psychiatric facilities. The reasons for this are complex, to do with issues such as quality of life for women and social expectations put on them as well as the enormous loss of opportunities experienced by them in today's society. In addition women are very often the emotional carriers in their relationships and families. In heterosexual relationships this can mean that the female partner 'carries' the depression of the male partner. Treatment offered to the female partner means that both partners miss out – the female has been wrongly labelled and the male has not had his need to express his feelings of sadness and despair recognized and facilitated. All too often male clients can have their need to express vulnerability, dependency, weakness and any emotion other than anger overlooked. This is even more striking in services offered to older men.

> My own experience is of individuals who had had very little
> opportunity to discuss deeply troubling experiences, for example, of
> coming to terms with having to kill or be killed in the second world
> war. They may have been offered 'practical' services or been
> psychiatrically assessed, but as men, their emotional concerns seem
> to have been considered to carry even greater illegitimacy for
> intervention than those of older women. They themselves often share
> this view in part and will not press the issue on an apparently
> reluctant confidant. (Bowl, 1985: 31)

2. Interactions

Workers can encounter the influence of gender issues operating in many situations brought by consumers. Many of these involve one party appropriating the right to control, label, abuse, demean, make decisions for, another. **Child abuse** and abuse and rape of women (see *violence towards women*) express the assumed right of one (or more) person(s), usually male, to exercise power, control and violence over others. Marital/couple/family issues brought to workers can also show the effects of long-term dominance by one partner over the other, or in families the scapegoating of one member by others. In all such situations, workers need to be alert to the gender dynamics involved, and to be aware of their own gender-based assumptions and attitudes so as not to get caught up in the perpetuation of inequality. In interactions between worker and consumer some involve greater danger of perpetuating abusive experiences; the male worker–female consumer with sexual abuse issues, male doctor–female patient with gynaecological or **sexual difficulties**, older male worker–younger female client working on dependency issues. For example, having male and female co-workers, adequate supervision and further training in gender issues can all help to counteract tendencies to ignore unexamined attitudes and assumptions, or to return to former more abusive patterns through complacency.

A generally unacknowledged issue is that of the effect on workers of being confronted by gender dynamics. Having to work with situations that emphasize the abuse of male power affects both men and women

workers at a deep level, and frequently contaminates their relationships with their own partners and families (Perry, 1992: 80; Perry,
1993: 74). **Supervision** of workers has a vital role to play here.
Supervision in the helping professions should consist of three elements
– the normative, formative and restorative (Hawkins and Shohet, 1989:
42). Too often, any supervision that is offered covers only the first of
these functions – the managerial and quality control aspects of the
work being done. The second is the educative function, the facilitation
of the professional development of workers. The third one enables
workers to examine their own reactions and responses to their work and
is vital in combating the **stress** and burn-out which lead to less effective
workers.

3. Language and recording

Language is a strong force in moulding the ideas and views of children
about their own and others' gender roles. It is an obvious starting place,
since language is the main tool of helping professionals. Care must be
taken to use inclusive language: words can marginalize women by the
act of non-inclusion. Obvious examples such as mankind, manpower
can be avoided: people and personnel can be used instead. Similarly,
terms with obvious gender connotations attached, such as gossip, nag,
dear, dick-head, should be avoided. Regional variations in terms of
female endearment, such as lass, duck, ducky, hen, pet, hinny, sweet-
heart, lovely, should also be avoided. Such terms are rarely used
towards men. The growing practice within the helping professions of
addressing consumers by their first names on first acquaintance can
feel very uncomfortable; this is especially so for women who might find
any status and respect dwindling away by being addressed by their first
name as if they were a child. This practice should be avoided unless it is
made clear that both professional and client are on first-name terms
and that it has been checked out as being to the client's taste. A practice
which grew from the desire to make helping professionals more
approachable too often feels like one which is in existence to underline
the power differential between helper and helped, leaving the helped
feeling disempowered.

Attention has been paid to recording is used by people working
within the helping professions in terms of pathologizing clients. Too
often, the impression can be given that consumers are one big problem
themselves, rather than people temporarily in the position of asking for
help or a particular kind of service. This is likely to increase as
resources decrease, so such resources are only likely to come the way of
clients who are defined as having major problems. Sandra Butler and

Problem characteristics: stereotypical responses to women's group members

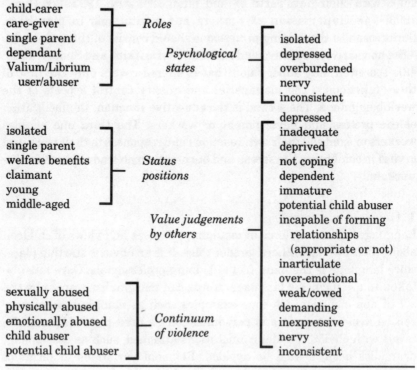

child-carer
care-giver ⎤
single parent ⎱ — *Roles*
dependant
Valium/Librium
    user/abuser ⎦

Psychological states

isolated
depressed
overburdened
nervy
inconsistent

isolated ⎤
single parent
welfare benefits
claimant ⎱ — *Status positions*
young
middle-aged ⎦

depressed
inadequate
deprived
not coping
dependent
immature
potential child abuser

Value judgements by others

incapable of forming
    relationships
    (appropriate or not)
inarticulate
over-emotional

sexually abused ⎤
physically abused
emotionally abused ⎱ — *Continuum of violence*
child abuser
potential child abuser ⎦

weak/cowed
demanding
inexpressive
nervy
inconsistent

(From Butler and Wintram, 1991: 35)

Claire Wintram, writing about services offered by social services departments to women who are mothers, produce a table of problem characteristics of such clients.

They point out that women only qualify for services in relation to someone else and, if that someone else is a child, they must be seen to fail in their capacities as parents in order to qualify for help. Referrals never recognize a woman's strengths and fortitudes. Further, the catalogue of value judgements reveals a depth of sexism which is never challenged. How often do such value judgements remain on referrals, case-notes, case conference minutes without a second thought being given to them?

4. Organizational structure
Almost the most striking, yet seemingly the least acknowledged, way in which gender issues are relevant within the helping professions is within the organization of the agencies themselves. The agencies might very well be overtly committed to an equal opportunities policy. It is a

common experience, however, that consideration of anti-sexist practice lags behind that of anti-racist practice (Perry, 1993: 58). When consideration is apparent it seems to apply only to how many women are able to get into senior management, rather than any deeper considerations about the services on offer or how the agencies are organized, that is, female as well as male friendly. It has been accepted for some time (Sturdy, 1987: 31; Perry, 1993: 89) that when women run organizations they do so in a different way from men. Organizations dominated by male attitudes and values are characterized by task and problem orientation, goal setting, fast results and competitive practice; whereas organizations created by women consciously expressing female attitudes and values are process orientated, emphasize co-operation and connectedness, and are characterized by exploration of feelings and individual experience as part of the method of evaluation. Such organizations also take into account the different patterns of work for female employees, which have to incorporate their role as carers or families.

Even though the public and voluntary sectors are likely to have more women in senior management positions than the private sector, it is still the case that women are very much under-represented in management. It is also likely to be the case that women achieve management positions in the public sector in those agencies in which the positions are thought of as female jobs. Women can be promoted to manage women but are less likely to be promoted to manage men (Alban-Metcalf and West, 1991: 161), as it is felt this is too difficult for men to adjust to. Additionally, in a comparison of female and male managers, it is still the case that women are more highly qualified than men at the same level and are more likely to have fewer family responsibilities (i.e. are more likely to be childless) than men. So much for equal opportunities.

(g)   Chaplin, J. (1989) 'Counselling and gender' in W. Dryden, D. Charles-Edwards and R. Woolfe (eds) *Handbook of Counselling in Britain*. London: Tavistock/Routledge; Lerner, G. (1986) *The Creation of Patriarchy*. Oxford: Oxford University Press; Perry, J. (1993) *Counselling for Women*. Buckingham: Open University Press.

JANET PERRY AND RICHARD WOOD
    (See also *racism and prejudice*)

Groups, use of

(a) The group may be defined as a gathering of individuals collected together for a specified purpose. Numbers may vary according to its function, but in general any gathering of people of three to nine in number may be considered to be a *small* group, from ten to twenty to be a *median* group, over twenty to be a *large* group.

For each of us the group is the primary unit of socialization; society may be viewed as a series of interlinking groups based upon the family, the first group to which most belong. All groups, whatever their nature or purpose, manifest the same phenomena, the same processes and the same developmental stages.

Much of the care that is offered is given by or within groups. The hospital ward and the residential home inevitably carry out much of their work as a group and in group situations. The organization providing care is a group, or collection of groups; and shows similar processes to therapy groups, making an impact upon the work of its members, and upon their feelings and their sense of themselves. Consequently, at least a basic understanding of groups, how they work and what happens in them is essential to all who work in the field of care, even if individual workers choose one-to-one contact with their clients.

(b) The uses to which groups may be put are virtually limitless and it is not possible to provide an exhaustive list here. The main uses of groups, for treatment or training are listed below. A more complete description follows in section (d).

Training
supervision
staff support
team building

Treatment
therapeutic communities
group analytic and psychotherapy groups
counselling groups
psychodrama

problem-specific groups:
   anxiety management
   social skills training
   assertiveness training
   alcohol and other substance abuse

survivors' groups:
   survivors of sexual and physical abuse
   groups in the wake of disaster

(d) There are two basic requirements that pertain to most, if not all groups:

1. **Confidentiality:** information brought to the group and all experiences within the group remain in the group.
2. Attendance: for the benefit of the group all members are required to attend regularly, and to make the group their first priority when it is scheduled to meet.

Groups for training

1. Supervision: Elsewhere I have suggested that a good definition of **supervision**:

> in its simplest form . . . is a meeting between two or more people who have a declared purpose in examining a piece of work. The work is presented and together they will think about what was happening and why, what was done or said, how it was handled – could it have been handled better or differently, and if so how? (Wright, 1989)

This basic definition applies equally to individual supervision and to supervision groups. The latter may be undertaken with peers: fellow workers who have experience and training to the same or similar levels, who meet together to bring wider views and perceptions to the piece of work under discussion.

Often such groups are convened by a colleague who has acknowledged expertise in a particular sphere. Most usefully supervision is undertaken in small groups of no more than three or four members so that each member does not have too long to wait between presentations of her work, thus enabling continuity.

Supervision of group work is best undertaken within groups, if only because it offers a model for understanding group situations. A supervision group affords each individual a live experience of groups which furthers the understanding of what it is to be in one.

2. Staff support: There is often confusion between support and supervision. This may have to do with the value of the supervision group in supporting not only the work of the supervisee, but the individual worker, who often feels *held* by colleagues and by their understanding.

The difference between the two is in the aims. A supervision group focuses on a piece of work and considers what was done and why. A support group more usually addresses the experience of the workers, the stresses and difficulties they face, and their emotional life as it relates to and is affected by those in their care and by the employing organization.

Staff support groups are also convened to provide a forum in which colleagues can confront and intend to resolve interpersonal difficulties that arise as a consequence of the work they undertake. Often they aim to address both the needs of the individual and the needs of the group. They usually, and most helpfully, have no more than eight or nine members. Small groups are more facilitative of this kind of work.

3. *Team building:*   Many organizations periodically engage in *team building* exercises, particularly at the inception of a new service or work group, or when circumstances are difficult. The work group is helped by a facilitator (most usually and arguably most helpfully an outsider) to identify common goals, individual and team skills, experience and talents; while at the same time noting and working with any difficulties within the team.

There are sometimes extravagant hopes and omnipotent claims made in the name of team building. Most usually it is a brief, focused intervention which relies upon a variety of techniques, e.g. games which intend to inspire trust, brainstorming to highlight strengths and weaknesses and so on. But where there are real problems then it takes a different kind of involvement, and longer commitment before they can helpfully be addressed.

Groups for treatment
With the exception of therapeutic communities all treatment groups can and do take place in both residential and non-residential environments.

1. *Therapeutic communities:*   The term was first used by Dr Tom Main in 1946 when writing about the work at Northfield Military Hospital. It is a term whose original, clear meaning has been distorted so that it sometimes comes to be something of a catch-all. The characteristics of therapeutic communities are listed below:

- communalism
- democratization
- flattening of the authority pyramid
- philosophy, based upon psychodynamic principles
- permissiveness
- reality confrontation.

The way in which these characteristics are interpreted is extremely varied. Mistaken understanding can mean that a so-called therapeutic community is anything but. There have been communities where democratization has meant that each has equal authority and none is responsible, where permissiveness has meant that no-one has a right to challenge anything, where communalism has meant everyone owns everything and privacy becomes a crime, and where reality confrontation subsides into bullying. But where the characteristics listed above are properly understood such communities have tremendous treatment potential.

People remain in therapeutic communities for roughly nine months to two years, depending on the nature of individual difficulty and the type of community. Some communities are very successful in their work with people with extreme problems (both individuals and, in some cases, families), e.g. borderline personalities (see *psychosis and severe mental disorders*), abusing families (see *child abuse*) or people with extremely challenging behaviours (see *learning disabilities*).

Much of the work is undertaken in groups, either therapy groups (described below) or work groups such as cooking and cleaning, maintenance and so on. In this way every aspect of daily life becomes the focus of thoughtful consideration and is available for modification over time. It can be a very intense, powerful and extremely worthwhile, holding yet challenging experience.

2. *Group analytic and psychotherapy groups:*   The most influential, widely available, psychoanalytically based form of group psychotherapy in Britain is group analysis. Developed by Foulkes and others, group analysis is a therapy *in* the group, *of* the group, *by* the group.

The conductor will follow the processes of the group, its patterns of interaction and emerging themes as they reveal underlying, influential, unconscious elements. These are worked through as they become available to the group in conscious form. Most particularly the facilitator or conductor of group analytic and psychotherapy groups will work with *transference phenomena.* Many argue that it is this central focus that enables change at the deepest, most profound level.

Psychotherapeutic and group analytic groups usually have a maximum of eight or nine members and a minimum of five. If there are more than eight or nine then intimacy and the necessary establishment of trust may be impaired; if there are less than five the group may behave as two pairings or as a couple with one left out.

These types of group meet usually once or sometimes twice weekly, for an hour and a half. They may be established as time limited groups for a year or two with a closed membership, but it is quite usual for them to be 'slow–open' in character: that is, the group may continue for years with a slowly changing membership as those who have benefited leave and others join.

Such groups work with people with a whole range of problems including **alcoholism**, **sexual difficulties**, anxiety states (see *phobias* *and anxiety*), **depression**, borderline personalities, **adult survivors of abuse** and so on, usually in a thoughtful and carefully established mix of membership. It is essential that those who would work in this way are properly trained, and continue in clinical **supervision** into qualified practice.

3. Counselling groups: There is a wide range of counselling undertaken in groups. Some are problem specific and have a partly educative role, e.g. counselling in illness. Others operate in ways similar to psychotherapy groups. Many are psychodynamically based. There is great variation in the duration of counselling groups, some lasting for a number of weeks, others 'slow–open' as described above.

While all groups pay attention to interpersonal relationships in the group, and to what is happening in the here and now, some (including counselling groups) attend to the 'there and then' (i.e. the influence of past experiences on the individual today). Usually psychotherapy groups work within the transference situation and deal directly with other unconscious phenomena. This is, perhaps, the main or most significant difference between psychotherapy groups and counselling groups (although some group counsellors also claim to work with the transference). Other types of counselling group are of a more prescriptive nature where the facilitator offers suggestions and recommendations, or information on specific issues. Again, people who work in this way should be properly trained and supervised.

4. Psychodrama: This is a very specific way of working. The therapist (director) works to assist a group member (protagonist) to recreate a current conflict or problem area as a sort of play, in which other group members act as characters who are significant in the situation depicted. In this way current difficulties are examined, alternative solutions sought and earlier similar experiences are brought to the surface, becoming available to be worked through in the psychodrama.

The protagonist is not the only member to benefit from the psychodrama. Other members gain from the resonances the protagonist's experiences evoke in them. The therapist is very visible and directive, in contrast to other types of therapy in groups. But, as in all forms of therapy, he or she remains sensitive to the needs of the individual and the group.

It is an emotionally powerful way of working that requires great skill, training and experience. It is undertaken in a variety of settings, both in the hospital and in the community, and often takes place weekly, lasting for about half a day, or an evening, for each session. Numbers vary, but normally range between 8 and 15, although sometimes they can be much larger.

5. Problem-specific groups: These include anxiety management, social skills and assertiveness training groups, and groups for those who misuse alcohol or other substances (see *alcoholism; substance misuse*). Usually such groups are time limited, lasting for a pre-defined period, often six to ten weeks; and they are highly structured. They provide a packaged programme that may begin with a definition, description and discussion of the problem in order to identify the target of the group; to enable its members to understand the causes of physical effects, the responses of others; and to establish *universality* – there is relief in finding one is not alone with the problem.

Many make use of cognitive approaches to re-define problems, and other more active techniques (such as role play and relaxation programmes) to address specific areas of difficulty. There is often a practice element encouraging members to take newly learned behaviour into the world outside the group. Members may be required to keep a diary of daily experiences in order to clarify which situations lead to difficulty and to help them to differentiate more clearly between states of mind. For example, it is quite common for anxious people to consider themselves anxious at all times, but when the diary is examined variations in levels of anxiety become apparent (see *phobias and anxiety*).

Such groups do not usually attempt to work with underlying causes, preferring to aim for a change in thinking and behaviour; or they have a more limited, still useful purpose of offering strategies that help the individual to cope better.

There is much variety in how this sort of group is conducted. Some include an interest in working with underlying issues; some offer a supportive group experience that continues after the initial programme has been completed. The type of work undertaken varies with the presenting problem. For example, social skills training groups may use techniques of role play and evaluation more intensively than an anxiety management or substance abusers' group.

Groups in the wake of disaster: As far as possible the role of the therapist in this situation is to enable established community or work groups themselves to do the work of supporting each other, grieving with each other (see *bereavement*), and facing the horrific experience of the disaster and its consequences. The notion of 'debriefing' is central; survivors of disaster are not dealing with long established problems of mental health. They are responding in ordinary human ways to overwhelming circumstance. Where debriefing can be quickly established, recovery rates are more rapid and the number suffering long-term emotional effects is reduced.

Of course, some are more vulnerable than others and may need longer-term help in a survivors' group led by a trained group therapist, since other problems have surfaced and require working through in a different setting (see *major incidents*).

Survivors' groups: There is some current research that suggests that victims of physical and sexual abuse may be considered to be suffering from **post-traumatic stress** syndrome. It is for this reason that they are considered here with survivors of disasters.

There are important differences. Recent research suggests that 'debriefing' work, undertaken immediately in the wake of disaster, is very effective in limiting the debilitating effects of the disaster upon the individual, especially when offered within the established work or community group. Clearly there is an important difference in cases of abuse; it often takes years for abuse to come to light.

Survivors of abuse: There is a notion that the only way one can work with survivors of sexual abuse in groups is by confining membership to those who have been abused. Some people (both genders can be victims) find great difficulty in talking about the abuse they have suffered with others who have no experience of it. Individuals should be given the choice. Beginning in an exclusive group may be the only way, initially, that help can be sought.

Group analysts and others have worked successfully in broadly based therapy groups with a mixed membership, of those who have been abused and those with other difficulties. The limitations imposed upon a group through confining it to one type of experience may impair or inhibit other possible curative experiences, and other views of the world and of relationships.

The duration of such groups varies, from an hour and a half weekly for ten weeks, to about two years.

Self-help groups
These groups develop like all groups, reveal the same phenomena and undergo the same processes. Those who work in these, and other groups, often benefit from an introductory, if not longer, training in group-work (see *self-help groups*).

(e)   Organizations offering training and treatment:
The Cassel Hospital (1 Ham Common, Richmond, Surrey. Tel: 0181 940 8181) offers training to qualified health care professionals, including specialized courses for nurses; in-patient treatment for families and individuals in the therapeutic community; out-patient groups, family work and individual psychotherapy.

The Institute of Advanced Nursing Education (The Royal College of Nursing, 20 Cavendish Square, London W1M 1AB. Tel: 0171 409 3333) offers training to nurses and others in therapeutic community practice.

The Association of Therapeutic Communities (The Courtyard, Howton Place, Bushey Heath, Watford, Herts WD2 1HX. Tel: 0181 950 9557) offers information on training and treatment and the location of member therapeutic communities.

The Institute of Group Analysis (1 Daleham Gardens, London NW3 5BY. Tel: 0171 431 2693) and Group Analysis North (c/o Miriam Jones, Administrator, 2 Brixton Avenue, Withington, Manchester M20 8JF. Tel: 0161 445 8176) both offer training at various levels, from introductory courses in groups, to qualifying courses in group analysis. They are also able to recommend qualified practitioners to those seeking treatment or consultation. A number of group analysts also offer consultation to organizations.

The Scottish Institute of Human Relations (The Garrethill Centre, 28 Rose Street, Glasgow G3 6RE) offers the General Group Course (IGA recognized) and a number of other related courses; and has information on available treatment.

The Tavistock Institute and Clinic (120 Belsize Lane, London NW3 5BA. Tel: 0171 435 7111) offers treatment and training in family, individual and group work.

The Holwell Centre of Psychodrama (East Down, Barnstaple, Devon) offers training and treatment, and information on both.

(g)   Jacobs, E., Harvil, R. L. and Messon, R. L. (1994) *Group Counseling, Strategies and Skills* (2nd edn). Pacific Grove, CA: Brooks/Cole Publishing; Wright, H. (1989) *Group Work: Perspectives and Practice*. London: Scutari Press; Wright, H. and Giddey, M. (eds) (1993) *Mental Health Nursing, from First Principles to Professional Practice*. London: Chapman and Hall.

HARRY WRIGHT
(See also *self-help groups*)

Guilt and shame

(a)   'Shame' relates to feelings about who one is. For the person who feels shame, her or his very self is of little or no worth. 'Guilt' refers to a feeling that what he or she has done or omitted to do is wrong: guilt thus relates to doing, shame to being.

Shame and guilt imply that one's being or one's actions are unworthy, although both shame and guilt have healthy and unhealthy forms. Healthy guilt pertains to the capacity for concern not to harm others, and to wish to make reparation where one is responsible for harm. Unhealthy guilt involves the sense that one's wishes or actions are unworthy or destructive. A healthy sense of shame pertains to giving up illusions and achieving a more realistic sense of self. Unhealthy shame pertains to a mistaken sense that the self is worthless, and may well be the outcome of being shamed or humiliated by others.

A further definition is 'existential guilt': this is a healthy state. Nevertheless it often leads the person who is experiencing it to seek help. The term refers to guilt or shame at having failed to fulfil one's potential.

(b) *Shame* is provoked by experiences that call into question our view of who we are, by making us see ourselves through the eyes of others. Healthy shame is dealt with by facing up to such perceptions and giving up illusions about the self. Denying shame develops a shell of defensiveness. In contrast, unhealthy shame means that self-worth is more or less crippled by shaming. However, shame is often not a straightforward conflict between objective truth and subjective illusion, and it is complex to disentangle what is helpful and what is crippling.

An example of healthy shame is the man who, believing himself to be a composer of genius, spends all his resources on his talent, neglecting his wife and family, and throwing tantrums if challenged. However, when his compositions are rejected by a composer he highly respects, he realizes he has been deceiving himself. He feels ashamed as he grasps his mediocrity, and his previous lack of insight into himself. His wife and family, throughout this difficult process, treat him warmly and continue to accept him for who he is; with this support, he comes to a more accurate sense of himself. He becomes a successful church organist and teacher, enjoys music as he never had before and, renewed and refreshed by his musical activities, is able to be more loving and attentive to his family.

We can rewrite this story to make it one illustrating unhealthy shame: Suppose that our composer is an unrecognized genius, who has had to summon up all his courage to show his distinguished colleague his work. The established composer is envious, and his judgement is not truthful, but an attack on something good. Suppose further our genius's wife and children are bitter and resentful at the years of emotional absence, at the poverty which has led to humiliating treatment by school fellows and neighbours. The husband shows his wife the distinguished composer's letter; she calls in the children and denounces him: 'This is what a *real* composer thinks of your stupid, puny father'; and she says to him: 'How dare you show off this letter, after what you've done to us? You should be ashamed. We're leaving you for good, you wastrel.' Abandoned, he burns his manuscripts and ends up destitute. His sense of worth has been destroyed by others.

I consider below the implications of these examples for the understanding and treatment of shame.

A sense of *guilt* is wholesome for individual development if it is realistic. It is unwholesome if it is not: where, for instance, it is so exaggerated as to lead to constant terror of punishment, or in other ways makes it impossible for the guilty person to live effectively, such as **obsessive-compulsive disorders**.

A helpful way of understanding guilt is provided by the psychoanalyst D. W. Winnicott. For him, morality is a question of the ability to follow one's own values, not of complying with imposed rules. The healthy person makes some compromise between his personal values and what society requires. He or she will have achieved a 'capacity for concern', which includes guilt, which is derived from anxiety: this concern includes an awareness of one's own power to harm as well as to sustain others. Where the sense of actually causing or potentially causing harm is not tempered by a sense of being able to do good, unhealthy guilt often results: people see themselves as 'bad' and destructive, because they cannot feel that the harm that results from pursuing their selfish needs can be made good by making reparation, for instance by loving or creative acts.

Winnicott emphasizes that a mother must be able to survive the neediness and destructiveness of her infant if a healthy sense of guilt is to arise in the growing child. Thinking of our composer and his family, we see how a healthy outcome could result either from his wife's tolerance and forgiveness of his self-delusion, or from his ability to survive her rage; we can also see how unhealthy guilt is shown in his collapse, perhaps because his family's departure convinces him that he has destroyed their love, and there is no opportunity to try to make up for it.

Existential guilt is powerfully portrayed in Camus' novel *The Fall* (1963): a judge fails to prevent a suicide when he was in a position to do so. Unwilling to respond to a drowning woman's cries, he betrays his own integrity. He renounces his position of judge, with its implication that he himself is above crime, and adopts the role of penitent. He can imagine no true reparation but to live the event again and respond to the drowning woman's cries for help, and even if this were possible, he knows he might still not take the risk. There are elements of reparation in his refusal to be a hypocrite, but in the main what seems to be portrayed is a disillusioned human being trying to live with the knowledge that he does not have it in him to make good the damage he has done.

His existential guilt is triggered by actual guilt at his initial failure to respond. This failure opens up for him a sense which is rooted in the developmental struggles of infancy, and belongs to the ordinary life of adult human beings, maybe especially to maturity. In the face of death, which gives rise to existential anxiety particularly in mid-life (see *mid-life crisis*), we realize how we have fallen short of what we hoped to become. Although there remains the chance to continue to fulfil one's potential, there is also the need to mourn and accept its loss.

(c)   Healthy shame comes from confronting self-deception. Such illusion often results from attempts to defend oneself against an awareness of personal inadequacies, as in our composer's need to behave as if he were a genius, thus covering up his real ordinariness. He might also have felt inadequate in other roles as well, currently those of husband and father: with his incompetence in that part of his life perhaps justified as the result of absorption in a 'higher' task.

Unhealthy shame, shown in the second version of the story, is often suffered by those who have been bullied, or otherwise oppressed, for example for their gender, race or physical appearance; or for their religious or political beliefs. The most extreme shaming attempts to destroy any sense of self, as in the systematic persecution of the Jewish people by the Nazis.

Perfectly healthy people may succumb to shaming by others. Those whose early experiences in the family have led to a weak or unformed sense of self are most susceptible. Inadequate parents, though not deliberately attempting to humiliate, may fail to convey to a child a sense that they understand and value him or her. They may be unable to perceive how vulnerable and sensitive their infant is, or have little capacity to tolerate her or his neediness and unorganized nature. Such parenting may lead to a deep feeling of worthlessness in the child, which in extreme cases is covered completely by a false self: a stance in life that is based on fitting in totally with the perceptions and wishes of others, in place of recognition of and inclusion of one's own essential humanity.

Guilt commonly originates in a sense that one's actions towards others are destructive. As we have seen, insofar as this is accurately perceived, it leads to a concerned response to others. But often, in its attempts to preserve the faith that parents or other important caring figures are good and powerful, infants and children perceive that the bad things that happen in relation to their parents are all their own fault. Great suffering can result from such infantile thinking, which often seems to arise particularly where the threat to the child's faith in others is extreme: for example, when parents divorce, or where a parent sexually abuses a child. Such guilt feelings are quite disproportionate to any role the child has played, yet they are felt to be real and may endure in the adult as a continued belief in their own wickedness.

(d) People who come for help with feelings of shame have lost support both from others and from within themselves. What is needed to guide such people through their feelings is a careful exploration that is based on the helper's provision of understanding, respect and genuineness. This must be demonstrated through patience, reliability and an abstinence from retaliatory words or actions, even where these might be provoked by the person seeking help. In other words, what the helper tries to provide is what we might presume was lacking in the sufferer's previous environmental support.

Where guilt is the issue, particularly existential guilt, it is important to support the person's honest enquiry, and to allow painful feelings to come through. Helpers and carers have to have an ability to distinguish when guilt and shame are realistic, and therefore need to be heeded, and when they are unwarranted and need to be given up. However, it has to be said that letting go of inappropriate guilt or shame is seldom straightforward. Helpers need to have dealt sufficiently with their own sense of shame and guilt, otherwise they are likely to retreat defensively into using their expertise by moralizing, teaching, judging and condemning, or even colluding with and reassuring those who ask for help. The essential factor in caring in such instances is the provision of adequate (but not excessive) environmental support, so as to enable the sufferer to find and reach into her or his internal resources.

(e) Potential helpers dealing with people experiencing shame and guilt will benefit from training in counselling skills, and from themselves having had counselling or psychotherapy. **Supervision** from an experienced counsellor or psychotherapist is also advised. Deep-seated and resistant shame and guilt need referral to professional counselling or psychotherapy. Referrals can be made to those listed in the directories published by the British Association for Counselling (1 Regent Place, Rugby CV21 2PJ) and the UK Council for Psychotherapy (Regent's College, Regent's Park, London NW1 4NS).

(f) Confidentiality is of the utmost importance in dealing with guilt and shame. Where absolute confidentiality cannot be guaranteed, its limitations should be made clear to the client, and where it seems important to disclose confidential material in a client's interest, her or his permission must be obtained.

(g) Dass, R. and Gorman, P. (1985) *How Can I Help?* London: Rider; Kirschenbaum, H. and Land, H. (eds) (1990) *The Carl Rogers Reader*.

London: Constable; Winnicott, D. W. (1986) *Home Is Where We Start From*. London: Penguin Books.

JOHN WHEWAY
(See also *adult survivors of abuse; violence towards women*)

Holistic medicine

(a) Holistic models attempt to comprehend and describe whole organisms and systems as entities greater than and different from the sum of their parts. Holistic medicine sees health as a dynamic continual process of self-restoration in response to a fluctuating and challenging environment. Disease occurs when the ability to maintain internal equilibrium in the face of environmental challenge or internal distress breaks down.

(b) Evolution reminds us that adaptations in form, structure and function arise as a result of complex interactions between environment and organisms. Within the organism itself a constant internal milieu has to be maintained despite a fluctuating external environment, from which the organism receives a constant flow of air, food and information. The processes of homoeostasis ensure that integrity and internal equilibrium are maintained.

The central nervous system is a key co-ordinator regulating these physiological systems, and homoeostasis depends on the mutual influences of both psychological and physical factors. The holistic model, integrating psyche with internal physiology, opens up an enlarged perspective on illness, where biological, psychological and social demands may all call up physiological (and potentially pathological) responses in the organism. This bio-psycho-social model of medicine sees the individual not as an isolated and fragmented bio-machine, but rather as a body–mind immersed in and interacting with a complex and holistic ecosystem.

Scientific inquiry has now developed to a point where narrow perspectives and single solutions are seen as inadequate to the complex problems we face. Until the 1970s, the supremacy and unbounded progress of conventional medicine – or biomedicine – were rarely questioned. Then the flow of spectacular discoveries slowed down: little has changed in the treatment of common diseases since the 1960s. Chronic and stress-related illness, environmentally mediated illness, diseases of mood and desire, 'mental' disorders, addiction states – are only partially helped by biomedicine. Medical expenditure is still increasing rapidly in all developed countries. Despite this, life expectancy for someone who has reached middle age is much the same as it was at the turn of the century; and we now have to face the likelihood that the 'magic bullets' approach may prove ineffective against the epidemic diseases affecting adults in Northern societies.

Many people now look to holism as an antidote to the mechanistic reductionism of the prevailing sciences, and in the field of health care its appeal is particularly due to a growing sense of fragmentation and over-specialization. There is an equally growing awareness of biomedicine's side-effects: over-medication, a fragmentary pattern of health care and a growing sense among both health-care professionals and their clients, of dehumanization, dependency and disempowerment.

(d) Holistic medicine's underlying idea is the concept that health is influenced by mind, body and spirit in the context of a social and physical environment. Characteristically, holistic approaches to health care respect the innate capacity for self-healing, and encourage clients to be active partners, not simply passive recipients of treatment. Emphasizing health promotion and education for self-care and stressing the importance of nutrition, exercise or relaxation and attitude change, holistic approaches use a broad range of interventions that tap homoeostatic potential for self-regulation. In this broader view of what makes and keeps people well, therapy is only a small part – friends, nutrition, spirituality, community, art, education, love, etc. all make up a much bigger part of the picture.

1. A new model for health care
First, the 'whole person' is acknowledged to be multi-dimensional, responding to and developing within a social and environmental context. The whole person is a hierarchy of natural systems, each level of which is simultaneously a component in a higher system (von Bertalanffy, 1968). The unique characteristics of each level are described in the language of separate disciplines – molecular biology, psychology, sociology, etc. – and consequently there seems a gigantic gulf between mind and molecule. Research, however, is beginning to show how feelings and experiences change us even at a cellular level (Locke and Hornig-Rohan, 1983).

This is the central theme of holistic medicine – that all these systems influence one another – change one and potentially you change them all. So the balance between health and illness can be maintained or disturbed at any level. In these terms, diagnosis involves identifying the most appropriate level on which to make an effective intervention.

The other axis of holistic medicine is developmental, because we live in time, continually adapting (Ornstein, 1975). How people relate, consciously and unconsciously, to their own and their cultural past, what knowledge skills and attitudes are at their disposal and how they imagine the future, will all influence the way they live in and cope with the present moment.

2. *A wide range of interventions*

Holistic medicine stresses the importance of context. A diseased organ exists within a whole person; a sick person within a social and physical environment. Where then is the most appropriate level to intervene; and what methods are effective? 'Orthodox', 'complementary', social and psychological work, environmental and political approaches all have their place. Working at these different levels demands critical openness to a broad range of therapies and health maintenance strategies. Therefore the range of knowledge, skills and attitudes actually needed for holistic health care will perhaps generally be provided by multidisciplinary teams, rather than by exceptionally gifted individuals (Bennet, 1984).

Such teams need to develop a common humanistic core to their work. Perhaps by bringing together the different professional groups – including medical students, nurses, social workers and occupational therapists – for part of their training, the foundations of co-operative interdisciplinary practice, so necessary for holistic health care, will be created.

In managing chronic disease and disability, health care should aim to prevent sequelae, whether physical, social or psychological. Sufficient evidence has accumulated to suggest that there may be an important role for complementary therapies – both 'mind–body' and 'alternative medicine' – as well as for self-help and a more psychosomatically informed approach to rehabilitation. Their potential for making a valuable cost-effective contribution to mainstream health care should now be investigated as a priority in the NHS's research programme

3. *Self-help, self-healing and prevention*

In health, body and mind maintain self-regulation. This ongoing process of homoeostasis can be encouraged. Diet and exercise can make an important contribution in changing risk factor profiles. However, research in *behavioural medicine* indicates that self-regulation can be enhanced using a variety of techniques akin to relaxation training and auto-hypnosis (Pelletier, 1978).

Biological approaches to health care can be augmented by these highly cost-effective methods, which are simple to teach and could be offered to patients in both general practice and hospital care. Their role is well researched in the prevention and rehabilitation of cardiovascular disease, in pain management and in common functional disorders such as migraine, asthma and irritable bowel syndrome. Nurses, occupational therapists and health visitors have a vital part to play in disseminating these techniques.

Self-help includes these new approaches to health promotion – mind/body techniques like relaxation response training as well as the cognitive and behavioural skills underpinning **stress** management. Rehabilitation (including support for the adaptation stresses of the whole family involved (see *families, working with*)) has a central part to play particularly in **cancer** care and after cardiovascular disease. In the long term it is likely to offer a buffer against secondary pathology and so result in more cost-effective medicine.

Many major diseases are preventable either by altering personal lifestyle or the external environment. Although we are free in varying degrees to make individual choices, collective action may be required to deal with relevant social, educational and environmental factors (Black et al., 1982).

Individuals have to be motivated if they are to change their ideas, behaviour and attitudes. Because health and illness are not separate from the society in which they occur, politicians, educationalists and health professionals must all consider how to make *healthy* choices *easy* choices.

4. Caring, clarity and the need for staff support

What most patients want from practitioners is kindness, sympathy, patience, tolerance and understanding (Balint, 1968). Disease is always a crisis, not only for the sufferer but for those – family and friends – who are in support. Although disease will often trigger a breakdown of coping and communication, it can also be a powerful motivator for change and an opportunity for development. The adequate provision of **counselling** can overcome the sense of helplessness that may accompany illness, help prevent the spread of emotional illness and encourage natural healing processes that might otherwise be swamped. The value added benefit of training professionals to handle any illness with some psychological awareness is that it also buffers *them* against some of the consequences of their stressful work (see *stress*).

The awareness and 'wellness' of the practitioner obviously become crucial components in the practice of holistic medicine. However, available evidence suggests that the self-care habits of health professionals are often poor, and they and their relationships often particularly prone to breakdown.

The NHS's own organizational health, and the health of many individuals working in it, is far from ideal. Although the situation is bound to be exacerbated wherever rates of change are high, it is an endemic problem because nurses and doctors usually work under considerable pressure. A large body of research shows how their maladaptive behaviour, poor stress management and communication skills put them at risk.

Stressed staff are less able to perform their tasks well, while stressed organizations have high levels of client damage and staff wastage. Policies that can break this vicious cycle will encourage practitioner well-being in spite of what may be unavoidably high stress occupations. At the same time, it will be important to develop more healthy corporate structures which can encourage personal qualities known to provide a buffer against stress-related disease. A sense of challenge, of choice and commitment, individual stress management skills and access to social support in the work setting are all important protective factors that a corporate culture can either encourage or stifle.

5. Complementary therapies

To a considerable and perhaps surprising degree, there is already a working consensus amongst many doctors as to what constitutes effective non-conventional therapy, and some confirmatory research exists for major complementary therapies such as osteopathy, acupuncture and homoeopathy. Access to a broader range of non-conventional therapies – including aspects of complementary medicine as well as mind–body techniques – could be highly cost beneficial to the NHS through improved management of stress-related diseases, functional disorders, musculo-skeletal disorders (especially the back) and other persistent pain.

Those who can afford to seek help from these therapies are doing so in large numbers. Yet many more might benefit. Their ongoing management – often relatively ineffective, possibly harmful and costly – might usefully be complemented or even replaced by non-conventional approaches. They remain disenfranchised of the choice that the 1948 Act was intended to offer them. Ironically, in many cases their own GPs who would like to refer them on to appropriate NHS units where suitable therapies could be tried, feel equally helpless.

Amidst the apparent welter of oddly named specialisms in alternative medicine it is important to distinguish systems, diagnostic methods, therapeutic modalities and self-care techniques (see opposite).

6. Complementary systems

Systems have their own internally consistent approaches to aetiology, diagnosis and treatment, whereas treatment techniques can be separated off from their system and used in a way consistent with conventional consideration of aetiology and diagnosis. A system is more

Complete systems	Diagnostic methods	Treatment techniques	Self-care
traditional Chinese medicine	iridology	acupressure	meditation
chiropractic	Kirlian photography	manipulation	relaxation
homoeopathy	hair analysis	reflexology	exercise
Ayurveda	dowsing	massage	co-counselling
anthroposophical medicine	pulse testing	kinesiology	imagery
osteopathy		healing	
naturopathy			

complete if it includes in its map not only body, mind and feelings, but also how these interact with the environment; and how all this relates to a social world and spiritual life. For any system to be an *alternative* to another it would have to be entirely comprehensive, and able to deal with every possible problem. Until such a system emerges, all systems are provisionally complementary to one another. Although Western conventional medicine may only now be starting to grasp the importance of the wider picture, there are times when surgery, drugs and life support have their place.

Generally speaking, whatever level good treatment is aimed at, it has an effect at other levels. Such approaches can justifiably be called holistic. Whatever the system, the way practitioner and client relate to each other is often as important as the treatment used, because whole person care is an ideal to be striven for, not an off-the-shelf package available simply by looking in Yellow Pages for a well-qualified practitioner.

Generally in conventional medicine treatment is in the hands of doctors, who take *responsibility* for getting the patient better. The treatment process usually involves *confronting* a disorderly body chemistry or an invading infection, and works at the *physical* level – surgeons on organs, drugs on biochemical pathways, etc. Still there is a good deal in conventional medicine that *catalyses* wellness too; for instance, rehabilitation work by physiotherapists and occupational therapists; a counsellor helping someone cope with loss; psychologists using cognitive and behavioural therapies; a social worker endeavouring to alleviate a housing problem. Even setting a bone is working *with* the healing process. Increasingly, conventional medicine sees that changing life-style and self-care can prevent disease and promote health.

It is relevant that complementary systems, while they aim to cata-lyse the healing processes, are usually as reliant on the external control of the expert practitioner as is the conventional system. But a good practitioner – conventional or complementary – also helps people understand issues around the meaning of health and illness *for them*, and will explore what *they* can do to get better.

Non-conventional systems have much in common. In one way or another, they all talk about energy, and attribute qualities to different kinds of energy. They all try to consider a person's mind–body make-up, assessing *constitution* (body) and *temperament* (mind). When looking for a cause they often identify the *context* in which the person lives – social or environmental. Different systems understand the *organs* as depending for their health on a proper *dynamic balance* between different *qualities* of energy. All attempt to identify and treat problems before organs have been physically damaged; and often in diagnosing these they study build, posture, face, tongue or pulses.

Chinese, Tibetan, Ayurveda *systems* are all Eastern in their origin, and all of them have highly developed philosophies of mind, body and spirit interaction. Energy and its dynamics within the body–mind are diagnosed by looking, listening and feeling. Diet, herbs, massage and exercise form a large part of the treatments used, together with the use of needles for acupuncture in Chinese medicine. While these systems have an understanding of health based on very different notions to conventional medicine, homoeopathy, naturopathy, chiropractic and osteopathy all lean much more closely towards conventional ideas about causes and pathology.

Anthroposophical medicine is a Western system of whole person care. Initiated under the direction of Rudolf Steiner, drawing on his own profound knowledge of world spiritual traditions, and developed by subsequent generations of practitioners, the anthroposophical (mean-ing 'wisdom of mankind') approach is considered an extension of con-ventional medicine. It is practised by qualified doctors who base their diagnosis on an understanding of the human constitution as physical, energetic, sentient and spiritual. How these elements interweave in health and illness determines treatment, which may involve not only medicines – often homoeopathically prepared – but also artistic thera-pies and **counselling**.

Homoeopathy is a European development. According to which trend within homoeopathy you care to look at, it is wide open to ideas about mind, body and spirit. Unfortunately it can appear over-attached to solving big problems by giving 'remedies'; but only the most partisan practitioner would fail to question this position and look for factors that lead to illness or which maintain it. Although highly adaptable to a wide range of philosophical positions, it has become the medical system of choice for certain fundamentalist Christian sects, a large proportion of the Indian sub-continent and committed New Agers. It is also widely used in families who might buy at the chemist retailing chain Boots, showing that homoeopathy has achieved serious market penetration. Its basis is appealing: symptoms are the mind–body's way of letting you know what it needs. However, this language is coded. To crack the code you need to identify the poison that would create similar symptoms; and to treat it, simply give a small dose of it back to the mind–body.

Diagnostic methods   include Kirlian photography, medical dowsing, allergy pulse testing, 'bioenergetic' investigations such as Vega, or applied kinesiology tests. Some non-conventional practitioners use them. Their efficacy is not proven.

Treatment techniques   can be used without a whole system to explain the detailed cause of problem and how they work: e.g. massage, reflexology, aromatherapy, therapeutic touch, acupuncture needling.

Self-care methods   exemplify those approaches that work '*internally*'. Often they are the type of methods that people decide to embark upon themselves: nutritional, exercise, relaxation, yoga. Often, as in the case of meditation and prayer, they work at a psychological or even a transpersonal level.

(e)   Further information can be obtained from:
Holistic medicine: The British Holistic Medical Association, Royal Shrewsbury Hospital, Mylton Oak Road, Shrewsbury, Shropshire SY3 8XF; Marylebone Centre Trust, The Education and Training Unit, 33 Queen Anne Street, London W1M 9FB (Tel: 0171 255 3550).
Ayurveda organizations: The International Society for Ayurveda, 7 Ravenscroft Avenue, Golders Green, London NW11 0SA; Ayurveda Seminar, 27 Lanker's Drive, North Harrow, Middx.
Tibetan medicine organizations: The Tibet Foundation, 43 New Oxford Street, London WC1A 1BH (Tel: 0171 379 0634); The Tibetan Medical Centre, Dharamsala Cantonment, District Kangra, Himachal Pradesh, India.
Traditional Chinese medicine organizations: The Council for Acupuncture, 179 Gloucester Place, London NW1 5DX.
Anthroposophical Medical Association: Rudolf Steiner House, 35 Park Road, London NW1 6XT. A full list of fully qualified anthroposophical physicians can be obtained from this address – enclose s.a.e.
Homoeopathy: The Faculty of Homoeopathy, Powis Place, Great Ormond Street, London WC1 (Tel: 0171 837 3091) (for doctors); Society

of Homoeopaths, 2 Artisan Road, Northampton NN1 4HY (Tel: 01604 21400) (for non-medical homoeopaths).

(g) Fulder, S. (1988) *The Handbook of Complementary Medicine.* Oxford: Oxford University Press; Pietroni, P. (1990) *The Greening of Medicine.* London: Gollancz; Stalker, D. and Gilmour, C. (1985) *Examining Holistic Medicine.* London: Prometheus Books.

DAVID PETERS

Homelessness

(a) Homelessness is more than 'rooflessness'. It is about being unsettled, on the move even if friends have temporarily provided a sofa or a charitable agency has provided a bed. It is to feel unable to go back or to move forward. What blocks the way back may be domestic violence, abuse, betrayal or rejection. What blocks the way forward may be inadequate financial resources or insufficient points on a housing waiting list.

In human terms, the condition of homelessness carries with it the loss of any sense of belonging (the very word 'home', etymologically, referred not so much to a building as to an area of which one was part). Without this sense of belonging, a person is left to drift, emotionally and physically, unable to form significant relationships or undertake meaningful commitments. It is essential for helpers to appreciate from the outset that such symptoms should not superficially be interpreted as personality traits (unfeelingly referred to by terms such as 'disaffiliation', 'fecklessness', etc.) but as reflections of what happens when people are deprived of such a basic human need as a home.

(b) Nothing could be more unhelpful than to brand the wide range of people in this situation with the common label 'the homeless'.

In the first place, it is essential to look first at the person rather than at her or his homelessness. This means not only taking account of the individual's strengths and points of vulnerability but also appreciating the relevance of gender, age, class, ethnicity, etc.

But beyond these basic personal differences, there are also important differences in the nature of homelessness itself. Is the homelessness a recent occurrence? If so, the person may still be trying to cope with the trauma of homelessness but will often have a high degree of motivation to take action and to accept advice. If not, the person may be moving towards the point where the prospect of change is actually more threatening than trying to cope with the vicissitudes of homelessness. A further question: is the person from the local area? If so, there is likely to be an invaluable network of informal resources – workmates, school friends, neighbours, etc. – which it is imperative to tap. If not, then the person may need the help of agencies which, while bringing to bear professional skills, may lack insight into the lived reality of the person they are seeking to help.

(c) Homelessness does not occur in a vacuum. Leaving home, or being asked to leave home before alternative arrangements have been made, is such a desperate measure that it is safe to assume that homelessness is the latest of a series of troubles which the person has been experiencing.

More often than not, there is a chain of interconnected factors. For example, the person may have lost her or his private sector flat for having fallen behind with the rent. This may have been due to no fault of the tenant, but to delays with housing benefit. Dependence on housing benefit in turn results from the lack of regular well-paid employment, a by-product of which may be a sense of failure, for which solace may have been sought in drink.

(d) The first task of any helper is to enable a person to sort things out. This means listening rather than judging. The willingness to listen can be communicated by simple gestures – offering a cigarette, a cup of tea, a quiet corner, a comfortable chair. What the helper is listening for is, of course, not just facts but also feelings, not just weaknesses but also strengths, not just disappointments but also hopes. In some cases, for example where violence or abuse has repeatedly been inflicted, leaving home was the right and courageous course of action and should be affirmed as such. In other cases, it may have been a dreadful mistake. In either case, particularly for someone homeless for the first time, the experience is likely to be tremendously disorienting. All the things one valued, relied on, took for granted are gone. Confusion, panic and trauma may be not far below the surface. And below that may be feelings of shame, anger, bitterness and even hatred. And still deeper may lie buried feelings of failure, rejection, loneliness too painful to be borne in their consciousness. One of the most common yet most pathetic of feelings on the part of homeless people – contrary to public opinion – is the sense of blame and failure they attach to themselves for being homeless. The failures of other people and of our housing and employment systems become internalized and transformed into a sense of personal inadequacy.

Listening, while refusing to making hasty judgements, is the easy part of responding to homelessness. Less easy is the task of overcoming homelessness itself. Here the question that must be wrestled with is: what does it mean to find a home? Of course it includes finding a reasonably secure and comfortable dwelling. But it also means finding a place where one will feel able to belong. This may well mean returning to the area which one has left, with or without a reconciliation with the people with whom one has previously shared one's life. But in many cases such a course of action may simply be out of the question. A new start may need to be made. And that may mean rethinking what one wants to do with one's life. Where will one, in time, be able to sink roots?

None of these answers can be rushed. Meanwhile, how is one to survive? Practical action must be taken urgently because, without a home, a person is clearly at risk. This makes it essential to distinguish between short-term and long-term action.

Short-term action is oriented essentially towards simple survival – a place for the night, a meal, possibly a shower and a change of clothes. But this all costs money. So, does helping entail the 'loaning' or giving of money? Rarely. Far better to arrange, in consultation with the individual themselves, overnight accommodation. But what kind and where? Although the routine answer might seem to be a night shelter or a hostel in the centre of town, a moment's reflection will indicate why this could actually place some homeless people in even greater risk. Displacing a person from the very area where he or she has a range of informal support networks, and plunging them into a sub-culture of street-wise people will most likely deepen rather than alleviate his or her sense of alienation and despair. Much more sensible, therefore, to try to find either a local resource (even a local guest house or hotel) in the area with which he or she is familiar, or an agency which is run for (and preferably by) people with a background similar to theirs.

Once emergency accommodation has been secured, space may have been opened up for getting into some of the longer-term issues. In many cases the people providing the emergency accommodation may be best placed to offer this sort of help. But there may be times when it seems right to build upon the relationship which may have developed with the helper who made the referral. One way of making this possible is for the helper to accompany the homeless person to the place where accommodation has been arranged and ensure that he or she knows how best to get back in touch.

Whoever is involved should be clear that the next step involves assistance with both the personal and the practical needs of the homeless person. It is quite mistaken to assume that homeless people have a host of deep-seated personality defects. Homeless people resent being seen automatically as social work cases. The starting point must be basic human empathy and down-to-earth practical help. But homelessness does tend to shake a person's self-confidence. And a loss of self-confidence can erode hope and lead to an inability to make a fresh start. And where a person has hardly any savings, little training and few friends there may be quite valid reasons for lacking confidence. The task at this stage is about the discovery of their own resources.

The most obvious need for someone who is homeless is for permanent accommodation. Having decided on the desired locality, the next step is to contact the nearest housing advice centre or, failing that, a Citizens Advice Bureau. Although the government is reviewing the legislation, the current position is that any family (one- or two-parent) with dependent children, any woman who is pregnant and any single person who is 'vulnerable' because of age, mental or physical illness or disability enjoys a right to housing. Other single homeless people do not, but they are still entitled to advice and assistance.

A final area to be explored is that of longer-term support. Many homeless people are perfectly able, once settled, to form their own networks of friendship and mutual support. Others may never have had the experience of living on their own and would find life in a flat or a bed-sit little better than a prison. For them the solution may lie in shared accommodation or in a group home. And still others may be damaged as a result of their experiences and may need regular professional care from health and social services departments. The fact that they have been homeless does not deprive them of the rights to assessment and to a personalized care-package under local authority Community Care responsibilities. Complementing all this and helping people who have been homeless establish links with the locality are a range of community-based agencies – day centres, luncheon clubs, community groups, churches, etc. – whose merit is precisely that they do not operate under a specialist social work banner.

(e)   Amongst the more basic sources of help for homeless people are housing advice centres, homeless persons' units, social services departments (which, in addition to accepting responsibilities under the Children Act and the Community Care Act, will normally have a duty officer available on the telephone at all times) and day centres.

In order to make best use of these resources, helpers should bear in mind that one of the trials of being homeless is being shunted about from agency to agency, which can involve complicated journeys, lengthy queueing, repeated filling in of forms and provision of personal details, and occasionally being sent either to the wrong place, or to the right place but at the wrong time. This can sap what remaining energy people have left and can be greatly demoralizing. Helpers can spare homeless people this unnecessary burden by keeping at their disposal an up-to-date list of local resources with accurate details of telephone numbers, opening hours, target groups, services on offer, charges, etc. There is nothing to prevent each carer drawing up her own list, but there are some very good reasons for seeking to have this done by some local co-ordinating body. Not only is this likely to be more efficient and comprehensive; it might also enable the local community to identify gaps in services for homeless people.

(f) Liaison with the agencies – housing departments, social services, health authorities, etc. – should not normally be undertaken without the consent, and where feasible the participation, of the individual concerned. It is still the case that statutory authorities at times seem unaware of their full range of duties towards homeless people. For this reason, helpers may need from time to time to assume the role of advocate (see *advocacy*).

(g) The present period of profound economic and social change means that increasing numbers of people from a wide diversity of backgrounds are faced with the threat or the reality of homelessness. As in other areas of social need, there have also been frequent and often profound changes in social policy and social services. Literature, therefore, can quickly become dated. Among the organizations which provide up-to-date and relatively inexpensive material are: CHAR, 5–15 Cromer Street, London WC1H 8LS (which produces regular guides to homeless people's rights); SHAC, 229–231 High Holborn, London WC1V 7DA (which produces a regular resource sheet for housing advisers, although mainly oriented to Greater London); and Health Action for Homeless People, c/o The Print House, 18 Ashwin Street, London E8 3DL (which produces good practice notes on enabling homeless people to have access to health and community care services).

PATRICK LOGAN
(See also *community politics*)

Home visiting

(a) For the purposes of this article I define the term 'home visitor' as applying to one whose visit to a person, in their own home, is intended to promote well-being, and to facilitate appropriate, necessary change.

(b)   The term 'home visitor' can be used to describe a very large group of people. However, this group can be roughly divided into four categories according to whether their prime task in visiting is to meet:

1. spiritual needs, e.g. clergy, elders, befrienders from local churches of all denominations;
2. medical needs, e.g. GPs, district nurses, health visitors;
3. emotional needs, e.g. post-bereavement visitors, victim support, psychiatric nurses, social workers, befrienders from the local churches and community;
4. practical needs, e.g. volunteer bureau workers (decorators, gardeners, etc.), social workers, community care assistants, meals on wheels, carers from the local churches and community.

The aim of all these people is to promote some kind of change: e.g. spiritual – peace, belief, understanding; medical – healing, reassurance, 'coming to an acceptance of'; emotional – encouragement, validation, 'to make sense of', building up self-esteem and worth; practical – removal of anxiety, sense of pride returning.

I do not imply that these four categories are mutually exclusive. Experience shows that, for example, meeting medical needs, can also address the emotional need of support and reassurance; meeting emotional needs can reduce stress levels thus offering the potential of preventative medicine. Moreover, it is important to note that all home visitors can be instrumental in promoting sound, effective networking with one or more of the categories.

(d)   In *A Guide to Pastoral Care* (1976), White concludes that sound, effective pastoral care is facilitated and enabled by the practitioner (home visitor) adhering to a series of appropriate guidelines: 'Though detailed rules are impossible, in pastoral experience certain general principles do emerge which can increase efficiency and avoid blundering or wasted effort'.

My own conclusions are gleaned from my own study, from practical experience as a pastoral carer, counsellor and as a trainer of listeners and lay visitors for the Diocese of Southwell. I have also received valuable input from groups of people who are actively undertaking visiting as a result of their training, and also from discussions with individuals who are experienced, professional carers from all the categories mentioned above. Whenever I use the word 'professional' I am not only referring to those who are professionally trained and qualified, and who earn their living through their caring, but also to all those who can be regarded as embracing professional practice in their work, i.e. the competent use of appropriate specialist and general skills.

I have been heartened over the last few years by the growing number of volunteers who seek training in order to become competent in the skills and knowledge needed in their particular field of caring. There is a growing number who are realizing that part of this professional practice also includes a willingness to be accountable, and where necessary to be supervised. Like their paid colleagues, they also need the sound support structures that accountability and **supervision** offers. Voluntary agencies and churches are becoming better at offering this type of support to their carers.

The following guidelines inevitably have to be generalized. I appreciate that specific guidelines may not be appropriate to members of all the categories.

Preparation to be undertaken before visiting

1. Make sure that you are very clear about, and in accord with, the *primary* task of your visit. (This may be dictated by the agency you represent.) Be prepared to respond appropriately to whatever else may come up in the course of the visit.

2. Be prepared to offer appropriate **confidentiality** and respect for the person visited. The degree of confidentiality required is going to vary enormously from one situation to another but it is essential that this is thought through beforehand, and practised.

3. Be clear in your own mind what the boundaries of the relationship are going to be, and make them clear to the person visited. Do you contract to adhere to the agreed boundaries? e.g. may they contact you at any time of the day or night? May they call on you in a crisis? Do you promise to come at the 'drop of a hat'? Do you specify firmly the amount of time you have available?

4. Understand/consider your motivation for undertaking this work. As we all need to be needed and valued, none of us can claim pure motivation, but honest self-evaluation will discern whether our motivation is based primarily on meeting our own needs rather than meeting the needs of others.

We therefore need to be sure our *primary* aim in visiting is not in order to meet our own needs, e.g. to alleviate our own loneliness, to make us feel good (virtuous), to bolster our own image of ourselves; or to impose on others our belief and value systems, e.g. our own prejudices, feminism, racism, political views, **religious belief**, morals. Any of these examples could be experienced as abusive.

5. Are you aware of (i) your professional needs; and to this end, have you an adequate support system? e.g. how is supervision offered, and accountability required? Who/what is available for you to consult or to use as a resource? (ii) your own personal needs; and to this end, have you established an adequate personal support system? e.g. are you

ensuring that all your needs are being met, emotional, physical and spiritual? To whom/what do you turn to for these?

6. Do you feel adequately equipped for the visiting you are about to undertake? Has the training you have received and/or your life experience given you the personal confidence, skills and knowledge that you need in order to accomplish the given tasks in a sound professional manner?

7. Do you acknowledge and celebrate your skills/gifts while recognizing and owning your limitations?

8. Do you refer on when you have reached the limit of your competence? If this is adhered to, it will promote damage limitation, i.e. by taking appropriate responsible action, the possibility of harming those visited is minimized. This is essential.

9. Do you have an established referral network to which you can turn when you reach the limit of your competence/experience?

10. Are you willing to take appropriate responsibility for yourself? i.e. ensuring that your preparation is adequate for tasks to be approached.

Once we have prepared ourselves in the most appropriate way for the tasks ahead, then we need to consider the *conditions* which will promote a sense of safety and well-being of the person we visit.

Carl Rogers (founder of person-centred counselling) offers the following conclusion – that three core conditions need to be offered before trust, openness and the required change can take place. These are:

- a deep acceptance of the person visited, for whoever he or she is;
- a wish to understand that person;
- a commitment to being real in that relationship.

I suggest that these are all observed when the skill of effective, active listening is offered. Roger Hurding writes of this:

> Learning to listen is a prerequisite for *all* caring relationships. However effective listening needs to have two components: a *mental* element which observes, takes note and remembers, and a *social* element which responds appropriately to what is heard. (1992: 104)

A common factor in the training and practice of *all* home visitors is one which promotes the sound use of listening skills. For the purposes of home visiting it is valuable to consider the guidelines for listening and responding offered by Jacobs (1985: 13–14):

Guidelines for listening
1. Listen with undivided attention, without interrupting.
2. Remember what has been said, including the details (the more you listen and the less you say, the better your memory).
3. Listen to the 'bass line' – what is not openly said, but possibly is being felt.

4. Watch for non-verbal clues to help you to understand feelings.
5. Listen to yourself, how you might feel in a described situation, as a way of further understanding – empathy.
6. Try to tolerate pauses and silences that are a little longer than is usual in conversations (and avoid asking lots of questions to break silences).
7. Help yourself and the other to feel comfortable and relaxed with each other; keep calm even when you don't feel calm.

Guidelines for responding
8. Be as accurate as possible in describing feelings/ideas that you perceive (not just 'depressed' or 'angry').
9. Use your empathic understanding, again making this accurate, although also tentative (you may be wrong).
10. Keep questions to a minimum, unless:
    • you need precise information (in which case ask precise questions);
    • you want to open up an area (in which case use open-ended questions);
    • you wish to prompt (when rhetorical questions help);
    • and avoid at all costs questions beginning 'why . . . ?'.
11. Use minimal prompts 'mm', 'yes', or the last few words.
12. Paraphrase or reflect accurately as:
    • a way of prompting;
    • an indication that you have been listening;
    • a way of checking out that you have heard correctly.
13. Avoid making judgements or loaded remarks.
14. Where possible link reported experiences, events, reactions and ideas.
15. Avoid changing the subject or interrupting unnecessarily.
16. Avoid speaking too soon, too often, or for too long.
    And finally, when you have responded:
17. Return to the listening mode, to watch and listen for the reaction to your own response, as well as anything new that emerges.

Although some of the categories of home visitor do not necessarily need listening skills in order to attend to their *primary* task, e.g. the practical helpers, these skills are still of enormous benefit in enabling appropriate responses to whatever else may come up.

The following story illustrates the way two carers, whose primary task in visiting was to care for the practical needs of the elderly, were able to accomplish so much more, through the skilful use of effective, active listening:

One day, two carers from the local church knocked at the door of a very elderly couple. The wife of 85 answered, with tears streaming down her face. She was in a state of high anxiety: 'I just don't know how we're going to manage', she whispered. With some trepidation the offer was made – 'I wonder if we could help?' It transpired that the lady and her 92-year-old husband had managed between them the Herculean task of taking down their heavy front room curtains, and put them on the line to freshen up. Now, they were both distraught because their combined efforts – they both had arthritic fingers and hands – had not been nimble enough to connect the curtains and curtain hooks again. They had convinced themselves that they were facing the prospect of living in a goldfish bowl – their window looked directly on to the street. The feelings of frustration and irritation had almost reached despair when the knock came on the door. The curtains were quickly hung; a cup of tea was made as a thank you. As skilful listening and responding were offered, and they received the reassurance needed, the panic and fears subsided and life began to be experienced as good again. The carers were able to ensure that the couple were regularly visited. They were also able to link them up with domiciliary services for assessment, and put them on the gardening rota run by the local volunteer bureau. It was a good example of networking.

While acknowledging that much of what I have written is of particular importance to volunteer home visitors, it also serves as a valuable reminder to professional visitors of the way in which they might approach visiting clients in their own home.

(g)   Egan, G. (1990) *The Skilled Helper*. Pacific Grove, CA: Brookes/ Cole Publishing Co.; Jacobs, M. (1985) *Swift to Hear*. London: SPCK; White, R. E. O. (1976) *A Guide to Pastoral Care*. Glasgow: Pickering and Inglis.

SUE HOPTON

Hospital visiting

(a)   This article is concerned with the principles and techniques of visiting patients in hospital. The focus is primarily upon the needs of those who visit in the context of relationships which are professional and broadly pastoral (and sometimes voluntary) rather than of those who visit within the bonds of family and friendship.

(b) Different groups may find themselves engaged in hospital visiting for professional and/or pastoral reasons each with their own aims and objectives. Lawyers may have important business to transact; representatives of social service agencies or of self-help groups may try to help patients come to terms with their illness or have a concern for their aftercare and support; ministers and priests of local congregations and members of church-based lay pastoral care groups may seek to bring support and encouragement in the context of a shared religious faith.

(d) Those who wish to visit patients in hospital should first make sure that a visit would be welcomed by the patient and ascertain when it is convenient to do so. Patients have a right to receive visitors; visitors do not have a right to visit! Hospitals are busy places and patients may be out of the ward having tests, or be exhausted recovering from various procedures, or they may just not be feeling like having visitors. One should also consider whether it is best to visit during normal visiting hours (when it will be possible to see other members of the family) or whether normal visiting times should definitely be avoided. It is also possible that some aspects of ward routine (e.g. rest hours, doctors' rounds) may make visiting inappropriate. Phone calls before visiting can save much frustration.

Prior to visiting, the use of the *imagination* can be of great value especially where the visitor has not met the patient before. Much more may be known about the patient than the visitor realizes. Careful reflection upon all that is known about the person to be visited may allow a picture to begin to form. In what kind of ward is the patient? Medical or surgical? Orthopoedic or gynaecological or oncology? Each type of ward brings its own stresses and anxieties (quite apart from those which are peculiar to the individual). A young man recovering from a broken leg after a motorbike accident is in a different emotional state from a woman having a hysterectomy, or again from someone embarking upon a second or third course of chemotherapy.

On arrival at the ward, it is again important to check with the nurse in charge that it is convenient to visit. This is not only common courtesy, but a recognition that the situation of wards and patients can change very rapidly.

As one approaches the patient it is important to use one's powers of *observation*. How does the patient look? Bright? Unwell? Unconcerned? Connected to a number of drips and drains (and therefore possibly post-operative)? The bedside locker can also provide clues. A locker covered in get-well cards indicates a person with many friends; a bare locker may indicate the opposite – or that the patient has just been admitted or is about to go home or be transferred to another ward. The presence of a Bible or of a crucifix or some other religious symbol on the locker may give some clues concerning the patient's faith orientation. While the development of one's powers of imagination and observation can enhance visiting skills it is also important not to jump to premature conclusions based on inadequate evidence.

Approaching the patient, it should be remembered that the patient is host and the visitor is guest (even when the visitor works in the hospital). It is normally better to sit by the bedside facing the patient so that the visitor is not standing over the patient and talking down to him or her. The patient's permission should be sought to bring a chair alongside the bed. Sitting on the bed is not normally encouraged by either patients or staff. Hospital wards are not usually conducive to confidential conversations. Partial privacy is possible by drawing curtains but curtains are not walls and sound travels easily. If privacy is essential and the patient is well enough, it may be possible to move with the patient to some more suitable place (again checking with staff).

All conversations with patients should be conducted with the realization that they are in hospital for a reason. They may be quite ill physically; it has been said that for patients there are no 'small' operations; and even if they are only in for tests, they are likely to be experiencing a degree of anxiety about the results, no matter how cheerful they appear on the surface. The experience of hospitalization can have the effect of constricting the world-view of patients so that the only reality is what is happening to them or to others within the ward. It is therefore important to identify oneself clearly and to state one's reason for visiting, particularly if one has not met the patient before and/or if the patient was not expecting a visit. An article in an American journal entitled 'The first three minutes in the sick room' makes the important point that it is necessary to make some kind of early contract, even an implicit one, with the patient (though the effect is somewhat spoiled by the author, a chaplain, taking the three minutes to list the various services offered by the chaplaincy).

Sometimes visits are made with a specific task in mind. Lawyers may visit to discuss legal matters or social workers to explore arrangements for discharge from hospital or even doctors to discuss diagnosis and prognosis. In such cases the agenda of the visitors will give structure to the conversation. When specific decisions are required by the patient, visitors should be aware of the fact that there is often a gap between what is said and what is heard and that there may be some advantage in having a third person, such as a relative or friend, present who can check that the patient has assimilated the salient points in the conversation. This is especially so in cases where the patient is elderly, which the majority of hospital patients are.

Where visits are made with a more general supportive or pastoral intent, different approaches are needed. The visitor may need to take the initiative but will do so with sensitivity and integrity, encouraging the patients to share as much as they wish but at the same time respecting their privacy and emotional boundaries. While the gentle use of open-ended questions may facilitate this process, control of the conversation should not be wrested from patients. It is comparatively easy to identify those techniques that will almost certainly not be found helpful. A totally client-centred approach (or rather a caricature of this approach) is unlikely to advance the conversation very rapidly. On the other hand, if the visitors attempt to fill awkward silences by talking about their own concerns or sharing their own experiences of illness, this too is likely to prove less than helpful – it is not unknown for patients to take some hours to recover from their visitors. While visitors may have had similar experiences of illness they do *not* 'know exactly how you feel' because the experience of illness is unique to the sufferer. (On the other hand, as in the case of the use of imagination, common human experiences do give clues as to how others *may* be feeling – but these clues need to be checked out.) Visitors should also be aware of the danger of offering easy reassurance, frequently done to allay their own anxieties. What patients sometimes want are visitors who will not discount their very real worries, but who rather will stay with them as they contemplate all the possibilities that lie before them.

A common concern among potential hospital visitors is a concern about what they will say. Yet this conceals a misapprehension about the nature of visiting because a primary task may be to encourage the patient to talk about his or her concerns. And even this idea bears witness to the fallacy that hospital visiting is always about talking and listening. The shared, intimate silence of friends can be deeply support- ive, and the ability to 'be', comfortably and silently, with another human being is a gift to be used with wisdom and discernment. The sensitive use of touch, such as holding hands, can be very effective in conveying human care and compassion, though it is important to be aware when this is appropriate and when it is not.

Pastoral visiting: Much hospital visiting of a supportive nature is undertaken by clergy and by representatives of churches. While all that has been written above is applicable, visiting in a pastoral or spiritual context has its own peculiar dynamics. When people are hospitalized, issues of faith and doubt, of sin and guilt, of hope and fear, of life and death may be very near the surface. It can happen that church represen- tatives, perceived by patients as representatives of God, find ideas and feelings inappropriately directed towards them. In the pastoral conver- sation transference is alive and well! Yet there is also room for a proper exploration of faith issues of importance to patients and an appropriate pastoral response. Sometimes pastoral visitors are concerned about whether or not they should pray with patients. In general, patients will indicate in their conversation whether this is important to them. In cases of doubt the visitor should always ask, but ask in such a way as to leave the patient with a genuinely free choice in the matter. While 'Would you like me to say a prayer with you?' does not present a free choice, to add the words 'or would you rather continue to say your own prayers?' leaves the decision firmly with the patient. In any case, if prayer is offered, it should be natural rather than formal; and in its content give expression both to the feelings and anxieties expressed by the patient and to the peace and presence of God in the midst of suffering. On occasion, patients may ask for prayers for some kind of miraculous healing in apparently hopeless situations. In such cases it is important to explore with patients their understanding of the nature of such prayers before proceeding to raise expectations which may not be fulfilled.

(e) Many Christians, particularly those who belong to traditions emphasizing the centrality of the sacraments, value the opportunity of receiving Holy Communion or the Anointing of the Sick while they are in hospital. Hospital staff are invariably helpful in facilitating this but again prior consultation, where this is possible, leads to good co-operation.

Sometimes, either by using one's imagination or through clues picked up during the visit, it will become obvious that the patient's family are in need of support. While such follow-up visits are usually much appreciated by patients and their families, it is important to pause and to make sure that one is operating within the bounds of **confidentiality** and to check how much of the conversation with a patient can be shared with the family. The fact that someone is a patient in hospital is itself an item of confidential information and it is not unknown for women to be in gynaecological wards for reasons which they wish to keep from their families.

(g) Lyall, D. (1995) *Counselling in the Pastoral and Spiritual Context.* Buckingham: Open University Press; Speck, P. (1988) *Being There: Pastoral Care in Time of Illness.* London: SPCK.

DAVID LYALL

(See also *pain and illness; recovery from major surgery; terminal illness*)

Infertility

(a) Infertility means the inability of a woman to achieve a pregnancy or carry a child to term, or of a man to create a pregnancy with his partner. In medical practice it is widely regarded as appropriate, assuming no known pathology, to consider that a couple has a fertility problem if they have not achieved a pregnancy within one year of regular, unprotected sexual intercourse. It would be more precise to speak of subfertility in most of these cases, as the ability to achieve pregnancy has not been demonstrated, rather than proved impossible. Clinics sometimes prefer the term 'fertility' with its arguably optimistic ring; others dislike this as a euphemism, capable of confusion with contraceptive clinics. The term 'sterility' – demonstrated complete lack of fertility – is avoided for its pejorative ring.

Community surveys about the frequency of infertility are as yet unclear, because it is very difficult in such surveys to distinguish those who have chosen not to have children, the 'childfree', and those who are delaying having children from those who are unable to do so, the 'childless'. It is estimated that one in six couples experience infertility.

(b) The primary settings in which couples or individuals present with concerns about infertility are medical, whether GP surgeries or at hospital clinics, both general and specialist. The social composition of referrals favours the higher socio-economic groups as in much elective medicine. The extent to which infertility is accompanied by emotional distress and pain is increasingly well documented (Monach, 1993). This distress reflects the extent to which our society expects couples to have children and fails to prepare them for infertility. The childless may experience their situation as akin to grief or **bereavement**, albeit for the loss of an unknown, never conceived child. Such couples may be seen elsewhere presenting with concerns about their relationship or **sexual difficulties**, which might prove to have a fertility component which has not yet been diagnosed or accepted.

Adoption and fostering services in many cases consider infertile couples as substitute parents. Specialist infertility services are in short supply everywhere, and increasingly rely on the private sector, especially for the assisted reproductive techniques (ARTs) like in-vitro fertilization (IVF), donor insemination (DI), egg donation, surrogacy, tubal microsurgery, etc. (For details of the range of conditions and treatments see Winston, 1994.) Patients with infertility problems may as a result also have severe financial problems caused by the high cost of repeated attempts to become pregnant via ART: one cycle of IVF costs £1,500 or even more; a surrogacy (child carried by another woman to be relinquished by prior agreement for adoption) £12,000. The motivation to parent may be so strong, and the treatment centres so enthusiastic to assist them, that couples can take enormous emotional and financial risks.

Success rates of many of the ARTs are very low and such couples may need the help of an independent counsellor to reach a realistic decision for themselves as to how far to go in their quest for a child. Some of the treatment options present very difficult emotional and ethical choices for the couples concerned. Will the child conceived from another man's sperm or another woman's egg or both really feel like their own child and be treated as such? What if the surrogate mother changes her mind? What if the child eventually conceived is not 'perfect'? What if all the anguish, time and expense leads to no child in the end? Parliament created the Human Fertilisation and Embryology Authority (HFEA) to oversee the provision of ARTs; this requires clinics to offer counselling to couples being treated. Concern remains, however, as studies have found that one-third or even half of patients at a clinic did not recall **counselling** being offered.

(c)   The most frequent physical causes of infertility appear to be sperm defects, ovulatory disorders and tubal problems. Infertility clinics usually report finding a fertility problem in about one-third of the women, one-third men, and in one-third both partners. This varies between clinics. The science of fertility evaluation, especially of the man, is developing all the time, such that, for example, semen samples previously thought to be adequate are now seen to have subtle defects adversely affecting the ability to impregnate. There is some evidence that fertility is decreasing, especially amongst men, in all societies. Reasons for this are being sought in pollution (radiation, herbicides, etc.), drug taking (including prescription drugs, tobacco and alcohol), contraceptive measures and surgical interventions (Winston, 1994).

While there is abundant evidence accumulating (summarized by Monach, 1993) that infertility *causes* psychological problems, there is still considerable controversy about the extent to which psychological factors actually *cause* infertility. Attempts to demonstrate personality differences between the infertile and the fertile, usually based on *a priori* psychodynamic 'insights', have not succeeded. **Stress** does undermine fertility, especially in sperm production and ovulation; however, the evidence that this is more than temporary for most people is weak. Research indicates that stress reduction programmes alone do not substantially aid conception rates, welcome as they might be for their own sake. **Sexual difficulties** may accompany infertility. Here again the evidence suggests that for the vast majority this is a problem consequent upon the stresses of infertility investigation and treatment rather than a primary cause. Monach (1993) and Edelmann et al. (1991) both reviewed the literature for psychologically caused (i.e. psychogenic or functional) infertility, and found little support for this being a significant reason for couples failing to conceive.

(d) A holistic approach, including attention to the physical, emotional and social needs of couples, is essential if treatment is to be most efficacious and least harmful.

Most societies, like ours, are pronatalist; that is, the status of parent is highly valued, and those who might be expected to become parents, who do not do so, may find themselves socially disadvantaged and sometimes stigmatized. Many childless couples report these social expectations, coming from friends, colleagues and family as significantly exacerbating their own distress. Children at school usually learn about contraception and the dangers of early pregnancy, but rarely that they may not have the choice of pregnancy at all. The loss of choice, is described as peculiarly hard. It is rare to hear the question asked 'why have children?', only 'when?' and 'how many?'

The personal pain of infertility affects individuals and their immediate social networks. It should not be assumed, as some professionals do, that all childless people are uniformly 'desperate' to conceive, nor that all are willing to go to the same lengths. In requiring the availability of counselling in ART clinics, the HFEA recognizes the difficult decisions which might face the infertile and the possibility of significant personal distress. HFEA requires several approaches to be available in the clinic or on referral elsewhere: implications counselling to help patients understand the full implications of any proposed treatment plan; support counselling to help cope with the emotional pressures of treatment; and therapeutic counselling for those in whom deepseated emotional and psychological problems may be raised by the experience of infertility. Counselling will be offered in this context, but concerns about the independence of an attached counsellor might indicate the advantages of seeking help elsewhere.

Childlessness is usually presented by a heterosexual couple. Indeed most clinics are very reluctant to work with the unattached or homosexual couples, although these people may experience their lack of children as painfully as anyone.

The model of understanding often used for the distress is that of **bereavement**: the loss of the ability to reproduce 'naturally', and fear that this might spell the end of all hope for their own children, genetically speaking. As in the classic model, this grief may appear in several manifestations, representing in some ways a series of stages: surprise (surely not me?); denial (can't be me!); isolation (only me); anger (why me?); guilt (what have I done?); depression (poor me);

acceptance (it's my lot). Most experienced counsellors now doubt that most people proceed through these stages in a simple linear fashion, but the ideas are very relevant. The inability to conceive, experienced uniquely, may particularly be perceived as a **loss** of one or more kinds: relationship with their own child; status or prestige of being a parent; personal self-confidence and self-esteem; one's stake in the future – genetic immortality; vicarious fulfilment of parenthood; healthy self-image; expectations of security in sickness or old age; symbolic value of parenthood; fertility and potency; actual experience of pregnancy and childbirth; pleasure of parenting; security in the fertile relationship.

In some of the ARTs, difficult moral, emotional and ethical choices face the childless (McWhinnie, 1992). Use may be made of donated gametes – eggs or sperm. This requires acceptance that one partner (or even both) will not be genetically related to the child conceived. How will this be handled? Who will be told? Will the donor prove compatible, whatever the clinic said? Will the non-genetic parent feel the same about the child? Will the child be told? When? It is obvious that however good the counselling offered at the time of the treatment, the dilemmas will go on into the future, and difficulties may re-emerge requiring skilled help: the analogy with adoption is clear. Surrogacy involves similar difficult questions and the prior fear: will the host mother actually go through with it? Will she allow us to adopt her child?

The impact on a relationship can be very severe, although evidence suggests that the effects are to exaggerate existing patterns, that is, poor relationships founder while good ones prosper. **Sexual difficulties** are common, although usually temporary, reflecting the stress of 'performing to order'.

There is increasing concern that the pains of infertility bear more hardly on the woman than the man, not just because of any variation in commitment to reproduction, but because wider society, including infertility services, treat men and women differently, and demands different levels of commitment and investment (Stanworth, 1987). Women-only support groups are one of the ways in which services are responding helpfully. The impact on men may also be intense, and is possibly less well documented (Mason, 1993).

There is some evidence in my own research that minority ethnic communities are under-represented amongst those receiving the scarce infertility services, which suggests that more attention to their particular concerns is required. Some of the major religions e.g. Islam, Judaism, have moral objections to much that is required by Western reproductive medicine. Such patients may require especially sensitive responses from involved professionals (see *faith differences*).

A range of services both within and without the structure of infertility clinics themselves is needed (Daniels, 1992). These will include professional individual counselling, networking by self-help (see *self-help groups*), campaigning and **advocacy** interest groups. All of these services have a part to play.

(e) Specialized counselling is available in HFEA licensed clinics. Social workers and counsellors are attached to hospital reproductive medicine or obstetric and gynaecology clinics. Local **self-help groups** exist for specific problems e.g. miscarriage or endometriosis. For information about infertility counsellors available in the United Kingdom: British Infertility Counselling Association, Charmian Russell, Reproductive Medicine Unit, Withington Hospital, Manchester (Tel: 0161 447 4231). Information and advice services for childless people: 'Child', Suite 219, Caledonian House, 98 The Centre, Feltham, Middlesex TW13 4BH (Tel: 0181 844 2468); 'Issue', 509 Aldridge Road, Great Barr, Birmingham B44 8NA (Tel: 0121 344 4414).

(f) Counselling offered alongside infertility investigation has a very specific focus. Couples may be very anxious about preserving the **confidentiality** of their treatment, and thus the genetic origins of any child conceived. This will need to be handled with considerable sensitivity by other professionals. As treatment may extend over a period of years, so might the need for counselling. One of the hardest decisions facing any infertile couple may be the decision to cease treatment.

(g)   Monach, J. H. (1993) *Childless: No Choice*. London: Routledge; Stanworth, M. (ed.) (1987) *Reproductive Technologies: Gender, Motherhood and Medicine*. Cambridge: Polity Press; Winston, R. M. L. (1994) *Infertility* (Positive Health Guides). London: Optima.

JIM MONACH
   (See also *adoption*)

Learning disabilities

(a) Every child and adult experiences learning difficulties from time to time throughout life. Each one of us will remember the challenge of discovering how to tie our shoe-laces, how to tell the time, or even how to read complicated books without pictures. As we become older, we invariably confront a series of daunting hurdles such as driving a car round a busy roundabout, contending with a set of geometry problems at school, or developing the skills to become an accomplished parent or professional. Most people have to endure a certain amount of anxiety and humiliation when undertaking new tasks, and if we fail in our efforts, we no doubt experience a certain degree of embarrassment and perhaps a feeling of stupidity as well. At such times, we might be described as temporarily disabled or incapacitated. Fortunately, with patience, persistence and perseverance, most people are able to cope with their handicaps and often overcome them entirely with the aid of parents, teachers, family members and friends.

Sadly, for many individuals, the degree of handicap and disability is much more extensive, and infinitely more difficult to surmount; and the afflicted person will reveal evidence of considerable intellectual impairment. Traditionally, such human beings have become the focus of considerable derision. In previous generations, professionals and non-professionals alike referred to the disabled as dumb, stupid, cretin, idiot, feebleminded, subnormal, imbecile, moron and a whole host of other euphemisms and insults (Sinason, 1992). As our knowledge and compassion has become more pronounced, we have abandoned these jibes, and now refer to such individuals as suffering from a mental handicap or from a learning difficulty or learning disability. At the Tavistock Clinic in London we prefer to use the term 'mental handicap', as we believe this phrase captures the full sense of anguish and impairment with which our patients suffer; whereas the more mild and often more popular 'learning difficulty' often ignores the full extent of the problem.

Irrespective of the terminology, mental handicap might be defined as a condition that afflicts both children and adults, characterized by a marked impairment of cognitive or intellectual capacities. An otherwise capable child who begins to display difficulties with mathematics at school following the divorce of her parents might suffer from a temporary learning difficulty; but such a turbulent patch in the life of a child would not warrant a formal diagnosis of mental handicap. By contrast, the child who can never concentrate adequately, and who displays signs of delayed language development and communicational skills, would be suspected of a mental handicap. Such people tend to score only 70 points or less on standardized Intelligence Quotient (IQ) tests; and they may also reveal behavioural disturbances such as violent acts against themselves or against others. Mental handicap may develop as a result of organic illness, or as a consequence of profound environmental trauma. Some forms of handicap may be alleviated or ameliorated with psychological treatment. In any case, handicapped individuals inevitably require an enormous amount of compassion, emotional support and practical assistance from family members and professional workers alike.

(b) The label of mental handicap actually refers to a very broad spectrum of people. Diagnosticians and classificationists have traditionally divided the population of handicapped patients into four separate categories, differentiated by respective IQ scores:

1. mild mental handicap   IQ score: 50–70
2. moderate mental handicap   IQ score: 35–49
3. severe mental handicap   IQ score: 20–34
4. profound mental handicap   IQ score: 0–19

Psychiatric practitioners often identify a fifth group known as Unspecified Mental Handicap, a condition which describes patients who offer clear evidence of poor intellectual ability, and further cannot sit through a battery of psychological tests which would determine more precisely the exact nature of the learning disability. Roughly 2 to 3 per cent of the global population suffers from the more mild form of mental handicap, whereas only 0.3 per cent of the population suffers from more extensive handicaps in the moderate, severe or profound range (Graham, 1986).

From a descriptive point of view, experienced clinicians have noted that handicapped people not only display signs of cognitive dysfunction, but many may also be characterized by delays and impairments in speech and motor skills, immaturity of the personality, self-absorption, passivity, repetitiousness and a preference for familiar routines. Mentally handicapped patients may also suffer from related physical handicaps or even from formal mental illness (Menolascino, 1990). Other patients behave in what most people regard as an inappropriate manner, particularly, in more extreme cases, patients who have spent a good deal of time in institutional settings or in abusive homes. Such behaviours might include eye-poking, head-banging, self-mutilation, spitting, smearing faeces, urinating and masturbating in public, and so forth. Valerie Sinason, consultant child psychotherapist in the Child and Family Department and convenor of the Mental Handicap Workshop at the Tavistock Clinic, has identified a further important feature that describes many such patients, a facial characteristic – the handicapped smile (Sinason, 1992: 132; Sinason, 1988): an unsettling grin that many handicapped people wear. Traditionally, many professionals have regarded the often ubiquitous smile as an indication that the handicapped person suffers no pain or emotional anguish. It would be comforting to believe this observation. Sinason has discovered, by contrast, that her mentally handicapped patients often fear being injured, attacked or even killed because of their disability, and so they force themselves to paint on a smile as a defensive manoeuvre to protect themselves from potentially hostile and abusive caretakers.

A brief sketch of two handicapped patients from my own practice will help to illustrate how these men and women present themselves. Miss A, a mildly handicapped woman in her early fifties, entered psychotherapeutic treatment many years ago, upon the advice of her social worker. A psychologist had assessed Miss A's IQ score as 67 points. She lived in a residential community setting with two other handicapped women, and a care assistant would visit them on a daily basis to help them cook their meals and pay their bills. Miss A smiled a lot whenever she saw me, and she also walked with a noticeable bounce which meant that people would stare at her in the streets. She spent her time collecting aluminium cans from rubbish tips in order to raise money for a local mental handicap charity; she also went to a soup kitchen every day along with the homeless people to have a free meal. She felt very comfortable with the homeless, as her own parents had put her up for adoption shortly after her seventh birthday.

In psychotherapy sessions, Miss A often referred to me as 'John', even though I had introduced myself clearly as 'Brett Kahr'. She often used words inappropriately or inaccurately, describing our meetings together as 'pysoferasee' instead of 'psychotherapy'. Miss A had the capacity to treat my consulting room and my person with respect. She would arrive on time to sessions, having mastered the bus route to my office. She sat in the chair, and she paid her bills punctually. Miss A did not work at a job, but during treatment she managed to forge a sexual relationship with a mildly handicapped man which has proved both loving and long lasting.

By contrast, Mr B, a 19-year-old teenager, had to contend with a very profound handicap, his IQ assessed at only 15 points. Unlike Miss A, who lived in the community with a moderate degree of support from social services, Mr B had spent most of his life as an in-patient in a special hospital for the handicapped and retarded. Although he suffered from no overt physical disabilities, Mr B could not read or write, and he had no capacity to feed himself or to toilet himself. He spent most of his time in hospital exposing his penis to female members of staff, and he also enjoyed hitting fellow residents on the head with his clenched fists. Mr B did relish painting very much, and he managed to attend some art therapy sessions in the hospital. Because he had experienced various complications at the time of his birth, he could barely speak, and this additional handicap caused him considerable despair.

This patient required two hospital porters to escort him to my consulting room. He spent much of his session time spitting on my furniture, scribbling on the carpet with crayons and jumping up and down on the psychoanalytical couch. Occasionally, he would masturbate in my presence or urinate on the floor, although he did manage to stop when I imposed a boundary and told him that he would not be permitted to engage in those activities in my office. After six years of treatment, Mr B still had to contend with the reverberations of his handicap, but he managed to contain all of his seemingly inappropriate and violent behaviour, especially after we had discovered that much of his sexualized and aggressive activity resulted from early experiences of anal rape by a family member. Because Mr B had no speech, he needed to resort to dramatic forms of non-verbal communication in order to indicate to the staff what had happened to him as a child.

(c) Handicapped behaviour can result from a number of different causes, ranging from organic disease to psychological traumatization. Unlike some illnesses such as dementia or glaucoma, which tend to afflict people at a particularly late stage in the life-cycle, the seeds of handicap can take root at any time, either during the preconceptual period, the pre-natal period, the perinatal period or the postnatal period. From the purely biological point of view, many cases of handicap begin long before the birth of the damaged child. The majority of individuals suffering from moderate, severe or profound handicap will have inherited a faulty genetic structure. These inherited anomalies may take the form of chromosomal defects, in other words, an abnormality in either the number or the shape of the chromosomes, which might be described as the vessels in which we store our genetic material. The most common chromosomal defect, Down's syndrome, previously known by the pejorative and unhelpful name of mongolism, accounts for a large proportion of mental handicap, roughly one baby out of every 600 or 700 live births. It is caused by the presence of an extra chromosome (trisomy 21). The clinical features which stem from this chromosomal disturbance include a very low IQ, delayed motoric development, delayed language development, diminished physical stature, decreased muscle tone, almond-shaped eyes, poorly aligned teeth, poorly developed nasal bone structure, protruding tongue and shortened fingers and toes. Needless to say, such an endowment predisposes most babies to considerable physical, cognitive and psychosocial disadvantage. Other well-known chromosomal anomalies apart from Down's syndrome include trisomy D syndrome, trisomy E syndrome, fragile X syndrome, Turner's syndrome, Klinefelter's syndrome, cri du chat syndrome and hermaphroditism. All of these conditions cause the patient to suffer from bodily disturbances, and often cognitive dysfunction as well (Menolascino and Egger, 1978).

In addition to the varieties of mental handicap or learning disability caused by faulty chromosomal transmission, investigators have also discovered forms of handicap which derive from defects within single, individual genes. These conditions include tuberous sclerosis, neurofibromatosis, phenylketonuria, Wilson's disease, galactosaemia, Marfan's disease, Laurence–Moon–Biedl syndrome and many others besides.

Handicap often emerges from the aforementioned genetic liabilities, but there can be many other biological triggers, most especially viruses and other forms of trauma. Pre-natal causes include maternal infections such as congenital syphilis, rubella, toxoplasmosis, cytomegalic inclusion disease, or even the Acquired Immune Deficiency Syndrome (see *AIDS/HIV*); furthermore, the use of drugs or alcohol may also predispose the foetus to the development of mental handicap. Additionally, maternal diseases such as diabetes mellitus or toxaemia may contribute, as does foetal radiation. Perinatal factors might include birth trauma or injury, anoxia, prematurity or maternal anaesthesia; and postnatal triggers might be head injury, encephalitis and other forms of cerebral infection, meningitis and other forms of meningeal infection, rheumatic fever, coccidiodomycosis, lead poisoning or intracranial tumours. In many cases, grotesque forms of child abuse can account alone for mental handicap, as in the case of a four-year-old boy whose mother bludgeoned him on the head repeatedly with a heavy iron frying pan, thus inducing profound and irreversible mental retardation in an otherwise healthy and sturdy child.

As for the psychological factors involved in the genesis of states of mental handicap, Sinason has reviewed these data extensively in her pathbreaking volume *Mental Handicap and the Human Condition* (1992), essential reading for anybody working in this field. She concurs with the view that most handicap results from organic factors, but that trauma and abuse may also play a key role in the exaggeration and maintenance of handicap. In other words, in addition to the primary handicap, some people develop a non-organic *secondary handicap* where they appear more disturbed and dysfunctional than they may be in reality (Sinason, 1986, 1992). As Sinason has noted: 'Individuals compliantly exacerbate their original handicap to keep the outer world happy with them. For instance, some handicapped people behave like smiling pets for fear of offending those they are dependent on' (1992: 21).

At the Mental Handicap Team of the Tavistock Clinic, we have found that patients often present themselves as stupid in the early stages of treatment, sometimes pretending that they cannot speak. As psychotherapy progresses, this secondary handicap begins to disappear as the patients trust us much more and no longer need to protect themselves from us. Sinason (1992) has reported the staggering finding that 70 per cent of all handicapped children referred to the Mental Handicap Team, as well as 40 per cent of all handicapped adults, have experienced documentable or suspected episodes of abuse. Handicapped individuals can be ideal victims for abusive parents or paedophiliac members of hospital staff teams because, in most cases, the handicapped patients can neither protect themselves nor offer a formal protest, ever fearful of retribution. The abuse of handicapped people occurs not only intra-familiarly, or in care settings, but also in the context of satanist rituals and other forms of organized ritualistic abuse (Beail, 1994; Bicknell, 1994; Charleson and Corbett, 1994; Morris, 1994; Sinason and Svensson, 1994). In spite of the range of abuse to which handicapped children and adults may be subjected, we now have very good evidence that as psychoanalytically orientated treatment progresses, patients abandon their secondary handicap, and act more intelligently. Sinason's patients have had their IQ tested both before group psychotherapy treatment and afterwards. After patients reveal details of sexual abuse in the course of therapeutic treatment, the mind becomes clearer, and their IQ scores will rise dramatically, often by as many as 15 points (Sinason, 1994). One cannot easily concentrate on an IQ test when preoccupied by painful memories, but after the patients have discussed these memories in psychotherapy, they can think more clearly. Such patients still suffer from a primary handicap, but less so from the defensive secondary handicap.

(d) Handicapped babies, children and adults require considerable care from family members and from residential and non-residential staff workers alike. Many mildly handicapped and moderately handicapped people live at home with minimal support from care workers, but the more severely impaired often cannot function at all well without a great deal of practical support as well as emotional support. In many situations, family members have abandoned their handicapped relatives, and it remains for the members of staff in hospital or hostel settings to assume many of the functions of the patient's relatives. Living with a handicap presents many special problems for patients, and the care-workers are often the first people to deal with particularly anxiety-provoking situations. For instance, who will break the news to Miss C, a 30-year-old handicapped hostel resident, that her aged mother has just died, and how should this sad message be conveyed? Which staff member in the mental handicap hospital will clean up after Mr D, a 63-year-old man who continuously defaecates in the corridors? How will the staff team respond to Miss E and Mr F, a young handicapped couple who met at a dance sponsored by MENCAP, and who have now begun to engage in sexual intercourse? Which staff worker will discuss contraception with them, not to mention AIDS, genetic counselling and related topics? Often staff members feel awk-ward and confused in their jobs, and we regard this as an accurate reflection of the difficulties of working with the handicapped; we also regard such feelings as an understandable counter-transference reac-tion which staff in this field experience on a regular basis. Patients often respond to our wish to help by mocking us or by ridiculing us; in this way, we end up feeling like the stupid or handicapped person, and the patient enjoys the rare moment of feeling more competent and more intelligent.

At the Tavistock Clinic we recommend clear, honest and forthright communication between staff and residents, and among staff members themselves. Above all, we urge that professional workers strive to adopt a thoughtful, psychologically-oriented approach to their work with handicapped people. Consider the following illustration: Mr G, a moderately learning disabled man in his middle years, began to aggra-vate the staff in the hostel where he lived because he had suddenly started to play his radio at full blast. The staff in Mr G's hostel asked whether they could meet with me to discuss how best to manage this situation, as all their attempts to encourage Mr G to turn down the volume on the radio had failed miserably. The enlightened staff members did not wish to confiscate Mr G's radio, but they certainly felt sorely tempted to do so. Together, we explored *why* the radio playing had suddenly become so unruly at this *particular* point in time, and in the consultation, it soon became clear that the radio disturbances had begun shortly after the keyworker at the hostel had entered Mr G's bedroom to inform him that his long-lost mother had just died of a stroke. It occurred to me that Mr G, an electively mute patient, could not bring himself to scream or cry upon hearing of his mother's death, and that perhaps the screams of the radio expressed this function for him. It also struck me that if Mr G played his radio at an unbearably loud volume, then he could not hear anybody speaking to him, and in this way, he would be unable to listen to any further bad news. I suggested that the squeals of the radio served a protective role. My tentative interpretations seemed to make some sense to the hostel workers, and they spoke to Mr G at dinner and told him that he must be very frightened of hearing more bad news from them, and that perhaps he turned on the radio to block out any further disappointments or shocks. This seemed to do the trick, and Mr G began to cry for his mother for the first time. He then spent more time in the company of the staff, rather than hibernating in his room with the noisy radio.

(e) Counselling and psychotherapeutic services for people with learn-ing disabilities have become increasingly more widespread within recent years as mental health professionals have begun to understand more about the psychodynamics and the inner world of these patients. The Tavistock Clinic in London offers the most comprehensive assessment and treatment service for children and adolescents with learning disabilities, as well as for family members. We also maintain close contacts with private practitioners to whom we can refer adult patients for intensive psychoanalytically-oriented psychotherapy. The Mental Handicap Team and the Mental Handicap Workshop also provide a range of supervisory and consultational packages for interested members of staff from mental handicap facilities; additionally, the Tavistock Clinic offers several specialist training courses in mental handicap for psychologists, psychiatrists, social workers, art therapists, music therapists, drama therapists, occupational therapists, psychotherapists, teachers, residential staff and related professional workers. Information about these services may be obtained by writing to the Mental Handicap Team at the Tavistock Clinic, The Tavistock Centre, 120 Belsize Lane, London NW3 5BA (Tel: 0171 435 7111). Another organization, Respond, offers intensive psychotherapy and counselling to adults with learning disabilities, including a specialist service for learning disabled patients who have also committed sexual offences. Additionally, the staff offer training to professional workers. They can be contacted at 170 Garratt Lane, Wandsworth, London SW18 (Tel: 0181 877 9992). Care-workers should also investigate services offered by local hospitals and clinics.

(f) Work with the handicapped often involves several different professionals and organizations. Every worker must struggle with important issues such as **confidentiality**, particularly when patients may be involved in complicated court cases involving allegations of sexual abuse. Sinason (1992) has addressed some of these topics. Once again, clear and honest communication is paramount. I never reveal information to staff members that I have not already discussed explicitly with the patient in question. For example, Miss I, a 23-year-old woman with Down's syndrome, attended my office once weekly for psychotherapy sessions. Because she could not transport herself, a keyworker from her community mental health setting acted as escort. Although I said 'Hello' and 'Goodbye' to the keyworker at the start and finish of each session, I had no other contact with this staff member, in the interests of confidentiality. Should I need to clarify the dates of future sessions, I did so in the presence of Miss I. My forthcoming book on the psychoanalytical psychotherapy of the severely handicapped addresses these matters in greater detail.

(g) Sinason, V. (1992) *Mental Handicap and the Human Condition: New Approaches from the Tavistock*. London: Free Association Books; Sinason, V. (1993) *Understanding Your Handicapped Child*. London: Rosendale Press; Sinason, V. (ed.) (1994) *Treating Survivors of Satanist Abuse*. London: Routledge.

BRETT KAHR
(See also *advocacy*)

Legal advice

(e) Clients who require legal advice in addition to or as a part of the issues they bring to the professional or volunteer carer may in some circumstances be able to afford a consultation with a solicitor. Some solicitors offer the first appointment free, although thereafter charges are normally made.

Those who are unsure about the legal help they require, or are unable to afford solicitors' fees, have a number of alternative sources of legal advice:

1. Community law centres are able to offer free advice in a more ongoing way than is possible with a solicitor's initial free first appointment.
2. The local Citizens Advice Bureau will know of any community law centres in the neighbourhood, and of other avenues of legal help. Some of the Bureaux have a duty solicitor on a regular basis, although since this is only, for example, one session a week, appointments are usually necessary.
3. Solicitors, through the auspices of the Legal Aid Board, operate a system of free legal assistance known as the 'Green Form' – a form that is given to the client at the conclusion of a first appointment. Legal aid pays for this appointment and for work necessarily to be done from the information received by the solicitor at that time. Like all other forms of statutorily-derived legal financial assistance, eligibility has been steadily eroded over the last ten years. This form of assistance is confined to persons earning no more than £70 a week, plus additional average allowances of £25 for each dependent partner or child. Such people should also not have capital of any more than £1,000, with an average of £300 for each additional dependent. Generally speaking the scheme is for the benefit of those in

receipt of statutory benefits. (All figures quoted in this article are correct only at the time of going to press.)

4. Legal aid is difficult to come by. In order to qualify for free legal aid, a person must not earn more than £2,382 a year, plus an average of about £1,100 for each dependant; and have no more than £3,000 in capital. Legal aid where the recipient makes contributions towards legal expenses is available to an upper income limit of £7,060 a year, with similar allowances for dependants (the contribution is 1/36 of annual income between £2,382 and £7,060). People on income support automatically qualify for legal aid, and for those in receipt of a retirement pension, income and capital are disregarded.

5. The small claims court is an inexpensive way of taking a civil action, but is confined to cases where the amount of compensation is no more than £1,000. The types of action likely to be taken to such a court are probably not those associated with the particular issues outlined in this guide. There is a booklet (available from the County Court office) explaining how to use the small claims court; and County Court clerks will advise on procedures. Those who take cases to such courts on their own need to recognize that it is not quite as straightforward as the literature leads them to believe, since there is nothing to stop the other party choosing to be legally represented, even if the litigant chooses to appear in person (the intention of the system). However, the small claims court is relatively informal (no wigs, gowns or witness boxes) and the deputy judges who preside over the court generally make allowances for litigants in person who, not being trained lawyers, might make some procedural mistakes. Nevertheless, there are stresses involved in taking a case through on one's own, and even if legal representation is not necessary, some kind of personal support (see *advocacy*) is desirable. A claimant in the small claims court who does not have much faith in their own powers of advocacy can take along a more articulate friend to put their case for them. This is allowed in the inferior courts, such a person being called 'a Mackenzie friend', although they need not necessarily be named Mackenzie!

MICHAEL JACOBS

Loss

(a)   Loss is a situation where there is a current *absence* of something to which, in some sense, an individual was previously attached; used as a noun it means 'that which is lost', the *object*, which can be a person, a physical object or an abstract concept. There is now a *separation* from the object, and a continued state of non-restitution provides the emotional experience that the loss is, or may be, permanent. Even very young babies experience loss as *deprivation*, long before they develop cognitive ideas of permanence, irreversibility, object-constancy and continuing future. An experience of loss can be felt even when there never was, and maybe never will be, an actual prior attachment (i.e. lost potential). Even if the object is recovered, restitution to the original perceived state may be only partial because either it, or the deprived individual's experience of it or attitude towards it may have changed temporarily or permanently.

(b)   All transition and change involves losses, whether these changes are sudden or gradual, normal or abnormal, predictable or unpredictable. Even positive and voluntary change situations – buying a better house or car, promotion, marriage, childbirth or winning the pools – contain losses amongst the gains, though they are rarely presenting issues in counselling. Pain from these losses is often denied or its source unrecognized, because people commonly assume that they ought to be either happy or sad, and that 'good' outweighs 'bad'. Guilty ambivalence needs to be acknowledged and explored, and permission given to grieve the losses.

Clients will have incurred losses while facing virtually all the situations in this book, and losses are inherent in the counselling process itself because clients change while being helped to move forward. Those unable or unwilling to attempt conscious voluntary changes, behavioural and cognitive, are unlikely to benefit from counselling, though crisis-intervention, support and befriending could help while they are forced, involuntarily and passively, to experience losses during life transitions and traumatic situations. The table opposite shows the ubiquity of life's losses.

(c)   Feelings about separation and loss originate during a child's earliest relationship with a primary *object/attachment figure*, usually, but not necessarily, the biological mother.

Separation implies:

	Objects of attachment	Loss situations
Self	body	birth, cutting umbilical cord, security *in utero*, terminal illness, own dying
	body parts (thumb sucking mother substitute)	surgery, loss of hair, limbs, teeth, breast, uterus etc.
	organs	organ/blood donation
	healthy functions	illness, accidents, handicap, sight, hearing, mobility
	appearance	ugliness, obesity, slimming, birthmarks, scars, figure
	sexuality	menopause, infertility, celibacy, virginity, impotence, rape
	abilities	'failure': exams, sport, criticism, reputation, dignity, memory, lost aspirations
	self-actualization	unfulfilled potential, low self-esteem/ self-confidence, retirement, redundancy
People	family (parents, grandparents, partner(s), siblings, children)	death, illness, dementias, hospital, prison, moving away
		weaning, enter school (especially boarding school), adolescence, college, leaving home ('empty nest'), graduation, marriage, living abroad, entry to monastery/convent, taken into care, military service, war, drug/alcohol addiction
	partner(s)	jilted, separation, marital breakdown, quarrels, divorce, working away
	pregnancy	infertility, miscarriage, abortion, still-birth, adoption, cot-death, handicapped child
	friends, colleagues, peers, neighbours, boss, role models, heroes, doctor, royalty, clergy	moving house, changing job, leaving neighbourhood community
	counsellor	termination or disruption of therapy, referral
Things	food, air, water, light	food chains, animals slaughtered, pollution
	landscape, trees, vegetation	hurricanes, tree felling, harvesting, fuel combustion
	wildlife	hunting, pesticides, herbicides, antibiotics
	pets	'putting down', losing, dying
	house/home, contents, view, garden	fire, flood, burglary, accidents, repossession, moving, homesickness
	'special objects' e.g. jewellery, engagement/wedding ring, child's toy/blanket/dummy – irreplaceable (these are linkage objects, an emotional substitute for a key person)	losing, theft
	photos, videos, grave memorials	damaged, lost, vandalized, stolen
	clothes (an expression of self)	wear out, wrong size, damaged, etc.
	uniform	reflects role, status, function, organization, which are lost after leaving school, work, college, ministry
	books, pen, money, wallet, handbag, address book, glasses, hearing-aid, false teeth, tools, keys, alcohol, tobacco, medical drugs, passport/visa church, college, office, laboratory	losing, theft
	native country	immigrants, refugees, living abroad
Abstract concepts	beauty, security, love, education, freedom, justice, ideals, sin/evil, truth, salvation, forgiveness, meaning, purpose, hope future, trust, faith, heaven/hell	change of faith/beliefs/values loss of ideal self in guilt/sin self-view/world view after crisis/disaster meaningless, fear, insecurity, despair, injustice, betrayal, trust 'not-being' after death

1. the normal development *process* of gradual psychological differ-
    entiation from the mother following physical detachment after
    birth;
2. an *event* – the mother's absence from the child.

Brief age-appropriate separations cause transient anxiety, but can be healthy and growth-promoting. The child can explore, develop indepen-dence and self-awareness, and learn that instant gratification of needs is rarely available. Nevertheless, major separations, especially those experienced between one and four years, can be so distressing and damaging that permanent relationship difficulties and feelings of inse-curity persist throughout adult life.

Various people's studies of responses in young children (and other animals, e.g. Rhesus monkeys) to separation from their mother led Bowlby (1971) to propose his *attachment theory*. He concluded that attachment behaviours are an adaptive response which is essential to maintain safety in a potentially dangerous environment. They reduce the risk of becoming lost or harmed and therefore had survival value during human evolution. A child's attachment behaviours – seeking, grasping, clinging and following – are elicited in circumstances which arouse feelings or wariness and fear. They ensure that the child remains close to their mother in whose presence they feel secure, protected and safe. Absence of the mother provokes *separation anxiety* in the child, who responds with a consistent predictable sequence of behaviours reflecting a *mourning-like process*, even when other adults are present and no actual danger exists:

- *protest*: angry distress; crying loudly; flailing arms;
- *searching*: being near door and trying to open it; seeking, calling, asking for mother; listening intently for noises signal-ling her return;
- *despair*: decreasing crying or activity; little interest in sur-roundings, people or toys; few demands made (indicating a preoccupation with mother's absence and increasing hopeless-ness about her return);
- *detachment*: renewed interest in surroundings and people; no attachment behaviour towards mother when she returns; fai-lure to greet, stay near, interact or even recognize her. This is a defence against the pain of separation and a protection against feeling further anxiety should mother be 'lost' again;
- *reunion*: detachment continues for hours/days; then ambivalent alternation between renewed clinging, searching, crying at further separations and hostile defiant rejection;

- *new normality*: behaviour similar to original pattern in familiar settings; heightened anxiety and fear in separation-threatening situations or towards surrogate carer from earlier separation.

People from a securely-based childhood usually negotiate successfully the mourning of losses during normal developmental changes in self-image, work and sexuality. They gradually become independent of parents, and are able to make satisfying, trusting and emotionally-committed relationships. They are also less likely than insecure people to mourn excessively during current loss situations or to develop reactive depression, though normal grief pains are inevitable.

Children experience parental separation, absence, or abandonment threats as a deliberate desertion. They feel responsible and tend towards self-blame and **guilt** throughout their life. This is not simply internalized rage, but is a defence against the even more painful reality of feeling like a helpless abandoned victim, unable to control external events. They fear further rejection and loss, and are likely to experience grief more painfully and to maintain low self-esteem even though their attachments to people may be shallower than those of more securely-based people. Adopted people usually feel permanently rejected at the deepest emotional level, regardless of why their mother 'gave them away' or the quality of their subsequent upbringing (see *adoption*).

Various characteristic adult behaviours and relationship styles reflect significant early loss trauma. Some are more extreme than others, presumably because the degree of trauma, personality and subsequent experiences also determine their present coping style:

Avoidance
- inability to trust or commit emotionally to any person, remaining distant and aloof
- alienating people
- children preferring to draw things, not people
- commitment anxiety, or emotionally unavailable in marriage
- cannot express painful emotions; even idyllic childhood memories might be screening the memory of a concurrent painful loss event
- early memories few or absent
- under-attachment even to objects and places, sparse furnishings, 'forgetting' or frequently losing things, travelling light

Sublimation
- over-investment in things and ideas – mathematics, philosophy, science, etc.

- children sent to boarding school, or with other losses, avoiding intimacy but investing energies into sport, hobbies, academic or practical achievement
- deep emotional resonance with sad themes; maybe highly creative at music, art, poetry, writing
- driven workaholic

Over-attachment
- dependent, immature, fear-based clinging relationships, jealous, suspicious, possessive
- hysterical outbursts/suicide threats if dereliction is likely (partner leaves/terminally ill)
- 'be prepared' hoarding or storing emergency supplies; heavy luggage
- stealing
- over-eating, obesity, addictions
- excessive love towards animals
- commitment anxiety; cannot make decisions because cannot relinquish alternatives
- excessively religious

Passive into active (controlling now to avoid risk of being helpless again)
- rigid, dictatorial, uniform-wearing authority-giving job (police, military, some teachers and ministers, lawyer)
- fundamentalism (political or religious)
- child/partner abuse
- angry campaigning
- passive aggression towards partner while idealizing internalized lost mother (marital breakdown likely)
- manipulating partner to behave 'badly', enabling person to reject first and keep control
- challenging provocative behaviour to 'test' the reliability of partner's/parents' love

Guilt/self-blame (can be protective by being less painful than helplessness or meaninglessness)
- permanently low self-esteem
- suicidal tendency
- unconsciously re-enacting circumstances and relationship styles that recapitulate traumatic loss
- permanent victim (difficult to counsel because cannot/will not get better)
- serial abusive relationships
- compulsion towards frequent house or job moves (reflecting similar childhood instability, e.g. in military families)

Searching

- serial relationships; broken marriages (searching unconsciously to replace lost person)
- frequent job-moving
- some promiscuity is a regressive search, not for sex, but for contact, closeness, oral gratification, security of warm arms
- 'marrying mother': older woman, large-breasted, nurturing type (even though actual mother was not necessarily nurturing); marrying older men ('father surrogate')
- religious quest

Developmental arrest

- if a major loss trauma occurs at any stage of childhood or adolescence, the person may fail to mature beyond the stage reached at that time, retaining mannerisms, behaviours, interests and even girlish/boyish appearance and clothes appropriate to that earlier time (emotional immaturity and overreaction to current losses are likely).

(d) 'Loss-scanning antennae' are useful while listening to a client's story, whatever the presenting issue. If major unresolved grief underlies the client's behaviour, it is rarely effective to deal only with current difficulties. The traumatic effects of losses are not only cumulative from earlier experiences but also interactive from various recent and current ones. If loss is the presenting problem, it is important also to explore other concurrent losses, both those relating to the main issue and other coincidental ones. The presenting issue may be quite a minor problem, but the client's resources might be reduced by ill-health or too many current pressures.

If a loss theme is indicated and sufficient rapport and trust are established, the client could be asked to write a chronological list, with dates and ages, of personally significant life-events. The preparation and emotional memories elicited while doing this can help the client to recognize connections between widely separated events, recurrent emotions and behaviours. It should help the counsellor to identify major key events and themes, and to focus upon potentially crucial issues. List making must be voluntary, and clients may need time to think and prepare before attempting it; others might do it privately, unable to talk about the most painful issues until they feel safe. Some clients are too vulnerable even to attempt such a threatening task, so obviously sensitivity, caution and loss counselling experience are essential.

Worden (1991) summarizes the *tasks of grief work* necessary while mourning a death. These can be applied equally well, in principle, to mourning any loss:

Task

1. To *accept the reality* of the loss
2. To work through the *pain* of grief
3. To *adjust to the environment* in which the lost object is missing
4. To *emotionally relocate* the lost object (i.e. internalize it) and move on with life (i.e. letting go).

This dynamic approach can help both counsellors and clients to navigate change processes with greater insight. It explicitly indicates the necessity of experiencing pain as an integral part of the healing process. It is important to acknowledge this because neither a caring counsellor nor a vulnerable client would otherwise consciously choose to enter into issues which are obviously going to increase painful feelings. Clients need to have this explained before they prepare a life-event list or explore loss issues in counselling. It also helps if they understand that emotional grief work *is* work, and is immensely tiring; therefore, if they do feel tired this is not in itself a 'bad' sign. Some feel relieved even at being told that their grief feelings are natural and normal, and that any losses, not only death, elicit grief. Others have already felt a jumbled mixture of painful emotions but had not realized either that they were grief or that they were triggered by experiences of loss during life-change traumas.

In practice these four tasks are accomplished in conjunction with each other, sometimes simultaneously. The reality of the loss is reinforced because pain is felt while trying to adjust to the changed environment. The discrepancies between the former and the current situation are painful but they cannot be denied permanently. Loss-related absences force people eventually to change behaviour, cognitive processing and future aspirations until they develop a new integrated reality-based perception of life.

Carers who are inventive, practical or unable to face people's pain often try to help with adaptations and changes (Task 3) before the person has grieved enough for what is lost (Task 2). For example, a new amputee saying 'I used to be so active until I lost the leg' is not yet ready to talk about wheelchair design, or the Paralympics, but does need to remember and grieve for their formerly active self (e.g. 'What sort of activities did you enjoy doing?'). 'Put it all behind you now' (Task 4) is also likely to be premature and grief-denying.

A large component of grief is not for what was, but for what never was and never will be. If this is recognized and expressed, people in unsatisfactory or ambivalent relationships and marriages are less likely to suffer from unresolved grief, whether or not the relationship is ended.

Expressing their pain and understanding its source may not change the situation but could help their attitude towards it.

Even if a person chooses a loss (**abortion**, having a baby adopted, being celibate, etc.), grief is still necessary, though **guilt** might prevent its expression.

It is often a shock and surprise to feel so much pain after what was thought to be only a minor loss situation. This could be displaced grief from another loss source, but it might simply reflect the fact that the attachment was much stronger than was ever realized before the loss. Attachments are not necessarily only positive. Most are partially or strongly ambivalent (e.g. towards abusive parents), while others are strongly negative (e.g. towards dictators and tyrants). Even giving up grieving is a loss for those unable to relinquish things.

Termination of a counselling or helping relationship always needs careful handling, but is even more significant for insecure people. Those being counselled after loss are even more likely to re-experience separation anxiety when termination is imminent. They may attempt to control renewed feelings of helplessness by preventing the ending, perhaps by introducing complex new loss-related issues. Others keep control by angry denial of the value of counselling received, being late or being absent from a final session. They might now have enough insight to understand the link between their earlier experiences of abandonment and their current feelings and behaviours; and some could try to handle this ending in a less regressive way.

(f)   Because losses are universal it is inevitable that counsellors and other professionals will always have their own unresolved griefs. Even when their current life involves major changes and losses they may not always be able to stop working with people who are also facing losses, sometimes very similar ones.

Self-awareness is essential when working in this field. Counsellors and helpers need to have achieved as much recognition and resolution of their past losses as possible, and to be especially aware of their own vulnerabilities and age-correspondences when listening to clients. **Supervision** should reduce the risk of over-identifying with a client, but this risk should not be allowed to inhibit the natural empathy and mutual recognition of pain from losses which are an integral part of the human condition.

(g)   Holmes, J. (1993) *John Bowlby and Attachment Theory*. London: Routledge; Simos, B. G. (1979) *A Time to Grieve – Loss as a Universal*

Human Experience. Milwaukee: Family Service America; Viorst, J. (1986) *Necessary Losses*. New York: Simon and Schuster.

KAY CLYMO
   (See also *bereavement; children's experience of loss and death; death of a child; depression; funerals*)

Major incidents

(a) A typical county emergency plan would define these as incidents

   which, by the nature of the hazard, the number and seriousness of casualties, and/or the amount of disruption caused to services, are beyond the capacity of the uniformed emergency services to clear up unaided, and which require the mobilisation and co-ordination of the non-uniformed local authority services and/or other organisations and agencies. (County of Cleveland)

Each disaster has its unique features but common to all are large numbers of distressed people who have unexpectedly been caught up in a situation of danger and who are trying to cope with their reactions to death, bereavement, injury and terror. Their support and care is an important part of a local authority emergency plan. Such plans have been influenced by a Department of Health Working Party report: *Disasters: Towards a Caring Response* (HMSO, 1991). This recommended that the social services department should be the lead body in planning and implementing the local provision for social and psychological care for major incidents. Emphasis was laid upon advance organization of various types of support and therapy with thorough co-ordination of statutory and voluntary agencies involving assignment of roles, selection and training, supervision and support for workers. It is hoped that carers drawn into the response to a disaster will have the advantage of this preparation.

(b) The immediate reactions to disaster are varied. Many will be calm, able to answer questions but dazed. A few will be in total shock, unable to communicate. Some will talk incessantly about what has happened. There will be sudden weeping or outbursts of rage and moods will change rapidly. For the carer this can be a stressful period, wanting to help but unsure what to say or do. Following these first reactions certain symptoms may become intrusive and create further difficulty. These comprise the three clusters of symptoms identified as **post-traumatic stress**: re-experiencing, avoidance and hyper-arousal.

As time passes these symptoms create separate problems which may be the first indication of disaster stress. Family relationships suffer as someone normally loving and relaxed becomes irritable and distanced from partner and children. Performance at work may deteriorate and lead to disciplinary action. There may be more frequent visits to the GP as physical illnesses occur. The excessive use of alcohol and drugs to allay anxiety or blot out memories is a common presenting problem (see *substance misuse*).

Other survivors feel unsure about their identity. **Guilt** about what they failed to do to rescue others or shame at their weakness undermine self-esteem. Their trust in the world as a place of reliable order is shattered and they say they do not recognize the person they have now become. These questions will need addressing on the road to recovery.

A final group of survivors will not make a normal recovery because the incident has activated severe and unresolved conflicts from the past. Unmourned losses, other experiences of trauma, childhood abuse and developmental crises of which there may be no conscious memory, all necessitate longer and specialist treatment. For a small number there will be no improvement and chronic **post-traumatic stress** disorder will require continuing support (Scott and Stradling, 1992: 168).

(d)   The care of survivors and the relatives of all involved starts in the hours following the incident. The range of experiences is broad, stretching from the shock of a near death experience, through additional sights, sounds and smells which are horrific, to multiple bereavement of family members. Relatives may be waiting to know if a loved one has survived, feeling an acute tension between hope and dread. The period spent at or near the incident site may be called the *impact phase* when the main task is to provide support. The presence of support team workers is appreciated both for their calming human presence and for the practical help they provide. Practical assistance has great psychological value in reducing chaos. People need information, telephone contact with their family and help with physical needs like clothing, money or accommodation. The comfort skills used by carers include being a calming influence by eye contact, touch and clear, even speech. Sensitive listening with brief, appropriate responses has a containing effect. Anxiety in the carer will be transmitted by uncertain gaze, over-reassuring, offering sympathy or giving advice. This is not the time for counselling. Support is designed to meet people where they are, accepting their emotions and statements without comment in order to help them face what must be done in the next few hours. One demanding task will be accompanying relatives to the mortuary for identification of the body. Additional training for this is helpful (Wright, 1991: ch. 5).

The quality and credibility of the experience of support often enables survivors and others affected to overcome their fears of stigma and accept later offers of professional help.

A good number of those involved in the incident will have a strong network of support from family, friends, clergy, doctors and other trusted confidants. It is important when offering help not to damage or disable this preferred resource of help.

A second, *intermediate phase*, starts with the setting up of an Assistance Unit which will co-ordinate the main response to those affected by the incident. It will disseminate information about care, provide for assessment of those seeking help and set up a pro-active approach to all survivors and bereaved relatives. A telephone helpline (see *telephone, use of*) will be established and manned by statutory and voluntary workers. A newsletter, like the Hillsborough *Interlink*, allows feelings and information to be shared. Assistance will be given to mutual support groups with facilitators offered. Some groups (see *groups, use of*) will emerge with a focus on action to prevent similar disasters recurring. The Assistance Unit will encourage community responses for services of remembrance and other commemorative events. Carers may find a role in supporting such activities and being available to individuals who may need help.

An early treatment which aims to prevent the onset of **post-traumatic stress** disorder is a form of stress debriefing which is used commonly for smaller traumatic incidents. This crisis intervention strategy is more readily used with groups who work together or are involved in the incident as a team. It is harder to reach the random individuals in a disaster although its methods can apply to them (Hodgkinson and Stewart, 1991). Survivors of the Hillsborough incident disliked a structured approach and preferred empathic listening (Newburn, 1993: 57).

Assessment by mental health professionals will lead to referrals for various kinds of help. The issue of bereavement may be foremost and grief counselling (see *bereavement*) is appropriate (Worden, 1991). Persistent symptoms may be relieved by cognitive/behavioural strategies (Scott and Stradling, 1992). Relationship difficulties arising from disaster are expected by Relate, who can help couples to recognize the effects of stress. Group therapy enables many to accept their symptoms as normal (see *groups, use of*). A positive experience of sharing restores confidence to socialize again. Some will not have dramatic reactions to the incident but slowly become more depressed (see *depression*) with active thought of self-harm or **suicide**. Here psychiatric assessment of risk and consultation with their GP is important.

Whatever role carers have in helping those recovering from a major incident certain considerations can be kept in mind:

1. Trauma undermines trust; time must be allowed for the helping relationship to be established.
2. An experience of massive forces of destruction causes a profound sense of helplessness. The goal of all therapies is to restore autonomy. Enabling a person to control intrusive thoughts or panic attacks helps them feel responsible for their own healing.
3. Recovery involves reviewing the incident in detail so that it can be assimilated. Such reviewing can be intensely painful and frightening and needs to proceed in manageable steps (Herman, 1992: ch. 9). The helper accompanies a client on his journey as a witness to his story so that it is anchored in reality.

A third, *long-term phase* of care concerns those whose problems do not respond to standard treatments and procedures. This may indicate longer psychotherapeutic involvement. At practical levels rebuilding a new life-style can take several years. Ending a marriage (see *divorce*) finding less stressful work, coping with unemployment or facing permanent disability complicate the recovery from disaster. As public interest in the incident will have faded there may be little sympathy or support. There is a case for befriending, which is offered freely at the impact phase, to be continued throughout the recovery period. A care strategy which has several concurrent strands commends itself. It does depend on the various professional and personal supports being aware of each other and seeing the value of interdisciplinary co-operation.

During the third, long-term stage, there will be first-time referrals arising from delayed reaction to the incident or from a new diagnosis taking post-traumatic stress disorder into account. Many years elapse before some seek help and there is evidence of traumas from war and abuse coming to light after decades (Parkinson, 1993: 21).

(e) The main treatment specialisms after a major incident will be mobilized by the local hospital's emergency plan. Psychological triage of distressed survivors will be carried out. Access to clinical psychologists and other medical staff able to help with persistent symptoms is possible through normal GP referral. There are agencies with teams of debriefers who can be contracted to give support to a local authority in emergency situations. Beside the telephone helpline the Samaritans always handle a large increase in calls after disasters, often from emergency staff seeking confidential support.

Bereavement agencies like Cruse and the Compassionate Friends take on extra clients and can help with training volunteers. Loss of religious faith poses problems which may be referred to hospital chaplains (see *religious belief*). Suitable counsellors may already be listed in the local authority emergency plan. The British Association for Counselling has a listing of counsellors able to help in major incidents and can also supply details of debriefers, supervisors, trainers and experts, for example, in the care of children after disaster. Carers working with the Disaster Assistance Unit will have access to supervision. Independent counsellors and other helpers need to recognize the extreme stressfulness of this work and to make arrangements for their own support. A group of such counsellors might well meet with a consultant for supervision and support.

(f) A major source of support is derived from one's peers or fellow team members. Working in a team for such incidents is to be preferred to working alone. Major incidents have produced examples of inter-agency rivalry and insufficient co-operation. Those who manage responses to emergencies are themselves under stress and this affects decision-making. The move towards a thorough co-ordination of all statutory and voluntary agencies with a definition of roles and agreed protocols for call out and deployment will help eliminate most of the tensions. With so many different groups involved there need to be clear rules for the compiling and sharing of information about people helped. The normal standards of **confidentiality** in records need to be observed and any exceptions defined beforehand. The extreme vulnerability of people in major incidents must be protected from exploitation. Prevention of media intrusions into private suffering should not obscure the positive role which the press and broadcasting can play (Hodgkinson and Stewart, 1991: 98).

(g) HMSO (1991) *Disasters: Towards a Caring Response*. London: HMSO; Hodgkinson, P. and Stewart, M. (1991) *Coping With Catastrophe*. London: Routledge; Raphael, B. (1986) *When Disaster Strikes*. London: Unwin Hyman Ltd.

IAN COOPER
  (See also *groups, use of; post-traumatic stress*)

Marriage customs, preparation, etc.

(a) Marriage has been basic to human societies since earliest times. While the understanding of marriage differs widely across the world, the instinct to give it public recognition and honour derives from concerns common to all societies: to offer a secure environment within which to bring up children and so safeguard the future of the race; to regulate sexual activity (especially to protect against incest); to provide an economic unit upon which the well-being of the community can rest; and, not least, to satisfy the companionate needs of women and men. So central have these concerns been that the instinct to interpret marriage in religious terms and see it as God-given for the good of the human race has been almost universal.

Even in today's Western secular societies, marriage remains a central and popular institution. In the early 1990s, up to 83 per cent of the adult population either is or has been married. Around 350,000 weddings are celebrated annually in the UK. Despite criticism of the nuclear family, marriage remains high on the agenda of political parties of both left and right, who see in the value placed on it an indicator of society's own humaneness and concern for human relationships. At the same time, the rising divorce rate (now running at around 175,000 per annum, on the basis of which one marriage in three can expect to end in divorce) constitutes a colossal toll in terms of economic cost as well as human misery (see *divorce*). Clearly, marriage education and the pastoral care of those are married or preparing for marriage is likely to be a sound investment.

This article concerns marriage as currently practised in Britain. It is restricted to monogamous marriage between persons of the opposite sex. (For same-sex relationships, see *gay men and lesbians*.)

(b) The marriage ceremony is a celebration, both for the couple concerned and (because of its public nature) for the whole community. Nevertheless, the process of becoming married can also be a period of real stress for a couple and their families. Reasons include:

- *change of role* from 'single' to 'married', with its new commitments and obligations;
- *merging of two families*, possibly from different locations, cultures or backgrounds;
- *establishing a new social/domestic/economic unit* requiring a different approach to life-style, money, decision-making, use of leisure time, etc.;
- *moving away from the parental home*, or if not, continuing to share it as a married couple;
- *emotional and psychodynamic factors* such as the models of marriage each partner brings from his or her own parenting; also anxiety about sexuality, or gender identity, or whether the proposed marriage is even likely to be viable.

Many of these issues are common to all who marry. However, the effect of some of them is greatly exacerbated in certain cases:

1. *Pregnancy*. Whether or not the couple are marrying at the instigation of parents or grandparents, a marriage entered into *solely* on account of pregnancy is often at risk.

2. *Marriage of minors*. Statistically, marriages contracted in the teenage years are at greater risk of ending in divorce than those entered into later in adulthood.

3. *Unemployment* places considerable financial stress on a marriage at a time of particular vulnerability.

4. *History of mental illness, violence, sexual difficulty or alcoholism*. Couples often expect such problems, when they emerge during courtship, to disappear after the wedding day. Almost always, they do not (see *alcoholism; psychosis; sexual difficulties; violence towards women*).

5. *'Mixed' marriage* of people from different ethnic or religious backgrounds can be highly creative and satisfying. Help is often needed, however, to establish the shared values and beliefs on which the relationship will be built. Problems can arise when the marriage is arranged, as is usual in Asian communities. The form of the wedding ceremony itself can be a contentious issue (see *faith differences*).

6. *Second and subsequent marriage*, especially where there are children from a former marriage, and where the reasons for the failure of a previous marriage have not yet been understood or properly worked through.

7. *Cohabitation*, where the question of what is expected to *change* as a result of getting married is often not properly addressed, especially if the relationship is a long-standing one.

(d)

1. Meanings of marriage

Every marriage is unique. Marriage is as old as the human race, yet each couple discovers it afresh, and invests it with their own vision and hope. The 'task' of marriage is different for each couple, as is the unique satisfaction and fulfilment they find in it.

No amount of theoretical knowledge can compensate for an understanding of marriage that arises from within the relationship itself. Marriage education is essentially experiential in character. The skills of a minister of religion, marital counsellor or therapist will be to help clients recognize and articulate this for themselves. The 'meaning' of marriage is the lived meaning a particular man and woman find in it. It is a lifelong exploration, if not for the lifetimes of the couple, then at least for the lifetime of the marriage. Meaning does not emerge without effort, struggle, even pain. Arguably, the fact that it has to be fought for is in the long run enriching.

Nevertheless, this 'meaning' is informed by the ways in which theology, social science and human experience have reflected on marriage down the centuries. Marriage rites are a good indicator of how marriage has been perceived by particular communities at particular times. The revised Church of England marriage ceremony in the Alternative Service Book (1980) for example, understands marriage as 'a gift of God in creation and a means of his grace, a holy mystery in which man and woman become one flesh'. In other words, marriage is a source of wholeness for human beings, intended for growth and happiness. In it, we find not only another person, but also ourselves, 'I' and 'Thou', in a covenant of interdependent, self-giving love. It is not surprising that the Judaeo-Christian tradition should locate the origins of marriage in paradise.

This new rite understands the threefold aims of the marriage covenant as being companionate relationship, sexual expression and the bringing-up of children. This reverses the order in which the older (1662) service spoke of the marriage aims, illustrating the significant shift in understanding that has taken place over the last three centuries. Today, the expectation of a 'companionate marriage', meaning a fulfilling human relationship lasting a lifetime, probably overrides all other considerations, at least in Western society. Similarly, the tone in which the new service speaks about sex ('that with delight and tenderness they may know each other in love') is far removed from the language of the traditional rite ('ordained for a remedy against sin, and to avoid fornication'). That, too, is to echo the more positive view of human sexuality which our present century has rediscovered.

These three aims of marriage are probably held by most married people, whatever their religious beliefs. This underlines the crucial insight that marriage is an institution that belongs to humanity. That marriages are solemnized (even sacramentalized) in places of worship does not take away from this central point. Marriage in a religious building is no different from one entered into anywhere else. To that extent, the register office is as holy a place as synagogue, mosque or church; its vows as solemn and binding.

2. *Marriage ceremonial*
'Getting married' is an extended process usually lasting many months. It comprises a string of ritual acts from the *engagement* or betrothal through the ceremonies of the *wedding* itself, to the *consummation* of the marriage on the honeymoon, and the final public *recognition* of the couple (usually in their own home) as husband and wife.

This catena of rituals, both public and private, formal and informal, is a classic example of a *rite of passage*. Such rites involve a *pre-liminal phase* in which old roles and relationships are left behind; a *liminal* period of transition and change (*limen* = 'threshold') and a *post-liminal phase* in which the new status is publicly affirmed, and the subjects of the rite are re-incorporated into the community in their new role. In the case of marriage, a man and a woman relinquish the roles of single (or widowed, or divorced) people in order to become married; in the biblical phraseology they leave their father and mother to become 'one flesh' (Genesis 2:24). Similarly, parents become parents-in-law; and if there are children by a previous marriage, step-relatives are created. These far-reaching changes of role and relationship created by the marriage rite give it a clearly *performative* character.

Every culture has its own way of enacting this fundamental human process. It is perhaps surprising that in today's secularized Britain, around 53 per cent of marriages are solemnized in a religious building, 66 per cent of those in Anglican parish churches. Many more (including second or subsequent marriages) include a service of prayer and dedication in a church following a civil ceremony at the register office (the usual practice in many countries of continental Europe). Space forbids even a rudimentary description of the marriage rites of the British churches, let alone those of the other faith communities represented in this country. The following general points are however worth making.

(i)   The celebrants of the rite are the couple themselves.

(ii) The 'blessing' of the marriage in a religious building is ritually separate from the making of the marriage contract. There is no essential difference between a marriage solemnized in a religious building, and a civil ceremony followed by a religious service of blessing.

(iii) The couple must publicly affirm that they are free to marry, and not under legal impediment (see below). They must also affirm their mutual consent, i.e. that they enter willingly and freely into the marriage, either as part of the marriage vow, or as a preamble to it.

(iv) The giving of the wedding ring(s) and joining of hands are not required by law, although they are integral to most religious ceremonies.

3. The law of marriage in the United Kingdom

Because of the public, social character of marriage, the law exercises an active interest in its regulation. Marriage law is an aspect of family law, and there will be cases where it impinges on pastoral work with those getting married. The following is a summary only of the chief points.

The conditions for a marriage to be valid in English law are as follows:

(i) *Each party must have attained the age of consent*, i.e. 16 years. Parental consent is needed in the case of minors, but a marriage is not invalidated if this has not been obtained.

(ii) *Each party must be free to marry*, i.e. not bound by an existing marriage that would render the new contract bigamous.

(iii) *The parties must not be within the prohibited degrees of affinity*. The 'Table of Kindred and Affinity' in the Book of Common Prayer sets out the traditional prohibition of marriage between close relatives. The law has been modified this century by various Acts of Parliament permitting, for example, the marriage of a man with his deceased wife's sister. First cousins have always been allowed to marry under English law.

(iv) *Each party must be capable of entering into the marriage contract*, i.e. of sound mind and able to understand the meaning of the marriage vow.

(v) *There must be mutual consent*, i.e. the couple must marry out of free choice, and not under duress.

(vi) *The couple must intend to consummate the marriage.* Where consummation can be proved not to have taken place, either through incapacity or through refusal on either side, the marriage may be annulled.

(vii) *The civil or ecclesiastical formalities must be complied with.* Traditionally, English law permits marriage only in a licensed place of worship or in a register office, although from 1 April 1995 certain other buildings (e.g. hotels, stately homes and historic monuments) may apply to be licensed for the celebration of civil marriages. Preliminary formalities required are the publication of banns of marriage or the issue of an ecclesiastical licence or superintendent registrar's certificate. The law lays down strict residence requirements for the parties, and specifies that the ceremony must take place between 8 a.m. and 6 p.m. These conditions can be dispensed with only on production of a special licence, issued by the Archbishop of Canterbury, which also permits marriage other than in a licensed building. The marriage must be solemnized before a competent person (licensed minister of religion, registrar) and in the presence of at least two witness.

(viii) *'Common law' marriage* or cohabitation, whatever the intention of the couple to be committed to each other, is no longer recognized in English law.

Scottish law differs from English chiefly in the matter of the formalities. Marriages may be solemnized anywhere (including the register office), provided that the requisite notice has been given to the district registrar, and been publicized for the statutory period. The ceremony must be conducted by a minister of religion, registrar or other authorized person. Irregular marriage 'by habit and repute' may in certain circumstances be recognized under Scottish law.

4. Marriage education and pastoral care

Education for marriage begins at birth. The best preparation for marriage is what children perceive as being modelled by their parents: not a perfect marriage, simply one that is 'good enough' for the growth and fulfilment of each person, and that provides a context of love and support within which to raise their family. Alongside this, the role of schools, churches and voluntary organizations in preparing young people for adult human relationships cannot be overemphasized. This is especially important in the area of sex education, where sexuality needs to be learned, not just as a biological drive, but as the expression of a committed human relationship.

More specifically, a couple approaching marriage are in particular need of skilled support. This is partly because the transition phase of engagement involves coming to terms with profound impending change. Alongside the expectation and hope for their marriage may lie uncertainty about what lies ahead, doubt about whether the relationship is truly based on love, a growing sense of the loss of personal freedom and a realization that to take on a lifelong commitment to another person is indeed an awesome prospect.

Marriage preparation is largely a matter of helping the couple recognize these emotional states as entirely natural. Often, however, concerns about *marriage* are submerged beneath concerns about the *wedding ceremony*, with its endless opportunities for family disputes, inordinate expenditure and romantic fantasy. The skilled carer will want instead to focus on how ready for marriage the couple are, what illusions they retain, how effectively they are beginning to communicate with and listen to each other; in short, how well they know each other and themselves. Separate, as well as joint, interviews often enable the truth about a relationship to emerge helpfully. Group sessions of several couples at a similar stage in their preparation have also been found useful. A full medical examination may also be appropriate (and reassuring).

The marriage ceremony is a complex occasion. Most weddings entail months of preparation, including dress, flowers, catering, transport and honeymoon arrangements. Each of these areas brings the couple into contact with professionals wanting to sell their services. The civil or religious ceremony is not simply one such service out of many. It is the heart of the celebration. So the interface between the church or register office and the couple is crucial at every stage. On secretaries, clerks, vergers, organists, clergy and registrars are projected, to some extent, the couple's aspirations for the future; they symbolize what marriage represents to them as hope and opportunity. All those involved in the ceremony have the chance of contributing to the care of the couple which is the ultimate aim of the rite.

Beyond the wedding day itself, pastoral care of the married has tended to mean helping couples whose marriages are running into trouble. Often, problems become apparent in the first few years, when marriages are at their highest risk of breaking up. It is not only clergy and marriage counsellors who then find themselves in the front line. General practitioners, solicitors, schoolteachers and, most of all, family and friends are inevitably drawn into a situation affecting an ever-widening circle of people. They need to know what kind of support they can realistically offer, and (always a key skill) when to refer the couple to professionals who can either help them repair their marriage and establish a satisfactory *modus vivendi*, or else take the decision to separate responsibly (see *divorce*).

In recent years, more holistic forms of pastoral care for married couples have evolved. Mostly working within the church context, 'marriage enrichment' has concentrated on helping couples celebrate what is good in their marriage and enhance it. The style of working is often group-based.

(e) Local clergy, registrars and marriage counsellors provide a local fund of knowledge and expertise. Citizens Advice Bureaux are a useful source of information on practical aspects of family law. Many of the organizations listed below have regional or local branches.

1. Marriage preparation, education and enrichment
Association for Marriage Enrichment, Westminster Pastoral Foundation, 23 Kensington Square, London W8 5HN (Tel: 0171 937 6956); Christian Action Research and Education Trust (CARE), 53 Romney Street, London SW1P 3RF (Tel: 0171 233 0455); Family Life and Marriage Education Network (FLAME), 11 Mundy Street, Heanor, Derbyshire DE7 7EB (Tel: 01773 761579); Growing Together in Marriage, Cross Keys, Hemingford Abbots, Huntingdon, Cambridgeshire PE18 9AE (Tel: 01480 68600); Marriage Encounter (Anglican), 4 Redclose Avenue, Morden, Surrey SM4 5RD (Tel: 0181 646 1217); The Mothers' Union, Mary Sumner House, 24 Tufton Street, London SW1P 3RB (Tel: 0171 222 5533); Worldwide Marriage Encounter (Roman Catholic), 14 Lutton Road, Hatch End, Pinner, Middlesex HA5 4RH (Tel: 0181 428 0302).

2. Marriage guidance
Catholic Marriage Advisory Council, Clitherow House, 1 Blythe Mews, Blythe Road, London W14 0NW (Tel: 0171 371 1341); Catholic Marriage Advisory Council (Scotland), Archdiocese of Glasgow Office, 196 Clyde Street, Glasgow G1 4JY (Tel: 0141 204 1239); Relate (National Marriage Guidance), Herbert Gray College, Little Church Street, Rugby, Warwickshire CV21 3AP (Tel: 01788 573241); Tavistock Institute of Marital Studies, The Tavistock Centre, 120 Belsize Lane, London NW3 5BA (Tel: 0171 435 7111).

3. Special needs
Asian Family Counselling Service, 74 The Avenue, London W13 (Tel: 0181 997 5749); Association of Inter-Church Families, Inter-Church House, 35 Lower Marsh, London SE1 7RL (Tel: 0171 620 4444); Family Planning Association, 27–35 Mortimer Street, London W1N 7RJ (Tel: 0171 636 7866).

(g)   Carr, W. (1994) *Brief Encounters: Pastoral Ministry through the Occasional Offices* (rev. edn). London: SPCK; Clulow, C. (ed.) (1993) *Rethinking Marriage: Public and Private Perspectives*. London: Karnac Books; Scarf, M. (1987) *Intimate Partners: Patterns in Love and Marriage*. London: Century Hutchinson.

MICHAEL SADGROVE

Menopause

(a)   The menopause is a natural and healthy process, the final phase of a woman's reproductive cycle. The effects of the profound internal changes are physical, sexual, emotional and psychological, and frequently also spiritual: the 'change of life' can bring to the surface long-buried concerns about mortality, purpose and meaning.

The signs can appear at any age from the late thirties to the early sixties. About 25 per cent of women have started it by the age of 45, and 40 per cent between 45 and 49 (Fairlie et al., 1987: 13). In some cases it can be much earlier, usually because of a previous medical condition, chemotherapy, radiotherapy or surgery, in particular 'total' hysterectomy. An important consideration for health practitioners is to make certain that the signs do indicate the menopause, rather than a developing health problem which has similar symptoms.

While hormone replacement therapy (HRT) has made an incalculable difference, especially to younger women who have had ovariectomy and/or hysterectomy, it is rarely a simple matter of choice (Shapiro, 1989: 191). HRT requires medical management, can mean the continuation of periods and does not suit all women. Its benefits need to be balanced against any health risks, side-effects and a later menopause. The major concern is osteoporosis – the thinning and weakening of the bone structure – which affects women to a much greater degree than men. There are several factors to take into account when assessing the risk, including heredity. Women with denser bones, for example many black women, have a lower risk of fracture as a result of osteoporosis than small-boned white and South-East Asian women (Kahn and Holt, 1989: 64). No woman should be pressurized to take HRT, and her decisions should be based first on a thorough health check, and secondly on full information – written by women users or issued by women's committees of health education authorities, rather than pharmaceutical company pamphlets which may be biased towards HRT.

(b) A client may present with clinical concerns about proposed surgery or HRT, or with sexual, emotional or psychological signs. Sometimes she does not associate these with the menopause.

1. Physical signs
Early signs of the menopause often feel like highly-exaggerated PMT (see pre-menstrual syndrome, although there are specific differences. A blood test can confirm changes in hormone levels. The most common signs are menstrual irregularities and 'hot flushes'. Others are vaginal dryness or itching, blood pressure changes, palpitations or faintness, anaemia, tiredness, difficulty in concentrating or memory lapses. These are caused by the body's adjustments to the different ways in which hormones are produced. There might be weight gain caused by fluid retention and a natural increase in fatty tissue, muscle spasms or cramps, skin dryness and some weakening of the pelvic floor muscles. Dark spots or moles may appear.

Even if there are no obvious signs, a woman is aware of inner changes in her body. She may experience restlessness or a need to focus on herself, increased sensitivity to others or low back pain. She may want a healthier diet or need certain foods (especially those rich in carbohydrates and calcium). For this reason, some women believe that they might be pregnant. It is possible to become pregnant during the early menopausal years, and many women in any case need to change their contraceptives.

2. Moods, *feelings and beliefs*

Hormonal changes can create mood swings, and are often confused with emotional feelings. One of women's greatest needs during the menopause is to make sense of these unexpected and contradictory sensations and feelings.

Women describe their experiences very differently (Kahn and Holt, 1989). Mood swings can create a sense of being out of control, especially when the woman feels tearful, impatient, anxious or aggressive for no obvious reason, or finds herself unable to concentrate. She might temporarily lose interest in sex. 'Hot flushes' can be alarming, irritating or embarrassing, and cause loss of sleep, especially when accompanied by heavy sweats.

Emotional feelings associated with mid-life – awareness of starting the transition to ageing – can range from **depression** to exhilaration, grief to relief. A woman may experience **guilt** at wanting more freedom and independence, or about wanting to improve or change her sex life. The menopause can feel like a second adolescence, the more so because of a simultaneous longing to be irresponsible, and to challenge socially-designated roles. Women exploring their sexuality may meet resistance, or find that their sexual needs are unmet. Lesbians more certain of and more open about their sexual identity may experience hostility as they face a new set of stereotypes about older women's sexuality (Neild and Pearson, 1992: 12).

A frequent issue is complicated **loss** of youth, employment, sexuality, partner, identity as a woman, fertility (see *infertility*) or choices about having children, and purpose in life. The reality of mid-life means that friends or partners are ageing and dying, parents or primary carers becoming elderly, debilitated or dying, and children becoming adults.

Women born outside the United Kingdom, who are experiencing grief about relatives who have died at home, can become intensely aware of the loss of families left behind and of their culture, especially cultures where older women are cared for and respected by their communities. Long-term experiences of **racism** and accompanying social factors – **stress**, poverty, experiences of the mental health system and isolation – can mean that black and Asian women show signs of ageing earlier. **Mid-life** is therefore a time to build support structures for the future (Phillips and Rakusen, 1989: 475).

(c) Ageist, sexist, heterosexist and religious/cultural beliefs have resulted in several myths, social taboos and stereotypes about the menopause. The ability to deal with these is dependent on a woman being prepared for the menopause, the strength of her identity, the extent to which she has internalized the stereotypes and the attitudes of people close to her. The menopause tends to be blamed for all women's emotional reactions, so concerns about other issues are often dismissed. Menopausal women are sometimes believed to be incapable of rational thought or reliable behaviour. Beliefs still remain about 'hysteria' and 'melancholia' – the latter only recently dropped from lists of psychiatric disorders (Phillips and Rakusen, 1989: 453). A woman may present with feelings that she is 'not a real woman any more', or that she is sexually 'on the shelf', or is 'having a breakdown'. She may feel embarrassed discussing her problems with a stranger, especially a man, or someone from a different culture. Psychiatric admissions increase at this age (Barnes and Maple, 1992: 87).

It is essential to take such stereotypes into account, without assuming that they are applicable to all cultures. Other related factors include parental status, relationships issues, disability, learning difficulty, mental health, class and economic status.

1. Physical causes
Medical and surgical history must be considered, and other possible causes of menopausal symptoms eliminated (Shapiro, 1989: 190). There are realistic concerns about increased risks of ovarian or uterine cancer during the menopausal years. There are several contra-indications for HRT (Kahn and Holt, 1989: 98).

Several health factors may suppress, contribute to or exaggerate the ordinary signs of the menopause. These include medication; addictive substances (prescribed or otherwise) (see *substance misuse*); caffeine-rich foods; foods which heat the body; foods low in protein and vitamins and high in sugar and additives. A dietary check is particularly important for women who experience **eating disorders**, and for women with digestive problems or conditions including liver or kidney disease, diabetes, ME, candida, food allergies, asthma and HIV (see *AIDS/HIV*) infection.

2. Sex and sexuality
In a sense, all women presenting with menopausal issues are exploring their sexuality, often needing to express it differently. While HRT can offset many of the physical problems, vaginal dryness or itching may result in painful penetration, worsened if, for instance, a male partner cannot or is unwilling to change his sexual behaviour. Tiredness, irritability and 'hot flushes' can mean that even if desire is strong, the woman is physically incapable of full sexual enjoyment. Women who are unassertive about their sexual needs or who have inconsiderate partners find the menopause difficult. Others may be delighted to have a reason to 'switch off'.

The menopause is a natural part of a woman's sexuality, a time of adjustment; desire usually returns. Many women report increased sexual pleasure once the risk of pregnancy is eliminated and the most distressing symptoms reduced.

Lesbians who have had opportunities to explore their sexuality in all its variety may have developed the emotional and psychological resources to deal with the menopause, and find partners and friends supportive (Bradford and Ryan, 1991). The opposite can apply for those who are isolated, without a partner, who are single parents, whose community is dominated by younger lesbians, or who need to maintain well-being and fitness because of work, parenting/caring demands and the desire to remain independent. A lesbian who has recently come out may feel cheated by what she perceives as limitations on exploring her sexuality, or feelings of losing her newly-acquired right to control what happens to her body (Young, 1995). If the menopause results in her first experience of formal counselling she may not want to mention her sexual orientation.

Care professionals therefore need to ensure an environment in which women feel comfortable discussing every aspect of their sexuality. It should also be remembered that the present generation of older women is the first to come to terms with the realities of **child sexual abuse** and domestic violence (see *violence towards women*). The menopause may present the first opportunity for some to bring these issues into the open.

3. Emotional factors

Mood swings and emotional feelings are real and need acknowledgement and expression. Underlying causes of, for instance, **depression** could be changes in dietary needs or blood pressure, a sense of multiple **loss**, lack of sleep or undischarged tension or anger. Depression and anxiety can also result from a fear of ageing and a need for purpose and meaning in life. A combination of issues can result in a **mid-life crisis**. A woman may feel abandoned by those close to her if they are intolerant or unwilling to support her. Work and caring responsibilities may feel overwhelming. She may resent them, and want to give up or at least share responsibilities. Women who have delayed decisions about having children, and find that it is too late to get pregnant, may go through a particularly intense period of grieving and self-criticism.

As the menopausal years often coincide with a daughter's first sexual experience, the illness, debility or death of partner, friends and older relatives, and other health problems of her own, a woman can feel that life is fraught with difficulties. She may feel that she is not allowed her sexuality, or is trapped in a supportive role. Professional help is invariably offered to enable women to cope with caring responsibilities, rather than express their own needs (Barnes and Maple, 1992: 75). A partner of a similar age may be experiencing mid-life problems and be unable or unwilling to offer support. **Redundancy** or 'early retirement' is, unfortunately, a frequent additional crisis factor at this age.

4. Beliefs

Associations with ageing and ageism (social or internalized) mean that the menopause can come as a shock to a woman who feels in her prime at the age of 45. The present generation of menopausal women is unique: the pre-Pill generation, the first to have spent their adolescent years exploring their sexuality and physical development in secret (sometimes accompanied by shame), their adult years experiencing or creating the considerable social changes brought about by feminism. However, many carry within them the effects of their younger days, which can be revived during the menopause, especially if they remember a mother's difficult menopausal years. Myths about sexuality can produce problems for a woman whose self-esteem depends upon her being sexually active, or who feels it is sex that holds relationships together.

(d)   The practitioner's role is to enable a woman to make choices which are most empowering for her. These can include enabling her to explore her self-image in wider terms than the usual expectations of motherhood (or potential fertility), caring and being a sexual partner.

Information and research in the past 30 years has concentrated on the physical changes, the development of HRT and the needs of the average, healthy, able, white woman. The more recent women's health guides originating in the USA have included the experiences of women from different races and cultures (Hepburn and Gutiérrez, 1988, and section (g)).

Practitioners working with women who have **learning difficulties** or are **physically disabled** need access to information about sexuality which includes menopausal issues. Mental health workers need to take into account the effects of existing and long-term medication, and the woman's ability to tolerate present doses without worsening the side-effects, as tolerance decreases with age.

Care should be taken to avoid problematizing the menopause, at the same time confronting its realities. Simple self-help techniques such as wearing natural fibres and layers can reduce the 'hot flushes'. Dentists can be asked to reduce the volume of adrenaline in injections. Preventive postural exercise is especially important. There is a wide choice of **holistic therapies**.

Many women experience the menopause as a transition which gives them opportunity to focus on their own needs and their futures. Help can acknowledge the feelings associated with **loss** and enable their expression, while realistically supporting the woman's preparation for a new, creative and possibly exciting phase of her life.

Issues for practitioners: Many issues have been covered above: the prejudices and the resultant myths and stereotypes about the menopause. A multidisciplinary approach means a 'whole woman' approach, rather than, as frequently happens, splitting a woman's needs among different sectors of the care professions.

Women are often at their peak during the menopause years, making considerable contributions to society. Their life experiences need to be validated and channelled. However, not all women have benefited from feminism (or, in the case of lesbians, from the gay liberation movement); or even been exposed to its ideas. Practitioners need to be aware of this and of their own issues around sexuality, sexual orientation and gender role expectations (see *gender issues*).

(e)   Health resources include GPs, well-woman and menopause clinics, gynaecologists and dieticians. Personal resources include relationship or family therapy (see *couples, working with; families, working with*), and **bereavement** counselling. Women's health networks can provide up-to-date information or book/tape lists on the menopause and HRT, and other possible problems such as hysterectomy, cervical cancer or breast problems.

(g)   Kahn, A. and Holt, L. H. (1989) *Menopause: the Best Years of Your Life?* London: Bloomsbury; Phillips, A. and Rakusen, J. (eds) (1989) *The New Our Bodies, Ourselves.* London: Penguin; Shapiro, J. (ed.) (1989) *Ourselves Growing Older.* London: Fontana.

VAL YOUNG

Mid-life crisis

(a)   The study of mid-life process is part of a wider stream of interest in developmental psychology that has emerged since the publication of Levinson's seminal book of 1978, *The Seasons of a Man's Life.*

Although the precise age of mid-life varies considerably in the literature, the period of middle life is generally taken to begin not earlier than 40 and to end not later than 55, with transitional stages happening either side of those years. The period 35–60 therefore contains the whole of the mid-life stage, although the period 55–60 is as much to do with entering late adulthood as it is with completing the mid-life period.

Levinson identifies four life stages, each lasting roughly 25 years and overlapping, 'so that a new one is getting under way as the previous one is being terminated' (1978: 18). These life stages are:

1.   childhood and adolescence: age 0–22
2.   early adulthood: age 17–45
3.   middle adulthood: age 40–65
4.   late adulthood: age 60 onwards

It should be noted that Levinson's original age classification (as set out immediately above) has generally shifted in the professional literature, which refers more readily to 'mid-life' rather than 'middle adulthood', mid-life having the slightly earlier span of 35–60 rather than the middle adulthood span of 40–65.

The concept of 'mid-life crisis' first occurred in a formal sense in a paper by Elliott Jacques called *Death and the Mid-life Crisis* (1965), although the work of Freud, Jung and Erikson is extensively concerned with matters that could be characterized as mid-life crises. Jacques was especially interested in an observation that he made in looking at the lives of over 300 famous painters, writers, sculptors, poets and composers, to the effect that there was a sudden jump in the death rate between ages 35 and 39, the rate being far in excess of the expected norm. Mozart is an especially vivid example.

The focus of Jacques' interest in creativity and mortality, with death occurring during the transitional period 35–40, has tended to concentrate the popular conception of mid-life as being inevitably bound up with conflict and crisis. This is not a helpful confusion. It has led to a general assumption that a 40th birthday creates an inevitable downhill slide in energy, attractiveness, occupational performance and marital happiness. Men are often depicted as bored with jobs, lives and wives. Mid-life men are then thought to be anxious, full of conflict and crisis-ridden. In a similar vein, women are depicted as menopausal (see *menopause*), fretful and depressed.

An alternative mid-life scenario is of men entering the most creative and powerful period of their lives, enjoying being in charge of themselves and others and with an increasing supply of material resources; while women, after the initial childbearing/rearing years, feel increasingly confident and free, especially in late-emerging sexuality and employment opportunities.

It is thus extremely difficult to characterize 'mid-life crisis'. As the following sections show, the crises that happen in mid-life may be weathered in a variety of ways. It may also be that the concept of 'mid-life crisis' should be restricted to events of a turbulent kind happening only in the transitional periods of 35–40 and 55–60; with the 15 years 40–55 being viewed as the consolidated period between the transitional and potentially crisis-ridden phases. It is our view that adopting these rather more rigorous and well-defined criteria when talking about mid-life process and crisis would be professionally appropriate. At the same time, we cannot but acknowledge that the unfortunate looseness of the concept 'mid-life crisis' is unlikely to be tightened up, although we strongly recommend that it should be.

For practical purposes, processes of change should not be immediately equated with the concept of crisis. Helping professionals tend by definition to see individuals who are distressed or dis-eased, and may well have an inclination to over-generalize their observations to the population at large. A strong body of research suggests that no more than 5 per cent of (white American middle-class male) individuals experience what they define as a crisis during mid-life.

(b)   In its broadest sense the whole of life could be construed as a continuing transitional process from birth to death. It is the special characteristic of being a human being to manage change in response to the external stressors of the world. Accomplishing this successfully creates a feeling of being effective and being in control. Crisis seems to be experienced when an individual finds that his or her strategies for coping are, for one reason or another, no longer effective. Thus only those life events which leave an individual feeling disempowered, and which occur in the age periods 35–40 or 55–60, should properly be classified as mid-life crises. There may, however, be an argument for distinguishing between transitional crises (which are likely to be the most acute) and crises which happen in the consolidating 15 years of 40–55. There are likely to be less acute but in some ways more surprising in that they occur in what should be otherwise experienced as a more settled phase.

Within the age limits as defined, the common core characteristic of all mid-life crises is the individual's sense of not being able to summon up sufficient or appropriate (internal/personal) resources with which to meet the demands of external stressors.

The psychological literature about mid-life crisis has come largely from attempting to understand the mid-life processes of white middle-class American heterosexual males. This creates substantial difficulties in generalizing across gender, ethnic, sexual and class boundaries. This difficulty may be of more concern when trying to anatomize mid-life process than when coping with manifest mid-life crises; for the core characteristic described above is free of these limiting concepts. In practice, though, crises tend to cluster within the following seven categories:

1. existing relationships (including extra-marital), marriage and family matters including children, parents and previous marital and dependent relationships;
2. health, functional abilities, sexuality (functional as well as orientation) and gender;
3. personal and economic security in the context of current socio-economic climate;
4. career and work;
5. race;
6. class;
7. spiritual convictions.

These issues are of significance to women as well as to men, although what is often especially apparent about the differences in the mid-life crises of men and women is that the man begins to be concerned with the inner world, while the woman begins to be more concerned with the external world. Both of these are of course likely to be the relatively unexplored sides of the individual's first half of life.

O'Connor (1981) has another way of classifying mid-life crises into groups although also by reference to context, as follows:

1. the social context;
2. the individual context;
3. the family context;
4. the occupational context;
5. marriage and the mid-life crisis.

Whichever of these two classifications one adopts, the issues that present are likely to be coloured by one or more of the fundamental psychological themes that resonate throughout human experience – attachment, **loss**, separation, hope and the various manifestations of fear, anger, hostility and love in particular.

(c) So far as precipitating factors are concerned, it is useful to distinguish between matters of recent origin and those that are more remote or historical within a person's life experience. The first are what various authors call life events, external stressors or triggers. The second arise from the emotionally laden life experiences which form part of the uniqueness of the individual. Mid-life crises can often be seen to create echoes within the person's emotional memory; and these echoes in turn resonate into the present. It is often because the earlier experiences were poorly resolved that, when they appear in a different guise in mid-life, a sense of not having the capacity to cope with them is so acutely felt.

> Jane, a training manager in a multinational corporation, decided to
> become an independent consultant at the age of 32. In difficult

trading circumstances, and with the help of a contract from her original company, she established herself successfully over a six-year period. She then began to feel bored, found herself less and less enthusiastic, and became increasingly anxious about her earning capacity.

These feelings had been triggered by undertaking a training contract in which she had had to cope with an extremely hostile client. Over three months of regular meetings with the departmental manager in question, she had felt her best endeavours were continuously invalidated. Somehow her natural resilience had been severely undermined. The focus of enquiry was upon why, in a person who appeared to be usually full of energy and zest, this one encounter had had such a deleterious effect.

She began to realize that her effectiveness as a trainer was based upon an underlying wish to please people, which was itself based upon a wish to please her mother's second husband, her own father having abandoned his wife and Jane when she was five. The unsuccessful attempts she had made to please an unduly hostile figure triggered very early anxieties about rejection and loss, and they in turn had resonated upon her current life situation, creating the fears of loss of income and future incapacity to sell her services.

This would properly have been characterized as a mid-life crisis in the work and career category. The influence of underlying psychological themes is very evident.

In the following account, George was very clear about the underlying themes, having worked them out for himself. What puzzled him was that knowing the causes did not help his crisis. He came for help to manage the crisis.

Aged 39, George had pursued a career as a teacher of young children. A kind and gentle man, unassertive in his own interest and dedicated to his job, he had watched his wife's career in law substantially outstrip his own in its earning potential and demands on time. Over 13 years of marriage he had become the domestic centre of their lives. His infertility had prevented them having children.

George's crisis had arisen when a new headmistress had replaced the previous headmaster. Younger than himself, she had set about a managerial reorganization of the school, reducing George's influence over many out-of-school activities in favour of a philosophy she espoused of teachers not being seen to work for hours for which they were not paid. George felt a great sense of grief at the loss of time spent with children for whom he cared, and in his own musings about what was happening to him had made a powerful association with his own family's grief when a late-arriving brother had died aged 2 when George himself was 14.

Enquiry suggested that these events bore the echo/resonance relationship which is so characteristic of the true mid-life crisis. A programme of behaviourally-based delayed grief therapy was instituted. Over a period of six weeks, George's mood lifted. A programme of assertiveness training was then begun, and George started reasserting his own values within the school common-room and, more directly, to school governors. He struck a sympathetic chord among parents and some other teachers and for the first time in his life found himself leading a minor and (with advice) well-managed crusade.

(d) Recognizing mid-life crisis is relatively easy. Finding the echo/resonance relationships which typically underlie them requires an understanding of psychodynamic and biographical processes. Making decisions as to what treatment processes might be effective requires access to a wide range of counselling and psychological resources. The diagnosis and management of mid-life crisis should not, therefore, be lightly undertaken.

There are many stressful events which will happen across the middle years of life which, when they occur, feel like crises but which do not provoke a mid-life crisis. The loss of a job by **redundancy**, for instance, will, for the vast majority of individuals, be a worrying, painful, financially embarrassing and eventually rewarding experience which is properly regarded as a crisis but, in that it does not trigger any incapacity to cope, is not a mid-life crisis.

Divorce is the most difficult of the events which often occur in the mid-life period to classify as a mid-life crisis. The threat of divorce within a relationship often produces periods of great uncertainty, feelings of helplessness and various manifestations of rage. It is clearly, in life event terms, a crisis. Unless, however, the individual concerned is unable to move his or her life forward, it is not usefully seen as a mid-life crisis.

Although we have not used it here so far, the concept of 'identity crisis' or 'existential crisis' is often used about mid-life crises. The middle years are often the time when the great questions about 'what am I doing with my life?' arise; often in the face of aspirations not being borne out by reality, or early perceptions of mortality. We find it more helpful to classify the focus of a mid-life crisis within the seven categories that we have listed above rather than use the broad-band ideas of existential identity. Individuals typically present within a context which is more narrowly defined than the infinity of existence. It is within the narrower context that helping resources can more usefully be brought to bear.

If, however, the existential question proves to be so insistent that no other focus will do, it is likely that the individual will most benefit from longer-term analytical psychotherapy; for when the existential anxiety has no here and now focus its roots are likely to be very deep within the individual's psychic development. In these circumstances analytic psychotherapy would be the treatment of choice.

(e)   It will be apparent from the above that the professional skills required to manage mid-life crisis will come from formal trainings in counselling, psychotherapy and psychoanalysis. Current life problems which are crises but not, in the sense that we have defined them, mid-life crises will respond then to sensible and sensitive practical advice.

Many individuals who have crises in their middle years that are not identifiable as mid-life crises will benefit in the first instance from contact with problem-solving agencies such as Citizens Advice Bureaux. What is needed in such circumstances is well-founded practical advice and support. The worker who wishes to engage seriously in the management of properly-defined mid-life crises must expect to be a well-trained person of recognizable professional expertise. A directory of counsellors and therapists is available from the British Association for Counselling, 1 Regent Place, Rugby, Warwickshire CV21 2PJ (Tel: 01788 578328) and a register of psychotherapists is available from the UK Council for Psychotherapy, Regent's College, Inner Circle, Regent's Park, London NW1 4NS (Tel: 0171 487 7554). Professional societies for psychotherapists normally have information on their members in any particular area – details of such societies are also available from the UK Council for Psychotherapy.

(g)   Hunter, S. and Sundel, M. (eds) (1989) *Mid-Life Myths: Issues, Findings and Practical Implications*. Newbury Park, CA: Sage Publications; Levinson, D. J. (1978) *The Seasons of a Man's Life*. New York: Ballantine; O'Connor, P. (1981) *Understanding the Mid-Life Crisis*. Sydney, Australia: Macmillan.

PAUL BROWN AND ANNE ABEL SMITH
(See also *menopause*)

Money advice

(b)   Handling finances and repaying debt may sometimes be an issue faced by people as a result of difficulties referred to elsewhere in this book (see *alcoholism; gambling*); while clearly for others lack of reliable or sufficient income may lead to problems with money (see *adolescents; divorce; old age; redundancy and unemployment, single parents*).

(e) In all instances specialist help is called for and referral is recommended, although a preliminary step is to encourage the person to talk to their creditors, telling them what the problems are, since creditors may be able to make arrangements that take off immediate pressure to repay the debt.

The first port of call in any area is usually the local Citizens Advice Bureau, where at the very least basic information on money advice is held, and can be used by all workers. Some bureaux have specially trained workers who can deal more thoroughly with the problems. The local Citizens Advice Bureau also holds information on any other independent resources in the area. Money advice workers are sometimes to be found in local authority departments, e.g. housing, or at county council level in some social services departments. A few areas in the country (e.g. Leicestershire) have an independent money advice centre, sometimes with a local helpline. There is a National Debtline on 0121 359 8501.

It is probably only independent advice that puts the client first. While creditors accept that people have problems, inevitably they are anxious about their own money. Their recovery procedures do not always take the wider picture into account. This is a good reason for seeking independent help first.

Those who are having money problems related to unsecured loans (credit cards, mail order repayments, personal loans) need to be made aware of the consequences of consolidating their debt with finance companies, since this is generally done through securing it against their house. Where loans remain unsecured, they are non-priority and easier to deal with. Once they are secured in this way, the finance company becomes a priority creditor, and default puts the home at risk.

(g) Wolfe, M. and Ivison, J. (1993) *Debt Advice Handbook*. London: Child Poverty Action Group.

MICHAEL JACOBS

Mothers and infants

(a) Mothers and infants are here taken together because in many ways they cannot be separated. D. W. Winnicott said that there is 'no such thing as an infant' (1965: 39). What he meant by this enigmatic phrase is that in a baby a cohesive 'unit self' has not yet been formed. Some of the functions of separate individuality, such as a knowledge of the boundary between self and other, are provided by the mother. Mother and child together thus make a whole unit. I follow Winnicott, therefore, in taking mother and baby together as, psychologically, they cannot initially be parted.

The biological mother of the child is most usually the person who fulfils this role of primary caretaker but this is by no means necessarily the case. The role may be taken up by a nanny or an adoptive or foster-mother. It may also be the child's father who is primary caretaker. I use the word 'mother' but do not wish to imply that the biological mother is necessarily in this role. Also, in using the word 'father' I am implying a person who primarily supports the 'mother'. This person could be another woman – particularly in the case of a lesbian family. So, by mother I mean someone who fulfils a permanent mother function. Indeed it is 'mothers' who will usually present for help. Babies can only make their presence felt to helpers via another person. I also look at the role of father in relation to the mother–infant duo.

(b) If we wish to make an effective intervention on behalf of this age group, it is essential to focus our attention on the mother. I therefore concentrate on the needs of infants in relation to their mothers, and the needs of mothers in relation to the stresses on them carrying such an onerous and important task. I also include those who are pregnant and in labour. Research (Verney and Kelly, 1982) has shown that babies as yet unborn are also affected by the emotional state of their mothers; and certainly women start to be mothers at the beginning of pregnancy.

As those who intervene on behalf of mothers and young children, we need to know that we cannot affect one without the other. Broadly speaking it is not possible to intervene on the child's behalf completely independently of the mother or make any lasting difference to the child's life without the mother. The child lives and breathes and has its being within the realm and orbit of the mother. She provides what Winnicott called a 'holding environment' in which the child thrives or fails to thrive. Mothers are usually very aware of the crucial importance of their role and are often very sensitive to criticism particularly as that criticism can be highly charged. It may be hard for her to draw attention directly to any difficulty she may be having with her child. It is necessary for care providers to be aware of quite subtle signs of distress which they may meet when the mother comes into contact with them in a routine way, such as a pregnancy check, or when they are sought out, such as for housing benefit, or through physical illness.

Pregnancy is often a time when a woman needs a great deal of help, even if it is not a first pregnancy. There are often anxieties surrounding her thoughts, feelings and experiences. In fact it is unlikely that any mother is totally free of them. Much can go wrong and she is well aware of that. She may well need to be listened to with special attention. Fears for the welfare of the growing child may not spring from realistic knowledge of physical problems, but can reflect the mother's own feelings of destructiveness or inadequacy. Alongside loving feelings for the child, the mother may find that she has destructive or hateful fantasies which may be born of envy or jealousy.

These feelings may well disturb her even if she is not consciously aware of them. They can result in seemingly irrational or overstated fears of being out of control, fears for her own health or for the well-being of her child. It is important for doctors, nurses or others who encounter these worries to understand the depth of disturbance that might be present. No mother is likely to be exempt from them. The same sort of worries may beset her after the birth. Sensitive listening and support from those she comes into contact with may be all that she needs at such a time.

A mother's insecurity about her ability to look after her child may manifest itself in many ways. She may become depressed and unable to carry out her tasks in relation to the child. She may become obsessional in her determination to do everything well and so become exhausted and depleted. The baby may be the one who manifests the distress by, for instance, having feeding or sleep disturbances. While physical causes may be discovered, there is often an underlying psychological situation which needs to be understood if the mother is to be effectively helped.

(c) As care-givers we need to understand that a human infant is not ready to go into the world without the physical and psychological support of another. We must therefore consider what the needs are and how they are best met – who can best meet these needs and what happens if they are not met. I look first at the optimal situation: one in which the baby's needs are met on the whole well enough by what Winnicott calls the 'good enough mother'.

Both the physical and the psychological survival of the baby are impossible without adult intervention although, as I show below, it may be artificial to divide the physical and the psychological. The baby seems totally unable to influence the likelihood of their survival on either count – but is this so? Although human babies are born in a state of complete vulnerability, they have their own part to play. The baby can make an appeal either by crying, or by simply looking appealing. Babies seem to engender a protectiveness in us that means that we know by identification with them their feelings of utter vulnerability. We therefore, in response to such identification, desire to provide what the baby needs.

Winnicott (1958) said that biological mothers are particularly well placed to provide this role as they have been prepared throughout the pregnancy and birth. They feel a particular identification with their baby. They have a sensitized knowledge of the baby's needs. He calls this 'primary maternal preoccupation' which he says is a little like madness. For a while the mother drops her own needs in order to care as well as possible for those of her child. (Although others may be able to provide for the baby in this way, they might find it more onerous.)

Winnicott (1958: 160) describes how the baby at first needs the attunement of the mother to be very accurate so that she seems to know what is wanted intuitively. As time goes by the mother inevitably fails in this task and the baby, when he has become psychologically strong enough through the comparative reliability of the mother, is gradually enabled to bear her failures without overwhelming distress. The baby is then able to become aware of his own needs. This brings with it a gradual realization of individuality. 'I am me, with my own particular needs; and she, being a separate person, might be able to meet them.'

Providing for physical needs therefore provides the backdrop for psychological ones. In feeding her baby the mother also provides warmth and contact through skin and gaze. Various researchers including Bowlby (1979) have shown that this human contact is more important than the actual food. The child may need the food to stay alive, but starved of empathetic contact the baby may well fail to thrive and die anyway. It has been shown that monkeys who were deprived of a mother but given either a hard machine which produced milk or a soft dummy 'mother' chose the soft object in preference to the food. Winnicott said that babies cannot be 'fobbed off' with a good feed (Winnicott, 1958: 163). By this he meant that much more is needed than just the food.

One might also say that babies cannot be fobbed off with a good cuddle. There is something further needed, which has probably best been described by Kohut (Ornstein, 1985). This is the need to be mirrored and to be able to idealize and identify with caretakers. In looking into the mother's eyes there needs to be a message from the mother which tells the child 'I see that you are beautiful and I love you for who you are'. In other words, a baby's acceptance is not conditional on meeting his mother's needs. Where bad feelings are experienced, which inevitably they are, the child does not have a strong enough sense of self to hold them and needs to give them to mother. The mother will then be able to hand these back in a manageable form. Their non-verbal conversation goes something like this:

Baby: I feel bad, I'm in pain.

Mother: You had a tummy ache and I was out of the room but it is all right now. I am back and I can help you to get rid of the pain. I will hold you until you feel better.

In providing these needs, an almost superhuman effort is expected of the mother. It is probably the most demanding physical and psychological work that is ever done. Most women do it often unsupported and usually unsung. Many of the supports that were once provided in our culture are now missing, such as extended families and close knit communities. Various professionals often have to fill this gap. How they can do this I describe below. Before that I look at the kinds of things that can go wrong.

Most basically and importantly the mother may not have the external or internal resources to provide well enough for her child. Caring for a baby is a very tiring job. Sleep is interrupted. There is little, if any, time off. If no one is able to take over for a little while, a mother's resources can be almost entirely depleted. If there is little money the difficult job is made even harder.

As indicated above, the presence of a baby often has the effect of our identifying with him or her. We remember our own babyhood, often in a bodily and unconscious way. In mothering a baby how we were ourselves mothered is echoed in us. If we were not well mirrored as babies we may well continue to look for this throughout life. It is, of course, natural to continue to need this sort of affirmation. We all need some narcissistic gratification to feel at one with ourselves and the world. However, if we are very needy it is hard for us not to look for this gratification in our children, so that they provide this for us rather than we for them. In that case, when the baby looks into the mother's eyes, he sees not his own beauty reflected, but the mother's neediness. A mother of a young child may be acutely aware of this and may need enough support for herself to provide well enough for her child. In an optimum situation there is another involved adult – possibly the father – who provides for the mother. Winnicott described this as the 'nursing triad'. The father holds the mother, who holds the child. When this is not available it can often put unbearable stress on the mother, who simply does not have enough resources for the job.

We can see then that, due to difficulties in her own early experiences or due to insufficient present-day support (or both), the mother may be unable to nurture her baby well enough. She may neglect or abuse the child either emotionally or physically. This may mean rejection at one extreme, or suffocating possessiveness at the other.

Although we can look separately at external situations such as poverty, and internal situations such as the mother's emotional needs, they cannot always be separated. A good enough external situation may provide well enough for the mother to find the resources within herself to meet those of the child.

As an example of something seemingly external, take the circumstances of the child's birth. This provides a pivotal situation in setting up a benign or difficult context for the subsequent path of the mother/child relationship. Optimally the birth follows a normal course. The contractions are not so painful or protracted that the mother needs anaesthetics or analgesics. The child is held immediately by the mother, who can put him or her to the breast when it seems right. The lights are not too bright; the child is not taken for protracted medical examinations; and mother and child are taken care of in such a way that they concentrate on the business of being with each other.

Many things can go wrong with this. The labour may be difficult. It may be lengthy and painful beyond toleration. The child may be distressed when born and taken away for medical care. Removing the child for examinations may be hospital policy in any case. Mother and child may not be sensitively cared for in a relatively stress-free environment. When any or all of these things happen the mother may find it difficult to bond with her child. She may become depressed and unable to provide care in the way I have described.

(d) The delivery of a baby as described above may provide us with a prototype of a situation in which a professional intervenes, either in a useful or a damaging way. Such intervention can support the mother in bonding with her child; or it can undermine the mother's confidence.

In a limited way the importance of a good birth experience is better recognized, with an increase in home births and hospital policies that take into account the importance of the mother–child bond. Although much has been improved, sometimes it seems that the far-reaching effects of these experiences are not always well enough appreciated. Hospital administration and first-line staff have their part to play in facilitating an optimum environment for mother and child at this important time.

After the birth the same principles apply. The professional should optimally take a role which supports the mother in providing for the child, not in taking over her role. Only in the case where the mother is so damaged that she is unable to care for her child at all does the helper need to take over the mothering functions herself.

(e) For many, the time of life that involves having small children is the time when they have most contact with professional carers of one sort or another. This in itself may well reflect, particularly in white families, the breakdown of traditional support systems such as communities and the extended family which potentially can support mother and child. Almost all mothers have contact with doctors and nurses or midwives in antenatal check-ups and during the birth. After the birth all mothers have several visits from a health visitor. Various other professionals may have contact with mother and child during this time. They include birth teachers, breast feeding counsellors, social workers, community psychiatric nurses, as well as counsellors or psychotherapists.

Good routine provision for women at this time and in pregnancy is not, however, a universal panacea. Some are so disturbed that more specialized help is necessary. Although a woman can be referred to a psychiatrist, it may be more effective to suggest a counsellor or psychotherapist who can help her understand her feelings and provide the depth of support necessary. This may provide a better prognosis for a good bond between mother and child. The very strength of the difficult feelings may well lead to a traumatic birth, **depression** in the mother and a tenuous bond between them.

Optimally the intervention of professionals in the care of mothers and infants provides a supportive framework in which the mother and father can provide the sensitive and demanding work of nurturing the very young. As it is now well understood that very early experiences are vital for the future mental and physical health of the individual, resources well used by professionals at this time are a sound investment both for individuals and for society at large.

(g)   Kitzinger, S. (1978) *Women as Mothers*. Glasgow: Fontana; LaChance, C. (1991) *The Way of the Mother*. Shaftesbury: Element Books; Winnicott, D. W. (1969) *The Child, the Family and the Outside World*. Harmondsworth: Penguin Books.

JUDY RYDE
(See also *abortion and miscarriage; adoption*)

Obsessive compulsive behaviour

(a)   Many of us experience, at some time in our lives, intrusive, unacceptable thoughts and impulses which typically we can dismiss with relative ease. Indeed, in a survey of the general public only 20 per cent claimed never to have had such an experience. In a small proportion of people (perhaps about 3 per cent of the population) these ideas or images cannot so readily be discounted and in psychiatric parlance are labelled 'obsessions'. An obsession is a recurrent idea, thought, impulse or image which is experienced, at least initially, as intrusive, unacceptable or frightening. Obsessions are not voluntarily produced, but are experienced as events that invade a person's consciousness. They can be worrying, repugnant, blasphemous, obscene, nonsensical or all of these. The person neither wants nor welcomes them and typically makes efforts to resist or nullify them, sometimes in the form of a compulsion.

A compulsion is a repetitive and seemingly purposeful behaviour that is performed according to certain rules or in a stereotyped fashion, and is designed to reduce the discomfort caused by an obsession. It may not be connected in a logical or realistic way with what it is intended to achieve (for example, silently counting in multiples of three when engaged in any child-care activity in order to ensure that no harm comes to the child); or it may be clearly excessive (such as washing hands for hours on end to get rid of germs). Usually there is a desire to resist. The person recognizes the senselessness or irrationality of the behaviour, and does not derive any pleasure from carrying it out, except that it may ward off feelings of tension.

(b) Although obsessive-compulsive disorder (OCD) is classed as an anxiety disorder there are similarities between OCD and **depression**. Many people with OCD suffer from depressed mood or from full-blown depressive disorders, and their preoccupations with **guilt**, failure and worthlessness also resemble the themes that are characteristic of depressed patients. For both OCD and depression the issue of personal responsibility is perhaps of importance here. Depressed people will often feel responsible for an event in the past. Those with OCD may feel that they might be personally responsible for a catastrophe in the future (for example, if I do not check my daughter's moles every day I might miss the onset of cancer, and it will be my fault).

Repetitive and stereotyped behaviours are sometimes found in people with acute, chronic and progressive brain pathology and with organic diseases of the central nervous system, but in these conditions there is an absence of the subjective feeling of compulsion, which distinguishes them from compulsive behaviours. It is also the sense of compulsion and desire to resist the behaviour that reveals the misnomer of the 'compulsive personality'. This personality type is characterized by traits of thoroughness, consistency, punctuality, and the like. However, the associated behaviours do not occur against the will of the individual.

It is perhaps worth reiterating that the experience of unpleasant thoughts and the performance of certain rituals (for example, taking one's lucky mascot into an examination room) is not unusual in the general population. Similarly in day to day conversation we will often hear people described as being obsessed with their hobby, work or partner. As with many other psychiatric diagnoses obsessive-compulsive disorder is not a discrete entity but is rather a label applied to people at one end of a continuum. What characterizes people with obsessive-compulsive disorder is the degree to which they are 'stuck' with their thoughts and the distress caused by them and the associated compulsions. The American millionaire Howard Hughes perhaps illustrates the extent to which OCD can affect someone's life. Hughes gave detailed instructions to all his staff for every activity relating to his fear of germs and contamination. For example, even when handing him a spoon, his attendants were required to wrap its handle in tissue paper and seal it with tape. A second piece of tissue was then applied over the first protective wrapping, and on receiving the spoon Hughes would use it with the handle still covered.

(c)   Psychoanalysts tend to view obsessions and compulsions as symptoms of some deeper problem in the person's unconscious mind. Certain memories, desires and conflicts are kept out of consciousness, or repressed, because they would otherwise cause anxiety. Within this perspective particular attention has been focused on the anal-sadistic stage of psycho-sexual development and claims have been made that OCD is the long-term result of conflicts aroused in the child during toilet training.

There exist a number of cognitive theories of OCD. One suggestion is that obsessive-compulsives overestimate both the probability and the cost of the occurrence of undesired outcomes. Another area which has received attention concerns the degree of personal responsibility that a person feels when confronted by an unpleasant thought. Within this formulation the focus is not so much on the initial thought (for example, 'an accident will befall my husband if everything on the mantelpiece is not in order') but on the sense of personal responsibility that a person has for the thought ('and it will be my fault'). Such ideas of responsibility can extend to having had the thought itself: that is, if the person believes that they are responsible for their own thoughts, the content of which is abhorrent to them, then they might regard themselves as being responsible for being a bad or evil person, unless they take steps to ensure their blamelessness. As has been suggested many people experience unpleasant thoughts and it is perhaps this issue of responsibility which influences whether they are readily dismissed or not.

Attention has also focused on the biological basis of OCD and in particular on serotonin, a chemical messenger within the brain. Drugs (like clomipramine) which increase its supply by preventing its re-uptake have been shown to be effective in the treatment of OCD.

The learning view argues that an individual may learn, through association with a painful or terrifying experience, to become anxious about certain things which are really harmless. He or she may also learn that certain behaviour reduces anxiety, and this then becomes strengthened. Consider, for example, a person frightened by the thought of contamination. Subsequently he or she will avoid certain things and places considered to be contaminated. If contact with a contaminant is unavoidable, the individual will become extremely anxious. Relief is achieved by sustained and repeated washing, in the mind of the sufferer the likelihood of infection is thereby reduced, and feelings of anxiety decrease. When the fear of contamination arises again the likelihood of vigorous and prolonged washing will be even greater because this behaviour has been rewarded in the past through its effects on lowering anxiety.

There are, however, many people with OCD who do not recall any initial painful experience at the starting point of their problems. Also, the theory gives no explanation as to why only certain kinds of things – for example, dirt and germs – and not others commonly become the subject of concern and lead to obsessions and compulsions. It also fails to explain the origin of the obsessions themselves, particularly those that are senseless – for example, order, patterns and symmetry. Though these can be meaningful in themselves, they appear to have no immediate relevance to the person's history or present life.

(d) Although as we have seen the learning view is not a totally satisfactory explanation of OCD it has nevertheless suggested some straightforward treatment strategies which have been demonstrated to be effective.

Exposure and response prevention involve asking a person to confront the source of their anxiety by resisting the urge to perform their compulsion. Somebody who fears being responsible for harming others and engages in compulsive checking might, for example, be helped to stop checking, thereby forcing them to face their fears. In time and with repeated practice it would be expected that the discomfort would subside, in turn reducing the necessity to check. In the technical jargon the person is said to 'habituate' to the anxiety and the desire to perform the compulsion is 'extinguished'.

There are a number of strategies that helpers can employ to assist someone with a response prevention programme. As in the treatment of phobias (see *phobias and anxiety*), exposure can be made easier by tackling it in graded steps. Typically there are a range of situations that can trigger an individual's rituals and the degree of anxiety associated with these may vary. The list below is a hierarchy from someone with a contamination obsession:

- touching the soles of my shoes

- using a public toilet
- touching the neighbour's dog
- using the door handle of the toilet
- putting the dustbin out
- using a public telephone
- touching loose change.

Once a person is confident that they can manage the easiest item on their hierarchy while resisting the urge to perform their compulsion, they can move to the next stage. To make an item more manageable it might be necessary to specify when and for how long a person can perform their compulsion. In the example above the first step could perhaps be made easier by allowing the person to wash their hands for two minutes, one minute after touching the money. Once this is accomplished the various timings can be altered. In this way the sufferer works at their own pace and hopefully has repeated experiences of success as they work their way up their own personal hierarchy. A helper may wish to model the task that has been agreed, doing it in a calm and controlled way, with no signs of discomfort.

One aspect of care that is often very important to people is that of reassurance. It can be an enormous relief for people to learn that they are not the only ones experiencing particular symptoms or that they are not going 'mad'. However, reassurance for people with obsessional problems can sometimes be unhelpful. When asked to perform a particular task a person with OCD might say something like 'I know what I've got to do to get better, but no harm will come to anybody as a result, will it?' It might be tempting for a carer or counsellor to reply 'Of course not'. If this reassurance is given there is a danger that the obsessional person does not take full responsibility for his or her own actions thereby reducing their anxiety and discomfort. Although comforting in the short term it means, as with the performance of compulsions, that the person is not confronting their anxiety. Similarly, modelling should not be done to excess, as in certain circumstances it may act to provide inappropriate reassurance.

Some people complain of obsessions without an accompanying compulsion. For such individuals repeated exposure to their upsetting thought may result in decreased anxiety. This can be achieved by getting someone to talk about, or write down, their thoughts. Alternatively, they can be recorded on a 'loop tape' so that the thought is repeated about every 30 seconds. (A loop tape, as its name implies, simply goes round and round, repeating whatever has been recorded. They are available in audio shops.) By using a personal stereo, an individual can walk around, exposing him or herself to an obsessional thought in a controlled and predictable way. The incessant repetition of the upsetting thought should also discourage the listener from performing neutralizing, anxiety-reducing rituals.

Carers can perhaps be reassured that although obsessional thinking and behaviour used to be considered as a defence against more catastrophic mental illness, notably schizophrenia, there is no evidence for this outcome from follow-up studies. However, there is some evidence that the procedures outlined do not have the same impact when people are significantly depressed. Given the co-incidence of OCD and depression it is perhaps sensible to monitor levels of mood and refer on should a person become too depressed (see *depression*). It is perhaps also worth remembering the degree of incapacitation that OCD can cause and also its effects on the families of sufferers. Some individuals will require particularly intensive treatment, perhaps away from a home setting, and carers need to be sensitive to this possibility.

(e) Within the National Health Service clinical psychologists and nurse behaviour therapists may have particular expertise in helping people with OCD and advising care-givers. Some doctors may be knowledgeable about psychological therapies and may, in addition, wish to prescribe medication.

(g) de Silva, P. and Rachman, S. (1992) *Obsessive Compulsive Disorder: the Facts*. Oxford: Oxford University Press; Tallis, F. (1992) *Understanding Obsessions and Compulsions: A Self-help Manual*. London: Sheldon Press.

JOHN ORMROD
(See also *psychosis and severe mental disorders*)

Old age

(a) Old age is an ambiguous term. It is generally taken to mean the final stages of life but its onset is not clearly defined. For some old people it is a case of 'old age is ten years older than I am' and they are reluctant to identify themselves as old until they are physically frail; 'old age' equals ill health. Conventionally, age is defined in chronological terms and old age commences with the statutory retirement age of 65 or 60 (for men and women, respectively). This definition is used in the health and social services and other public sector agencies. However, it is worth bearing in mind the huge variation in onset of physical, mental and social conditions associated with old age, and the negative connotations of the term, which make people uncomfortable about their personal ageing, and inclined to avoid using the term in relation to themselves for as long as possible. Within the literature of gerontology (the study of the ageing process) variation is acknowledged in the proliferation of sub-categories: young old (60–75), old old (75–85), the oldest old (85 plus), those in deep old age and so on.

(b) A major reason for the closer attention to variations in the ageing population is that it has grown as a proportion of the population as a whole. In 1987, 18.2 per cent were over pensionable age. Within the elderly population, the oldest old are growing at the fastest rate of all, baby boomers from many decades ago. In 1991, those aged 75 and over formed 3.6 per cent of the population but by 2031 they are expected to account for 6.1 per cent (OPCS Monitor PP2 93/1).

Terms with negative associations are sometimes regarded as suspect in themselves. Following the view that language can both reflect and create stigma, it is currently fashionable to refer to older people in particular terms and to avoid others. 'Older people', 'older adults', 'old people' or even 'elderly people' are preferred to 'the elderly'. The term 'the elderly' is impersonal and discounts the adulthood of older people. Political correctness might not seem important though the issue of terms does need to be taken seriously. It has been suggested in relation to services for older adults that even the term 'frail' will have to be abandoned in favour of something with stronger implications, such as disabled, before this client group gets a fair deal.

The view of ageing (this is the English spelling; in American literature the 'e' is omitted) as a negative experience was given credence in the early gerontological literature. The decrement model of ageing has given way to a more positive model which acknowledges the gains as well as the losses in individual experience over time. However, policy-makers and practitioners still subscribe to the notion of older people as dependent and needy, engaging in lop-sided transactions with younger generations. 'The burden of the elderly' is used to explain and justify other inequalities in provision. Concepts such as the dependency ratio are used to promote the idea of older people, like young dependants, as recipients of benefits supplied by the rest of society.

The view of older people as burdens on society has been challenged. The notion of independence as a normal condition of ageing, inter-generational solidarity and help flowing both ways across age lines has gained ground. But even here, generalization is unwise. Variation is a feature of old age. Several distinct birth cohorts are contained within the 30-year period we think of as 'old'. They represent two or three distinct generations, the oldest born at the turn of the century, young adults during the general strike and the depression, experiencing the call-up for the 1939–45 war, benefiting from the Beveridge reforms in middle age and having spent a third of their lives in retirement. The youngest old have been exposed to very different circumstances. Their value systems are closer to those of currently middle-aged and younger people, products of the welfare state and post-war affluence. Viewed in a life course perspective, 'old age' can be unpacked and the different conditions and needs of older people fully appreciated.

(c) Differences in chronological age lead to another important source of variation. We need to distinguish between age *changes* and age *differences*. Age changes refer to developments over the individual life course. In terms of health and welfare we can say that an individual is likely to experience normal physiological changes: there is a reduction in skin elasticity, brain weight, muscle mass, bone density, hearing, eyesight and so on. In other areas of functioning, capacity increases. Vocabulary scores, insight and judgement often improve with age. A gradual loss of immunity over the life course creates health problems. Those commonly associated with age are cardiac disease and circulatory problems, diseases of the joints and muscles such as arthritis and rheumatism, respiratory problems such as bronchitis, bone disease such as osteoporosis, and organic brain disease such as dementia. Age changes, both normal and pathological, affect every individual over time. Older people tend to suffer from a range of chronic and acute conditions. The former result in long-term physical impairment, experienced as disability and handicap.

In 1985, more than 50 per cent of retired people had a long-standing illness, and two-fifths said that they had a health problem that limited their lives significantly. However, rates of disability were low. Thirteen per cent needed help to go out of doors and walk down the road on their own; 2 per cent needed help to get in and out of bed; 9 per cent needed help to negotiate stairs; and 2 per cent needed help to get to the toilet. Those needing help are concentrated in the oldest age group, where the percentages are higher.

Age *differences* refer to people of different ages and birth cohorts. A birth cohort – people born at the same time, occupying the same slot in history and moving through time together – is exposed to common conditions which distinguish them from other cohorts. This means that people might age differently: middle-aged people today might expect a different kind of ageing experience from that of cohorts born before the introduction of the NHS, and environmental changes leading to clean air, improved diets and the eradication of certain childhood illnesses. Similarly, patterns of ageing in future might show the influence of preservatives in food and other negative trends.

Certain health conditions in later life are based on cohort differences as much as individual ageing. Trends in tooth loss, for instance, indicate a clear difference over time, occasioned by such things as childhood diets, dental technology and the introduction of fluoride. In 1968, 60 per cent of men in late middle age (55–64) had no natural teeth left. Twenty years later the percentage had halved: in 1988 only 30 per cent of late middle-aged men lacked all their teeth (Department of Health, 1992a).

The distinction between age changes and age differences (sometimes described as ageing-related and age-related differences) is relevant to work with individual old people. Knowledge of what is normal and to some extent predictable, and what is inevitable or treatable, is important in dealing with old people whose expectations are low. Expectations are themselves a product of differential ageing, reflecting the different conditions of childhood, family-building and retirement over time.

(d) In the current political climate, older people receive mixed messages about what they are entitled to expect. Alongside notions of 'the burden of the elderly' is current social policy rhetoric with its emphasis on user empowerment and consumer-led services. The NHS and Community Care Act implemented in 1993 seeks to promote independence through community-based services which enable clients to remain in their own homes. Delivery is ideally needs-led. 'Needs', like old age, is an ambiguous term which seems to bear little relation to wants and desires. Needs are defined by providers of services and provision is still resource-led. Older people – like other client groups – are subjected to lengthy and dehumanizing assessment procedures which determine the level of service they ultimately receive (Hobman et al., 1994).

The subject of needs and wants, desires and expectations is a complex one. Old people respond in a variety of ways to adverse circumstances. Objective and subjective realities do not always coincide. For instance, people with chronic health conditions which cause significant levels of impairment often describe themselves as 'well' if not 'fit'. Using a model of health and illness which relies on functions rather than symptoms they define themselves as well if they are able to lead what for them is a normal life-style: attending club meetings, going shopping and so on. Health and illness are not just physical conditions. There is a sense of virtue in coping, and weakness in 'giving in'. Health is a moral category.

Morality is an aspect of culture. Old age must be considered in its cultural context if the needs and preoccupations of older people are to be understood. The social and cultural conditions of old age in contemporary British society make ageing a difficult experience. There are core values which underpin relationships and social life – independence, autonomy, sociability, family, productivity, individualism. Conformity to these values is difficult. Older people are among those groups who are particularly disadvantaged by the cultural requirement to be independent, sociable, to participate in family life and couple relationships.

The stresses involved in ageing affect health in a variety of ways. Mental illness is recognized as a leading cause of physical illness and disability at all ages, and elderly people are recognized as a vulnerable group (Department of Health, 1992b). Severe mental illness is as prevalent in elderly people as younger (see *psychosis and severe mental disorders*). **Depression** – the most common mental illness – is more common in older adults than any other group. A significant percentage of older people consult GPs for anxiety states and other nervous disorders, the percentage rising with age. Depression accounts for roughly a quarter of first admissions to psychiatric hospitals among young old women (Department of Health, 1992a).

Older people suffer from a variety of emotional problems. Like younger people they are concerned with roles and relationships, health and illness, sexuality and body image, power and autonomy, and income, housing and physical security. Ageing brings additional problems and changes the character of existing ones.

Parent–child relationships change as the people involved move along different pathways. There is the loss of long-term relationships. The environment over which the older person seeks control comes to include the activities of caretakers (professional and informal). The ageing body loses power and opportunities for sexual expression. Opportunities for creativity and influence in public life, including the world of paid employment, are limited. Impending death creates the need for closure and acceptance of life as it has been lived.

Adopting a life course perspective again, it is possible to see how contemporary problems develop out of earlier experience. Successive cohorts reach old age with problems reflecting a variety of work, marriage and parenthood strategies.

Problems brought to counselling and psychotherapy fall into three categories: emotional states, inter-personal states and existential states. Emotional states include **guilt**, sadness and **depression**, unresolved grief (see *bereavement; loss*) and anger. Interpersonal states include dependency, loneliness and patterns of loving and caring. Existential states include frailty and nearness to death. None of these is exclusive to older people but they are exacerbated by time and maladaptive functioning over many years.

A common problem encountered by professionals and one which has received attention in recent decades is the strain of caring and being cared for in the family setting. In 1985, of those people who received care from family members, friends and neighbours, 76 per cent were over retirement age. This number included 23 per cent who were aged 65–74, 38 per cent between 75 and 84 and 15 per cent who were over 85. Amongst carers who devoted at least 20 hours a week to caring, 43 per cent were late middle-aged and 26 per cent were over the retirement age (Age Concern Fact Sheet, July 1989).

Emotional, physical and cognitive states influence each other at any age. They are particularly difficult to disentangle in older clients and patients. A range of professionals is involved in working with this age group. Before the implementation of the NHS and Community Care Act, of people aged 64 and over, taking a month in 1985, 34 per cent had seen their doctor, 5 per cent had seen a nurse, 1 per cent had seen a health visitor, 7 per cent had seen a chiropodist, 9 per cent had seen a home help, 2 per cent had meals on wheels and 5 per cent had been to a day centre. These services are currently co-ordinated by social workers or administrators after an assessment of needs and the allocation of a priority rating.

(e) Professionals concerned with the needs of older people include health visitors, community psychiatric nurses, specialists in geriatric nursing and medicine, occupational therapists, community service managers, care staff in residential and day care facilities, clinical psychologists and counsellors, paid and voluntary workers in charitable organizations such as Age Concern, adult educators and ministers of religion. Each has an area of specialist knowledge although boundary problems arise of an organizational and professional nature.

In some cases the needs of the old person are clear and unambiguous. Physical tending and caring and the provision of practical information are relatively straightforward. In other areas, though, boundaries are blurred. **Advocacy**, **counselling** and befriending overlap in ways that cause role conflict for the worker involved. Befriending involves supplying warmth, intimacy, emotional and practical support in an empathic way. It benefits from counselling skills though it is not counselling. It is not really friendship either, if that is characterized by choice, mutual attraction and mutuality.

Advocacy involves the promotion of interests. The advocate works either on behalf of the person whose needs are threatened, facilitating meetings, making a case, applying pressure on his or her behalf, or indirectly by offering moral support while the person negotiates on her own behalf. The advocate encourages assertive behaviour and acts as a witness to the person's attempts to defend her interests. Again, counselling skills are helpful and in its assertiveness-training aspect it comes close to counselling. **Counselling** is different from befriending and advocacy, though it has its own variations. Some varieties of counselling are at the interface with befriending and advocacy. Counselling can be either supportive or exploratory, or both. Supportive work helps the client to survive a difficult transition or change in external events. Exploratory work helps the client to recognize personal processes which are unhelpful, repetitive or destructive, and change them.

(f) It is sometimes argued that older people are more concerned with the maintenance of self than development of a new self: exploratory work is inappropriate with them. Such a view is advanced to justify the conventional lack of interest in dealing with the issues of later life. Opportunities for therapeutic help for older adults with emotional problems is limited by ageist professional attitudes which have inhibited service development. According to early developmental theories, the early years are the most significant and older people are incapable of change. Mental health provision has traditionally concentrated on organic brain disease such as Alzheimer's and on affective disorders such as **depression**, treated mainly by drug therapy. Psychological therapies are less often made available. This parallels the decision to withhold treatment for physical conditions on grounds of limited life expectancy.

It is important to be aware of attitudes which deter potential workers from engaging with the issues of ageing and interfere with the performance of people who are drawn into this area of work. There might be difficult family relationships of the worker's own which are transferred into the relationship with elderly clients and patients. **Guilt** and resentment in relation to one's own parents and adult children might influence work with clients and their families. Hatred and fear of frailty and death – not always conscious – and anxiety about one's own ageing and potential decline, can create difficulties in recognizing the real needs of older patients and clients. Work is thus influenced by what workers bring from their own past and what they respond to, a process described as counter-transference.

Not all the difficulties lie on the worker's side. There are reasons belonging to the older person for the low take-up of those services that do exist. A major practical problem is access. Mobility problems, coupled with confusion and hearing impairments which interfere with recall and reflection, make some psychological therapies in agency settings difficult to sustain. The attitudes of older people themselves must also be borne in mind. Generational differences in the acceptability of professional intervention, ideas about complaining behaviour and prejudice against (or unhealthy deference towards) certain types of professional, prevent some people from seeking or accepting help.

(g)   Bond, J., Coleman, P. and Peace, S. (eds) (1993) *Ageing in Society*. London: Sage; Genevay, B. and Katz, R. (eds) (1990) *Countertransference and Older Clients*. Newbury Park, CA: Sage; Victor, C. (1991) *Health and Health Care in Later Life*. Buckingham: Open University Press.

DOROTHY JERROME

Pain and illness

(a)   In contrast to many of the other topics addressed in this book, comprehensive definitions of pain and illness are difficult to articulate. Medical books on pain offer variable definitions. A classification/ vocabulary test (Melzack and Torgerson, 1971; Lowe et al., 1991) attempts to devise some consensus in words which describe pain. Pain is viewed as puzzling with no clear definitions, only perceptions of effects. This is not surprising. Individual experience of pain cannot be shared or known for certain by others. Pain remains a private experience, often described as lonely and isolating for the sufferer. In this context, perhaps definitions seem irrelevant; what is important is the diverse *meaning* given to the pain experience by *everyone* involved.

Illness, on the other hand, is more amenable to definition. It is interesting to reflect on the origins of the term 'patient'. This derives from the Latin *patior* which means *endure pain and suffering*. Illness is defined by the absence of health, a state of sickness or disease of body or mind (some would add spirit), which generally curtails the life and capabilities of a person.

(d)   I am particularly interested in the way in which pain seems recursively linked with illness. As one who lives with chronic pain, I do not describe myself as ill. This distinction is shared by many others who live with pain. This duality, predominantly arising from a medical model, is one which I would challenge. While there may be some similarities in respect of *effects* of living with pain and illness, the conditions are not synonymous. For professionals as well as those affected in whatever role, this is worth remembering. Notwithstanding, the constraints of this article inevitably reflect this duality.

When invited to contribute to this volume, I began to reflect on the nature and diversity of the many conversations both personal and professional that I have had in relation to this topic. These have produced a richness of ideas and options – particularly *increased choice* in terms of living with pain and illness. As a psychotherapist, I have become increasingly interested in the variety of meanings and beliefs that surround persons who become ill or who live with pain. I believe that we each bring many different stories, myths and beliefs about pain, illness and suffering. These may derive from family, society or culture. These beliefs shape and influence our actions when in contact with pain or illness. The following case example illustrates some of these connections:

> Maria was in her fifties, part of a close Italian family. She had severe back pain resulting in redundancy. She spent days in bed – too frightened to move. Family, doctors, friends, religious community, were all in some way organized around the pain and incapacity engendered. Some dominant beliefs surrounding Maria and her family included notions of 'serious illness', 'unwilling to help herself', 'lacking in religious faith', 'neurotic/fraudulent'. Not surprisingly, the future seemed desolate.

Working with Maria to create for herself choices in 'going on with life', we questioned these meanings and their effects. I mapped the influence of pain in her life and relationships:

- 'How has pain been successful in preventing you from being understood as you would like to have been by (family, doctors, church, etc.)?'
- 'Have there been times when, despite pain being very strong, you *have* managed to be understood?'
- 'How did this come about? What does this say about *your strength over pain*?'

Following several conversations, Maria decided to 'reclaim' something for herself and fight back, asking for a referral to a pain clinic. Although unable to work, Maria joined a local **self-help group**, becoming very active within that community. For Maria, the ability to create different *options and choices* for herself in relationship to pain enabled her to experience her life more positively.

Since each of us is unique in our experience and response to living, each experience of pain and/or illness will be unique. There are no right or wrong responses – just different. For those involved with a sick person, in whatever capacity, it may be useful to consider the context in which persons find themselves and the stresses that pain and illness engender.

The medical community

When a person becomes ill, the first contact is with their general practitioner. Depending on the severity of the illness, persons may then become part of a potentially complex system of medical care. Within this context, he or she is assigned the role of 'patient' which brings with it a whole range of expected behaviours – most of them passive. This can be confusing and disempowering.

Medical systems have their own particular jargon, rituals and ways of operating which can frequently be experienced as inaccessible by the patient. Severe illness is a testing time for both patients and their doctors. Society has created powerful stories with high expectations of medical science – a belief shared by doctors and patients. 'Failure' to cure still presents everyone with a sense of failure, frustration and loss despite rational awareness of human limitations.

For the one designated 'patient', it can be a real fight to establish some sort of identity that does not focus on pathology. The individual and family may experience themselves organized and overtaken by pain and illness. Conversations become pain or illness saturated. Sufferers become irritable and weary; carers and family may experience anger and frustration at their inability to help. Understandably, feelings of fear and anxiety may become paramount.

Most of us live as though we will live for ever, and as though illness is something that 'happens to others'. Faced with our own mortality, responses are variable. Some find that it is impossible to question what is happening to them. They may be unable to retain much of what they are told. Anger at misunderstandings, the feeling of being 'just a number' may all contribute to the sense of loss of control that many people experience. Others may want to understand in great detail what the treatments are, the options available and the prognosis. Often there may be a worry, articulated or not, that 'they won't tell me the truth'. This can be a fertile ground for miscommunication!

In this context, the challenge for 'patients' would seem to involve wishing to he heard and understood in terms of their situation. The challenge for doctors might be how to listen sensitively to patients as well as making accurate diagnoses. Doctors have myriad roles to fulfil. Treatment plans, tests – all within the space of a short consultation, possibly one of a hundred that week. Jonathan Douglas's light-hearted book (1992) about the doctor–patient relationship contains many useful ideas and questions for both patients and doctors caught in this experience.

One forward thinking consultant I know offers the possibility to patients of tape-recording the consultation so that they can replay his explanations. Alternatively, write down the concerns you have prior to the consultation. It is useful to remember that what *we* as *patients* might want to tell a doctor is not necessarily what he or she needs to know in order to be helpful. Honesty is usually appreciated, for example: 'I am rather concerned just now, and would like to ask you some specific questions. I wonder what it is you need to know particularly from me to help you in deciding how we go on from here?'

The effects of pain and illness

The Western world pays considerable homage to health, wealth and 'the good life'. Vulnerability in ourselves or in others is not given much space. Pain and illness is often compounded by a crushing sense of helplessness. Part of this may be understood as a fear of becoming 'dependent' in some way – of losing control of our destinies and being marginalized in society. This is a stressful experience. Families may also experience unemployment, disability, financial concerns and losses (see *redundancy and unemployment; physical disabilities; learning disabilities; loss*).

One distinction that may relate to pain more than illness is that often, persons in pain feel that they have to 'prove' their pain. Illness usually carries with it symptoms which are recognizable, socially acknowledged and valid (apart from some illnesses such as ME and HIV: see *AIDS/HIV*). Pain, however, is much more difficult to recognize. This increases the sense of isolation and depression which many chronic pain sufferers experience. Continual pain brings a particular kind of exhaustion that is hard to appreciate unless experienced first-hand.

Depression and anxiety are responses to the realization that one's life and expectations of life – both in terms of aspirations and duration – need to be re-evaluated. Curtailment of life-style, whatever form this takes, brings with it readjustments of goals, abilities and future hopes. **Guilt** and resentment may be experienced by both sufferers and families: The desire 'not to be a burden', the sense of feeling trapped and that your life is 'on hold', the attendant guilt because it is somehow 'not right' to blame the sick one. This can culminate in profound difficulties for both patients and families.

These diverse responses can be understood as part of the mourning process (see *bereavement*); part of coming to terms with the losses of a life or life-style, hopes and dreams previously held. This can be a lengthy process. These 'little deaths' are painful. They must be allowed space to be resolved. Mourning *is* a natural response to loss, but need not go on for ever! It can be tempting to feel 'a victim' when facing illness or pain. I have found it helpful when in that position to think 'What options (however limited) do I have in response to this? What choices do I wish to make *now* to influence what happens next?' – actively taking responsibility to move on. **Counselling** can be a valuable resource in this process.

In my experience, it is important that space is opened for increased choice in 'going on' with living. Emphasis needs to be placed on finding alternative ways of 'being' in the world – whatever the limitations. Although difficult, there are options to explore.

(e) Most family health service authorities have access to a pain clinic – doctors can refer. Research shows these to be highly effective in offering pain control and management techniques. Alternative treatments – osteopathy, homoeopathy, acupuncture, hypnotherapy, visualization and relaxation courses – are now more widely accepted as having an important role when living with chronic pain or illness. Only accredited practitioners should be consulted (see *holistic medicine*).

Additional resources include **self-help groups, counselling** or **spiritual direction**. Lists of qualified counsellors can be obtained from the British Association of Counsellors (Tel: 01788 578328) which provides lists of counsellors working within a pastoral setting. The United Kingdom Council for Psychotherapy (Tel: 0171 487 7554) has a directory of psychotherapists and agencies offering specialized help including supervision for workers. Addresses of local and national organizations in particular conditions are held at libraries, Citizens Advice Bureaux and by local authorities.

(f) For professionals, it is important to be clear about the responsibilities and boundaries of any particular role. It is easy for systems in stress or transition to become confused and overstretched – perhaps reflecting the confusion experienced by the individual and their immediate family. If many agencies are involved in caring and planning, it is vital that each knows the remit and boundaries of their particular contribution – and works within it! Helpers and volunteers should be aware of where they connect with these services to avoid unnecessary duplication and confusion. Working within a multi-helper context presents particular ethical questions, for example, client **confidentiality**. I make it a practice, as part of an ethical posture, to share with clients *all* information which I am asked to give to other professionals. Wherever possible, I encourage the *client* to share information or give informed consent for this to be done.

Working and living with chronic pain or illness presents challenges whatever the involvement. In the face of a chronic condition, professionals and carers can feel daunted by the seeming endless cycle of events. It is worth reflecting that this is probably an experience shared by the client. In my experience, the most useful conversations have been those which offer realistic understanding together with *manageable goals and options*, actively involving the individual in the decision process. I am aware of the many limitations such a brief space entails in reflecting the diversity of pain/illness experience. I invite the reader, in whatever context you are, to reflect on the connections this article makes for you. My hope is that this will access different ways of 'going on' with the unique experience of pain and illness.

(g) Cook, D. (1993) *Patients' Choice*. London: Spire (Hodder and Stoughton); Douglas, J. (1992) *How to Get the Most from Your Doctor*. London: Bloomsbury; Shone, N. (1992) *Coping Successfully with Pain*. London: Sheldon Press.

PENNY LEWIS

(See also *cancer; old age; recovery from major surgery; terminal illness*)

Phobias and anxiety

(a) *Anxietas* (Latin) means 'being troubled in mind'. Few of us go through a week of our lives without experiencing anxiety. Although generally an unpleasant experience, it often serves some useful function, preparing the mind and body for adaptive action. Sometimes it may even be enjoyable – people will flock to a new horror film; and some may actively seek anxiety and, like parachutists, get great pleasure from their mastery of dangerous situations. It is clearly a complex experience with different kinds of impact on our thoughts, feelings and behaviour.

For some people, however, the occurrence of anxiety is so regular, extreme or disabling that they may be categorized as having an anxiety disorder. The next section considers four examples of this in more detail.

(b) A phobia is a disrupting, fear-mediated avoidance, out of proportion to the danger posed by a particular object or situation, and indeed recognized by the sufferer as groundless. Phobos (Fear) was a Greek god who frightened his enemies and to the suffix 'phobia' there are a host of Graeco-Latin epithets ranging alphabetically from acrophobia (fear of heights) to zebraphobia (fear of zebras), added to indicate the source of the anxiety. Most, however, belong to one of three groups – the simple phobia (fear of a specific object or situation, for example, a snake or spider phobia): agoraphobia (literally 'fear of the market-place' but taken to include fear of open spaces, crowds or being in places from which escape is difficult); and social phobia (fear of social situations).

The Greek god Pan, with the face of a man but the body of a beast, used to delight in scaring humans by jumping out from behind trees and then disappearing equally quickly. The acute anxiety and terror felt by these individuals were labelled 'panic' after their originator. In panic disorder there is a sudden, and often, to the sufferer, inexplicable, attack of a host of frightening symptoms – laboured breathing, heart palpitations, chest pain, feelings of choking and smothering; dizziness, sweating and trembling; and intense apprehension, terror and feelings of impending doom. De-personalization and de-realization, feelings of being outside one's body and of the world not being real, and fears of losing control, of going crazy, or even dying may dominate the individual. Such panic attacks may occur frequently, perhaps once weekly or more often, and usually last minutes rather than hours.

The individual with generalized anxiety disorder is chronically and persistently anxious. So pervasive is the distress that it is sometimes referred to as 'free-floating' anxiety. Typically, there are numerous somatic complaints – sweating, flushing, pounding heart, upset stomach, diarrhoea, frequent urination, cold, clammy hands, dry mouth, a lump in the throat or shortness of breath. The person may also report muscular tension and aches, trembling, tiredness and difficulties relaxing. They are generally apprehensive, often imagining and worrying about impending disasters, such as losing control, having a heart attack or dying (Davison and Neale, 1990).

In **post-traumatic stress** disorder (PTSD), a person has experienced an event that is outside the range of usual human experience: one that would be markedly distressing to anyone (for example, rape, combat or a natural disaster). The person with PTSD re-experiences the event, perhaps through nightmares or flashbacks. Efforts may be made to avoid situations associated with the trauma, and there may be problems of memory and concentration, a loss of interest in significant activities and a sense of detachment. There may also be signs of increased arousal such as sleep difficulties and irritability.

It is perhaps worth adding that people rarely present with specific symptoms that enable them to be easily pigeon-holed into a discrete diagnostic category. Someone, for example, with a fear of social situations might also worry a great deal and have the occasional panic attack. Equally a person with generalized anxiety disorder may also have agoraphobia and perhaps certain **obsessive-compulsive** symptoms.

There may often be an association between an anxiety problem and **substance misuse**. It has been a popular and long held view that anxiety and alcohol consumption are closely wed (see *alcoholism*); for example, Hippocrates suggested that 'wine drunk with an equal quantity of water puts away anxiety and terrors' and today we often hear of people drinking for 'Dutch courage' or to 'unwind' at the end of a long day. Support for this relationship between alcohol and anxiety also comes from the scientific literature. Surveys of people with phobias have revealed a high incidence of alcohol problems. Similarly, studies of 'alcoholics' have suggested that they frequently have anxiety problems. Certainly, the majority of 'alcoholics' subscribe to the view that their drinking functions to lower levels of anxiety. Ironically there is evidence to suggest that in the long term excessive alcohol consumption actually increases anxiety levels. Abusers of other substances also frequently suggest that the function of their behaviour is to reduce feelings of tension.

Given that anxiety can have such a profound effect on the body (the 'anxiety' or 'fight or flight' response typically triggers increases in heart rate, blood pressure and rate of breathing; the liver releases a large supply of sugar into the bloodstream; the blood vessels of the limb muscles and other skeletal muscles dilate; and blood vessels of the stomach, intestines, skin and brain constrict) many people will present initially with concerns about physical symptoms. Also there is growing recognition that almost all illness has a psychological component and for many disorders (for example, irritable bowel syndrome) anxiety may be a particularly important component.

(c) Psychoanalysts contend that anxiety disorders are the product of unconscious conflict so that in a phobia, for example, by avoiding the feared object which has some symbolic significance, the person is able to avoid dealing with the repressed conflict. In a celebrated case, for example, Freud felt that a small boy's phobia of horses could be attributed to the fear of his father.

Learning theorists argue, as their name implies, that anxious behaviour is learnt. Thus a phobia might arise when someone experiences a traumatic experience with the phobic stimulus: the subsequent behavioural avoidance develops because of its rewards (i.e. the person avoids experiencing anxiety). Since not everyone with a phobia can recall an initial frightening experience the theory has been extended to include the possibility that anxious behaviour can also be learnt from observing the behaviour of others. To explain the frequency of some phobias, for example, those of snakes and spiders, and the relative scarcity of others, it has been argued that humans are predisposed to learn certain phobias and that this propensity may have conferred a genetic advantage on some of our ancestors.

Those from a cognitive perspective would suggest that it is how we construe ourselves and our environment that influences our emotional response. Thus it is not public speaking itself that makes someone anxious but their thoughts about such an activity (for example, 'I will make a fool of myself' or 'I might lose control and faint').

At the biochemical level a chemical messenger called GABA has received attention. Drugs that block or inhibit the GABA system lead to increases in anxiety and benzodiazepines (the so-called 'minor tranquillizers') reduce anxiety by enhancing the release of GABA.

(d) Education can be a valuable tool in helping the anxious individual. Many people are shocked to discover the physical impact that anxiety can have. Often people having a panic attack will believe they are having a heart attack, or that they are dying and will (not surprisingly given this construction of events) present to accident and emergency departments. They may be caught in the vicious circle outlined below:

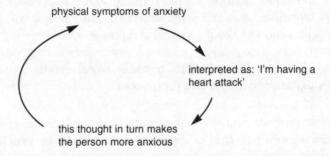

physical symptoms of anxiety

interpreted as: 'I'm having a heart attack'

this thought in turn makes the person more anxious

Each revolution of this circle, by producing more and more somatic symptoms of anxiety, may simply serve to confirm the individual's initial hypothesis that they are seriously ill.

For other people, anxiety triggers a fear that they are about to experience a catastrophic loss of control, or that they are about to faint and they become anxious about their anxiety. This again can be self-fuelling. One way to break these circles is to escape from a particular situation, and this may in certain instances be how behavioural avoidance develops (see opposite).

It can be extremely enlightening for people simply to learn that anxiety is a normal healthy response of the human body; that experiences like panic are just an extension of the 'fight or flight' response; and to have a 'model' to understand the interrelationship between thoughts, feelings and behaviour. In addition to providing reassurance it may also help them to modify their erroneous assumptions about what is happening to them when they are anxious.

Since many people are relatively secretive about their problems they may miss the opportunity to discover that others experience similar

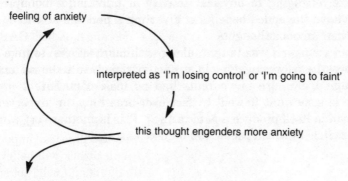

feeling of anxiety

interpreted as 'I'm losing control' or 'I'm going to faint'

this thought engenders more anxiety

escape (this may be accompanied by thoughts like 'if I hadn't run out of the shop then I would have lost control and perhaps passed out')

feelings. This isolation may further reinforce their belief that there is something profoundly wrong with them. Given this, education can sometimes make even more impact in a group setting where it is likely that many people will share similar experiences.

One exception to some of what I have described concerns blood phobics. Many people with acute anxiety believe they are about to faint, but in fact their anxiety is accompanied by increases in blood pressure making such a response highly unlikely. However, the reverse is true of blood phobics. Studies have found that exposure to blood-related stimuli is associated with near or complete fainting in about 15 per cent of college students and new blood donors. It has been argued that this could be an adaptive response evolved in circumstances where immobility produced less risk of further injury than did flight.

Teaching muscular relaxation can sometimes give the anxious individual a valuable coping skill. A number of commercial tapes are available and the recommended books in section (g) all give detailed instructions. In teaching relaxation skills it is perhaps worth emphasizing that learning to relax is a new skill for many people and that, as with any other skill, continued practice is likely to be required before significant benefit is derived.

It is perhaps also worth noting that for a significant minority of people the onset of relaxation actually makes them more anxious. Possibly for some individuals being physically relaxed provokes fears of not being in control. For this reason it is advisable for the carer to be present when teaching relaxation so that issues such as this can be addressed. Clearly if muscular relaxation is not found to be useful there may be other ways in which a person can be helped to relax. For example, engaging in physical activity or pursuing a hobby, which might have the added benefits of diverting a person's attention away from their anxious thoughts.

When younger I was taught, along with many others, to take some deep breaths before engaging in any activity likely to make me anxious. Although I am sure my parents had no malevolent intentions this advice is somewhat flawed! In fact over-breathing, or 'hyperventilation', can in itself produce a panic attack. This is another very common vicious circle in which people can become entrapped.

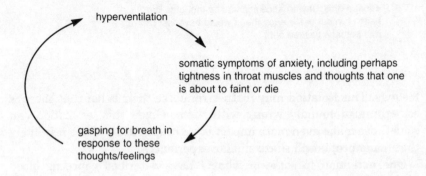

hyperventilation

somatic symptoms of anxiety, including perhaps tightness in throat muscles and thoughts that one is about to faint or die

gasping for breath in response to these thoughts/feelings

To cope with hyperventilation some doctors recommend their anxious patients to breathe into a paper bag when stressed, thereby increasing the amount of carbon dioxide in subsequent breaths and so countering the effects of over-breathing. Given that many anxious people are already sensitive to how they appear to others, this technique has perhaps only limited utility. Far better to teach controlled diaphragmatic breathing, instructions for which appear in the recommended books.

An old Chinese proverb states 'Go straight to the heart of the danger, for there you will find safety'. Avoidance is a feature of many anxiety problems. Thus, the person with **post-traumatic stress** will avoid situations that may trigger memories of a traumatic event and phobics will avoid the object or situation that they fear. Indeed some people with phobias are so 'successful' in their avoidance behaviour (for example, the agoraphobic who never leaves the house) that they never actually experience any anxiety. One strategy for dealing with avoidance is to be gradually exposed to the feared situation. Freud stated:

> One can hardly ever master a phobia if one waits until the patient lets the analysis influence him to give it up. One succeeds only when one can induce them to go about alone and to struggle with their anxiety while they make the attempt.

According to learning theorists, confronting a feared situation leads individuals to 'habituate' to their anxiety, so that the urge to engage in avoidance behaviour is reduced.

There exist a number of ways in which an anxious individual can be exposed to a feared situation. Flooding therapy forces exposure to the source of the phobia at full intensity. A spider phobic, for example, might be asked to endure having spiders crawl all over their hands and arms until their anxiety subsided. Not surprisingly the extreme discomfort that is an inevitable part of this procedure deters many people from choosing it, except perhaps as a last resort. Systematic desensitization entails getting the person to relax and confront the feared situation in imagination. Graded exposure is the most common and arguably the most effective form of intervention.

In graded exposure the individual draws up a list of feared situations and assigns an anxiety rating perhaps out of one hundred to each. Below is a hierarchy for an agoraphobic:

- staying in supermarket on my own for half an hour   95
- catching a bus to supermarket but not going in   80
- going around supermarket with a friend for twenty
  minutes on a weekday   70
- walking to local shops on a Saturday and buying something 55
- catching a bus into town with a friend on a Saturday   40
- walking to local shops in the morning on my own
  but not entering   25
- staying in the garden for half an hour on a week day   10

The therapeutic task is for the anxious individual to complete the task that evokes the least anxiety on their hierarchy, and only to move on to the next task when this has been successfully mastered. It is noteworthy that each step is fairly clearly described. This is done in order to facilitate evaluation. The danger of an unclear goal is that success can be discounted (for example, 'Yes, I went to the shops, but it was a Tuesday and they weren't very busy and I only stayed a couple of minutes'), whereas if a task is very clearly defined neither carer nor sufferer can be in any doubt as to whether it has been achieved or not. It is worth emphasizing that success in this context should simply be related to whether the task was performed. The fact that someone feels anxious when performing a goal is not indicative of failure: indeed, according to the learning theory view, experiencing such anxiety is a necessary requirement of therapy.

If an individual fails at a particular task then the challenge is to break it down into easier steps. If, for example, they cannot manage to walk to the local shop in the morning perhaps they can manage to walk half the way, or are able to go in the evening.

To facilitate exposure the anxious individual might wish to learn some relaxation skills. In contrast, blood phobics may need to learn to tense muscles or induce other feelings such as anger when exposed to the relevant stimuli. Building in a system of rewards might help someone achieve their goals, and particularly in the early stages of treatment the presence of a carer who models particular tasks and offers support and encouragement may be particularly useful.

It may be sensible to advise people to cut down their intake of caffeine since its consumption, particularly if it is excessive, may increase feelings of anxiety. Habitual users who cease their intake rapidly may experience withdrawal symptoms such as irritability and mood changes.

There exist a number of medical conditions (e.g. thyrotoxicosis, hypoparathyroidism and various neurological conditions) that produce anxiety symptoms and it is sometimes wise to encourage people to have a medical check-up prior to embarking on any therapeutic work. I remember being asked to help someone with writer's cramp learn to relax the muscles of their forearm. Referral to a neurologist revealed her difficulties in writing were in fact the product of a wasting disease of the nervous system.

As with **obsessive compulsive disorder** there is a close association between anxiety disorders and **depression**. Many people with an anxiety disorder will also be depressed. There is a need for particular caution (highlighted in the article on depression) when working with these individuals.

(e) Many venues now run stress or anxiety management groups or relaxation groups, which may be a useful resource for care-givers. A significant number of people experiencing problems with anxiety will also be addicted to tranquillizers and many areas may also have 'tranx' groups for people contemplating or undergoing withdrawal. Many of the strategies outlined here may also be applicable in helping an individual to stop taking tranquillizers, although appropriate GP liaison is recommended (the interested reader is referred to Curran and Golombok, 1985; or Trickett, 1986). Given the prevalence of anxiety problems many professional groups including occupational therapists, community psychiatric nurses, doctors and psychologists have developed expertise in their treatment. Regions vary as to which group is most relevant and easiest to access for further help. Certainly in areas covered by community mental health teams these should be able to supply information about local resources.

(g) Breton, S. (1986) *Don't Panic: A Guide to Overcoming Panic Attacks*. London: Macdonald and Co.; Butler, G. (1985) *Managing*

Anxiety. Oxford: Oxford University Press; Marks, I. M. (1978) *Living with Fear: Understanding and Coping with Anxiety*. New York: McGraw-Hill.

JOHN ORMROD
(See also *psychosis and severe mental disorders*)

Physical disabilities

(a) Physical disabilities present in many ways. Arthritis, blindness, deafness, multiple sclerosis, polio, facial deformities, cerebral palsy, spina bifida, road or sporting accidents and many other disabling conditions all bring their own challenges to the person who has them and to those meeting them for the first time or getting to know them over a longer period.

Some, such as walking difficulties, may be glaringly obvious: others, such as pain or the fatigue or neurological conditions, may be hidden. Some involve illness: others do not. Some disable the client; some may disable a helper. Some are constant, some variable. Some are congenital or began a long time ago, others are of recent onset. Many will have brought with them a shattering of hopes and expectations: others may have provided new opportunities. Some are known to the helper or carer; some are new and unknown and may be shocking or startling.

People with physical disabilities may seek help with the disability itself or with a trauma which caused other losses too. Practical or emotional support may be needed, perhaps involving other members of the family. For example, a woman facially damaged in a car crash which killed her baby may have terrible conflicts grieving both for her own looks and for her lost baby. A nurse, social worker or counsellor may be directly involved in the aftermath of an accident (see *post-traumatic stress*) or at a time of diagnosis of a disabling illness: an occupational therapist, trained to help people come to terms with disability, may find themselves dealing with **losses** which have never been confronted before (Segal, 1989).

However, a disability may not be the focus of a problem. Someone who cannot hear may seek help to obtain a baby alarm, or they may simply want help finding a flat. Someone who is approached for information about visible or vibrating baby alarms may be expected to know how to communicate with people who are deaf. A housing worker or member of the Citizens Advice Bureau, however, may have no such experience and may themselves be totally disabled when faced with a non-hearing client.

Other family members of someone with a disability may also seek practical or emotional help. The strains of living with someone whose personality or mind has been affected by a disabling condition can be considerable (Klein and Schleifer, 1993; Parker, 1993). Changing physical difficulties can cause trouble too, with other family members often feeling guilty at even recognizing their own loss or suffering.

Whatever the disability and whatever the character or situation of the person who has it, the attitudes and approach of professionals or volunteers may affect the outcome of the relationship and if only in a small way contribute to the quality of life for the client (Segal, 1991a). In section (c) I look at difficulties people have when faced with someone else's impairment.

(b)   People with disabilities have to learn to cope not only with their own feelings and practical difficulties, but also with the difficulties other people have, faced with their condition.

'I must keep cheerful' is one way of coping. It may be reinforced by the belief that positive thinking is the solution to all of life's problems. Someone who struggles to keep cheerful at all times sometimes presents as 'crying all the time', or having difficulty controlling their anger. They may secretly feel isolated, bad, perhaps resentful or guilty, afraid to share their fears or any 'disabled' or 'negative' part of themselves because they know no-one really wants them to. Not wishing to make a fuss, some may fail to obtain basic assistance which a more aggressive person would get.

There are many ways of attempting to overcome a disability. (See Segal, 1986, for the case of multiple sclerosis; and Morris, 1989, for spinal injury.) Some people seek information, plan and prepare in advance. Others wait and see, refusing help of any kind. Some maintain unrealistic hopes long after everyone else has given them up, as a means of keeping themselves going. Some feel that accepting help would mean they had 'given up'; that 'acceptance' means lack of faith and no miracle cure; others that it is a sensible solution to a practical problem. For some the label 'disabled' means being a non-person, despised, to be avoided and rejected: for others it is a badge to wear proudly, or a means of access to useful services.

It can take two years or more for the mind to get used to a change in bodily functioning; people are not being slow or difficult if they do not immediately order a wheelchair even three months after they first have difficulty walking. Particularly if there is uncertainty about the long-term prognosis, it may take two years before a loss is recognized as permanent.

While the personal meaning given to a disability may be highly significant for an individual and for the strategies they use to deal with it (Segal, 1991b), the sheer practical difficulties of living with a disability should not be underestimated (Campling, 1987). For some people it may take several hours to get up in the morning; whereupon they may feel tired enough to lie down again. It takes time and effort to prevent pressure sores, caused by immobility, which can kill. Obtaining help from social services may take years and involve numerous phone calls, forms, broken appointments and changes of worker. A helper who is full of ideas about things someone could or should be doing may need to take some time to try to understand why the person has not already done them.

Being a parent with a disability or a child with a disabled parent is not easy. A child, particularly a teenager, may be looked on as a carer and their own conflicting needs be neglected. Anxieties about being good parents may be compounded by fear of losing children to someone more able-bodied. Children's anxieties about their parent's condition are often unrecognized: children may fear telling their parents their troubles in case the worry literally kills them. Such anxieties (e.g. unrealistic fears that a parent is about to die) can often be sorted out by parents or someone else when uncovered (Segal and Simkins, 1993).

(c) There are many underlying causes of difficulty between people which result from disabilities of one kind or another. Here I pick up a few of the most important.

One way people use to understand disability is to split themselves into a 'disabled self', which naturally includes all their faults and weaknesses, and an 'able-bodied self' which has all their virtues and strengths. For example, people may assume that an ugly person is bad or insensitive: or a crippled person envious or incapable of selflessness. The 'disabled' self, child or adult, may be assumed not to be able to cope with bad feelings, or to be able to think at all, and so be excluded from important and relevant information, such as 'you make me angry', 'granny has died' or 'your husband has found another woman', when everyone else around knows. Disabled people may have been treated as part-people by strangers all their lives: even more disturbingly, they may see themselves in such ways. Part of the role a good helper can play is to uncover and challenge such assumptions in both the client and themselves (Segal, in press).

Someone who was born with a disability may have been denied normal family life, and in particular, normal development of sexual relationships. Many have been 'kept in cotton wool' by loving parents who wanted to protect their children from cruelty. Others have been rejected or even abused by one or both parents. Their relationships as adults may show the marks of an unusual childhood. Sexual feelings, for example, may emerge in relations with helpers in ways which helpers find difficult.

Contrary to what many people think, children born disabled do not automatically 'accept' their situation. One boy born without arms thought he would grow some when he grew up. A woman with learning difficulties struggled to understand what had gone wrong with her brain when she was born, which she knew had upset her mother so much she could not talk of it.

Given the difficulties faced by many children born disabled – many imposed by a society which finds them unbearable to look at or talk to directly – it is perhaps surprising how many manage to make good relationships, including marriage. Disabled children can have a good childhood: in spite of difficulties many become caring, creative adults. In the author's experience, surprisingly few disabled adults are angry and bitter, 'difficult' or 'manipulative'. Love, affection, tolerance and good humour are as common amongst the disabled population as amongst the able-bodied.

(d)   In general, both professionals and volunteers may be unsure of their own competence when faced with a disability they have not met before. They may justly fear giving offence, without knowing how to avoid it. There seems to be a fine line between admitting to discomfort in a way which opens up communication, and thrusting one's own difficulties on a client who is really not interested.

'Everyone is really like me' is a common fallacy. A helper may like a friendly touch and find it difficult to understand someone who does not. Someone who likes to be offered help may offer help to a person who wants to be left to do something in their own time and manner. Some carers may think nobody could want to marry them if they had a disability, and extrapolate to the whole population. Their own fears of a wheelchair may not allow them to discover that a newly disabled client is more afraid of being alone or of not being able to help others. Clients often have similar difficulties and cannot understand why others do not behave towards them as they think they would behave themselves in similar circumstances.

Carers need to be firm that they do not know and cannot know how someone wants to be treated, or what their disability means to them. Normal boundaries between helper and helped may be challenged and may have to be broken, for example if a client requests help in the toilet.

This situation is disturbing for an inexperienced helper and needs to be acknowledged as such, though not necessarily with the client. It may cause a helper to withdraw emotionally while feeling both guilty and angry. Discussing the situation with a colleague may help.

One of the normal rules of social life is that one does not discuss other people's appearance if it is strange. In a professional situation this may not apply: if an odd appearance or a disability is relevant to the problem in hand it has to be discussed. This skill may be practised with a colleague.

Helpers sometimes find their anxieties about a disability come between themselves and client. They may fear that emotional or practical demands will cause stress and be dangerous for the client. They may recommend a 'cure' (yoga, psychotherapy, positive thinking, diet) as a means of saying 'this cannot be incurable'. They may trivialize symptoms ('I have difficulty with my eyes too'), or label the client ('she's denying her disability') as a means of distancing themselves. All of these prevent the helper getting close enough to hear the client's agenda or to understand the client's situation.

If a client's speech is not clear it is generally better to admit this than to pretend. Using an alphabet to spell out words; seeking a translator; setting up a series of signs to indicate 'yes' and 'no' may be used if repetition (however embarrassing) is not sufficient. Where understanding cannot be achieved it is better to terminate the interview and acknowledge that the client has not received what he or she was seeking.

Recognizing that the client is probably the expert on their own condition and its effects on them may help.

In general British people are not good at handling grief. Exhorting people to 'think of the good things' and forget the bad, or to 'think positively' makes those who mourn into failures. Initial feelings of grief may include highly unrealistic, exaggerated anxieties about having lost everything, of being deservedly abandoned. Where such feelings are not shared freely they may never be challenged and changed.

In the right circumstances a non-family member may be the person best placed to help a person to grieve for their losses. In this situation the carer needs to be able to tolerate sharing someone else's grief, sorrow and despair without bringing it prematurely to an end. Time needs to be allowed and the frightening ideas be brought to the surface where they can gradually face the light of day. Helpers may need to practise this skill, or to recognize where they cannot do it and need to refer someone to a person who can.

Very often helpers can help more than they think they can. They may feel they are no use for several reasons. They may be really unable to solve the problem – particularly if this means getting rid of the disability. Often there are no solutions: this may be checked with a colleague. The client may feel they themselves are 'no use' because of their disability, and evoke this feeling in the helper. A helper who can admit and share a feeling of uselessness can sometimes give a client sufficient space to find some means of helping themselves.

A helper may be really unable to help if they have too negative expectations and fears in connection with a particular condition. A desire to find a more competent helper for the client may be realistic – though it may be an attempt to get rid of a disturbing problem. Support from outside may enable the worker to give real help in spite of their own difficulties (which may turn out to be difficulties the client shares and therefore a source of deeper understanding).

(e) There are some specialist services. A relevant self-help group or charity may provide useful information: the client may know of one. DIAL UK, the National Association of Disablement Information and Advice Services (Victoria Buildings, 117 High Street, Clay Cross, Chesterfield, Derbyshire S45 9DZ, Tel: 01246 864498) is a source of useful information, including the whereabouts of local disability groups and disability rights groups. ParentAbility is the National Childbirth Trust network for parents with disabilities and can be contacted through the NCT (0181 992 8637).

Self-help groups can provide support, advice, education and political action, for clients and helpers alike (see *advocacy; self-help groups*). If 'counselling' is offered 'counsellors' may or may not be well selected, trained and supervised. Professionals such as social workers or occupational therapists may know of local resources. There may be a disability team.

The present author, Julia Segal, offers some consultancy for counsellors or others working with people with disabilities. She can be contacted at the CMH MS Unit, Central Middlesex Hospital, Acton Lane, London NW10 7NS (Tel: 0181 453 2337).

(f) Charities for people with disabilities can be excellent sources of money: however, people sometimes complain of the older charities' patronizing attitudes, or of their subservience to the medical profession and neglect of the point of view of those most directly affected by the condition. Few provide professional counselling for members or consultancy to professionals.

Doctors have emotional difficulties with disabilities like anyone else: in addition, a disability may be evidence of medical failure. A general practitioner may have limited experience of any particular disability; the specialists involved may also not know enough. In addition, the doctor may be a focus of disappointments with the outcome of therapy. It can be very important to take seriously a client's criticisms of care received without taking sides.

Social workers are another common focus for discontent. Even very good social workers may turn out to be on holiday or maternity leave just when they are most needed. Bureaucracy, delays and lack of resources can be very frustrating. Difficulties may be compounded by the personality of the person with the disability, or by changes of mind or situation mid-stream. There may be political disagreements over the rights of people with disabilities as well as conflicts arising over priorities: issues of fairness are complex and disability services tend to have low priority.

Many people with disabilities do not want to be defined as 'disabled': others are militant in their struggle for rights to access to the normal things which most people can take for granted. There may be conflicts between these groups, as well as other differences of opinion within the politicized disability movement. Able-bodied people may occasionally meet rudeness or high-handed treatment from some people with disabilities on a tit-for-tat basis; however, tolerance can often be greater than deserved.

The 'peer counselling' issue is one arena where people with disabilities sometimes argue for their own superiority over able-bodied people (see *advocacy*). This can discourage competent able-bodied people from offering their services to people with disabilities.

While it is certainly true that direct experience of anything gives much better understanding, we do not normally demand that professionals of any kind work only with experiences they know directly. There is no reason either, for example, why a counsellor with no legs should be naturally more receptive towards someone with cerebral palsy or learning difficulties than an able-bodied counsellor who is willing to learn from the client.

(g)   Morris, J. (1994) *Independent Lives, Community Care and Disabled People*. London: Macmillan Press; Parker, G. (1993) *With This Body: Caring and Disability in Marriage*. Buckingham: Open University Press; Segal, J. and Simkins, J. (1993) *My Mum Needs Me: Helping Children with Ill or Disabled Parents*. London: Penguin Books.

JULIA SEGAL
      (See also *advocacy; old age*)

Post-traumatic stress

(a)   A traumatic incident, anything from a minor accident or event to a
major disaster, affects all those involved. This includes not only survivors and victims, but also rescuers and helpers. It also includes
onlookers, witnesses, families, friends and colleagues. Post-traumatic
stress can be defined as:

> the development of characteristic symptoms following a
> psychologically distressing event which is outside the range of
> normal human experience.

(b)   Although not everyone will suffer the symptoms, those who do are
reacting normally. Post-traumatic stress is the normal reaction of
normal people to abnormal events. These 'abnormal' events include
major disasters, road, rail and air accidents, shootings and bombings,
war experience, witnessing or finding **suicides**, rape (see *victims of
crime; violence towards women*), rescue attempts (especially unsuccessful), industrial accidents, armed or other robberies, being attacked or
beaten up, **divorce**, **abortion**, surviving sexual, physical and psychological abuse (see *child abuse*), **redundancy and unemployment**,
retirement and having a home broken into or burgled – or any incidents
where shock, pain, violence and fear are generated. Although such
reactions are normal, it is impossible to predict the actual ways any one
person will be affected. Characteristic symptoms of post-traumatic
stress are:

1. Re-experiencing
Sensations, emotions and feelings associated with the traumatic event
can be re-experienced, as if the incident was happening again. Such
feelings can either be triggered or emerge 'out of the blue'. Triggered
reactions can come at any time and may be caused by:

- sights – TV, video, photographs, media reports
- sounds – police or ambulance sirens, bangs, crashes, voices
- smells – petrol, rubber, disinfectant, dampness, sweat, food
- tastes – food, water, petrol, alcohol, sweat, dry mouth
- touching – rubber, metal, skin, water, being touched.

The anniversary of an event or a court case can also act as a trigger for
symptoms. Other previously experienced traumatic incidents can be
resurrected. 'Out of the blue' reactions can come at any time and
without any trigger or warning, at home, at work, while shopping,

relaxing, resting or anywhere, and because they have no apparent cause, may be extremely frightening or overwhelming.

2. Avoidance

Those involved can seek to avoid anything or anyone which might remind them of the incident, even those with whom they were involved; e.g. fear of flying, getting into a car or on to a ferry, reunions, anniversaries, birthdays, meeting certain people, family or friends. They might try to avoid thoughts, feelings or situations. There can be loss of concentration and even of acquired skills, loss of feelings or emotions, or an inability to express or show feelings of love and affection. Some avoid thinking about the future and may not expect to live long, believing that life is without purpose or meaning. Some become depressed and sad, and experience intrusive thoughts and images, nightmares and sleep disturbances and feelings of regret, irritability, shame, anger and bitterness. Some are afraid of closed or open spaces, or of crowds and even family gatherings. Some feel guilty about having survived.

3. Arousal

There can be an increased sensitivity to noise and the slightest sound may cause people to 'jump' nervously. This might involve inability to accept the usual events of work, home or family life. Children playing or a friend or partner talking can lead to outbursts of anger or even violence, or sufferers can retreat into isolation. There may be impulsive actions such as changing a job, life-style or relationships. Some incessantly talk about the incident, keep a diary or collect newspaper cuttings and articles. There can be an expectancy that something dreadful is going to happen at any time and without warning. There can be feelings of sympathy for any aggressors involved, especially during and after hostage situations. There may be sleeplessness or difficulty in concentrating and some may become hyper-vigilant.

4. Physical symptoms

There are often physical effects such as headaches, stomach pains, tightness in the chest and generally feeling unwell. People may be tired and listless, excitable or hyperactive or turn to alcohol, tobacco or drugs (see *alcoholism; substance misuse*). There can also be changes in values or beliefs. Some discover a new faith or reject a faith they already have. There can be feelings of vulnerability and the belief that life is not safe or secure and is without meaning or purpose, and some lose a sense of self-respect, self-worth and value.

On the positive side, there can be an increased sense of worth. Some come to see life, people, relationships and even objects as more precious and of even greater value. Some will feel that it is good to be alive and have a sense of real achievement.

(c)   Reactions depend on a number of factors. There are personal and personality factors such as previous experiences of traumatic events and previously learned behaviour, upbringing and childhood experiences, as well as the coping strategies developed and used at the time. Research suggests that people who have a family or previous history of psychiatric, psychological or social problems are less likely to cope. External factors include the traumatic nature of the event and the length of time people were involved, whether or not there were fatalities or injuries, and how prepared or otherwise they were for the incident. The involvement of children is particularly distressing.

However, what might seem an insignificant incident for one person can be devastating for another. The individual, the families, partners and children can be caught up in changes beyond their control. These can cause problems at work, marital stress and the breakdown of relationships, ill health and sometimes the development of deeper and more disturbing symptoms. When the symptoms persist or intensify, generally for more than a month, a condition called post-traumatic stress disorder (syndrome), or post-traumatic stress reaction, may develop. There is some disagreement about the length of time taken for symptoms to develop – some say four to six weeks and others extend this to six months or more. What is not disputed is that symptoms can emerge days, months and even many years later and vary from being mildly disturbing to incapacitating.

(d)   At the time of the incident and shortly following it a process known as 'defusing' is important. This includes previous training and preparation for the critical event and the support offered and given at the time. During the incident, support comes from the presence of colleagues, supervisors, psychiatric and counselling support teams, medical staff, chaplains and others. These helpers, as well as immediate victims and members of the emergency services, may also be trauma casualties either at the time or later.

The best way that carers can help is through using techniques familiar in grief counselling (see *bereavement*). The reality of the situation must be faced in order to counteract defences of denial. The incident has happened, it is real and must be faced. In some cases victims can be helped by returning to the scene of the incident. Rest is important and those involved should be made as physically comfortable as possible. Reassurance should be given, especially that reactions are normal and that feelings and emotions can and should be expressed.

Where appropriate, short- or long-term support should be offered. Allowing people to talk is essential and should confirm and emphasize that symptoms are not signs of weakness or personal inadequacy. Victims and helpers should be encouraged to look for support mechanisms both within themselves and from whatever external resources are available.

Immediately after **major incidents** there is usually an operational debriefing which deals largely with practical matters; however, further help can be given through a process known as critical incident debriefing. This is usually a group meeting which reviews the impressions and reactions of those involved (Dyregrov, 1982). The main aim is preventive: to normalize effects and to reduce the possible development of any unnecessary and distressing psychological after-effects. It does not take place at the time of the event, but some two to three days later and, on some occasions, up to eight weeks or so afterwards. It is a highly structured meeting which encourages those involved, either an individual or a group, to talk through the incident from facts to feelings and then to look at the future (Parkinson, 1993: 143f.). It is widely used in the emergency and armed services and with banks and building societies, but is equally useful with victims of any violent or traumatic incidents from rape (see *violence towards women*) to **divorce**. Those who develop deeper symptoms may need the services of a psychiatrist. psychologist or trauma counsellor.

Treatment of post-trauma stress reactions varies. There are behavioural treatments such as desensitization and exposure to the fear, flooding techniques and training in methods of relaxation. In cognitive therapy the aim is to correct unreasonable, distorted or unhelpful beliefs. Psychotherapy attempts to deal with the anxiety caused, the defence mechanisms generated and the hidden feelings and emotions. Group therapy sometimes involves the use of residential care and outdoor activities. Medication is also frequently used, often in conjunction with other treatments. There are also trauma reduction techniques which largely originated in the USA following the Vietnam War.

(e) Finding professionals for referrals who understand the nature of post-trauma stress and who have the skills necessary for helping can be difficult. Some believe that because carers are professionals they will not suffer symptoms, while victims can be put into pigeon-holes. Sometimes only individual symptoms such as **depression** and anxiety (see *phobias and anxiety*) may be recognized and treated. County emergency planning officers, responsible for co-ordinating and organizing for major incidents, and social services can offer help, but the first resource for victims should be through the local medical services and GP. Most areas have clinics where psychiatrists, psychologists, community psychiatric nurses and clinical nurse therapists work together and some major hospitals have trauma clinics. Two NHS hospitals in London with specialist clinics are the Middlesex Hospital (Tel: 0171 380 9462); and the Maudsley Hospital (Tel: 0171 919 3122). A private hospital in East Sussex offering a similar speciality is Ticehurst House Hospital (Tel: 01580 200391). Military hospitals have trauma clinics and take referrals of ex-service personnel and, occasionally, of emergency service workers: RN: the Royal Naval Hospital, Haslar, Gosport (Tel: 01705 584255); Army: Queen Elizabeth's Military Hospital, Woolwich (Tel: 0181 856 5533); RAF: Princess Alexandra's Hospital, Wroughton, Swindon (Tel: 01793 812291).

A number of organizations specialize in giving support, advice and information about treatment: Victim Support (Tel: 0171 735 9166) has a nation-wide network of volunteers (see *victims of crime*). The British Association for Counselling (Tel: 01788 550899) gives information and advice about training and counselling. The British Association of Social Workers (Tel: 0121 622 3911) publishes a booklet, *Search – the Community Care and Consultancy Training Directory*. The Ex-Services Mental Welfare Society (Combat Stress) has a network of welfare officers offering support and advice.

Carers should also use local resources for particular problems. To deal with the trauma a specialist should normally be consulted, but where the problem has other effects people might need to be referred to the relevant agency: Cruse – for bereavement; Relate – for marital and personal problems. However, without dealing with the basic trauma other presenting problems might not be resolved.

(f)   Denial, a defence mechanism typical of loss and grief reactions, is one problem for helpers and can cause difficulties between carers and organizations. It can prevent people from asking for or seeking help. It is a defence found especially in male-dominated institutions where emotional reactions can be viewed as a threat to discipline, leadership and authority and where a macho-image sees traumatic reactions as signs of weakness. There can also be problems of inter-organizational conflict and rivalry and a retreat into parochialism. Carers and helpers, where possible, need to be pro-active in their response in order to confront this denial. Individual carers and helpers should also be aware that they too can be affected and influenced by their involvement with both victims and other helpers and therefore should seek help and support through personal **supervision**.

(g) Hodgkinson, P. and Stewart, M. (1991) *Coping with Catastrophe*. London: Routledge; Parkinson, F. W. (1993) *Post-Trauma Stress*. London: Sheldon Press; Scott, M. and Stradling, S. (1992) *Counselling for P.T.S.D.* London: Sage Publications.

FRANK PARKINSON
(See also *bereavement; groups, use of; loss; major disasters*)

Prayer and ritual

(a) Prayer is communion or conversation with God. The soul, a biblical word used in spiritual direction (see *spiritual direction*) and virtually synonymous with 'person', communes with the divine by expressing attitudes of love (adoration), of sorrow (confession and a desire for reconciliation), thanks and need. The last is referred to as intercession, petition or supplication. The sheer multiplicity of words indicates how much asking for gifts for another, or the self, is often understood to be the essence of prayer. In fact, adoration and thanksgiving are the more important parts.

Prayer is primarily a corporate activity, secondarily a personal or private one; hence the importance of ritual. Ritual, the formalization of acts within a liturgy or action, is the means by which human beings celebrate powerful emotional occasions in a manageable and creative way. The ordering of public worship, the meaning of 'liturgy', the corporate addressing of God in music, word and silence, always has a form; without it the occasion easily slips into banal and often comic chaos, or more rarely into the emotional frenzy of an uncontrolled mob. Ritual is especially important at the cardinal moments of transition in personal life, at birth, marriage (see *marriage customs*) and death (see *funerals*), as much as in corporate life, as for example, at the signing of a peace. There are many more opportunities than are normally taken for marking significant moments in life by a celebration in a form of worship.

Corporate prayer within the Christian tradition is of two main types, the office and the Eucharist, word and sacrament. The word is primarily the Word of God, God addressing the people in the words of the Bible, and in His Word Jesus Christ. It is the emphasis of the more Protestant Churches, and has a markedly masculine feel.

Sacrament in the classical Anglican description refers to outward and visible signs which convey inward and spiritual grace. Thus bread and wine in the Eucharist are the outward and visible signs by which the participants receive the inward and spiritual grace of the body and blood of Christ. The sacraments are pre-verbal in their appeal, addressing the soul by way of symbols at a deep level of the being. They are the emphasis of the more Catholic and Orthodox Churches and have a more feminine feel.

Office: this is from two Latin words *opus facere* – 'to do the work'. To do the work of God was required of the early Benedictine monks, who met in the monastery chapel seven times a day for prayer; at dawn, at the hours of 9, noon and 3, at sunset and before going to bed. Apart from the third hour (9 a.m.) Islam expects the same; the faithful are called as a body by the muezzin to prostrate themselves on their prayer mats in adoration of the one God.

In the Christian tradition, *The Rule of St Benedict* (McCann, 1952) is one of the most important foundation works of Western spirituality and civilization. Guiver has studied the development of the Western Office in his *Company of Voices* (1988) which has strongly influenced a new work called *Celebrating Common Prayer* (1992) developed for the Anglican Franciscan order and now widely adopted by many English Christians. The Roman Catholic Office and the French ecumenical Taizé office are two other important forms. Many Christians prefer a less obviously ordered form of prayer, although again such prayer stems from the same early Jewish synagogue pattern of psalms and readings. It usually follows a regular order, albeit with extempore prayer and choruses.

Eucharist: This term is from the Greek and means thanksgiving. Another word for the Christian celebratory meal is 'mass', derived from the final words of the Roman Catholic Latin rite, *ite missa est*, the phrase referring to the sending of the people out into the world.

The first part of a Christian Eucharist is in the office form. The second is sacramental: the Christian community together presenting itself in thanksgiving to God by celebrating the sacrifice of Christ on the cross. It is marked by a fourfold action of offering by the gathered body for reception by Christ, a long prayer of thanksgiving, the breaking of the bread and the sharing of the community in the consecrated body and blood of Christ. The action celebrates the Christian vocation of commitment to the way, thanksgiving for all that God does within the whole body, the wounding and pain of the way and the nourishment, encouragement, grace and strength for the sending back on to the way.

(b)   Private prayer can take a number of forms, many of them nurtured by corporate formulations like the office. There are those today who are looking for a more personal communion with God by meditation and contemplation.

Meditation: Traditionally this is a more formal way of reflection than contemplation, which came to prominence in the years preceding the reformation. Early teachers were St Ignatius of Loyola who taught a formal way of meditation in the *Spiritual Exercises* (Puhl, 1951), and much later St Francis de Sales in *An Introduction to the Devout Life* (Day, 1961). These teachings provide a framework for ordering thoughts as they move into silent reflection on a passage or scene from the Bible.

Contemplation is silent looking at God without reflection, without distraction: simply being there, as St John of the Cross puts it, like the glass of a window receiving the rays of the sun. It is an expression of love and delight in the beloved.

Meditation, like the Eastern discipline of yoga, is used widely today as a means of relaxation. Both, however, are first of all spiritual disciplines, means of training the mind to be self-controlled and attentive as preliminaries to prayer. They are never merely physical exercises, if any exercise can be called that (witness ballet dancers who refer to their daily bar exercises as their prayers). They lead the soul towards prayerfulness and, even if the divine is not named or perhaps not even considered comprehensible, they lead into something which inclines towards prayer. For someone who does not admit to prayer, it is a way of doing so acceptably.

Meditation, particularly what is happening to the body while meditating, has been the subject of research. EEG readings show that the concentrating meditator's brain is functioning on long alpha waves and even theta rhythms normally associated with drowsiness; and an ECG similarly shows a rather slower heart beat. The body is relaxed, while paradoxically attentive.

Many people in the West have been unfamiliar with Western teaching about meditation so that the spiritually gifted have turned more to the East for inspiration. The Western mystical tradition is, however, important. In England it has been strongly influenced by the affective writings of the eleventh-century Cistercian St Bernard, and the example and vision of the twelfth-century Franciscan founder St Francis. The richest vein is that of the four fourteenth-century mystics, Walter Hilton, Julian of Norwich, Richard Rolle and the anonymous author of *The Cloud of Unknowing* (all in the Penguin Classics series).

To study spiritual writers such as these is to realize that meditation and contemplation can never be used merely as a therapeutic technique. They are silent forms, and the unsuspecting person may not realize just how many thoughts, fantasies and feelings, some of them very alarming, will emerge from the unconscious. Christian teaching emphasizes prayer within the love of God, so that growing self-knowledge develops within an ambience of forgiveness and acceptance.

St Catherine of Siena, the fourteenth-century Dominican mystic, spent a three-year moratorium in her late teens in a private room in her parents' home. In profound prayer she encountered God and her self, and discovered that if she dwelt on God alone, she felt ecstatic and inflated, while if she simply concentrated on her shortcomings, she felt the stirrings of despair. It was only in the combination of both that she came to know the depth of God's love for her, and the extent of her own alienation from herself and from God.

In a remarkable encounter she describes a conversation or colloquy she had with God about the reality of her being in this alienated human state. The Lord said 'Do you know, daughter, who you are and who I am? If you know these two things you have beatitude in your grasp. You are she who is not, I am who is' (Fatula, 1987: 79).

(c)   Prayer is a natural response of the human being to the divine, the unknown, 'the unheard of' as Dag Hammarskjöld calls it in *Markings*:

> Now. When I have overcome my fears – of others, of myself, of the underlying darkness: at the frontier of the unheard-of. Here ends the known. But from a source beyond it, something fills my being with its possibilities. (1964: 77)

Prayer is almost universally practised, by some 44 per cent of the general English population, 55 per cent women, 32 per cent men (Argyle and Beit-Hallahmi, 1975: 12, 73), and in cases of emergency as a cry to someone or something by almost everyone – 72 per cent of men on going into battle (Argyle and Beit-Hallahmi, 1975: 52). At its most primitive, prayer tends always to be petition, a plea to the Lord of the universe to do something about the supplicant's need, or an ongoing inner dialogue with what the person understands to be God, an approximation no doubt, partly ego-ideal, partly super-ego, but still to a greater or lesser extent the Holy Spirit.

(d)   Prayer is usually learnt at a very young age in the intimacy of the family. The future Pope John XXIII described his uncle leading his extended family in the daily recitation of the rosary. Many people pick up prayers they like, or find short expressions of prayer which express their inclinations. For many the difficult point is making the transition from the prayer they valued as a child to a more mature form as an adult.

Position is important. Eastern meditators sit cross-legged in the lotus position like the Buddha, a pose as good for the hips as it is for stillness. For those who are less supple, the Carmelite position is easier. The person sits back on the haunches or on a very low stool, the legs beneath the seat, the bottom upon it, the back straight and the person attentive. There are seats available, designed ostensibly to help a bad back, which seem purpose built for this kind of prayer. A third possibility is to sit back on an upright chair, both feet firmly planted on the ground, and the hands laid peacefully in the lap. One of these positions is essential for listening prayer, and they are of value in all prayer.

Men and women of prayer report that there is wisdom in praying each day in the same place; it helps the process of quietening the mind. In contemplative prayer where there are no words to occupy and direct the mind, the major task is remaining still and attentive and open.

A beginning is usefully made by listening to and identifying the sounds around, before withdrawing into a now stilled interior. An alternative is to become familiar with the body, ascending and becoming aware of the tight muscles and tensions of the different parts as the soul rises from the toes to the crown, and once more moving gently into an interior stillness. A third alternative is to breathe slowly from the diaphragm, in, out and deeply for a number of breaths until peace has settled within the soul.

If the meditator is using a passage from the Bible, or a spiritual text, it needs to be brief. The author of *The Cloud* emphasizes the value of limiting the subject to one word, for example the name of the divine, 'God'. Modern teachers similarly encourage the use of a *mantra* as it is called in the Eastern tradition. The writings of John Main (1977) are important in this respect. The meaning of the word or phrase used is unimportant, but it is probably better to use a word appropriate to the praying person's tradition. Words have a spiritual effect.

The Jesus prayer 'Lord Jesus Christ, Son of God, Have mercy upon me a sinner' is used widely in the Russian Orthodox Church, and is valued elsewhere (French, 1986).

Whether the person praying uses words, or is totally silent, the aim is to listen and be open to the Spirit. It is demanding, Baron von Hügel says, speaking of the neural cost, and it is wise to begin gently. A little time well used is of much greater benefit than a longer time occasionally.

Ending should be as simple as beginning, a short sentence of offering, a quiet parting before starting the next task.

There are many pitfalls, and three can be noted; distraction, and as subgroups of that, fantasies, and boredom or sleep.

The mind is normally so alert that it darts away at the first sight of an association of curious interest. It can be equally diverted by the delights of a forthcoming breakfast. The position of the body, and the use of a focus, a symbol, an icon, a lit candle on which the attention can dwell, are initial aids, and an interior focus is of value at later stages.

Distractions still regularly come. The best way of dealing with them, once the person is aware again, is simply to bring the soul back to attentiveness, and continue unconcernedly on.

Strongly sexual or violent fantasies are more difficult. Sometimes there may be a case for entering into the fantasy, listening and befriending it as one might a dream, to explore within a prayerful context its meaning, especially if it is a regular fantasy. At other times there is value in returning to a focus gently and unless there is cause for penitence, without guilt.

Both boredom and sleep are signs of the soul withdrawing from the fray. The former may be a sign of depression; the latter a simple statement that the person is tired, but equally it may be an escape. Since prayer is costly the time chosen to pray needs to be when the soul is fresh. Each person has to work out his or her own rule, but experience suggests that prayer is usually an early morning activity.

Boredom might also be a sign that ritual has become stereotyped, and has lost its meaning. While the Office and Eucharist and similar prayer of other faiths can bear endless repetition, gathering new depths as the years go by, equally the exciting new ritual can in a few years time become empty and dull if it is not regularly examined.

Prayer, in leading to truth in the inward parts in communion with the source of love, is the servant of reality.

(e)   Spiritual aspirants of all traditions have looked for guides to help them on their way. In the East, the postulant has to prove real commitment and desire, even to the point of beating down the guru's door to plead a case, before a spiritual guide will begin to contemplate taking the soul on (Trungpa, 1973 – the writer is a Tibetan Buddhist). In the more docile West direction is more available, though spiritual writers through the centuries have deplored the standard of wisdom they have been given. The guide, like any counsellor of relationships, endeavours to help and deepen the communication between the soul and God (see *spiritual direction*).

Jungian psychology has had a considerable influence on spiritual direction through the Myers–Briggs Type Indicator, a test which helps determine personality types. Keating, in *Who We Are Is How We Pray* (1987), gives ideas for prayer to suit each of the personality types.

One of the most difficult aspects of prayer is finding the time to do it. It is an exacting, demanding exercise, which is not always exciting. As T. S. Eliot puts it in *The Dry Salvages* after describing spiritual moments in and out of time: 'the rest is prayer, observance, discipline, thought and action' (1969: 190).

(g) The reader in prayer could do no better than turn first to classical spiritual writers like St Teresa of Avila and St John of the Cross as well as the following: Clément, O. (1993) *The Roots of Christian Mysticism.* London: New City; De Mello, A. (1978) *Sadhana: A Way to God.* Gujarat, India: Gujarat Sahitya Prakash; Guiver, G. (1988) *Company of Voices: Daily Prayer and the People of God.* London: SPCK.

DAVID GOODACRE
(See also *faith differences; religious belief; spirituality*)

Pre-menstrual syndrome

(a) The term 'pre-menstrual syndrome' is often used interchangeably with that of 'pre-menstrual tension'. 'Syndrome' has become more widely used, as it encompasses the many different experiences a woman might have during her menstrual cycle, rather than solely the tension she might feel. It is important to recognize that descriptions vary from woman to woman. The symptoms, feelings, thought patterns and behaviour she describes as being affected by her pre-menstrual state need to be examined in the context of her life in general. Broadly speaking, a description is that of any major mood change that affects a woman's life during her pre-menstrual phase, which does not seem explicable by any other factor in her life at that moment.

(b) The commonest aspect of the syndrome (giving rise to its more popular name) is the tension, emotional and physical, and the irritability that women experience. However, other changes and problems that women may describe include the following (and it is important to recognize that no two women's symptoms are the same and that they may vary for each woman from month to month): mood swings, increase in feelings of anger, violent feelings or the commission of acts of violence, anxiety, depression, forgetfulness, confused thinking, sleep disturbance, suicidal thoughts, disorientation, agoraphobia, clumsiness, shaking and trembling, weight gain, water retention, tender breasts, hands and feet swelling, headache, migraine, increase in appetite, increase in craving for sweet foods, tiredness, dizzy spells and fainting, increase in pulse rate, loss of interest in sex, increased physical activity, aching legs, bad breath, increase in thirst, increased sensitivity to noise and light.

It is important to look at what is happening in a woman's life overall, and how her physiological experiences link in with her emotions. The problems may be presented as relationship issues; as difficulties with self-esteem and self-image, even with body image related to diet. They may be presented as specific areas of concern such as regular attacks of migraine or anxiety or nightmares. The woman herself may not have linked her experiences to her pre-menstrual phase. In working with a woman who may be trying to live with any of these problems, building up a picture of pattern and regularity is vital. The keeping of a diary in whatever form (i.e. writing, audio-tape, drawings – whichever is easiest) will help build up a picture of whether what happens is an isolated event or cyclical.

(c)   There are differences of opinion between members of the main-stream medical profession and complementary therapists and workers in this field on what are the precipitating factors. As the name suggests, pre-menstrual syndrome occurs before a period, at any time from three to 14 days beforehand, i.e. from ovulation onwards. Some women also complain of the psychological symptoms *after* menstruating, even though the physical symptoms have been relieved. From a medical point of view, contributory factors are seen to be an excessively high level of the hormone oestrogen and/or low levels of the hormone progesterone. It is thought that some women have difficulty excreting oestrogen before their period and that the effects of this on the nervous system create the problems. There are also connections with vitamin B deficiency which again can be caused by the body being overloaded with oestrogen before a period. Treatment with vitamin B can relieve some pre-menstrual symptoms and heavy bleeding during the period itself. Treatment with progesterone supplements has been used extensively after the pioneering work of Dr Katharina Dalton (1984) in this field from the 1950s onwards.

More recently, the entire social context within which a woman's menstrual experiences occur, and the attitude she and those around her have to her place in the world, have been investigated. The impact of her own and others' negative or positive responses to her emotions and behaviour has been evaluated (Shuttle and Redgrove, 1986). Since the 1970s, there has been an extensive investigation into the impact of diet and stimulants on women's menstrual health, and the ways in which changes in diet can bring about relief from symptoms.

(d)   Many women can recount instances where their feelings, views and statements have been discounted and belittled because they are in the pre-menstrual phase of their cycle. Jokes are made constantly at women's expense, about an essential aspect of life which becomes trivialized or demonized. There are several dangers in this, namely: that women themselves internalize these attitudes and do not seek support for their own distress and pain, and consequently do not offer support to other women, on the basis of 'if I put up with it, why can't she?'; that sensitivity towards women's differential needs is not demonstrated in the workplace, at home, within friendships, and that women's behaviour is misinterpreted; that women's behaviour is seen as a mental health problem and not something that could be susceptible to change with attention paid to the appropriate elements of life; that the problem gets 'medicalized' exclusively with women being offered mainstream treatment that may not work and then being blamed if it does not; that women are told it is their lot to suffer in this way; that women sometimes believe they are going insane because there is no rational explanation for sudden surges of rage and violence or unhappiness and everyone else in their lives just wants to keep out of the way.

Another issue is the conflict between recognizing that your body *does* go through changes on a regular basis, and learning to identify and integrate these into acceptable experience, and not feeling that you are totally at the mercy of an organism over which you have no control. There are implications in this for how much in tune different women feel with their bodies. It is likely that a woman who recognizes the interaction between her mind and emotions and her physical well-being will be more inclined to engage in discussion about her menstrual life than one who feels she should just steel herself to the distress. Some women will feel happier putting their fate in the hands of a practitioner of whichever discipline, hoping that they will find relief or a cure. Any woman is likely to benefit more from a process that gives her more control over what is happening to her than one which numbs her responses. Women have been and still are treated with anti-depressants for mood changes, or indeed with hysterectomy to get rid of what is seen as the source of the problem – after all, no periods, no pre-menstrual syndrome! While there may be some instances of chronic and severe distress that are not susceptible to anything but the most drastic measures, it is to be hoped that all non-invasive and non-psychotropic methods will be considered first.

It is important to point out that there is not widespread knowledge amongst the mainstream medical profession (Stewart et al., 1992) about the significance of diet in women's experience of pre-menstrual syndrome. It may be that a woman approaching a counsellor/therapist for help has been met with scepticism when trying alternative and complementary methods. It is important that she is able to pursue what is right for her. Pre-menstrual syndrome, as so many aspects of women's lives, has been subject to so many inaccurate pronouncements by 'experts' that women have often lost confidence to stick with what they feel is right for them. Again, many of the medical breakthroughs have been invaluable, but not every woman will benefit from one specific approach. It is probably reasonable to assume that a woman is going to have to make certain adjustments to her life-style if she is to experience relief from symptoms, rather than taking pills. This inevitably involves taking more responsibility in life and might feel threatening. Sometimes the symptoms are so severe that women will try anything. If a woman's self-confidence has been so undermined both by her own feelings about what is happening to her and by other people's reactions to her behaviour, she may find it very hard, and need a lot of support to believe that she has the right and the capacity to try to change things for herself.

A woman may be terrified and confused by her experiences and feel that she is the only person going through such awful times. She may find herself having destructive thoughts and feelings towards herself and others and indeed, may act on these. She may feel as though she undergoes a complete personality change, for the worse, during this part of her cycle. This may lead to feelings of **guilt and shame** about things she has said, done or thought. These need to be explored, and encouragement given for finding ways of changing this behaviour which do not apportion blame. There is no doubt that a woman is far more likely to be motivated to improve her situation if she has support – whether from a partner, other family members or from a group.

Working alongside more specialist services (see section (e)), it is necessary for the therapist/counsellor/care-giver to encourage the woman to build up her self-esteem and self-awareness. It is important to offer the woman ways of recognizing her own needs, of acting on these and of giving them value. There is one theory (Shuttle and Redgrove, 1986) that during the pre-menstrual phase, the strong emotions women experience, whether they are rage, distress, sadness or creativity, are how women really feel all the time. During everyday life, women are constrained in the expression of such strong feelings, because of social convention. But women and those around them, because they expect and tolerate changes in women's behaviour during the pre-menstrual phase, give permission to 'let rip'. So maybe women need to listen to what their bodies and minds are telling them at such times – not so that acts of violence or self-destruction are committed, but so that women recognize and name the anger, **pain** or creativity that is locked up inside at all the other times. Ways of giving these expression on a more regular and productive basis need to be found.

(e)   Several towns have support groups for women who experience pre-menstrual syndrome. This can be checked out through Citizens Advice Bureaux, social services departments or registers of local voluntary and self-help groups. Some hospitals may also have information of this nature. It is always worth encouraging women to talk to each other and to break the silence and the taboo that there may be around discussing this subject. It is vital to take into account the different cultural approaches (see *cross-cultural awareness*) there are to discussing menstruation and pre-menstrual syndrome, and that some women may need a lot of time and encouragement before they feel they can broach the subject at all.

In many instances, women have found relief with progesterone treatment which can only be given by a doctor. Other women have found that eliminating certain substances from their diet has made a rapid and overwhelming difference (Stewart et al., 1992). These include: caffeine (tea, coffee, chocolate, cola-type drinks), yeast, sugar, alcohol, salt, a reduction in dairy products, cutting down on or giving up smoking. These, alongside regular exercise, relaxation and sufficient sleep, have in some trials brought about almost total disappearance of symptoms. The theory is that although period pains and discomfort and the sequence of events around pre-menstrual syndrome have been with us for a very long time, both women's willingness to talk about what happens and a possible increased incidence have made people more aware. This increased incidence is seen in some circles as caused by changes for the worse in many women's diets and is therefore susceptible to relatively easy change. Women need to consult a nutritionist, however, to ensure that they are getting a properly balanced diet.

(f) Any woman presenting with problems related to pre-menstrual syndrome needs a sympathetic hearing, reassurance that she is not mad and support to find the approach that is right for her. This might involve staying with her through trying different methods. Whatever the case, she needs to know that it is not all in her mind, as she may have been told, but that it is in her body, too, and that something can be done to help.

(g) Shreeve, C. (1992) *Pre-menstrual Syndrome*. London: Thorsons; Yudkin, J. (1986) *Pure, White and Deadly*. London: Viking Press.

CLAIRE WINTRAM
        (See also *depression; menopause; pain and illness; self-help groups; sexual difficulties*)

Prisoners and ex-offenders

(a) Prisoners and ex-offenders are affected by association with 'crime'. The word 'crime' comes from the Greek *krinein* meaning to sift facts, to adjudicate between right and wrong, and particularly to bring to a 'crisis' or trial. The lives of prisoners and ex-offenders – together with their families – are engulfed in troubles as a result of these processes.

Pastoral helpers offer support to people drawn into these formalities which can be protracted and depressing. This support is sometimes perceived as standing on its own although closely relating to other areas of need. It calls for special self-understanding in the helper and particular awareness about the people who are offered support.

(b) Helpers have to act objectively and impartially in assessing complicated background factors. They must understand their own feelings about bizarre behaviour. They can benefit from building on experience. Helpers must respond sensitively to law and order officials who have to abide by regulations, yet also react compassionately towards prisoners and ex-offenders who might be burdened by shame, inadequacy or self-centredness. To avoid burn-out, disillusion or cynicism helpers need constant personal development to enhance realism, vision and sensitivity.

The individuality of offenders is equally important. It can be overshadowed by the impersonal character of criminological studies, statistics and glib stereotyping. Personal relationship with offenders can be hindered by class perceptions and by obligations imposed by authority figures. Attitudes towards offenders can be prejudiced or moralistic, everyone having opinions, few speaking from close contact with them. The panoply and rituals of the law and harsh indignities in 'locking up' prisoners also inhibit person-to-person rapport. Ultimately natural openness with those in serious trouble with the law is crucial for initiating and sustaining help.

Opportunities for helping prisoners and ex-offenders are affected by their position in the system. Prisoners are held by an organization which can appear tightly enclosed. Community helpers wanting contact often feel excluded. Outsiders should, however, realize that their position offers potential for 'bridge-building'. The Prison Service's policy is to break down the isolation of prisoners and prepare them for 'a law-abiding life . . . after release'. When prisoners become ex-offenders they are more accessible and assistance changes in emphasis.

(d)   There are three phases for helping people passing through the system – first, time after arrest on *remand*, secondly, time after *conviction* serving a sentence, and thirdly, time after *release*. Issues arising in one phase also appear elsewhere.

1. Remand   is stressful. People are usually surprised to have been caught and held in custody. Few who commit crime are resigned to the consequences of arrest – as, for instance, with peace protesters whose equilibrium and clarity of intent contrast with turmoil in those more commonly encountered in the initial stages of serious legal trouble.

Many arrested for the first time are ignorant about **legal advice**. Legal assistance is not the purpose of pastoral care and helpers should remain neutral. However, the accused may want to change a legal adviser obtained in the heat of arrest. Helpers could provide a list of solicitors offering legal aid and leave the defendant to choose a name. They may also find it useful to obtain permission to communicate with the solicitor in the future. Etiquettes about **confidentiality** make such permission essential. Solicitors sometimes find that helpers can assist the defence case.

Offering help to those held in police stations raises delicate issues. People are usually taken suddenly into police custody feeing frightened and bereft when other professionals are not available. Pastoral visits in police stations may be viewed warily by the police because matters are 'sub judice'. However, independent, non-statutory, community-based accredited help is an important feature of democracy. Those held in police stations should be aware of their current rights to have pastoral visits, to remain silent and to have a legal adviser present when questioned. If they need medical care this should be responded to and noted for future defence. The delicacy of assistance offered in a police station is enhanced by the need for the helper to stand on impartial ground between the police and the person questioned.

The immediate domestic consequences of detention in police custody might require attention – for instance, notification of relatives or employers may be more tactfully handled by those who offer pastoral help than by police officers. It might be possible to organize bail – although this may be fraught with difficulties because of current charges and previous convictions. Inexperienced helpers should be extremely careful not to act naïvely. Advice from the local probation service can be useful. Any contact made at this sensitive juncture with a person in trouble can beneficially affect subsequent trust and openness.

The first few days on remand can be difficult. Prisoners have to adjust to arraignment by the press and public disapproval, to family separation and to institutional routines, to uncongenial company and to deep future uncertainty. Many of them are the least equipped to cope with such experiences.

Contacting imprisoned people at this time – even if only by letter – can help ease feelings of condemnation and isolation. Offering significant relatives travelling assistance to the prison – or on occasions encouragement to overcome past antagonisms – can be appreciated. Frequently it is helpful to talk through the strains of a 'bad visit' with all concerned. Pastoral visits to the home and workplace – and to the prison – offer potential 'bridge-building' opportunities. Family meetings in prison are often not ideal situations for pastoral visits.

Listening skills are important. When immediate problems seem intractable prisoners can value pouring out anxieties on topics like innocence or guilt, marriage tensions, domestic finance, informing on others, long-term work prospects, anger, self-justification or self-worth.

Problems arise over compromise and **confidentiality**. Hearing about illegal activity hitherto unknown to the police could draw listeners into compromising situations. Helpers must not convey messages to people who may be victims, potential witnesses, criminal associates or those subject to court protection. Helpers might, therefore, be wise to establish boundaries to avoid complications. Listening is generally less dangerous than taking action.

Many remand prisoners consume energy reading legal depositions, working out defence strategies and agonizing about their plea. Consequently, they do not anticipate dilemmas in plea-bargaining at their trial. Difficulties then arise in rapidly balancing family opinions and self-esteem with a sense of fairness. Voluntary helpers may be better placed in this situation than lawyers.

Pastoral helpers in criminal justice need a considered attitude towards judgementalism. Truth is elusive. Law and order is characterized by black and white, guilty or not guilty decision-making. Sometimes troubled people seek truth at a level more akin to integrity than facts – as, for example, in the case of many men accused of rape where they believe they were enticed into the alleged attack. Helpers must balance condoning with condemning, leading prisoners to judge themselves alongside spiritual or human values which they respect – especially in matters like forgiveness and assurance about the meaning of life. Many prisoners find support in religion – some by discovering it anew, others by returning to previous roots. While helpers must maintain a neutral stance to avoid being judgemental about facts they may well find prisoners are appreciative of encouragement to develop spiritually.

Outside pastoral helpers need to understand prison access procedures. Church connected helpers can usually visit through chaplaincy services, and accredited voluntary agencies through probation or health-care services. These visits are customarily arranged in advance with the prisoner's agreement. They do not reduce domestic visit entitlements which are daily on remand and at least fortnightly after conviction. Visits on other pastoral bases are at the governor's discretion. Helpers are ill-advised to travel distances to visit prisoners without telephoning on the day to ensure that they are present. Despite firm arrangements prisoners suddenly disappear for surprising reasons!

2. *After conviction*   the scene is more settled. Apart from possibilities of appeal prisoners know the terms on which they will be in custody. The perspective is different for long-termers as opposed to short-termers.

Prisoners have to adjust to anxieties. They have concerns about the location in which they are held in relation to their homes. They may be fearful about association with other prisoners because of crimes or ethnicity. Painful feelings relating to attachment and **loss** are commonly experienced. Most problems relate to families – to partners in particular – and to welfare of children. Many prisoners have to go through a **divorce**. Five per cent of prisoners are women – many of whom have special problems in retaining their babies in prison. Poignant situations arise over death and dying of loved ones. In **bereavement** prison authorities often facilitate extra family contact and value liaison with pastoral helpers based near home.

Some prisoners become conspicuously depressed and are liable to attempt or commit **suicide**. If outside helpers suspect either of these possibilities they should immediately disclose the fact to the prison authorities – notably to the governor.

Prisoners can be encouraged to seek inside assistance in dealing with difficulties. Among many problems encountered are **alcoholism**, **gambling**, **substance misuse**, **sexual deviation**, as well as poor physical and mental health. Custody can be used to pursue therapeutic opportunities to come to terms with past difficulties – especially in programmes based on group work (see *groups, use of*), creative art and drama as well as sports, all of which are offered in most prisons. These programmes are especially important for the high proportion of young prisoners who are impressionable and need encouragement to avoid recidivism.

Surprisingly to outsiders, prisoners have strong codes of values about crimes – sometimes expressing views intolerantly in relation to sex offenders. Many prisoners talk about moral problems associated with their activities. In large groups they may be influenced by 'machismo' stances making them hesitant to talk sensitively. But in smaller groups and one-to-one meetings headway can be made in sharing moral awareness. In some prisons this has resulted in victim/offender encounters.

Outside volunteers can enter officially arranged befriending relationships as prison visitors. Their important contributions are to help prisoners feel valued as people and to keep them in touch with wider life. People interested in offering time for this should write to a local prison governor. Caution is needed; prisoners may hope that such introductions develop into long-term emotional relationships.

3. *After release*   the stigma of prison poses difficulties. The Rehabilitation of Offenders Act (1974) should be known to all ex-offenders because it protects their rights. Some people shake off prison more easily than others, but difficulties are obvious because two out of every three prisoners return to prison. It is hard for many not to resort to the security of 'old friends'.

Ex-offenders have to find accommodation. In the UK no-one should leave prison without lodgings – although it is unrealistic to imagine that this always happens. Local probation services, NACRO and churches are in touch with hostels and some work possibilities (see *homelessness*).

People who have been in prison could be encouraged to join groups that may help them with specific problems – like HIV, addictions and loneliness. These groups can be contacted through public libraries, local health clinics or probation service 'drop-in' centres. Prisoners sentenced to over one year are released on licence to probation officers, but ex-offenders usually want to disassociate themselves from officials after release. Others leaving prison might be encouraged not to renew contacts that led to trouble – especially when trade related.

Most prisoners find the 'crisis' experience continues after they have passed out of the criminal justice system. Immediately after imprisonment they often face a lengthy readjustment with bitterness, impoverishment and scant opportunity. Those staying out of trouble do so usually because they grow out of criminal habits and find a settled life. Throughout this period non-statutory pastoral help can be greatly appreciated and a positive influence.

(e)   An assisted prison visits scheme (P.O. Box 2152, Birmingham B15 1SD) provides financial assistance for families on low income. Further domestic advice is obtainable from Prisoners' Wives and Families Service, 51 Borough High Street, London SE1 1NB (Tel: 0171 403 4091). The National Association of Prison Visitors is based at 46b Hartington Street, Bedford MK41 7RL (Tel: 01234 356763). 'The New Bridge', 27a Medway Street, London SW1P 3BD (Tel: 0171 976 0779) recruits and trains volunteers and provides an employment service for ex-offenders in London. NACRO is based at 169 Clapham Road, London SW9 0PU (Tel: 0171 582 6500) and the Prison Reform Trust at 59 Caledonian Road, London N1 9BU (Tel: 0171 278 9815).

(g) Atherton, R. (1987) *Summons to Serve: The Christian Call to Prison Ministry*. London: Geoffrey Chapman; *Prisoners' Information Pack*. The Prison Reform Trust (price £1); Zehr, H. (1990) *Changing Lenses: New Focus for Crime and Justice*. London: Metanoia Press.

ALAN DUCE

Psychosis and severe mental disorders

(a) The term 'psychosis' has been criticized because it covers a large number of conditions that differ widely in their presentation and causes and whose natural history and treatment are heterogeneous. Nonetheless 'psychosis' broadly signifies states of mind of a different order to those commonly understood to be normal within a particular culture. These differ from neurosis in that the individual experiences a range of phenomena which distort external reality through interfering with the mental processes involved in thinking, feeling, perceiving, interpreting, integrating and acting.

It is frequently stated that psychotic people have little or no awareness of their condition, described as a 'lack of insight'. In practice there is an enormous variation in awareness and acknowledgement of such experience as abnormal and in seeking help or treatment. The capacity for insight has a profound effect on the way the psychotic person relates to others, and vice versa.

The law and society regards psychoses as forms of mental 'illness', raising questions as to whether judgement and personal responsibility are diminished as a consequence. The medical profession, especially psychiatrists, and other mental health professionals, are charged with holding the expertise in discerning mental disorder and with taking a view about appropriate treatment. This is recognized legally in the Mental Health Act. For counsellors and other carers the use of a medical model implicit in the Act may run contrary to their own belief system, concerning clients' responsibility for making decisions about their own lives. However, the Mental Health Act also makes clear a concern for the health or safety of the individual or the protection of others, and the responsible counsellor or carer will recognize an implicit duty of care which is of a different order from that appropriate to other forms of mental distress.

What follows is a guide to the more common clinical presentations. The most florid present little difficulty in diagnosis. The more subtle may elude even the most experienced psychiatrist.

(b) Although major classifications no longer make the distinction, it is useful to differentiate 'organic' and functional' psychoses – based on whether or not there are known underlying physical causes.

Organic psychoses   are mental disorders attributable to underlying bodily disease, such as structural changes within the brain, e.g. Alzheimer's disease, cerebral tumour, cerebral haemorrhage, etc; or alteration of brain function because of more general physical illness or toxicity, e.g. diabetes, thyrotoxicosis, pneumonia, various forms of **substance misuse, alcoholism**, etc.

A large number of physical conditions can cause altered mental functioning. The brain has a limited reservoir of options in responding to organic assaults and while there is much overlap, two main types of reaction tend to result.

Acute brain syndromes   are states of delirium or confusion in which the person misconstrues her or his environment, often with clouding of consciousness. A range of perceptual misconceptions occur leading to hallucinations (often visual), delusions and paranoid interpretation. Thought is usually incoherent and may be accomplished by change of mood, varying from the euphoric to the depressed. Most notably there is impairment of the higher cognitive functions. Disorientation in time and place, poor attention span and impairment of short-term memory are very noticeable. The sufferer looks perplexed, and often irritable and distractible, possibly through trying to make sense of a world in which he or she has been acutely let down by the organizing functions of the mind.

This acute picture, which if undiagnosed and untreated may lead to death, contrasts with the slower onset and course of *chronic brain syndromes* to which the word *dementia* is frequently attached. This features usually in older age groups, again with loss of cognitive functions, especially memory. Initially memory for only recent events is affected, but gradually a recollection of past events becomes hazy, with inability to integrate the present with the past, resulting in confusion and loss of meaning. The individual tends to restrict activity, and avoid situations which demand use of memory. The capacity to organize daily living becomes increasingly difficult. Greater disorganization takes place with loss of self-care. Repetitious activity such as telling the same story over again is common. Thought content is restricted and delusional ideas emerge, often of a paranoid or hypochondriacal type. These are often fleeting, simple and poorly sustained. Mood varies from irritability and excitement to apathetic withdrawal and depression and may be difficult to differentiate from depression from other causes. The loss of cognition also leads to a range of misperceptions and illusions and occasional hallucinations.

The behaviour observable in dementing conditions is in part a reaction to loss of intellectual function, an attempt to organize internally and give meaning to an increasingly disorganized and bewildering world. Under such circumstances, a temporary catastrophic reaction may result in loss of even those coping capacities that have been so far retained. Most dementing disorders reflect underlying physical conditions that are progressive. Some are treatable and require thorough medical investigation.

Functional psychoses   was a term used for psychotic phenomena which could not be explained by an underlying physical condition. However, the International Classification of Diseases of the World Health Authority (ICD-10) has rendered this term obsolete. These conditions are now broadly grouped as either one of the sub-categories of *schizophrenia*, or one of the *mood* or *affective* disorders. The mental health specialist ultimately has to decide which category best fits any one person. The non-specialist dealing with a severely mentally disordered person needs some idea of the differing nature of these conditions, since they present differently, run different courses, carry different risks and have different treatment options.

Because of the very many ways in which *schizophrenia* can present, considerable difficulty has been experienced in providing sub-categories that do justice to the phenomena. Taking a broad view, the illness is characterized by fundamental distortions of thinking and perceiving, associated with alteration of mood. As a consequence a range of abnormal behaviours result, which are frequently bizarre, or inappropriate.

Although there is considerable overlap, there are two main forms – *acute* and *chronic*. Acute forms are characterized by a range of florid or 'positive' symptoms, developing over a period of weeks or months, usually in young adults. The process of thinking is disordered, and may appear meaningless. Delusions are prominent. These are false ideas which cannot be altered by an appeal to reason – bearing in mind the culture from which the person comes (see *cross-cultural awareness*). An ordinary event may be believed to have special significance. Thoughts may be experienced as put into the mind by some external source; alternatively, they are being broadcast to the world at large, so that others know what the person is thinking. Other examples include the feeling that adverse comments are being made, or that the person is being referred to on TV or radio.

The stream or form of thought is often affected. There may be loosening of associations, with bizarre or illogical association of ideas, so that vagueness or loss of meaning ensues; or poverty or blocking of thoughts, sometimes associated with a sense that thoughts are taken out of the mind by an alien force. The person may feel that they are controlled by such external forces.

An hallucination is a perception experienced in the absence of an external stimulus, experienced as both real and emanating from the external world. In schizophrenia a range of hallucinations occurs, usually auditory, taking the form of voices discussing and commenting, or repeating, or controlling thoughts and actions. Secondary delusions which appear to explain such phenomena (e.g. hidden radio transmitters) are common.

Mood is frequently labile, suspicious, blunted or incongruous. Excitement or its reverse, stupor, may occur. Attention and concentration is usually impaired. Associated depression is not uncommon.

The acute schizophrenic may appear quite normal, but some demonstrate a variety of abnormalities such as withdrawal, perplexity, bizarreness with inappropriate smiling, laughter or tears, without apparent causes. Behaviour may be noisy, hostile, occasionally violent and unpredictable. There is an increased risk of **suicide**.

This acute picture is contrasted with the *chronic* syndrome, characterized by slower onset and so-called 'negative' symptoms of withdrawal, apathy and lack of drive. Self-care suffers, with loss of social skills and behaviour, often leading to downward social drift. There tends to be restricted thinking, often associated with delusions. Affect is usually blunted. Hallucinations occur commonly, and are often intractable. Behaviour, sometimes with mannerisms, may be bizarre.

Paranoid states are usually classified with schizophrenia, but can occur in association with affective disorders and organic conditions, or as an enduring feature of personality. Paranoia is a morbid distortion of beliefs concerning the relationship between the individual and others. It frequently takes the form of a persecutory relationship, but may include delusions of love, grandeur or jealousy. Paranoia can occur as a primary state, or be associated with features of other psychotic states. Fixed delusional beliefs often emerge first in middle life, usually associated with considerable preservation of personality. More frequently other features of schizophrenia, especially hallucinations, are present. Especially when persecutory delusions are associated with commanding hallucinatory voices, the potential dangers of the person acting under their influence must always be taken very seriously.

Of special importance are states of pathological jealousy. The main feature is a conviction that a sexual partner is unfaithful. The condition is diagnosed when the evidence for such behaviour is missing. The belief has the strength of delusion, and can be associated with subjective feelings of anger, irritability and apprehension. The condition is often intractable, and usually only resolved by separation of the parties. It may lead to serious violence or even homicide.

The other main group of psychoses and severe mental disorders is called *affective disorders*. There is considerable disagreement about classifying them. The World Health Organisation describes common clinical presentations and introduces grades of severity. They are subclassified into manic episodes, bipolar affective disorder, and various types of depressive episodes, with or without psychotic symptoms. The more severe end of the spectrum is described.

In differentiating affective from other psychotic disorders, change in the individual's mood is the central focus. In older terminology, depressions were divided into 'endogenous' and 'reactive', implying the former are constitutionally determined, as opposed to those that are reactions to stressful events. However, some individuals with clinical features of endogenous depression develop the condition after a precipitating life event, usually involving loss or major stress. Many psychiatrists maintain the old endogenous/neurotic nomenclature partly because of different treatment approaches.

A moderately severe *manic* episode is characterized as follows: mood is nearly always elevated beyond explainable circumstances; there is usually an acknowledged and infectious cheerfulness often leading to a state of excitement. There is evidence of increased energy and over-activity including speech. The capacity to attend is reduced, with a tendency to flit from subject to subject. Over-activity extends into hours of sleep with no initial exhaustion. There is loss of social inhibition linked to ideas that are grandiose. This may lead into behaviour in keeping with such ideas: e.g. spending sprees, sometimes beyond the capacity to pay. Risky or reckless life decisions may also result. The general loss of inhibition together with increased self-esteem and sense of omnipotence may be expressed sexually, or in overbearing attitudes and unrealistically ambitious schemes.

With increasing severity, psychotic features may appear. These are essentially extensions of all the features mentioned earlier, but reality testing is impaired. Grandiose or religious delusions may emerge, extending to personal identity or role. Speech may become rapid and difficult to follow, flitting from idea to idea, often with tenuous but usually understandable associations. Puns, rhymes and alliterations are common. Excitement may increase to exhaustive severity, with acts of aggression resulting, if the person feels thwarted as irritability becomes more marked. Self-care can be neglected and lack of sleep may lead to dangerous states of exhaustion and dehydration. Hallucinations can occur, usually in keeping with the elevated mood, e.g. voices commenting on the individual's special powers. Generally at this stage there is little or no insight, although some measure of personal control can be maintained for short periods. If the illness has reached this stage, treatment within the security of a hospital is usually essential.

Depression is the other main form of affective disorder. Unfortunately the name is also given to states of mind that could be called unhappiness or sadness. Depressive symptoms occur in conjunction with many psychological and indeed physical disorders. At the more severe end of the spectrum, depressive states tend to show a rather similar constellation of symptoms, although the features may not all be present in one person. There are considerable variations with respect to the natural history, and response to various forms of treatment. Because of these different characteristics the World Health Organisation classifies depressive illnesses as mild, moderate and severe, with or without psychotic symptoms, noting whether or not the condition is recurrent.

A central clinical syndrome exists which tends to be common to all forms. It features depressed mood, loss of interest and enjoyment, tiredness, reduced energy and activity. Concentration and attention are impaired so that the person may complain of a poor memory although there is little objective evidence in most cases to sustain this. Self-esteem and self-confidence are reduced. Feelings of guilt or unworthiness are prominent. There tends to be a pessimistic view of the future, which may be associated with ideas or acts of self-harm or **suicide**. Typically symptoms are worse in the morning and improve during the day.

A cluster of symptoms sometimes called 'biological' are common in moderate or severe depression. Typically disturbance of sleep occurs: a tendency to wake in the early hours with subsequent difficulty in dropping off again. The person lies awake with brooding pessimistic or agitated thoughts, often associated with a sense of helplessness or hopelessness, or is preoccupied about actual or imagined failure. Other patterns of sleep disturbance also occur. Appetite is impaired and there may be considerable weight loss. Slowing up, sometimes called 'psycho-motor-retardation', also affects the bowels with actual and/or preoccupation about constipation. Worries about health lead into hypochondriacal ideas. Libido is low. Women may experience absence of periods.

States of anxiety are frequently associated with depression, especially in the elderly. The accompanying restlessness leads to a state of 'agitated depression'. Irritability with the self or others is common. Phobic, obsessional and hysterical symptoms may be associated, even dominating the presenting picture so that the depression is masked, especially where a low mood is denied. The sense of helplessness and hopelessness can lead to suicidal rumination, planning and eventually suicidal action.

All these symptoms leave their mark on the appearance. There may be self-neglect, so that the person appears shambling or dishevelled. Facial appearance is also changed, with a tendency to look worried or down-at-mouth. The demeanour of the person is often stooped or slowed down. Sometimes, however, just the opposite is the case with a smiling denial of depression, despite many of the features described earlier.

In more severe forms of depression some or all of the above functions are exaggerated. Depressive ideas become depressive delusions so that contact with reality is lost. It is correct then to term the condition *psychotic depression*. Symptoms of worthlessness, guilt, worries about health or money become converted into delusional systems, e.g. of having done wrong and deserving punishment. Hypochondriacal or physical preoccupations become delusions of major physical illness with hopeless outcome. Delusions of poverty or occasional persecutory delusions may occur. Depressive delusions can become projected into hallucinatory phenomena, typically rather short and unelaborated, in which voices are heard making derogatory comments, commenting adversely and sometimes indicating that the person deserves to die. Risk of suicide in the presence of such phenomena is extremely high. Psycho-motor-retardation can also become exaggerated to a state of gross retardation, which can proceed further to a state of depressive stupor: the person becomes mute, not taking in any nourishment and totally unable to care for themselves.

For all forms of depressive disorder the course is very variable. It is likely that most depressions are essentially self-limiting although episodes can be aborted by appropriate treatment. There is a tendency for affective disorder to be recurrent, but single episodes do occur. Different types of disorder are likely to occur at particular times of life. The mean age of onset in manic depression is about 30 but there is a wide variation, with some cases starting in early adulthood, and others much later. In contrast what used to be known as *involutional melancholia* is a depressive syndrome that occurs for the first time in middle life, often associated with agitation and hypochondriacal delusions. Immediately following childbirth is a particularly vulnerable time, and a range of psychotic phenomena, including those resembling schizophrenia, may become apparent in that immediate period.

(c) How can these severe mental disorders be understood in terms of their causation and precipitating factors? Psychiatrists and research workers agree that the matter is highly complex. Medicine is accustomed to considering multi-factorial causation of illness, and that there are agent, host and societal considerations. Similarly in mental disorder we have to consider a multiplicity of causes, and weigh up in any individual what factors seem of greatest significance. Increasingly causes are unravelled through objective research, usually on a number of subjects demonstrating common patterns of disorder. No less important, but far more difficult to evaluate, are subjective accounts based on personal experience, often gleaned in the course of the psychodynamic psychotherapies.

A single cause may lead to several effects, e.g. early maternal deprivation has been cited as a causal agent in affective disorder, schizophrenia and disorders of personality. Conversely, a single effect can arise from multiple causes. Multiple causation can be considered under a number of headings and divided into predisposing, precipitating and perpetuating factors.

Predisposing factors   determine vulnerability to a condition. Genetic influences operate from the moment of conception and contribute to the constitution of the individual. Constitutional factors also include very early environmental influences including intra-uterine life. Following birth the nature of the facilitating environment and early life experiences are thought to be important. Together with genetic endowment they lead to the development of a particular type of personality with specific vulnerabilities. There is now no doubt that genetic factors play an important role in the development of schizophrenia, affective disorders and certain organic conditions, such as Huntington's disease or some forms of Alzheimer's disease. In the functional psychoses, however, it is thought unlikely that genetic environment alone explains the manifestation of the condition. Other factors need to be taken into consideration.

There has been much research into the contribution of biochemistry and neurophysiology to the cause of major mental illness. A number of interesting hypotheses derived largely from psycho-pharmacological research have been suggested reflecting the improvement possible through various forms of physical treatment, especially drug therapy. The mechanisms whereby mental states are transformed into brain physiology are not known. That such mechanisms exist must be obvious from everyday life where the experience of stressful life events can be seen to have profound physiological effects on the working of the body and vice versa. We know that certain stressful life events precipitate psychosis and there may be analogous mechanisms.

Sociological factors have also been cited as predisposing to major mental illness although these are likely to be mitigated through psychological pathways. Thus it has been shown that vulnerability to depression in women is increased when there is a history of death of the mother before the age of 11, more than three children under 14 years in the family, where the woman has no work and feels isolated at home, and where there is no confiding relationship with a partner. Similarly a number of studies show an increased incidence of schizophrenia in migrants, although there are complex underlying reasons.

A range of psychological factors also contribute. Psychoanalytic theories and observations of family systems have been used to explain vulnerability to psychosis. Thus in schizophrenia a number of themes concerning the role, style of communication and personality types of key family members are thought relevant. These theories link reasonably well with descriptions of faulty bonding, disturbed early relationships and the absence of a good enough facilitating environment in the first years of life that have been put forward as causes as a result of psychoanalytic findings. Such factors lead to a vulnerable personality organization that regresses to primitive modes of functioning with massive denial, splitting and projection, in an attempt to reconcile the intolerable split between internal and external worlds. Thus schizophrenia is seen as an attempt to manage overwhelming emotional forces. Although it is extremely difficult to verify such theories, the intensive method of investigation used in analytic and allied techniques requires respect.

Alternative psychological theories derive from learning theory and cognitive theory. The role of beliefs and systems of thinking in depressive disorder has been particularly studied. It is postulated that in depression a low mood results in a pessimistic appraisal of the self and the world, fuelled by selective memories of past failures. This further lowers mood, and a vicious circle is established which tends to lead to further patterns of faulty thinking. Improvement takes place through the therapist drawing attention to and attempting to reverse these attitudes.

Precipitating factors   are events which occur immediately before the onset of a condition and are thought to have induced it. Common psychological precipitants are **loss** or major personal change, e.g. **bereavement**, **redundancy**, **divorce** or a **major disaster**. Physical factors such as viral infections, brain injury, drugs, etc. can also precipitate breakdown.

Perpetuating factors   are those which prolong a condition and require modification to help control it. Thus it has been shown that in the families of some schizophrenics a high level of expressed emotion may both precipitate and prolong the illness. Separation from the stressful environment or attempts to explain and alter the attitudes of family members may improve the outlook.

(d) Certain features in an encounter with a client may be taken as possible warnings of psychosis or serious mental illness, and further clarification obtained by sensitive exploration.

A number of the conditions described above carry increased risk of **suicide**. The possibility of such intent must always be borne in mind. Asking clients whether they feel so despairing that they have thoughts of suicide is likely to give responses that guide further intervention by the carer or counsellor. Severe guilt, self-reproach, deserving punishment and a sense of helplessness against powerful forces are important pointers.

Clients may make statements that suggest they are out of touch with reality. These can be taken up by staying with clients' ideas. Suggestion that the client has hallucinations or is deluded or persecuted can be asked about: whether they feel got at, talked about or looked at, often follows on naturally from clues in the client's statements. Further enquiry might reveal that they feel talked about on radio and television, or that they hear voices talking about them. Clients in greater touch with reality acknowledge that the world feels changed or different in some way. They may have heard or seen unusual things. Some feel they have themselves changed, and now have special powers; that their bodies have changed; or that their minds are no longer under their control. Asking about difficulty in thinking may reveal that thoughts are muddled, absent, interfered with or being broadcast to others. Organic disorders are often suggested by subjective and objective evidence of memory disturbances. Evidence of real, as opposed to apparent, memory loss comes to light through asking more about areas of difficulty and tactfully asking questions that test memory. Especially where there is other supporting evidence of mental disorder, any threats of harm or violence to others must always be taken seriously (see *suicide; violent clients*).

The carer often has a key role in facilitating co-operation with treatment plans, based on the capacity to develop a trusting therapeutic relationship. The passport is to listen attentively and to stay with the client's experience while trying to understand its meaning for them. By doing this the carer provides a continuing interest in the client as a human being and encourages a sense of safety.

The people we are considering are to a greater or lesser extent out of touch with reality. Their experiences are real to them, and it is important to confirm their personal reality, without agreeing or colluding with it. To confront a delusion, for example, by an appeal to reason is almost invariably misguided, as it leads to the client feeling misunderstood, more isolated or alienated, and hence more confused, angry or despairing. It is better to investigate how a particular conviction makes the client feel, and the implication of those feelings. This frequently opens up wider concerns.

Whether or not they retain some insight, psychotic people are frequently deeply perplexed or distressed by their experience. Ventilating their fears to another who is tolerant and not judgemental relieves anxiety and fosters trust. It is part of ordinary human experience that if anxiety levels are too high it is difficult to think coherently. When a person feels understood, anxiety falls and the capacity to think improves. It is very easy when dealing with psychotic people to forget this and treat them as totally unable to think or take responsible action for themselves. Yet it is precisely the maintenance of a responsible working relationship that needs to be preserved, to effect co-operation and help the healthy part of the individual to function.

If attention to the client's experience is the central function, this is also true of monitoring one's own experience. Used constructively, the acknowledgement and investigation of one's own reactions can be very helpful both diagnostically and in establishing a therapeutic relationship. The experience of finding it difficult to think clearly, of feeling confused or not being able to grasp meaning, and an overall sense that it is you, the helper, who is 'going mad' may be a useful indicator of thought disorder in the client.

Similarly, noting one's own feelings about presenting material gives important clues to the client's feelings. To find oneself feeling elated, jocular and somewhat disinhibited is a powerful clue to the presence of manic experiences in the client. Manic processes are, however, the obverse of depression and can be seen as attempts to avoid disturbing depressive ideas, often related to major **loss**. Understanding this and tactfully not colluding with the client is helpful in keeping the illness in bounds.

Conversely, finding one's thinking slowed, or feeling sad, guilty or useless about the client may be an indicator of depression, and facilitate engaging with how depressed the client feels and whether there are suicidal thoughts. Feeling anxious and defensive in answering client's questions is often an indicator of paranoid traits and profound mistrust by the client, who may be frightened of their own impulses and of going out of control. These personal experiences, often disturbing when first encountered, help the carer understand the client's world, and facilitate a response which encourages a relationship in which the client feels supported.

The capacity and motivation of people in the grip of psychosis to think about their experiences in psychological terms is usually very limited, especially when the illness is in an acute phase. There is therefore only a limited role for deeper psychotherapeutic interventions, except by the very skilled and experienced. Nevertheless attempts to understand the meaning of hallucinatory or delusional material is important in trying to understand something of the core dilemmas in the client's life. Discussion of such material in supervision or with an appropriately trained psychiatrist can sometimes be extremely helpful in maintaining a supporting role.

(e) Once psychosis or severe mental illness is recognized there is invariably an implication that others with specialist mental health skills need to be involved. Treatment is always a complex issue, usually involving the client, their family or those in their immediate circle. A range of professionals with particular skills and roles in the various aspects of mental health can be called upon to aid client and carer. How and when to call on their services depends upon the type of disorder, and the manner of its presentation. This does not mean automatic referral to psychiatric care, but rather careful consideration of the options available in obtaining access to such opinion. Discussion in **supervision** is the first step.

The next is likely to be contact with the client's general practitioner. GPs are trained in the recognition and diagnosis of mental illness and are usually able to initiate treatment. They have links with the local mental health services. Such contact may, however, give rise to difficult ethical and technical difficulties where the client is fearful or reluctant for contact to be made.

Apart from such general supportive measures, treatment of psychosis tends to rely on drugs and occasionally electro-convulsive therapy (ECT). A wide range of drugs, known as psychotropic, has become available, with a beneficial effect on psychotic symptoms. The responsibility for prescribing lies with the medical profession. However, when people are unconvinced that they are ill, or do not wish to recover, or when they are frightened of the effect of the drugs on them, there may be great difficulty in obtaining compliance. It is around such issues that admission to hospital, sometimes against the person's will, needs to be negotiated. When there are real concerns for the health and safety of the client or others, compulsory admission under one of the sections of the Mental Health Act must be pursued further. These are seldom easy issues for carers who may find themselves in a conflict of loyalty between understanding the need for treatment, feeling for the client, and fearing a breakdown in the tenuous relationship with the client. Discussion of such dilemmas in supervision, and with the mental health team involved, often helps to place them in a helpful perspective.

(f) Discussion with the general practitioner will help to clarify whether it is in the best interests of the client for the counsellor or carer to continue their present link, whether it should be modified or move towards termination. These discussions will also take into account whether specialist mental health workers should be involved. Whether it is decided that the carer will stay involved or not, good communication is essential, as is agreement on the goals each party is aiming for. Organizations which are likely to encounter psychosis fairly frequently need to anticipate problems arising, and have ongoing arrangements for consultation with an appropriate mental health professional. The carer's capacity to extend knowledge and skill in relation to psychotic disorder will grow with experience and study. The books listed below are all useful in guiding the non-specialist.

(g) Betts, T. and Kenwood, C. (1992) *Practical Psychiatry*. Oxford: Oxford University Press; Gelder, M., Gath, D. and Mayou, R. (1994) *Concise Oxford Textbook of Psychiatry*. Oxford: Oxford University Press; World Health Organisation (1992) *The ICD-10 Classification of Mental and Behavioural Disorders*. Geneva: World Health Organisation.

PETER AGULNIK

Racism and prejudice

(a) Britain has long been a multi-cultural society, with evidence of racism and prejudice. The relatively well-integrated co-existence today of those of Celtic, Anglo-Saxon and Norman origin belies the successive upheavals in many communities of accommodating either immigrants or invaders of different cultures, race and religion. Anti-racism awareness may be new, but racism and prejudice are not. Religious persecution in the past has included that of Catholics and Protestants, while those fleeing religious and ethnic persecution abroad include the Huguenots and the Jews. Slavery may have exacerbated racist attitudes, although prejudice about the so-called 'primitives' may have been one of the contributing factors in the mass exploitation of African peoples through the slave trade. Although post-1945 Britain may have experienced a huge immigration of Afro-Caribbean and Asian families, a similarly large influx of Irish and of Jews occurred in the nineteenth century.

It is generally agreed that 'race' itself is almost impossible to define since it is a term that is contextually variable in its use. 'Racism' is hardly any easier, since it too is a culturally determined and highly subjective concept. An early working definition was that 'racism is the dogma that one ethnic group is condemned by nature to congenital inferiority and another group is destined to congenital superiority' (Benedict, 1940). The definition reflects a particular debate at a particular time – namely questions about intelligence in black and white people, based upon genetic difference. It is clear that racist attitudes continue to exist even when such congenital differences have been shown to be a false basis for distinction between races. A later definition of racism is that it

> results from the transformation of race prejudice and/or
> ethnocentrism through the exercise of power against a racial group
> defined as inferior, by individuals or institutions, with the
> intentional or unintentional support of the entire culture. (Jones,
> 1981:28)

Allport's (1954) definition of prejudice has been widely accepted: it can be negatively defined as 'thinking ill of others without sufficient warrant'; or it can incorporate a positive and negative component as in 'a feeling, favorable or unfavorable, toward a person or thing, prior to, or not based in actual experience'. Each of these definitions includes both an attitude and a belief: 'the attitude is either negative or positive, and the attitude is tied to an overgeneralized or erroneous "belief" ' (Ponterotto and Pedersen, 1993: 110). Allport's definition of negative ethnic prejudice is also helpful: 'Ethnic prejudice is an antipathy based upon a faulty and inflexible generalization. It may be directed toward a group as a whole, or toward an individual because he [or she] is a member of that group' (1954: 9).

(b)   Although issues of racism at first appear related to a black versus white attitude, racism (or ethnic differences) is much wider, involving significant cultural variations and therefore the potentiality for intense hostility *within* groups of blacks and whites. Thus there are ethnic conflicts in the Indian sub-continent, in Africa, in former Yugoslavia and in Northern Ireland even though colours of skin and facial appearances look deceptively similar to the outsider. Prejudice need not be based upon ethnicity alone; for example, an Indian educated and naturalized in Britain may find his tolerance towards his peers in India as stretched as a white British national does in Britain. While race-based distinctions are used to categorize people, there are in fact more differences within racial groups than between them. One of the problems of all prejudice is the ease with which people with an obvious similarity are thought to be the same in every other respect.

Racism and prejudice therefore take many forms, and involve different groups and individuals. Simplistic 'black and white' thinking is unhelpful either to an analysis of the problems or their solution. It is also important to recognize that no single racial or ethnic group can escape the charge of prejudice and racism. What tends, especially to the white liberal, to be seen as the problem of white society, is apparent in racist attitudes in most societies.

By its very nature racism itself can only take root when it is supported by the whole culture, so that the caring professional or agency worker has to remember that he or she functions in that context. There may be agency or institutional attitudes that can be identified as problem areas (see *cross-cultural awareness*). In working with individual clients and working alongside colleagues, the carer is likely to encounter three different presentations of racism or prejudice. First there is the person who is a victim of racial abuse, religious intolerance or some other form of prejudice. Secondly, there is the person who demonstrates blatant aggressive racism or prejudice towards certain groups, or individual representatives of those groups. Thirdly, more subtle, and much less easy to bring into the open are those who reveal racist or prejudicial attitudes through biased judgements and statements, despite the fact that they declare that they are 'not racist' and see no need to examine their awareness. Such people may resist the requirements of institutions or agencies to monitor practice and to ensure that both the agency itself and the individual workers within it are not discriminatory against minority groups in their behaviour or attitudes, either actively or through neglect.

(c)   There are various explanations of the reasons for and the perpetuation of racism and prejudice, none of which are mutually exclusive, and each of which may help begin to identify ways of reducing such problems. Sociologists point to the significance in race relation situations of *social stratification*, particularly (in Rex, 1970) divisions such as:

1.   a more organized political group meeting one whose levels of technology are lower;
2.   class conflicts where there is confrontation between groups holding different degrees of market power;
3.   caste systems;
4.   groups interacting for limited purposes only, but leading separate communal lives.

Thus for example immigrants are perhaps classed as 'colonials' and therefore already cast into past socially inferior roles; they take up employment which may carry deprived status; and they may settle in a deprived housing area, gradually creating or re-creating their own community. However much they improve their own situation, housing and other conditions, they become a 'pariah' group, and therefore open to scapegoating for any hardship suffered by the dominant domicile group, as happened, for example, to Afro-Caribbeans in Britain in the 1950s. Where there is high unemployment particular groups such as immigrants or women can be blamed for taking jobs, when in fact government policies, world economic factors and other factors are to blame.

Social stratification alone is not a sufficient explanation for racism. Belief systems also play an important part. Other reasons have also been identified: for example, *historical* (e.g. contemporary prejudice has its roots in slavery) or *personality dynamics*. The psychodynamic model suggests that child-rearing practices give rise to internal processes and personal dispositions that may result in specific prejudices. According to this theory, only certain people develop prejudice as a major feature in their lives – perhaps insecure, anxious personalities need to adopt an authoritarian and exclusionist way of life rather than a relaxed or democratic way. Such an explanation carries some hope for change, since racism is seen as having its roots in individual deviations from the norm. Allport (1954: 216) puts forward a *phenomenological* explanation, that 'a person's conduct proceeds immediately from his view of the situation confronting him. His response to the world conforms to his definition of the world.' This is the most immediate level of causation.

A further explanation is that of *stimulus and response*. Here, although there may be real differences between groups, giving rise to hostility, the differences are much less than they are imagined. Reputations are not earned, but 'gratuitously thrust upon a group' (Allport, 1954: 217). More plausible still is that the combination of real and imagined differences leads to a sometimes lethal interaction, reinforcing prejudice. Where there are differences between people anxiety can be aroused, and reasons are sought to explain this anxiety: 'myth and theology, philosophy and science, all provide us with systematic ways of meeting this need' (Rex, 1970).

In trying to unravel the tangled knot of causation – situational, cultural, historical, psychological – it is helpful to examine the process of *stereotyping* (Hamilton and Trolier, 1986: 127–58). Categorization is endemic in us, important to the way we perceive, understand and adapt to the many stimuli with which waking life presents us. In meeting new situations we look for identifiable features that help us distinguish what might be safe and what might be threatening. The gender, race and age of other people are immediately obvious distinctions, as well as their occupation, economic and social status, revealed sometimes in their behaviour, the way they dress, etc. Accents and dialects also reveal differences and similarities. Although there are many ways in which people differ from each other, we tend to establish clear-cut categories: black and white, men and women, young and old. People are therefore first seen as members of a group rather than as individuals.

We tend to believe those who are different, have certain common characteristics: stereotyping springs from such belief systems – that Afro-Caribbeans are always late, that Scots are mean with their money, that Jews are avaricious, that women are illogical or that men are unfeeling (see *gender issues*).

In making these statements we make the original categories into groupings that become even more homogeneous – people within them are seen as more alike, and those outside as more different. In-groups and out-groups are formed. This in turn can lead to attribution of racial or religious reasons for differences in behaviour: 'Well, they're Muslim, so what do you expect?' Polarization is increased. Where a person or a group is viewed positively, the perception grows more favourable; where they are viewed negatively, the perception grows less favourable. Prejudice, as Allport defined it, can be positively charged as well as negative. Whole thinking processes are then distorted, so that explanations for behaviour are made along stereotypical lines, with positive features identified as arising from being a member of the 'in-group' and negative features arising from being one of the 'out-group'.

This explanation of racism and prejudice is rather less hopeful for change than that based upon integral psychodynamic difficulties. The cognitive explanation suggests that stereotyping is a universal phenomenon, wherever different groups meet; and therefore much more difficult to eradicate. Nevertheless it also provides the hope (and indeed some evidence) that there is a way of changing behaviour and attitudes through processes that are similar to desensitization. By getting people of different groups to mix and work together on common tasks, their perception of the members of the other groups are often tested and found wanting. Thus prejudice towards women in certain occupations grows less, as men (or some men) realize that their previous views of women's abilities were based on prejudice rather than on reason. Religious groups that differ can find they have more in common than there is that divides them. Those of different races who collaborate on equal terms can find the same feelings and anxieties beneath some of the culturally determined behaviour patterns.

(d)   In this article suggestions for dealing with the wider dimensions of the problems of racism and prejudice are clearly inappropriate. Nevertheless there are ways in which individual helpers can promote better race relations and reduce stereotyping and prejudice in colleagues and clients.

Education and employment play a key role. Multi-cultural education recognizes cultural diversity and promotes integration of these values in and amongst students. While there are obvious major advances in anti-racism awareness in schools, similar opportunities can be exploited in **adult learning** and professional training. Teachers and trainers who represent different cultures are clearly desirable, although both will depend upon 'student' enrolment, or volunteer selection that reflects the true ethnic mix of an area, since it is those who start as students who in the end become those who teach, train and select. Anti-racism should not be a 'bolted-on' part of the syllabus, but lived through (and talked through) in the normal course of staff–student and peer interactions, as well as in reflecting on different parts of training. Gaertner and Dovidio report that 'cooperative learning groups were among the activities most related to positive interracial attitudes' (1986: 325). They describe one study where even the seating arrangements in a small group (mixing up different ethnic groups, as opposed to keeping them in two halves of the circle) significantly altered perceptions of the way both the group worked and leadership by someone from a different ethnic group could be accepted. Other suggestions for improving relationships and looking at prejudice are discussed in the article on **cross-cultural awareness**.

It is important that the most self-perceptive liberal helper examine her or his own attitudes to racism. Clients of other ethnic groups may be seen by some helpers as solely the victims of racism, and their individual contributions to situations minimized. Other helpers may so minimize the differences between people that they become 'colour blind', and fail to acknowledge the real cultural differences of which their clients may justly be proud. Some helpers think they understand other cultures when their knowledge has simply come from books. Obviously too there are more blinkered helpers who fail to acknowledge the realities of the external world, and attribute the client's problems to internal difficulties, seeing paranoid features in the client where others would recognize actual prejudice. Helpers need also to acquire a comfort with racial and cultural differences as part of their repertoire of personal skills. In addition, d'Ardenne and Mahtani (1989) comment that

> counsellors working across cultures have many tasks in establishing
> their credentials with their clients. But they need also to be careful
> of overemphasising cultural or racial factors to the exclusion of other
> variables. (1989: 53)

In working with the individuals who present issues of racism and prejudice the most common element is that of building up trust – this is equally vital whether helping someone who is the victim of prejudice, or working with someone who demonstrates obvious racist attitudes, even though in the latter case these attitudes are probably not seen as a problem. Clearly the most testing, yet also potentially productive, situation is where the helper and client come from different ethnic groups. The persecuted client is faced with yet another person who could be persecutory. If the client has had no choice in the gender and race of their helper this is clearly a situation where the helper needs to be alert to any sign of suspicion and mistrust. The use and abuse of power and authority in such situations is also a matter for the utmost consideration. Curiously the same applies where the client exhibits racist attitudes, because the caring situation nearly always assumes a helper in the position of power, and a client in an inferior, supplicant role. For someone whose view of other races or groups has been one of his or her own superiority, now to be 'at the mercy' of the 'inferior' person will be an anxious and embarrassing position. The differences between helper and client may at some point need to be acknowledged, although not always at the first session, unless they are clearly interfering with making a working relationship. It may be helpful to acknowledge early on how strange it must be talking to 'an outsider'.

Again with both the persecuted and the persecutors it is important to acknowledge the pain and emotional damage – even though in the case of those who are racist the helper may feel less sympathetic to the defences that promote and the fears that at least partially underlie such attitudes. The impact of prejudice and racism is probably an overt part of the agenda of the client who is suffering from its effects. It is probably not so obviously part of the agenda of the client who exhibits racist views, yet even here, once sufficient trust has been established, such ideas can be acknowledged, particularly through reflecting back loaded phrases: 'You say that all Italians are crooks?' By repeating what the client has said, since they are the client's words, the client cannot object, except perhaps by qualifying what they then can hear to be a prejudiced statement. Reflecting back is (at least on the surface) non-judgemental, yet it confronts the client with what he or she appears to think. A client's hostile response to such a reflection will indicate whether it was too early to bring it forward, although the difference between helper's views and client's views can still be observed: 'I can hear that is what you think, although I differ from you there'. The helper may even ask how the client feels about that. In the end, of course, the helper is trying to encourage the client to assimilate differences between people. Tolerance of difference between helper and client is a not insignificant step, even though one difference of opinion is a long way from accepting those of a different colour, country, gender or set of beliefs.

Ultimately, in working individually with racism and other forms of prejudice, as Bagley and Verma conclude, 'we can only assess the real meaning and roots of prejudice by considering people as individuals, and by knowing a great deal about them' (1979: 199). All the roots and causes examined above may be relevant in disentangling the belief systems of any one person.

Since helpers cannot retaliate when there are racist or prejudicial attacks upon them, but have to contain them until such time as the client is ready to face them, this can impose its own stresses. Feelings aroused should be shared with sympathetic colleagues or in **supervision**.

(e) Resources for counselling, psychotherapy and/or support, as well as social needs, can be found in London and major metropolitan areas for a variety of ethnic and religious groups; and nearly every city also has some facilities. Particular expertise on cross-cultural therapy is available from Nafsiyat (Inter-cultural Therapy Centre), 278 Seven Sisters Road, London N4 2HY (Tel: 0171 263 4130) and Race and Cultural Education in Counselling, BAC, 1 Regent Place, Rugby, Warwickshire CV21 2PJ (Tel: 01788 578328).

In cases of racial harassment, or where other advice on race relations or local ethnic groups is required, the Commission for Racial Equality (Elliott House, 10–12 Allington Street, London SW1E 5EH; Tel: 0171 828 7022) has offices in Birmingham, Edinburgh, Leeds, Leicester, London and Manchester. In some other places there may be a Racial Equality Council, part-funded by the CRE but autonomous. The local telephone directory will list a contact point, where one exists, under either Commission for Racial Equality or Racial Equality Council. Community law centres are another source where legal advice is required.

Other useful addresses include: British Refugee Council, Bondway House, 3–9 Bondway, London SW8 1SJ (Tel: 0171 582 6922); Confederation of Indian Organisations, 5 Westminister Bridge Road, London SE1 7XW (Tel: 0171 928 9889); Jewish Care, 221 Golders Green Road, London NW11 9DW (Tel: 0181 458 3282); Joint Council for the Welfare of Immigrants, 115 Old Street, London EC1 9JR (Tel: 0171 251 8706).

(g) Allport, G. (1954) *The Nature of Prejudice*. Cambridge, MA: Addison-Wesley Publishing; d'Ardenne, P. and Mahtani, A. (1990) *Transcultural Counselling in Action*. London: Sage Publications; Ponterotto, J. G. and Pedersen, P. B. (1993) *Preventing Prejudice: A Guide for Counselors and Educators*. Newbury Park, CA: Sage Publications.

MICHAEL JACOBS

(See also *cross-cultural awareness; faith differences; fanaticism; gay men and lesbians; gender issues; menopause*)

Recovery from major surgery

(a) What is major surgery? To the patient and the patient's family almost all surgery appears major, as it involves a process that raises anxiety and that they would naturally rather avoid. For professionals it is also difficult to define because rapid advances in medical science have significantly altered the danger levels and recovery times for many kinds of operation. Twenty years ago the length of time spent in hospital following surgery and the use of a convalescent hospital would have been good indicators of major surgery. The development of more sophisticated anaesthesia, of surgical skills and of technology which limits the extent of invasiveness – e.g. lasers, keyhole surgery, robotic aids – and the ever-increasing range and power of drugs, all mean that patients can be returned home in hours rather than days or weeks. Stitches (clips or staples) can be removed at home or at the local GP surgery or health centre, or as an out-patient. For the purpose of this article my working definition of 'major surgery' is where any intervention is made that involves a significant level of support (medical, nursing and technological) following the operation.

(b) The need for surgical intervention comes through three major routes, congenital disorder, disease and accident. Congenital problems may be known or identified before birth (indeed some surgery is carried out *in utero*), or diagnosed in the early part of life. This creates a partnership between the parents and the doctors in deciding the acceptable level of intervention. As a child grows older he or she becomes increasingly involved in this decision-making process. The second route is through disease. Here particular symptoms or a spell of being 'out of sorts' have led the patient to the GP and from there to hospital. When a disease is diagnosed it leads to a process in which either immediate surgery is required, or a partnership is established to determine the appropriate stage for intervention (which may also be affected by waiting lists). Thirdly, the need for surgery may follow an accident; in this case there may be little or no time for consideration.

(d) Although I focus on *recovery* from major surgery it is not possible to discount the time *before* surgery takes place. Anticipating major surgery has an impact which is sometimes very profound, as the thought bites deep of putting oneself in the hands of someone with a knife. It gives rise to a range of consequent fears. A number of people also have fears related to anaesthesia: not only 'Will I wake up again?' Fear of pain, and also of the consequences of the surgery on future life, may also be present. These are examined more closely below. For the professionals involved, the waiting time is an opportunity to establish rapport and trust which may be significant later, even if that time is only very brief, e.g. the accident patient taken to theatre quickly after initial assessment. Where the time factor is limited, a smile or holding a hand on the way to theatre may have a seemingly disproportionate impact on the patient. Where there is more time, empathic listening and sensitive response to patients and their fears may forge an important relationship of trust for the recovery time. This can be in stark contrast to the response the patient may have had from the family, who because of their own anxieties cannot allow the patient to express fears, especially doubts about the outcome. Professionals similarly should be aware of the needs of families and friends and be empathic in their response to them. This has importance for the recovery time, especially when the patient returns home. Delays in carrying out the surgery sometimes raise anxiety levels and cause anger. It can be extremely draining for the patient and family to prepare for surgery on a particular day only to find that emergencies have caused a delay. An apology and an explanation can help to assuage the anger, and help diminish the feeling that 'I'm not important'.

Following surgery the recovery process can be divided into four broad bands:

1. the acute or immediate recovery time;
2. the professionally managed recovery time;
3. the home recovery time; and
4. re-emerging into 'normal' life.

1. After the completion of the operation the patient enters the immediate or acute recovery time. From the operating theatre he or she is moved to a recovery room and from there back to the ward; or in the case of very major surgery or the weak condition of the patient, to an intensive care unit. If the patient is taken to an intensive care unit a high level of technology will be evident, often including the use of life-support systems. In this situation the patient's ability to respond verbally will be very limited or non-existent. Awareness levels may also be very limited depending on condition and levels of drug control, but it should be noted that hearing and sensitivity to touch may well be present. Thus talking to the patient and explaining what is happening is important, together with encouragement to the family to use touch and to speak to the patient. Families frequently need a lot of support at this stage, both because of what is happening to the patient, and also because of the impact of seeing their relatives attached to so much unfamiliar equipment (they can become mesmerized by the monitors). As soon as possible the patient will be transferred to the ward.

The majority of patients are returned directly from the recovery room to the ward. Here, as in the intensive care unit, there will initially be a high level of intervention: e.g. the patient is likely to be attached to a range of equipment – drips and drains which need constant attention; as well as constant monitoring of her or his condition 24 hours a day. At this stage disorientation may be experienced by the patient as a result of the trauma of surgery, the effects of the anaesthetic and the effects of powerful drug regimes. Again limited ability or desire to respond verbally should be expected. Alongside this there may well be underlying levels of fear and the need for basic reassurance. The carer requires not just the ability to be with, but that most difficult of skills, to be with in silence or relative silence that is not intrusive and does not make unnecessary demands on the patient. Similarly the ability to use gentle, sensitive and reassuring touch is of great value. The families here often need a lot of support and help to understand these skills.

2. The majority of patients move very quickly into the second stage, i.e. the professionally managed stage. Here there are many milestones of recovery obvious to patient and family alike, including the early mobilization of the patient, accompanied by the removal of monitors, drips and drains; the return to taking liquids and then solid food: and the lengthening of time between routine observations: e.g. temperature and blood pressure. During this stage the patient is heavily reliant on the professional input not only for the management of the recovery, but also for information about what was discovered during the operation, what surgery was carried out and what the likely prognosis is.

When they are faced with the implications of what has happened, for many patients this involves putting together a jigsaw puzzle, the pieces of which are their own hopes and fears, what they feel, what they observe in their own body, what has been communicated by the professionals and what is being communicated by the family. At the same time a patient is still very debilitated by the effects of the anaesthetic, the trauma of surgery and the ongoing impact of pain, discomfort and the effects of drugs. Heavy demands – often the patient thinks of them as *too* heavy demands – are made on limited energy resources as the patient is remobilized and given exercises, to prevent complications settling in. Sleep patterns may be difficult to re-establish, and this is not helped by the inevitable level of activity on a busy surgical ward.

Clearly at this stage there is an increased ability to respond, but professionals and visitors (whether family, friends or volunteers) need to be very sensitive to the patient's wishes and strength. A conversation, particularly one focused on the agenda of the visitor, is very demanding and can be very intrusive. The value of simply *being with* should not be forgotten. To allow the patient to set the agenda for interaction is less demanding to the patient, and allows the professional or visitor to be responsive to needs (see *hospital visiting*).

The patient is likely to be struggling with huge questions at this stage. Fears and anxieties may be exercising them, together with a struggle with those threats to selfhood that often follow major surgery. The first and obvious threat is to body image. By its nature invasive surgery creates an inevitable disfigurement – at its lowest level a scar which may well be hidden but is known to the patient. Some forms of major surgery involve major changes in body image: e.g. amputation, breast removal (which is also amputation, particularly to those who undergo it), colostomy, ileostomy. This is an area which frequently causes a divide between patient and carers (professional, family or volunteers) as each sees the situation from a different angle and with a different agenda. The patient is focused on what has been lost (see **loss**), both in terms of physical ability ('I won't be able to play football again') and also body image ('I won't wear shorts or a bikini again'). The carers are focused on the 'success' of the operation and look forward to what the patient *will* be able to do. Desperate attempts can be made to help the patient 'be positive', accompanied by intrusive and often offensive platitudes: e.g. following an accident to a young undergraduate, who was a good sportsman, he came round to find he was a paraplegic, only to be told 'You're lucky to be alive!'; 'It could have been worse'; 'Miracles do happen'; 'Cheer up, you will soon be out in a wheelchair'; 'Looking back won't help'.

Carers are often threatened by the essential process of looking back. The patient is focused on what has been lost and needs to explore in that direction first. He or she should be allowed to do so openly, as well as be affirmed and accompanied in that painful exploration. This critical stage of coming to accept what has happened can then lead into an examination of the present, and further into an exploration of what may be possible in the future. The process of accompanying this may well forge an important support relationship for the future. The carer does not need answers, but a willingness to explore the questions and the darkness. This exploration moves into self-image and the implications relating to work: will it be possible to go back to the same job? or will a new direction need to be sought? Home life may also be examined, because there can be implications for roles at home: for some there will be major adaptation or indeed complete loss of certain roles, which not only affect the self but also family relationships. Social life too may need to adapt to a greater or lesser degree.

3. This process of exploration is continued when the patient returns home. Recovery milestones tend to be further apart, which can be frustrating to patient and family alike. Patients can feel quite depressed when they see little evidence of recovery from day to day. This may be exacerbated by the frustrations of being at home, unable to

carry out traditional roles and watching others carrying them out. For some patients a significant loss of self- and body image includes the loss of, or limitation of, sexual functions. The importance of this for patient and partner should not be underestimated (see *sexual difficulties*).

4. The final stage of re-engagement with 'normal life' is again a gradual process, first focused on little excursions or walks from home, then social visiting and finally back to work. Confidence may be very fragile at this time with many patients exhibiting irritability. This is a time for encouragement but also acceptance of the cost to the patient, in terms of mental, physical and spiritual tiredness. It is important to encourage the fullest possible return to normality. For a significant number this means to a full life.

(e)   There are literally hundreds of support groups and agencies available. Wards dealing with particular forms of surgery usually have a list of contacts for such groups. Most county councils, or councils for voluntary organizations, produce a comprehensive list of groups within their own area.

(g)   Speck. P. (1978) *Loss and Grief in Medicine*. London: Baillière Tindall; Stoter, D. J. (1995) *Spiritual Aspects of Health Care*. London: Mosby.

DAVID STOTER
    (See also *cancer; hospital visiting; loss; terminal illness*)

Redundancy and unemployment

(a)   Redundancy and unemployment are difficult to define because there are differences between being made redundant and feeling redundant and being unemployed and feeling unemployed.

Being made redundant normally means having had a job and then the job or position ceases so the individual becomes unemployed. There are also people who apply for voluntary redundancy, and who may or may not get or look for another job. They too can be classed as redundant although some might be reasonably satisfied, especially if they are given a pension or gratuity. However, being made redundant is not necessarily the same as feeling redundant. Some who volunteer for redundancy discover that they develop strong feelings which are difficult to cope with and which adversely affect their lives and relationships. Even those who are re-employed can still speak of having been made redundant and feel redundant, especially if their next job is not what they really want. Others feel redundant when the state or position they occupy, not necessarily in paid employment, ceases. Some women feel redundant if they never marry or cannot have children, after a hysterectomy, when the children have left home or during the **menopause**. Men can feel redundant after a vasectomy or following the birth of a baby into the family. Some may feel redundant after losing a limb or their sight, speech or hearing. People retiring or in **old age** may feel redundant when they realize that their mental and physical faculties are decreasing.

Being unemployed means either having had a job and losing it, for whatever reason, or never having had one. Someone who does not want a job may still consider themselves unemployed, although they might not have registered as such or qualify for unemployment benefit, or are not seen as 'job seekers' by those in authority. There can be differences between official definitions of unemployment and the experience of losing a job and wanting to work, and feeling or thinking that you are unemployed. A woman looking after a home, children and partner can feel unemployed. She may be a qualified teacher or nurse or just want to work outside the home, but be unable to do so. A self-employed person who has not enough or any work coming in may feel unemployed. Statistics do not take these factors into account. We are dealing with perceptions and feelings in a society where the expectation is that everyone who can, should work. It seems easier to say 'I have been made redundant' rather than 'I am unemployed'. People are more likely to be offered sympathy in the former than the latter case. It is seen as misfortune or bad luck to be made redundant, but saying you are unemployed seems to give you a lower status. 'You must be lazy and it is your own fault. You haven't looked hard enough. You must be unemployable.' Such attitudes can be associated with a person's perceived position in society. If you have long hair, are poorly dressed and unemployed, you may be thought of as a parasite and 'waster'. If you live in a 'respectable' area, are smart and wear a suit, others are more likely to feel sorry for you. Some professionals and others use the term 'resting' or 'between jobs'. Attitudes can also be influenced by numbers. A few people unemployed or redundant may seem acceptable. When there are millions, it must be somebody's fault, and the fear of losing your own job can make you defensive and unsympathetic. In looking at what is meant by unemployment and redundancy we are dealing with real people and their situations, reactions, attitudes, feelings and emotions rather than definitions.

(b)   Being made redundant and being unemployed are often traumatic and reactions can be typical of **loss**, **stress** and trauma. There is a loss of status and security because regular employment gives a person an established and acceptable role, place and value in society. It can lead to the loss of a sense of worth and self-esteem. Work gives meaning and purpose to life as well as an income and should produce feelings of being appreciated and useful. Often work is closely tied to a person's self-image and public image. Work is sometimes not just a means of earning money but an integral part of a person's life and identity. Some see work as a life-time commitment in a 'service' or 'vocation'. When redundancy or unemployment comes there can be a loss of stability and feelings of uncertainty and anxiety. It can mean not only the loss of a job and lower income, but also of a home and relationships, friends and family. Children are also affected for they may have to move schools, change houses and lose friends. They can experience the same reactions as adults, but are unable to verbalize them as well and might only show them through behaviour. Children may even blame themselves for what has happened. The loss of income results in further insecurity and can produce poverty and dependence. There can be much wider effects. When a coal mine or factory closes it can affect and destroy not only individuals and their families, but whole communities. Shock, and the belief that it cannot have happened, causes some to close their minds and ears to the inevitable. Feelings of unreality result: 'They can't get rid of me, surely?' or 'I'll find a job soon'. Some are upset and feel sad and numb while others feel they are not wanted. Some become anxious and feel vulnerable and victimized and develop sensitivity to criticism or to pressure from other people. They may also have difficulty in making decisions.

There can be anger: at those who are considered responsible; at those who are not redundant or unemployed; at self; and at the world in general. It can also be directed at carers and helpers. There can be feelings of **guilt** and self-blame and of having failed self or one's family. Some feel regret about the past, and anxiety about both the present and future. Some act impulsively or become irritable and are unable to concentrate. There may be sleep disturbance and dreams or night-mares. Some withdraw from families and friends and cannot feel or show love or affection. There can be feelings of rejection – 'I am not wanted and have been pushed aside'. Some may experience a great sense of relief, especially after periods of uncertainty, and may even feel a new sense of purpose. Others will be devastated and some may commit or attempt **suicide**.

Depression is also common. Applying for a number of jobs, often receiving no reply, being unsuccessful or not even interviewed can be extremely depressing. Many lose the will to carry on applying. Some console themselves by thinking that they have not been made redun-dant – the job has. Sometimes, organizations run courses for those made redundant and they may be told not to take it personally. However, it is often impossible to separate an individual from their work. Often the feeling is 'The job has gone and so have I'. Some may cry when they are given the news about redundancy, and others may cry later. Crying and despair may also be reactions of the unemployed and redundant at any stage. There may be feelings of helplessness, loneliness, isolation and pointlessness and some experience a loss of identity and believe that life is totally unfair and unjust. Some lose acquired skills or expertise, and some change their faith, beliefs or political outlook. Others find that their self-image has altered and they may reject their families and friends and seek a new life and different relationships. There may be physical reactions with non-specific illnesses, headaches, stomach pains, tightness in the chest and reliance on alcohol, tobacco or drugs (see *alcoholism; substance misuse*). Unfortunately, there can be the expectation that any feelings generated will soon go away and, as in bereavement, that 'you'll soon get over it'.

Hopefully, the outcome of grieving is acceptance and healing, but this is not always the case. This is also true of the redundant and unemployed who may move into a kind of limbo, existing in a world where it seems that nobody cares and nothing matters. There is no hope and no purpose. Some eventually give up hope of finding work and, in order to cope, evolve a way of life which is not acceptable to others. Some develop a false sense of self-confidence in their own abilities which may temporarily boost their morale. Once the state makes decisions about what support they should or should not receive, this also influences how they react, cope and survive.

(c)   The causes of unemployment and redundancy are complicated, because there are external as well as personal factors involved. Having a job is considered to be the 'norm' in a society with the legacy of the 'Protestant work ethic', where it is believed that an individual earns a place in society through work. People go to school, move into a job and contribute towards their own welfare and the welfare of others. However, some people leaving school now might never work even if they want to. There might not be any jobs available. Deliberate government and economic policies may keep some people unemployed, but those affected may still think of themselves as being disadvantaged especially if they receive low allowances and status. Some become disillusioned and stop looking for work and some might decide not to work even if jobs are available. Other practical causes can be various: someone has a job and leaves, or leaves because the employer can no longer afford them, or the business ceases, or they have made a mistake and are dismissed; some voluntarily apply for redundancy or early retirement; some are considered unemployable because of lack of skills, education or mental or physical ability; others are unable to find a job because of pregnancy or because of looking after a home or children or a sick, elderly or handicapped person. Some may decide to stay unemployed because their allowances are more than they would receive if they worked. More personal problems such as **depression**, anxiety (see *phobias and anxiety*) and **stress** may also cause unemployment. Conditions such as agoraphobia, claustrophobia, compulsive and **obsessive disorders** and other psychological conditions may also result in redundancy or unemployment. Under present rules, those who are sick and off work, for whatever medical reasons, are under threat of unemployment or dismissal and may become unemployed for being non-productive.

(d) In order to help, carers should view the experience of being made redundant or unemployed as similar to that of **bereavement** because many of the reactions are the same as those of grief and **loss**. Helping strategies are largely based on the bereavement counselling model of coping with the reactions of shock, anger and depression mentioned in section (b) above. The carer can offer support through giving information, practical help and advice, through helping them to accept what has happened, by encouraging people to talk and express feelings and by helping them to look to the future. They should be encouraged to work through the experiences and emotions generated by the shock, anger and depression and not avoid them. Sympathy in the form of 'I'm sorry' may be seen as patronizing and will sometimes result in rejection or scorn. People need to feel that someone cares and is trying to understand and help. The carer should move beyond sympathy to offer deeper empathy by trying to know how they feel deep inside. Support can take the form of **careers guidance** and encouraging self-appraisal or through suggestions about re-training and adjusting and of looking at possible new areas of work. People should be encouraged to go to the various government agencies set up to help them to find out what entitlements and benefits they are allowed. They may need advice about finance, either because they have very little money or because they have a pension or gratuity. They might even need help or advice about investments and pension plans (see *money advice*).

Carers can suggest various strategies which might help. These are often outlined in official leaflets and booklets.

1. Face the fact of your situation. Denial – 'It hasn't happened' – can be a powerful reaction; accepting the reality of what has happened and knowing how you and others might react can be helpful. Here the intention is to encourage acceptance, but not a surrender to despair.

2. Be aware of how this might affect health and relationships with families and friends and allow expression of your emotions. Talk to someone about how you feel.
3. Seek emotional, physical and personal support, especially from families and friends.
4. Make a plan about applying for work and keep records. If possible, have a set time and place for doing this.
5. Do not stay in bed in the morning but live as though you are still working. Do not change your personal standards of hygiene or dress.
6. If possible, learn new skills and maintain present ones.
7. Look for voluntary work.
8. Join a local **self-help group**.
9. Take regular exercise and meals.
10. Discover what local resources are available for help and advice and use them.

(e)   The Jobcentre is the first place to start when looking for a job or for advice, but there is also the Employment Service office, the careers office and the Social Security Department. The Employment Service offers 'Job Search Seminars' which give advice about interview techniques, 'Job Review Workshops' which look at possible career changes, 'Restart Programmes' and 'Restart Courses' offering information, 'Jobclubs' encouraging positive thinking, 'Job Interview Guarantees' ensuring interviews are offered, 'Work and Employment Trials' testing suitability for a particular job and 'Training for Work' offering job experience. For the long-term unemployed there are 'Job Plan Workshops' and 'Community Action Initiatives'. Help and advice can also be obtained from Training Access Points (TAPs) – databases found in libraries and Jobcentres. These give information about training and education. Advice and assistance may also be available from Training Enterprise Councils (TECs), the Citizens Advice Bureaux and, for the disabled, from Placing, Assessment and Counselling Teams (PACTs). These encourage people to look for work although they tend to assume that jobs are available. Obviously these initiatives and resources may change according to government and agency policies.

Because the experiences of redundancy and unemployment are traumatic and affect individuals and families as well, the services of particular agencies or groups may be required. Some problems need careful **counselling**, and referral and co-operation between clients, carers and agencies may result in difficulties over **confidentiality**. Specialist help may be available for there can be: chronic **depression** and other illnesses; personal and marital breakdown; **child abuse**;

violence; financial problems (see *money advice*) and poverty; **home-lessness**; crime; **substance misuse**, especially drugs; **alcoholism**; **phobias and anxiety; suicide and attempted suicide**. Carers and helpers should be aware of local, national and specialist agencies offering counselling, help and advice such as Relate, Cruse, the Samaritans, Victim Support, Age Concern, Alcoholics Anonymous, local drugs councils and support agencies, Community Service Volunteers, the National Council for Voluntary Organizations and many other charities and groups. The local Citizens Advice Bureaux can provide information about what is available. Medical and psychological help from GPs, hospitals and clinics may also be necessary. (See also: Bainham and Cox, 1992; Bainton and Crowley, 1992; Corfield, 1993; Doherty and Tyson, 1993; Jackson, 1994).

(f) Because of the possible defences used, the reactions of those involved and the problems which can result, carers should be pro-active in offering help. Some may be experiencing shock or feel angry and embarrassed and will decline any offers of help. Where possible, carers and helpers should work with families and family groups as well as with individuals. The individual might be made redundant or unemployed, but it is the family which may also suffer and has to cope with the distress, anger and depression often generated in the parent, son or daughter (see *families, working with*).

The strategies for helping, outlined above, may seem helpful, but there might not be any jobs available and, consequently, may result in feelings of helplessness and impotence for both clients and helpers. Staff in Jobcentres and carers are usually in paid employment, and this can result in deeper feelings of rejection, anger and resentment in and from the unemployed. It can also produce feelings of guilt, frustration and anger in helpers. Carers will need to try to maintain confidence and self-esteem, not only in clients, but also in themselves. Also, policies and benefits often tend not to confirm a worthwhile status for the unemployed and this can exacerbate symptoms and reactions. Helpers and carers can be seen as representatives of a corrupt and oppressive society who are attempting to keep the unemployed happy and content. They offer strategies, advice and information which can be viewed as nothing more than 'sops' in a society where there is no work and no hope. Consequently, some unemployed may become vagrants, 'bag-ladies' or dwellers in 'cardboard cities' or 'squats' and some turn to crime or drugs. Some leave home in despair and may become 'New Age travellers' (see *homelessness*). Any of these can be the result of a desire to rebel against the conventions of a society which they believe has rejected them and purposely kept them unemployed. However, such reactions can be positive and may help people to survive and, to some extent, maintain their self-esteem and dignity.

Working with the unemployed and redundant can be extremely distressing and stressful and produce some of the same symptoms in carers as experienced by those amongst whom they work. Carers should be aware of their own need for help and support, especially through regular contacts with colleagues and the helping agencies and through personal **supervision**. Carers need to take care of themselves.

(g)　Allen, S. (1986) *The Experience of Unemployment*. London: Macmillan; Bolles, R. N. (1993) *What Colour Is Your Parachute?* Berkeley, CA: Ten Speed Press; publications from the Department of Social Security, Employment Service Benefits Agency.

FRANK PARKINSON
　　(See also *careers guidance*)

Religious belief

(a)　Religion has been defined as

> recognition on the part of man of some higher power as having control of his destiny, and as being entitled to obedience, reverence and worship; the general mental and moral attitude resulting from this belief, with reference to its effect upon the individual or the community. (Oxford English Dictionary)

This already wide definition has been enlarged by those who study the phenomenon of faith. 'Religion' is thought by some to mean 'that which binds'. There are other belief systems that do not have to include 'some higher power' for them to be binding. The belief system itself becomes a higher power' which to a greater or lesser degree 'dictates' how a person thinks and behaves. Thus a belief system has also been described as 'people's orientation to the ultimate environment in terms of what they value as being most relevant and important to their entire lives' (Kohlberg, 1981: 323). Faith need not include belief in a God. Some Eastern religions clearly do not have such a clear-cut concept; and there are people within traditional theistic religions whose more radical faith questions the existence of a supernatural being. These, and many others who apparently do not profess conventional religious faith, nevertheless have beliefs by which they live, which similarly to a greater or lesser degree (both consciously and unconsciously) 'bind' them, as religion does, to particular ways of being, thinking, feeling and acting. Freud recognized that certain psychological states do the same (1907). In this article, although religious belief provides the main illustrations, such a wider view of a person's faith (whether in a religion, a political ideology, ethical codes or even core intellectual tenets) is also relevant. Some studies appear to show a common pattern of development and similar difficulties in any system of belief.

(b)   There are probably few people who directly present difficulties about belief itself, although loss of meaning and questions about their life's purpose can emerge in the course of helping. Questions about the content of a set of beliefs are more commonly presented to clergy or leaders of religious groups, through 'factual' questions such as: 'What is the teaching on . . . ?'; 'Am I permitted to . . . ?'; 'How do you reconcile . . . ?' Such questions may hide moral or faith dilemmas of a deeper nature, as someone struggles to reconcile what he or she has been taught, or has always believed, with new experiences (often a personal or family crisis); or there are new ideas that challenge old patterns of belief. Because in many religious circles it is felt 'unfaithful' to question the roots of a belief system, such as the existence of God, it is rare for faith to be presented except as an intellectual issue. Yet real loss of faith can be accompanied by crushing **guilt** at no longer holding what you have been told you should believe. It is also difficult to tell someone else within the faith that you no longer believe – it is like a divorce. Loss of belief (whether in a religious object or any other ideology) can be devastating, like any other **bereavement**; and yet the person feels responsible for the **loss**, so these are matters that are not readily shared. It may also be thought that those who do not share a belief cannot understand why losing a faith is so difficult to bear.

In fact 'loss of faith' is a misnomer. A person may be losing one type of faith, but is in the process of replacing it with another. As in all transitions, this intermediate space is filled with anxiety and insecurity, even if in the end a faith that is more open to doubt and questioning can prove a relief. Since changes of belief and loss of particular types of faith often accompany other life changes this is an area that is worth listening out for in any helping context.

There are other difficulties about religious belief, although they are similarly seldom presented as the obvious issue. Some people express a particular kind of faith through highly obsessional, ritualistic acts (see *obsessive compulsive behaviour*). They have to perform certain religious rituals, or ensure that they are performed correctly; they must be unfailing in their attendance at public service; in their private devotions they must say certain prayers or read a certain portion of their holy book, often at set times; they have a predilection to confess minor 'sins' that constantly beset them (see *forgiveness*). Since such people

often experience great **guilt** should they fail to perform these obser-
vances, or great anxiety should another fail to perform them correctly,
they are likely to present more with the consequences of such failures
than with any questioning of the validity of their actual beliefs and
behaviour. It can be very difficult to get them to question their beliefs,
and often impossible to change their obsessive behaviour, since both
normally serve to keep them free from anxiety and guilt. Only when
such defences break down might it be possible to offer help.

Another common disturbance is **fanaticism**, an intense and extreme
belief that seeks to convert and control others. This again is one which
such believers seldom themselves experience as a problem. It is generally third parties (including sometimes their families) who suffer. It
may take a religious form, or may be an equally intense political
ideology, sometimes reflected in **racism and other prejudice**.

To a lesser extent all belief systems, because they seem to serve such
a central psychological purpose, are difficult to adapt and re-think. Any
questioning of core ideas or habitual behaviour is seen as an attack. In
the case of belief systems such challenges, even when they are
expressed in a mild way, appear to threaten not only the individual as
such (although this is obviously where it really pinches) but also the
object of the individual's devotion. Deeply held beliefs are perhaps the
most heavily invested 'objects' in a person's life. They may even die for
them, however mistaken others think they are.

(c)   To suggest reasons or causes for belief (religious or any other) may
seem presumptuous. For many who have a particular belief their faith
is self-explanatory and circular. It does not have to be justified. 'The
Lord wants me to do this . . . '; 'It tells me in the Bible'. Those who look
deeper into their faith may suggest that believing is an innate tendency
in human beings (which it may be), and that seeking the spiritual is as
much part of being human as seeking food or shelter, and as much a
driving force as genetic reproduction. Jung (1961), for example, sees the
spiritual dimension (see *spiritual direction*) as one of the mainsprings of
existence, as distinct from Freud's stress on the sexual drive. Transpersonal psychology accords an equal standing to the 'Spirit' as part of
both the human and the universal psyche.

Others suggest, especially when looking at its extremes, that religious belief and behaviour are essentially defensive. Freud views
religious beliefs as 'illusions, fulfilments of the oldest, strongest and
most urgent wishes of mankind' (1927). Others are less negative.
Winnicott, for example, believes (and such a word justifies significance
of a broader interpretation of belief) that

> the individual . . . can enjoy in the exercise of religion or the practice
> and appreciation of the arts the rest that human beings need from

absolute and never-failing discrimination between fact and fantasy.
(1988: 107)

Few would seriously question the accuracy of Freud's analysis that religious belief contains much projection in it (that is, people's views of God, for example, reflect their views of significant others or parts of themselves, or their wishes for an idealized parent). Another researcher affirms the hypothesis, yet broadens it: 'Projection is not pathological, but normal. Everyone projects, always and necessarily' (van Belzen, 1992).

People can employ religious belief as a defence – against anxiety, guilt and insecurity, against fears of human closeness and vulnerability, and as ways of coping with extreme **pain** and other overwhelming situations. Defences serve a valuable purpose. It is axiomatic that defences should not be dismantled until a person is ready to face that which they have previously been avoiding. It is normally pointless to try to change a *belief* (except through equally undesirable 'brainwashing' techniques), although it may be necessary to try and change *behaviour* if a person is damaging either themselves or others by their attitudes or actions. Beliefs as such, as long as they remain within the head and heart, are normally harmless enough – it is when they are acted out that they assume different dimensions. Intolerance is not confined to the religious.

(d) A helpful model when working with problems about belief is that of faith development – a relatively new area of study, which provides some convincing descriptions of the variety of expressions of belief and types of faith. It owes much to the work of J. W. Fowler (1981), whose model combines Erikson's analysis of psycho-social stages, Kolhberg's study of moral thinking and Piaget's model of cognitive development. While there is room for criticism – particularly the linear pattern or life 'stages' which such models describe – the typology is helpful. It is possible to trace a person's belief system as 'progressing' from one stage to another. Such development is a result of both natural growth (particularly in childhood), and of other circumstances, external and internal, in adult life.

Helpers cannot force progression but can encourage the *idea* of movement and change to become common currency in religious and faith circles, in contradistinction to much religious belief that appeals because it is seen as essentially unchanging, and therefore stable and reliable in an otherwise vulnerable human existence. It is also important to recognize that while faith development can be progressive, it moves at different times and at different speeds in relation to different ideas in a person's belief system. In other words, people can be much more free in their beliefs about certain areas of life than others, and more at ease with questioning some articles of faith than others. Under stress anything can happen!

Fowler's stages of faith start with primal faith – the symbiotic relationship between mother and baby that lays down the basis of all trust and faith in later life. If the relationship is poor or virtually non-existent this may give rise to an inverted faith – the belief that you cannot trust anyone or anything. The stages that follow pass through 'the blooming, buzzing confusion' of infancy where fantasy and illusion abound, to childhood beliefs around stories, myths, images and symbols, gradually consolidating into more sustained stories. They help children make sense of experience, but without anxious questioning or self-consciousness. This can be called 'simple faith', accepting things at face value, often in a very trusting way, although on occasion full of primitive dread. There are also adults who have this type of belief, which (when positive) often serves them very well.

Just as children's questions become more complicated, and they seek answers and authorities, so much religious faith (and other forms of belief) moves in this direction. Particular sources of authority are looked to as providing rules and interpretations of rules, dogmatic teaching and creeds, together with explanations – often of the contra-dictions – of religious beliefs. Assuming a progressive model, this stage of faith provides much of the 'raw material' which people need in order to begin to develop a more personal faith for themselves. It is important for communicating the conventions and traditions of the culture and the community in which a person lives. But it is also a stage of belief that can turn into conformity, sometimes backed up by guilt-inducing threats to those who challenge the community in their thinking, or in behaviour which 'breaks' the rules.

Even without such threats, it is sometimes necessary, if people are to question more deeply, for them to break away from any group to which they have been attached. It is often a personal crisis that triggers questions which traditional belief systems fail to answer. The centre no longer holds. Some throw everything out at this point, to their great relief. Others find themselves at a complete loss. For those who find freedom within a new belief system, there is always the risk of the new set of beliefs in turn becoming a conventional set of ideas. This is perhaps the most fluid stage of belief, one where the helper is most welcome, especially to those who feel either guilty or bereft (or both) in thinking they have no faith. For them to know that this is part of a developmental sequence can be very reassuring. Nevertheless, the linear model of development is not the only perspective, since many people do not reach this stage, and there is no reason to think of them as being necessarily disadvantaged.

Those who move beyond this stage of isolation, and do not return to the necessity of a precise belief system, can find themselves able to combine the child-like pleasure in symbols, images, stories and myths with the ideas and traditions of their own and other communities, providing a rich treasury of thought and belief. In this 'stage' beliefs are never so firmly fixed that they become obsessionally held. Doubt holds the promise of new insights. Those who differ from oneself provide enriching perspectives – it is more than tolerance; rather it is learning from difference. Fowler suggests that such a stage of faith also embraces unconscious as well as conscious. In fact he proposes a seventh stage, which includes self-sacrifice for the universal principles, but others see this as an extension of this 'conjunctive' stage – where many previously disparate strands are woven together.

To those who are deep into the conventional stage of belief, these further stages are an aberration rather than a progression. The problem with faith development models is that they are only relevant to those who have moved beyond either unquestioning faith on the one hand, or conventional faith on the other. While it provides a useful tool for those who work with people at different points of their belief, it may be particularly helpful at points of transition: for example, for those moving from 'simple' faith into preliminary questioning (the point at which some dogmatic belief systems 'pounce'); or for those who have begun to see through their (sometimes self-imposed) slavery to authority and dogma; or for those who have tired of reductionism (which can become equally dogmatic) and individualism, and may be encouraged to dip into the mine of wisdom and creativity that is to be found in other faiths, in art, in music, in the unconscious and in dialogue with others.

(e) While there is clearly expertise available in matters of belief amongst those who are the leaders of faith communities, it has to be said that the position they may adopt varies as much as it might in those whom they lead. Since they are trained to fulfil a faith-leadership role one can assume they fall into one of two 'stages' of faith: there are those who see their task as guardians and interpreters, providing answers to those who question, and likely to defend their faith against anything that might undermine traditional beliefs and values. They sometimes suggest that doubt, for example, is part of faith, but in practice regard it as a temporary going into shadow before moving back into the true light. There are other religious guides who have no particular axe to grind: they seek only to assist the individual find her or his own path. They do not impose standard beliefs and values, although they may point to some of the rich resources that can inform and enlighten. It is my assumption that those who are looking for clear answers and a definitive faith will have little difficulty in finding what they seek – they will need no assistance from the helper, even if the helper were willing to make such a referral. What is more difficult is to find the religious leader or the faith community that is open to debate and doubt at a profound level.

It is impossible to provide a list of resources that will suit each individual presenting issue in this area. In some cases counselling or psychotherapy may be used for other difficulties, in the course of which questions of belief may arise. In other cases there may be alternative or more radical religious groups for those who seek a particular way. Sometimes a period 'in the wilderness' is essential for the development of a more personal faith. Some churches or other traditional religious communities will be just right: safe and stable but not oppressive.

(f) Religious belief is often a problem area for helpers. Perhaps because of their own bias, sometimes based on experience of conventional belief systems and communities, they think this is an area they should avoid. They are afraid of getting into a debate they do not understand, or fear that they will cause offence by questioning what a person believes. Other helpers, particularly those who are part of a religious community, or who are approached because they are known to have such connections, assume that religion is not an issue, or only to be answered in religious way. It is confusing when some people ask their helper to refer them to a 'Christian (or other) counsellor'. They may be afraid that a secular counsellor will undermine their beliefs, or they want a Christian who will understand their faith. The danger is that either will collude with such defensiveness, by disregarding beliefs as a contributory factor to, or as an expression of, other difficulties.

Helpers need to be open to different forms of belief, and where possible have some understanding of faith stages. Whether they hold a religious belief or not, it might be helpful to refer to a person's faith as 'You believe that ... ' or 'Your God is ... ', neither owning nor disowning the client's view as the correct one. Introduction of the idea that beliefs can change may also be useful in any set of issues where religion plays a part.

(g) Cracknell, K. (1986) *Towards a New Relationship*. Manchester: Epworth; Fowler, J. W. (1981) *Stages of Faith: The Psychology of Human Development and the Quest for Meaning*. San Francisco: Harper and Row; Jacobs, M. (1993) *Living Illusions: A Psychology of Belief*. London: SPCK.

MICHAEL JACOBS
(See also *faith differences; fanaticism*)

Self-help groups

(a) The basic idea behind a self-help group is very simple: that individuals come together to pool resources and to solve common problems to their mutual benefit. It is one of the basic organizing principles of human community (see *community politics*): the trades unions on the one hand and insurance companies on the other had their origins in such small groups; and local government itself has been described as 'the first-line defence thrown up by the community against our common enemies – poverty, sickness, ignorance, isolation, mental derangement and social maladjustment' (Holtby, 1954). Self-help is not new.

However, in the 1970s many came to see institutions such as local government, and the so-called 'helping professions' which had begun to proliferate, as part of the *problem* rather than part of the *solution*, in dealing with these 'common enemies'. Vulnerable people often experienced professionals as remote, bureaucratic and authoritarian, pushing their own agendas. People formed self-help groups as a way of empowering themselves, and of defining their own needs and getting them met, often within a vision of a transformed, less individualistic society. 'This corporate action is based on recognition of a fundamental truth about human nature – we are not only single individuals, each face to face with eternity and our own separate spirits; we are members one of another' (Holtby, 1954).

In a self-help group, we jointly create something that helps us all. It is about creating a 'wider we'. Mutual aid is the opposite to my helping myself at your expense.

(b) A full picture of self-help groups today is woven of many strands. One strand is the many and various dissenting political groups who have strongly embraced self-help and mutual aid as principles, and made small leaderless groups a part of various conscious strategies against oppression, e.g. feminism's consciousness-raising groups or the peace movement's 'affinity groups'. Such groups have an ideological function: they demonstrate alternative, more egalitarian models of organization. They also provide moral and emotional support to activists. Another strand is the development of self-help groups to provide services for those who would not otherwise have access to them, or to provide a different kind of service to the official ones; e.g. the 'Saturday schools' set up by black parents to teach their children subjects that were not taught at all in state schools, such as black history, or subjects that were not well taught to black children, such as maths. Other groups of parents have set up 'free schools', such as those which flourished in Liverpool, London and Manchester in the 1970s; or 'Education Otherwise', to support parents in educating their children without schools at all. In the field of housing, groups of homeless people have collectively squatted blocks of flats or derelict pieces of land, often in the process providing community services, such as music festivals, wholefood cafés or community gardens. In the field of finance, there is the well-established Afro-Caribbean tradition of credit unions, to provide credit to those to whom banks deny it. Another example is the local food co-op where bulk buying enables food to be distributed more cheaply round a neighbourhood. In such examples the focus has been more practical than ideological. There is a need – for housing, education, credit or cheap food – which is ignored by the established providers. People have organized together to provide for their needs and to meet them in their own way, on their own terms.

Yet another strand is the plethora of self-help groups in the field of health. Some organize around an issue, such as birth; others take as their focus a specific medical condition, such as multiple sclerosis or **AIDS/HIV**. These groups vary widely: some see their main aim as providing and/or facilitating the sharing of information, and practical, emotional and moral support for sufferers and their families. Others aim to raise funds to improve research and equipment for treatment. Some campaign for changes in medical practice, such as for active birth or for more hospices. Some groups are loosely structured support networks; others are formally constituted societies with elected officers. Some are registered as charities. Their common focus is a basic need shared by all those affected by the particular condition, their families and carers: to meet with others in the same position, and to share resources for their mutual benefit.

A similar need brings others to self-help groups such as Unemployed Workers' Unions, Women Who Love Too Much or Alcoholics Anonymous groups, seeking support through specific difficulties. They may be structured around a particular pattern of activities for each session. They may or may not have a formal leader or facilitator, or enjoy the support of a national organization.

There is also the increasing application of self-help principles to rites of passage: 'do-it-ourselves' ceremonies for 'handfastings' or 'weddings' (legal, heterosexual and otherwise), naming ceremonies for babies, menarche rituals and **funerals** (Spottiswoode, 1991). This is not an exhaustive list – I merely give an impression of the vast range of activities that can be covered by the title.

(c) People usually form self-help groups to bring about change, and to meet needs not being met elsewhere. They may feel some anger towards professionals, whom they perceive as having failed them; or they may be indifferent to or ignorant of the existence of the relevant professionals. By the same token, the professionals may see the setting up of a self-help group as a challenge to their power or a criticism of their practice. There can be real power issues between the professionals and the 'volunteers' over access to decision-making, money and other resources. Such issues are more sharply felt where the two groups are also divided by differences of gender, class, race or physical ability.

But relations between these two sets of people, professionals and members of self-help groups, do not have to be hostile. There are many examples of good partnerships where both sides have benefited; for example the Mary Ward Centre in Central London has long promoted self-help groups as part of its work in adult education; the London Borough of Haringey employs an officer to promote and support credit unions; ICARE, an Islington-based centre for people affected by the HIV virus, works closely with a self-help group of African men, women and children with AIDS.

(d)   The best way to illustrate some issues about self-help groups is to describe some of my own experience. I have been a member of various self-help groups, mainly in the context of feminism and left-wing politics. My core training in counselling was on a self-directed course; and before I embarked on that I was in a women's self-help therapy group for six years. I spent ten years supporting self-help therapy groups in the London area under the auspices of the Women's Therapy Centre. I am currently in four self-help groups, two of them for women, two mixed: a writing group; a spiritual group; a Domestic Theatre group, and the Woodcraft Folk. The women's self-help therapy group and the Woodcraft Folk illustrate contrasting experiences of how such groups might function (see *groups, use of*).

The self-help therapy group started in 1980. It grew out of an eight-week workshop at the Women's Therapy Centre called 'Gestalt for Women', led by a therapist. It settled down to a core of five members and ran for six years in total, with fluctuating membership: only three were in the group from beginning to end, although about ten women were members at one time or another. Most stayed for at least a year.

My motivation in suggesting the formation of the group was partly distrust of the ability of professionals to meet my needs, partly excitement and the desire to create something new. My distrust was based on bad experiences with personal and institutional father-figures, and a deep alienation from patriarchal capitalist society. I had been influenced by authors such as Illich (1971) with his general critique of professionalism, as well as by feminist writers such as Chessler (1973), Daly (1979), Millett (1979) and Morgan (1974). I had had experience of working collectively in editing journals, and had been excited and inspired by the pamphlet produced by the Red Therapy collective about their development of a model of therapy congruent with left-wing political values.

Although most of our group did not share my political beliefs or reading habits, we were wary of most professionals in the field of women's mental health. We felt vulnerable and in need of help in dealing with our inner worlds, but did not wish to entrust ourselves to anyone who might try and impose on us views of how 'proper' women ought to behave and feel. Two of our number had had abusive sexual relationships with male psychoanalysts, although this took a long time to emerge. We also shared the excitement of creating something new: a new kind of group experience, a new way of relating to other women, a new way of doing therapy.

There were other important advantages in the self-help model. It was cheap – where there are no 'experts', there are no fees. It was flexible – not tied to any one school of thought or practice, but seeing all schools as offering both advantages and disadvantages for women. And it was fun! There was a large element of play, especially in the way we used psychodrama and gestalt.

Most importantly such a group was empowering – we claimed 'We are our own experts', and based our work on trust in ourselves, our own bodies and our own experience. We went at our own pace. Each was recognized as the ultimate authority on her own experience; others offered supportive feedback, but no interpretations. In this we could be said to be embodying Rogers' 'self-actualising tendency' (Rogers, 1961). We put into practice that basic tenet of humanistic psychology, 'each one of us is a centre of awareness and power'.

It was not all fun, nurture and play. Conflicts arose, and we learned how to resolve them, often surprising ourselves in the process. (For a full discussion of the processes of development in a self-help therapy group, see the article by Chaplin and Noack in *In Our Experience*, listed in (g).)

A major factor in the success of our group was our relationship with the Women's Therapy Centre (WTC), which acted throughout as a support and a resource, promoting and encouraging but always in the background. Their workshop programme had links to self-help groups: several of the first workshop leaders had been members of the original Red Therapy group. The Centre's ground-breaking work on compulsive eating included setting up self-help groups, especially in conjunction with the theatre group Spare Tyre (Chapman, 1987; Noble, 1987). There were workshops specifically designed to help women set up self-help groups and keep them going.

It was very important when we started to know that the Centre was there, and that we could call in workshop leaders to run sessions for us if we needed them. In the event we did this only once, to teach us some skills in working with dreams. It was more important to us that group members could attend workshops at the WTC to learn new skills, which they then brought back into the group to share with the rest of us. This was particularly helpful in reconciling our need to rotate the role of leader with the fact that some of us had more experience and skills than others.

Being in the self-help group was life-changing. I eventually came to co-ordinate groups and run workshops on the topic at the Centre – it was my way into my current work. Other transformations made by members since the group include moving out of London and writing a novel, giving up social work in favour of practising Shiatsu, ending an abusive relationship and seeking healing for the abuse, and studying successfully for an MA. One of the group died: at her request I conducted her funeral.

I have had a less helpful experience in my local group of the Woodcraft Folk. This is a long-established national youth organization, with strong links to the Co-operative Movement. Its aims are to promote peace and co-operation in the world, and among its members. Meetings and activities for the children are run by the parents on a rota system. Local groups are managed by parents who are exhorted to 'form a strong collective'. Such features make it a type of self-help group.

In a particular period of three years in which my daughter and I belonged to a local group, my perception is that the group was in crisis. Its activities bore very little relation to the stated aims of the organization: the adults had not formed a 'strong collective'. None of us had experience of the Woodcraft Folk as children: we differed in our approaches to organizing activities, in our experiences of working collectively and in our understanding of what it means to run a group containing both girls and boys, committed to equality and co-operation. We varied widely in our incomes, and several of us were parenting alone: we differed in the resources we brought to the group. Yet these issues were never discussed.

The result was a small group of busy mothers doing most of the holding-together; children often behaving badly, reflecting the unaddressed tensions between the adults; and the more vulnerable children – the youngest, weakest, smallest, shyest – having a bad time and eventually leaving. Activities were sometimes cancelled at short notice. Meetings were called and only a few turned up. These were all signs of crisis.

One factor in all this was the lack of any support. There was no 'good parent' in the background, to act as a resource in times of trouble. The national headquarters seemed to our group to be a bad parent, sending regular demands for money, and occasionally requesting participation in fund-raising or publicity activities for the national organization. It did not feel like a nurturing, encouraging, good parent.

Contrasting these two experiences, the relationship between self-help groups and the professionals is like that between young adults and their parents. Young adults need to leave home and may need to reject their parents' ways as part of this process. At the same time they lack experience and resources, and sometimes confidence that the wider world will welcome them and their gifts. In this situation parents need to be positive and encouraging about a young person's attempts to leave. They must be prepared to give their blessing to their children's independence. What is required is not just the letting go of control, but positive welcoming of a young person's increasing powers and possibilities: a recognition that: 'Your children are not your children. They are the sons and daughters of Life's longing for itself' (Gibran, 1980: 20).

In our self-help therapy group, we felt that we had that good, nurturing 'parent' in the background – the WTC. Beyond that was the wider movement for women's liberation of which the Centre was a part, and which provided inspiration for us all. We not only felt supported, but part of something bigger and creative – the 'wider we', 'life's longing for itself'.

The Woodcraft Folk group on the other hand appeared to have a very different 'parent' – hard-pressed, under-resourced and ageing, and therefore non-nurturing and demanding. The wider political currents – of socialism, peace, international co-operation and solidarity – which it needed to sustain it flowed weakly. The climate was more hostile to new growth and to good parenting.

(e)   There are so many self-help groups, and so many different kinds, that there is no one way to find one. There is no national organization or directory, although some local authorities publish local directories which include self-help groups of various kinds. If you would like to be a member of a self-help group of any kind, there are two possibilities: search all the local and national lines of communication you can think of; or start one yourself.

(f) Most self-help groups get along quite happily without any professional help at all. But if professionals are to be of any help to them, it is
important to recognize that:

1. The initiative must come from the group: this appears obvious,
    but is easily overlooked. The group must define what is needed,
    and control the formation of the relationship until trust has
    been built up. This sensitive process can easily be ruined by
    arrogance, lack of imagination or over-controlling attitudes.
2. Professionals control resources which self-help groups may
    need: money, premises, knowledge of how particular systems
    work (the NHS, benefits, housing departments) or access to
    decision-makers. The group may value these more highly than
    other knowledge or skills that the professionals may want to
    offer. Resources need to be shared in a spirit of solidarity and
    generosity.
3. A positive attitude towards self-help groups means willingness
    to share power, and to learn from them. Professionals may have
    to trust groups to manage things their own way, outside exist-
    ing structures, while at the same time demanding that the
    groups be accountable for any public money they receive. I have
    been told by experts that certain people are 'unsuitable' for a
    self-help group – women with bulimia, or incest survivors, or
    single parents. Yet I know such people who have gained from
    membership of a self-help group. Self-help challenges the boun-
    daries of what is possible.
4. Finally, what it is *not* about is letting the state off the hook over
    resources. Self-help has often been used as a pretext for cutting
    resources, and to cover under-funding. It can be appealing to be
    offered control of the budget of your local school – until you find
    that a group of untrained governors with jobs and other respon-
    sibilities are expected to do the work formerly done by full-time
    administrators. That is not self-help.

(g) Ernst, S. and Goodison, L. (1981) *In Our Own Hands*. London: The
Women's Press; Krzowski, S. and Land, P. (eds) (1988) *In Our Experience*. London: The Women's Press; Proctor, B. (1993) 'In the counsellor's chair', *Counselling* 4(4). Rugby: British Association for
Counselling.

PENNY CLOUTTE
(See also *community politics; groups, use of*)

Sexual deviation

(a)   If it is true, as Bancroft suggests, that deviance is behaviour 'that contravenes the norms of society' (1983: 177) then it should not be too difficult to formulate an agreed list of behaviours that fall into this category. The list would have to include the more serious deviations (so serious they are punishable offences) like paedophilia, rape and possibly incest. But what else would the list consist of? Presumably it could include such diversities as fetishism, sado-masochism, perhaps voyeurism. But should it include oral sex or masturbation?

The difficulty is that something like fetishism hardly contravenes the norms of society, for there are few men who are not moved by a glimpse of, say, high heels, black stockings or suspenders. If the preference is for a sexual object that is separate or incidental to the actual person, then it becomes a fetish; and such preferences abound, at least with men, in normal society.

Again, sado-masochism, at its extreme, involves cruelty which to most would be clearly unacceptable. Yet in its milder form, it describes the preference for being either dominant or submissive. There are few sexual relationships which have not, at least, some nuance of this kind of interplay. Similarly, though voyeurism at its worst can be an intolerable invasion of privacy, there are perhaps few who, given the opportunity, would resist taking a second look.

Is oral sex a deviation? Some include it and some do not. On the basis of the most recent and reliable survey (Wellings et al., 1994: 151) 55.6 per cent of men and 49.5 per cent of women have had some experience of oral sex in a twelve-month period. It is of course possible to regard behaviour as contravening the norms of society even if it is practised by the majority, but in doing so we would be getting close to the hypocrisy of which we widely accuse former generations.

We can only guess at the prevalence of masturbation. It is certainly an argument for its normality to consider that Bakwin (1973) observed masturbation, obviously to the point of orgasm, in children of both sexes, as young as six months. However, inhibition develops with age, as also eventually a loss of interest. For whatever reason, it would seem that 'wanking' is not the most talked-about subject for couples even before middle age. This reticence relates to its practice as well as to its choice as a conversation piece. The fact is that it is still taboo for many adults and resisted by those who see it as harmful or superfluous to an ongoing sexual relationship.

The norms of society are not easy to identify, especially in a pluralistic society of quite different if not opposing cultures and traditions. There is the added variable of fashion. What is acceptable today might not have been so yesterday, and might not be tomorrow. This might be determined by the fickle vagaries of human nature, or by more serious health concerns, such as the scare about the spread of HIV (see *AIDS/HIV*).

However we view sexual deviation, and whether we choose other terms like 'unusual sex' or 'paraphilias' or, more pejoratively, 'perversions', what is helpful in care and counselling is for the helper to have a recognition of her or his own sexual predilections, and to have assimilated them. Without this, they are defended against, and there is a greater chance of the client being experienced as threatening. When that happens, too great a distance may be maintained, which is less than helpful for the client who is concerned about such matters.

The following is a tentative list of some known sexual deviations:

Offending
  exhibitionism (indecent exposure)
  frottage (touching)
  incest
  necrophilia (sexual contact with a dead body)
  paedophilia and child abuse
  rape
  voyeurism
  zoophilia (sex with animals)

Non-offending
  anal intercourse
  asphyxophilia
  bondage
  coprophilia (sexual play with faeces or urine)
  CP (spanking rituals)
  fetishism
  putaphilia (sexual attraction to an amputee)
  sado-masochism
  transvestism/trans-sexualism
  voyeurism

(b)   When help is sought it is most often for one of three reasons: First and most commonly, it has become a problem because it is threatening a relationship. The deviant behaviour of one partner is not appreciated by the other. Sometimes there may have been considerable persuasion to take part in unusual behaviour, and at first there may have been some attempt to meet such requests. To the unenthusiastic partner it can seem that there is no end to the increasing demands. Schemes might become more elaborate. As the 'deviant' partner never seems to be satisfied, so the resentment and feelings of personal rejection might grow in the other. Although the sharing of adventurous sex can produce a blissful harmony for some couples, for others it produces tension and increasing anger on both sides. Eventually there has to be a choice between continuing the unusual behaviour or continuing the relationship.

The second group of clients are those whose sexual interests are satisfied without a relationship and who therefore can become increasingly isolated. On the one hand separation is seen as preferable to closeness, but on the other too much separation becomes irksome and hard to bear. If this group includes women, then very few of them seem to look for help. It seems more likely that secretive sexual practices are a strongly male preoccupation. They usually have some contact with like-minded others, but the underlying problem, of which the deviation is only one symptom, is an inability to establish close relationships with anyone.

The third, by far the smallest group, is those who have come into contact with the law or fear doing so. The client may have a genuine desire to change, or he may be concerned to be seen in this light. He is likely to be very scared of the consequences of being found out. Such men do not have many friends, either in or out of prison (see *prisoners and ex-offenders*).

(c) It is not known why sexual preferences vary so much. There clearly has to be a reason why it is nearly always men who are the more deviant. There is often a vague feeling of inadequacy or fear for men when faced with the prospect of sexual intimacy, and a reliance on other impersonal procedures might be seen as a defence against this. The sexual drive cannot be ignored, and if it cannot find expression within a close, loving relationship, then it has to surface in other guises. On the whole, women tend to have less trouble with intimacy.

Hudson and Jacot (1991) write about 'the wound' which men have suffered as a result of having to detach themselves from their mother. They attribute many of the peculiarly male characteristics to this stage of development. Friday (1993: 7) refers to the pre-Oedipal mother as a forbidding shadow who for men is behind every woman to whom they are attracted, and from whom they have to escape.

It seems as though the same causes, whatever they are, lie behind a range of preferences or a mixture of several of them. Masochistic tendencies are common amongst transvestites and fetishists. Fetishes are common amongst sado-masochists. Occasionally there is a variety of unusual preferences affecting the same individual, which indicates that the conditions necessary for the development of one type of preference may facilitate the development of others. Efforts have been made to isolate biological causes, either neurological or from the effect of pre-natal hormones; but these have to be placed alongside environmental factors, and in particular Marshall (1993) has stated clearly how poor-quality attachment bonds between the male infant and his mother are a likely explanation.

(d) If the helper is working with a couple then the generally recommended ways of working will apply (see *couples, working with*). One particular difficulty might be for the helper to remain neutral if, as is likely to happen in these instances, one partner is making what seem to be unreasonable and yet persistent demands upon the other. It might not be easy to avoid pairing with and feeling protective towards the passive partner. Moreover, a male counsellor might find himself becoming angry with a male client, not just because he feels protective towards the woman, but because the client's behaviour resembles his own conscious or unconscious wishes. Revulsion is sometimes a defensive response to that which is secretly attractive.

One way of working with the couple might be to help them achieve a greater sharing of control, so that the sexual needs of each of them have equal attention. Some allowance can be made for any practice which is difficult for either of them, without that practice being eliminated. For instance if the male partner enjoys tying up the woman, and chooses to do this on most occasions, but the woman feels pressurized and chooses never to do it, an agreement to include it only occasionally, say, once a month, might protect both interests. On the other hand, if a practice like coprophilia is completely repugnant to the other partner, then they may agree that this should be satisfied elsewhere, outside the relationship. This kind of management is nevertheless hard to sustain.

There are some practices, especially fetishism, which appear more compulsive as the relationship becomes less satisfying. What then happens is that the increased reliance on the fetish makes the relationship even worse. This repeated pattern of failure can be seen in a normal heterosexual relationship which produces alternative, deviant behaviour. For this reason, if the motivation for change is genuine enough, it is advisable to continue working with the couple, rather than separating them and working with the man on his own. The focus has to be the relationship.

For men on their own, the second group of likely presenters, a psychodynamic approach can be very helpful if the client has the capacity to work in this way. The therapeutic task might be to enable the client to become more accepting of himself. Being in a therapeutic relationship that offers warmth and understanding rather than fear and hostility can provide the client with a unique opportunity for learning how to live more easily with himself and, consequently, with others. Clearly this involves the helper experiencing genuine understanding for the client, and overcoming feelings of fear and anger.

A cognitive/behavioural approach can also be appropriate, and with this there are different ways of working. One way aims at helping the client to restructure his understanding of his behaviour and its consequences (Lang, 1993). It is a direct approach and is concerned to heighten the client's awareness of his victim (if any) and ways in which he might avoid further relapses. Another approach aims at working in a more general way on heterosocial skills, thereby reducing the isolation of the client (Leiblum and Rosen, 1989). Other procedures, like orgasmic reconditioning (using fantasy to fade out unwanted behaviour and replacing it with more acceptable ideas) and covert sensitization – fantasy of unwanted behaviour paired with aversive fantasy (De Silva, 1993) – are probably too specialized for most helpers although they are used by those trained in such matters.

Whatever approach is chosen, much depends on the helper's experience, natural ability and supervisory support.

A word of caution has to be given about working with those clients in the third group, clients whose practices constitute a serious offence. Thankfully it rarely happens, but in these circumstances it is necessary to inform the client that social services have to be contacted in order to provide protection for the third party, often a child. This needs to be made clear to the client as soon as possible, certainly within the first interview. It is useful if the helper, in whatever capacity he or she is working, has some built-in access to someone in social services in the event of this happening. Although this might seem severe, there has to be this limit on **confidentiality**, and when this is pointed out to the client it is often appreciated. The client coming for help suggests that this might represent the only way he or she knows of stopping further offences being committed. There can be some relief for the client when the helper takes this amount of control. If social services have to be brought in, it does not mean that the counsellor has to stop seeing the client who continues to need help in managing a very harrowing experience. However, the precise degree of co-operation should be discussed with social services before agreeing this with the client.

(e) Contact with social services should be made by telephoning the duty officer at the local office. Other sources of referral can be advised by: the British Association for Sexual and Marital Therapy, PO Box 62, Sheffield S10 3TS; the local office of Relate (Marriage Guidance), who may have trained sex therapists working with them; the Institute of Psychosexual Medicine, 11 Chandos Street, Cavendish Square, London W1M 9DE.

(g)   Bancroft, J. (1983) *Human Sexuality and Its Problems*. Edinburgh: Churchill Livingstone; Rosen, I. (1979) *Sexual Deviation*. Oxford: Oxford University Press; Storr, A. (1964) *Sexual Deviation*. Harmondsworth: Penguin Books.

GUY DEANS

Sexual difficulties

(a)   Within normal sexual activity there are three identified stages: 1. desire; 2. arousal/excitement; and 3. orgasm. Sexual difficulties occur when one or more of these stages do not happen reliably. The extent of the difficulty is determined by the amount of anxiety this impairment produces. What is horrendous to one person or couple might be easily tolerable to another. If anxiety is produced, there is normally hesitation and uncertainty. The likelihood of failure increases and the anxiety worsens.

(b)   1. In normal functioning, desire is stimulated by sexual thoughts, images or fantasies. Women tend to be less occupied with these than men and it is lack of desire which is the most common problem for women. However, if a couple present this as a problem, it may be an unusually strong sexual need in the male that is more the cause of the difficulty. In matters of responsiveness it is not easy to establish a norm; neither might it be helpful to try and do so.
2. If desire is impaired it can affect the next stage of arousal and excitement. The usual signs of this stage, for a woman, are extra vaginal lubrication and genital swelling. If a woman has been through the menopause, these signs might be less obvious. A sustained erect penis is the very obvious sign in a man, so much so that he is likely to be self-conscious when it does not happen. The inability either to gain or keep an erection is the most common problem for men.
3. Difficulties with the third, orgasmic stage are typified by men who do not have sufficient control over ejaculation and by women who are dissatisfied about rarely, if ever, reaching orgasm.

Other, less common difficulties which can be experienced by women are vaginismus (the inability to allow any penetration of the vagina) and dyspareunia (painful intercourse).

All sexual difficulties can be either primary or secondary. A primary condition is when normal functioning has never been achieved. A secondary condition is when there has been normal functioning but this has been lost. Another distinction is that a difficulty is either global or sporadic. If global, it is a difficulty in all circumstances. If sporadic, it occurs in only some situations, perhaps with one particular partner. These are important distinctions to make as they affect the kind of help that is appropriate.

When single clients present, the difficulty might not fall into any one of the above categories. Men, in particular, often present unusual sexual preference as the cause of their problem rather than sexual dysfunction (see *sexual deviation*). For figures showing the incidence of sexual difficulties presented to therapists see either Bancroft (1983: 204) or Cole (1988: 36).

The helper needs to be aware that what appears as a straightforward sexual problem may not be the case. One possible reason for this is that some clients prefer to present complicated issues under one neat heading, because they imagine that only by doing so are they likely to gain admission to therapy. While this happens in counselling generally, it seems more often the case in sex therapy. It is not just a matter of improving their eligibility for therapy. The process of simplifying problems and putting a label on them can somehow make it more manageable for the client. It is easier for a man to say he has 'premature ejaculation' than to say that because of a mother whom he saw as domineering, he is now frightened of allowing any woman to get too close to him, and that he therefore wants to have sex while avoiding threatening intimacy. Few men would present in this way, but if there is such a background, then it is clear that a behavioural approach aimed at modifying the sexual behaviour might not be wholly adequate.

The cloaking of deeper emotional and marital problems by a conveniently labelled sexual difficulty is nowhere more apparent than with the most frequent presentation in women, of lack of desire. Underneath this symptom there is often a backlog of distress and anger in the woman, who has over the years been trying desperately to achieve some kind of emotional contact with her partner. The sexual symptom might be used to hide anger and the need to punish, or it could reflect the battle over power and control. It can be an expression of grief or **depression**. None of this is to say that a helper should ignore the presenting sexual difficulty, but that it should not necessarily be taken at face value.

Another tendency with couples who present is for one partner to carry the sexual problem – the other partner being quite happy with this arrangement! Things begin to change after some progress has been made with the presenting problem, and the 'well' partner does not have that original problem to hide behind. Rarely does a sexual difficulty belong to one partner only. When it changes hands in this way, the helper might begin to wonder whether it is really a sexual difficulty at all.

Another consideration that is useful to make is how the presenting sexual difficulty is reflected in the client's behaviour generally. Sometimes it is clear that impotence or lack of interest or failure to reach orgasm, is part of a general pattern. If this is the case, it is again inappropriate to focus on the sexual problem in isolation.

(c) Underlying causes of sexual difficulties are either organic or psychological.

Organic causes
There are a number of conditions, neurological, vascular or endocrinal, that might affect sexual performance. Several drugs might also have an adverse affect – for a comprehensive list of these see Kaplan (1974: 80–5, 98–103). In certain cases, most obviously in primary erectile dysfunction, it is clearly appropriate to refer for medical advice. It might also be appropriate with a secondary difficulty, although a simple test is to establish whether or not erections are achieved either at night-time or on waking, or through masturbation.

If an erection problem is diagnosed as organic there are a number of surgical or non-surgical treatments. The surgical procedures, penile implants, are expensive, and the non-surgical devices, plastic vacuum sheaths, are rather cumbersome. But they usually work. The use of the drug papaverine, administered by injection intracavernosally, has proved effective in producing lasting erections. It seems a simple and reliable solution, but Virog (1985) believes that the high incidence of prolonged and painful erections may limit its potential value. There is concern amongst therapists about the way this treatment is being offered to men who become eager patients/customers, but for whom such recourse might not be necessary.

It is possible for there to be an organic cause for retarded ejaculation; and, in the case of loss of interest, a therapist might be on the look out for any debilitating kind of illness which produces **depression** or tiredness.

It seems that women are less likely to be affected in their sexual response by organic factors, though this might only seem to be the case because female response is less obvious. Clearly, a debilitating condition can affect sexual interest in the same way as it does for a man. In addition, fluctuating hormonal levels might have an adverse effect. One might suspect organic causes for vaginismus or dyspareunia, but although medical examination is advisable, most often the cause is psychological.

Psychological causes
These can be divided into five groups:

1. Relationship (dyadic):   Sexual difficulties sometimes occur with other changes in the relationship: e.g. after the 'falling in love' stage when the harsher facts of reality are being faced; or when a commitment has been made, such as a couple getting married after living together for a time. Another significant change might be pregnancy or the birth of the first child, or when the family has become complete. All such changes (and there are more affecting the woman than the man) can potentially affect the sexual responsiveness of either partner.

An ongoing difficulty might be the way one partner transfers feelings, often hostile ones, from earlier relationships to the other. This can develop into a punitive withdrawal of sexual favours. It is likely to be experienced as personal rejection by the receiving partner who, in turn, also becomes hostile. The vicious cycle that develops is similar to that when a couple is engaged in a power struggle and sex is seen negatively as a symbol of compliance. Either or both partners might be caught up in behaviour that avoids feelings of being dominated.

These are some ways in which discord in the relationship might affect sexual activity. When clients are in a relationship, the helper needs to ask how the sexual dysfunction is being affected by such struggles. A resolution of the relationship problem might alleviate the sexual difficulty.

2. Immediate: These include any concerns which get in the way at the time and which prevent either partner from becoming comfortable in or abandoned to the erotic experience. They include a preoccupation with responsibilities like children or work, fear of failure, anxiety about performance, ignorance of what is wanted, feelings of **guilt** or the kind of intellectual detachment which produces 'spectatoring'. Some therapists concern themselves with the reasons behind these dispositions. Others find it is enough to intervene in a way to remove such obstacles.

3. Intrapsychic: The wish to enjoy sex and the unconscious fear of doing so produces a conflict which can have powerful destructive effects on sexual and non-sexual attitudes and behaviour. Old childhood fears of punishment might be re-evoked by adult sexual expression. Having chosen the parent of the opposite sex as the initial object of erotic aims, thereafter feelings of guilt, frustration, anxiety and conflict persist.

The sex therapist introduces experiences which help the client get in touch with those loving and erotic feelings against which he or she has been defensively alienated. This contrasts with the traditional psychotherapeutic approach which is more lengthy and consists of gradually raising the unconscious conflicts and working them through, on the assumption that the sexual symptom will thereby be relieved.

Deep-rooted sexual conflict might produce ambivalence, fears of intimacy and confused sexual orientation.

4. *Learned:*   Conditioning and reinforcement are the processes by which negative learning takes place. Unpleasant early sexual experiences, especially if repeated, might easily produce negative attitudes later on, sometimes without the person being aware of the association. While some experiences of abuse are entirely negative, others, which also have a positive component, produce the kind of intrapsychic conflict described above.

5. *Other causes:*   Finally there are other conditions which are common enough but which do not fall easily into the above categories. These are **depression**, **stress** and grief (see *bereavement; loss*). These invariably have an effect on sexual interest and it is of little use trying to effect any change in sexual behaviour while they persist. In fact such efforts might only serve to intensify the symptoms.

(d)   The main concern of helpers might be to decide whether counselling or referral to sex therapy is appropriate. As a general rule, sex therapy is for those couples who have a specific sexual dysfunction (other than inhibition) and whose relationship otherwise is reasonably trouble-free and balanced. Such clients are actually a small minority of those presenting a sexual difficulty. The majority can be helped by counselling.

In the first place, enabling the client to talk about his or her own sexuality can be enormously helpful. It may be the first time they have ever done this. Sexual cravings, fears or inhibitions, all of which are quite common, assume huge proportions when they remain closeted. Airing these feelings, accompanied by the realization that they are not so unusual, can reduce shame and uncertainty.

When working with a couple the aim is to help them talk about such matters to each other rather than to the counsellor (see *couples, working with*). It is not unusual for a couple to have engaged sexually throughout their relationship in silence, making assumptions about what the other likes and dislikes, and being unable to state clearly what their own preferences might be. Such silence may have contributed to sex always being serious and repetitive. There has been no fun, no laughter, no chatter about it. Thus when clients present for counselling, they will do so anxiously and cautiously. The helper might acknowledge this anxiety without getting drawn into it and without perpetuating the silence through collusive avoidance.

It goes without saying that if a helper is going to enable others to talk more about their sexuality, he or she needs to be relatively at ease with his or her own. This is not to say that the helper needs to be totally uninhibited. This could be as threatening to the client as obviously being inhibited. But it does mean that the helper should be able to talk about sexual matters, and parts of the body, comfortably. This might need some practice and is best achieved through the use of role play in training programmes.

It really does help also if the counsellor knows what she or he is talking about! Even today, when we might assume that sex education has cured so much ignorance, misapprehensions still abound. Counselling does not have to become a lesson in biology, but reliable information can bring relief as well as enlightenment. Engaging in the process of talking about genitalia and what happens through the stages of sexual activity can also contribute to the process of de-inhibiting. It can be particularly useful to recognize the similarities between male and female responses.

The use of terminology is important. Clients have their own and provided it is not wildly inaccurate, there is little reason why it should not be adopted by the helper.

What counselling can achieve more than anything else is the reduction of anxiety. Although for some people anxiety stimulates arousal (Cole, 1988: 342), it seems this is unlikely for those who are experiencing difficulty (Barlow, 1986), for whom the opposite is more likely to be the case. In addition to the process described so far, a very effective strategy is to encourage the client to put on hold, perhaps for a period of months, that part of sexual behaviour which produces the most anxiety, and to enjoy that with which they feel more comfortable. So often, when people get into sexual difficulties, they adopt the approach of persisting with what is awkward as if by trying harder they will eventually succeed (a legacy of childhood?). In fact, failure and frustration are more likely to be intensified. It is more helpful for them to take time out and start again, gradually rebuilding step by step.

Masters and Johnson (1970) and Kaplan (1974) have introduced a way of working with couples which can be seen as partly behavioural, partly educational and partly 'permission giving'. It is an open way of working which encourages clients to participate. A ban on intercourse has to be agreed by the clients. Instead the clients are invited to explore and enjoy each other sensually. The behavioural programme known as sensate focus continues over a period of several weeks, perhaps months.

Each step is agreed by the clients and has to be seen as manageable so that it remains free from anxiety.

Towards the end of the programme, when the clients are feeling more confident and fears of intimacy have been reduced, special techniques can be introduced for dealing with specific dysfunctions. To practise this kind of sex therapy requires specialized training and without it the untrained helper is not advised to dabble with these procedures. However, the notion of avoiding that part of behaviour that produces most stress and helping a couple find ways of enjoying intimacy without feeling threatened is one that helpers might usefully bear in mind. The more the clients themselves are able to initiate such changes in behaviour the better. It might only need gentle support and encouragement from the helper, and a careful watch that partners maintain equal control.

Contrary to the way we might have been conditioned, it is not helpful for partners to be occupied with the need to give pleasure to the other. A man might be desperately concerned to turn his partner on, but this may be for the sake of his own self-esteem. This need he has for her to become aroused by his efforts can be difficult for his partner to manage. It is also based on a questionable assumption, because her arousal is far more dependent on her own predisposition. A woman may be similarly concerned to give pleasure to the man, and when both partners are occupied with this, it can produce a stalemate! There is a great deal to be said for pleasing ourselves without too many expectations of our partner. It may be difficult for clients to become assertive or to relinquish their dependency on their partners, but if each of them can clearly determine with integrity what they want and what they do not want and put this into practice, it saves misunderstanding and resentment.

Of course this may highlight possible differences which it is hard to reconcile, but it is a more honest approach and it helps to define what it is they have to work with. It does not have to produce a rigid, uncompromising situation. Sexuality allows for variation and inexhaustible exploration, and if a relationship is trusting and equal, this can continually unfold, so that the partners increasingly become fully sexual.

(e)   Names of sex therapists can be obtained from: Relate – local office, or Herbert Gray College, Little Church Street, Rugby CV21 3AP; British Association for Sexual and Marital Therapy, PO Box 62, Sheffield S10 3TS; Institute of Psychosexual Medicine, 11 Chandos Street, Cavendish Square, London W1M 9DE; family planning clinics; general practitioners.

(f)   The question sometimes arises about counselling clients who are simultaneously receiving sex therapy. As sex therapy also involves some counselling this is not advisable. A common and agreeable practice is for clients to complete counselling before engaging in sex therapy. It is often preferable for there to be a gap of some months between them.

(g)   Bancroft, J. (1983) *Human Sexuality and Its Problems*. Edinburgh: Churchill Livingstone; Cole, M. and Dryden, W. (1989) *Sex Problems; Your Questions Answered*. London: Macdonald Optima; Hawton, K. (1985) *Sex Therapy: A Practical Guide*. Oxford: Oxford University Press.

GUY DEANS
      (See also *menopause*)

Single parents

(a)   In 1992, 21 per cent (that is one in five) families with dependent children in Great Britain were headed by a lone parent. Approximately 91 per cent of these were headed by a lone mother, which largely explains why single parents are usually thought of as single women. It is important to recognize this: for instance, an important consequence is that poverty amongst single parent families actually means poverty amongst mainly women and children.

About 20 per cent of all children live in a one-parent family. Approximately 40 per cent of lone mothers are under 30, compared with only 7 per cent of lone fathers. This is mainly because a high proportion of lone fathers are widowers, whereas mothers are alone for different reasons. A breakdown of the figures shows that 53 per cent are divorced or separated women; 6 per cent are widowed mothers; 32 per cent are single women; and 9 per cent are lone fathers.

In 1992 just over 31 per cent of live births were outside marriage. However, this group should not be confused with single-parent families as over half of these children were registered by both parents living at the same address. This group represents couples who are choosing not to get married, but nevertheless at the time of the birth are mutually committed to one another and the child.

Sufficient money is a concern to everyone, but the figures demonstrate why this is such a concern to so many lone parents. In 1992 the gross weekly income of one-parent families was just under 40 per cent of the income of two-parent families with two children. A typical single parent with one child received £73.60 a week from Income Support with an extra £15.05 for a second child under the age of 11. Their gross weekly disposable income including housing benefit was £180.23, whereas the corresponding figure for a man, wife and two children was £470.20.

There are also enormous discrepancies in housing. Only 36 per cent of one-parent families live in owner-occupied property compared to 77 per cent of other families. Nearly 60 per cent of one-parent families live in council housing compared with only 20 per cent of two-parent families. A recent survey showed that contrary to claims that single parents walk into the best council housing, 20 per cent of local authorities expect a lone mother and child to share a bedroom. Larger three-bedroom properties are much more likely to be given to couples with one child than to a lone parent with one child.

Over half of lone fathers work full time compared to only 17 per cent of lone mothers. One survey shows that the age of the youngest child relates closely to employment for single parents: only 9 per cent with a child under five work full time whereas half with teenage children have jobs. Most people say they want a job, but key obstacles to this include lack of affordable child care and the 'benefits trap', whereby single parents who find work can end up with a smaller income. The survey shows that those in full-time work earn around £130 per week. Fewer than one in ten earn over £160, and many of these are lone fathers who average considerably more – nearly £200 a week.

(b) Single parents may present with a range of issues and difficulties although those relating to finance and housing are often central. Over 60 per cent of calls to the National Council for One Parent Families are about housing. As far back as 1974 the Finer Committee Report on single parent families noted that housing problems closely rival money problems as a cause of hardship and stress to one-parent families. It seems this has not changed. Anxieties about money are considerable, and the implications of lack of money extend to all areas of life (see *money advice*). Single parents on low incomes struggle to provide the basics for themselves and their children, and do not always manage even to do that. If money is borrowed, it is inevitably often from expensive sources; the vicious circle of lack of money becomes increasingly tight as demands for repayment combine with ongoing expenses. Living in a highly consumerist society is difficult on a very limited income. Single parents experience considerable anxiety and guilt about not providing for their children as they would wish. When providing the basics is hard, providing extras for school trips, swimming lessons and days out becomes impossible.

The introduction of the Child Support Agency, operational from April 1993, has caused considerable anxiety to some lone mothers. Some may feel they will be better off, but others fear punitive measures if they do not co-operate with the agency.

Single parents suffer other forms of stress too. They may feel socially isolated and unacceptable in what is still a couple-oriented society. There is little respite from child care when there is no other adult to share this with. Illness, either of a child or a lone parent, can be an especially difficult and worrying time, while the serious illness of the parent presents very real child care problems. Lone parents who are also disabled experience particular difficulties. Single parents who have recently lost their partner through **divorce**, separation or death have to grieve the loss of the relationship and face a major transition in life. This is one point when they may present for help: not only are they having to cope with their own feelings, but they have to deal with their children's as well (see *children's experience of loss and death*), at a time when income may have dropped considerably and moving house may be necessary. Furthermore, difficulties over access arrangements may loom large when divorce or separation is involved.

Single fathers, although they tend to be financially less poor than single mothers, can feel disadvantaged in other respects. They may present with particular problems of isolation, often feeling excluded from the world of mothers and children. Women are still the primary carers of children, particularly when they are small; and many activities and centres that draw together mothers and children may not be experienced as father-friendly. If fathers wish to retain primary care over their children after divorce they may fear this will not be upheld by the courts especially if the children are young. A similar anxiety is often experienced by lesbian mothers.

(c)   Single parents have always been part of society, sometimes as a result of the death of one parent, sometimes when a child is born outside the context of a permanent relationship and – especially in more recent time – as a result of divorce. To some extent there has been a change in societal attitudes. Unmarried mothers are no longer consigned to the workhouse or to mental hospitals; nor hidden away from public gaze until after the birth, when their child would more than likely be placed for adoption. Legal abortion and contraception have given women more choices over having a baby. More relaxed attitudes have made it easier for a mother, who is not attached to a man, to care for her child.

However, attitudes are still ambivalent. Single parents continue to get a bad press from many quarters: in 1987 Rhodes Boyson was quoted as saying that 'one parent families were bringing up hooligans and muggers'; in 1988 Nigel Lawson was quoted as saying that the benefit system was contributing to the rising tide of family break-ups. There have been governmental suggestions that young girls are deliberately getting pregnant in order to get council accommodation, despite a report (Clarke, 1989) showing this is not the case.

(d) It should not be assumed that single parenthood is in itself a problem. Several studies have found that, despite all the difficulties outlined above, for many women single motherhood has been a positive move. Itzin (1980) states that 'despite the hardships, these single parents are – without exception – happier as single parents than they were married'. Sharpe (1984) notes: 'Women also experience a sudden and rapid precipitation into what for many is a hitherto unknown level of independence. The realization that decisions have to be made and tasks carried out and that there is no one else to do it but themselves can be a daunting prospect, but also a stimulating and exciting challenge.'

In offering help to single parents it is therefore important to ascertain their own perception of their difficulties and to respond accordingly, without making assumptions or falling into stereotyped misperceptions. Single parents are not a homogeneous group. It would be unhelpful to offer psychological counselling to someone who has financial difficulties, although a specialist debt counsellor might be appropriate. Similarly, if poor and overcrowded housing conditions are causing **depression** or inability to cope with children, it is the housing needs that should be addressed (see *homelessness*). In dealing with local authorities, housing associations and other relevant bodies a single parent may need an advocate to help them put and stress their case (see *advocacy*). However, if depression is caused by the **loss** of a relationship through death or **divorce**, or other internal factors, then practical approaches are unlikely in themselves to be sufficient. This may leave the person feeling that the helper cannot cope with their pain or distress and is turning to practical matters as a means of avoiding their unhappiness. Neither is it helpful to minimize the difficulties the single parent is facing by false reassurance that one day things will be better.

It is evident that single parents may need very specialized help in certain situations: finance (see *money advice*), housing (see *homelessness*) and **legal advice** are obvious ones. So the helper needs to have a sound local knowledge of where this specialist advice can be obtained and to refer on as appropriate. In addition the helper needs to recognize the distress that single parenthood can bring, especially in the early days. Although many single parents ultimately discover that taking sole responsibility has its advantages, it may not seem so at first, particularly when the loss of a partner has been involved.

Of course not all single parents suffer a personal loss in this way as they will not have been in a close partnership: a few have made a conscious decision to become a mother and remain single; many more have experienced unplanned pregnancies, and from the beginning have had to face the fact that the father was not prepared to take any active role as a parent.

As already noted, for some a key difficulty is social isolation. It can feel as if no-one else understands or is in the same position. Since many in fact are, and women single parents are particularly good at offering mutual support and child care, it can be very beneficial to help someone to locate others in the area, who are also alone with their children. The most appropriate help may be **self-help groups** that can organize babysitting, holidays and play-schemes, as well as others to talk to. In these groups the single parent can have a valuable role to play: she has something to give others, as well as having some of her own needs met. Consequently her self-esteem is likely to increase. Groups have the added and significant advantage of acting as pressure groups to campaign for a better deal for single parents. They have considerable knowledge of local and national resources. Single parents alone have little power, but by joining together they have a more effective voice, which can be empowering in a situation that all too often silences them.

(e)   The National Association of One Parent Families has been campaigning vigorously for the rights of single parents since its inception as far back as 1918, although then under a different name. It can be contacted at 255 Kentish Road, London NW5 2LZ (Tel: 0171 267 1361). Gingerbread is another national organization for single parents, which has local groups offering a variety of resources including social events. The National Office is at 35 Wellington Street, London WC2E 7EN (Tel: 0171 240 0953). See also your area phonebook for local groups. Citizens Advice Bureaux also hold details of what is available in your area. Home-Start is an organization through which volunteers befriend families with pre-school age children. Although not specifically aimed at single parent families it can be useful to them, particularly as it offers a home visiting service aimed at offering both support and friendship, and practical advice to young families. Home-Start is organized in local groups, which should be listed in the phone book. Its National Office is at 2 Salisbury Road, Leicester (Tel: 0116 255 4988).

(g)   Itzin, C. (1980) *Splitting Up*. London: Virago; Macaskill, H. (1993) *From the Workhouse to the Workplace: 75 Years of One-parent Life 1918–1993*. London: National Association for One Parent Families; McKay, S. and Marsh, A. (1994) *Lone Parents and Work*. DSS Research Report: No. 25. London: HMSO.

MOIRA WALKER

Spiritual direction

(a) Spiritual direction is concerned essentially with a person's relationship with God. That relationship will be dependent upon a person's particular understanding of the nature of God. For instance, there are those who perceive God as a supernatural being with whom one can have a personal relationship, whereas others would see God as metaphor, a symbol or signifier of that which ultimately concerns us. Both theological understandings of the nature of God demand a response on the part of a believer. What is my relationship to God – in my home, at work, in recreation, within marriage or partnership, in the family, within the neighbourhood, in friendships, in my prayer life, within the corporate life of the church or religious congregation? These are the questions addressed by spiritual direction, which is concerned with the whole of life, not just the 'religious bits'. Nevertheless, what is offered by a spiritual director needs to be appropriate to a person's pattern of belief and their particular understanding of the nature of God.

At the risk of stating the obvious, although all human beings have a spiritual aspect to their personhood, not all believe in God. Spiritual direction is best offered to those who do have a belief in God, however residual that belief might be.

Whatever a person's understanding of the nature of God, spiritual direction is concerned to enable a person to draw closer to God, union with God being the purpose of the spiritual journey. Drawing closer to God entails drawing closer to oneself. As Anthony De Mello SJ says, 'You will experience nothing closer to God than yourself' (De Mello, 1978: 49). Drawing closer to oneself poses problems for most of us but especially for those who have a seriously damaged or diminished self-image, yet it is critical to the process of spiritual direction. For God is at the very centre of our being, around which all other aspects of reality revolve. Not to acknowledge this central reality is to be estranged from God (whether perceived as a personal being or as the summation of one's ultimate concerns) and from oneself, and thereby to become estranged from other people. For there appears to be a direct connection between one's ability to draw closer to oneself and one's ability to relate well to other people. Hence the Christian commandment, 'Love God and your neighbour as yourself' (Luke 10:27); the essence of love is the giving and receiving of acceptance. Therefore although spiritual direction finds its primary focus within the life of the individual, there are also social implications which have to be taken into consideration.

In our pluralist and multi-cultural society it also needs to be recognized that the concept and practice of spiritual direction is not limited to

the Christian tradition. Within ancient indigenous cultures the sha-
man or holy man exercised the function of spiritual direction or guidance, very often linked to healing. The spiritual guide also plays a
significant role within major world religions other than Christianity.
There is the presence of the Guru within Hinduism, the Sant in
Sikhism, the Sheikh in the Islamic Sufi tradition, monks (Sangha) in
Buddhism and Roshi or Rebbe within Chasidic Judaism.

(b) In what ways might a client's need for spiritual guidance present
itself?

For those carers who work under the auspices of a religious organization such a need often arises quite naturally as an outcome of religious
experience or within the context of pastoral care. For those who work in
the secular field the need for spiritual guidance is likely to manifest
itself in counselling or psychotherapy sessions (see *counselling, suitability for*), or within adult education, personal growth or human potential
groups (see *adult learning; groups, use of*). Disillusionment with Western post-war values and institutional religion in the 1950s and 1960s
led some young people to experiment with drugs in order to attain
spiritual enlightenment. There was also a turning towards Eastern
mysticism, all of which was at its best a search for meaning, but at its
worst was a form of escapism. *Homo sapiens* is a meaning-seeking and
meaning-making species. The 'Who am I? Where am I going? What's it
all about?' type questions do not go away, and when they are asked very
often indicate the presence of real spiritual hunger. Such a hunger can
present itself in counselling sessions or group work and is as much to do
with a yearning for purpose and structure in life as it is to do with
personal spiritual understanding.

Unfortunately, there are those who exploit this human desire for
meaning by subjecting gullible and vulnerable people to what can only
be called religious or spiritual abuse. The more horrific and shocking
examples find their way on to the front pages of our newspapers, but
there are many more less spectacular cases of people being deformed
rather than transformed by religion. Such deformation can present
itself in individual counselling or group sessions, more than likely in
the form of hostility towards religion or guilt. Guilt, induced or exaggerated by religion, is particularly pernicious. Guilt (see *guilt and
shame*) serves a not dissimilar function to pain in that they both act as a
warning. They indicate something is wrong. But there is no virtue in
enduring either of them beyond the time of warning. It is for this reason
that within the Christian Church provision has always been made for
guilt to be dealt with by some form of confession of sin followed by the
absolution of forgiveness (see *forgiveness of sin*). Confession may take
place in private with a priest or minister administering absolution, or

during public worship in the form of a general confession and absolution. For the person who cannot 'quiet his own conscience', as the 1662 Book of Common Prayer expresses it, and who requires the authoritative assurance of guilt assuaged and sins forgiven by God, a formal experience of confession and absolution is essential. For those severely afflicted by guilt such an experience might be offered as the culmination of an extended period of counselling or psychotherapy. But for others it will just be a normal part of the maintenance of their spiritual life in relation to God.

(c) Guilt can indicate the presence of a poor self-image. Such a diminished sense of self-worth can also be caused by a number of other factors. For example, lack of parental love, absence of appreciation or affirmation at school or at work, career failure, marriage collapse (see *divorce; redundancy; bereavement*) and so on. That an impaired self-image is a predominant phenomenon in the lives of many people is indicated by the considerable interest shown in self-help books and personal growth courses, which proliferated in the 1960s and 1970s and are still popular today.

(d) As far back as Old Testament Judaism, it is interesting to note there was a resistance to human spiritual direction because traditionally it was thought that God (Yahweh) was himself guide and director: '*You* guide me by your counsel' (Psalm 73:24). This reservation over the need for a human intermediary between human beings and God resurfaced in the life of the Western Catholic Church at the time of the Reformation in the sixteenth century. The Eastern Orthodox Church was hardly affected by the Reformation and continued to place its confidence for spiritual guidance in the hands of the Startzi (Holy Monks). The proponents of reform sought to review the beliefs and practices of the Catholic Church in the light of Biblical scholarship and authority. The rejection of the proposed reforms by the Papacy led to the establishing of the Protestant or Reformed Churches, which itself led to a Counter-Reformation within the Catholic Church some years later. One of the abuses in need of reform was that associated with sacerdotalism – the undue exercising of excessive authority and influence by the ordained priesthood. The principal function of a priest is to act as mediator between human beings and God. For the power of that function to be abused, as was the case in the sixteenth century, and at other times in the Church's chequered history, is to seriously undermine confidence in the priesthood and what it has to offer, not least in relation to spiritual direction. This suspicion of the priesthood resulted in the Protestant Churches discouraging spiritual direction, which was perceived as being a Catholic priestly practice, especially when linked to sacramental confession (see below). However, in recent years there has been a rediscovery within the Protestant tradition of the riches of Catholic and Orthodox spirituality, including the concept and practice of spiritual direction or guidance. Despite this recent development, members of the caring professions and those working in the voluntary sector need to bear in mind that the suggestion a client be referred to a spiritual director is more likely to be received sympathetically by a Catholic than by a Protestant.

Within the Christian tradition there are different expressions of spiritual direction but they all have one thing in common: that is the belief and conviction it is the Holy Spirit of God who directs and guides, not the spiritual director. The spiritual director is a channel, an instrument of God's grace, discerning and enabling the directee to 'read the breathings of the Spirit' (Carter, 1973: 117). For this reason a spiritual director strives not to come between the directee and God. Unfortunately in times past, and it has to be said, in times present, there are those directors who do not strive with sufficient vigour in this respect and fall into the trap of spiritual hubris by 'playing God'. Such directors can become tyrannical, a tendency noted by the nineteenth-century priest and director F.W. Faber who says that whereas 'spiritual direction must be free as air and fresh as the morning sun', it can have 'a desperate proclivity to become tyrannical' (Faber, 1960: 150). For this, and other reasons, the title of spiritual 'guide', 'companion', 'personal consultant' or 'soul friend' is preferred to that of 'director' which has an authoritarian ring to it, quite inappropriate to the role as it is practised today.

Latterly, a good deal of interest has been shown in the Myers–Briggs Type Indicator (MBTI), not least within the Christian Church. The MBTI is a Jungian-based temperament indicator designed by Katharine Briggs and her daughter Isabel (see Briggs Myers, 1980). It is used widely throughout education, industry and commerce especially in relation to career counselling and team building.

Within the Church it has found an application in spiritual direction in that it emphasizes the validity of individual temperaments and how they relate to a person's prayer life. There are many pathways to God and the MBTI helps ensure this is recognized. It is all too easy to assume that 'my way is the only way', thus leading to spiritual arrogance. A considerable number of people have been 'spiritually disenfranchised' by such arrogance and lack of sensitive discernment. It is therefore of crucial importance to assure people who have a desire to pray, i.e. to communicate with God, that just because they are unable to do it in accordance with a particular spiritual 'convention' does not mean they cannot do it at all. For instance, there are those for whom the exercising of the five senses in prayer is important, whereas others prefer a more intellectual approach. There are those who prefer traditional patterns of prayer while others are more committed to exploring new ways to God. Some prefer silence in prayer and worship, others find noise helpful, and so on. There is a spiritual understanding of *chacun à son goût*, one might say. The task of helping a person discover what their particular prayerful way to God might be is central to the process of spiritual guidance.

Furthermore, the MBTI also promotes an 'I'm OK, you're OK' approach to life as distinct from the poor self-image version of 'You're OK, I'm not OK' (Harris, 1973). Not only do the MBTI and other models of human understanding such as Transactional Analysis, Gestalt, psychodynamic counselling, etc. promote self-acceptance, but with MBTI's 'I'm OK, you're OK' philosophy it also promotes the acceptance of others. In this respect it ties in well with spiritual direction which has, as was suggested earlier, a corporate and social dimension to it. It is not merely a matter of 'myself and God' but also 'myself, God and neighbour'. Spiritual guidance seeks to promote an engagement with and not a flight from the reality of other people and the society in which we live. It is the antithesis of withdrawal.

For this reason, one of the most influential and currently popular models of spiritual guidance is that offered by St Ignatius Loyola (founder of the Society of Jesus, 1491–1556). The Ignatian method is about engagement with oneself and the world and can be summarized as involving awareness, discernment, freedom of action and service. As Broderick explains, 'Ignatian spirituality begins with an awareness of one's inner life, then moves on to sifting that inner experience, discerning what comes from one's authentic self and what comes from one's inauthentic self. This discovery of one's authentic self leads to freedom and the power to make sound decisions' (Broderick, 1993: 37). It is the task of the spiritual director or guide to assist that process of growing awareness, discernment and decision-making.

(e) When it comes to referring a client for spiritual direction or guidance to whom should such a referral be made? What are the qualifications and qualities one is looking for in such a person?

Unfortunately, for many years it was assumed that the offering of spiritual direction was the exercising of a gift from God given to very few people. Some monks, nuns and clergy were seen as possessing this gift, as was the very occasional lay person. This highly elitist attitude effectively prevented many holy men and women possessed of great spiritual discernment from exercising this ministry. Fortunately the situation is changing. More and more people, both clergy and lay, are being trained and/or having their confidence restored in their spiritual capabilities. The qualities one is looking for in a spiritual guide or director can be summarized as follows:

1. experience of life
2. the ability to discern spiritual needs
3. a capacity for exercising sound but gentle judgement
4. a willingness to continue to learn
5. a desire for holiness of life under the inspiration and guidance of the Holy Spirit of God.

One would also expect such a person to be able to maintain **confidentiality**. If the director is a priest, and spiritual direction includes sacramental confession, then confidentiality is mandatory as all that is said in confession comes under the 'seal of the confessional' which a priest may not break. This can lead to difficulties over referrals from other professional colleagues, especially if there is a case discussion element to their co-operation. Hence the need for clarity of understanding regarding colleagues' expectations over referrals.

A number of Anglican dioceses now have training courses for spiritual directors, and some keep a register of practitioners. Unless stated otherwise in the diocesan year book (or its equivalent), the person to contact would be the bishop of the diocese. It is important to remember that as far as the Church of England is concerned a person does not have to be a member in order to benefit from its ministry. (In fact one Archbishop of Canterbury, William Temple, remarked that the Church of England was a unique organization in that it existed primarily to serve its non-members!) Anyone at any time therefore has a right to call upon that ministry, in connection with spiritual guidance or any other felt need. With respect to other Christian denominations, Roman Catholic bishops would also be willing to help, as would the Chairman of the Methodist District or the Provincial Moderator of the United Reformed Church. The Orthodox priest who services the needs of local congregations would also be co-operative. Names and addresses of the different denominations can be found in the telephone directory.

(f) Those practised in the skills of counselling may ask what the difference is between counselling and spiritual direction. Clearly there are similarities and overlaps between the two disciplines, but one obvious difference is that counselling does not normally concern itself with a client's relationship with God. This relationship may well arise in conversation but it is not necessarily essential to the counselling process, whereas for spiritual direction it is axiomatic. Furthermore, counselling tends to be crisis or problem focused and relatively short-term, whereas spiritual direction is a growth centred 'continuous process, the movement to God and in God' (Leech, 1977: 96). There will of course be occasions when, in the process of spiritual direction or guidance, a problem is encountered which is best dealt with by **counselling** or therapy. Conversely, counselling sessions may well unearth a need for spiritual guidance in a client's relationship with God. There are counsellors who can cope with this new expectation. Likewise there are spiritual directors who can offer counselling. But in a number of cases, especially those involving deep-seated psychological or spiritual problems, a wiser and more prudent course of action would be a referral to a fellow professional working in the other discipline.

(g) Jeff, G. (1987) *Spiritual Direction for Every Christian*. London: SPCK; Leech, K. (1977) *Soul Friend*. London: Sheldon Press; Merton, T. (1975) *Spiritual Direction and Meditation* and *What is Contemplation?* Wheathampstead: Anthony Clarke.

TONY CHESTERMAN
    (See also *faith differences; forgiveness of sin; guilt and shame; menopause; prayer and ritual; religious belief*)

Stress

(a) A universally accepted definition for stress has yet to be found. Each profession uses the word differently, from psychologists to engineers, biologists to musicians, astronomers to counsellors, and each highlights different aspects of this complex subject. The significant factor in any situation is how the individual responds to perceived demands. For some people it is more than they can cope with to cross the road without help; others thrive on crossing countries on their own. There is no one stressor (that which causes stress) which produces a constant degree of stress in all people equally – even death itself is welcome in some circumstances – and so the 'stress' lies in the reaction of the perceiver. Stress is about a pattern of responses to a pattern of challenge, each perceived differently by different individuals. As long as someone feels there is nothing that can be done, in particular about what comes at him or her from 'outside', there is a sense of being trapped and helpless; people frequently talk of their horror at not being able to cope. Stress management consists of enabling individuals to recognize their own responses, and to harness skills and attitudes which put them in charge of their own choices. Self-recognition on the part of each person is of primary importance.

Increasingly, all professions and all industrial managers (Coe, 1994) are acknowledging the significance of stress to the nation. It is claimed that as much as £26 billion is lost annually in stress-related illness and absenteeism (NASS, 1992); that the British 'epidemic' of coronary heart disease is due to risk factors which include stress; and that the stress resulting from poor housing, unemployment and the growing rift between those who have and those who have-not is dramatically raising the rate of suicide. Nonetheless statistics that are gathered over a number of years are hard to come by, and improved quality of life is notoriously difficult to measure.

The more our society admires and rewards the dedicated Type A citizen disproportionately as compared with the competent but relaxed, flexible worker, the more we will carry high levels of stress.

(b)   The variety of ways in which over-stress shows itself is almost unlimited. *Stress-signs* can be experienced in the body, or the mind, or the emotions, or in that little-aired area of things of the spirit – or in any combination of these areas. Too much stress can affect the total living and behaviour of a client, or simply show itself in an occasional and uncharacteristic display of bad temper. Over-stress can produce stress-signs at opposite ends of many normal functions. For instance, in different people the effects of stress can be seen in over-excitability or in withdrawal; it can result in either compensatory overeating or punishing under-eating; in either constipation or hurried bowel syndrome; in either over-religiosity or disillusionment. With that in mind, the most commonly cited stress-signs are:

of the body	*of the mind*
muscular pain or spasm	taking too much on
headaches that persist	confusion
tightened tummy/dysfunctioning	inability to make decisions
digestion	insistence on directives
self-comforting practices	hurry sickness
fast talking/walking/eating	spiralling mental activity
sleeplessness	lowered resistance to challenge
heightened risk to all illnesses and	control must be seen and overt
accidents	reduced concentration and memory
skin problems, breathing problems	being 'in a fog'

of the emotions	*of the spirit*
irritability	coldness
overwhelming disproportion of any emotion	lack of purpose or meaning
	difficulty with laughing/playing
self-hatred; self-denigration	absence of self-worth
hosltility towards others	fury at 'fate', or God
unrealistic expectations of self	irrational and wild beliefs
over-dependency on others, or external substances	rigid application of external religious observances
difficulty with personal relationships	difficulty with authority

All these can lead towards an 'inability to cope' syndrome, or even actual breakdown.

(c) To describe 'precipitating factors' in relationship to stress implies some sort of breakdown, and indeed over-stress is a factor in breakdown of any sort. It is a recognized risk in diseases of the heart, of the digestion, of the respiratory system, of the immune system and virtually any physical dysfunction. The presence of constant stress threatens relationships and jobs. But to concentrate on this sort of excessively high stress discounts the need to counteract the everyday experience of stress that is now common to us all – we do not all break down, but it is commonly acknowledged that in the Western world we are exposed to the highest levels of stress yet known to mankind. That is not to say the highest levels of poverty or disease or exploitation or war, but the greatest and continuous amount of challenge in our minute-to-minute living. This is brought about by many factors, each of which can stretch our resources to their limits:

- increases in physical speed and change in our lives;
- the vast overload we bear in information, communication, competition and alternative life-styles;
- the way in which we can now compare ourselves with other people around the world;
- the presence of images of horror and despair in the heart of our homes through the media;
- the availability of over-stimulation in our concepts of 'entertainment';
- the high emphasis put on personal decision-making in the light of multiple choices;
- choices are made in a climate where traditional guidelines have been diminished. Generally speaking, moral frameworks are now considered to be the property of individuals; it is not simply that individuals have the proper freedom to choose their own

constructs, but that they have taken on the right to make them
up as they go along;

- in addition, since the Enlightenment the ability to reason and
control and achieve has been admired and fostered to the
detriment of our powers to wonder and play and intuit. Our
reward systems and our education lead us to develop the Type A
personality as one that is desirable and should be applauded.
Our present day ideas of worth are based on external things
which can be measured and possessed, to the detriment of
'beyond reason' things like inwardness and caring.

We so easily become hooked on to striving and achieving and controlling and living in the *highs*. Too often this means we neglect the *deeps*,
where we give over control in order to ponder and receive and listen. We
are busy making ourselves into human *doings*, having forgotten we
were created human *beings*. I expand this theme in a practical way in
People Need Stillness (Nash, 1993).

Life-event scales can be used to indicate the external occasions which
consistently add to the presence of stress, but such scales are now being
discounted in the understanding that different individuals react to the
same circumstances in different ways. For some, moving house is a
process from which it needs two years to recover, for others it is an event
eagerly looked forward to and enjoyed. For some, an uneventful and
consistent lifestyle is seen as boring and stress provoking, while to
others it is the zenith of relief. Some people can take momentous
happenings in their stride, but show signs of great stress when their pet
becomes ill. It is important for each individual to recognize the factors
that increase their own stress, and then to pick and choose their own
battles, as well as their own weapons (Sapolsky, 1994). It is unreliable
to suggest that there are objective scales against which to measure the
whole person.

In specialist terms, psychologists use questionnaires to gauge levels
of anxiety and depression; cardiologists use electronic and chemical
tests to gauge heart and circulatory activity; exercise biologists use
mechanical means to gauge the expenditure of energy; physiologists
use chemical tests to gauge metabolic activity; and all these contribute
to the objective calculation of the effects of stress. But for the ordinary
assessment of how much I myself can take of stress, it is up to me to
listen to my own body, and mind, and feelings and spirit.

In the context of who is *least* likely to fall under an excess of stress,
some research findings are useful. A certain characteristic identified as
'hardiness' is shown to be prominent in the personality make-up of
those who deal constructively with stress. This is made up of resilience,
confidence and cheerfulness. Another valuable attribute is that of being

able to tolerate ambiguities without too much discomfort or threat. A third is the attitude which sees the locus of control as being within one's own responsibility – especially when things go wrong – rather than resting with an outside authority (fate or the doctor or boss or 'the government'). Those people who are without these various attributes have been shown to be more vulnerable to the effects of stress than those in whom these attributes are developed.

People who display an ability to cope are described as 'togethered', or having a clear sense of their 'centre'.

(d) The most important first step in dealing with anyone under stress is to listen to their description of how they see their situation. It may well be that at first they insist their difficulties are due to something outside themselves: the lack of money, the impossible working conditions, the council tax, a nagging partner, the clamorous children, the scheming workers, the bad housing, the distress on television, the recurrent illness – all these and more are initially seen as bearing the blame for the person's predicament. And they all play a part; if, however, the carer colludes with the idea that external factors are the total cause, then this reduces the opportunity for the client to see that it is the response made to these irritants that is largely in their control, rather than having to modify the whole world outside.

Recovering the skills to deal with these contributing factors starts by identifying the specific stress signs. Then the client must decide whether to undertake some change and development in their own behaviour, or whether they are content to stay at the place where they are 'done to'. Obviously, medical symptoms must be taken to their doctor; **phobias** or neuroses, and signs of pathological depression or self-destruction, must be dealt with using psychiatric or psychotherapeutic help; and sometimes the client should be encouraged to see, for instance, the personnel officer at their place of work to help sort out difficulties to do with working practices. But outside of these more obvious solutions, there is a range of palliative strategies available to the ordinary person who is feeling over-stressed. There is a wealth of personal skills that can be developed to enrich anyone's life, but especially those who are aware that their response to the stressors that come at them is in their own hands. Taking charge of my own behaviour and attitudes is perhaps the most empowering and fully human activity I can engage in. These stress-skills are available in each of the areas of body, mind, emotions and spirit.

These are laid out in Figure 1 on p. 429.

What is equally important, however, is the central part of Figure 1, where there is clearly a gap in the middle. Some people are expert in the

Stress-skills of the body
Taking responsibility for what I eat, drink and enjoy;
how I keep exercised;
how I get regenerated and sleep.
Practising deep relaxation.
Listening to body language, my own and others';
understanding my own physiology.
Learning appropriate breathing.
Using medicines and treatments;
seeking appropriate professional help.
Knowing my own biological clock;
bio-feedback.
Valuing pleasurable activities.
Finding like-minded support.

Stress-skills of the mind
Taking charge of my choice;
using reason and logic.
Planning; prioritizing; organizing; deciding.
Managing my time.
Setting goals with realism.
Delegating tasks.
Making use of advice.
Rehearsing for change and conflict.
Objectifying and distancing.
Knowing when and how to say 'No'.
Valuing stability zones.
Mind stilling.
Finding like-minded support.

Stress-skills of the emotions
Allowing them! taking responsibility for them.
Owning them – recognizing my own self-talk.
Managing my own joy, anger, grief, guilt,
without harming others.
Relationships – listening, building rapport,
adjusting my expectations of myself and others.
Knowing what rewards and refuels me,
without relying on external approval.
Recognizing when to be assertive.
Learning when and how to let go.
Counting my blessings.
Laughing – especially at myself.
Finding social support.

Stress-skills of the spirit
Discovering my own values –
what is *really* important to me?
Recognizing significance:
what is the direction, purpose, meaning of this experience, now?
Should I make space for God?
Centering, finding my own ground.
Practising meditation and stillness.
BEING, as well as DOING.
Valuing non-rational mysteries.
Giving place to hope, creativity,
good cheer, confidence.
Finding like-minded support.

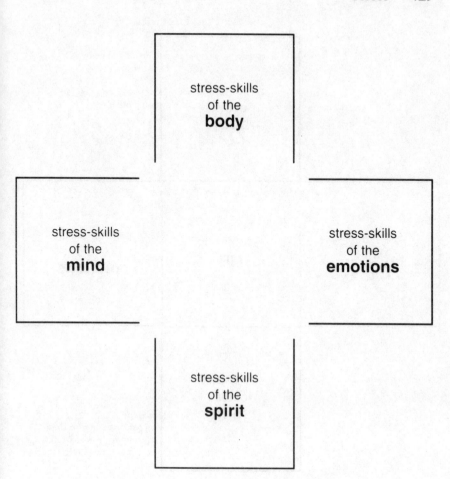

Figure 1

stress-skills of the body but are out of touch with, perhaps, skills of the mind. There are those who are expert at all the rational skills but are out of contact with, perhaps, the skills of the emotions. And some are expert in their ivory towers of spirituality, but neglect their bodies. All these areas can be connected by including the central issue of 'Recognizing who I am', which involves:

recognizing me,
recognizing my own capacities,
my strengths, weaknesses and limitations;

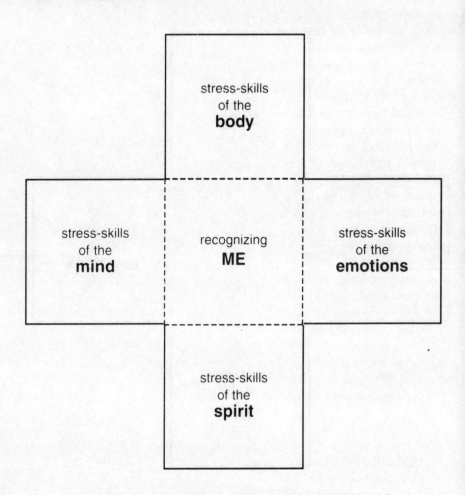

Figure 2

accepting that I am unique;
allowing my own self-worth,
knowing that I make mistakes, and can recover from them;
affirming that part of the image of God that is within me
and in each other too.

In practice, the greatest value of recognizing the central me is that I can act out of what I really want to do. Skills have to 'fit' the person I am: the things I long to do, prefer to do, like to do, yearn to do, to which I will dedicate my best energy and galvanize my most authentic drive. Things that I choose to do because I want to do them will always be more effective – more rewarding for myself and more constructive for others – than those things I do out of duty and because I have 'got to do them'. Because 'I want to' is too often associated with selfishness, I prefer to speak of my 'wannas' – the working out of my deepest convictions, and most authentic attributes; in contrast to working from my 'gottas' – the hand-me-down imposed set of values that I have inherited. If I work out of what I have got to do, those duties become 'oughts' and 'musts'. The things I have brought into my present from the past, which have deteriorated into 'shoulds', do not engage my whole-hearted being.

Each of us is unique. It cannot be stated too strongly that the particular 'wannas' and 'gottas' in each of us are different. An inordinate amount of stress stems from the way one person imputes or imposes their personal 'wannas' and 'gottas' on other people, without valuing their personal distinctiveness. On the other hand, the more I can work towards becoming the Me I was created to be, rather than the Me others tell me to be, the more I will be of genuine use to others by giving them space to be themselves. And the less stress I will spread around me.

Today we are all bent on finding instant solutions for our problems, but the management of stress is a long-term process, and it is just as well that we have been given a lifetime to tackle it. No sooner do we manage to establish one set of skills, than we will find another with which to enrich our lives.

(e) Similarly, the practitioner who provides stress management will always be able to add to their personal and professional development. Those familiar with biology can increase their awareness of the dimensions of psychology for instance, and those familiar with education strategies can grow in awareness of the contribution of the social services. Where the competencies of one practitioner end, the knowledge and skill of another professional will slot in, so networking within the provision of stress management is vital. Hands-on carers will need to know when to advise their clients to take their problem to their general practitioner, and those highly qualified in their own field, like dentists, need to acknowledge there are others such as relaxation therapists who can help their clients as it becomes appropriate. There will be times when agencies such as Relate, or a housing association, the parish clergy, community workers, the organizers of charitable concerns and many others may be turned to for advice and help.

Aromatherapy is popular, and with its use of massage, its intimate atmosphere, its acceptance of the body and use of neglected senses it is very valuable. Reflexology and acupuncture offer similar occasions for individual attention and therapy; and hypnotherapy has been used for the development of self-confidence in the face of fear of flying, pre-examination nerves, smoking-stop and diet control (see *holistic medicine*). Enjoying non-competitive exercise and learning the conditioned skill of deep relaxation are fundamentals to stress management.

Classes for the development of deep relaxation can be found throughout the country; some are privately run, some are attached to GP surgeries or hospital departments, and some are in the form of courses at leisure centres or adult education centres. Enquiries about these various provisions can be made to health visitors, or to the General Secretary, International Stress Management Association (via the South Bank University, LPSS, 103 Borough Road, London SE1 0AA).

There is a rash of commercially-based concerns that claim to have quick-fix remedies, discounting the need for each client to work on their own self-development. Until an academically-based and evaluated profession of stress management has been established, carers must be wary of extravagant statements put out by inadequately qualified practitioners to vulnerable people.

(g)   Nash, Wanda (1994) *At Ease with Stress*. London: Darton, Longman and Todd. Relaxation tapes are available to accompany this book. For specific work-related stress: Warren, Eve and Toll, Caroline (1994) *The Stress Work Book*. London: Nicholas Brealey. *The Stress Pack: A Positive Approach to Stress* (1993) is produced by the Derbyshire Health Authority in conjunction with K. Childs, H. Fender and S. Stone. This is a book of information and plans for group discussion, together with photocopiable material for groups, leaflets, relaxation tape and booklet of useful addresses. The complete pack costs £30 and can be obtained from the Derbyshire Family Health Services Authority.

WANDA NASH
   (See also *loss; post-traumatic stress*)

Substance misuse

(a)   Drugs have been used for both medicinal and recreational reasons for at least 5,000 years and probably long before that. The Sumerians used the poppy (from which opium is derived) as a medicine and chose a word which means 'joy' or 'rejoicing' to refer to the drug. Drug use, though more prevalent today than at any other time in the recent past, was far more popular 150 years ago. Within the United Kingdom during the middle of the nineteenth century, the average consumption of opium-based drugs per head of population was equal to 150 standard doses of morphine per year (Royal College of Psychiatrists, 1987: 1).

For our purposes, a drug can be defined as any substance which is taken to control pain, change consciousness or mood. Unlike alcohol (also a drug – see *alcoholism*), which is legal in most circumstances, most drugs are illegal and this adds a whole new dimension to their use and misuse. To complicate matters even further, some drugs are available on prescription from a physician and are legal as long as they are used by the person to whom they are prescribed; but they can become illegal if sold or given to someone else.

A working definition of drug (or substance) misuse can be similar to that used for alcohol: drug misuse is the use of any drug which causes physical, psychological or social harm to the drug user or to others.

(b) Drugs come in a variety of forms and their effects depend on a number of factors. These factors include:

1. the pharmacology of the drug, i.e. how it affects the brain and other organs;
2. the personality and expectations of the drug user;
3. the health, mood or mental state of the drug user;
4. the presence of other drugs including alcohol and the previous experience of that class of drug, i.e. tolerance.

Most drugs, when taken repeatedly, can induce tolerance, which is the body's adaptation to the constant presence (usually a week or two of continuous use) of the drug. The higher the dose and the longer the repeated use of the drug, the higher the tolerance. In practice this means that the drug user needs to take more of the drug to achieve the same effect.

Drugs are classified according to their main action and how most people experience them. Not all drugs easily fit into the categories below. Some have the properties of two or more categories.

Opiates.   These drugs are extracted from the opium poppy or synthetic equivalents of the naturally occurring substances:

examples: heroin, morphine, methadone, codeine.
main effects: opiates will reduce pain, cause drowsiness, relieve anxiety and distress. They will also cause a pleasant or even euphoric mood, and when taken intravenously cause a 'rush' – a sudden overwhelming feeling of well-being and euphoria. Problems can be ignored as they lose their emotional impact.
withdrawal symptoms: sleeplessness, cramps, aches and pains, sweating, diarrhoea, restlessness, anxiety, craving for the drugs and frustration are common symptoms. These symptoms are uncomfortable but

not life-threatening and can to a degree be controlled by gradual rather than sudden withdrawal.

Stimulants.   These drugs stimulate the nervous system:

examples: amphetamines, cocaine, crack (a short-acting form of cocaine which is smoked), Ecstasy (which also produces hallucinations).
main effects: they can cause sleeplessness, rapid heart-beat and rapid breathing, loss of appetite, hyperactivity, restlessness, anxiety and sometimes paranoia. They can also lift depression, and give people energy, confidence and cheerfulness.
withdrawal symptoms: in the short term prolonged sleep followed by insomnia, weight gain, craving, depression and lethargy can be expected.

Depressants.   These are drugs which depress the central nervous system:

examples: alcohol, barbiturates like Tuinal, Seconal, Nembutal and benzodiazepines, such as Valium (diazepam) and Ativan (lorazepam).
main effects: sedation, impaired motor skills and memory, relief of anxiety, feelings of calmness and relaxation. Paradoxically, sometimes they can appear to cause stimulation as a result of disinhibition.
withdrawal symptoms: insomnia, anxiety, tremor, irritability and sleeplessness. Hallucinations, confusion and convulsion can occur in severe cases.

Hallucinogens.   These are drugs which cause visual and other sensory hallucinations:

examples: cannabis, LSD, magic mushrooms.
main effects: these drugs can cause hallucinations and a heightened appreciation or distortion of sensory experience. Sometimes anxiety, panic and paranoia are present. More usually in milder forms such as cannabis, there is a pleasant elevation of mood, relaxation, feelings of dissociation and heightened enjoyment of food, sex, etc.
withdrawal symptoms: there are few physical withdrawal symptoms but some people complain of mild sleeplessness, cravings and anxiety.

Solvents.   The effects, in many ways, are similar to being drunk on alcohol. Users sometimes feel sick, drowsy, disorientated, confused and euphoric. Like alcohol, solvents are disinhibiting. 'Pseudohallucinations' (the user knows the visions are unreal) are reported by some. When the user stops, the effects wear off in 15 to 45 minutes. Many readily available products can be inhaled including solvents, glues and paints. Some products, such as petrol, propellant gases in aerosols and fire extinguishers, cigarette lighter gas, are more dangerous than others. Accidents and the use of more dangerous products account for a large proportion of solvent-related deaths.

Anabolic steroids.   These drugs are mainly used in body building and sports. If taken in large doses when performing heavy exercises such as weight lifting, they probably increase strength, size and weight. Some users report feeling more aggressive and belligerent when taking steroids. There is some controversy over the existence of 'steroid' or 'roid rage' – uncontrollable violent outbursts – which is reported by a minority of users. Steroids are not illegal under the Misuse of Drugs Act. Long-term use for men can include side-effects such as over-development of breasts, increased sex drive followed by decreased sex drive, hypertension, sleep disorders, depression and paranoia. For women it can cause increased sex drive, menstrual irregularities and growth of facial or body hair. Most users do not report unwanted effects but the more steroids that are used and the longer they are used the more likely that such effects will develop.

Drugs in fashion.   Drugs, like clothes and music, come in and out of fashion. Newer drugs on the scene are:

Ecstasy – an amphetamine with hallucinogenic properties and the capacity to induce empathy, often found at raves.

GHB ('GBH') – a long-acting anaesthetic which sedates and causes disinhibition and increased libido.

Mixing drugs is more dangerous than using one drug; the effects are often difficult to predict. Most problem drug users use more than one drug and may switch their drug of choice from time to time.

Drugs and the law.   The possession, unlawful supply, intent to supply, import or export, or the production of a whole range of drugs is illegal under the Misuse of Drugs Act, 1971. Drugs are placed under three 'classes' and each class has a range of penalties according to whether the conviction is for possession, unlawful supply, etc. Class A drugs (carrying the harshest penalties) include heroin, cocaine (crack), LSD and methadone. Class B includes amphetamines (besides those prepared for injection which are Class A) and cannabis. Class C includes most of the benzodiazepines.

In practice, despite the fact that more and more people are prosecuted under the Misuse of Drugs Act every year, it has become common for the police to use their discretion and issue a formal 'caution' instead of prosecution. This is often the procedure for people who are found in possession of cannabis for the first time but in some areas it is used for those in possession of Class A drugs. There is widespread variation on how 'cautions' are used throughout the country.

Possession of solvents, even those for under 18, is not against the law. However, it is unlawful to supply solvents to those under 18 if you have reason to believe that they will be used for the purpose of 'sniffing'. The police are entitled to remove a child to a 'place of safety' (such as their home or police station) if they find them intoxicated in a dangerous place.

The Home Office Index.   The Misuse of Drugs (Notification of and Supply to Addicts) Regulations 1973 make it a legal requirement that any doctor who attends a patient whom the doctor considers to be or has reasonable grounds to suspect is addicted to (not just using!) one of fourteen drugs (broadly Class A drugs but not LSD) must write to the Chief Medical Officer of the Home Office. The Index is supposed to be available only to doctors and for research purposes. However, many drug users believe that the Index is available to the Home Office or police and for this reason some are reluctant to come for treatment.

(c)   Most people use some kind of drug; alcohol, tobacco, tranquillizers, anti-depressants, cannabis or heroin. They use drugs for a variety of reasons, which include:

- pleasure: drugs make us feel good;
- social reasons: to conform with our friends and as an adjunct to social activities such as parties;
- to help us forget our problems;
- to ward off uncomfortable withdrawal symptoms (if used regularly to excess).

As most of us use some form of drug, why do some take enough drugs to develop problems? There are a number of explanations:

1. Social and economic problems cause problem drug use.   There is ample evidence that areas of high unemployment (see *redundancy and unemployment*), poor housing (see *homelessness*) and social deprivation have higher rates of problem drug use than more affluent areas. Did the drug users lose their jobs and social status and move to deprived areas, or is it that deprivation, unemployment, etc. make the individual more susceptible to problem drug use?

2. Problem drug users have a genetic predisposition to this problem.
There is far more research about the genetics of alcohol problems (see *alcoholism*) than drug problems, but it is often assumed that the mechanisms are similar. Most explanations for the genetic link suggest a 'personality type' which is inherited rather than a specific gene. The

question then is: how much of what we commonly consider to be personality is inherited and how much is learned?

3. *Problem drug users are trying to mask psychological distress.*   Most problem drug users have a whole range of personal problems, some of which have childhood roots and others arise from more recent experience. Did the problems precipitate the drug use or did the drug use cause or make worse the problems?

4. *Problem drug users have simply developed a strong appetite for the positive effects of the drug or are avoiding withdrawals.*   Some psychologists claim that problem drug users are simply seeking to repeat the pleasurable experiences which drugs give. We choose the drug we most like. The other side of the coin is that once we take enough of the drug to suffer withdrawal symptoms as a result of not having it, we are doubly reinforced to take it again, not only to achieve the desired effect but to avoid the discomfort of the withdrawals.

(d) People use drugs in a variety of ways, from relatively harmless, occasional use to chronic, life-threatening use:

- experimental drug use: this denotes occasional, less risky and social drug use for pleasure. Most drug use falls into this category.
- casual drug use: this signifies recreational or intermittent use which may be causing some, but not severe, problems.
- chronic or habitual drug use: this type of drug use is characterized by daily (or nearly daily) consumption of drugs, the accumulation of severe drug problems, physical and/or psychological dependence and time-consuming drug-seeking behaviour.

Getting started: making the assessment
In any assessment it is important to get a feel of who the client is and what they are like, not just a history of their 'problem'. Not every problem drug user will want to give a full history. If all they ask for is information or relatively simple advice, that should be provided. When you are at the stage of talking to them about their drug problem, you need to know the following:

1. What exactly is the problem? Are they having specific health, legal, relationship, work or school, financial difficulties?
2. What drugs do they use and how (i.e. smoke, inject, orally) do they use them? How often are they used? What drugs (and alcohol) have they used in the past?

3.   What help do they want?

Offering help
Not every problem drug users wants to become abstinent immediately.
It is good practice to set goals with your client soon after the assessment. Goal setting must be a joint activity between client and
counsellor.

Setting goals and harm reduction
Most drug workers believe that avoiding **AIDS/HIV** must take a
higher priority than immediate abstinence. Therefore, most drug agencies accept the following hierarchy of goals:

* the cessation of sharing needles and syringes
* the move from injectable to oral drug use
* a decrease in drug misuse
* abstinence

These goals were recommended by the Advisory Council on the Misuse
of Drugs (1988). In general, these measures have been called 'harm
reduction'. It may mean helping people to reduce their drug use or refer
to a needle/syringe exchange. It may also mean helping a problem drug
user find a physician in order to discuss a prescription for methadone (a
heroin substitute) to decrease his or her reliance on illicit supplies.
Methadone may be prescribed on a short-term de-toxifying regime or on
a more long-term basis to help problem drug users stabilize their drug
use. For young people who are using solvents and do not want to stop, it
may mean advising them on avoiding dangerous practices.

How to do it
Most drug workers find that they spend most of the time talking to their
clients about issues other than drugs. These may include practical
issues such as helping clients with financial difficulties, accommodation or legal problems (see *homelessness; legal advice; money advice*).
They may also include more personal problems such as child care,
relationships, anxiety or depression. You may find that simply helping
your client to find work, advance their education, find new hobbies is of
great value in helping them to change their drug habits. Though these
issues are vital, do not expect that a resolution of other problems will
automatically lead to abstinence.
  Problem drug use is a complex blend of pharmacology, behaviour and
attitude. Most problem drug users have been problematically using
drugs for years before they come for help. It may take months or years
for their behaviour and attitude to change. Along the way they are

likely to relapse, go back to old habits, but this is by no means the end of the advances they may have made. If this occurs it is wise to see what can be learned from the relapse, the offending, the unsafe drug use, etc. Try not to always relate a relapse or 'binge' to a new or old problem.

Remember, drug use (problematic or not) is the result of many factors, not just problems! While problem drug users must see the disadvantage of aspects of their behaviour in order to change, it does not follow that they must undergo a 'cathartic' revelation about their past or present situation in order to make the necessary changes to achieve their goals. Many problem drug users change their habits as a result of finding other interests, a new relationship, a job or further education, or simply by growing old.

(e)   Since most drugs are illegal or at least thought to be unacceptable by most people, drug users may be reluctant to come forward for help. Not every drug user needs help. Most people who use drugs experience few if any problems as a result of their drug use. They do not think that they have a problem though others may. Sometimes drug users may recognize problems but not recognize that they may be drug related.

Compulsory psychiatric treatment under the Mental Health Act is rare, as alcohol and drug misuse alone are specified as insufficient reason for compulsory admission or treatment without consent. Someone with mental illness who uses drugs or alcohol or someone who has a mental illness caused by drugs or alcohol, e.g. amphetamine psychosis, may be admitted compulsorily if their mental state warrants it.

It is important to respond early to requests for help and not to be judgemental. **Confidentiality** is a key issue but limits to confidentiality should be explained. It is also important to recognize different views on drugs which may be held by ethnic minority and religious groups (see *cross-cultural awareness; faith differences*).

When dealing with **adolescents** it is best to involve parents if possible but not to deny services if parents cannot be involved. Drug users who are parents will often be concerned about the local authority being made aware of their drug use. These days, most local authorities do not view parental illicit drug use as sufficient reason to take a child into care. A careful assessment needs to be made of the risks to the child. Check with your local authority about their policy but be aware that they may not have one!

Nearly all health authorities have either a Community Drug Team or Drugs Advice Centre which can be contacted on a confidential basis. Some welcome self-referrals and most take referrals from any agency.

Many of these agencies offer a range of help including **counselling**, advice, information, prescribing and medical advice. There is a variety of residential rehabilitation services, which are intensive programmes aimed at heavier drug users. Most programmes last about a year but shorter programmes are being considered. Most people who attend these programmes require local authority financial support in the form of community care.

Problem drug use (as well as problem alcohol use) is covered by local authority community care procedures. Clients who have problems as a result of their drug use may be eligible for help in the community or financial support to attend a residential programme. Advice can be obtained from local social services departments.

Needle and syringe exchange programmes provide clean injecting equipment, information and advice. Some are based in local pharmacies and others have their own premises or use community facilities.

Self-help groups, parents/family groups, etc. are more common in some areas than in others. The local Drugs Advisory Service or Community Drug Team will be able to provide information.

(g) *Drug Abuse Briefing* (1993), London: Institute for the Study of Drug Dependence (5th edn); Ghodse, H. (1989) *Drugs and Addictive Behaviour: A Guide to Treatment*. Oxford: Blackwell Publications; Glass, I. (ed.) (1991) *The International Handbook of Addiction Behaviour*. London: Routledge.

IRA UNELL
(See also *AIDS/HIV; alcoholism*)

Suicide and attempted suicide

(a) Suicide is a self-inflicted, life-threatening act resulting in death; it is deliberate, self-initiated and done consciously with the person's knowledge and expectation of its fatal outcome. Attempted suicide is a conscious, deliberate self-inflicted act intended to be, or to appear to be, life-threatening, but the person does not actually die.

Suicidal people usually have ambivalent emotions. They act suicidally but their intention varies between total expectation of dying and healthy survival after conveying their 'message'. It is difficult to classify their acts unambiguously because their intentions vary, and chance discovery and resuscitation might change the outcome.

(b) *Higher risk situations*

1. Demographic: male (more actual suicides); female (more attempts, especially 15–40 years); age: over 45, with rates rising in under-25s; occupations: doctors, vets, dentists, pharmacists, students, sailors, military, farmers, retired.

Residence: homeless, bedsit, boarding-house, hostel, rural isolation, living alone, prison, immigrants, refugees.

2. Social:

(i) *isolated/alienated*: little family contact, few friends, family conflict, outsiders, withdrawn, introverted, homosexual, newcomer, drop-out, non-religious

(ii) *public 'failure'*: academic failure (or fear of), redundant, unemployed, professional under-achievement/stagnation/misconduct, bankrupt, debt, prosecution (or fear of), criminal, public figure exposed (sex/shoplifting/corruption), media-hounded, 'failed' suicide

(iii) *broken relationships*: jilted, rejected, single, separated, divorced, marital problems, bereaved, recent quarrel, problems with parents, siblings, children

(iv) *suicide in peer group, public figure, TV*: 'copy-cat' cluster (using same method) in school, college, friends.

3. Behaviour: preoccupation with past; revisiting birthplace, old friends, sentimental places, interest in old music, photos, memories; making will; destroying letters and diaries, reorganizing finances, buying life assurance, instructions about future, distributing money and precious possessions; talking of funeral, hymns, grave; interest in death, tragedy, sad things, after-life; increased intake of food (bulimia or obesity), drugs, alcohol, tobacco; decrease in eating, self-care, productivity, concentration, work, sex, former interests, school performance and attendance; visiting GP (over 70 per cent of suicides and attempters visited in previous month – sometimes for 'only trivial' symptoms); uncharacteristic behaviour, overspending, odd purchases; indecision, crying, hostility, agitation, irritability; withdrawal, isolation, emotional deadness, slowness; self-mutilation, 'accidents', dangerous behaviour, suicide threats, blackmail, indirect hints; talking about suicide (which does *not* mean they will not do it).

4. Mental and physical health:

(i) *past*: insecure, unhappy childhood; death or loss of parent(s) before 15 years; other bereavements; abuse: physical, sexual, emotional; parents threatening, fighting, arguing, alcoholic, grieving; previous psychiatric illness, suicide attempts in self or family, major losses, marital breakdown;

(ii)   *present*: painful, terminal or debilitating illness; epilepsy, hypo-
chondria, insomnia, fatigue, 'trivial' complaints; fear of illness;
imagined cancer, AIDS; puberty, pregnancy, menopause,
'empty nest'; mood: hopeless, fearful, anxious, betrayed, let-
down, humiliated, ashamed, lonely, worthless, angry, revengeful, guilty.

5. Mental disorder (may be obscured by concurrent physical illness):
depression; manic-depression; schizophrenia; organic brain, personality or anxiety disorder, compulsive-obsessive, impulsive, paranoid (at
least 33 per cent of suicides have verified mental illness).
6. High risk periods: just before and after time in mental hospital; when
therapist/counsellor changes, cancels appointment, has holiday, termi-
nates therapy; before treatment becomes effective (anti-depressants
can take one to three weeks to give relief); when mood lifts (person
seems more relaxed and has more energy to organize the suicide).
7. Age/date correspondence: when person reaches same age as important relative was when they died; on anniversary of death or of other
significant event (the connection is often unconscious).
8. Pre-suicidal syndrome: thinking narrowed and rigid; 'tunnel vision';
polarized 'either/or' thoughts; focus entirely on self or anger/aggression
at particular person; disturbed perception of reality; flight from reality;
emotional and social isolation.

(c)   No single factor 'causes' suicide. Many aspects of a person's past
and present life situation contribute to their decision to act now (see
(b)).
Suicide is a hostile act. Violent methods like shooting or mutilation
reflect this, but the hostility is frequently denied or masked by depression. Freud believed that suicidal persons unconsciously turn upon
themselves their unexpressed anger and revengeful fantasies towards
an ambivalently-loved significant person. Conscious motives are
usually mixed. Some can be inferred from suicide notes, previous
conversations and behaviours; others are reported by survivors after
suicide attempts. Some attempters did not intend to die and their
motives differ from those of successful suicides.
Common *motives* are:

- guilt, self-punishment, atonement
- fear or shame from actual or anticipated public humiliation
- escape from a situation perceived as intolerable
- to manipulate, frighten, or get revenge on someone
- to show desperate feelings
- to get attention, sympathy, better diagnosis and treatment
- fantasies of rebirth and fresh beginning after death

- compensation and consolation in afterlife for current deficiencies
- desire for reunion with a dead person, or identification with them
- to control this one last decision in otherwise impotent situation
- to cease being conscious – not necessarily to be dead.

The suicidal *process* develops from suicidal thoughts, through imagined and actual plans, to suicidal action. These are all differing expressions of a fundamental suicidal tendency, which may begin early in life, associated with unsatisfactory parenting and subsequent relationships. Early **loss** or inadequate parenting may leave an individual with permanent emotional insecurity and social instability. These may predispose him or her to suicidal behaviour during subsequent crisis periods, perhaps throughout life.

Indirect suicide: Many people feel ambivalent about being alive. They 'want' to die, or be dead, but do not act consciously to kill themselves. They use chronic life-shortening behaviour which they rationalize or intellectualize, and usually deny any suicidal motives. They may be very manipulative as they use their long-suffering martyrdom to express hostility indirectly. They invoke sympathy and attention and may seek help, seeming to want to get better. Attempts to help them receive a 'yes, but . . . ' response, and counsellors themselves may feel frustrated as they experience the passive hostility, and their efforts remain unsuccessful: e.g. 'accident-proneness'; dangerous driving, work, sport; **substance misuse**; obesity; malnutrition; anorexia and bulimia nervosa (see *eating disorders*); over-working; some altruistic bravery; refusing or 'forgetting' to take medication, to visit GP, or receive treatment.

(d)   Of those who attempt suicide up to 60 per cent repeat and 10–15 per cent eventually succeed. Of successful suicides a large proportion are known to have attempted before, although numbers are underestimated because some attempts are not recorded.

All attempts and threats should be taken seriously, however minimal the self-harm. In 60–80 per cent of cases suicides have directly or indirectly indicated their intention beforehand. Clients seek counselling for innumerable reasons and there is no fool-proof way of recognizing suicidal individuals or of preventing determined people from dying.

Suicide risk assessment in crisis counselling:

1. keep them talking;
2. listen, while noting suicide-risk indicators;

3. do not confront or argue. Offer non-judgemental supportive relationship, to encourage client's trust and willingness to receive further help;
4. ask directly about suicidal ideation and planning. (This will not 'put ideas into their head': it could actually give relief and permission to talk honestly);
5. establish their address and availability of support;
6. decide whether it is safe for them to leave unaccompanied;
7. consider referral for assessment and treatment (GP, hospital, specialist agency);
8. arrange an early follow-up appointment if you choose to continue offering support;
9. realize that encouraging trust and confidences and then 'rejecting' the person may reinforce their feelings of worthlessness and enhance the suicide-risk.

Non-crisis assessment can be done while collecting information suitable for most case-histories. New clients may not feel trusting enough to disclose mental illness or previous suicide attempts in either self or relatives, so pace sessions comfortably and explore less threatening issues, while establishing sufficient rapport to allow exploration of vulnerable areas. The following format could be adopted, and data entered in any order. High-risk situations (using information from section (b)) may be highlighted in case-notes for subsequent exploration.

1. *Identity*: Name, age, place of birth/date. Marital status. Address, type of accommodation, number in household (ask about recent changes; newcomer, live-alone, last child departed).
2. *GP*: Name. Last visit: date/reason. Current treatment/drugs. Relationship quality.
3. *Religion*: Upbringing; current beliefs; attitude to suicide, death, afterlife.
4. *Education*: History. Interests. Achievements. 'Failures'. Regrets. (Recognize any low self-esteem, or not fulfilling parental expectations.)
5. *Employment*: Present job, duration, attitude, problems at work. Previous jobs, dates, reasons for leaving.
6. *Personal history and dates*: Childhood. Major life changes. Physical and mental illnesses: past, present. Significant relationships: deaths, abused? Marital history. Children (including miscarriages, stillbirths, abortion, adoption). Broken loves, rejections, losses. Crises. Hopes/fears for future.
7. *Family (dates)*: Next of kin (name, relationship, address and telephone). Relatives: physical/mental illnesses. Losses,

divorces, separations. Deaths, suicides or attempts (age, date, method). Note age/date anniversary – correspondence with client's present age. Past and current state of relationships.

8. *Support*: Friends: in whom to confide? Colleagues, neighbours, church, clubs. Has suicide of anyone known, admired, read about, had strong effect?

9. *Appearance/manner*: Clothes, presentation, expression, eye contact, posture, agitation, tremor, movement, alertness, hostility, evasiveness.

10. *Speech*: Amount, flow, intonation, volume, slurred (alcohol?).

11. *Mood*: Depressed, anxious, hopeless, afraid, ashamed, guilty, angry, revengeful, worthless, lonely. (Be alert as mood lifts – the person may be expressing relief at having decided to commit suicide now.)

12. *Recent changes*: In moods, relationships, behaviour, performance, job-satisfaction, decision-making, finances, eating, sleeping, weight, alcohol/tobacco/drug use, interest in sex, leisure activities, social life, beliefs.

13. *Thinking*: Self-image, reality basis, rigid, constricted, illogical, contradictory, delusions, problem-solving, memory.

14. *Suicidal issues*: Perceived main and other current problems. Suicidal thoughts: frequency, duration, trigger-situations, content, motives. Plans: theoretical, practical. How? When? Previous attempts: dates, methods, motives, outcome. Any alternatives to suicide? Have you tried them? What stops you killing yourself now? Likely effects on others? What gives (or could give) your life meaning now?

Any suicidal person should be encouraged to consult their GP. They should be encouraged to talk not only of physical symptoms but also of their desperate feelings and of any earlier suicide attempts or mental illness. Suicidal people are often mobile or rootless, so the GP may know little about the person and nothing of any family history of suicide and mental illness. Frequent monitoring is necessary, especially if anti-depressants (the most commonly-used 'overdose' drug) or other high-toxicity drugs are prescribed. The person may feel worthless and need encouragement to return. It helps to be given a specific appointment.

Some people feel unbearable **guilt** after surviving a traumatic incident. They commit suicide months or years later, sometimes when illness diminishes their defences, or on the anniversary of the incident. They feel 'performance guilt' ('I should have done more') or 'survivor guilt' after others die. Life seems futile and meaningless and they feel worthless and tormented. Watch for self-punishing, self-mutilating behaviour, self-neglect, addictions, over-protection of remaining family and inappropriate acts of expiation. Explore possible ways of reparation and the concept of forgiveness. The fact that you now know and accept their guilt and 'failures' and still continue to give support and affirmation could be the beginning of the long ascent towards self-acceptance and inner peace.

Help a suicidal person to talk about the current situation and why it feels so hopeless. Prioritize its different aspects and then focus on each separately, starting with the most urgent or worse feared. Explore together what might happen if those fears were realized; possible ways of responding; and what coping resources would help implement an effective response. Discuss the relative merits and envisaged outcomes for each response and show that there are alternatives to suicide, possibly by making major changes like re-training, job change, or ending a relationship.

Because suicide is a hostile act it is essential to explore feelings of aggression, repressed anger and revenge. Current situations and relationships may trigger emotions which elicit memories of earlier childhood conflicts. Only immature reactions like fear and 'flight' were possible then, but now help may be given to develop more effective strategies and better techniques like social skills, anger and anxiety management, problem-solving and more open and honest ways of communicating and relating. Deeper issues like unresolved grief or **child abuse** may need specialist referral.

Eventually some people find it unnecessary to use further manipulation, violence or suicidal blackmail. More satisfying relationships reduce their loneliness and isolation and improve their confidence, self-esteem and hopes for the future.

Grief after suicide   is similar in its overall adaptive processes and emotions to that after any death, but certain aspects usually make it even more complex and painful:

- Timing: grieving usually takes longer and may never be well resolved if:
  - motives were never known or unacceptable;
  - the body was never found, discovery delayed, or not viewed;
  - denial was maintained until inquest;
  - the fact of suicide was not disclosed until later.
- Inhibition of mourning:
  - the stigma (even though suicide has not been a criminal offence in Britain since 1961);
  - the police investigation and manner (guarded; it might have been murder);

- the inquest and verdict. Family conflict about motives (may be unsympathetic). Sudden deaths allow no good-bye, and leave unfinished business. Full grief sometimes begins only after the inquest.
- Mode of death:
  - violent: shooting, jumping, self-castration;
  - special place: birthplace, honeymoon site;
  - contents of any suicide note.
- Discovery of body:
  - mutilated, decayed;
  - anyone finding body may suffer stressful memories (police, neighbour, dog-walker, social worker);
  - **post-traumatic stress** in friends or relatives who discover body could inhibit normal grieving;
  - distressing memories impair balanced reality-based internalization of the entire relationship;
  - if suicide occurred inside home or garage, family may move from house and neighbourhood (more major losses), losing support from community network. They may never grieve fully;
  - relatives, neighbours or professionals feel guilty if body lay undiscovered for long period.
- Family stresses: these may have contributed to the death and will impede grieving:
  - ambivalent relationship: quarrels, blaming, marital breakdown, extramarital partner involved;
  - absences: hospital, prison, abroad;
  - mental illness;
  - abuse: violence, emotional (suicide blackmail), sexual, drugs, alcohol.

Role crisis: because the relationship ended in suicide, which feels like a conscious rejection, its whole meaning and value is now questioned and doubted. Anyone involved has difficulty in retaining any confidence that they were effective (or could ever be) as spouse or sexual partner, parent, brother or sister, counsellor or social worker ('why didn't they contact me?'). There may be fears of contagion. Feeling a worthless person may lead to suicide. (The risk is high in all bereaved people.)

Some *anger* is usually felt towards the dead person even in normal bereavement. Recognizing that some of it is irrational exacerbates the pain. After suicide, however, such anger is not irrational. Most people cannot help dying, but suicide is consciously chosen and sometimes planned with cold-blooded precision. Victims feel the full effects of this hostile act and some have even been forced to witness it directly after a shooting.

Anger is an energetic emotion: it gives some sense of power and tension-relief to the otherwise impotent griever. Anger both towards the dead person and displaced towards God, 'incompetent' politicians, social workers, doctors and other carers needs to be expressed and heard. The grieving person needs permission to feel it, and to understand that it is a normal emotion after **loss**. Once the anger and its targets have been acknowledged and explored, the pain of the person's underlying sense of dereliction, emptiness, isolation and failure can be reached. Denied or unexpressed anger may lead to **depression** which is even more common after suicide than other deaths.

Guilt after suicide may be so severe that the bereaved person may feel too unworthy to warrant seeking help. Some sources of guilt are:

- the victim feels inadequate and responsible for having 'caused' the suicide, almost as a murderer;
- the police investigation, publicity, invasion of privacy, and the inquest increase guilt;
- they should have noticed warning signs and prevented the death;
- their sense of relief after the death, perhaps because the relationship had deteriorated and the person had been alcoholic, violent, repeatedly threatening suicide, or mentally ill;
- a child or adolescent may feel responsible if a father, uncle or stepfather, etc. kills himself after their disclosure of **sexual abuse**;
- if the victim's religious beliefs still condemn suicide as sinful they will feel even more guilty and have no spiritual relief from absolution.

To say 'you shouldn't feel guilty' is unhelpful: the person feels it. Their guilt must first be heard, explored and accepted. Then its components can be examined separately. Some are 'rational' and reality-based: things the person regrets saying, doing or thinking. Some are irrational and can be challenged where appropriate: believing that one adult can control and be responsible for another's chosen action; or keep watch over someone day and night; or they could have acted on information known only in hindsight. They may concede intellectually that they were not responsible, but deeper emotional exoneration takes much longer. Assure the person that relief feelings are natural and normal and that it is 'permissible' to feel both relief and the pain of loss, and that neither emotion annihilates their underlying love.

There could be major causes for guilt. Listen non-judgementally to the person's story if the relationship was turbulent: e.g. abuse, marital conflict, affairs, quarrels, emotional blackmail, addictions, teenage rebellion, family dysfunction or criminal offences. Ambivalent relationships are associated with complicated mourning even without suicide complications.

Support and supervision are essential for those dealing with suicide. Although the counsellor believes that clients take responsibility for their own decisions and progress, unless they are in crisis or need admission to hospital, some professional and personal guilt is still often felt after a client's suicide. Debriefing (individually or in a group) should be available as soon afterwards as possible:

- to examine exactly what happened and assess standards of care and communication between the professionals involved;
- to study possible ways to prevent such a death in the future;
- to explore and share experiences, emotions, behaviours and thoughts about the death. This is especially important for anyone finding the body, whatever state it was in. It could prevent persistent intrusive images and long-term **post-traumatic stress** if done within days of the discovery.

Such debriefing also helps prepare for giving evidence at an inquest.

(e) Specialist help is available from: Samaritans: 24-hours telephone befriending; Cruse Bereavement Care (Tel: 0181 940 4818): It could be helpful for relatives after suicide, carers working with suicide, or suicidal people (not currently in crisis or deep depression) with death-related unresolved grief. Local branches offer counselling (free) and social groups. Some have groups specifically for those bereaved after suicide. Community mental health teams, youth counselling (see *adolescents*) and MIND (Tel: 0171 637 0741) may have self-referral services.

Ministers of religion may conduct the **funeral** and mention suicide explicitly if requested and appropriate. Some support and relief for guilt could be given. Ministers of various faiths and some Christian churches and sects still condemn certain (or all) suicides and may refuse to give their services, so an exploratory telephone enquiry could protect a bereaved family from further rejection and pain.

(f) Counsellors and other helpers should not collude with secrecy and offer absolute **confidentiality** to a suicidal person. When there is believed to be a serious and *imminent* danger of suicide they should request that the client discloses the situation to their GP and perhaps to family or anyone *in loco parentis*. If this is refused or not done quickly, request permission to disclose on client's behalf. Counsellors should also disclose unilaterally to obtain assessment and mental health care (voluntary or compulsory admission to hospital may be necessary). Obtain support for yourself and share responsibility. Remember that any relative can request a mental health assessment if they believe the person may need further medical treatment.

(g) Hawton, K. and Catalan, J. (1987) *Attempted Suicide*. Oxford: Oxford Medical Publications; Retterstol, N. (1993) *Suicide: A European Perspective*. Cambridge: Cambridge University Press; Wertheimer, A. (1991) *A Special Scar: The Experiences of People Bereaved by Suicide*. London: Routledge.

KAY CLYMO

Supervision

(a) Supervision is an essential component of ensuring that every caring professional and volunteer is supported in continuing to maintain their own health, effectiveness and development. Supervision can be briefly defined as the process by which a person is helped to explore their work and the effect it is having on them, in order to increase their understanding and effectiveness. The purpose of supervision is to both protect the interests of the client and to develop the person being supervised.

(b) Anyone who works in the caring professions is daily exposed to distress, dis-ease and disturbance. If professionals are truly caring, then they respond to these situations with empathy. That is, they find the place within them that can resonate with the experience and distress of the client. This may be a health visitor dealing with a cot death, a social worker forcibly taking children into care, a nurse looking after a terminally ill cancer patient who is frightened of death or a counsellor helping somebody work through their heroin addiction. Constant exposure to such emotions either leads to **stress** in the worker or to shutting down the channels of empathy and becoming less empathic and available to the client in distress. In her now famous study, Isobel Menzies (1970) showed how whole hospital systems could become bureaucratic and avoid close relationships with patients, as a defence against the anxiety and feelings inherent in the work. In consultancy work with caring organizations one not only comes across organizational defences and individual distress and burn-out, but also collegial abuse, where the various professionals relieve their pent-up feelings by taking it out on their colleagues. Teams of caring professionals that have become dysfunctional by not containing their distress and having support and supervision systems in place can become very uncaring and persecutory places to work.

Providing time for the caring professional to work through how they have been affected by the distress, disturbance and dis-ease, is only one of the three main tasks of supervision. Kadushin (1975) and Proctor (1988) have described these three tasks, using slightly different terms but describing similar processes:

Kadushin	Proctor
managerial	normative
educative	formative
supportive	restorative

The managerial or normative aspects of supervision provide an important quality control process. Supervision can ensure that there is consistency in the standards of practice delivered by a helping agency or indeed by an individual. This is not only to protect the organization, but more importantly to help protect the clients from either poor or abusive practice. It also supports the worker, as anybody in the caring professions is at times bound to be prone to acting in a reactive way or with blind spots, where they can be helped by another professional also being aware of what is happening in the relationship.

The educative aspect of supervision provides the most valuable learning forum for most helping professionals. Historically, training in social work, nursing, medicine, etc. would precede practice, with some form of internship or apprenticeship linking the theoretical training and full practice. More recently it has been recognized that good professional practice can only be sustained where the practitioner is constantly learning from experience. Learning from experience requires a skilfully facilitated space in which the practitioner's experience can be reflected upon and digested. This is the third important function of supervision.

Many new supervisors find it quite complex to balance these three different but interconnected functions of supervision (Hawkins, 1982). The supervisor has to serve the interests of the client, the supervisee and the agency, even when these seem to be in conflict. This complexity makes it essential that there is a good contracting process between the supervisor and the supervisee, in which there is a clear negotiated agreement on each of the following:

1. times and frequency of meeting;
2. who is responsible for making sure it happens;
3. the place of meeting;

4. the different functions and how the balance will be managed;
5. the parameters of the process, what can and cannot be talked about and what is confidential;
6. the style of facilitation that will be most helpful for the supervisee;
7. when the supervision will be reviewed and re-negotiated.

(d)   If we take each of these contractual elements in turn it is possible to draw out the key factors that affect supervision.

1. Times and frequency of meeting

It is important to decide whether the supervision will be on a regular basis, with appointments arranged in advance, or whether it will be ad hoc, or on demand. The danger in having an ad hoc arrangement is that it leads to a crisis orientation, that is, supervision is seen as something that only takes place when things go wrong, or when remedial action is needed. Under such an arrangement the educative and supportive elements of supervision become less developed. In my own experience it is often when I think that I have no issues to take to supervision that some of the most important issues emerge, as I do not have a pre-set agenda.

Some trainee supervisors have said that they find having regular times difficult as they do not know what to do when there are no obvious issues to focus on. This is normally the sign of an inexperienced supervisor rather than over-frequent supervision, or of a supervisory relationship in which the options and choices within supervision have not been adequately explored.

2. Who is responsible for making sure it happens?

It is also important that responsibilities are clearly agreed in the contract, that is, who is responsible for arranging the times of meetings, what will happen if one or other of the parties cannot come to the session and what sort of events will take precedence over supervision and cause the meeting to be cancelled. Supervisees can feel very let down and unsupported by a supervisor who makes a habit of cancelling their supervision meeting for 'more pressing business'.

3. The place of meeting

Supervision needs to take place in a relaxed and private space without interruptions. It is important to ensure that the phone is re-routed to be dealt with by somebody else and that other staff know that both parties are doing supervision for the allotted time span. It is best to avoid doing supervision across a desk or even around a formal table. A private interview room with a couple of armchairs provides the best sort of environment.

4. The different functions of supervision

I have described the different functions of supervision above. It is important in the contracting phase to explore each of these functions and the roles and responsibilities of both the supervisor and supervisee in relation to each function. Within the managerial function it is important that the supervisor is clear about what quality control functions they have to undertake as part of the supervision, and what these demand of the supervisee in terms of reports, both verbal and written.

In relation to the educative function, the supervisor should explore with the supervisee their learning needs and how these relate to any training the supervisee is undertaking or has recently completed. For both these two functions it is important that the relation of the supervision to any assessment procedures be clarified, whether this be writing a supervisor's report for a training course or carrying out an appraisal for the employing organization.

In the supportive function, the contractual exploration could usefully include a discussion of the supervisee's past experience of supervision, what they have found useful and what they have found unsupportive or difficult. This discussion could also include the general areas of the work where supervisees believe they want most support.

5. The parameters of the supervision process

The two most commonly asked questions in training courses for supervisors are: 'What are the boundaries between supervision and personal counselling or psychotherapy?' and: 'Should supervision be confidential?'

If we take the first of these two old chestnuts, it is important that it is clear that supervision is work-focused, even though at times work issues may involve a good deal of personal exploration. When working so intimately with personal problems and distress, it is inevitable that the worker will have their own emotions and past or present difficulties restimulated and their personal blocks reactivated. These personal areas are a necessary and important focus for supervision, as the main tool or instrument that the helping professional is using in their own person, with all its flaws and imperfections. However, it is important that these are handled sensitively by the supervisor; and that the level of personal exploration takes regard both of the level of relationship and trust that has been established, and how ready the supervisee is to discuss their own issues.

One easy way for the supervisor to handle the boundary is to ensure that the supervision session starts with what has been happening in work since last having supervision, and ends by looking at what the supervisee is going to take away from the session and use in their work in the forthcoming period. This ensures that all personal exploration is clearly within a framework of work-based issues.

Confidentiality is another complex boundary issue. If the session has no confidentiality boundary the supervisee may feel very reluctant to share personal issues or their difficulties, in fear that it may be used against them outside of the session. However, if the session is entirely confidential, supervisors may then find themselves hearing information that they know they should professionally report to other people, but they are constrained by a promise of confidentiality. One of the clearest ways of handling this dilemma is for the supervisor to explain to the supervisee that they undertake to avoid gossip about any issues that the supervisee indulges. Further, only material that is professionally important should be taken out of the session and the supervisee should always be told first. If necessary, examples of the type of material that the supervisor would take elsewhere and to whom can be cited. This may include the supervisor maintaining the freedom to discuss the supervision that they give in their own supervision.

6. The style of facilitation in the supervision

In *Supervision in the Helping Professions* (Hawkins and Shohet, 1989) we outline six different modes of focus that can be adopted in supervision.

(i) Reflection on the content of the work session: Attention is concentrated on the actual phenomena of the work sessions; how the clients presented themselves, what they chose to share, which area of their life they wanted to explore and how this session's content might relate to content from previous sessions. The aim and goal of this form of supervision is to help the worker pay attention to the client, the choices the client is making and the relatedness of the various aspects of the client's life.

(ii) Exploration of the strategies and interventions used by the worker:
The focus here is on the choices of intervention made by the worker; not only what interventions were used but also when and why they were used. Alternative strategies and interventions might then be developed and their consequences anticipated. The main goal of this form of supervision is to increase the worker's choices and skills in intervention.

(iii) Exploration of the work session process and relationship: Here the supervisor pays particular attention to what was happening consciously and unconsciously in the work session process; how the session started and finished; what happened around the edges; metaphors and images that emerged; and changes in voice and posture. The main goal of this form of supervision is the worker having greater insight and understanding of the dynamics of the work session relationship.

(iv) Focus on the worker's counter-transference: Here the supervisor concentrates on whatever is still being carried by the worker, both consciously and unconsciously, from the work session and the client. The counter-transference may be of four different kinds: personal material of the worker that has been restimulated by the work session; the transferential role that the worker has been cast into by the client; the worker's unconscious attempt to 'counter' the transference of the client; projected material of the clients that the worker has taken in somatically, psychically or mentally (see also Casement, 1985: 92–3).

(v) Focus on the here-and-now process as a mirror or parallel of the there-and-then process: Here the supervisor focuses on the relationship in the supervision session in order to explore how it might be unconsciously playing out or paralleling the hidden dynamics of the work session (Mattinson, 1975: Searles, 1955). Thus, if the client was covertly acting in a passive-aggressive way to the worker, this might emerge in the supervision by the worker becoming unconsciously passive-aggressive to the supervisor as they discuss that particular client.

(vi) Focus on the supervisor's counter-transference: Here the supervisor primarily pays attention to their own here-and-now experience in the supervision; what feelings, thoughts and images the shared work session material stirs up in them. The supervisor uses these responses to provide reflective illumination for the worker. The unconscious material of the work session which has been unheard at the conscious level by the worker may emerge in the thoughts, feelings and images of the supervisor.

We argue that good supervision in any of the helping professions uses all six modes, but the balance depends on the type of work and the supervisee's needs and developmental level. Poor supervision only uses a limited number of foci, and these are dependent on the supervisor's preferred ways of working. This model was originally written to provide a language for supervisees to use in negotiating with their supervisor for the style of supervision they most wanted.

7. *Review and renegotiation*
Forming a clear contract can never be a once and for ever process as the needs of both parties will change and develop over time. Thus it is essential that regular feedback is built into the supervision process and that from time to time there are more formal times for reviewing the contract and negotiating changes. Clear structures and skills for giving and receiving feedback in both directions are an essential component of quality supervision. Such skills and structures are outlined in Hawkins and Shohet (1989: 83–4).

(e)   Names of possible supervisors can be obtained from either:
    British Association of Counselling, 1 Regent Place, Rugby, Warwickshire CV21 3PJ (Tel: 01788 578328); or United Kingdom Council for Psychotherapy, Regent's College, Regent's Park, London NW1 4NS (Tel: 0171 487 7554).
    Training in supervision is available from:
    Centre for Staff Team Development, c/o Bath Consultancy Group, 24 Gay Street, Bath BA1 2PD (Tel: 01225 333737); Metanoia, 13 North Common Road, Ealing, London W5 2QB; Roehampton Institute, Department of Psychology, Digby Stuart College, Roehampton Vale, Roehampton, London SW15 5PU; the Tavistock Clinic, 120 Belsize Lane, London NW3 5BA; University of Leicester Department of Adult Education, University Road, Leicester LE1 7RH (Tel: 0116 252 2471); Westminster Pastoral Foundation, 23 Kensington Square, London W8 5HN (Tel: 0171 937 6956).

(f)   Issues of overlap occur between the practice of supervision and managerial issues on the one hand, and personal issues on the other. I refer the reader to sections (b) and (d.5) above.

(g)   Brown, A. and Bourne, I. (1995) *Supervision in Social Work and Community Settings*. Buckingham: Open University Press; Dryden, W. and Thorne, B. (eds) (1991) *Training and Supervision for Counselling in Action*. London: Sage Publications; Hawkins, P. and Shohet, R. (1989) *Supervision in the Helping Professions*. Buckingham: Open University Press.

PETER HAWKINS

Telephone, use of

(a)   The telephone has become a key piece of communications technology in the 1990s and has influenced developments across the board in
the caring professions. From simply being used to make appointments
for a range of services, the telephone is now seen by many as a valid
mode of delivery of most helping services including bona fide counselling. It has become a major component in the human services network of
the developed world. The growth of telephone helplines or hotlines can
be seen as a sign of the acceptance of the telephone as the medium of
choice for many people and services. This article will look briefly at a
number of uses of the telephone in caring work, but will concentrate on
the implications for the core helping relationships at the heart of the
services offered by the majority of individuals and agencies. As technology changes so rapidly in this field, it is to be expected that the
associated issues will change and develop accordingly. Agencies should
not expect policy or practice to reach a state of completion or competence, but rather be in a constant state of development and revision.
This article does not offer solutions: it raises new issues and offers
points for consideration when contemplating using the telephone in
caring work.

(b)   Use of the telephone by clients has many implications for helping
relationships in the caring professions. This use generally falls into two
categories: 1. delivery of the helping service, and 2. supporting the
delivery of the helping service. The latter, although frequently carried
out by administrative staff, still requires thoughtful preparation and
appropriate training. Unfortunately there is not the space to deal with
this latter area in this article.

While the above categories are largely 'agency-centred', it is also
helpful to look at telephone use from the point of view of the client.
Since the client's or agency's reasons for choosing the telephone shapes
the nature of the helping activity, the possible advantages of using the
telephone in helping situations and relationships are briefly described.
Understanding the reasons why clients may prefer to use the telephone
also helps us to respond sensitively to callers, and begin to empathize
with them.

Advantages to the client

Convenience: Many clients have restricted mobility or freedom, e.g.
single parents with young children, disabled people, those living in
remote/unpopulated areas, those caring for infirm relatives, people who
find transport difficult, those whose personal freedom is restricted, e.g.
children, old people, abused women.

Cost: The telephone is becoming the cheapest way of gaining access to a service or to make contact with others, if one compares the cost of a cheap local call with a bus/train journey or petrol and parking.

Control: This manifests itself as giving power to the client over several relationship factors which are usually determined by the physical realities and social conventions of face-to-face relationships; e.g. clients may feel more in control if they can put the receiver down and withdraw from the session without public embarrassment or explanation. The telephone is also a low-risk, low-commitment way of checking out the agency and its service.

Anonymity: The telephone gives power to the client to remain anonymous. This cloak of anonymity was used by Davis (1982) when a role player called a selection of British hotlines to evaluate their listening skills.

Image: For some people, going to get help, even help to which they are legally entitled from a statutory agency, carries a social stigma which effectively excludes them from access to that help.

Fear: Some clients are just too frightened to go to a counsellor or agency for help. The telephone is a safe way of making contact with strangers or specialist helpers without having to meet them.

Advantages to the agency or helper

Accommodation: There is no need for private interview rooms or reception areas. Location of premises and environment is less important. In extreme cases, when helpers work from home, the need for accommodation is almost eliminated altogether.

Counsellor/helper safety: Agencies can achieve a degree of anonymity for their workers and since they do not meet clients face-to-face, they are at reduced personal risk.

Staffing: Fewer staff are required for a telephone service and they can be more flexibly employed. Some agencies employ staff as 'home workers' although this raises other issues dealt with below.

(d) *Skills:*   The notion of 'telephone manner' is familiar to us all and conjures up images which vary from the caring 'Samaritans, can I help?' to the unnatural sing-song of the corporate receptionist. We all have a telephone manner and a 'telephone voice' which are significantly different from our face-to-face ways of communicating. In counselling and helping we often talk about the 'baggage' we bring to helping relationships and how we might become aware of this so as to not let it get in the way of our helping. It is a good idea to develop the same attitude regarding the 'baggage' we bring to each telephone helping relationship. It is therefore worthwhile looking at why we behave differently on the phone. Exploration of the personal meaning of the telephone for each of us should be the beginning point of any telephone training for helpers. Perhaps we associate the telephone with bad news, or good news. Perhaps we see the telephone as an irritating intrusion into our private lives, or perhaps it is a life-saving link to the outside world. The skills of telephone helping are grouped around understanding relationship dynamics without sight of the client and in a changed power structure, e.g. clients can keep their identity secret and can terminate the relationship without undue embarrassment.

Technology: Any comments on technology are destined to be either out of date as soon as they are printed or predictions that are simply wrong. Recent and proposed developments in communications and technology offer varying opportunities and threats to telephone helping. While the use of answer-phones is now commonplace, they can still put off the less motivated or more anxious out-of-office-hours caller. Caller identification is a facility which will show the number of the phone making the call as it is ringing. Introduced as a security and 'convenience' measure in the USA (i.e. you can pretend to be out when certain people call), it is seen by helplines to threaten the essential anonymity of the caller which is central to the service they offer. Itemized bills pose a similar threat; imagine a woman abused by her husband, kept effectively housebound, who calls a 'confidential' helpline, only to find that the call is presented on the next itemized bill. While some large agencies might be able to afford the use of 0800 toll-free or other ways of avoiding this trap, the majority of low-budget services may find this a problem.

On the positive side, some agencies use automatic call-diversion (available on digital exchanges) to feed the call from their central office number to volunteers working from home. Others (e.g. some employee assistance programmes) use a central control or operator to divert calls with a 'personal touch' to the appropriate home-based counsellor. These devices protect the volunteer or on-call home-based worker from having their private phone number given out to clients.

Access: Issues of opportunity of access are as relevant for telephone service users as they are for face-to-face users. All providers of helping services should ask: 'Who is this service for?' with a view to making it as accessible as possible or in order to limit access to those entitled to use the service. Sensitivity to **gender** of helper, provision for non English-speaking users, acknowledgement of other cultural issues, should be familiar to all service providers and should be carried through to any telephone services. Service providers should also consider what special provision they wish to make for callers with hearing problems and whether to operate a toll-free number or local rate number. Some local authority funded agencies may be 'allowed' to provide a service only to those within a certain geographical area, so a respectful way of turning some callers away must be developed.

Boundaries: The telephone provides unique opportunities for helping relationships. Because we often do not view the telephone as a valid relationship-building medium, we might also discount the powerful effect that telephone-based relationships might have. Counsellors engaged in face-to-face helping might have concerns if their client seeks help from another counsellor in parallel to their own helping relationship. Are such concerns legitimate when the client seeks additional help from a telephone counselling agency? How do we monitor this boundary between helpers?

Most counselling and caring work includes some notion of confidentiality of the client's material. When working on the telephone it becomes clear that confidentiality and privacy (often thought of as inseparable when working face-to-face) are different. Some public settings can be confidential – sitting on a park bench with no-one else within hearing range, while some interviews in a private room are not confidential – the helper may tell others afterwards. A large proportion of highly confidential telephone work can be done in a large room occupied by many helper/operators with a fair amount of background noise, conditions which would render most face-to-face work impossible.

Problem calls: Many people entering the world of offering caring relationships over the telephone are unprepared for what I have come to identify as 'calls we would rather not receive'. Some people refer to such calls as 'problem calls' but it is clear that there are many types of call which fall into this category and not all of them are a problem to everyone. This category of calls includes: abusive, violent and threatening calls, calls from people (mostly men) who want to talk to someone (mostly women) while they masturbate, silent calls, calls from people who are threatening self-harm or **suicide**, callers asking for help or action on behalf of a third party. Helpers need careful selection and preparation if they are to feel confident in dealing sensitively and appropriately with this range of calls. Whenever a phone number is given out offering help, advice, assistance or simply information (even customer services lines) it will attract its share of hurt, distressed, angry and damaged callers. There is no way to avoid such calls, so helpers must be prepared through training to deal with them so as to not damage the caller further and to protect themselves from needless distress.

Support: Whenever an individual telephone helper receives a call they would rather not have received, they will suffer varying degrees of distress and their immediate need is for support. This can be in the form of formal debriefing, spot supervision, time out in a quiet room to gather their thoughts or someone with whom they can let off steam. Readers not familiar with supervision will find the article on **supervision** helpful. Agencies must not think they can get away with no support for telephone workers. Debriefing and time out away from the phone lines should be offered. Debriefing can follow a pre-determined structure if necessary and may be conducted by a colleague or line manager.

Training: It is now accepted that specialized training for telephone helpers is necessary, from customer relations through to bona fide counselling. Training needs to address the key issues raised here, and should give an opportunity for helpers to practise the skills, using real telephone equipment, preferably with tape-recording facilities. It is not enough to prepare helpers by giving them training in face-to-face helping, then putting them straight on to the telephone. There are a few consultants and trainers with the experience and skills to enable them to help with this training.

(c)   Organizations and agencies with experience of using the telephone in caring work may be able to offer advice and information on setting up and training: Samaritans, 17 Uxbridge Road, Slough SL1 1SN, and local telephone directories; Broadcasting Supporting Services (providers of telephone helplines to support telephone and radio programmes), 21 Manor Street, Ardwick, Manchester M12 6HE and 252 Western Avenue, London W3 6XJ; Childline, Freepost 111, London N1 0BR; National AIDS Helpline, PO Box 1577, London NW1 3DW; Parentline (support to parents under stress), 106 Godstone Road, Whyteleafe CR3 0EB.

(g)   Sanders, P. (1992) *An Incomplete Guide to Using Counselling Skills on the Telephone.* Manchester: PCCS; The Telephone Helplines Group (1993) *Telephone Helplines: Guidelines for Good Practice* (2nd edn). c/o Broadcasting Support Services, 252 Western Avenue, London W3 6XJ.

PETE SANDERS

Terminal illness

(a) A terminal illness is one where medical assessment concludes that death is inevitable and no realistic possibility of recovery remains. The time between diagnosis and death varies enormously.

(b) The medical implications after a terminal diagnosis are necessarily that it is futile to continue treatments aimed entirely at cure. Those like chemo- and radiotherapy have major side-effects (nausea and fatigue) though radiotherapy still controls symptoms in some cancer patients. Otherwise they could impair the quality of life, reduce stamina, and even shorten the time remaining, especially in those requiring hospital admission or tiring and painful long-distance travel for specialist outpatient care. Stress from these now unnecessary further disruptions could contribute to family problems like neglect of others' needs and marital breakdown. Stopping, or not offering, such treatments (e.g. if exploratory surgery has already revealed a hopeless situation) means that the only realistic medical help now is *palliative care*. Its holistic approach and creative philosophy, pioneered by the hospice movement aims at:

1. giving effective symptom relief
2. retarding the disease's progress, perhaps prolonging life
3. treating concurrent diseases (e.g. secondary infections and depression)
4. improving the quality of life
5. helping the patient's emotional, social and spiritual needs
6. supporting the family emotionally and practically
7. giving bereavement support after the death.

If patient and family can accept the painful prognosis, they may feel immense relief at no longer having to plan precious remaining time round hospitals and treatment. They can then make a realistic choice of a care-plan best suited to their needs, illness and circumstances. Local facilities vary enormously but usually include:

Hospital: in/outpatient; some have palliative care wards, Macmillan nurses and social workers

Hospice: respite care: day centre; counselling; assessment and symptom control; dying in final phase; bereavement support

Home care: using GP, district nurse, Macmillan, Marie Curie and other nurses, home care (social services) and equipment loans.

Modern methods of symptom relief, e.g. sustained-release drug formulations and variably controlled syringe-driver delivery, reduce anxiety and enable families to cope better. Dying at home is becoming more common again, because it retains, wherever possible, an atmosphere of familiarity, normality, peace, freedom and comfort. Hospital or hospice admission may still be needed at various times, so it is unethical to guarantee that a patient will remain at home.

Patients may refuse treatment for secondary infections and make a 'living will' recording wishes in case mental function deteriorates: not to be resuscitated, permission given or refused for organ donation, or disposal of the body (e.g. medical research). Discussing such painful matters certainly reduces denial in everyone affected.

People vary in their balancing of hope and despair. This may be affected daily or even hourly, by the severity of current symptoms or the context of their conversation. Many seem to accept that they are dying but actually talk that way to convince themselves.

Some people have no discernible symptoms, their illness having been diagnosed only after routine tests or screening. Since they do not feel or look ill, they and their relatives understandably have difficulty in believing that they have any disease, let alone a fatal one. This is also true for patients in healthy remission (e.g. leukaemia). Unfortunately, many cancers cause no noticeable symptoms until they are untreatable.

Unless denial is rigidly maintained, terminal illness usually allows some preparation for death. Sometimes, however, patients with degenerative disease deteriorate gradually but die unexpectedly from an infection. Unprepared relatives experience the death as sudden, though also a release from further distressing deterioration. With good symptom control, a quite seriously ill person may continue to deny that death is near. Patients sometimes choose to retain some pain to remind them of this underlying reality.

AIDS is not itself a terminal illness; death is caused by opportunistic infections by which the body's ineffective immune system is now overwhelmed. Emotionally, however, it must feel terminal to everyone involved even though infections are usually treated until death. Dementia and Alzheimer's disease also feel emotionally terminal to relatives watching the person they knew and loved 'die' within their healthy body-frame.

In counselling, it probably matters less about an exact definition of 'terminal' than people's reactions to serious life-threatening illness. People need help whether they know, believe or deny the prognosis and seek at least a second opinion as they cling tenaciously to a '15 per cent chance'. A few do recover, against all expectation, and even this could be difficult if patients have enjoyed the secondary gains of being ill, or lose the support of terminal-care facilities. Relatives have grieved since the diagnosis and may already have 'let go' both emotionally and functionally. Everyone's grief process must now operate 'in reverse' and it takes time for full acceptance even of good news. This is true also when someone's 'growth' is diagnosed as benign, or after a false positive diagnosis when relief is compounded by anger and litigation if aggressive treatment was given.

(d) Kübler-Ross (1969) proposed a five-stage model to reflect the dying process during terminal illness:

- denial
- anger
- bargaining
- depression
- acceptance

Nurses are taught this, but when taken too simplistically it can demean and depersonalize – e.g. nurse telling patient 'You're in the angry stage'. Its components are certainly observed, but people rarely progress in such a linear sequence; they display various emotions simultaneously and oscillate between widely variable behaviours.

After the diagnosis, both patient and close relatives face death with various degrees of realistic acceptance while negotiating the ever-increasing changes which the illness, dying and prospects beyond require. While certain aspects are more prominent for the patient, and others for the relatives, their overall change process is similar. These are its main components:

1. moving from ignorance, disbelief and denial towards accepting the reality of each new issue and its likely implications, and eventually of death;
2. grieving at various stages of the illness for all the **losses**:
   - self as a conscious person (patient)
   - potential
   - each body part and healthy function, as new symptoms develop
   - freedom, privacy, dignity, sexual expression, appearance, independence
   - formerly-active role in family and outside life
   - future after the death.

This involves feeling and expressing emotions: anger, irritability, sadness, guilt, remorse, despair, hope, fear, anxiety. **Depression** may need treatment;

3. developing behavioural and cognitive ways of avoiding or facing realities:
   resisting – withdrawal, distancing, avoidance, regression, rigidity, overactivity, unrealistic optimism, alcohol/drug abuse;

evaluating – seeking medical information; enquiring about care facilities;

accepting – trying new skills, inventing practical aids, fundraising, valuing each new day. Planning finances, funeral, saying goodbye;

4. continually adjusting self-view, world-view and belief-system to accommodate increasing discrepancies between what was, what now is and what will be;

5. retaining inwardly a balanced, realistic view of the past;

6. wondering about dying. Many people are more afraid of dying than of being dead, mentally extrapolating their current symptoms to a terrifying fantasy of unbearable pain and suffocation. (Reassurance that modern methods of pain relief are very effective for most patients could help here);

7. examining ideas and fears of what lies beyond death. Whatever their previous beliefs, or fantasies that death happens only to others, it is now necessary to re-explore unknowable issues: not-being, judgement, heaven, hell. Since major illness often results in emotional and behavioural regression, earlier naïve or child-like ideas may give more hope and comfort than courageous adult agnosticism;

8. accepting the inevitable with reluctance, resignation, optimism or hope.

Acceptance is not always achieved and should never be regarded as everyone's only goal. Patients who fight hopefully seem often to outlive those who resign themselves prematurely.

Within the same family people handle change at different rates and with variable effectiveness, perhaps feeling similar emotions but with different responses reflecting each person's personality, coping style, past experiences and future perspective. Their individual losses vary according to the illness and the type and quality of the relationship. When you lose your parents you lose your past, your partner your present, and your children your future.

Family dynamics, roles and rules also determine how a member reacts. 'Vulnerable' ones (often children and sometimes the patient) are not told the true diagnosis (the conspiracy of silence), making honest communication and reality-based support difficult or impossible. Some families cannot express feelings freely; someone has to be 'strong' and cope. Family changes will vary depending on the dying person's role: scapegoat, victim, organizer, boss, communications link, breadwinner, listener, nurturer, etc. Sibling order and status will change if a child is dying, while remaining children may have to act out alien roles – being 'clever' or 'good' – and many continue to do this for the rest of their life (see *children's experience of loss and death*). If a parent is dying, children (especially the eldest) may be forced to take responsibilities beyond their age and lose their remaining childhood. Some rebel or seek attention while others work desperately hard at school or college to please their dying parent.

Some religious people cannot reconcile their painful feelings with their current understanding of faith (see *religious belief*). Their prayers for recovery have obviously 'failed' and they feel guilty and inadequate when seeing others apparently casting their burdens or 'accepting God's will'. Their concept of resurrection, hope or God's love gives no consolation as they watch themselves or their loved one dying. A crisis of faith may then alienate them from their church or family, increasing further their isolation and inner loneliness.

Some relatives feel strongly ambivalent towards the patient if their illness was self-inflicted (**AIDS**, lung cancer, liver cirrhosis). Heart failure from a partner's driven workaholism may elicit anger at years of lonely neglect as feelings of incipient dereliction resonate with those from earlier experiences.

Uncaring behaviour towards a dying parent might reflect anger and bitterness after **childhood abuse**. Sometimes only now do siblings discover that they had this same experience, gaining relief by sharing details of their guilty memories.

An unsatisfactory relationship involves grief for lost potential. Any remaining hope for reparation, however irrational, must now be abandoned and grief for what was not needs to be expressed and explored.

Dying **adolescents** may resent or reject their mother's help with intimate body functions. They are forced to be dependent just when they were becoming private, autonomous and perhaps rebellious, so many prefer to confide in and receive care from an outsider.

Ex-family members, homosexual or extramarital lovers may grieve privately and be unable to communicate with the dying person, or attend the funeral. There could be problems about wills, property distribution or burial arrangements, and common-law or homosexual partners might have legal difficulties about home-ownership or inheritance.

Fear underlies many emotions and behaviours, especially anger. **Guilt** often contains fear of not being respected, loved or accepted were the truth known. Many people cannot mention deep fears explicitly, so helpers need to detect them in hints, gallows humour, reasons for introducing a topic, double messages, or parting remarks. If an immediate response is impossible or inappropriate, significant remarks should be noted and reintroduced at a more suitable occasion. Saying 'Don't worry' is not helpful, but these interventions could be:

- help the person to acknowledge and name a specific fear;
- discover what is believed, known or fantasized;
- reassure or correct misunderstandings and outdated ideas (e.g. about uncontrollable pain);
- ask about past experiences as a possible source for this fear;
- explore worst imagined scenarios;
- explore any realistic ways of coping with or preventing the feared issue;
- share thoughts and feelings about unfathomable or unknowable aspects.

Entering more deeply and honestly into fear seems unnatural and cruel when someone is suffering already, so most people avoid such pain. Nevertheless it can give enormous relief to explore and share these lonely feelings even when reassurance is impossible and nothing can be done about them. Help with exploring specific fears could enable the person to move further from denial towards reality.

The terminal illness period can be a surprisingly enriching time for enjoying deeper, perhaps more honest relationships, reconciliations, celebration of ordinary things, setting realistic goals to maintain hope and self-esteem, solving some problems, re-appraising priorities and values, spiritual growth and deeper self-understanding. Most people, whatever their philosophy, need to believe that their life had unique value and meaning. Helping to validate their life by exploring these aspects can give mutual interest, satisfaction and pleasure

childhood memories/photos	achievements/proudest
growing up	moments
happiest/saddest/difficult times	wartime
family relationships	unfulfilled hopes
school, college, jobs	regrets/mistakes
enthusiasms	valuable things learnt.

Video/audio talks or interviews can be recorded or letters written (perhaps including a poem or gift) to be read later by children now too young to understand – confirmation day, 18th birthday, wedding, graduation, childbirth.

Both patient and relatives may become increasingly detached, especially after a long illness when most grieving and letting-go has been done and the patient even wants to die. Another person's presence or touch may be their last life-link; if that person leaves, however briefly, the patient may cease engaging and die quickly. This happens frequently, leaving relatives feeling guilty; they need to understand that their absence perhaps gave final 'permission' to die.

As energies dwindle, defences are lowered, and many dying people regress physically and emotionally. Being fed and bathed elicits memories of their childhood experiences. It is interesting that many call to their mother at this final insecurity and the almost universally-reported 'light at the end of the tunnel' in people's near-death experiences could be a recapitulation of their original birth-journey and first visual image.

(e)   Information about resources for terminal care may be available from any local hospice, Citizens Advice Bureaux, social services and Macmillan nurses.

(f)   Other factors that need to be borne in mind are:

* the conspiracy of silence: whose wishes are being honoured? There are issues about communication between the family and professionals about 'who knows' and 'who doesn't know' the prognosis;
* religious and cultural needs, which may include the handling of the dead body and last rites;
* in cases of **AIDS** there will be special need for confidentiality about the diagnosis;
* support for professional and other carers, especially those who visit homes. They could benefit from debriefing and sharing feelings after the death and the funeral.

(g)   Buckman, R. (1992) *How to Break Bad News: A Guide for Health-Care Professionals*. London: Macmillan; Moorey, S. and Greer, S. (1989) *Psychological Therapy for Patients with Cancer*. London: Heinemann Medical Books; Robbins, J. (1989) *Caring for the Dying Patient and the Family* (2nd edn). London: Chapman and Hall.

KAY CLYMO

Transvestism and trans-sexualism

(a)   *Transvestism* is dressing up in clothes of the opposite sex – literally, cross-dressing. As such it is not a phenomenon we are unused to. Publicly women's fashions often include conventional men's wear. Men, though on the whole more reticent, often take delight in cross-dressing when the occasion allows it.

Cross-dressing is common enough, but the term 'transvestite' also refers more particularly to men who cross-dress, initially in private, but then sometimes in public, for sexual excitement. The handling and wearing of female clothes can be a type of fetish and like other fetishes is confined almost entirely to men.

Trans-sexualism can be defined as the way in which people assume a gender identity which is opposite to that which is indicated biologically. When the term was first used (Benjamin, 1953) it referred not simply to those who happened to behave like their opposite gender but who, despite a biological identity with one sex, were convinced they belonged to the other sex. This belief is held from an early age and it intensifies with age to the point when such people are offended by their own genitalia. A sex change operation (sexual reassignment) becomes seen as the only way they are likely to obtain a more complete and satisfying identity. It contrasts with transvestism in that it is about sexual identity (gender) rather than genital excitement (sex).

(b)   There are five different kinds of transvestites:

1. The *fetishistic* enjoy wearing a few female garments or a whole outfit and do so to become sexually aroused. They either masturbate on their own or invite their partner to engage sexually while they are cross-dressed. These men are heterosexual and quite happy about being male. Prince and Bentler's survey (1972) found that of 504 cases more than three-quarters had been married and about two-thirds were still married. Three-quarters of them were fathers.

2. *Trans-sexuals* cross-dress, not for sexual arousal, but because it feels more comfortable to do so.

3. *Male homosexuals* sometimes cross-dress to attract heterosexual men, either for their own pleasure or for prostitution. The impersonation might be a crude caricature of the male view of a sexy woman.

4. The *mixed group* have attributes of more than one of the above: a complex mix of fetishistic, trans-sexual and homosexual tendencies. Within this group might be the man who initially cross-dresses occasionally as a fetish, but who moves towards a stronger need to cross-dress as he gives way to a latent desire to adopt a female role.

5. The *entertainers* are a part of a long tradition, common enough when there were no female actors. It is a device that is used for comic effect and perhaps on another level to present an intriguing sexual illusion.

Transvestism is rarely presented as a problem unless the fetishistic urge increases and begins to threaten a relationship. Helpers who counsel couples report a common scenario: the man who is discovered wearing female clothes (not necessarily accidentally) by his partner. After the initial shock, the woman may come to terms with this occasional variation. But he becomes less discreet and more persistent in his demands, and eventually, even though the relationship might be good in other aspects, the woman finds his behaviour intolerable.

Trans-sexualism is even less likely to be presented as a problem apart from within a specialized clinical setting. Pauly (1969) estimates the prevalence of male trans-sexualism at 1:100,000 of the general population. Women trans-sexuals represent about a quarter of that number. Over a period of four years Tully (1992) worked with 200 applicants for gender reassignment at the Charing Cross Hospital Gender Identity Clinic. Nearly 30 per cent of this group received surgery, the majority male to female. To seek this radical surgery may seem extreme. By some it is seen as mutilation and a part of the controlling of gender stereotypes (Raymond, 1980).

There are many people who would not go to this length but who nevertheless have mixed feelings about their identity. It may be that they are physically one sex while mentally the other; or more unusually, it might be that physically there is some confusion because of congenital organ defects. Whatever the reason, the confusion is likely to make it difficult to relate confidently to other people whether they are seen as the same sex or the opposite. It might produce feelings of exasperation because there is no clear purpose in life. It is hard to integrate in society or in themselves. There is the feeling of being the odd one out, of being rejected and misunderstood. There may be acute self-consciousness or self-loathing which could either produce the need to withdraw into a private world, or a reactionary self-flaunting, an attempt to be the centre of attention.

(c) *Transvestism:*   A psychoanalytical understanding of the need to cross-dress as a fetish is that it is a reaction to the fear of castration. Freud considered that no men were spared the fright of castration at the sight of female genitalia. The wearing of women's clothes overcomes this fear by creating a woman who has a penis. So, 'the horror of castration has set up a memorial to itself in the creation of this substitute' (Freud, 1927). It is argued that most of the attention in cross-dressing is not on the penis which is hidden but on the clothing. There is, however, no denying the penis is still there, even in secret.

For some cross-dressers, women's underclothes might be seen as an extension of the female body. The first erotic experience might have been the contact with clothes belonging to mother and cross-dressing might therefore reflect incestuous desires. Wearing female clothes enables them to create another woman over whom they blissfully have control and who is therefore not threatening.

Trans-sexualism: Stoller (1979) offers a comprehensive explanation for what he calls 'primary trans-sexualism' i.e. those who have always behaved as if they were the opposite sex.

He describes how the mother of the male trans-sexual has strong masculine attributes. The father is passive and distant. When the mother bears a son she feels she has become complete for the first time. She lives in and for her son who becomes an extension of her own body, never really separate. Father is kept out and so, unlike other male children, the child experiences no Oedipal conflict. As the mother identifies with her son so he identifies with her. He does not want to possess her erotically. Instead he wants to be like her.

Green (1974) finds that amongst boys who are confused about their gender, there has always been the tendency to play the female role and that this has been allowed or encouraged by parents. He finds that mother is over-protective of her son and discourages rough-and-tumble play. Like Stoller he identifies excessive maternal attention and physical contact resulting in a lack of separateness and 'individuation' of the boy from his mother, although Green only recognizes this with any certainty in a minority of cases.

Other predisposing factors might be the loss or absence of father, lack of male playmates, or a physical beauty that encourages others to treat him like a girl.

Female trans-sexuality might be produced by the opposite circumstances, that is, by the girl having a mother who is not able to function as a mother in the first few months or so. The girl's masculinity might be born from pain and conflict, not bliss; from premature separation from mother rather than symbiosis. One way of trying to reach mother might be in her masculinity, attempting to stimulate father's maleness. The relationship with father might be much closer and it might have promoted masculine behaviour (Pauly, 1969).

It must, however, be emphasized that there is generally very little understanding of the causes of either transvestism or trans-sexualism. Any aetiology can only be tentative.

(d) *Transvestism* is rarely a problem in itself. Like other fetishes it may be regarded by some as abnormality, but by its adherents it is seen as a satisfying way or expressing their erotic life. Typically it starts as an experiment around puberty or in adolescence. The induced sexual excitement might be stronger than before, and it quickly becomes an experience indulged in whenever there is an opportunity.

Few transvestites ever reach the point therefore when they would wish to eliminate this behaviour. It is not against the law, though sometimes it leads to offences like stealing clothes or soliciting.

It is likely therefore to be raised in counselling as an incidental rather than as the presenting problem. If this is so it is not helpful if the counsellor's attention is drawn towards it disproportionately either by natural curiosity or prejudicial assumptions.

The exception is when cross-dressing has become intolerable for the female partner. In this circumstance there are two points worth bearing in mind.

Firstly, even though the transvestite may appear to be amenable to giving up the behaviour, the prognosis for successfully doing so is poor. If the cross-dressing is purely fetishistic without any trans-sexual elements and the motivation for change sufficiently strong then behaviour therapy might justify more optimism. Aversion therapy, though generally unfashionable, has been used with some success (Gelder and Marks, 1969). Unless the transvestite is willing to undergo this kind of treatment there is little hope for change, and any decision the couple are having to make about the future of their relationship is best made in this knowledge.

Secondly, and perhaps more hopefully, there do seem to be fluctuations in fetishistic behaviour. More particularly, the reliance on fetish objects can vary according to the state of the relationship. If this pattern is recognizable then it would clearly be helpful to focus on the relationship between the couple, especially sexually. The need to cross-dress might be reduced as the relationship becomes more satisfying.

Trans-sexualism: Primary trans-sexuals are unlikely to present to unspecialized helpers. Usually they are only interested in becoming more completely the gender they see themselves.

For all counsellors and helpers however, the phenomenon of trans-sexuality challenges attitudes towards gender differences (see *gender issues*). If we have a view of behaviour that clearly distinguishes male and female roles then we could regard many people as behaving trans-sexually. Within present-day Western culture, especially amongst younger people, there is evidence of stereotypical gender roles being questioned and dismantled. Yet the demands for conformity to a male/ female dichotomy largely persist. How we respond to those who are having difficulty with gender identity is largely determined by the extent to which we are influenced by those demands. The term 'trans-sexualism' suggests crossing over from one sex to the other, implying there are no gradations in between. To live with uncertainty and ambiguity is not easy, but like Brierley (1984: 85) it might be more accurate to speak of 'variation in gender identity' rather than trans-sexualism.

Degrees of ambiguity are common enough and helpers will be faced by men and women who find they are somewhere in between being male and female. If this is an issue it may be quite frightening for the client, especially for the young client who feels pressurized to establish some identity against the risk of isolation. Help may be needed to overcome these fears and to make a choice which is compatible with prevalent feelings; or to tolerate the ambiguity. If the choice is made there is then a process of learning to live with it. This includes learning how to cope with the reactions of other people, especially parents and family. Adjustments may have to be made to personal or others' expectations in much the same way as for the homosexual person.

The whole process requires a gentle but encouraging approach. It is likely to include the management or hostility which is felt towards an alien society or punitive parents.

(e) The Beaumont Society offers counselling and support for transvestites and their families: the Beaumont Society, BM Box 3084, London WC1N 3XX (Helpline: Tel: 0181 756 1782); The Gender Identity Clinic (Charing Cross Hospital, London) offers counselling and advice for trans-sexuals (Tel: 0181 846 1234).

(f) At the Gender Identity Clinic, counselling is an important part of the process. If clients are referred there the question arises whether the counsellor should continue to work with the client. There may have to be some liaison with the clinic to resolve this. The same might apply with clients being referred to the Beaumont Society.

(g) Hirschfield, M. (1991) *Transvestites: The Erotic Drive to Cross-Dress*. Buffalo, NY: Prometheus Books; Tully, B. (1992) *Accounting for Transsexualism and Transhomosexuality*. London: Whiting and Birch.

GUY DEANS

Victims of crime

(a) Victims are those who suffer directly as a result of a crime, or are indirectly affected, e.g. family, colleagues, witnesses. I use the term to cover both direct and indirect victims unless stated otherwise. By crime I mean unlawful acts against property or persons, whether reported to the appropriate authority or not. In general the victims of the following crimes are offered the services of Victim Support: theft, criminal damage, burglary, actual or grievous bodily harm, robbery, aggravated burglary, sexual assault, rape and relatives of murder victims (see *violence towards women*). Local Victim Support schemes have their own individual policies within the guidelines issued by the National Association of Victim Support Schemes.

Maguire and Corbett (1986) found that 25 per cent of victims of serious crimes – burglary (with loss), 'snatch' theft, robbery and serious assaults – and 10 per cent of all victims of recorded offences against individuals, can be shown to be in need of some sort of psychological support or reassurance. Furthermore, if practical needs are added, which were often intertwined with emotional needs, about 30–40 per cent of victims of more serious offences are in need of support. Nicolson (1993) confirms that 25 per cent of victims experience acute distress immediately after the burglary, with 65 per cent of victims showing persistent effects four to ten weeks later. She also finds that many people assume that their reaction to the crime is not serious enough to merit the help of Victim Support.

While each crime brings its own difficulties, it should be remembered that its impact is greatly affected by the individual circumstances of each victim, e.g. what happens to the victim immediately after the crime, and the way others such as family, friends, professionals and colleagues respond to them in a more general sense. Other factors include the current life situation, previous life experiences, personality, coping strategies, personal networks, etc.

Common reactions to all crime are:

- disturbed eating patterns and feelings of nausea; actual sickness may be experienced;
- fear of being watched;
- fear that offenders will return because they now know what there is in the house, or that they will return after replacement by insurance;
- fear of leaving the house and of returning to the house; yet also fear of staying in the house. This impossible set of dilemmas often leads to the desire to move house;
- feelings of being unclean or contaminated, with a need to scrub the whole house, or to throw away items that have been touched;
- sleeping difficulties, including dreams and nightmares, may be experienced over a period of time.

Alongside these reactions victims initially suffer shock, disbelief about the crime. This can result in them feeling confused, unable to concentrate, disoriented, lacking energy and motivation, or depressed. They may be upset and weep, be angry and belligerent, or blame self and others such as family members, the police or society. Others may make light of it, joking or diminishing what has happened.

In instances of offences involving property, theft – such as the loss of a radio from a car – may be inconvenient and present practical or financial difficulties; whereas a purse containing a personal memento of a deceased parent may be the last straw, which releases the flood-gates of intense grief (see *loss*). Criminal damage can range from being a minor irritation to indicating deeper relationship problems within the family or the neighbourhood. Racial harassment may be an issue here (see *racism and prejudice*). In cases of burglary of a home, the strength of feelings varies from being an inconvenience to being personally violated. The impact is greater where damage as well as theft has taken place (Maguire and Corbett, 1986).

Where there is violence against the person the impact generally is as it is in burglary and other crimes. There are, however, some significant differences. These crimes (assaults, robbery, sexual assault, rape and murder) cover a variety of situations from mild verbal threats of violence to use of weapons, with or without loss of property. They may result in victims being frightened, having minor cuts or bruises, being near to death from multiple injuries, or loss of life. Presenting symptoms and difficulties from any of these follow a recognizable pattern (Worden, 1981), although the intensity and timing are unique for each individual. When a victim is faced with threats of or actual violence, they experience the feeling of helplessness, fear and vulnerability. They face the possibility of their own death. This may be at a conscious or unconscious level and may be only fleeting or over a period of time.

Few young people have seriously considered the prospect of their mortality, and this is the age group, particularly males, most at risk from assault (*Digest of Information on the Criminal Justice System*, 1991). It is common for them to say things like 'I've changed', 'I feel as if I have aged years' or 'I am not the same person any more'. This is true. It is as if their maturational processes have been accelerated. Death is something most of us come to an awareness of over several decades, but for these victims it is overnight. They will never again be without the knowledge that existence is fragile, whether it is their own or that of their families.

Physical injuries give victims a space in which to recover, as they will not be expected to carry on as usual with, for example, broken limbs. However, 'psychological injuries' cannot be seen so clearly, and recovery is expected to be much quicker, both by the victim and by the outside world. It is a common expectation that a victim of an armed robbery, who is not physically hurt, will be able to return to work in a day or two. 'Weren't you lucky?' or 'Nothing really happened' is what some might say. The victim's internal response may be one of agreement, which leads them to question why they feel as they do; or their response may be one of disagreement and rage that what they experienced is dismissed or diminished by others. One victim reported friends saying 'I hear you had a bit of excitement at your shop the other day'. Her immediate response was to scream 'No, it was not excitement: I thought I was going to be shot'. What she actually said was 'Oh yeah', and walked away.

Most crimes happen unexpectedly while victims carry out their everyday routines, e.g. a purse is stolen while shopping; a robbery takes place at work; a milkman is on his rounds; someone is walking home after an evening out with friends; or having a meal out with a girlfriend; or opening their own front door. Most of us live with the basic premise that the world is a safe place. For victims this is no longer true. The world becomes an unpredictable place – somewhere you can be hurt for no good reason. For a while it is difficult for them to take anything for granted. Often they are unable to trust their own judgement. They question what they failed to notice, or whether it was their behaviour that caused the attack. Initially they become more vigilant both of themselves and their surroundings. For most victims this soon settles into a healthy alertness or a common-sense approach to living, e.g. parking in a well-lit area, not leaving a handbag in a shopping trolley, eg. For others it is difficult to risk any activity. They live in a world where anything can happen, at any time, to anyone. This may seriously affect their ability to work or make relationships and cause them to question their existing relationships. The question they are left with seems to be 'Who am I?'. Changes in facial appearance may add to this. 'When I look in the mirror, I don't see myself. And who does my wife see? I am not the man she married.'

For young male victims of violence particularly, the effect on their perception of themselves can have a deep impact on their everyday life. It may raise doubts about their ability in any of the following areas:

- family provider – reduced income may be a fact due to injuries of long term disability
- protector – how will he behave in the future? can he protect his family? is he a coward? etc.
- father – anxieties about himself as a role model to his own sons, whether he currently has children or not; anxieties about his own father's image of him, whether he is currently alive or dead
- sexual partner – some degree of disturbance can be experienced within sexual relationships (see *sexual difficulties*).

For older men the reality of ageing can also be thrust upon them. They recognize that they are no longer as physically strong as they were. The need for dental work, for example, might feel premature and can therefore be deeply resented. All these aspects may affect the balance of relationships, which is keenly felt by both partners.

Victims are bothered by 'what might have happened', and it is important to explore this fully. A lady who had thwarted an attempted armed robbery, and who at no time had left herself exposed, eventually said 'Every time I close my eyes, I see myself on the floor in a pool of blood'. Her family was unaware of this and could not understand why she was unable to forget the incident. She was unable to tell them about the image, because she was not sure that it was normal. A victim of burglary may also have fears of what might have happened if they had returned home, had they woken up, had the children been in, etc.

The response of other people at the time of the crime and immediately afterwards also has a major effect on the level of impact that victims may experience later. If a victim appeals to members of the public for help and no help is forthcoming the sense of isolation is increased. Their new image of the world as an uncaring place is reinforced. Alternatively, if someone responds positively this immediately starts to redress the balance. The response of the emergency services is also critical. Victims are greatly reassured by a speedy and sympathetic response to their call for assistance. If this is not the case, victims can feel angry, resentful and very frustrated. The image of the uncaring world is extended. Sometimes of course the professional services are handy targets for displaced feelings.

As time goes by responses from friends and family, colleagues and other professionals can be difficult to deal with. Many people want to tell a victim what they would have done in the situation; or they ask how they are, only to tell them their own feelings about what happened. Family and friends naturally want the victim to recover, and may put pressure on them to return to 'normal' as a way of seeing them recovered. The pace of recovery is idiosyncratic – it is a process that takes time.

Victims may be put in touch with aspects of themselves that are very difficult to accept; for example, they may experience intense rage, bitterness or strong feelings of retaliation towards the offenders. They may discover stronger prejudices, and become very intolerant, when they had normally been easy-going and accepting of other people. This can make the acknowledgement and expression of these feelings particularly difficult. It again raises the questions of personal identity.

(d) It is obvious therefore that the most recognizable pattern is the state that follows an actual or a perceived **loss**, whether it is loss of property, personal safety, security, self-esteem, mobility, limbs, personal looks, personal beliefs or life. Recovery is the process by which victims work through the losses to regain a sense of balance, so that the trauma becomes a more tolerable memory. This may take anything from three to four weeks to several years, depending on the crime and the individual. It is important to re-emphasize that there is no direct correlation between a particular crime and its impact. In caring for victims of crime it is useful to have in mind the stages of mourning as described by Elisabeth Kübler-Ross (1969), or Worden's four tasks of mourning (1981). Together these provide a framework within which to work with victims so they can understand and come to terms with the impact of what has happened to them. Often they are trying to make sense of something that does not make sense. There is neither rhyme nor reason to becoming a victim. The reactions described above are normal responses to an abnormal event. The fact that this trauma is suffered at the hands of another human being puts it apart, I believe, from many other experiences.

Victims of violence experience symptoms similar to those described in **post-traumatic stress** disorder. In common with other victims of trauma and loss, they need to regain control over their own life. It is important therefore to follow their natural pace of recovery. In Victim Support, within a confidential relationship that may take time to develop, general information is offered about the possible range of feelings, thoughts and physical symptoms victims may experience, and the possible time scale, at the same time stressing the individual factors in these situations. Information concerning the legal system is available. In general terms it is helpful if victims are able to talk confidentially about the crime itself and the events surrounding it. It is useful to establish the facts, and their thoughts and feelings at the time of the crime; and to identify what has been lost as a result of the crime. Central to recovery, and possibly the most difficult area of work, is to encourage and enable the victim to identify and express feelings that may be very intense and frightening both for them and their helper. It is necessary to ascertain what these feelings are connected to. It is helpful to test their reality with them; e.g. 'I should not have opened the door'. Possible responses are: 'Are you telling me it was irresponsible of you to answer your door bell at lunch time?' or 'Are you telling me that nobody else you know would have done this?'

Adjusting to life after suffering as a result of crime needs to be at the victim's own pace. Small steps, with possible points of failure allowed for, will help to rebuild confidence. If the offence took place in a crowded shopping centre and it is difficult to return there, plan short outings to different uncrowded places with a trusted friend. Slowly extend the time spent there, and eventually return to the original shopping centre, at a quiet time of the day. Gradually increase the time spent at the scene of the crime, and then begin to make visits at a busier time.

Repeat the sequence, this time without the friend. Be prepared nevertheless to abandon any of these plans if they prove too stressful; you can always try again tomorrow. Similar plans can be worked on with children who regress, or who behave in ways that are more appropriate to a younger age; e.g. sleeping with parents, or with the light on, bedwetting, etc. Small attainable goals and confident attitudes will usually give positive results, if not today then maybe tomorrow.

Although I have not addressed children as victims of crime specifically, they are affected both as direct and indirect victims (see *child abuse*).

(e) The National Association of Victim Support Schemes has affiliated 371 local schemes covering most of England and Wales. In addition there are court witness schemes in approximately half of the crown courts and a few racial harassment helplines.

For further information, or a local contact number, contact the National Association of Victim Support Schemes, Cranmer House, 39 Brixton Road, London SW9 6DZ (Tel: 0171 735 9166; Fax: 0171 582 5712).

Related organizations: Victim Support Scotland, 14 Frederick Street, Edinburgh EH2 2HB (Tel: 0131 225 7779); Irish Association for Victim Support, Room 16, 29–30 Dame Street, Dublin 2 (Tel: 00 353 1679 8673).

(g) Hodgkinson, P. E. and Stewart, M. (1992) *Coping with Catastrophe*. London: Routledge; Maguire, M. and Corbett, C. (1986) *The Effects of Crime and the Work of Victim Support Schemes*. Aldershot: Gower; Worden, J. W. (1981) *Grief Counselling and Grief Therapy*. London: Tavistock Publications.

MAGGIE GARSIDE
(See also *violence towards women*)

Violence towards women

(a) Women are subjected to many forms of violence both within the home and outside it. No single source of information can accurately be used to estimate the numbers of women who suffer in this way. Estimates partly differ because definitions of violence vary, but also because no official statistics, for instance of reports to the police of rape,

sexual assault and domestic violence, accurately reflect actual incidence. Many women do not report these crimes for many reasons.
Surveys of the general population show varying results, again partly
depending upon definitions used. Whatever definitions or studies are
examined, violence against women remains a pervasive problem.

Both women and men can suffer violence but there are certain forms
frequently experienced by women and rarely by men. These are firstly
rape; and secondly domestic violence, that is violence occurring within
the confines of the home. Research testifies to the fact that the vast
majority of victims of domestic violence are women and the perpetrators men. It is these two situations upon which this article focuses.

Rape is a more frequent crime than is often recognized because of the
low incidence of reporting it to the police. I have worked with many
girls and women who have been raped or assaulted; practically none
have reported it, fearing the trauma would be further intensified,
particularly if it would involve a court appearance.

It is crucial to recognize that domestic violence, rape and sexual
assault are not limited to certain sections of the population, any more
than is child abuse. Popular misconceptions and myths suggest otherwise, but rape can happen anywhere, including the victim's own home;
at any time of day or night; the victims are both young and old. The
victim may be a young child out playing or an elderly resident asleep in
bed in a residential home. Although girls and women are warned of
attacks by strangers many rapes are perpetrated by boys and men
known and trusted by their victims. Similarly, domestic violence occurs
in mansions with large grounds as well as in maisonettes in inner city
areas. Perpetrators cut across class structures. Men who attack their
partners may be highly successful in the professions or in business, or
unskilled and unsuccessful. Money and status does not protect women
from violence. Some research (Pagelow, 1981) suggests that middle-
class abusers are more likely to use techniques that leave less visible
bruises and injuries. Other research (Goolkasian, 1986) reminds us that
violence is more likely to come to the attention of public agencies when
it is among disadvantaged socio-economic groups; and that a third of
women reporting domestic violence have also been raped by their
partners (Frieze, 1983).

(b)   Women who have suffered rape or sexual assault may present for
help immediately. Some women may come for help years later, sometimes having told no-one in the meantime. As with abuse in childhood,
their experience has become a carefully guarded secret, until it is
triggered into renewed consciousness.

Women who present immediately after rape are in a state of shock
that can manifest itself in many ways. Symptoms of **post-traumatic**

stress are frequently experienced. For some the shock is so great that the experience cannot be taken in: women describe how they just returned home, took an aspirin, had a bath and went to bed, only to recognize the full horror later. They may describe the rape as a nightmare or a bad dream, or as if it is something that has happened to someone else. They may experience out-of-body experiences at the time, as if they were looking down on the scene of the rape and not part of it. Others may try to deny the rape or attempt to minimize the experience in order to deal with it. Statements may be made such as: 'I'm not going to let it get at me. It's going to be as if it never happened. Life must go on. I was lucky he didn't hurt me. I'm just grateful to be alive. It could have happened to a youngster. I'm older so I can cope. Awful things are happening to women all over the world: it's nothing really compared to all that.'

For others the reality of the horror of rape is immediate. They experience extreme distress, grief and absolute terror, often accompanied by irrational but very real feelings of **guilt and shame**. Women often ask the question 'Why me?' They wonder if they in some way caused the attack, and can feel as if they are bad and dirty. The converse is of course the truth: rapists are responsible for rape. The badness is theirs and not their victim's; but it will often not feel this way for the women.

After being raped a woman commonly cannot bear to be alone: the world has suddenly become a totally unsafe place in which her trust has been demolished. Particularly if the rapist is a friend or colleague, all close relationships with men are thrown into doubt, and her own sense of judgement challenged.

Anger as a result of rape is a normal and healthy reaction but it often occurs at a later stage. Paradoxically some rape victims either experience anger, or fear it, from other people. This, combined with their sense of shame, is often a factor in preventing women, particularly girls and younger women, telling anyone about the rape. Many victims have reported comments made to them by friends, families, doctors, solicitors, judges, police, who suggest that somehow the woman was at fault: 'What were you doing there anyway?', 'Are you sure you said "no"?', 'Why didn't you fight or scream?', 'I told you not to wear short skirts', 'Did you lead him on and change your mind to tease him?', 'Why did you let him stay in the house?' These are a few responses that have been reported to me.

There are many reasons why women might present for help years after a rape. They may have recognized that their attempts to deny or minimize the effects have not worked. They may be haunted by nightmares and flashbacks. They may be unable to form trusting relationships with men. Sexual difficulties may persist, as may ongoing feelings of **depression**, anxiety, panic attacks and lack of self-worth. Such women are unable to progress with their life as they wish, and are forced to see what enormous and destructive consequences the rape has had.

Women who are or who have been victims of domestic violence may present this as the main difficulty, or it may emerge via another presenting problem, such as depression, extreme anxiety or low self-esteem. They do not always connect this causally to the violence, especially if it has been going on for many years, and they have felt powerless either to prevent it or to leave. Others come acknowledging what is happening; wanting to find a way either out of the relationship, or of stopping the violence. Some have made previous attempts to leave that have failed for a variety of reasons. Others come out of concern for their children; they may have tolerated violence to themselves for many years, but the trigger for seeking help is when their children are also assaulted. Some who come for help are women who have left violent relationships, but leaving has been difficult: they still carry the scars and can take many years to recover, needing considerable help to do so. They are faced with reconstructing their whole life and self.

(c)   The vital question is why men, whether by rape, sexual assault or physical abuse, violate women, including women in close relationship to them. There is no straightforward answer, but it is important to acknowledge that 'rape is motivated more by retaliatory and compensatory motives than sexual ones; it is a pseudo-sexual act, complex and multi-determined, but addressing issues of hostility (anger) and control (power) more than desire (sexuality)' (Groth, 1979).

The idea that men have irresistible sexual impulses that they cannot control no longer attracts much credence, although it appears that in situations where normal social controls are removed (for instance, in wartime), the incidence of rape, including gang rape, rises dramatically.

The theme of the significance of power and control by men over women is central to much understanding of rape, although not all writers, clinicians and researchers state this as categorically as Brown-miller (1975), who writes: 'From prehistoric times to the present, I believe, rape has played a critical function. It is nothing more or less than a conscious process of intimidation by which all men keep all women in a state of fear.'

When exploring the reasons for male violence historical factors are significant, emphasizing the significance of male power. A man's right to beat his wife was firmly entrenched in British law until the late nineteenth century. The only controversial issue until then was the acceptable limit of such treatment. Similarly, regarding a wife as her husband's possession has a long social and legal history.

Societal myths abound, represented by some of the responses I have quoted above, regarding women and rape, and women and domestic violence. Hopefully these are lessening, although they have not disappeared. Perhaps such myths are comforting for both men and women. For men it moves responsibility conveniently elsewhere, away from the perpetrator towards the perceived or imagined behaviour and attitudes of their victims. For women, myths may offer the comfort that they will not be hurt if certain rules are obeyed, such as 'Do not go out alone at night' – even if these rules restrict freedom and impose a virtual curfew on half the population.

In recent times the debate relating to domestic violence has shifted ground. Many of the studies published in the 1960s and 1970s emphasized the masochism of women who stayed in violent relationships. They were labelled as somehow deviant, and their resulting symptoms were further evidence of this, rather than being seen as understandable responses to continuous abuse. Other research profiled abused women as helpless and passive victims, also failing to recognize the effect of violence on them. Studies influenced by feminist perspectives focused on violence as a means of controlling women who are in essentially unequal power relationships. What is generally agreed across the research is that violence escalates in frequency and intensity over time. If violence occurs once it is likely to happen often.

(d)   It is essential to understand that rape is an appalling violation of a woman's whole self and body, which has long-lasting and severe consequences.

When a girl or woman presents shortly after a rape she will be in considerable crisis. This demands a particular response. Very careful attention must be given to her so that her needs are heard and recognized. Assumptions about the right course of action should not be made, because any intervention that ultimately aids recovery must be geared to the individual's expressed needs. She may need help to decide about police involvement. If she has not received medical advice she may want someone to make appropriate arrangements with, and to accompany her to, a sympathetic medical practitioner. She needs to decide whom she tells and how; and if she is very young she may need particular help in telling her parents. It is crucial that she is with someone with whom she feels comfortable, who can cope with her distress without in turn becoming overwhelmed.

She must be supported in whatever decisions she takes. This can be hard for the helper, if she decides against police involvement, for instance, particularly when she knows the identity of the rapist.

Helpers need accurate information about services and personnel in their area. For instance, it is useful to know the police procedures in your locality. Some police forces have specially and highly trained women officers available, who deal sensitively and well with rape cases. Others do not. It is not a good time to discover this when you are with a highly distressed and traumatized woman in need of help.

The woman should control the helping process throughout. She should not feel that things are done to her, or around her, without her consent. In the days and weeks after a rape it is helpful to make frequent and regular times available and to ensure that sufficient support systems are in place. If all this is quickly in evidence a woman will begin to rebuild her self, and re-establish a sense of safety and trust. For some time she may need constant companionship. Although helpers cannot themselves provide this, they can assure her that hers is a normal reaction to an abnormal and horrific situation, and explore with her who might best meet this need. At the same time as needing companionship the rape survivor can find closeness hard to tolerate and accept. It may sometimes make her angry and even aggressive. This fluctuating need for closeness and distance again needs to be understood as a normal, if confusing, response.

Although some may block out events from conscious memory, nightmares and flashbacks to the rape are commonly experienced. As with other forms of trauma, recalling the detail of the assault, often repeating it over and again, is helpful and necessary. This is not just an immediate need, but one that can continue. The event may be recalled or triggered by a particular event or situation years afterwards, particularly if the woman is again made helpless or frightened, or events are once more out of her control. Helpers can offer reassurance and encouragement (although never pressure) for the woman to repeat what has happened to her as often as she needs.

Many who work with rape victims are confused by the apparent lack of anger shown initially towards the perpetrator. This often emerges later, when it is a very positive sign that the anger, instead of being internalized, has begun to be directed outwards. Helpers can assist its expression, and validate a woman's right to do so; but they cannot make her feel anger before she is ready. This again can be difficult for the helper, who may be eaten up with rage and accompanying fantasies about what *she* would like to do to the perpetrator. Similarly women who are so traumatized that they feel nothing for a long while may continue to remember and recall the event, but without emotional affect. Time and patience is again needed, combined with an understanding of why she is reacting in this way.

The most facile, unhelpful comment to a rape victim that I have heard was from a doctor who told the woman that she should just put it all behind her and get on with her life: talking about it would simply prolong the agony. However, I have also worked with women who have found a strongly anti-male stance similarly unhelpful in some agencies, particularly if they are in a relationship with a man, or are themselves trying not to generalize from their experience. To be clearly anti-rape is helpful, as is firmly placing the responsibility where it belongs – but to argue that all men are potential rapists is not helpful to most women. These examples emphasize that those who work with rape victims must take enormous care to be respectful and caring, never minimizing or rationalizing what has happened, and never imposing their own views.

Women who have been raped, and who present quickly, need help for different lengths of time depending on many factors, especially how much other support is available. Ideally women should control the time they need themselves, saying when they feel able to cope alone. Help should not be withdrawn before they are ready. When women present at a later stage some issues are the same, but others are different. The immediate crisis is obviously not present, but there is a crisis of another kind. If the experience of rape, or the extent of its consequences, have been repressed for some time, any sudden and unexpected trigger of memories is itself deeply shocking. This needs acknowledging and working with. Others may seek help at this stage as a thought-out decision arising from an awareness that all is not well, and that the rape is significant in this. Women in this position may not experience shock, but still face considerable pain.

The need to recall and retell remains an important part of the process. This is particularly painful if it has never been spoken before. The decision of whom and how to tell takes a different form. It is very difficult to tell friends and family long after the event. Because rape is so traumatizing and devastating, for some women speaking about it becomes impossible: they cannot bear to voice it to themselves, let alone anyone else. When they reach a point where they can speak, their anxiety to be both believed and understood is considerable. One question they may have to face is why they said nothing before. A woman may fear disbelief or anger; but if she does not say anything she is left living with a painful secret and consequent isolation. Support from family and friends is crucial for her recovery, but it can be harder to find at this later stage.

Women who have suffered, or are suffering from domestic violence, can also present at different stages. For those who have left violent partners a large part of the struggle has been won. But there are other difficulties. Finance (see *money advice*) and housing (see *homelessness*) loom large as key difficulties. Obtaining protection from the abuser is also vital; many women are unable to leave violent relationships because they fear pursuit and reprisal, and in some cases this is tragically correct. This should never be under-estimated: violent men have real power over such women and they use it. The level of fear women live with is impossible to communicate adequately.

In addition to all the practical considerations, leaving any relationship represents a loss of hope and the loss of an actual or longed-for way of life. Leaving one marked by violence is considerably more complex. The process of rebuilding her own sense of self, often while dealing with needy and grieving children, demands enormous personal resources at a time when a woman may feel she has none left. Effective support needs to acknowledge all she has done, all there is still to do and the complexity of feelings that are inevitably aroused at this stage. It is important to recognize the interaction between the external world of practicalities that such a woman has to deal with, and her internal emotional world, which may be in considerable turmoil. Some approaches tend to emphasize one aspect or the other, offering either practical or psychological help. Both are necessary.

Women who remain in violent relationships can experience criticism. In one interdisciplinary meeting set up to explore violence to women a male senior worker in a social services department commented that if women really wanted to leave violent men they would. The implication was that if they did not they must be content with their situation. This grossly simplistic way of understanding is extremely worrying, particularly coming from someone with real power over women's lives. Anyone working in this field needs to understand why it is so hard for women to leave.

Factors referred to above such as housing, finance and fear should not be under-estimated. If you have nowhere to go, and no money to go with, and you are frightened for your life, and you have children, leaving may seem like an unrealistic dream. The difficulties of making the transition are enormous, even for women who can potentially adequately support themselves and their children. For many others the prospect seems impossible. Women generally earn less than men, and child-care facilities for single parents are woefully inadequate.

It also has to be remembered that violence within the home is a private horror in a setting that most people regard as their safe retreat. Because it takes place in private it is frequently not acknowledged by others. It is also denied by the abuser. The victim is thus frequently left feeling both responsible and ashamed. These feelings conveniently reinforce the man, who then blames his partner for his own lack of control. Another pattern is that violent attacks are followed by an apparently deep display of remorse – until the next assault. All this is psychologically confusing and demolishing for the woman, who is left undermined, depressed and unable to tell anyone. Domestic violence is extremely alienating and isolating, and is further compounded if outside the home her partner presents a very different public image.

Those who are assaulted by strangers can receive support and sympathy. They are expected to be distressed and possibly unable to function normally for a time. But this understanding does not always extend to victims of domestic violence: they can be severely and repeatedly assaulted, with the added horror that the assailant is someone they believed they could love and trust. It is essential that helpers recognize that domestic violence attacks the core of the self and takes away the capacity for autonomous and independent thought and action, and yet to leave any relationship a strong enough sense of self is needed. Violence destroys that part of a woman she most needs to extricate herself from her situation. Perhaps it is surprising, given the psychological and the practical difficulties involved, that so many manage to make the break.

(e) Helpful agencies include:

Rape Crisis Centres offer a confidential counselling service for girls and women who have been sexually assaulted or raped; consult the local phone book; or contact 0171 278 3956 or 0171 837 1600 (24 hours). MIND offers individual counselling and group work and other local projects; the National Information line is 0181 522 1728. Victim Support schemes offer support and practical help to victims of any sort of crime (Tel: 0171 735 9166 for local schemes, or consult the local phone book). LIFELINE (PO Box 251, Marlborough, Wiltshire SN8 1AE) offers support and counselling for victims and abusers in domestic violence. Women's Aid have a network of refuges throughout the country (Tel: 0171 251 6537).

(g) Hopkins, J. (ed.) (1984) *Perspectives on Rape and Sexual Assault.* London: Harper and Row; Kirkwood, C. (1993) *Leaving Abusive Partners.* London: Sage Publications; Smith, L. (1989) *Domestic Violence.* Home Office Research Study 107. London: HMSO.

MOIRA WALKER

(See also *adult survivors of abuse, victims of crime*)

Violent clients

(a) Violent acts damage victims or property and involve physical aggression and force. Aggression can be limited to verbal expression of anger or threats, but violence always involves action. In violence, aggressive feelings are translated into behaviour. Angry thoughts or feelings do not always lead to violence. Violence may be directed towards a variety of victims including a spouse, family member, group, institution, carer, oneself or a stranger. It can be the result of a momentary loss of control or a deliberately chosen strategy for getting something the violent person wants (this is known as instrumental aggression). It can be a way of exercising power over others (e.g. bullying or intimidation), or of expressing disagreement (as in politically motivated violence). Sexual violence (rape or sadism) can be directed towards men, women and children.

Violence can occur in almost any setting. It takes place both in private (as in most domestic violence) and in public (as in football hooliganism or fights started on the streets). Professional carers may meet with it in their work in mental health settings, general practice, community centres, probation hostels, general hospitals, places of work, prisons, church group or schools. The violence may have occurred in those settings or elsewhere.

(b) Violent clients may themselves seek help, often after a violent incident. They may be afraid of losing control again or of the consequences of this. They may have already caused serious harm or injury and have been arrested or charged with assault or damage. Often they will have been referred by a partner, colleague, GP, probation officer, social worker or friend.

(c) *Background factors:*   Common background factors of violence in adulthood include the experience of violence in childhood, low self-esteem, **depression** or other mental illness (e.g. paranoia), acceptance of sub-group norms that value violence, habitual use of violence in adolescence, inadequate alternative means of self-expression and lack of assertiveness. It can be associated with a high level of social anxiety or with general anti-social behaviour and the absence of strong internal controls.

Immediate triggers: These may include disinhibition caused by alcohol (see *alcoholism*), drug or solvent abuse (see *substance misuse*), dementia, mental illness (see *psychosis*) or acute emotional stress (see *stress*). A recent stressful life event (e.g. **redundancy, bereavement**, moving, **divorce**, birth of a child) may increase the likelihood that a perceived humiliation, provocation or threat will trigger violence. The client's perception and interpretation of actions and events as dangerous or insulting affects their decision to respond aggressively.

Theoretical approaches: Two important theoretical approaches to understanding violence are: *personality-based theories*, which focus on long-standing characteristics of the individual, shaped by biological forces and developmental factors such as early parenting experiences; and *social learning theory* which emphasizes the situational factors that determine the acquisition, performance and maintenance of aggressive behaviour.

One example of a personality-based theory is the psychodynamic which sees the function of violence as ego-protection against perceived attack. Violence serves as a defence against perceived humiliation and the fear of attack. Fear is considered to be strongly linked with aggression and the violent client may have a suspicious world-view and distrust the continued stability of the environment. The violent client often has low self-esteem and uses violence to achieve a sense of power and control. In treatment the individual would explore the underlying fears and depression from which violence protects them.

Social learning theory stresses the need for detailed analysis of the antecedents of the violent behaviour in a given situation, the actual behaviour and the consequences of the behaviour. This theory highlights the central role played by early parental modelling of aggression, environmental factors and the consequences of violence in maintaining or diminishing behaviour. As violence is a learned behaviour it can also be unlearned through behavioural modification.

(d) *Key issues in the assessment interview*

A good assessment should include a family and personal history as well as exploration of background factors and triggers of the most recent violent episode. One of the most important questions is whether the carer's personal safety can be protected when assessing and working with the violent client. Measures to ensure some protection include a contract with the client not to use violence in the sessions, and a commitment not to attend the sessions when under the influence of disinhibiting substances such as alcohol, drugs, or solvents. It is important to ensure that the client is never seen when no one else is in the building. The layout of the room is also important; the carer should have unobstructed access to the door. Seeing the client in a room which has a window in the door is advisable. A statement of understanding from the client's point of view, such as 'It must be very frightening for you to have been so out of control', can help the task of setting the client at ease. Acknowledging their fears of enacting violent impulses is often reassuring to clients as it makes explicit what has previously been considered too frightening to mention.

The following questions about the client's violence might be addressed in the assessment: Is the violence organized or random? Have weapons been bought? – a serious indication of risk. Is the violence directed towards particular individuals or is it spontaneous and random? Has the client been violent in the past? – this is the best predictor of future dangerousness. What were the triggers of the violent episode? Is the client normally violent? Who were they with? Had the person been drinking or using drugs at the time? Can they identify specific triggers or precipitating factors that led to the violence?

It is important to evaluate the client's motivation and insight by considering whether the client has the capacity and genuine desire to change. It is worth asking about the secondary gains of continuing to be violent and exploring what function the violence serves.

The decision to work with the violent client should be based on a thorough assessment of the client's needs and motivation as well as on the carer's confidence that their setting is appropriate for such work. If in doubt, refer on, as the violent client may endanger the carer or have other difficulties that need to be addressed before counselling can be effective.

Offering help: the process of counselling
The first stage for many violent clients is to recognize that they have a problem and that they need help. It can be more difficult to admit to being violent than to being depressed or anxious and many violent clients deny and minimize the extent of their violence. They will often see themselves as victims and attempt to convince the carer of this by blaming external factors for their violence or regarding it as a justifiable response to stress and frustration. It is essential not to collude with this presentation of events. Violent clients may be distressed or emotionally damaged but they are also aggressors who need help in controlling violence. Carers should also avoid adopting a punitive or confrontational approach to violent clients as this will only reinforce the client's low sense of self-esteem and may lead to defensiveness or hostility.

Violent clients have often themselves been victims of violence. This violence may have been modelled by parents or other carers. Their own violence might mask an underlying depression perhaps caused by traumatic early experience. Violence may be a defence against depression. Violence is used because it serves a function in the short term (often to enhance self-esteem and provide a sense of mastery) and it is the task of client and helper to develop alternatives which will serve the same function, without injury to others.

Strategies for controlling violence
The following may be useful:

- agreeing that violence is not acceptable;
- helping the client to recognize signs of anger in themselves (bodily, cognitive, emotional) as described in Novaco (1975);
- teaching alternatives for coping with anger through relaxation and self-coping statements;
- setting targets for change;
- identifying and anticipating trigger events;
- educating client about the effects of alcohol and drugs on violent behaviour;
- using relaxation and distraction techniques;
- reinforcing good coping methods for reducing stress and tension;
- enabling the client to express their frustration, unhappiness and sense of powerlessness verbally rather than through violence; teaching them to be assertive rather then aggressive;
- facilitating victim empathy through an exploration of the client's own experience of violence.

Aggression towards the carer
If the client becomes aggressive towards the carer it is important to try to *defuse* the situation by acknowledging the client's feelings and pointing out the warning signs of escalating anger, remaining calm and non-confrontational, e.g. remaining seated and speaking calmly. The carer should suggest that the interview or contact be terminated if the client does not feel in control or safe enough to carry on. The carer might also suggest to the client that they may be displacing their anger towards other significant people on to the carer, and that this is creating difficulties in the counselling relationship.

Emotional issues for the person offering care
Strong counter-transference feelings can be generated through work with violent clients and these should be acknowledged and examined with colleagues, or in **supervision**. Violent clients can express attitudes and behaviour which evoke powerful feelings in workers and challenge their system of values – moral, political and personal. It is essential to maintain distance and professional objectivity, rather than becoming involved in hostile confrontation or tacit agreement. Violent clients may express angry sentiments which the carer shares but collusion is unhelpful.

Boundaries   are vital in work with the violent client, who is likely to be chaotic and to feel out of control. Underlying the violence there may be a profound sense of deprivation and desire to have emotional needs met through the caring relationship. When these needs are not fully met, as is inevitable, the disappointment can lead to intense anger. Clarity about the limits of help, the extent of confidentiality, the duration of the contact and the importance of interpersonal boundaries is essential. Supervision and discussion with colleagues is recommended, particularly when the carer feels boundaries are threatened.

(e)   These are some of the reasons for referring the client on to other agencies:

1.   the client has specialist problems such as drug or alcohol abuse, sexual deviation or severe mental illness which need treatment before their anger can be addressed (see *alcoholism; substance misuse, psychosis and severe mental disorders; sexual deviation*);
2.   the client repeatedly threatens the helper, damages property or threatens other clients in the organization;
3.   the helper feels the limits of help have been reached;
4.   the client requests specialist help.

The following organizations may be able to provide assessment, treatment, consultancy and supervision: the forensic psychology and psychiatry services, the probation service, the Portman Clinic, part of the Tavistock–Portman Clinic Trust (which also offers a range of courses in forensic psychotherapy with deviant or offender clients), the National Society for the Prevention of Cruelty to Children, Relate, Alanon, community drug and alcohol teams, social services. Rape crisis lines will advise victims of sexual violence (see *violence towards women; victims of crime*).

(f)   The conflict between client **confidentiality** and the carer's duty to inform the police in cases of **child abuse** or spouse abuse (see *violence towards women*) is a central issue in working with violent clients. It is especially problematic when the victims of violence are children. If the police are to be contacted, because of the policy of the voluntary organization or the statutory duty of the worker, this should be made clear to the client before they disclose sensitive information.

The carer should be aware of the child protection policies within their organization. In some agencies it will not be unusual to liaise with the police, social workers or probation officers; in others this will be exceptional. It is essential to be aware of the limits of confidentiality in the particular situation and to be clear about the extent of liaison with other agencies that may be required. For those working in the voluntary sector ethical issues about duties to protect other members of society versus the desire to preserve confidentiality should be discussed and resolved so that a clear and explicit policy exists.

(g) Howards, K. and Hollins, C. R. (1989) *Clinical Approaches to Violence*. Chichester: John Wiley; Novaco, R. W. (1978) 'Anger and coping with stress' in J. P. Foreyt and D. P. Rathgen (eds) *Cognitive Behavioural Therapy*. New York: Plenum Press; Winnicott, D. W. (1958) 'The anti-social tendency' in *Through Paediatrics to Psychoanalysis*. London: Tavistock.

ANNA MOTZ

References

(Authors referred to in the articles are listed in full here if they are not included in the short list of recommended further reading at the end of most articles)

Adirondack, S. M. *Just About Managing: A Guide to Effective Management for Voluntary Organisations and Community Groups*. London Voluntary Service Council, 68 Chalton Street, London NW1 1JR.

Advisory Council on the Misuse of Drugs (1988) *Aids and Drug Misuse*. London: HMSO.

Akbar, N. (1982) *From Miseducation to Education*. Jersey City, NJ: New Mind Publications.

Alban-Metcalf, B. and West, M.A. (1991) 'Women managers' in J. Firth-Cozens and M. A. West (eds) *Women At Work*. Milton Keynes: Open University Press.

Alinsky, S. D. (1969) *Reveille for Radicals*. New York: Vintage Books.

Alinsky, S. D. (1972) *Rules for Radicals*. New York: Vintage Books.

Alternative Service Book (1980) Oxford: Oxford University Press and A. R. Mowbray.

Argyle, N. and Beit-Hallahmi, B. (1975) *The Social Psychology of Religion*. London: Routledge.

Bagley, C. and Verma, G. K. (1979) *Racial Prejudice, the Individual and Society*. Farnborough, Hants: Saxon House.

Bainham, J. and Cox, D. (1992) *Job Hunting Made Easy*. London: Kogan Page.

Bainton, C. and Crowley, T. (1992) *Beyond Redundancy*. Wellingborough: Thorsons.

Bakwin, H. (1973) 'Erotic feelings in infants and young children', *American Journal of Diseases of Children* 126: 52–4.

Balint, M. (1968) *The Doctor, His Patient and the Illness*. Tonbridge: Pitman Medical.

Bancroft, J. (1983) *Human Sexuality and Its Problems*. Edinburgh: Churchill Livingstone.

Barlow, D. (1986) 'Causes of sexual dysfunction: the role of anxiety and cognitive interference', *Journal of Consulting and Clinical Psychology* 54: 140–8.

Barnes, M. and Maple, N. (1992) *Women and Mental Health: Challenging the Stereotypes*. Birmingham: Venture.

Bateson, G. (1972) *Steps to an Ecology of Mind*. London: Granada.

Beail, N. (1994) 'Fire, coffins and skeletons' in V. Sinason (ed.) *Treating Survivors of Satanist Abuse*. London: Routledge.

Beck, A. T., Rush, A. J., Shaw, B. F. and Emery, G. (1979) *Cognitive Therapy of Depression*. New York: Wiley.

Beckford Report (1985) *A Child in Trust*. London: Borough of Brent.

Benedict, R. (1940) *Race and Racism*. London: Routledge.

Benjamin, H. (1953) 'Transvestism and transsexualism', *International Journal of Sexology* 7: 12–14.

Bennet, G. (1984) 'The wounded healer in the twentieth century', *British Journal of Holistic Medicine* 1(2): 127–30.

Berger, P. (1969) *The Social Construction of Reality*. Harmondsworth: Penguin Books.

Bicknell, J. (1994) 'Learning disability and ritualistic child abuse: introductory issues' in V. Sinason (ed.) *Treating Survivors of Satanist Abuse*. London: Routledge.

Black, D., Morris, J. N., Smith, C. and Townsend, P. (1982) *Inequalities in Health: The Black Report*. Harmondsworth: Penguin Books.

Boscoli, L. and Bertrando, P. (1993) *The Times of Time: A New Perspective in Systemic Therapy and Consultation*. New York: Norton.

Boszormenyi-Nagy, I. (1986) *Between Give and Take*. New York: Brunner/Mazel.

Bowl, R. (1985) *Changing the Nature of Masculinity*. Social Work Monograph 30. Norwich: University of East Anglia.

Bowlby, J. (1973) *Attachment and Loss*. Volume 1: *Attachment*. Harmondsworth: Penguin.

Bowlby, J. (1980) *Attachment and Loss*. Volume 2: *Separation*. Harmondsworth: Penguin.

Bowlby, J. (1979) *The Making and Breaking of Affectional Bonds*. London: Tavistock Publications.

Bowlby, J. (1971) *Attachment and Loss*. Volume 3: *Loss*. Harmondsworth: Penguin.

Bradford, J. and Ryan, C. (1991) 'Health concerns of middle-aged lesbians' in B. Sang, J. Warshow and A. J. Smith (eds) *Lesbians at Midlife: The Creative Transition*. San Francisco: Spinsters.

Braun, M. J., and Berg, D. H. (1994) 'Meaning reconstruction in the experience of parental bereavement', *Death Studies* 18: 105–29.

Brierley, H. (1984) 'Gender identity and sexual behaviour' in K. Howells (ed.) *The Psychology of Sexual Diversity*. Oxford: Basil Blackwell.

Briggs Myers, I. (1980) *Gifts Differing*. Palo Alto, CA: Consulting Psychologists Press.

British Association for Counselling (1993) *Code of Ethics and Practice for Counsellors*. Rugby: BAC.

British Humanist Association (1984) *Guidelines for Officiants at Non-Religious Funerals*. Bradlaugh House, 47 Theobalds Road, London WC1X 8SP.

Broderick, W. (1993) 'A training course for spiritual directors – an ecumenical venture', *Journal of Religious Education* 5(3).

Brownmiller, S. (1975) *Against Our Will: Men, Women and Rape*. New York: Simon and Schuster.

Burgess, A. and Homstrom, L. (1974) *Rape: Victims of Crisis*. Bowie, MD: Brady.

Butler, S. and Wintram, C. (1991) *Feminist Groupwork*. London: Sage.

Cade, B. (1993) *A Brief Guide to Brief Therapy*. New York: W.W. Norton.

Cameron, P., Cameron, K. and Procter, K. (1989) 'Effect of homosexuality upon public health and social order', *Psychological Reports* 64(2): 1167–79.

Cameron, P. and Ross, K. P. (1981) 'Social and psychological aspects of the Judeo-Christian stance toward homosexuality', *Journal of Psychology and Theology* 9(1): 40–57.

Campling, J. (ed.) (1987) (1987) *Images of Ourselves: Women with Disabilities Talking*. London: Routledge and Kegan Paul.

Camus, A. (1963) *The Fall*. Harmondsworth: Penguin.

Cantwell Smith, W. (1979) *Faith and Belief*. Princeton: Princeton University Press.

Carter, B. and McGoldrick, M. (1989) *The Changing Family Life Cycle*. New York: Gardner Press.

Carter, E. (1973) *The Spirit Is Present*. Canfield, OH: Alba Books.

Casement, P. (1985) *On Learning from the Patient*. London: Tavistock.

Chaplin, J. (1989) 'Counselling and gender' in W. Dryden, D. Charles-Edwards and R. Woolfe (eds) *Handbook of Counselling in Britain*. London: Tavistock/Routledge.

Chapman, C. (1987) 'Putting the issue on the boards' in M. Lawrence (ed.) *Fed Up and Hungry*. London: The Women's Press.

Charleson, N. and Corbett, A. (1994) 'A birthday to remember' in V. Sinason (ed.) *Treating Survivors of Satanist Abuse*. London: Routledge.

Chessler, P. (1973) *Women and Madness*. New York: Avon.

Clarke, E. (1989) *Young Single Mothers Today*. London: National Council for One-Parent Families.

Cleveland Report (1988) *Report of the Inquiry into Child Abuse in Cleveland 1987*. London: HMSO.

Clulow, C. (1985) *Marital Therapy*. Aberdeen University Press.

Cockett, M. and Tripp, J. (1994) *Social Policy Research Findings* No. 45. York: Joseph Rowntree Foundation.

Coe, T. (1994) *Managers Under Stress*. Report of the Institute of Management. London: Institute of Management.

Cole, M. (1988) 'Normal and dysfunctional sexual behaviours: frequencies and incidencies' in M. Cole and W. Dryden (eds) *Sex Therapy in Britain*. Milton Keynes: Open University Press.

Corfield, R. (1993) *How You Can Get That Job*. London: Kogan Page.

Cracknell, C. (1986) *Towards a New Relationship: Christians and People of Other Faith*. London: Epworth Press.

Curran, V. and Golombok, S. (1985) *Bottling It Up*. Boston: Faber and Faber.

Dalton, K. (1984) *Pre-menstrual Syndrome and Progesterone Therapy*. London: Heinemann.

Daly, M. (1979) *Gyn/Ecology: The Meta-ethics of Radical Feminism*. London: The Women's Press.

Daniels, K. R. (1992) 'Management of the psychosocial aspects of infertility', *Australian and New Zealand Journal of Obstetrics and Gynaecology* 32(1): 57–63.

Davis, P. G. K. (1982) 'The functioning of British counselling hotlines: a pilot study', *British Journal of Guidance and Counselling*, 10(2): 195–9.

Davison, G. C. and Neale, J. M. (1990) *Abnormal Psychology*. New York: Wiley.

Day, M. (ed.) (1961) *St Francis de Sales: Introduction to the Devout Life*. London: Dent.

De Mello, A. (1978) *Sadhana*. Gujarat, India: Gujarat Sahitya Prakash.

Department of Health (1990) *Protecting Children: A Guide for Social Workers*. London: HMSO.

Department of Health (1991) *Working Together Under the Children Act*. London: HMSO.

Department of Health (1992a) *The Health of Elderly People: An Epidemiological Overview*. London: HMSO.

Department of Health (1992b) *The Health of the Nation*. London: HMSO.

De Silva, P. (1993) 'Fetishism and sexual dysfunction: clinical presentation and management', *Sexual and Marital Therapy* 8(2): 147–54.

Digest of Information on the Criminal Justice System: Crime and Justice in England and Wales (1991). London: The Home Office.

Dingwall, R. (1989) 'Some problems about predicting child abuse and neglect' in O. Stevenson (ed.) *Child Abuse: Public Policy and Professional Practice*. Hemel Hempstead: Wheatsheaf.

Doherty, N. and Tyson, S. (1993) *Executive Redundancy and Outplacement*. London: Kogan Page.

Dryden, W. (ed.) (1989) *Individual Therapy in Britain*. Buckingham: Open University Press.

Dyregrov, A. (1982) 'Caring for helpers in disaster situations: psychological debriefing', *Disaster Management* 2 (1989).

Edelmann, R. J., Connolly, K. J., Cooke, I. D. and Robson, J. (1991) 'Psychogenic infertility: some findings', *Journal of Psychosomatic Obstetrics and Gynaecology* 12(2): 163–8.

Education Act (1982, 1993). London: HMSO.

Eliot, T. S. (1969) *The Complete Poems and Plays*. London: Faber and Faber.

Ellis, A., McInerney, J., Digiuseppe, R. and Yeager, R. (1988) *Rational Emotive Therapy with Alcoholics and Substances Abusers*. Oxford: Pergamon Press.

Erikson, E. H. (1964) *Insight and Responsibility*. New York: Norton.

Faber, F. W. (1960) *Growth in Holiness*. London: Burns and Oates.

Fairlie, J., Nelson, J. and Popplestone, R. (1988) *Menopause: A Time for Positive Change*. London: Javelin.

Fatula, M. (1987) *St Catherine of Siena's Way*. London: SPCK.

Finer Report (1974) *Report of the Committee on One-Parent Families*. DHSS. London: HMSO.

Finneron, D. (1993) *Faith in Community Development: Case Studies of Church-Based Projects in Urban Priority Areas*. Manchester: Manchester Monographs, Centre for Adult and Higher Education, University of Manchester.

Firth-Cozens, J. and Payne, R. L. (eds) (1987) *Stress in the Health Professions*. Chichester: Wiley.

Freire, P. (1972) *Pedagogy of the Oppressed*. Harmondsworth: Penguin.

Freire, P. (1974) *Education: The Practice of Freedom*. London: Writers and Readers Cooperative.

French, R. (1986) *The Way of a Pilgrim*. London: SPCK.

Freud, S. (1907) 'Obsessive actions and religious practices' in *Standard Edition* IX, 115–276. London: Hogarth Press.

Freud, S. (1913) 'Further recommendations in the technique of psychoanalysis: on beginning the treatment' in P. Rieff (ed.) (1963) *Therapy and Technique*. New York: Collier Books.

Freud, S. (1927) *The Future of an Illusion*. Penguin Freud Library, Volume 12.

Freud, S. (1927) *Fetishism*. Penguin Freud Library, Volume 7.

Friday, N. (1993) *Men in Love*. London: Hutchinson.

Frieze, I. H. (1983) 'Investigating the causes and consequences of marital rape', *Signs* 8(3): 532–53.

Gaertner, S. L. and Dovidio, J. F. (1986) 'Prejudice, discrimination and racism: problems, progress and promise' in J. F. Dovidio and S. L.

Gaertner (eds) *Prejudice, Discrimination and Racism*. New York: Academic Press.

Gelder, M. G. and Marks, I. M. (1969) 'Aversion treatment in transvestism and transsexualism' in R. Green and J. Money (eds) *Transsexualism and Reassignment*. Baltimore: The Johns Hopkins Press.

Gibran, K. (1980) *The Prophet*. London: William Heinemann.

Gil, D. G. (1978) 'Violence against children' in C. M. Lee (ed.) *Child Abuse: A Reader and Sourcebook*. Buckingham: Open University Press.

Gilbert, P. (1992) *Depression: The Evolution of Powerlessness*. Hove: Lawrence Erlbaum Associates.

Gonsiorek, J. C. and Weinrich, J. D. (1991) 'The scope and definition of sexual orientation' in J. C. Gonsiorek and J. D. Weinreich (eds) *Homosexuality: Research Implications for Public Policy*. Newbury Park, CA: Sage Publications.

Goolkasian, G. A. (1986) *Confronting Domestic Violence: The Role of Criminal Court Judges*. Washington, DC: National Institute of Justice.

Gough, T. (1987) *Couples Arguing*. London: Darton, Longman and Todd.

Gough, T. (1989) *Couples in Counselling*. London: Darton, Longman and Todd.

Gough, T. (1990) *Don't Blame Me!* London: Sheldon Press.

Gough, T. (1992) *Couples Parting*. London: Darton, Longman and Todd.

Graham, P. (1986) *Child Psychiatry: A Developmental Approach*. Oxford: Oxford University Press.

Grayshon, J. (1987) *A Pathway Through Pain*. Eastbourne: Kingsway Publications.

Green, R. (1974) *Sexual Identity Conflict in Children and Adults*. London: Duckworth.

Groth, N. A. (1979) *Men Who Rape: The Psychology of the Offender*. New York: Plenum Press.

Halmos, P. (1970) *The Faith of the Counsellors*. London: Constable.

Halnan, K. E. (1982) *An Approach to the Treatment of Cancer: Past, Present and Future*. London: Chapman and Hall.

Hamilton, D. L. and Trolier, T. K. (1986) 'Stereotypes and stereotyping: an overview of the cognitive approach' in J. F. Dovidio and S. L. Gaertner (eds) *Prejudice, Discrimination and Racism*. New York: Academic Press.

Hammarskjöld, D. (1964) *Markings*. London: Faber and Faber.

Hardiker, P. and Barker, M. (1994) *The 1989 Children Act: Social Work Processes, Social Policy and 'Significant Harm'*. Leicester: University of Leicester.

Harris, T. A. (1973) *I'm OK. You're OK*. London: Pan Books.

Hawkins, P. (1982) 'Mapping it out', *Community Care* 22 July: 17–19.

Hawkins, P. A. (1991) *A Humanistic, Integrative and Psychodynamic Model for Short Term Counselling and Psychotherapy.* Working Paper of the Bath Centre for Counselling and Psychotherapy.

Hawkins, P. and Shohet, R. (1989) *Supervision in the Helping Professions.* Buckingham: Open University Press.

Hayman, A. (1965) 'Psychoanalyst subpoenaed', *The Lancet* 16 October: 785–6.

Hendrix, H. (1988) *Getting the Love You Want.* New York: Harper and Row.

Hepburn, G. and Gutiérrez, B. (1988) *Alive and Well: A Lesbian Health Guide.* Crossing Press.

Herman, J. (1992) *Trauma and Recovery.* London: HarperCollins Pandora.

Hobman, D. (ed.) (1994) *More Power to Our Elders.* Counsel and Care, Twyman House, 16 Bonny Street, London NW1 9PG.

Holtby, W. (1954) *South Riding.* Glasgow: Fontana.

Honey, P. and Mumford, A. (1992) *The Manual of Learning Styles* (3rd edn). Maidenhead: Peter Honey.

Hudson, L. and Jacot, B. (1991) *The Way Men Think.* New Haven: Yale University Press.

Hurding, R. (1992) *The Bible and Counselling.* London: Hodder and Stoughton.

Illich, I. (1971) *Deschooling Society.* London: Calder and Boyars.

Jackson, T. (1994) *Perfect Job Search Strategies.* London: Piatkus.

Jacques, E. (1965) 'Death and the mid-life crisis', *International Journal of Psychoanalysis* 46: 502–14.

Jones, J. M. (1981) *Prejudice and Racism.* Reading, MA: Addison Wesley.

Jung, C. G. (1961) *Modern Man in Search of a Soul.* London: Routledge and Kegan Paul.

Kadushin, A. (1976) *Supervision in Social Work.* New York: Columbia University Press.

Kaplan, H. (1974) *The New Sex Therapy.* London: Baillière Tindall.

Keating, C. J. (1987) *Who We Are Is How We Pray.* Mystic, CT: TwentyThird Publications.

Kempe, C. and Helfer, R. (eds) (1980) *The Battered Child* (3rd edn). Chicago: Chicago University Press.

Kennedy, E. and Charles, S. (1990) *On Becoming a Counsellor.* Dublin: Gill and Macmillan.

Kinsey, A. C., Pomeroy, W. B. and Martin, C. E. (1948) *Sexual Behaviour in the Human Male.* Philadelphia: W. B. Saunders.

Kinsey, A. C., Pomeroy, W. B., Martin, C. E. and Gebhard, P. H. (1953) *Sexual Behaviour in the Human Female.* Philadelphia: W. B. Saunders.

Klaus, D. (1993) 'Solace and immortality: bereaved parents' continuing bond with their children', *Death Studies* 17: 343–68.

Klein, J. (1987) *Our Need for Others and Its Roots in Infancy*. London: Routledge.

Klein, S. D. and Schleifer, M. J. (1993) *It Isn't Fair! Siblings of Children with Disabilities*. The Exceptional Parent Press, Bergin and Garvey, 88 Post Road West, Westport, CT 06881, USA.

Knapp, R. J. (1986) *Beyond Endurance: When a Child Dies*. New York: Schocken Books.

Knowles, M. (1975) *Self-directed Learning*. New York: Association Press.

Kohlberg, L. (1981) *The Philosophy of Moral Development*. San Francisco: Harper and Row.

Kolb, D. A. and Fry, R. (1975) 'Towards an applied theory of experential learning' in C. L. Cooper (ed.) *Theories of Group Process*. Chichester: John Wiley.

Kübler-Ross, E. (1969) *On Death and Dying*. London: Macmillan.

Lang, R. A. (1993) 'Neuropsychological deficits in sexual offenders', *Sexual and Marital Therapy*, 8(2).

Leon, I. G. (1990) *When a Baby Dies: Psychotherapy for Pregnancy and Newborn Loss*. New Haven and London: Yale University Press.

Lerner, G. (1986) *The Creation of Patriarchy*. Oxford: Oxford University Press.

Le Vay, S. (1993) *The Sexual Brain*. Cambridge, MA: Bradford Books.

Lieblum, S. and Rosen, R. (1989) *Principles and Practice of Sex Therapy*. New York: Guilford Press.

Locke, S. E. and Hornig-Rohan, M. (1983) *Mind and Immunity: Behavioural Immunology: An Annotated Bibliography 1976–1982*. Institute for the Advancement of Health, 16 E 53rd Street, NY 10022, New York.

Loizeaux, W. (1993) *Anna: A Daughter's Life*. New York: Arcade Publishing.

Lowe, N. K., Walker, S. N. and MacCallum, R. C. (1991) 'Confirming the theoretical structure of the McGill Pain Questionnaire in acute clinical pain', *Pain*, 46: 53–60.

McCann, J. (ed.) (1952) *The Rule of St Benedict*. London: Burns and Oates.

Mach, Z. (1993) *Political Symbols, Conflict and Identity: Essays in Anthropology*. Albany: State University of New York Press.

Mackie, K. (1981) *The Application of Learning Theory to Adult Teaching*. In P. Allman and K. Mackie (eds) Adults: Psychological and Education Perspectives series. Nottingham: University of Nottingham Department of Adult Education.

McWhinnie, A. M. (1992) 'Creating children: the medical and social dilemmas of assisted reproduction', *Early Child Development and Care* 81: 39–54.

Main, J. (1977) *Christian Meditation: The Gethsemane Talks*. Montreal: The Benedictine Priory.

Malan, D. H. (1976) *The Frontier of Brief Psychotherapy*. New York: Plenum Press.

Marshall, W. L. (1993) 'The role of attachments, intimacy and loneliness in the etiology and maintenance of sexual offending', *Sexual and Marital Therapy* 8(2).

Marty, M. E. and Appleby, R. Scott (eds) (1991–93) *Fundamentalisms Observed, Fundamentalisms and Society* and *Fundamentalism and the State*, published by The Fundamentalism Project. Chicago: University of Chicago Press.

Mason, M. C. (1993) *Male Infertility: Men Talking*. London: Routledge.

Masters, H. and Johnson, V. E. (1970) *Human Sexual Inadequacy*. London: Churchill.

Mattinson, J. (1975) *The Reflection Process in Casework Supervision*. London: Tavistock.

Meadow, R. (1989) *ABC of Child Abuse*. London: BMJ Publications.

Melzack, R. and Torgerson, W. (1971) 'On the language of pain', *Anaesthesiology* 34(1): 51–9.

Menolascino, F. J. (1990) 'Mental illness in the mentally retarded: diagnostic and treatment considerations' in A. Dosen, A. van Gennep and G. J. Zwanikken (eds) *Treatment of Mental Illness and Behavioral Disorder in the Mentally Retarded: Proceedings of the International Congress, May 3–4, 1990. Amsterdam, The Netherlands*. Leiden, The Netherlands: Logon Publications.

Menolascino, F. J. and Egger, M. L. (1978) *Medical Dimensions of Mental Retardation*. Lincoln, NE: University of Nebraska Press.

Mental Health Foundation (1993) *Learning Difficulties: The Fundamental Facts*. London: Mental Health Foundation.

Menzies, I. (1970) *The Functioning of Social Systems as a Defence Against Anxiety*. London: Tavistock Institute of Human Relations.

Millett, K. (1979) *Sexual Politics*. London: Virago.

Minchin, S. and Fishman. H. C. (1981) *Family Therapy Techniques*. Cambridge, MA: Harvard University Press.

Monckton, G. (1994) *Dear Isobel: Coming to Terms with the Death of a Child*. London: Vermillion.

Morgan, R. (1993) 'On women as colonised people' in *The Word of a Woman*. London: Virago.

Morris, J. (ed.) (1989) *Able Lives: Women's Experience of Paralysis*. London: The Women's Press.

Morris, S. (1994) ' "You will only hear half of it and you won't believe it": counselling with a woman with a mild learning disability' in V. Sinason (ed.) *Treating Survivors of Satanist Abuse.* London: Routledge.

Murisier, E. (1901) *Les Maladies du Sentiment Religieux.* Paris: Felix Alcan.

Nash, W. E. (1993) *People Need Stillness.* London: Darton, Longman and Todd.

National Association for Staff Support (NASS) (1992) *The Costs of Stress and the Costs and Benefits of Stress Management.* NASS.

Neild, S. and Pearson, R. (1992) *Women Like Us.* London: The Women's Press.

Neuberger, J. (1994) *Caring for Dying People of Different Faiths.* London: Mosby.

Newburn, T. (1993) *Making a Difference?* London: National Institute for Social Work.

Nicholson, P. (1993) *The Experience of Being Burgled: A Psychological Study of the Impact of Domestic Burglary on Victims.* Sheffield: University of Sheffield.

Noble, K. (1987) 'Self-help groups – the agony and the ecstasy' in M. Lawrence (ed.) *Fed Up and Hungry.* London: The Women's Press.

Novaco, R. W. (1975) *Anger Control: The Development and Regulation of an Experimental Treatment.* Lexington, MA: D.C. Heath.

Office of Population Censuses and Surveys (1994) *Mortality Statistics* (DH2 no. 19). London: HMSO.

Ornstein, P. H. (ed.) (1985) *The Search for the Self: Selected Writing of Heinz Kohut.* New York: International Universities Press.

Ornstein, R. (1975) *The Psychology of Consciousness.* Harmondsworth: Penguin.

Pagelow, M. D. (1981) *Woman-Battering: Victims and Their Experiences.* Beverly Hills, CA: Sage Publications.

Parkes, C. M. (1975) *Bereavement: Studies of Grief in Adult Life.* London: Penguin.

Parkinson, F. (1993) *Post-Trauma Stress.* London: Sheldon Press.

Parton, N. G. (1989) 'Child abuse' in B. Kahan (ed.) *Child Care Research, Policy and Practice* (4th edn). London: Hodder and Stoughton.

Pauly, I. B. (1969) 'Adult manifestations of male and female transvestism' in R. Green and J. Money (eds) *Transsexualism and Reassignment.* Baltimore: The Johns Hopkins Press.

Pelletier, K. R. (1978) *Mind as Healer, Mind as Slayer.* London: Allen and Unwin.

Perry, J. (1992) 'Who cares for the carers?' in M. Winfield (ed.) *Confronting the Pain of Child Sexual Abuse.* London: Family Service Units.

Perry, J. (1993) *Counselling for Women*. Buckingham: Open University Press.

Pitt, J. and Keane, M. (1984) *Community Organising? You've Never Really Tried It*. Birmingham: J. and P. Consultancy.

Prince, C.V. and Bentler, P.M. (1972) 'Survey of 505 cases of transvestism', *Psychological Report* 31: 903–17.

Prochaska, J. and Diclemente, C. (1986) 'Toward a comprehensive model of change' in W. Miller and N. Heather (eds) *Treating Addictive Behaviour*. New York: Plenum Press.

Proctor, B. (1988) *Supervision: A Working Alliance* (videotape training manual). St Leonards-on-Sea, East Sussex: Alexia Publications.

Puhl, L. (1951) *The Spiritual Exercises of St Ignatius*. Chicago: Loyola.

Ratigan, B. (1991) Personal communication to Dominic Davies.

Raymond, J.G. (1980) *The Transsexual Empire*. London: The Women's Press.

Renouf, J. (1993) *Jimmy: No Time to Die*. London: Fontana.

Rex, J. (1970) *Race Relations in Sociological Theory*. London: Weidenfeld and Nicolson.

Rogers, C. (1961) *On Becoming a Person*. London: Constable.

Royal College of Psychiatrists (1987) *Drug Scenes*. London: Royal College of Psychiatrists.

Rubin, S. S. (1993) 'The death of a child is forever: the life course impact of child loss' in M. Strobe, W. Strobe and R. Hansson (eds) *Handbook of Bereavement: Theory, Research and Intervention*. Cambridge: Cambridge University Press.

Rubinstein, H. (ed.) (1990) *The Oxford Book of Marriage*. Oxford: Oxford University Press.

Rudin, J. (1979) *Fanaticism: A Psychological Analysis*. Notre Dame, IN: Notre Dame University Press.

Russell, W. (1988) *Shirley Valentine*. London: Methuen.

Sang, B., Warshow, J. and Smith, A.J. (eds) (1991) *Lesbians at Midlife: The Creative Transition*. San Francisco: Spinsters.

Sapolsky, R. (1994) *Why Zebras Don't Get Ulcers*. New York: W. H. Freeman.

Scott, M. and Stradling, S. (1992) *Counselling for Post-Traumatic Stress Disorder*. London: Sage Publications.

Scott Peck, M. (1978) *The Road Less Travelled*. London: Touchstone Books.

Searles, H. (1955) 'The informational value of the supervisor's emotional experiences' in H. Searles (1965) *Collected Papers on Schizophrenia and Related Subjects*. London: Hogarth Press.

Segal, J. C. (1986) *Emotional Reactions to MS*. Available from The Multiple Sclerosis Resources Centre, 52a Silver Street, Stansted, Essex CM24 8HD.

Segal, J. C. (1989) 'Counselling people with disabilities/chronic ill-nesses' in W. Dryden, R. Woolfe and D. Charles-Edwards (eds) *Handbook of Counselling in Britain*. London: Tavistock/Routledge.

Segal, J. C. (1991a) 'The professional perspective' in S. Ramon (ed.) *Beyond Community Care: Normalisation and Integration Work*. London: Macmillan Education.

Segal, J. C. (1991b) 'Use of the concept of unconscious phantasy in understanding reactions to chronic illness', *Counselling* 2(4): 146–9.

Segal, J. (in press) 'The stresses of working with clients with disabilities' in W. Dryden and V. Varma (eds) *Stresses in Counselling in Action*. London: Sage Publications.

Seligman, M. E. P. (1973) 'Fall into helplessness', *Psychology Today* 7: 43–8.

Sharpe, S. (1984) *Double Identity: The Lives of Working Mothers*. Harmondsworth: Penguin.

Shernoff, M. (1989) 'AIDS prevention counseling in clinical practice' in J. W. Dilley, C. Pies and M. Helquist (eds) *Face to Face: A Guide to AIDS Counselling*. San Francisco: AIDS Health Project, University of California.

Shuttle, P. and Redgrove, P. (1986) *The Wise Wound*. London: Paladin.

Sinason, V. (1986) 'Secondary mental handicap and its relationship to trauma', *Psychoanalytic Psychotherapy* 2: 131–54.

Sinason, V. (1988) 'Smiling, swallowing, sickening and stupefying: the effect of sexual abuse on the child', *Psychoanalytic Psychotherapy* 3: 97–111.

Sinason, V. and Svensson, A. (1994) 'Going through the fifth window: "Other cases rest on Sundays. This one didn't"' in V. Sinason (ed.) *Treating Survivors of Satanist Abuse*. London: Routledge.

Skynner, R. and Cleese, J. (1983) *Families and How to Survive Them*. London: Methuen.

Society of St Francis (1992) *Celebrating Common Prayer*. London: Mowbray.

Spottiswoode, J. (1991) *Undertaken with Love: The Story of a DIY Funeral*. London: Robert Hale.

Stewart, M., Abraham, G. and Stewart. A. (1992) *Beat PMT Through Diet*. London: Vermilion.

Stoller, R. J. (1979) 'The gender disorders' in I. Rosen (ed.) *Sexual Deviation*. Oxford: Oxford University Press.

Sturdy, C. (1987) 'Questioning the Sphinx' in S. Ernst and M. Maguire (eds) *Living with the Sphinx*. London: The Women's Press.

Telford, A. and Farrington, A. (1991) 'Gender issues in couple therapy' in D. Hooper and W. Dryden (eds) *Couple Therapy: A Handbook*. Milton Keynes: Open University Press.

Thomas, D. H. (1983) *The Making of Community Work*. London: Allen and Unwin.

Trickett, S. (1986) *Coming off Tranquillisers and Sleeping Pills*. Wellingborough: Thorsons.

Trungpa, C. (1973) *Cutting Through Spiritual Materialism*. London: Robinson and Watkins.

Tully, B. (1992) *Accounting for Transsexualism and Transhomosexuality*. London: Whiting and Birch.

Tyler, B. (1958) *The Origins of Culture*. New York: Harper and Row.

van Belzen, J. (1992) 'The rise of Dutch psychology of religion', *Changes* 10 (3).

Verney, T. and Kelly, J. (1982) *The Secret Life of the Unborn Child*. London: Sphere Books.

Virog, R. (1985) 'About pharmacologically induced prolonged erections', *Lancet* 1: 519–20.

von Bertalanffy, L. (1968) *General Systems Theory*. New York: Braziller.

Walker, M. (1990) *Women in Therapy and Counselling*. Buckingham: Open University Press.

Walrond-Skinner, S. (1993) *The Fulcrum and the Fire*. London: Darton, Longman and Todd.

Warnock Report (1978). London: Department of Education and Science.

Walter, T. (1990) *Funerals and How to Improve Them*. London: Hodder and Stoughton.

Wellings, K., Field, J., Johnson, A. M. and Wadsworth, J. (1994) *Sexual Behaviour in Britain*. London: Penguin.

White, M. (1989) 'The externalising of the problem and the re-authoring of lives' in *Selected Papers*. Adelaide: Dulwich Centre Publications.

Winnicott, D. W. (1958) *Through Paediatrics to Psychoanalysis*. London: Tavistock.

Winnicott, D. W. (1965) *The Maturational Processes and the Facilitating Environment*. London: Hogarth Press.

Winnicott, D. W. (1988) *Human Nature*. London: Free Association Books.

Worden, W. (1991) *Grief Counselling and Grief Therapy* (2nd edn). London: Tavistock/Routledge.

Wright, B. (1991) *Sudden Death*. London: Churchill Livingstone.

Young, A. P. (1991) *Law and Professional Conduct of Nursing*. London: Scutari Press.

Young, V. (1996) 'Working with older lesbians in lesbian, gay and bisexual affirmative therapy' in D. Davies (ed.) *Pink Therapy: A Guide for Counsellors and Therapists Working with Lesbians, Gay and Bisexual Clients*. Buckingham: Open University Press.